TEXTBOOK ON
'A' LEVEL LAW

This book is dedicated to the memory of B.J.
A very dear friend.

TEXTBOOK ON

'A' LEVEL LAW

Second Edition

Patricia Hirst
and
Michael Hirst

First published in Great Britain 1996 by Blackstone Press Limited,
Aldine Place, London W12 8AA. Telephone 0181-740 2277

ISBN: 1 85431 845 4

First edition, 1996
Second edition, 1998

British Library Cataloguing in Publication Data
A CIP catalogue record for this book is available from the British Library.

Typeset by Montage Studios Ltd, Horsmonden, Kent
Printed by Livesey Ltd, Shrewsbury, Shropshire

Contents

The nature of law — Law and legal personality — English law and other forms of law — Law and morality — Historical development of English law — Common law and equity today

Civil courts and criminal courts — Superior and inferior courts

Magistrates' courts — The county courts — The High Court — The Court of Appeal (Civil Division) — The House of Lords

Modes of trial and the classification of offences — Magistrates' courts — The Crown Court — The Court of Appeal (Criminal Division) — Criminal appeals to the House of Lords

What is ADR? — Arbitration — Procedure — Other forms of ADR — Agencies offering ADR services — The courts and ADR — Limitations of ADR

Modern changes within the legal profession

Qualifications needed to become a solicitor — The work of solicitors — Repercussions following the abolition of monopolies

Qualifications needed to become a barrister — Work of a barrister — Rules of conduct for barristers — Junior barristers and Queen's Counsel (QCs) — Changes to the legal profession: the effect upon barristers — Complaints against solicitors — Complaints against barristers

Justices of the peace — Stipendiary magistrates — District judges — Recorders — Circuit judges — High Court judges — Lords Justices of Appeal — Lord of Appeal in Ordinary — Special judicial offices — The independence of the judiciary — Separation of powers

The costs of litigation — The Legal Aid Act 1988 — Legal advice and assistance: the green form scheme — Assistance by way of representation — Legal aid in civil cases — Legal advice and assistance in criminal cases — The duty solicitor scheme — Legal aid in criminal cases — Recovering costs of a successful defence — Paying costs of the prosecution — The problems of legal aid — Conditional and contingent fees

8   The Criminal Process   104

Prosecutions — Police powers of stop and search and question — Police powers of arrest — Procedure following arrest — Safeguards for persons in police custody — Detention for questioning, etc. — Questioning of suspects — Period of time for which the detainee may be kept in police custody — The decision to prosecute — Bail — Forms of trial — Pre-trial disclosure — Evidence at trial — Trial by jury — Miscarriages of justice

9   The Powers of the Criminal Courts   129

The purpose of criminal sanctions — The approach towards punishment today — Background information relevant to sentencing — Imprisonment — Detention and custody of young offenders — Community sentences — Fines — Absolute and conditional discharges — Disqualification and deportation — Confiscation, forfeiture and restitution orders — Compensation orders

10   Civil Procedure   141

Pre-trial procedure — Representative or class actions — The trial — Enforcement of judgments — Recommendations for reform of the civil justice system

PART TWO   INTRODUCTION TO CRIMINAL LAW   149

11   The Essential Elements of a Crime   151

The actus reus   152

Voluntary and involuntary conduct — Acts and omissions — State-of-affairs offences — Causation

Mens rea   160

Intention or intent — Maliciousness — Recklessness — Negligence — Coincidence of *actus reus* and *mens rea* — Transferred malice

12   Strict Liability Offences   169

The process of identifying strict liability offences — Arguments for and against strict liability offences — A half-way house? — Strict liability offences

Innocent misrepresentation — Rescission — Bars to rescission — Exclusion clauses and misrepresentation

Contracts to commit crimes or other unlawful acts — Contracts promoting sexual immorality — Contracts contrary to the administration of justice — Further consequences of illegality — Lawful contracts performed in an illegal manner

Preface

The two years since the publication of the first edition of this textbook have been filled with judicial and legislative activity. There are, in other words, many new cases and many new Acts of Parliament. Some areas of law have changed almost beyond recognition, and in places this new edition reads very differently from the old one. Quite apart from the changes brought about by new laws, we have rewritten and expanded certain passages in an attempt to improve the quality of analysis and the clarity of our exposition.

We are grateful for the many positive and constructive comments which have been passed to us following the publication of the first edition. The basic format of the book has not changed. It is not dedicated to any particular Board or syllabus, but attempts to cover those areas of law most commonly included in A level courses or in other courses which provide introductions to the basic principles of English law.

We have stated the law as of July 1998.

Patricia and Michael Hirst
Aberystwyth
September 1998

Table of Cases

Table of Statutes

PART ONE

Law and the English Legal System

ONE

An Introduction to Law and the English Legal System

The principal aims of this introductory chapter are:

   (a)   to examine what is meant by the term 'law' and the role which law plays within our society; and

   (b)   to consider some of the unique features and organisations of the English legal system.

The nature of law

The term 'law' may be used in a variety of different ways. For example, the term may be used to refer to the laws of physics, the laws of Church or the laws of nature. To a lawyer, the term law has a different meaning, but pinning down or defining that meaning is not easy. As the legal theorist, H. L. A. Hart, wrote in his classic text, *The Concept of Law*,

> Few questions concerning human society have been asked with such persistence and answered by serious thinkers in so many diverse, strange and even paradoxical ways as the question, 'What is law?'

We will look, later in this chapter, at some of the conflicting theories as to the nature of law. At a basic level, however, the question can be answered (in part at least) by stating that law regulates the conduct, rights, duties and relationships of those persons who are subject to it. Without a system of law, it would be most difficult, if not impossible, for any form of civilised society to function. To put it another way, without law, there can only be anarchy; and this usually means savagery and the law of the jungle.

The most basic kinds of laws are those forbidding certain kinds of dangerous, violent or antisocial behaviour. Such prohibitions will generally be backed by threats of punishments for breach, these punishments being imposed by or on behalf of the society in question. This is what we term 'criminal law'. A properly functioning society needs more than this, however. There must also be rules of 'civil law' governing the ownership and transfer of property, the enforcement of obligations, etc. The more complex the society, the more complex these rules must become. A modern, industrialised state, such as the United Kingdom, with its elected central and local governments and sophisticated banking and financial systems, necessarily requires elaborate and complex laws to regulate it.

Law and legal personality

Any system of law has its *subjects* and its *objects*. The subjects of a legal system are those who have rights and duties or obligations under that system. They will be expected to obey the law and may in return be able to invoke that law in support of their own rights. The subjects of English law, apart from the organs of the state itself, are primarily individuals (or 'natural persons') who live within, visit, own property within, or have some other connection with, England or Wales. 'Artificial persons' (or corporations) may also have such rights and duties (see below), but animals, houses, cars or trees can only be the 'objects' of that law. An animal or house may be bought or sold, protected or destroyed under the rules of English law, but cannot be prosecuted or sued under it, nor can it be required to 'obey' that law. Thus, a dog which chases sheep or fouls footpaths is not breaking the law, and cannot be prosecuted, although its owner may be.

This book is primarily concerned with English law, but there are many other systems of law, including public international law, which regulates the conduct and relationships of states and international organisations. States are the principal subjects of international law. Individuals may be the objects of international law (as where a state is held responsible for the misconduct of its officials) but are only treated as subjects of that law in very limited circumstances (as where the leaders of Nazi Germany were tried by the International Military Tribunal at Nuremberg after the Second World War). For most purposes, individuals in international law are like animals under English law: they may be affected by that law, but the law is not addressed to them, nor have they any right to enforce it.

Corporations and corporate personality
Corporations are important subjects of most legal systems, but could never exist outside the context of a legal system. In other words, if there were no legal

systems, there could be no corporations, because they are wholly artificial legal inventions.

In English law, corporations may take one of two principal forms, namely corporations aggregate and corporations sole. The former are more numerous and important than the latter. A corporation sole (such as a bishopric of the Church of England) has just one member, whereas a corporation aggregate may have two or more (and sometimes several thousand) members, but each type of corporation has a legal personality which is separate and distinct from that of its membership. Thus, the Bishop of London (as a corporation sole) is regarded as a different legal entity from the individual clergyman who holds that office at any given time; and the Universal Widget Company Ltd (as a corporation aggregate) is a different legal entity from the individual share-holders who are its members.

The importance of the separate legal personality accorded to corporations under English law can hardly be underestimated. Corporations can own property, enter into binding contracts, employ workers and incur debts. They can sue other persons, and be sued by other persons, in the courts. In the case of a company registered with limited liability, the members cannot ordinarily be called upon even to meet the unpaid debts of that company. This is a vitally important feature of our capitalist economy, because it enables an individual capitalist to invest various sums of money in the shares of several different companies, secure in the knowledge that, in the event of the failure of any one of those companies, the worst thing that could happen is that he may lose his stake in that particular company. As long as he has fully paid for his shares, he cannot ordinarily be held personally liable for any part of that company's debts.

Corporations must be distinguished from unincorporated associations, such as partnerships. Partnership, like marriage, is merely a relationship between those persons who are partners: it can have no existence independent of those partners, and the relationship necessarily changes or dies if the partners change or die. A partnership is not therefore a legal person, but a corporation is, and it can therefore outlive and in due course replace its original members, without having to be reconstituted.

Natural and positivist theories of law
Over the centuries, many philosophers, theologists and legal theorists have championed the concept of 'natural' law: law which has reason, morality and justice as its basis, and which derives its moral authority from its essential rightness. The philosophers of ancient Greece, who were arguably the first to investigate the essential nature of law, believed that there were objective moral principles which were part of the natural order of the world, and that civilised man developed these natural moral principles so as to enable himself to survive within the society of others. Primitive man could survive without law, but city states, such as those of Greece, could not survive without law. Plato suggested that civilised life in the city states became viable only once God (Zeus) had

bestowed on men a sense of natural justice and mutual respect. Later writers developed this theory into one under which 'natural law' was seen to be the basis of civilised life, and civilised life the natural, perfected form of human existence. In so far as law prohibits self-evidently wrongful actions, such as the killing or maiming of innocent persons, it may be seen to reflect natural law. Such acts are indeed prohibited under the laws of every civilised country.

Law making and legal reasoning were more highly developed by the Romans, and Roman law became the basis for many modern legal systems in Continental Europe. Roman law often prevailed by reason of might, rather than right, but Roman legal philosophy nevertheless included some highly developed natural law theories, the most famous of which was that advanced by Cicero, who wrote:

> True law is reason in agreement with nature ... To curtail it is unholy, to amend it illicit, to repeal it impossible; nor can we be dispensed from it by the order either of senate or of popular assembly ... one and the same law, eternal and unchangeable, will bind all peoples and all ages.

In another passage Cicero considered the position of 'wicked and unjust' man-made statutes. These, he said, 'put into effect anything but laws'. In other words, unjust rules, which offend against natural law, do not merit the title 'law' at all.

The early Christian approach to law was similar in some respects to that of Cicero (and may indeed have been influenced by some of his writings). Christians argued that divine or religious law (as embodied, for example, in the Ten Commandments) reflected 'God's will' and therefore overruled any other laws that might be inconsistent with it. If a man-made law conflicted with divine law, then the latter would have to prevail, because God's law was of a higher order than man's. One practical effect of such doctrine in early Christian societies was that religious leaders acquired considerable power as law makers or as arbiters of the validity of secular law, and secular leaders were often obliged to defer to their demands. A similar situation arguably exists in some modern day Islamic states, such as Iran.

In the early mediaeval period, the relationship between divine law, natural law and man-made law was reconsidered by the leading Christian philosopher, Thomas Aquinas. According to Aquinas, natural law was that part of moral or eternal law which man could develop through the exercise of his powers of reasoning, whilst other principles could be acquired from the teachings of the Bible. Aquinas acknowledged that divine laws could not by themselves cover the entire spectrum of human activity and that man-made laws were also required, many of which could be morally neutral; but in the event of conflict, man-made law was inferior to natural or divine law and could be overridden by it. Unjust law was inherently invalid. It 'had the quality, not of law, but of violence'.

There are still strong echoes of such thinking even in modern times. Muslim fundamentalists may argue that any law which conflicts with the Koran must be invalid. Most modern lawyers, however, follow what may be described as a 'positivist' theory of law, under which the validity of a law depends, not on its moral rectitude, but on its place within an effective system of legal rules. If a revolution or war overthrows the existing legal order, that legal order will cease to be valid, and if a new regime gains effective control, its laws will be valid from then on. The morality of those regimes or of their laws is not the issue.

The nineteenth century jurist, John Austin, offered one of the first developed theories of positivist law. He argued in *The Province of Jurisprudence Determined* that all laws are commands set by a superior being (a state or sovereign) addressed to inferior beings (or subjects), and enforced by sanctions or threats. The theory of sovereign commands proved problematic. The rules of criminal law do indeed take the form of prohibitions backed by the threat of criminal penalties ('Do not steal; if you steal you will be punished') and some civil rules can, up to a point, be regarded in such a way. Thus, if you want to make a will to govern the distribution of your property after your death, this document must conform to the requirements of the Wills Act, or (and this is the sanction) it will not be valid, and your property will be distributed amongst your nearest relatives as if you had never made a will at all. Many legal rules, however, are permissive, rather than mandatory, and some, notably the rules of public international law, result from agreement between equals, rather than from commands imposed on them by a sovereign power. If Austin was right, there could be no such thing as public international law. To put it another way, international law, being largely the product of agreement between equal and independently sovereign states (rather than a law imposed on them by some higher sovereign power) could not really be law at all.

As a result, no legal theorists now accept Austin's theory in its entirety, and some reject it almost entirely. On the other hand, Austin was surely right to emphasise that law can exist independently of justice, merit or morality. Bad law can still be valid law. Its existence and validity depend on the realities of power. As John Salmond later wrote in his *Jurisprudence*, law can be defined as 'the body of principles recognised and applied by the state in the administration of justice'. Whether any given proposition is part of English law depends on whether it can be shown to have originated from, or been adopted by, a recognised source of law within that particular system (see below).

Nevertheless, concepts of natural law still arise from time to time. In 1934, the Chief Justice of the Irish Free State declared (in a dissenting judgment in *The State (Ryan) v Lennon*) that:

> ... if any legislation ... were repugnant to the natural law, such legislation would be necessarily unconstitutional and invalid, and it would be, therefore, absolutely null and void and inoperative.

In 1968, a court in West Germany had to consider, retrospectively, the status of an overtly racist citizenship law that had been in force in the Nazi era. It held that this law had *never* really been valid, apparently on the basis that it conflicted with natural law or morality. The court's motives in so ruling were doubtless very noble, but its reasoning was suspect. From a strict positivist viewpoint, that law had once been perfectly valid, at least whilst the Nazi regime was in power.

English law and other forms of law

Legal rules are concerned with the regulation of human conduct, including the activities of corporations or states, which are controlled by human agency. One must distinguish, however, between those rules that form part of English law (or the law of England and Wales) and rules that fall outside it. The rules of a club, sport or association, or church may indeed regulate human conduct, but (with the exception of the laws of the established Church of England) they are not in any sense part of English law. Nor is the law of Scotland or Northern Ireland part of English law. Scottish law, in particular, differs from English law in many respects. We are concerned only with those rules that form part of the law of England and Wales, or which are incorporated within that law. How are such rules to be identified?

One can eliminate at once any rules which the courts of England and Wales would refuse to recognise or enforce. This largely depends on the origin of the rule in question. The courts will enforce rules laid down by Act of Parliament, or in regulations or orders made with the authority of an Act of Parliament. They will enforce rules previously created by the courts themselves (common law rules and rules of equity) and certain rules of international law or European Community law, which are deemed to be incorporated into English law. The rules of sports, associations or companies are not, on that basis, any part of English law. It should be noted, however, that the *members* of such associations or companies may have agreed to abide by those rules, and such agreements may be enforceable in the courts as contracts. They are not directly part of English law, but may indirectly be enforceable under that law.

Law and morality

The relationship between law and morality is arguably a loose and flexible one, as Austin and other 'legal positivists' have frequently pointed out. The relationship nevertheless raises some important issues, particularly for the person who may be minded to defy a particular law of which he strongly disapproves. Is it necessarily wrong to disobey the law? Natural lawyers of the Cicero or Aquinas schools would argue that unjust laws are not true laws in any event. In contrast, the ancient Greek philosopher, Socrates, is said to have accepted and suffered a sentence of death, imposed by unjust laws, rather than defy those laws by escaping when the opportunity to escape was available to him. His view, it seems, was that, having lived for many years under the protection of the laws of his city state, he could not then defy them when they operated against his interests or beliefs.

Many people would find it difficult to support either of these extreme positions, but would acknowledge that, in extreme cases (and perhaps *only* in extreme cases) it may be right and proper to defy the law. This must certainly be true of laws which are inherently monstrous: who could possibly criticise those subjects of Nazi Germany, or its empire, who risked their own lives by sheltering Jewish families in secret defiance of Nazi laws? At the other end of the scale, it may be right to defy basically just and reasonable laws, if special circumstances arise which justify such violation. In *Buckoke* v *Greater London Council* [1971] 2 All ER 254, Lord Denning MR argued that it would be right and proper for the driver of a fire engine to drive carefully through a red traffic light (in breach of the law) in order to rescue a person from a fire. In such a case, it is obviously better that the law should be flexible enough to *permit* such behaviour in emergencies (as it now does), but Lord Denning was surely right to hold that, even if such conduct *is* criminal, it may still be a cause for congratulation rather than condemnation and punishment.

There are very few absolute principles in this area, but persons who are minded to defy a law they disapprove of (e.g., by disrupting or wrecking some other person's lawful activities) must bear in mind that if everyone ignored or defied every law of which they disapproved, chaos and anarchy would not be far away.

The legal enforcement of morality or moral standards
One other area of great academic debate is the extent to which the law ought to enforce private morality. There are great difficulties associated with such an issue. Many moral issues bring forward a wealth of differing opinions. Which, if any, should the law then enforce? The issue of law (and in particular criminal law) being used as a method of enforcing morality has most frequently arisen in connection with sexual morality.

The libertarian viewpoint, of which the most famous exponent was John Stuart Mill, holds that the criminal law should only ever be used against a person to stop him doing harm to others. On that basis, for example, child sex abuse can justifiably be made criminal in order to protect children; but incest between consenting adults (e.g., brother and sister) or homosexual acts between such adults, should not be. The Wolfenden Committee in its 1957 Report on Homosexual Offences and Prostitution adopted this approach. In a famous and much-quoted passage from its final Report, the function of criminal law was declared to be:

> To preserve public order and decency, to protect the citizen from what is offensive or injurious and to provide sufficient safeguards against

exploitation or corruption of others, particularly those who are specially vulnerable because they are young, weak in body or mind or inexperienced or in a state of special physical, official or economic dependence. It is not ... the function of the law to intervene in the private lives of citizens, or seek to enforce any particular pattern of behaviour, further than is necessary to carry out the purposes we have outlined. . . There must remain a realm of private morality and immorality which is, in brief and crude terms, not the law's business.

This liberal approach was subsequently reflected in statutes such as the Sexual Offences Act 1967, which largely decriminalised private adult homosexuality. It has not, however, won unanimous support. The eminent judge and writer, Lord Devlin, argued in *The Enforcement of Morals* (1965) that the *primary* function of the criminal law was to maintain public morality. If such basic morality is not protected by the criminal law, he argued, this will undermine the very existence of society and society will disintegrate. An example of the law stepping in to 'protect public morality' through the use of the criminal law can be seen in the case of *Shaw* v *Director of Public Prosecutions* [1961] 2 All ER 446. In this case, the publisher of a booklet containing the names, addresses and photographs of London prostitutes was convicted of a previously unknown offence of 'conspiracy to corrupt public morals'. The House of Lords upheld his conviction. Viscount Simonds stated:

In the sphere of the criminal law ... there remains in the courts of law a residual power to enforce the supreme and fundamental purpose of the law, to conserve not only the safety and order but also the moral welfare of the State, and *it is* their duty to guard against attacks which may be the more insidious because they are novel and unprepared-for.

There are all kinds of problems with such an approach. What morality should the law be protecting? It is scarcely possible to identify a particular form of morality which is shared by the vast majority of society, save in so far as this deals with matters such as murder, theft, or other acts which involve identifiable harm to other people. Lord Devlin seems to have assumed that morality or immorality can be identified by reference to the feelings of ordinary people; but even if ordinary people can indeed be found to have a common attitude to certain conduct (e.g., a disgust of homosexuality or incest), how can it be assumed that their reaction is a moral one, rather than one of blind, irrational prejudice?

The European Convention on Human Rights, to which the United Kingdom is a party, broadly supports the principle of individual freedom from interference in private life, but nevertheless allows such legal interference 'as may be necessary in a democratic society . . . for the protection of health or morals'. In the recent case of *Laskey* v *United Kingdom* (Case No. 109/1995) the Court of

Human Rights held that the British courts had been entitled, for health reasons, to condemn and punish the behaviour of a group of homosexual sado-masochists who had engaged in mutual torture sessions for the purpose of sexual excitement. Whether such legal interference is really necessary is another matter, and will probably remain a source of dispute.

Historical development of English law

In order to understand how the English legal system exists as it does today, it is necessary to consider how it has evolved over the centuries. One point to note is that English law has been relatively little influenced by the doctrines of Roman law, which was the dominant influence on the development of legal systems throughout continental Europe. Instead, English law has been formed by a combination of judge-made law (which can be divided into common law and equity) and legislation (also known as statutes, or Acts of Parliament). Most modern law is heavily based on legislation, which has become progressively more important over the years; but legislation once played a secondary role to judge-made law, and to understand the development of English law, one must begin with the origins of the common law.

Origins of the common law
The development of the common law can primarily be attributed to the Norman conquest of England in 1066, and more particularly to the Normans' desire to impose a 'common' or unified government and legal system upon the country they had conquered; but its development was slow and uneven. Vestiges of the old Saxon courts and laws remained for centuries after the conquest. The Normans inherited and initially made use of a system of local administration built around the shire (or county) and the hundred. Each hundred held monthly courts, which were in part concerned with local administration, but which were also used to settle private disputes and to identify local criminals. These courts applied customary laws which could vary from one part of the country to another, as could the methods of trial.

The hundred courts and other local courts could not immediately be replaced, but were gradually overtaken in importance by the new royal courts (the courts of King's Bench, Exchequer and Common Pleas), which grew out of the *Curia Regis* (the royal court) during the thirteenth century, and by itinerant judges or commissioners who periodically visited different counties of the realm in order to dispense royal justice in what subsequently came to be known as Assizes: a system which lasted until the creation of the Crown Court in the 1970s. The itinerant judges originally applied local customary law wherever they went, but in time they standardised on a 'common' set of rules and procedures that could be applied throughout the realm. This became the common law.

The development of equity

Under English law, 'equity' is a distinct body of rules which was originally based upon broad principles of natural justice and fairness, but which over time became formalised as rules of law. The system of equity can be traced back to the thirteenth century, when it developed as a reaction to certain manifest defects in the common law system.

By the thirteenth century it had became clear that there were serious imperfections in the common law. Common complaints levelled against it concerned the problems associated with the writ system and the related forms of action and also the absence in many cases of adequate remedies for wrongs.

Problems with the writ system and the 'forms of action'

Civil proceedings could only be commenced through the issue of a writ. This need not in itself have been a problem, but the law relating to the issue of writs, and the 'forms of action' or procedural rules that had to be followed in connection with each particular form of writ, had become hopelessly rigid and technical. There was a specific writ and form of action for each particular type of legal wrong, and it was vital that the aggrieved party chose the right writ to fit his cause of action. If he used the wrong kind of writ (or the wrong kind of pleading to go with it) his action could be 'non-suited', and he would lose it, or at best have to begin it all over again. If there was no recognised form of writ available to cover his grievance, he might be left with no remedy at all.

Inadequate remedies

The only remedy which the common law could provide was that of monetary compensation, or 'damages'. In many cases, however, damages may be an inadequate remedy. For example, the plaintiff in a contract dispute may prefer that the defendant be compelled to perform his part of the bargain (e.g., to sell the plaintiff a particular house) rather than simply being required to pay damages for non-performance.

As a result of these and other imperfections, dissatisfaction grew and dissatisfied litigants began to petition the King for a remedy. Petitions to the King became so numerous that he had to delegate responsibility for them to his chief minister, the Chancellor. Petitions would typically conclude with the words 'and he (the petitioner) hath no remedy at the common law'. The Chancellor could then intervene to correct the harshness or inadequacies of the common law. There were no fixed rules which the Chancellor had to apply. His jurisdiction was thus very flexible. At all times, however, the Chancellor would decide the case as he thought fair. The fact that there were no strict rules meant too much depended on the personal opinions of the Chancellor. Equity, it was said, varied with the length of the Chancellor's foot. It was not really until the seventeenth century that equity began to be administered by a set of consistent and predictable principles. Eventually, a Court of Chancery was established to deal with such cases, but in due course this became as technical, ponderous and legalistic as any other court in the land.

Conflicts between the Court of Chancery and the common law courts
During the sixteenth century, a conflict developed between the common law courts and the Court of Chancery. The conflict can be attributed to a number of factors. First, the Court of Chancery had developed a series of alternative remedies to damages. For example, it developed the injunction and the order of specific performance, which were often more satisfactory from the litigant's point of view and made the Court of Chancery more popular than its competitor. An injunction was an order to refrain from doing a particular thing; whereas an order for specific performance positively required the performance of contractual obligations. Obviously the common law judges resented what they saw as competition and interference. More seriously, however, the Court of Chancery had begun to use its powers to restrain certain litigants from asserting strictly legal (but inequitable, or unfair) rights. This was a direct challenge to the authority of the common law courts.

This argument came to a head in 1615 in the *Earl of Oxford's Case*. In this case, judgment had been given by the common law courts, but it was held to be inequitable by the Court of Chancery which imposed an injunction against the party who had been successful in the common law courts. The injunction commanded him not to enforce the judgment he had just won. The King was asked to resolve the dispute, and he came down in favour of the injunction. Henceforth, if any conflict between equity and common law were to arise, equity would always prevail. The effect of that ruling can still be felt today, and is indeed enshrined in s. 49 of the Supreme Court Act 1981. The rules of equity and common law are now administered by the same courts as the common law, but where there is any conflict between the different principles, it is the equitable principles that the courts must apply.

Common law and equity today

In the nineteenth century, as a result of the Judicature Acts 1873–75, the common law courts and the Court of Chancery were fused or combined in one of the great legal reforms of that period. Although the courts were fused, the two systems still remain distinct systems, each with its own different principles. The main result of the fusion was that any court now acquired the ability to apply both equitable and common law principles and to award either common law or equitable remedies.

The courts are still able, to a limited extent, to develop new equitable principles, as can be seen in the development of the doctrine of promissory estoppel in the period following the *High Trees* case of 1947 (see Chapter 20). Even common law rules can be developed or modified, up to a point. Today, however, it is Acts of Parliament which form the major source of new legal rules, and the judges will often reject pleas to reform old common law rules by replying, 'Such reform is a matter for Parliament, if Parliament thinks fit to change it'. See for example the case of *C (a minor)* v *Director of Public Prosecutions* [1995] 2 All ER 43, where the House of Lords so replied on being invited to overturn the absurd old common law presumption (admittedly a rebuttable presumption) that a child between the ages of 10 and 14 is too young to possess criminal intent. (The Crime and Disorder Act 1998 will abolish that presumption.)

TWO

The Courts and Appellate System

This chapter will look at the English court system and the system of appeals. Chapter 4 will look at the impact which our links with Europe have had upon our court system and the procedure which exists for appeals from the decisions of our courts to the European Court of Justice or the European Court of Human Rights.

CLASSIFICATION OF THE COURTS

It is difficult to find an entirely satisfactory form of classification for the courts. The following classification nevertheless draws out most of the more important distinctions.

Civil courts and criminal courts

Civil courts are concerned with the resolution of disputes between private persons (whether individuals or companies), or between private persons and the state. Civil law deals with such things as contractual obligations, compensation claims following personal injuries, property rights, matrimonial disputes and taxation. It is not the aim of the civil law to punish defendants, but to protect and enforce rights and obligations. Criminal courts, on the other hand, determine whether defendants have broken the criminal law. If the defendant (or accused) is found guilty of a crime, he may be punished. Many courts can exercise both civil and criminal jurisdiction (authority). For example, magistrates' courts deal primarily with criminal cases, but also deal with matrimonial matters and with civil cases involving the collection of the council tax.

Superior and inferior courts

Courts may also be classified according to whether they are 'superior' or 'inferior'. The distinction is long established, but not very clear-cut. The superior courts include the House of Lords, the Court of Appeal, the High Court and the Crown Court. These courts have jurisdiction to deal with the most important and difficult cases. Inferior courts include the county courts and the magistrates' courts, which have more limited jurisdiction and deal with less important and less serious cases. There are limits, for example, on the maximum penalties that can be imposed in magistrates' courts, compared with those available in the Crown Court. The inferior courts are also subject to the 'supervisory jurisdiction' of the High Court, which can strike down decisions arrived at by improper procedures, etc. (see p. 20); but to a limited extent the Crown Court (a superior court) may also be subject to that jurisdiction. (It is exempt from it when trying criminal cases on indictment.)

THE CIVIL COURT STRUCTURE

We will look at the civil courts in ascending order of superiority. Remember that many courts deal with both civil and criminal cases. It may help at this stage to look at the diagrams provided at the end of this chapter in order to ascertain what jurisdiction each court has, and its relationship with others.

Magistrates' courts

The main role of the magistrates' courts is to deal with criminal cases (see below), but they exercise a limited jurisdiction over civil matters as well. Magistrates have the power to hear 'family proceedings', particularly under Domestic Proceedings and Magistrates' Courts Act 1978 and the Children Act 1989. They have jurisdiction to hear certain applications for residence and contact orders in respect of children, to make orders for financial provision, personal protection orders and exclusion orders in cases of matrimonial violence.

In addition, magistrates' courts may make orders for the recovery of council tax and non-domestic (or business) rates from those in arrears of such payments. They have the power to grant, revoke or renew licences for such things as the sale of liquor and the possession of shotguns.

Appeals from magistrates' courts
Appeals in family proceedings can be made to a Divisional Court of the High Court Family Division. Appeals relating to licensing applications can be made to the Crown Court. Complaints over incorrect procedures, or disputes as to the jurisdiction of a magistrates' court, may be resolved by invoking the supervisory jurisdiction of the High Court.

The county courts

The county courts were created by the County Courts Act 1846 in order to hear small civil claims. The reason for their creation was to provide cheap justice in small civil cases, as the courts which existed before that time were unable to do so. Originally their jurisdiction was limited by reference to the value of the claim. In 1991, however, the jurisdiction of the county courts was transformed and the principal deciding factor in determining their jurisdiction is now the complexity of the case (see below).

There are nearly 300 county courts. They are staffed by circuit judges and district judges (formerly known as registrars). The district judge can normally only hear cases involving £5,000 or less, but he can hear larger cases with the permission of the circuit judge and of the parties. As to the role of district judges in small claims arbitrations, see p. 18.

Limits on the jurisdiction of the county courts
The county courts are inferior courts, and their jurisdiction is limited in two main ways. The first limit upon their jurisdiction is geographical. Most proceedings must be commenced either in the county court for the district in which the defendant lives or carries on business, or in the county court for the district where the cause of action arose. Secondly, the county courts are restricted in what remedies they can grant. They cannot, for example, grant the prerogative remedies of certiorari, mandamus or prohibition (see below for further information on these orders); if such orders are required, an application must be made to the High Court.

In 1988, a Civil Justice Review was set up to examine the distribution of work between the county courts and the High Court. The review concluded that the High Court was weighed down with too many trivial cases and that the costs involved in bringing such actions were often out of proportion to the amounts being claimed. It concluded, therefore, that many of these cases would be more appropriately dealt with in the county courts. Most of the recommendations put forward by the Civil Justice Review were subsequently incorporated in the Courts and Legal Services Act (CALSA) 1990 and in orders made under that Act.

The allocation of cases between the county courts and the High Court
Under CALSA 1990, the county courts were given almost all the powers of the High Court. As a result, the county courts may now try the majority of civil cases. They have exclusive jurisdiction over cases concerning consumer credit agreements, sexual and racial discrimination cases (except employment cases, which go to industrial tribunals) and most kinds of mortgage possession proceedings outside London. In other cases (e.g., contract, tort or property disputes) the county courts will usually be preferred to the High Court where the action concerns personal injury under £50,000, equity and probate

disputes under £30,000, or any action under £25,000, *unless* the criteria established under CALSA 1990 suggest that the case is more suitable for trial in the High Court. The allocation of cases to the High Court is therefore no longer based simply on the financial value of the claim, but may be distributed so as to reflect the complexity and importance of the proceedings.

In deciding which court would be the most appropriate the following factors must be considered:

(a)   the value of the action;
(b)   the nature of the proceedings;
(c)   the parties to the action;
(d)   the degree of complexity involved with the case; and
(e)   the importance of any question likely to be raised in the course of proceedings.

There are certain types of cases which are considered unsuitable for trial in the county courts and which should instead be heard in the High Court. These include: professional negligence; fatal accidents; allegations of fraud or undue influence; defamation; malicious prosecution or false imprisonment, and claims against the police.

Special jurisdiction of the county courts under other statutory provisions
All county courts have the power to hear specific family proceedings under certain designated pieces of legislation. Some county courts are also designated as 'divorce county courts' and may hear petitions for divorce, nullity of marriage and separation orders. Other county courts can be designated by the Lord Chancellor to hear insolvency cases and to deal with the winding up of smaller companies.

Small claims arbitration in the county courts
The Administration of Justice Act 1973 created a scheme for the quick, informal and inexpensive arbitration of small claims using the personnel and facilities of the existing county courts. (See Chapter 5 for more information on the concept of arbitration.) At first, the new procedure was restricted to claims for amounts not exceeding £75, but this limit has been raised five times, not merely to keep up with inflation, but also to bring more and more cases within the small claims procedure. It was raised to £3,000 in 1996 and is likely to be raised to £5,000 during 1998. In the absence of special circumstances (such as issues of legal complexity) which may justify the holding of a full trial, a defended civil action will automatically be referred to small claims arbitration wherever the amount involved does not exceed the current limit.

Small claims hearings are normally held in private and proceedings are informal. The technical rules of evidence and procedure do not apply. Claimants merely have to complete a relatively simple claim form in order to commence proceedings. Court fees are low, and unsuccessful litigants can only be required to make a limited contribution (currently no more than £260) to the legal costs of the winning party. This has two consequences. The first is that the 'risks' of entering into such a procedure are relatively limited. The second is that litigants may be discouraged from hiring expensive lawyers, because they will then have to pay most of their own costs, even if they win. Legal aid will not ordinarily pay for representation at such hearings.

The parties in such proceedings often put forward their own cases, although they may choose to employ a lawyer or be helped by a friend or other unqualified representative. Trainee solicitors often 'cut their teeth' as advocates by representing clients at such hearings. The arbitrator, who is usually a district judge, may help an unaided litigant by putting questions to witnesses and explaining technical legal terms.

In a review of the small claims procedure in 1986, it was found that most cases brought under this procedure related to the provision of goods and services and the procedure was used to an equal degree both by traders or professionals and by ordinary consumers. Furthermore, most litigants expressed satisfaction with the procedure and cases were decided more quickly than ordinary cases in the county courts, although the enforcement of awards may be a problem (as with the enforcement of other civil court judgments: see p. 145 below).

Appeals from county courts
Most appeals from the county courts go to the Court of Appeal, although appeals may be made to a Divisional Court of the Chancery Division on bankruptcy matters.

The High Court

The High Court consists of three administrative divisions, namely the Queen's Bench Division, the Chancery Division and the Family Division. Judges of the High Court usually sit in the Royal Courts of Justice in the Strand in London, but by virtue of the Supreme Court Act 1981, sittings of the High Court may be held at any place in England or Wales, and judges of the Family and Queen's Bench Divisions regularly hear cases in major court centres outside London. The Lord Chancellor directs where such sittings may take place. The High Court's jurisdiction is mainly civil, although the Queen's Bench Division does have important appellate criminal jurisdiction.

The Queen's Bench Division (QBD)
This division has the heaviest workload and the most important part of its business is its original jurisdiction (i.e., hearing a case for the first time) in civil matters such as tort and contract. If the case involves a complex commercial dispute, it may be heard by the Commercial Court, which by virtue of the

Administration of Justice Act 1970 is deemed to be part of the QBD. Admiralty matters are heard by the Admiralty Court, formerly part of a different division, but now also part of the QBD. This exercises jurisdiction over such matters as loss of life or personal injury arising from collisions between ships, claims of ownership relating to ships, etc.

The QBD also exercises appellate jurisdiction, i.e., hearing appeals from the decisions of lower courts. When acting as an appellate court, it sits as a Divisional Court. This means that at least two judges hear the case, or sometimes three if it is a particularly important one. One of the judges will usually be a Lord Justice of Appeal.

Apart from its criminal jurisdiction (below), the Divisional Court also exercises an important supervisory jurisdiction over tribunals, inferior courts and governmental or other public bodies through the use of the procedure known as judicial review. The principal purpose of applying for judicial review is to question and scrutinise the validity of decisions of public bodies etc. The Divisional Court exercises control by means of the 'prerogative orders' of which the main ones are:

(a)   the order of mandamus, which is an order compelling a person or body to carry out some public duty;

(b)   the order of prohibition, which forbids a lower court or tribunal from exceeding its proper jurisdiction; and

(c)   the order of certiorari, which has the effect of ordering a lower court or tribunal to send a record of its proceedings to the Divisional Court.

In this way the actions of the lower courts or public bodies are scrutinised by the judges.

The Chancery Division

Most hearings before the Chancery Division take place in the Royal Courts of Justice in London. The Chancery Division deals only with civil matters and is the successor to the old Court of Chancery. The matters primarily dealt with by the Chancery Division today include the administration of estates of deceased persons, trust matters, mortgages, revenue matters, partnership disputes, bankruptcy, contentious probate, patents and trade marks, company law and the appointment of a guardian of a minor's estate.

A Divisional Court of the Chancery Division comprising two or more judges can hear appeals from the county courts on bankruptcy matters and land registration, and it may also hear appeals from the decisions of Special Commissioners of Income Tax.

The Family Division

The Family Division is concerned with all difficult divorce cases, nullity of marriage, decrees of judicial separation and orders as to the financial and property arrangements following such decrees. The Division also has jurisdiction over matters concerning children, such as issues arising from wardship, custody and adoption. A Divisional Court of the Family Division may hear appeals from the decisions of magistrates in family proceedings.

The Court of Appeal (Civil Division)

The Court of Appeal comprises two divisions, namely the civil division and the criminal division. The jurisdiction of each division is purely appellate. The civil division is presided over by the Master of the Rolls (although he cannot sit personally on every case) assisted by Lord Justices of Appeal and sometimes by co-opted High Court judges. Usually a case will be heard by three judges, but this figure may be increased to five in important cases.

The Court of Appeal hears appeals from all three divisions of the High Court and from the county courts. It also hears appeals from the restrictive practices court and from various tribunals. The method of appeal involves reviewing the case on the basis of legal argument and transcripts of proceedings in the lower court, and the Court will not normally admit fresh evidence, although it can do so in exceptional cases.

The House of Lords

The appellate committee of the House of Lords is the highest court in the United Kingdom. Judicial decisions of the House of Lords can only be overruled by statute or by the House of Lords itself. Until the nineteenth century, any member of the House of Lords was entitled (in theory) to sit and hear an appeal, but the Appellate Jurisdiction Act 1876 provided that lay peers may not participate in judicial sittings of the House of Lords. Most cases are heard by five Lords of Appeal in Ordinary (the 'law lords'), but the Lord Chancellor himself will often sit in important cases.

Appeals are heard in one of the upstairs committee rooms of the Palace of Westminster (or Houses of Parliament). Each law lord may deliver his own separate judgment, which is written but until recently was always called a 'speech'. Sometimes one delivers an agreed judgment on behalf of all, which makes life easier for lawyers who have to interpret it. No oral evidence is heard. The law lords base their decisions on counsels' arguments and on their own research into the law. A majority decision will often determine the outcome of the case.

Most civil appeals heard by the House of Lords come from the Court of Appeal. There is no automatic right of appeal. Instead, leave to appeal must be given either by the House of Lords itself or by the Court of Appeal. Under the Administration of Justice Act 1969, the House of Lords may exceptionally hear civil appeals directly from the High Court, thereby bypassing or leap-frogging the Court of Appeal. This very rare procedure may be followed, however, only if the High Court judge grants a certificate certifying that the case involves a point of law of general public importance which either relates to the construction of a statute/statutory instrument, or is one in respect of which the judge is bound by a previous decision laid down by the Court of Appeal or House of Lords.

The House of Lords also hears civil appeals from the Scottish Court of Session and from Northern Ireland, although these are fairly limited in number.

THE CRIMINAL COURT STRUCTURE

Modes of trial and the classification of offences

Before looking at the criminal jurisdiction of the courts, it is necessary to consider how criminal offences are classified as far as modes of trial are concerned. All offences may be classified as being subject to one of the following modes of trial:

Offences triable only summarily
These are mostly created by statute and are of a relatively minor nature. They can be tried only by a magistrates' court (or by a youth court, where juvenile offenders are involved). There are hundreds of summary offences, many of which are motoring offences. On conviction for a summary offence, magistrates may, in some cases, impose a prison sentence for a period not exceeding six months, or a fine not exceeding £5,000. In many cases, however, the maximum permissible sentence may be far lower, and may not include imprisonment at all.

Offences triable only on indictment
These include the most serious crimes, such as murder, manslaughter, rape and treason. These offences are triable only by a judge and jury in the Crown Court. Before a person can be sent for trial to the Crown Court, he must ordinarily be brought before a magistrates' court, which conducts a preliminary inquiry into the case. Such inquiries are known as 'committal proceedings'. The magistrates study the facts of the case to determine whether a *prima facie* (or apparent) case has been made out against the defendant. In most committal proceedings, the magistrates usually look only at the documentary evidence, and the proceedings are rarely disputed.

The Royal Commission on Criminal Justice acknowledged that the criminal justice system must be able to prevent hopelessly weak cases being sent to the Crown Court, but thought that there were more efficient ways of securing this goal than through the use of committal proceedings. Under reforms subsequently set out in the Criminal Justice and Public Order Act 1994, the magistrates' function of acting as examining magistrates *was* to have been abolished. Those reforms were never implemented, but fresh proposals set out in s. 51 of the Crime and Disorder Act 1998 will eventually restrict committal proceedings to offences triable either way. Crown Court judges will weed out hopeless cases where committal proceedings are not held.

Offences triable either way

These are offences which are listed in schedule 1 to the Magistrates' Courts Act 1980, or which are made triable either way by other statutes. Such offences may be tried either by a magistrates' court or by a Crown Court, depending upon established criteria. If an offence is triable either way, the magistrates must first establish whether the defendant intends to plead guilty. If he does not, they must decide (by conducting a 'mode of trial hearing') which form of trial would be better suited for this particular case. In other words, would it be better for the case to be heard in the Crown Court by a judge and jury, or would it be more appropriate to deal with it summarily themselves? When determining this question, the magistrates must consider a number of factors, such as the seriousness of the offence and the complexity of the evidence. For example, theft is an offence which is triable either way since thefts can vary in severity, ranging from those involving enormous amounts of money to the theft of a tin of beans from a shop. A theft of a tin of beans is rather trivial and could be dealt with summarily by the magistrates if the accused consents. The theft of a million pounds in a complex investment fraud is not trivial and is not suitable for summary trial under any circumstances. The magistrates' powers of sentencing are too limited when serious crimes are involved. For most purposes, the maximum sentence on summary trial is six months' imprisonment and/or a £5,000 fine. Heavier sentences (including up to a year in prison) are possible in cases where the accused is convicted of more than one 'either way' offence but this is the maximum available.

In appropriate cases the defendant will be informed by the magistrates that the case can be dealt with summarily, and if the defendant consents to this the magistrates will proceed with the case summarily, usually at a later date. If the defendant does not consent to this then, assuming that there is sufficient evidence to justify a trial at all, the case must be sent for trial by jury in the Crown Court. In contrast, if the magistrates decide that the charge can be dealt with only by a trial on indictment, their decision is final and the defendant cannot insist on being be tried summarily.

If the defendant is convicted summarily of an offence triable either way, he may be committed to the Crown Court for sentencing if the magistrates find that their powers of punishment are inadequate in the light of information about the defendant's antecedents (i.e., his criminal record, which they would not have known at the start of the trial).

Magistrates' courts

The office of magistrate or 'justice of the peace' is one which can be traced back to 1195. Originally magistrates had a number of administrative duties as well as judicial ones, but today the office is confined to judicial responsibilities. A magistrates' court is usually presided over by two or more unpaid lay magistrates or justices of the peace. Lay magistrates receive basic instruction on law and procedure when appointed and they are assisted in court by a legally qualified clerk. It is wrong to suppose, however, that all court clerks are fully qualified solicitors or barristers. Some are, but only the senior clerk (or 'clerk to the justices') must hold such a full qualification. In larger cities there are full-time paid magistrates known as stipendiary magistrates. Stipendiaries are appointed by the Lord Chancellor from individuals who have served as barristers or solicitors for at least seven years. (See Chapter 6 for further information.)

Youth courts

A person under the age of 14 is known as a child, while anyone over that age but under 18 is referred to as a young person. They are sometimes known collectively as 'juveniles'. They will normally be tried in a youth court (formerly known as a juvenile court). This is essentially a magistrates' court sitting for the specific purpose of dealing with youngsters, and the justices themselves are selected from a special panel. There must be three justices on the bench to hear the case. At least one of them must be a woman and one must be a man. These courts not only deal with criminal proceedings against young people, but also deal with care proceedings. Sittings of youth courts are arranged so that they are kept separate from any other court proceedings and members of the public are not admitted. The press are allowed access to the proceedings, but publication of the proceedings is very restricted. The juvenile's identity must not be made known by the press unless specific permission is granted, either by the court or by the Home Secretary. Youth courts deal with all but the most serious juvenile offences, including offences for which an adult would have to be tried on indictment in the Crown Court. Under s. 24 of the Magistrates' Courts Act 1980, however, a juvenile may face Crown Court trial:

(a) if he is charged with homicide;

(b) if he is charged with a grave crime and may deserve a long period of detention; or

(c) if he is charged jointly with an adult and it is thought necessary to try them both together.

Appeals from the magistrates' courts on criminal matters

An appeal from a decision by a magistrates' court may be made to the Crown Court if, for example, there is a dispute as to whether the decision is consistent with the weight of the evidence. The appeal will take the form of a complete rehearing of the case by a circuit judge or recorder accompanied by two or more magistrates, who will hear the parties and witnesses give evidence all over again. The appeal will then be either upheld or dismissed.

If the defendant has been found guilty, he may also appeal to the Crown Court against sentence. Lastly, an appeal on a point of law may be made to the Divisional Court of the Queen's Bench Division by way of 'case stated'. This procedure requires the magistrates to state the facts of the case as found by them and their decision in the light of those facts. The Divisional Court then decides whether the law justifies such a decision.

The Crown Court

The Crown Court was created by the Courts Act 1971. Until 1971, trials on indictment were tried either by Assizes or by Quarter Sessions. The more serious offences were tried in the Assizes and the less serious ones in the Quarter Sessions. There were, however, a number of defects in this system, one of which was that the courts did not sit continuously. Furthermore, the Assize system was outdated and too much time was wasted by judges and officials travelling between one Assize court and another. As a result, there were often terrible delays before defendants could be brought to trial, and High Court judges were forced to waste so much of their time in this way that civil hearings were also seriously delayed. Indeed, the civil delays were much worse, because criminal work was given priority. Much-needed reforms were subsequently brought in by the Courts Act 1971.

The Courts Act 1971

The Courts Act 1971 abolished the Assizes and the Quarter Sessions and the whole of their jurisdiction, including their limited civil jurisdiction, was transferred to the Crown Court. There is only one Crown Court, but it has 94 centres throughout the country. The Central Criminal Court, or 'Old Bailey' is now a branch of the Crown Court. Crown Court centres are arranged into six circuits, each with their own circuit administrator, headquarters and staff. Some centres are first tier centres. They are served by High Court and circuit judges, and these centres may also be used for civil sittings of the High Court. Then there are second tier centres, which are also served by High Court judges and circuit judges but which deal only with criminal cases. Lastly, there are third tier centres, which are served by circuit judges and recorders and which deal only with less serious criminal cases (those which do not need to be tried by High Court judges).

All trials on indictment (jury trials) are heard by the Crown Court and are divided into four categories. Class I offences include the most serious crimes (such as murder) which must usually be tried by a High Court judge. Class II offences are (in theory) normally tried by a High Court judge, although in practice they are more often tried by a circuit judge. Such offences include the crimes of manslaughter and rape. Class III and IV offences cover the less serious types of indictable offence, including all of those triable either way, and are almost always tried by circuit judges or recorders, rather than by High Court judges.

Jurisdiction of the Crown Court

The Crown Court hears all cases on indictment and such cases are heard by a single judge and a jury. It also hears appeals from magistrates' courts, against conviction or sentence or both (no jury is used in such cases). It can also sentence persons committed to the Crown Court for sentencing following their conviction for an 'either way' offence in the magistrates' court.

The Court of Appeal (Criminal Division)

Initially the Court of Appeal was set up simply to hear only civil appeals, but in 1966 the Criminal Appeal Act was passed, which created the Criminal Division of the Court of Appeal as a replacement for the old Court of Criminal Appeal, which had a somewhat different composition. The Criminal Division is presided over by the Lord Chief Justice who is aided by Lord Justices of Appeal and by the judges of the QBD. The Court hears appeals from the Crown Court against conviction, or sentence or both. There is an automatic right of appeal against conviction on a point of law, but leave to appeal must be obtained in order to appeal against sentence only or against a finding of fact. The Court of Appeal also hears certain cases referred to it by the Attorney-General or the Criminal Cases Review Commission (see below). Appeals in summary cases, as previously explained, go to the Crown Court or to the Divisional Court of the QBD.

An appeal will normally be heard by three judges, although an appeal against sentence may be heard by two. An appeal may now also be made by the prosecution against a sentence which they feel to be too lenient, but never against an acquittal by the jury, which is final even if it is demonstrably perverse. Appeals against conviction may be based on a variety of factors (including complaints concerning rulings made by the trial judge as to the admissibility of evidence or the interpretation of a statute), but will be allowed only where the Court of Appeal ultimately considers that the conviction is 'unsafe' (a change introduced by the Criminal Appeal Act 1995). If an appeal against conviction is allowed, the conviction will be quashed, but a re-trial may be ordered if the Court thinks this would be appropriate.

Criminal appeals to the House of Lords

The House of Lords also hears criminal appeals from the Court of Appeal (Criminal Division). There is no automatic right of appeal. The Court of Appeal must certify that a point of law of general public importance is involved and *in addition* either the House of Lords or the Court of Appeal must grant leave to appeal. Although hundreds of criminal cases go to the Court of Appeal each year, only a handful go on to the House of Lords.

The House of Lords also hears criminal appeals from the Divisional Court of the Queen's Bench Division, provided a similar certificate is given and leave to appeal is obtained.

MISCELLANEOUS COURTS

The Privy Council

The Judicial Committee of the Privy Council is a high-powered appellate court staffed primarily by the law lords. It is not strictly part of the English legal system, but hears appeals from British dependent territories, such as Gibralter, and from Commonwealth countries, such as Bermuda or Jamaica, which have chosen to retain it as their court of final appeal. In criminal cases, in particular, many of the leading precedents shaping the law can be found in decisions of the Privy Council

Coroner's courts

Coroner's courts enquire into the death of any person where there is reason to believe that the death was sudden, violent, or from unnatural causes. They also look into cases involving the finding of treasure, where ownership of that treasure may need to be determined. Coroners are barristers, solicitors or legally qualified medical practitioners.

Other courts

There are many other courts, which cannot all be considered in detail. They include the ecclesiastical courts, the restrictive practices court, naval and military courts (including courts martial) and the Court of Protection. The Employment Appeal Tribunal, despite its title, is in fact a superior court of record. These courts all feed into the civil or criminal systems at various points. Many provide appeals to the Court of Appeal. Appeals against the verdicts of naval and military courts martial are heard by a court known as the Courts-Martial Appeals Court. This has a similar composition to the Criminal Division of the Court of Appeal.

THE CRIMINAL CASES REVIEW COMMISSION

The Criminal Cases Review Commission was set up by the Criminal Appeal Act 1995, but did not come into existence until 1997. Although not a court, its members (of whom there must be at least 11) are tasked with the investigation of possible miscarriages of justice. These are cases in which innocent people may have been convicted or in which sentences may have been imposed which overlooked or ignored special circumstances concerning the facts of the case or of the convicted person himself. Any normal rights of appeal must ordinarily have been exhausted before the Commission can be required to intervene.

If the appointed members of the Commission (a minimum of three in any case) consider that there is significant evidence of a possible miscarriage of justice, they may refer the case to the relevant appellate court. The Commission need not confine itself to cases involving persons still serving sentences of imprisonment. One of the first cases it considered was that of Derek Bentley, hanged for murder in 1953. It referred the case to the Court of Appeal and in July 1998, his conviction was posthumously overturned.

System of courts exercising criminal jurisdiction

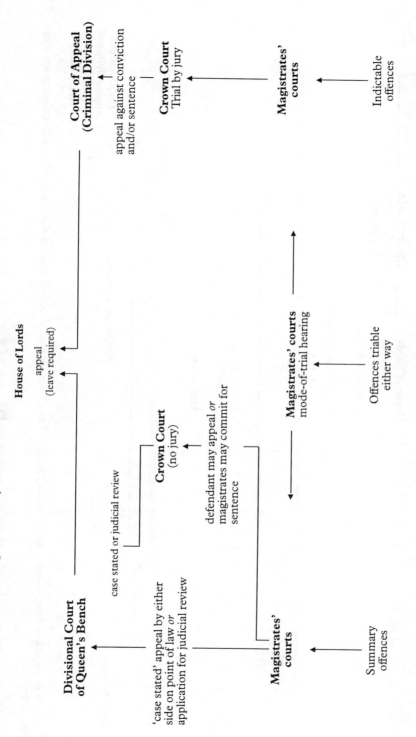

The civil court system (simplified)

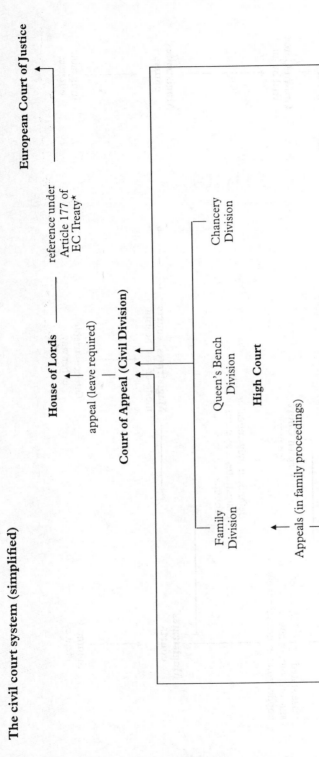

European Court of Justice

reference under Article 177 of EC Treaty*

House of Lords

appeal (leave required)

Court of Appeal (Civil Division)

High Court

Queen's Bench Division

Chancery Division

Family Division

Magistrates' courts

Appeals (in family proceedings)

County courts

Employment Appeal Tribunal (and other tribunals)

*References to the European Court of Justice under Article 177 may be made by any court or tribunal where a question of Community law arises. See Chapter 4.

THREE

The Sources of English Law

The law of England and Wales is derived from two principal sources, namely legislation (which has become the dominant source of law) and judicial precedent, which is otherwise known as case law. The two are not altogether separate. Some law is entirely the creation of the judges (into this category come both common law and equity), but the courts also have to interpret legislation and the decisions reached by the higher courts when so doing effectively shape the way in which that legislation is understood.

Precedent and legislation are not the only sources of English law. Custom still plays a small part, and is considered briefly at the end of this chapter. One must also note the ever-increasing importance of European Community law. This is now an important source of law in its own right, and is dealt with in Chapter 4.

The term 'source of law' is used here to mean a method by which new law is created or old law modified. The decisions of the courts may, for example, modify the way in which a long-established legal principle is understood in the future. Legal writers and textbooks are not ordinarily regarded as a 'source of law' in this sense, although they can of course be invaluable as means of ascertaining what the law actually is. In some cases, however, writers may have a more profound effect on the development and reform of the law, as will be explained at the end of this chapter.

LEGISLATION AND STATUTORY INTERPRETATION

The supremacy of legislation

Legislation is law made by Parliament and is the major source of law under the English legal system. In a typical year, Parliament passes between 70 and 100 statutes, which run into hundreds of pages. Under English constitutional law, the law-making powers of Parliament are supreme. In other words, Parliament has legislative supremacy. This has two important consequences: first, Parliament has the power to create an unlimited amount of law; and, secondly, no person or body can challenge the validity of an Act of Parliament, even if the Act is unreasonable or the Act's passage was as a result of some fraud or irregularity. An example of the latter principle can be found in the case of *British Railways Board* v *Pickin* [1974] AC 765. The respondent challenged the validity of an Act concerning British Rail on the grounds that British Rail had fraudulently concealed facts from Parliament. The House of Lords stated that the respondent could not challenge the validity of an Act of Parliament. Lord Morris of Borth-y-Gest summarised the attitude of their lordships as follows:

> The question of fundamental importance which arises is whether the court should entertain the proposition that an Act of Parliament can be so assailed in the courts that matters should proceed as though the Act or some part of it had never been passed. I consider that such doctrine would be dangerous or impermissible. When an enactment is passed there is finality, unless and until it is amended or repealed by Parliament. In the courts there may be argument as to the correct interpretation of the enactment; there must be none as to whether it should be on the Statute Book at all.

As to the impact of European Community law on this doctrine, see Chapter 4.

Advantages of legislation

Several advantages may be claimed for statute law, in comparison with judge-made law (or case law). One major advantage stems from the absolute power of Parliament. If new laws have to be passed, or if an area of law needs drastic updating, then it is through an Act of Parliament that this is most easily done. Parliament has the power to strip away existing law completely and replace it speedily with a new set of rules. In contrast, changes in the law through the case-law method can be effected only slowly and haphazardly. Judges cannot, by means of one case, update and transform whole areas of law, as they are restricted in what they can do by the facts in front of them.

Statute law is made in advance. It lays down the law applicable as from a given date. Case law can be known only at the same time the decision is made, and the decision necessarily involves facts that have already taken place. If there is no statutory provision covering a particular legal point, the parties may not know what their rights are until after the judge has decided the dispute between them; and if the courts seek to modernise and update the law (e.g., by rejecting out-dated notions devised by judges in previous centuries), any party who has relied on the law being applied consistently with the old precedents will find himself betrayed.

Lastly, it should be possible for statutory provisions to be expressed, not only in authoritative form, but more clearly and comprehensively than case law can achieve. Unfortunately, much of the potential for clarity in legislation is wasted, because too many statutes use language which taxes the understanding of lawyers and judges, and which is quite incomprehensible to lay people.

All statutes enacted from 1996 until the present are freely accessible on the Web (http://www.hmso.gov.uk).

The legislative process

Before proposed legislation passes through Parliament, it is introduced as a 'Bill'. There are two main types of Bill: public Bills, which affect the country as a whole, and private Bills, which are of personal concern to some major company or even (in theory) to an individual. Public Bills may in turn be divided into government Bills and private member's Bills. The vast majority of Bills (and the most important) are government Bills. Some are designed to effect political objectives (e.g., 'privatisation' of nationalised industries or institutions). Others may originate from law reform bodies, such as the Law Commission, and may be relatively uncontroversial, from a political viewpoint at least. Law reform Bills that are relatively non-political are often introduced in the House of Lords, whereas high-profile political legislation is always introduced to the Commons first. The detailed drafting is undertaken, in either event, by specialist Parliamentary draftsmen.

Private member's Bills are introduced into Parliament by individual MPs. Only a handful of private member's Bills ever become law, because of shortage of Parliamentary time, but they often cover topics for which the government does not wish to take responsibility. Private member's Bills which have become law include the Murder (Abolition of Death Penalty) Act 1965, which was presented by Sidney Silverman MP; the Obscene Publications Act 1959, introduced by Roy Jenkins MP; and the Abortion Act 1967, introduced by David Steel MP.

Before a Bill can become an Act, it has to pass through the House of Commons and House of Lords and receive the Royal Assent.

The details of this procedure need not be considered in any detail. Suffice to note that Bills may be amended or defeated during their passage through the House of Commons, and must then go on to the House of Lords, which may propose further amendments, which must be approved in turn by the Commons. The ability of the Lords to halt the passage of a Bill is limited. They may only delay a Bill for a year (or for just one month in the case of a finance or money Bill (such as the government's budget proposals)).

The granting of the Royal Assent, under which the Bill becomes a statute or 'Act of Parliament', is merely a formality. Although it may be given by the Queen, it is usually given by three Lords Commissioners acting on her behalf. The Royal Assent has not been refused since Queen Anne refused her assent to the Scottish Militia Bill in 1707, and there is now a constitutional convention that it will never be withheld. Withholding it would accordingly spark off a major constitutional crisis.

In most cases, the greatest influence on the content and character of new legislation is exerted, not by MPs, but by Parliamentary counsel or draftsmen, acting on the instructions of the government department responsible for promoting the Bill in the first place. Draftsmen and civil servants from the appropriate departments hammer out the basic structure of new legislation before it is ever set before Parliament, and although public debates in Parliament may lead to certain changes being made to a Bill, its overall structure and content is rarely more than dented.

Complaints as to the complexity and obscurity of legislative drafting have persisted for many years (see for example the Report of the Renton Committee on the Preparation of Legislation in 1975) but there is little sign of improvement. Indeed, it is arguable that modern legislation has become less intelligible than ever before.

A statute does not necessarily (or even usually) come into force on the day it receives the Royal Assent. Parliament regularly enacts statutes which cannot be implemented until the necessary resources are prepared and put into place. Not all of the Act will necessarily come into force at the same time. Different parts may be introduced on different dates, which may be specified in a 'commencement section' at the end of the Act itself. It is becoming increasingly common, however, to find an 'appointed day section', authorising a Secretary of State to implement the Act by means of orders made by statutory instrument (i.e., by a form of delegated legislation, as to which see below). The Act may therefore be passed before its commencement dates have even been worked out. This can be confusing. If legislation was merely implemented in coherent chunks (e.g., the first half of the Act on 1 March and the second half on 1 August), that would be tolerable; but instead the normal procedure appears to be for a few sections to become law on one date and a few more at some later date, and so on. Some statutes are brought into force by 20 or more different commencement orders over several years; and parts of many Acts seem never to be implemented at all. This is most unsatisfactory.

Delegated legislation

Parliament has increasingly delegated law-making powers to other bodies. Ministers of the Crown (or Secretaries of State) are regularly given the power to make regulations by means of statutory instruments, which may in theory be vetted by Parliament, but which are in practice so numerous, complex and technical that Parliament has no time to do any such thing. Local authorities and public corporations may be given the power to pass by-laws and regulations, all of which have the force of law. With delegated legislation, Parliament delegates the power to make law by means of a parent Act. The parent Act lays down general principles but delegates to the appropriate subordinate body (in practice, the civil service bureaucrats and lawyers employed in government departments) the task of filling in the administrative, financial or technical details (including, as we have seen, the commencement dates for the parent Act itself).

Statutory instruments (or 'SIs') vastly outnumber statutes in any given year. Many of these SIs are very short, but even allowing for this, the total volume of delegated legislation invariably outweighs that of primary legislation (i.e., Statutes) by a large margin each year. All SIs published from 1997 onwards are reproduced on the HMSO web pages (see http://www.hmso.gov.uk).

Reasons for delegated legislation

The vast extent and technicality of the delegated legislation enacted each year provides one very obvious explanation for its increasing use in today's complex and highly regulated society. Parliament itself scarcely has the time to give proper consideration to the government's primary legislative programme. There is no way in which it could find time to cope with much of the material which now finds its way into statutory instruments or other forms of delegated legislation. Delegated legislation may also cover areas which involve quite specialised technical knowledge, and few MPs have the knowledge required to deal with the details of technical legislation which is accordingly left to experts in government departments or public authorities. Further, the use of delegated legislation provides for far greater flexibility as it can be used to fine tune the legislation when it comes into force rather than amending it by another statute.

Criticism of delegated legislation

Delegated legislation can be criticised for a variety of reasons. The main criticism seems to be that Parliament ought not to delegate the power to make law to persons or bodies who are non-elected. This is a power which ought to be reserved to Parliament. A further criticism is that much delegated legislation is even more complex and impenetrable than the legislation itself, and the vast outpouring of delegated legislation makes the problem of understanding and keeping abreast of the law almost intolerable.

Parliamentary control over delegated legislation

Certain parent Acts require any delegated legislation made under them to be laid before Parliament and approved before it can be put into effect. Whether MPs actually find time to inspect the huge volume of technical material is another matter.

Control of delegated legislation by the courts

The validity of delegated legislation depends on whether its terms are consistent with the terms of the statute under which the power to legislate was delegated, and on whether the procedures used to enact it were consistent with any procedures laid down or mandated by that statute. If this is not the case, the courts may declare that the delegated legislation is *ultra vires* ('without authority') and thus invalid. The courts may also refuse to give effect to delegated legislation if it conflicts with European Community law.

Challenges to such legislation may be raised by means of an application for judicial review by the High Court but in the absence of any provision to the contrary in the parent legislation, *ultra vires* may also be raised as a defence in a criminal prosecution or in any other enforcement proceedings in which it is alleged that rules made under the delegated legislation have been infringed, as the House of Lords recently confirmed in *Boddington v British Transport Police* [1998] 2 All ER 203. The defendant in that case was charged with smoking in a non-smoking railway coach, contrary to a by-law made under s. 67 of the Transport Act 1962. He argued that this by-law was unlawful, in that it purported to ban all smoking on Network South Central trains, whereas the parent Act only authorised the 'regulation' of such conduct. The House of Lords held that the defendant should have been permitted to raise this argument before the court by which he was tried. He was not restricted to the alternative of instituting proceedings for judicial review in the High Court. He nevertheless failed to convince their lordships that there was anything unlawful about the 'no smoking' by-law, and his appeal therefore failed on its merits.

The courts may even declare a local authority by-law to be invalid if its terms are unreasonable. In *Strickland v Hayes* [1896] 1 QB 290, a by-law purported to prohibit the singing or reciting of obscene songs or ballads or the use of obscene language. The court held that there could be no justification for such a wide-ranging prohibition, which did not even distinguish between public and private activities, or require that any member of the public be annoyed.

Statutory interpretation

Although Parliament is the main law-making body, its powers cannot be isolated from the activities of the judiciary, who are responsible for the final enforcement of the legislation. As Parliament is legislatively omnipotent, the courts cannot challenge an Act of Parliament. Instead, their role is to apply the legislation to the facts of the cases before them. This will sometimes be a straightforward task, but if the statute is ambiguous or unclear, the judges must interpret it before they can apply it, and the task of statutory interpretation can often become difficult.

The language used in statutes is often unclear, imprecise or ambiguous, and in those circumstances the judge will have to choose an interpretation which is in line with the general tenor of the Act itself. Added to this problem is the fact that legislation is often used to govern notoriously complicated or difficult subjects, such as taxation and company law. Legislation governing specialised topics such as these will be littered with technical terms which the judges will have to interpret and apply, and this can lead to even greater difficulties.

One of the main functions of an Act of Parliament is to legislate for future eventualities. For many reasons, however, such as lack of foresight or scarcity of space, the legislator can never provide for every possible future eventuality. These gaps will have to be filled in by the judiciary when such cases come before them, and here again the interpretative skills of the judges become paramount.

Another reason why statutes can give rise to interpretational difficulties is that they frequently attempt to provide solutions to problems affecting different and conflicting interests. The problem of using language which is totally free from any ambiguity is difficult enough in simple situations where the parties are of the same outlook. As Harold Macmillan once pointed out, the simple sentence 'A met B and he raised his hat' is capable of being interpreted in several different ways. (Who raised whose hat?) The problem is exacerbated where the parties have an incentive to find different meanings in the words used. When highly paid lawyers are employed to find an interpretation which is favourable to their client, any ambiguity will be ruthlessly exposed. It is the judge who has to decide which interpretation is more in keeping with the true meaning of the Act.

Rules of interpretation

When a judge interprets a statute he may be assisted by certain 'rules' and presumptions, which are explained below. The supposed rules (namely, the literal rule, the mischief rule and the golden rule) are not rules in the strict legal sense, but might better be described as alternative (and to some extent contradictory) judicial approaches to the interpretation of statutes. In addition, there are some extrinsic and internal aids which may be of use in some circumstances. The various rules, presumptions and aids may collectively be referred to as the principles of statutory interpretation.

The literal rule
The literal rule was for many years the dominant principle of statutory interpretation, and even today, the language used in a statute must ordinarily be given its plain, ordinary or literal meaning. If the words used are perfectly clear in meaning, then the judge must apply those words, even if this leads to hardship for those affected by the legislation, even if the judge does not approve of the individual provision, and even if strict application leads to a highly unsatisfactory result. It is sometimes said that this risks ignoring the real intention of Parliament. In *Black-Clawson International* v *Papierwerke Waldhof-Aschaffenburg* [1975] AC 591, Lord Reid said: 'We are seeking the meaning of the words which Parliament used. We are seeking, not what Parliament meant, but the true meaning of what they said.' The literal meaning, however, is not necessarily decisive. The courts increasingly recognise that it may sometimes be necessary or desirable to look beyond this in order to understand and give effect to the will of Parliament. (See in particular *Pepper* v *Hart* (1993), below.)

The golden rule

Although judges may often state that they must give effect to the literal meaning of a statute, there will be circumstances in which the result of a strict literal interpretation would be so absurd as to make them hesitate. The golden rule, a modification of the literal rule, caters for this. The idea behind it is that the judge should apply a literal approach towards interpretation *unless* that leads to absurdity. The golden rule may be used in two ways so as to avoid such an outcome. First, the judge must consider whether any particular words involved have two or more meanings and apply whichever of those meanings makes the greater sense. If that approach fails to prevent an absurd result, the court may simply place an interpretation on the words which is sensible, rather than strictly accurate.

This is what the courts have always done with s. 57 of the Offences Against the Person Act 1861. That section provides that a married person commits the crime of bigamy if he 'marries another person' during the life of his existing spouse. Strictly speaking, this is impossible. One *cannot* in fact 'marry another person' while already married to someone else. Any attempt to do so can only be an invalid sham; it is null and void under all the civil laws governing marriage. On a literal interpretation of s. 57, bigamy is a crime which cannot ever be committed. If that section is to have any meaning at all, the crime must be one of *purporting* to marry another person during the life of one's existing spouse! That is not exactly what the section says, but it must surely be what it means.

How absurd must a literal interpretation be before the judges reject it? This is difficult to predict, because different judges may have different levels of tolerance to absurdity. In *Fisher* v *Bell* [1961] 1 QB 394, the defendant was prosecuted under the Restriction of Offensive Weapons Act 1959, which made it an offence to 'sell or offer to sell' weapons such as flick-knives. The defendant was charged with offering to sell such a weapon, which had been displayed for sale in his shop window. His defence was that under the law of contract, a display of goods in a shop window amounts *not* to an offer for sale, but to an invitation to treat (see Chapter 19). He had not 'offered to sell' anything. One might have expected the Divisional Court to reply that such an argument made nonsense of the Act, and that a slightly less precise interpretation was clearly the one Parliament intended. Some judges might have ruled in that way, but the judges in *Fisher* v *Bell* did not. They applied the literal meaning of the words, and the defendant was acquitted. As a result, the Act was amended, and now prohibits such weapons from being sold, offered for sale *or possessed for the purpose of sale*.

The mischief rule

The mischief rule (or the purposive rule as it is commonly known today) can be traced back to a case from the sixteenth century, namely *Heydon's Case* (1584) 3 Co Rep 7a. This approach (if followed) allows the court to look at the state of the former law in order to discover the mischief in it which the present statute was designed to remedy. In order to discover the purpose behind the statute it was held in *Heydon's Case* that the judge should consider four things:

(1) the ... law before the making of the Act;
(2) the mischief and defect for which the ... law did not provide;
(3) the remedy resolved upon by Parliament; and
(4) the 'true reason of the remedy ... the intent of the makers of the Act'.

The mischief rule also allows a judge to refer to evidence outside the statute, such as reports of Royal Commissioners and Departmental Committees on whose recommendations the statute was made, in an attempt to discover what mischief the statute was intended to remedy.

In the past, there were severe restrictions upon what extrinsic evidence judges could refer to when interpreting legislation. In recent years, however, the rules have been relaxed and external material is now often consulted in order to discover what mischief the Act was intended to remedy. Judges have looked at the reports of the Law Commission, Royal Commissions, the Law Reform Committee and other official committees.

For many years judges were not allowed to look at Parliamentary debates, as reported in *Hansard*, when interpreting statutes. Many judges (including, of course, Lord Denning) had for years disagreed with the restriction, but to no avail. The position, however, was finally abandoned in *Pepper* v *Hart* [1993] 1 All ER 42, where the House of Lords held that reference to *Hansard* would be permitted if each of the following conditions was satisfied:

(a) the legislation must be unclear, or its literal meaning must lead to an absurdity;
(b) the material relied upon must consist of statements by a Minister or other promoter of the Bill; and
(c) the statements thus relied upon must themselves be clear.

Lord Griffiths in that case said:

The days have long passed when the courts adopted a strict constructionist view of interpretation which required them to adopt the literal meaning of the language. The courts now adopt a purposive approach which seeks to give effect to the purpose of the legislation and are prepared to look at much extraneous material that bears on the background against which the legislation was enacted.

It appears from the case law reported after *Pepper* v *Hart* that the courts are now referring to *Hansard* even where there is no obvious or apparent ambiguity in the words used (see, for example, *Thomas Witter Ltd* v *TBP Industries Ltd* [1996] 2 All ER 573 which is examined at p. 311).

Presumptions

When a judge interprets a statute there are certain presumptions which he may rely upon. They are called presumptions because they are 'presumed' to apply unless the statute expressly states that they should not. There are numerous presumptions and some of the more important will be considered here.

Statute does not alter the law

This may seem to be a surprising presumption, but if Parliament intends to alter the common law it must ensure that the statute does so clearly and explicitly, otherwise the courts will presume that the statute does not have that effect. Similarly, it will be presumed that a statute does not amend or repeal an earlier statute unless this is expressly stated. Any amendments and repeals are therefore listed in schedules at the end of a statute, and any statute not so listed will be presumed to remain in force, even if it is difficult to reconcile with the new one.

Presumption against the deprivation of liberty

It is presumed that Parliament does not intend to deprive persons of their liberty. If it does so intend (as, for example, in some provisions of the Mental Health Acts) then clear, express words must be used, because those words used will be construed in a way which permits the least possible interference with such liberty.

Presumption against ousting the jurisdiction of the courts

Statutes sometimes provide that the decision of a tribunal or an administrative body 'shall be final'. If it is Parliament's intention to oust the jurisdiction of the courts then the words used must be clear and unambiguous.

Presumption against criminal liability without fault

The general rule is that a person can be convicted of a criminal offence only if he is proved to have been at fault. Even if a statute does not specify any fault element, the courts will usually presume that the accused must at least be proved to have been reckless. If Parliament wishes to create a 'strict liability offence' for which proof of fault is not needed, it must ordinarily make this clear from the words used. As explained in Chapter 12, however, this presumption is very easily rebutted in statutes which create 'regulatory' offences.

Statutory aids

The Interpretation Act 1978

This Act provides definitions of certain words which are frequently used in statutes, and these definitions apply to the statute being interpreted unless a contrary intention is expressed in the statute. For example, the Interpretation Act 1978 provides that words importing the masculine gender include the feminine; words in the singular include the plural (and vice versa); the word 'month' means a calendar month; 'writing' includes printing or photography; and 'person' includes any corporation or unincorporated body etc.

Interpretation sections in statutes
Most modern statutes contain a special 'interpretation' or 'definition' section, which explains the meaning of key words used in the particular statute, and individual sections or parts of statutes may contain further definitions. Indeed, the very first thing a lawyer should do when interpreting a provision in a statute is to look for guidance within the statute itself.

The creative role of the judge in statutory interpretation

The function often attributed to judges when interpreting statutes is to discover the intention of Parliament. This role reaffirms the principle of parliamentary supremacy. Today, however, there are few who would deny that the judges' role is wider than that, in the sense that they also exercise a creative function. Many statutes are far from perfect instruments; they can be full of ambiguities and can fail to cover certain future eventualities. This can be seen in such diverse areas as tax law and the law of theft. There is a vast amount of case law in each area, dealing with situations which the legislature never envisaged. Gaps and ambiguities in the relevant statutes have been plugged (or in some cases exacerbated) by reported decisions of the appellate courts. One image which may convey the idea of how judges exercise their creativity can be taken from Reed Dickerson's book, *The Interpretation and Application of Statutes*. Dickerson likens the creative function of the judiciary to that of the restorer of ancient vases. Much depends upon how much of the original vase remains. If there is merely a small part of the vase missing then the restorer can be

> guided by the adjacent contours, and, if he is skilful, the result blends well enough to attract little or no attention.... His job is harder if the vase has been decorated, but the difficulty is small if the decoration follows a discernible pattern.

Where the statute is vague or scarcely addresses the problem at all, the judge has little to go on and judicial creativity is likely to be at its highest. But even when the judge can exercise this degree of creativity, he must respect the language of the statute and not place a strained construction upon the meaning of the words used. The judge must use common sense. He must acknowledge that statutes are not perfect instruments and be prepared to interpret them with that in mind, but at the same time must respect the legislature and must not alter its meaning, merely because he does not approve of it.

JUDICIAL PRECEDENT

The doctrine of judicial precedent is the process whereby courts or judges apply legal principles laid down or applied in previous cases. Almost all legal systems require their courts to consider principles laid down in earlier cases. Previous decisions are treated with respect and will usually be followed, in the interests of consistency. No legal system can provide a satisfactory standard of justice if its courts cannot be relied upon to decide similar cases in a broadly similar way. In other words, courts and judges refer to or consult earlier decisions in order to help resolve the cases before them. This is true even in European countries, where almost all of the law has been codified (i.e., set out in the form of published legislation). The English legal system, however, applies the concept of precedent in a more significant way. In certain cases, past decisions constitute *binding* precedents and *must* be followed in subsequent cases, irrespective of whether the courts in those subsequent cases agree with them or not. This is known as the doctrine of binding precedent, or *stare decisis*.

Before any system of binding precedent can operate effectively, two important requirements must be satisfied. First, there must be a reliable system for the full and accurate reporting of judgments. Secondly, there must be a clear hierarchy of courts, so as to make it clear which court's decisions binds which other courts.

As far as the first requirement is concerned, many (but not all) decisions of the superior courts are now reported by barristers who specialise in such work, and some reports (the most definitive) are examined and corrected by the judges responsible before publication, in order to ensure their accuracy. Problems are caused, however, by the non-reporting or delayed reporting of some important decisions, and by the sheer volume of reported case law, which can be very difficult for lawyers or judges to keep up with.

Most modern case references in this book are to the *All England Law Reports* (All ER). These are not in fact regarded as the most authoritative reports, but they are the most widely used and widely available series of 'full text' reports, and some schools and sixth-form colleges subscribe to them. Where full text reports are not available, reference may be made to the law reports published in *The Times*. All House of Lords judgments since November 1996 are fully reported on the Parliament web site (http://www.parliament.uk) within a few hours of publication.

As for the necessity for a clear hierarchy of courts, the Judicature Acts 1873–75, as modified by the Courts Act 1971, established a relatively clear hierarchy, as discussed below.

The courts hierarchy

The House of Lords

The House of Lords is the highest court in the land and its decisions must be followed by all lower courts. Prior to 1966, the House of Lords was bound by its own previous decisions, and the only way in which a rule laid down by the House of Lords could be changed was by means of an Act of Parliament. In 1966, however, the Lord Chancellor issued a *Practice Direction* which stated that the House of Lords would no longer regard itself as absolutely bound by its own previous decisions. Although it has now been given this flexibility, it is clear from various pronouncements from their lordships that the House will not lightly depart from earlier decisions. This is to be welcomed. It is important that the law is applied consistently, and the interests of justice would not be served if the highest court in the land changed its mind on important issues every few months. In a few rare cases, however, it may be necessary for the House of Lords to admit that one of its previous decisions was wrong.

A rare example of the House using its power to depart from a previous decision can be seen in the case of *R* v *Shivpuri* [1986] 2 All ER 334, in which their lordships expressly stated that an earlier House of Lords decision given a few years before in the case of *Anderton* v *Ryan* [1985] 2 All ER 355 (on the interpretation of the Criminal Attempts Act 1981) was wrong. Lord Bridge in *Shivpuri* said:

> ... I am undeterred by the consideration that the decision in *Anderton* v *Ryan* was so recent. The 1966 *Practice Statement* is an effective abandonment of our pretension to infallibility. If a serious error embodied in a decision of this House has distorted the law, the sooner it is corrected the better.

The Court of Appeal (Civil Division)

The Court of Appeal is bound to follow the previous decisions of the House of Lords. Decisions of the Court of Appeal itself are clearly binding on the High Court and the county courts. A more difficult question concerns the extent to which the Court of Appeal is bound by its own previous decisions. The general rule is that it is indeed bound by them. Over the years, however, a number of exceptions to that general rule have been developed. In *Young* v *Bristol Aeroplane Company* [1944] KB 718, the Court of Appeal listed the circumstances under which it can refuse to follow one of its own previous decisions. First, if the previous decision conflicts with a later House of Lords decision, the Court of Appeal must obviously follow the House of Lords. Secondly, if there are two conflicting Court of Appeal decisions (which should never happen, but sometimes does!) then it will have to choose between them. The rejected decision would then lose any binding force it may previously have had on any of the lower courts. Thirdly, the Court of Appeal may depart from one of its previous decisions if it was made *per incuriam*, that is, 'through lack of care'. This may occur, for example, if the Court forgot to have regard to a relevant statutory provision in the previous case. In such a situation, the *per incuriam* decision will again lose any binding force which it may have had on the lower courts. No lower court can dismiss the decision of a higher court as *per incuriam*. In *Broome* v *Cassell & Co.* [1971] 2 QB 354, the Court of Appeal purported to reject an earlier decision of the House of Lords as *per incuriam*, but was reprimanded by the Lords for so doing.

Lord Denning, when he was Master of the Rolls, persistently argued that the Court of Appeal should have greater freedom to depart from its own previous decisions. He actively campaigned for the Court to acquire the same powers as those given to the House of Lords by the *Practice Direction* of 1966. One case in which Lord Denning MR defiantly pushed this idea was that of *Davis* v *Johnson* [1979] AC 264. He said:

> To my mind, this court should apply similar guidelines to those adopted by the House of Lords in 1966. Whenever it appears to this court that a previous decision was wrong, we should be at liberty to depart from it if we think it right to do so . . .

When this case went on appeal, however, their lordships made it quite clear that they were not going to accept any such proposition. Lord Scarman said:

> Lord Denning MR has conducted what may be described, I hope without offence, as a one-man crusade with the object of freeing the Court of Appeal from the shackles which the doctrine of *stare decisis* imposes upon its liberty of decision. . . This House should take this occasion to reaffirm expressly, unequivocally and unanimously that the rule laid down in the *Bristol Aeroplane* case as to *stare decisis* is still binding on the Court of Appeal.

The Court of Appeal (Criminal Division)
This Court is bound to follow the previous decisions of the House of Lords and its own decisions are binding upon all inferior courts. It is also normally bound by its own previous decisions and by those of the old Court of Criminal Appeal (which it replaced in 1968), but because this Court is concerned with the liberty of individuals, the doctrine of precedent is more flexible than in the Civil Division. If the Court thinks that its previous decision is wrong *and* that it may do injustice to the appellant, then it may depart from its own previous decisions in order to quash a conviction that appears to be wrong or unjust.

Divisional Courts
It will be recalled from Chapter 2 that Divisional Courts hear a range of appeals from lower courts. In criminal cases, the Divisional Court is bound by the decisions of the House of Lords and Court of Appeal. Like the Court of Appeal, however, it has claimed the right to depart from its own previous decisions if this is necessary to prevent an unjust conviction.

In civil cases, Divisional Courts are bound by the decisions of the House of Lords, the Court of Appeal (Civil Division) and by their own previous decisions, subject to the same exceptions as were laid down for the Court of Appeal in *Young* v *Bristol Aeroplane Co.*

The High Court

High Court judges hearing first instance cases are bound to follow any relevant precedents set by the House of Lords, the Court of Appeal or Divisional Court. A High Court judge will ordinarily follow the previous decisions of other trial judges, but is not strictly required to do so. This can quite often result in a series of conflicting decisions, which will perplex and unsettle litigants and their legal advisers until such time as the Court of Appeal lays down a binding precedent dealing with the point in question.

Other courts

The Crown Court, county courts and magistrates' courts are all bound by the decisions of the appellate courts and High Court, but do not themselves lay down binding precedents. Indeed, their decisions on points of law are rarely reported at all.

The Judicial Committee of the Privy Council

The Judicial Committee of the Privy Council hears appeals from Commonwealth countries. Its decisions are not, in theory, binding on English courts. In practice, however, the status of Privy Council decisions is so high that English courts treat them with almost as much respect as decisions of the House of Lords. Indeed, the judges who sit on the Judicial Committee of the Privy Council are usually law lords, sitting in a different capacity.

Conflicting precedents

Where conflicting precedents are laid down by the appellate courts, the problem for subsequent trial judges is one of deciding which precedent to follow. If the House of Lords has overruled previous decisions of its own or of the Court of Appeal, then there is no conflict, because the new decision of the House of Lords is clearly the precedent to be followed; but what if a decision of the House of Lords appears to have been misapplied or misunderstood by a *subsequent* decision of the Court of Appeal? Should a trial judge ignore this Court of Appeal ruling, and go back to the House of Lords case as the precedent to rely on; or should the judge regard himself as bound by the Court of Appeal's interpretation of what the House of Lords decided, even if he is sure it is wrong? The answer appears to be that he should follow his immediate superiors in the Court of Appeal. In *Miliangos* v *George Frank (Textiles) Ltd* [1975] 3 All ER 801, Lord Simon said:

> It is the duty of the subordinate court to give effect to the decision of the immediately higher court, notwithstanding that it may appear to conflict with the decision of a still higher court. The decision of the still higher court must be assumed to have been correctly distinguished (or otherwise interpreted) in the decision of the immediate higher court ...

What if a decision of the Court of Appeal has been disapproved by a powerful and authoritative ruling of the Privy Council? As explained above, the judges who sit on the Judicial Committee of the Privy Council are usually law lords, and under normal circumstances their rulings are treated with much the same authority. In *Doughty* v *Turner Manufacturing Co. Ltd* [1964] 1 All ER 98, the Court of Apeal followed a ruling of the Privy Council in preference to a much older decision of its own, but it appears that judges at first instance are obliged to follow a Court of Appeal ruling. In *Campbell* [1997] 1 Cr App R 199 Lord Bingham CJ warned judges of the Crown Court that they were obliged to follow the Court of Appeal's interpretation of the law relating to provocation in homicide cases, rather than the conflicting view of the Privy Council. (On this particular conflict of precedents, see p. 185.)

Which part of a judgment is binding?

Not every part of a judgment given by a court will be binding. It is only that part which contains the *reason* for the decision which can form a binding precedent. This is known as the *ratio decidendi*. Professor Cross in *Precedent in English Law* states:

> The *ratio decidendi* of a case is any rule of law expressly or impliedly treated by the judge as a necessary step in reaching his conclusion, having regard to the line of reasoning adopted by him, or a necessary part of his direction to the jury.

It is not always easy to ascertain what the *ratio decidendi* of a particular case may have been, as the judges do not always make this clear. Cases heard by the Court of Appeal and the House of Lords are heard by three or five judges, and in many cases each of those judges will give his own separate judgment. If each of the judges gives a slightly different reason for his decision, it can sometimes be difficult to discover any single *ratio decidendi* in the case as a whole. An illustration of this problem can be seen in *Hyam* v *Director of Public Prosecutions* [1974] 2 All ER 41, where by a majority of three to two the House of Lords upheld Mrs Hyam's conviction for murder. Each of the three majority judges gave a different reason. The disagreement arose from their different interpretations of the law of murder and of the meaning of intention in the criminal law as a whole. As a result of their failure to agree as to why Mrs Hyam was guilty, the law of murder was left in a considerable state of confusion for many years.

A judge may give two or more possible reasons for the decision, and each of them may form the *rationes* of the case ('I find for the defendant on the basis of reason A, and also on the basis of reason B'). In other cases, however, the judge will make it clear that the decision is based on A alone, and that although the judge suspects B would justify the same result, he does not seek to rely upon it. In such cases, the judge's observations on point B are *obiter* ('by the way') and are not binding on any other court or judge. In other cases again, the judge may unfortunately fail to make it entirely clear whether B is one of the reasons for his decision, or whether his observations thereon are merely *obiter*.

Furthermore, the judge may also discuss a number of matters in his judgment which may not be directly relevant to the case in hand. For example, he may speculate as to what the position would have been had the facts been slightly different. Such comments (or *dicta*) are also deemed to be *obiter*. *Obiter dicta* do not form part of any binding precedent, but they may sometimes be highly persuasive. They may, for example, be cited and applied in a later case in which the facts envisaged by the judge in the earlier case have actually arisen.

The *dicta* of judges in appellate cases may be very persuasive. An example may be seen in the landmark case of *Hedley Byrne* v *Heller & Partners* [1963] 2 All ER 575. The importance of *Hedley Byrne* v *Heller* was that the House of Lords recognised, for the first time, that a plaintiff might recover damages in tort for economic loss caused by reliance on negligent misstatements or advice (see further Chapter 39). The defendants in that case had been guilty of giving negligent advice as to the creditworthiness of a company with whom the plaintiffs were doing business. The plaintiffs lost money through reliance upon this advice, but the defendants had prefaced it with an exclusion clause in which they warned that their advice was given without liability, and it was held that this disclaimer was valid. This being the case, it might be argued that everything that was said about the existence of potential liability for negligent misstatement was *obiter*. If that is so (and it is a highly contentious point!) the *ratio* of the case is to be found in a couple of sentences at the end, and none of the rest is of any binding force. Worse still, it would mean that earlier decisions of the Court of Appeal, denying that liability could ever arise for such statements, would remain binding on lower courts. Although that may theoretically be true, the fact remains that a carefully considered analysis of the law by a unanimous House of Lords will be treated by ordinary judges as a statement of binding law. Cairns J so held in *W. B. Anderson & Sons Ltd* v *Rhodes Ltd* [1967] 2 All ER 850, where he stated:

> An academic lawyer might be prepared to contend that the opinions expressed by their lordships about liability for negligent misstatements were *obiter*, and that *Candler* v *Crane, Christmas & Co.* [[1951] 2 KB 164 — an earlier case which did not accept liability for negligent misstatements except under very limited circumstances] is still a binding decision. In my judgment that would be an unrealistic view to take. When five members of the House of Lords have all said, after close examination of the authorities, that a certain type of tort exists, I think that a judge of first instance should proceed on the basis that it does exist without pausing to embark on an investigation of whether what was said was necessary to the ultimate decision.

Avoiding precedents

A criticism which is often levelled against the doctrine of binding precedent is that it leads to rigidity in the system. There are, however, various ways in which judges may sometimes avoid following a previous decision.

Distinguishing

A judge may be able to distinguish an earlier case from the present case on its facts and thus avoid following it. No two cases will ever be wholly identical. The question is whether certain differences between them are material. If the only differences are trivial and immaterial, the existing precedent should be followed. If, however, the material facts in a later case are slightly different from those in the earlier one, then the earlier decision may have to be expanded or modified in order to accommodate this different set of facts. And if there is a very significant difference in the facts, the existing precedent may be wholly inapplicable.

A simple example may help. Suppose that A is attacked by B with a nine-inch knife. It is a warm sunny day and B is wearing blue shorts and a green shirt. Fearing for his life, A picks up a poker and hits B across the temple, whereupon B dies. A is found to have acted in lawful self-defence. In another case, two years later, the facts are that C is attacked by D with an eight-inch knife. It is a cold and miserable day and D is wearing jeans and a leather jacket. Fearing for his life, C picks up a brick and hits D across the head, whereupon D dies. Are the material facts of this later case similar to those in the previous case? The differences between them are: (i) the knives were of different lengths; (ii) the weather conditions were different; (iii) the attackers were different persons and were dressed differently; and (iv) the instruments used to strike the fatal blows were different. Are those differences material in this situation? Surely not! The cases remain remarkably similar in all material respects. If A was entitled to rely on self-defence, then C should also be allowed to, and should similarly be acquitted. If, however, C had been spat upon by D, and had killed or injured him in a sudden fit of temper, there would indeed have been a material difference, namely that C's actions, even if provoked, could not have been justified by the need to protect his own life.

The following actual cases are concerned with the issue of causation under criminal law. They illustrate how cases can be distinguished and how this leads to the growth and development of the law. In *Jordan* (1956) 40 Cr App R 152, Jordan stabbed Beaumont who eventually died. He was convicted of murder. Later, further medical evidence came to light and he appealed against his conviction. The evidence was that when Beaumont was admitted to hospital, he had been treated with a certain type of antibiotic to which he proved highly allergic. Despite his reaction to the drugs, Beaumont survived and began to make a good recovery. Unfortunately, a different doctor, who had obviously not read Beaumont's notes, prescribed a further large dose of the same antibiotic, and this killed him. The Court of Criminal Appeal held that Jordan's conviction for murder could not be allowed to stand. The repeated administration of the antibiotic had been an extraordinary and unforeseeable form of medical treatment and he could not be held responsible for that. In other words, the initial wound had ceased to be a substantial and operating cause of death and the negligent medical treatment had broken the 'chain of causation'. Jordan was clearly guilty of wounding, but he was not guilty of homicide.

The facts of *Jordan* can be contrasted with the later case of *Smith* [1959] 2 All ER 193. Smith was a soldier who became involved in a drunken fight with other soldiers in the barracks. He stabbed private Creed with a bayonet and Creed eventually died. As in *Jordan*, there was evidence that medical treatment (or mistreatment) had made matters worse. Creed's friends had dropped him twice on the way over to the medical centre and the army doctor had made a hurried and incorrect diagnosis of Creed's injuries. He failed to recognise that the bayonet had pierced Creed's lung. With proper medical treatment Creed would have survived. On the face of it, you may think that *Smith* is like *Jordan*, but the Court held that it was different from *Jordan* in that the bayonet wound was still a substantial and operating cause of death. The doctor had simply failed to treat it properly, but it was still the wound, not the doctor, which killed Creed. *Smith* does not overrule *Jordan*. Each case was correctly decided on its own facts. The facts, however, were materially different.

Overruling

If the Court of Appeal, Divisional Court or House of Lords refuse to follow the earlier decision of a judge or court which is not binding on them, it is said that the earlier decision has been overruled. The parties in the previous case are still bound by that decision (which must be very galling for the party which lost!), but when a case is overruled in this way, it loses its authority and will not be followed ever again.

One associated issue which is worthy of mention at this point is that of reversing. This is concerned not with a previous case, but with the same case which has gone on appeal. When a case goes on appeal, the first judgment may be reversed by the appellate court, and the party which originally lost becomes the winner.

Disapproval and refusal to follow

A court may sometimes express disapproval of a previous decision without going so far as to overrule it. (A High Court judge, for example, is not bound by the earlier decision of one of his fellow judges, but he cannot overrule such a decision.) The effect of expressing such dissent is to weaken the authority of the earlier case.

Advantages and disadvantages of the doctrine of binding precedent

Advantages

(a)   Precedent brings consistency to the English legal system, in that two cases with similar material facts will be treated in the same manner. No legal system can be perceived as fair unless everyone receives equal treatment.

(b)   A valuable effect of the doctrine of precedent is predictability. This enables lawyers to advise their clients with some degree of certainty. They can tell their clients, for example, that their proposed course of action would be upheld by the courts, or that they will inevitably lose their current lawsuit and should settle the other party's claims.

Disadvantages

(a)   It may be argued that the doctrine of binding precedent can lead to rigidity and inflexibility. (But note the methods which can be used by the judges to circumvent this.)

(b)   There is no doubt that the doctrine can lead to the perpetuation, often for long periods of time, of bad decisions. Sometimes, it is openly acknowledged that a binding precedent is a bad one, but the courts may be very slow to respond to rectify the problem.

(c)   Attempts to distinguish unwanted precedents, in order to avoid having to follow them, may sometimes lead to the drawing of vague or imaginary distinctions, which will only serve to confuse lawyers in subsequent cases. There is a saying, indeed, that 'hard cases make bad law'.

Do judges make law?

An issue frequently raised in the context of judicial precedent is whether judges make law. It is sometimes said that they do not, but merely decide cases in accordance with existing legal rules. In other words, they merely declare law which already exists. This 'declaratory theory' is, with respect, manifest nonsense, because the common law could never have developed on such a basis, and today there are few judges who would deny that they do in fact make, shape and develop the law.

Judges may influence the development of the law in a number of ways. For example, a judge may follow a previous precedent if he approves of the rule it embodies or may be able to distinguish it from the present case if he would prefer not to follow it. Distinguishing a particular case may have the effect of preventing or restricting the development of the law along a certain avenue.

Sometimes the issue before the judge may be an entirely new one. In such situations the judge may come to a conclusion by drawing analogies with cases that are similar only in certain limited respects. A rule for the present case may be created out of these. Furthermore, as we saw above, Parliament cannot legislate for every possible future eventuality and the courts frequently have to fill in the gaps left by statutes. The law of theft, for example, is stated only in outline by the Theft Act 1968. Much of the law is now contained within the many cases decided under that legislation, and the statute can no longer be understood without reference to those cases.

In summary, therefore, the generally held view today is that the judges do make law, both on a case-by-case basis and through their role in the interpretation of statutes. This prevents the law from stagnating, but does, unfortunately, introduce an element of unpredictability into the decision-making process. Lawyers may have to advise their clients that although the law as currently stated seems to give them no chance of success (or apparently *guarantees* them success), it is possible that the law will be overturned when the House of Lords next considers the issue; and this may be in the client's own case. This is not really satisfactory, even if the unpredictability stems from the judges' search for improvements to the existing legal rules.

CUSTOM AS A SOURCE OF LAW

Prior to the development of the common law, custom was a form of law-making. Custom develops within primitive legal systems by means of people developing a practice of doing certain things in certain ways. Through such common usage, it gradually develops into a proper custom which is regarded as having binding legal effect. A number of the principal rules of public international law developed in this way. (International law remains a primitive system of law, without any sovereign legislative body which can impose law on its subjects.) As a state develops, however, law-making becomes more advanced and custom as a form of rule becomes less important. Under today's English legal system, custom as a source of law is practically non-existent.

Local custom

The only way in which custom may still play even a very minor role is in terms of local custom. A local custom involves ancient usage which has obtained the force of law and is binding within a particular area or place upon the persons or things which it concerns.

Before a court will recognise the existence of a local custom, the court must be satisfied as to the following factors:

(a) the custom must have existed since time immemorial (i.e., beyond living memory and as far as published records exist);
(b) it must have been observed continuously and without interruption;
(c) it must not be unreasonable;

    (d)   it must not be contrary to statute;

    (e)   it must be certain or clear in its effect; and

    (f)   it must apply to a definite locality.

Customary international law

One can perhaps add customary international law to the above. Customary international law develops when states regularly behave in a certain way, and eventually come to consider themselves legally obliged to continue so doing. For example, the practice of affording diplomatic immunity to foreign ambassadors and their staff developed as a convenient form of state practice, but eventually (perhaps imperceptibly) hardened into a sacred (and very rarely infringed) rule of international law. Customary international law is recognised by the courts of England and Wales, and is deemed to be incorporated automatically within English law (*The 'Parlement Belge'* (1879) 4 PD 129; *Maclaine Watson* v *Department of Trade and Industry* [1989] 3 All ER 523). In the latter case, however, the House of Lords confirmed that, although rules of customary international law must be given effect to in the English courts as an integral part of English law, obligations created by treaties (or 'international conventions') can become part of English law only if legislation is passed to that effect. For example, the Treaties of the European Community and European Union could never have had effect in English law in the absence of legislation enacted for that purpose. Were this not so, the government could make new law merely by concluding treaties with foreign states, thereby usurping the role of Parliament.

SECONDARY SOURCES OF LAW

Legal textbooks or monographs and articles published in learned journals all have some effect on the development of the law. For most purposes, they can best be described as secondary sources. They do not, in theory, make the law, but merely explain (and perhaps criticise) the law as it is made by Parliament and the courts (the 'primary sources' of the law). The influence of textbooks and articles is usually subtle, but occasionally the courts openly decide a case on the basis of the view expressed in a published work. An example is provided by the House of Lords in the important case of *Shivpuri* [1986] 2 All ER 334. A previous decision of the Lords (*Anderton* v *Ryan* [1985] 2 All ER 355) had been savagely criticised in an article by Professor Glanville Williams of Cambridge University. He had argued that their lordships had completely misunderstood the true meaning of the Criminal Attempts Act 1981. In *Shivpuri*, their lordships, led by one of the principal 'offenders' from *Anderton* v *Ryan*, thanked Professor Glanville Williams for pointing out their error, and promptly overruled their earlier decision.

FOUR

The European Dimension

European law does not exist as a single concept, although it is sometimes incorrectly treated as such. One must distinguish between the European Community and the European Union, on the one hand, and the European Convention on Human Rights, on the other. Although the United Kingdom's membership of the European Community is closely linked to its membership of the European Union, neither has any connection with the Human Rights Convention, which is enforced by the European Court of Human Rights in Strasbourg.

THE EUROPEAN COMMUNITY AND EUROPEAN UNION

The European Community

By virtue of the European Communities Act 1972, the United Kingdom became a member of what were then three distinct entities, namely the European Coal and Steel Community (ECSC), the European Atomic Energy Community (Euratom) and the European Economic Community (EEC). The most important of these was the EEC, which was created by the Treaty of Rome in 1957. The ECSC and Euratom have now effectively been absorbed into the EEC, and since the Maastricht Treaty of 1992, this has been known (in the singular) as the European Community, or EC.

One of the main objectives of the Treaty of Rome was to develop stability throughout Europe by means of encouraging a closer union between member states. One way to achieve such a union was by developing economic unity through the elimination of trade barriers between member states (i.e., the

'Common Market'). Furthermore, the Community developed its own institutions and laws and became able to regulate the rights and obligations of member states, at least in the economic field.

The European Union

Throughout the 1980s and 1990s, attempts have been made to achieve ever greater unity throughout Europe by continuing the development of economic unity and striving towards the ultimate aim of both political and financial unity. Progress in these areas has been made through the implementation of the Single European Act (SEA) which was incorporated into United Kingdom law by the European Communities (Amendment) Act 1986; by the 1992 Treaty on European Union (the Maastricht Treaty) which was incorporated into United Kingdom law by the European Communities (Amendment) Act 1993; and by the 1997 Treaty of Amsterdam on European Union, which pushes member states into closer cooperation in areas such as foreign policy, defence and criminal justice.

The SEA's main aim is to realise the original objectives laid down in the original European Communities Treaties, namely the establishment of the true freedom of movement of goods and services within the European Community. The aims of the Maastricht Treaty, on the other hand, are more far-reaching. Its overall goal is to move the European states to a position of true European union. The preamble to the Treaty states that its aim is to continue the process of unification through means of economic and monetary union, including the development of a single common currency, common citizenship, common foreign and security policies, a common defence policy and common justice and home affairs policies. The European Union is a political concept to which many politicians in Europe are striving to aspire and of which the European Community will merely be a part. The European Community will still be regulated by the institutions of the Community, which will be looked at in detail below. In contrast, decisions affecting common foreign, security, home and justice affairs will be reached by way of inter-government cooperation. The Maastricht Treaty, however, has given rise to much controversy and it is far too early to say whether it will prove to be a success. In particular, it is doubtful whether the peoples of Europe really want such a degree of unity. If they do not, the whole enterprise may be doomed to failure.

Institutions of the Community

The principal institutions of the Community are:

(a)   the Commission;
(b)   the Council of Ministers;
(c)   the European Parliament (formerly known as the Assembly); and

(d)   the European Court of Justice (not to be confused with the Court of Human Rights).

The Commission

The Commission is at the heart of the Community and is concerned with all aspects of Community decision-making. Articles 155 to 163 of the Treaty of Rome deal with the Commission's powers. It consists of representatives drawn from member states, and each member state provides at least one (but not more than two) commissioners. Appointees hold office for five years, at the end of which they may be re-appointed. Commissioners are independent, and are not representatives of their governments.

The Council of Ministers

This is the principal legislative body of the Community and it also exercises executive powers. It comprises ministerial representatives from each member state, each of whom is authorised to act on behalf of the governments of their respective states and obviously is expected to defend their respective state's own interests. Each member state acts as President of the Council for rotational periods of six months. The Council of Ministers meets only at intervals as its members have responsibilities to attend to within their own member states. Therefore, in order to preserve continuity, a Committee of Permanent Representatives (COPERER) was set up which carries out much of the Council's routine work.

There are three basic methods by which the Council may reach a decision. Most issues merely require adoption by means of a simple majority vote, whereas others demand a unanimous vote, as for example where the Council wishes to implement a new policy or modify an existing one. In a third type of case, however, decisions must be taken by means of a 'qualified majority vote' which is linked to a system of weighted voting. The largest states, namely Germany, France, Italy and the United Kingdom, have ten votes each, while the smallest have only two. A minority group of larger states may therefore be able to outvote the rest.

The European Parliament

The European Parliament was formerly known as the European Assembly. It was given its new name by the SEA, but it is not a Parliament in the same sense as the British Parliament. It is not a supreme legislative body. Prior to the SEA, it had a purely advisory and supervisory role (although it has always played an important role in the approval of the Community budget, and actually rejected a proposed budget in 1979). The SEA and the European Union Treaty 1992, have, however, increased its legislative powers. It now plays a far greater role in the legislative process and in the scrutiny of the actions of other Community institutions. Indeed, the European Parliament's role in the legislative process is now one of its most significant features.

At one time, members were appointed from their respective national Parliaments, but since 1979 members have been directly elected by the voters of member states. Elections are held every five years and, as one would expect, the larger states supply more representatives than the smaller ones. There is not, however, any exact correlation between the size of a country and the number of members it elects. The United Kingdom elects only 14 times as many members as Luxembourg, but has 150 times its population.

The European Court of Justice

The European Court of Justice (ECJ) consists of judges nominated by each member state. These are assisted by six Community law experts, known as Advocates-General. The role of the Advocates-General is unlike anything we have in the United Kingdom. They are not judges of the Court, nor do they represent the parties, but instead they carry out independent reviews of the cases to which they are assigned, and present their own findings and analysis to the judges of the Court.

The Court's primary function is to ensure the legal enforcement of Community obligations and to ensure that Community law is uniformly applied throughout the member states, but it also has an increasingly important role in reviewing the legality of the acts of the Community's own institutions. Under Article 173(1) of the Treaty of Rome:

> The Court of Justice shall review the acts of the Council and the Commission other than recommendations or opinions. It shall for this purpose have jurisdiction in actions brought by a member state, the Council or the Commission on grounds of lack of competence, infringement of an essential procedural requirement, infringement of this Treaty or of any rule of law relating to its applications, or misuse of powers.

Under Article 174, the Court shall, if the action is well-founded, declare the act complained of to be void. This power enables the Court to strike down or restrain high-handed or irregular law-making activity on the part of the Council or Commission; much in the same way as the High Court may be required to strike down or restrain improper use of the power to make delegated legislation under English law.

Jurisdiction under Article 177

It is considered important that Community law should be applied and uniformly interpreted in all member states. To that end, cases raising issues of Community law can be referred to the Court of Justice, either by direct actions, which are normally available to the Commission or to member states, or through references by national courts of member states under Article 177 of the Treaty of Rome. Article 177 states:

(1)   The Court of Justice shall have jurisdiction to give preliminary rulings concerning:

(a)   the interpretation of this Treaty;

(b)   the validity and interpretation of acts of the institutions of the Community;

(c)   the interpretation of the statutes of bodies established by an act of the Council, where those statutes so provide.

(2)   Where such a question is raised before any court or tribunal of a member state, that court or tribunal may, if it considers that a decision on the question is necessary to enable it to give judgment, request the Court of Justice to give a ruling thereon.

(3)   Where any such question is raised in a case pending before a court or tribunal of a member state, against whose decisions there is no judicial remedy under national law, that court or tribunal shall bring the matter before the Court of Justice.

It follows that any national court or tribunal may refer a question which turns upon an interpretation of Community law for an authoritative ruling from the ECJ. Meanwhile, the case in the national court or tribunal will be suspended pending a ruling from the ECJ. The national court or tribunal is then obliged to apply the ECJ's ruling in reaching its decision. Where, however, a case is pending in a court or tribunal 'against whose decisions there is no judicial remedy under national law', no discretion exists and the case *must* be referred to the ECJ for a ruling. This provision obviously applies to the House of Lords (i.e., because there is no higher court in the country). This does not mean, however, that it is only the House of Lords to which this duty can apply. There are some types of case which cannot be appealed as far as the House of Lords, and Article 177 will therefore apply to the highest court to which that particular case can be referred. (See *Bulmer Ltd* v *J. Bollinger SA* [1974] 2 All ER 1226.)

Sources of Community law

The Treaties are the primary sources of European Community law, but the provisions contained within the Treaties are broadly framed, and usually require detailed implementation in order to take effect. Such detailed implementation can take a number of different forms. Article 189 of the Treaty of Rome (as amended) states:

In order to carry out their task and in accordance with the provisions of this Treaty, the European Parliament acting jointly with the Council, the Council and the Commission shall make regulations and issue directives, take decisions, make recommendations or deliver opinions.

Regulations and directives are properly described as sources of Community law, and are discussed below. Recommendations and opinions lack legal force, and are not therefore true sources of law. Decisions have legal force, in so far as they are binding on the states to whom they are addressed, but they are arguably administrative, rather than legislative, in character.

Regulations

Regulations have general application. They are 'binding in their entirety and directly applicable in all member states'. They must accordingly be given direct effect by national courts. Member states do not have to take any further action to bring them into force. Regulations may also confer rights upon individuals which can be enforced in the national courts.

Directives

Directives are more widely used than regulations. They are one of the most important instruments used by the EC for the purpose of harmonising the laws of member states. Like regulations, they are binding upon the member states to which they are addressed, but leave the appropriate method of implementation to be decided by the member state. This means that the member state may decide what form the implementation should take and the method by which it should be passed into law. Directives will usually be implemented into English law by means of statutory instruments, an example of which is provided by the Unfair Terms in Consumer Contracts Regulations (see Chapter 34); but implementation may sometimes require an Act of Parliament, an example of which is provided by the provisions of the Consumer Protection Act 1987, dealing with defective products (see Chapter 38).

Directives set time limits within which member states are required to implement them (although states sometimes fail to comply with those limits) and they may confer rights on private individuals, which may be enforced in the courts of member states (see below).

Rights of individuals and companies under Community law

Occasionally a provision will have the effect of bestowing individual legal rights upon individuals or companies within the Community. These rights will be enforceable by such persons in the municipal courts of their respective member states. They are known as directly effective rights. Most such rights arise out of directly applicable provisions, such as regulations, but they can also arise, under limited circumstances, from provisions in directives. Whether or not a Community provision has direct effect will normally be a matter of adjudication for the national court before whom the issue arises. If the national court requires guidance upon the issue, it may refer the question to the ECJ under Article 177.

Situations where provisions may have direct effect

Treaties

In *Van Gend en Loos* v *Nederlandse Administratie der Belastingen* [1963] ECR 1, it was established that individuals may, in limited circumstances, have rights conferred upon them directly under Community treaties. These rights may be enforced both against the individual's own state and against other individuals. A treaty provision will have direct effect, however, only if:

(a)   it is clear and precise;
(b)   it establishes an unconditional obligation;
(c)   it does not depend upon further state action for its implementation; and
(d)   it does not relate to inter-state relations alone.

A number of Treaty of Rome provisions have been held by the ECJ to have direct effect. Thus, Article 119, which states that men and women should receive equal pay for equal work, has been held to be directly effective (*Defrenne* v *Sabena* [1976] ECR 205).

Regulations and decisions

Many regulations have direct effect against both the state and other individuals. Decisions are directly binding on those to whom they are addressed.

Directives

Directives do not ordinarily have direct effect (hence the need for implementation by statute or statutory instrument) but they may nevertheless, under limited circumstances, give rise to directly enforceable rights. The ECJ so held in *Grad* v *Finanzampt Traunstein* [1970] ECR 825 and this was confirmed in the later case of *Van Duyn* v *Home Office* [1975] 3 All ER 190, in which the court held that the United Kingdom was bound by a directive on freedom of movement within the Community, even though that directive had never been implemented by the British government. In some circumstances, failure to implement a directive may lead to a claim for damages being made by an aggrieved individual against the state concerned. It would have to be shown, however, that the alleged failure of implementation caused financial loss to the claimant as in *Francovich* v *Italy* [1991] ECR I-5357 where the Italian government's failure to implement a directive on the rights of employees in insolvency cases deprived Francovich of payments of salary arrears to which he would otherwise have become entitled; and the government was required to compensate him for this loss.

Where a directive is deemed to have direct effect, it can only be enforceable against the member state or its organs, and not against private individuals or corporations. The concept of a state has been widely defined. In *Foster* v *British Gas* [1990] 3 All ER 897, it was held that a directive could be enforced against 'organisations or bodies which are subject to the authority or control of the state'. This would include any public bodies, which British Gas still was at that time (before privatisation), but only as long as they provide a public service. In *Marshall* v *Southampton and South West Hampshire Area Health Authority* [1986] 2 All ER 584, the plaintiff had been employed for many years by the health authority, but was forced to retire at the age of 62. At that time, the normal retirement age for women was 60, but it was 65 for men. She brought an action under the Equal Treatment Directive, on the basis that she had suffered discrimination on the grounds of sex. The health authority argued that the directive could only be invoked against a member state. The ECJ accepted that argument, but held that the health authority was an organ or agent of the state, even when acting in its capacity as an employer. The ECJ accordingly rejected the health authority's argument that the directive could not apply directly to it.

Community law and Parliamentary supremacy

Britain's membership of the European Community raises the constitutional issue of how this has affected the legislative supremacy of Parliament. The traditional principle of Parliamentary supremacy is that Parliament is legislatively omnipotent: it can 'make or unmake any law whatsoever; and no person or body is recognised by the law of England as having a right to override or set aside the legislation of Parliament'. The question then arises of the extent, if any, to which the United Kingdom has surrendered its Parliamentary supremacy as a result of joining the European Community.

The ECJ itself has made it quite clear in numerous cases over the years — such as that of *Costa* v *ENEL* [1964] ECR 585 — that in the event of a conflict between Community law and national law, the former ought to prevail. The European Communities Act 1972, s. 2(1), provides that all directly applicable and directly effective provisions are to be given effect in the United Kingdom, while other matters are to be dealt with either by statute or by statutory instruments. If an existing United Kingdom statute is followed by inconsistent directly applicable or directly effective provisions of Community law, the European Communities Act 1972 makes it clear that it is Community law which must prevail. But what if legislation is passed *after* the Community provision which is inconsistent with that legislation? If the wording of the subsequent Act is unclear or ambiguous, the courts will certainly attempt to interpret the Act and the Community provisions in such a way as to avoid any conflict. But what if attempts at reconciling the inconsistent provisions fail? According to traditional constitutional doctrine, primacy should be given to the subsequent statute. In the important case of *R* v *Secretary of State for Transport, ex parte Factortame (No. 2)* [1991] AC 603, however, the House of Lords accepted the supremacy of Community law. The case concerned a number of fishing vessels that were supposedly owned by British companies and counted against British fishing quotas. The companies, however, were themselves owned by Spanish shareholders. New regulations passed under the Merchant Shipping Act 1988 required applicants for fishing permits to show that their ships (or any companies that owned them) were at least 75 per cent British owned. This appeared to conflict with existing Community law, in so far as it discriminated against the nationals of other member states. The House of Lords recognised that if the regulations were indeed inconsistent with directly enforceable EC law, the EC law would have to be recognised as supreme and the regulations declared invalid. (This indeed is what the ECJ subsequently decided.)

Problems may arise where there is real doubt as to whether a new statute is indeed inconsistent with EC law. The courts will be slow to suspend the application of British legislation, pending the outcome of a reference to the ECJ, as the Court of Appeal held in *R v HM Treasury, ex parte British Telecommunications plc, The Times*, 2 December 1993, but where a statute clearly infringes directly enforceable EC law the courts will now hold it to be invalid. In *R v Secretary of State for Employment, ex parte Seymour-Smith* [1997] 2 All ER 273, the House of Lords held that certain provisions of the Employment Protection (Consolidation) Act 1978, which allegedly discriminated against female employees, were invalid if and in so far as they infringed Article 119 of the Treaty of Rome and related directives. The question as to whether Article 119 was infringed was referred to the European Court of Justice.

THE EUROPEAN CONVENTION ON HUMAN RIGHTS

The European Convention on Human Rights (ECHR) was drafted under the auspices of the Council of Europe, an international organisation composed of 25 European states, which was formed in 1949 as part of a post-war effort to promote unity in Europe. The major impetus behind its formation was to form a bastion against the spread of Communism and to prevent any reoccurrence of the horrific conditions and scenes witnessed by Europe during the Second World War. Many of the states which are party to the Convention are also members of the European Community and European Union, but it must be emphasised that the ECHR is not, in any other sense, connected to the EC or EU.

The ECHR came into force on 3 September 1953, and is mainly concerned with the protection of civil and political rights. Article 2 imposes strict limits on the right of any member state to execute criminals or use lethal force in upholding its laws; Article 3 states that no person shall be subjected to torture or to inhuman or degrading treatment or punishment; Article 4 outlaws slavery, servitude and (save in specified circumstances) forced labour; Article 5 protects personal liberty, outlawing detention or imprisonment imposed otherwise than in accordance with certain procedures prescribed by law; Article 6 guarantees everyone the right to a fair and public trial of any civil issue or of criminal charges against them, upholding the presumption of innocence in criminal cases, the right to legal representation (free representation if necessary), the right to call witnesses and the right of the defendant to cross-examine witnesses who give evidence against him. Article 7 prohibits the imposition of criminal penalties for acts which were not recognised as criminal when they were done; Article 8 states that everyone has the right to respect for their private and family life, their home and their private correspondence, etc; Article 9 upholds freedom of thought, conscience and religion; Article 10 upholds the right to freedom of expression; Article 11 upholds the right to freedom of peaceful assembly (subject to constraints which may be necessary for the protection of public safety, national security or civil order); and Article 12 upholds the right to marry and raise a family. Additional 'protocols' have been added which deal with matters such as the right to enjoy property, the right to education and the right to freedom of movement or residence within the territory of a member state. The above rights must all be secured without discrimination on grounds of race, sex, religion, etc. (Article 14 of the Convention). A further protocol abolishing the death penalty has not as yet been agreed to by the UK (although it is likely that the death penalty for treason, piracy and mutiny within the armed forces will soon be abolished in any event).

If any state which is party to the ECHR is found by the Court of Human Rights at Strasbourg to have broken its provisions, that state will be obliged to change its laws so as to comply with the Convention, or it will be in breach of its obligations under that Convention. It must be stressed, however, that offending laws cannot automatically be declared invalid, and improper convictions, etc, cannot automatically be set aside.

The ECHR can be enforced by means of both state and individual applications. Very few state applications have been brought, but two applications were brought by Ireland against the UK in 1971 and 1972, concerning the mistreatment of terrorist suspects by security forces in Northern Ireland. The UK subsequently modified its treatment of such suspects.

The majority of claims are brought by individuals. For example, in *Malone v United Kingdom* (1985) 7 EHRR 14, the applicant brought a claim against the UK over allegations that the tapping of his telephone conversations by the police was a breach of his right to privacy under the Convention.

The ECHR has led to many improvements to laws governing civil liberties in the UK. For example, before the Malone case, there was no official procedure or independent observer to deal with interceptions of mail and telecommunications by the police and security services. The procedure was totally secretive and free of any external scrutiny. When the Court held that such a system was inconsistent with Article 8 of the Convention, the British government felt obliged to introduce a properly regulated system in respect of mail and telecommunication intercepts, which it did through the Interception of Communications Act 1985. Under this Act, an intercept may only be legal if a warrant is authorised by the Secretary of State under any one of a number of specified grounds. Although the government did the minimum in order to comply with the Court's judgment, the Act nevertheless represented a significant step forward.

The Human Rights Bill 1998

Treaties or Conventions (unlike customary international law) do not automatically become part of UK municipal law. They can only be so incorporated by Act of Parliament. At the time of writing (April 1998) the United Kingdom was currently one of the few parties to the ECHR which had not adopted that Convention into their own systems of law. This largely explains the relatively high number of complaints brought against the UK in Strasbourg. The law of England (or Scotland or Northern Ireland) is not especially bad in this respect; but whereas complainants in most other states can have the Convention enforced within their own courts, this is not true of the UK. Where UK law infringes the ECHR, aggrieved persons have always had to take their complaints to Strasbourg. In many cases, they have succeeded there (to the public discomfort of the British government), but usually long after the event complained of, and often too late to compensate them properly for the injustice in question. It has often taken three or more years for cases to be heard by the Court of Human Rights, added to which will be a further time lapse of another year or two before the British government has enacted any necessary legislation to remedy the problem.

The Labour government which came to power in 1997 quickly declared its intention to pass a Human Rights Act, incorporating the ECHR into the municipal laws of the UK. At the time of writing, the Human Rights Bill was before Parliament, and may well have been enacted by the time that this book is published; but the exact form of the Bill may change during its passage through committee stages, etc., and the following discussion is necessarily confined to the original structure of the Bill.

The general scheme of the Human Rights Bill

The government might perhaps have chosen to put forward legislation which enabled the courts to declare invalid any law inconsistent with ECHR, much as they now do with any law which is inconsistent with EC law. This is not, however, the approach chosen for the Human Rights Bill, which continues to recognise the concept of Parliamentary sovereignty; it recognises, in other words, that Parliament may still, if it chooses, enact legislation which is totally inconsistent with the ECHR and that the courts would be obliged to give effect to such legislation. Instead, the Bill requires the courts to interpret legislation (primary or delegated; past or future) in such a way as to make it compatible with the ECHR, but only 'so far as it is possible to do so' (clause 3). It will enable the courts to reject previous (and otherwise binding) interpretations of legislation, if an alternative interpretation would avoid incompatibility with the ECHR; but if the legislation in question is quite clearly incompatible, the only option left for the courts is to apply it and make a 'declaration of incompatibility', drawing the government's attention to the problem. Only the 'higher courts', such as the High Court, Court of Appeal or House of Lords, will be authorised to make such a declaration, and it will not 'affect the validity, continuing operation or enforcement of the provision in respect of which it is given' (clause 4(6) of the Bill). The enactment of subsequent legislation contravening the terms of the ECHR is nevertheless discouraged: ministers presenting new Bills before Parliament will be required either to state that the Bill is consistent with the ECHR, or to acknowledge openly (and no doubt controversially) that it is not (clause 19).

Public authorities (including local authorities, the police and courts or tribunals) must act in accordance with the terms of the ECHR, unless primary legislation obliges them to do otherwise. Actions which are inconsistent with the ECHR may be declared unlawful by the High Court in judicial review proceedings brought by an aggrieved party. The Court may then grant 'such relief or remedy within its jurisdiction as it considers just and appropriate' (clauses 6–8).

The likely impact of a Human Rights Act

It is generally agreed that the passing of a Human Rights Act will have a significant effect on the administration of justice. This is not because English law is riddled with legislation that is manifestly inconsistent with the ECHR, the UK has been a party to the ECHR for many years, and has on the whole attempted to keep its laws consistent with its obligations under the Convention. The problem is that many of the key provisions of the ECHR, such as the rights to freedom of expression or freedom of assembly, are not simple and absolute, but may be qualified by competing interests (such as the need to maintain public order and safety), and in order to give effect to the relevant Articles of the ECHR, judges must balance one interest against the other, in a manner not ordinarily required by conventional techniques of statutory interpretation. It remains to be seen how the judges will adapt to the new regime.

FIVE

Tribunals and Alternative Dispute Resolution

The courts are not the only forum for the resolution of disputes. There is a variety of other approaches which may be considered, such as arbitration, mediation, conciliation and resort to tribunals. It should be pointed out, however, that potential litigants do not always have a choice of alternatives. In many cases, for example, a tribunal is the only available forum for the adjudication of a dispute. This chapter will look at some of the different methods of dispute resolution and consider the advantages and disadvantages of such procedures compared with the court system.

TRIBUNALS

The twentieth century has seen a huge increase in the use of tribunals as a means of settling disputes. There are now hundreds of tribunals in existence, dealing with a myriad of topics. The vast majority of them are created by statute, but some have been privately established by various organisations or sporting bodies with a view to dealing with internal disciplinary matters. There have been many criticisms levelled against the tribunal system, many of which were addressed by the Franks Committee of 1958, whose recommendations were subsequently enacted in the Tribunals and Inquiries Act 1958. Today, the relevant provisions are to be found in the Tribunals and Inquiries Act 1992. As a result of these reforms, it can now be said that the tribunal system plays an integral part in the English legal system.

Administrative tribunals

During the twentieth century the State has progressively taken greater responsibility over its citizens' welfare and as a result there has been a massive increase in social legislation in areas such as housing, health, education, discrimination etc. Legislation of this kind invariably involves the regulation of individuals and organisations and makes them subject to state schemes, which may lead to a variety of possible disputes. The main purpose of establishing administrative tribunals is to deal with the thousands of disputes which arise between private citizens and departments of central government over such issues. The court system would simply collapse under the pressure of dealing with the volume of such disputes. The use of tribunals as a forum for the settling of such disputes provides an informal and relatively cheap alternative to the use of the court system.

Some administrative tribunals, on the other hand, deal with disputes between private persons. For example, rent tribunals deal with disputes between landlords and tenants over issues such as the level of rent, security of tenure, etc. Further examples include industrial tribunals, medical appeal tribunals, mental health review tribunals, and many more.

The fact that there are so many different tribunals means that they can vary greatly in their procedure, in their degree of formality and in their composition. The Lands Tribunal bears the greatest resemblance to a court, whereas industrial tribunals are relatively informal.

Tribunal chairmen will often be legally qualified, but many tribunal members are lay persons with particular expertise in the area of dispute. (Note that lay persons also play a part in the legal system through the use of the jury and magistrates.)

In 1958, the Council on Tribunals was created on the recommendation of the Franks Committee. Its role is to review the workings of tribunals and to compile reports on their operation from time to time. The Council consists of between 10 and 15 members who are appointed by the Lord Chancellor and Secretary of State.

Administrative tribunals and the courts

One can identify a number of features that tend to distinguish administrative tribunals from courts. Some of these are listed below. It should be noted, however, that points of distinction are rarely clear cut. All courts are tribunals of a sort and in many respects administrative tribunals serve the function of lower-tier courts, exercising, as do the courts, the judicial function of the state. They may therefore benefit from the protection of the law of contempt of court (*Pickering* v *Liverpool Daily Post* [1991] 1 All ER 622). Some courts (notably the lay magistrates' courts) possess certain features more commonly associated with tribunals, whilst procedures in heavyweight tribunals such as the Lands Tribunal may at times seem hard to distinguish from those of the courts.

Subject to that *caveat*, if general points of distinction must be identified, they may be said to include the following:

(a)   Adjudicators in administrative tribunals are not usually as rigidly bound by legal precedents as are the mainstream courts. They may therefore have greater scope to reach decisions which will serve the ends of justice in the particular case before them. On the other hand, this can make their decisions harder for litigants or their legal advisers to predict.

(b)   Tribunals are usually credited with the advantage of an informal atmosphere when compared with the more formal atmosphere of the court-room. As a result, a claimant may feel more relaxed and better able to put forward his case in his own way. This informal atmosphere is aided by the fact that in most (not all) tribunals the strict and frequently technical rules of evidence and procedure associated with the civil courts do not have to be followed.

(c)   Tribunal proceedings are usually quicker and less expensive than court proceedings, and therefore involve fewer financial risks to litigants.

(d)   Tribunals often adopt an inquisitorial approach in their proceedings. This means that the tribunal members may themselves take an active role in determining the facts in issue. In contrast, the judge or jury in a court of law usually acts more as an impartial umpire, deciding between the merits of conflicting versions of the facts that are presented by the parties in dispute. Court proceedings, in other words, are usually adversarial. Here again, one must beware of sweeping generalisations. Some tribunal proceedings are adversarial, and some court proceedings (e.g., those concerning the welfare or custody of children) may involve elements that are inquisitorial.

Defects in the administrative tribunal system
Despite the reforms implemented following the Franks Report, there are still a number of criticisms levelled against administrative tribunals. Some of these are listed below:

(a)   Although legal representation is permitted in the vast majority of tribunals, there are some in which legal representation is not allowed. This helps keep costs down, but may cause problems for claimants who are uneducated or inarticulate.

(b)   Most tribunals are required to give a reason for their decisions, but there are some instances in which the tribunal is not required to do so, and this is a major source of criticism. The purpose behind demanding that tribunals give reasons for their decisions is that this gives the High Court an opportunity to review a tribunal's decision and to quash that decision for 'error of law on the face of the record' if the reason given is erroneous. It is worth noting, however, that juries in criminal trials, where a person's liberty may be at stake, are precluded from giving reasons for their decisions, save in exceptional circumstances. This is not therefore a criticism which can be made of tribunals alone.

(c)   Legal aid is unavailable for the majority of tribunal hearings, although legal advice and assistance (including ABWOR) may sometimes be received (see Chapter 7).

(d)   Normally there is a right of appeal to the courts on a point of law arising from the decision of an administrative tribunal, but there are still a number of tribunals against whose decisions there is no available right of appeal. Where there is no right of appeal, there may nevertheless be the possibility of an application for judicial review to the High Court. Such applications may be made on a variety of possible grounds, such as error of law, breach of natural justice, or improper exercise of jurisdiction.

Supervisory control over administrative tribunals by the courts
Tribunals are bound to observe the rules of natural justice, examples of which include the rules that both sides to the dispute must be heard, that the hearing must be fair, and that each side must have time to prepare its case. The Divisional Court of the Queen's Bench Division exercises a supervisory role over tribunals (as it does over inferior courts) through the process of judicial review. The court may where necessary issue prerogative remedies of *certiorari*, *mandamus* and prohibition in order to control the activities of such tribunals. (See Chapter 2 for further information.)

Appeals from administrative tribunals
A right to appeal from the decision of a tribunal to a court of law exists only if it is specifically provided for in the enacting statute. There is no general right to appeal.

Domestic tribunals

Domestic tribunals should not be confused with administrative tribunals. Most domestic tribunals are set up by trades and professional bodies to resolve disputes between their own members and to maintain discipline over them. These domestic tribunals differ from administrative tribunals in that the latter are established by statute to deal with matters of a public nature, whereas the former, even though they can be established by statute, simply regulate conduct in particular professions. Examples of domestic tribunals include the Disciplinary Committee of the General Medical Council and the Solicitors' Disciplinary Committee, each of which is established by statute. There are also domestic tribunals which are created by agreement between the members of the trade or profession itself, such as the Benchers and the Senate of the Inns of Court, which exercise discipline over barristers, or the Football Association, which exercises discipline over soccer clubs and over both amateur and professional players.

Domestic tribunals usually have the power to fine or suspend their members, or to expel them from their organisation. If the domestic tribunal has been established by statute then the member may have a right of appeal to the courts. In contrast, however, if the domestic tribunal was created by agreement, there can be no right of appeal. In either case, however, the High Court retains its right of supervisory jurisdiction over the tribunals and could, for example, quash a ruling that infringes the rules of natural justice or which involves the exceeding of the tribunal's own jurisdiction.

The remedies available to an aggrieved party as a result of an application to the courts will depend upon the status of the domestic tribunal, i.e., whether it has been created by statute or by private bodies for internal purposes. Domestic tribunals created by statute are public bodies and can therefore be made subject to the prerogative powers of *mandamus*, prohibition and *certiorari*, as these remedies operate in the area of public law. Where domestic tribunals are created by private bodies, on the other hand, their functions are purely private and thus the only remedies which can be pursued by the aggrieved party are private remedies such as injunctions, declarations or damages.

ARBITRATION AND ALTERNATIVE DISPUTE RESOLUTION

In an era of expanding but increasingly expensive civil litigation, which is still subject to long delays, there may be good reasons for potential litigants to consider some form of alternative dispute resolution, or ADR. It has long been known that it may be advantageous to the parties to a civil dispute to settle it without actually going to court, and the vast majority of civil disputes are indeed settled or abandoned before trial. Standard pre-trial procedures encourage this. But, whereas traditional pre-trial negotiation is conducted adversarially against a coercive backdrop of impending litigation, ADR may offer a different and arguably better way of resolving things. As Lord Woolf points out in his 1995 report, *Access to Justice*:

> ADR has the obvious advantage of saving scarce judicial and other resources. More significantly . . . it offers a variety of benefits to litigants or potential litigants. ADR is usually cheaper than litigation, and often produces quicker results. In some cases, the parties will want to avoid the publicity associated with court proceedings. It may also be more beneficial for them . . . to choose a form of dispute resolution that will enable them to work out a mutually acceptable solution . . .

What is ADR?

The label 'ADR' can be applied to a number of different procedures, and there is no universal agreement as to which procedures properly merit that label. Tribunals are sometimes included under this label, but in practice they usually function as forms of lower-level court, rather than as alternatives to the courts, and they are therefore dealt with separately in the first part of this chapter.

The most important form of ADR is arguably arbitration, but some definitions of ADR exclude it on the basis that arbitration is itself one of the standard forms of binding and coercive dispute resolution. Writers who take this view typically define ADR as 'dispute resolution without resort to binding or coercive rulings'. Lord Woolf, however, does include arbitration in *Access to Justice* as a form of ADR.

Mediation and conciliation are the universally recognised forms of ADR, and are considered later in this chapter; but there are certain other procedures (not usually thought of as ADR) which deserve at least a passing mention in this context:

(a)   Complaints of alleged malpractice in central or local government, or in various service industries (such as banking or insurance) can sometimes be directed to public or private ombudsmen, who have powers to investigate and recommend forms of settlement. Lord Woolf included these in his survey of ADR procedures.

(b)   The instigation of criminal procedures as a method of seeking individual redress is not ordinarily thought of as a form of ADR, and is certainly coercive, but it may in practice offer an aggrieved person a faster and (from his viewpoint) a much less risky method of obtaining compensation for what might otherwise be considered a civil wrong. Aggrieved consumers, for example, may find that a complaint (or even the *threat* of a complaint) to their local trading standards office will trigger a faster and more conciliatory response from delinquent traders than any threat of civil proceedings would achieve. Taking civil proceedings over (say) the purchase of an unsatisfactory used car may involve a plaintiff in significant risk, worry and expense; but if the car can be shown to have been inaccurately described by the dealer (as for example where it has been 'clocked') the dealer may instead be prosecuted for an offence under the Trade Descriptions Act 1968. The complainant does not then have to worry about the mounting of such a prosecution, which the trading standards authority will conduct, nor need he worry about its cost, but he may still expect to be compensated if he is proved to have suffered loss; and as previously noted, the mere threat of a criminal complaint may be a potent weapon in negotiations for the immediate rescission of the transaction.

Arbitration

Arbitration involves referring a dispute to a third party for a decision (which is usually termed an 'arbitration award'). This award is then binding upon the parties. Arbitration clauses are commonly found in commercial and partnership agreements, so as to achieve a speedy settlement of the point at issue. They may, for example, be found in contracts between businessmen or in contracts between trade associations and their consumers. In these circumstances, the arbitrator's jurisdiction is binding on the parties because they have contractually agreed that this should be the case. As to the so-called 'arbitration procedure' adopted as the method of dispute resolution of small claims in the county courts, see Chapter 2.

An arbitration clause or agreement normally requires that the parties should refer any dispute which arises between them to an arbitrator, whose findings as to the facts of the dispute will then in most cases be final and binding. This form of clause is considered perfectly valid and the courts will not interfere with it. Any arbitration clause which seeks to oust the jurisdiction of the courts completely, by denying their right to rule on the relevant *law* will, however, be invalid in that respect. In other words, there must always be a right to refer issues of law to the courts.

One of the main advantages of arbitration is that it is usually convenient to the parties involved in the dispute. The arbitration hearing can be fixed at a time which suits them and it can be held in private, which is often important in commercial dealings. Proceedings under arbitration can be much cheaper and quicker than if the dispute were heard in court. The subject matter of the dispute, if highly specialised, can be considered by an expert in that area. Such proceedings are not always cheap, however, as an arbitrator is a professional and will demand professional fees. If the award is appealed against, any cost advantage will almost inevitably be lost.

Procedure

The procedure for arbitration, other than statutory arbitration (which is to be found in the statutes themselves) is governed by the Arbitration Act 1996. Disputes are normally heard by a single arbitrator who may be a lawyer (especially where complicated areas of law are involved) or a specialist in the subject being determined. If the dispute is heard by more than one arbitrator and they cannot agree, the disputed question may be referred to a third party, known as the umpire.

An arbitrator has the power to examine witnesses, inspect documents, and order the discovery of documents, but the rules of contempt of court do not directly apply.

Supervision by the courts

The Arbitration Act 1996 provides that a right of appeal exists in relation to any question of law arising out of any award made on an arbitration agreement. To prevent frivolous appeals, the right only exists where both parties consent to the appeal or where the leave of the court is granted. The court will only grant a leave to appeal where it is satisfied that there is a question of law to be determined which could substantially affect the rights of the parties. In addition an application for judicial review may be made to the High Court and there is a limited right of appeal against that decision to the Court of Appeal.

Other forms of ADR

The principal non-coercive forms of ADR are mediation, conciliation and negotiation. A common feature to them all is that nothing is binding upon the parties. If it does not work, the parties are free to litigate or perhaps go to arbitration. There is nothing new about the idea of negotiation as a way of settling civil disputes. On the contrary, out of court settlements have always been the most common way of resolving such disputes, and negotiation has always played some part in that. There are, however, a number of newer approaches that have been taken to assist parties to come to some form of settlement.

Conciliation

Conciliation is a practice whereby the parties to a possible civil action are encouraged to discuss 'without prejudice' the issues involved. Conciliation in this context is often carried out by professional legal advisers, insurance companies or trade unions. Conciliation is particularly common in matrimonial cases relating to matters such as arrangements for the custody of and access to children, although it tends to be more informal than conciliation proceedings in other areas of civil law. Conciliation attempts informally to resolve or identify the issues at stake. A resolution reached at conciliation proceedings is not legally binding, but it may avoid the need for proceedings in court, or it may enable the parties to go to court with a mutually acceptable scheme for child custody, etc., which the court will usually be happy to approve. It would not, however, approve a half-baked scheme that appears contrary to the child's best interests, even if the parents have previously agreed to propose it.

Mediation

Mediation is similar to conciliation in many respects, and is similarly intended to guide the parties towards a mutually satisfactory resolution of their dispute. It can be defined as a process whereby a neutral person (the mediator) aids the parties to reach a common position. The mediator will in some cases be invited to express his own views as to the merits of the dispute (an 'evaluative' mediation) but in many cases he avoids doing so, whilst attempting to steer the parties towards common ground (a 'facilitative' mediation). In either case, the mediator's powers are limited to *suggesting* possible solutions, rather than imposing them on the parties.

Agencies offering ADR services

A number of agencies are now available to assist parties who may wish to avoid resorting to litigation. The Advisory, Conciliation and Arbitration Service (ACAS) is best known for its involvement in the settlement of strikes and other industrial disputes, but may also help parties to avoid litigation. Others bodies include the Centre for Dispute Resolution (CEDR); Mediation UK (an umbrella organisation which publishes the *Directory of Mediation and Conflict Resolution Services*); the British Academy of Experts; the Chartered Institute of Arbitrators and the City Disputes Panel.

The Centre for Dispute Resolution (CEDR)

CEDR was established in 1990 to encourage the settling of commercial disputes through alternative methods of dispute resolution. CEDR offers a range of methods for settling disputes, although mediation is the most popular. It has over 300 trained mediators and claims an 85 to 90 per cent success rate.

The City of London Disputes Panel

This panel was set up in order to address problems caused by the length, expense and complexity of proceedings before the Commercial Court. It provides arbitration and mediation services by means of a panel of experts, which includes retired judges and members of the financial services industry.

The courts and ADR

Far from resenting the ADR industry as a potential rival, the courts generally welcome and encourage it. Various reports commissioned from the judiciary, including the Heilbron/Hodge Report and more recently Lord Woolf's reports, have advocated extended use of alternative methods of dispute resolution in an attempt to encourage the most cost-effective method of resolving civil disputes.

A *Practice Direction* issued by the Lord Chief Justice ([1994] 1 WLR 1270) now requires lawyers acting for potential litigants to certify whether they have explored possible forms of ADR and to consider whether ADR might help either to resolve the case or at least to narrow down the issues in dispute. This requirement originated in the Commercial Court, and it is in cases before the Commercial Court that the pressure to adopt ADR remains strongest. The clerk to the Commercial Court keeps a list of ADR providers for litigants to consult, and judges of the Court may even adjourn proceedings where it is thought that ADR may be tried or retried.

Limitations of ADR

It must not be imagined that ADR necessarily offers the best form of justice in every case. There may be schemes, working practices or other ideas which could be copied or adapted by the courts, as Lord Woolf has pointed out in his recent reports into the operation of the civil justice system in England and Wales, but at present ADR suffers from the fact that legal aid is not available to fund such proceedings. According to Lord Woolf, this is a matter to which the Legal Aid Board should have regard. Furthermore, injunctions and mandatory orders, which may in appropriate cases be available from the courts, cannot be obtained by any form of ADR.

Tribunals and alternative dispute resolution

The courts are not the only forum for the resolution of disputes; there are alternative methods

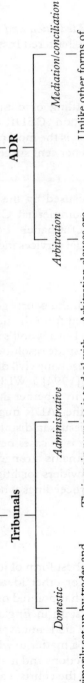

Tribunals

Domestic

Primarily set up by trades and professional bodies to resolve disputes between their own members and to maintain discipline over them.

They may be created privately or by statute. If created by statute, there is a right of appeal to the courts. If created privately, there is no such right of appeal, although the courts may exercise supervisory jurisdiction over domestic tribunals.

Administrative

Their main purpose is to deal with disputes between private citizens and departments of central government.

Tribunals are normally cheaper and more informal than the court system.

The courts may exercise control over administrative tribunals through the process of judicial review and the issue of prerogative remedies. There may also be a right of appeal, on a point of law, to the courts against a tribunal's decision.

ADR

Arbitration

Arbitration clauses are frequently found in commercial and partnership agreements. Their aim is to achieve a speedy resolution of disputes.

The dispute is referred to an arbitrator and his decision is known as an 'award'.

If the parties have included an arbitration clause in their contract then the courts will usually refuse to hear the case unless it first goes to arbitration.

Any arbitration clause which attempts completely to oust the jurisdiction of the courts will be void.

Appeals may be made to the courts on a point of law.

Mediation/conciliation

Unlike other forms of alternative dispute resolution, mediation and conciliation do not impose solutions on the parties but simply guide them to a solution.

Most disputes are settled out of court. Mediation and conciliation assist the reaching of a settlement.

SIX

Lawyers and Judges

THE LEGAL PROFESSION

The legal profession in England and Wales is unusual in that it is divided into two separate professions, namely, solicitors and barristers. In most countries there is only a single legal profession. English law is not, however, unique in this respect. A similar division is found in Scotland and in some Commonwealth countries which have modelled their legal systems on ours.

The separation of the legal professions in the United Kingdom has an ancient historical basis. The origins of the division can be traced back to the mid-fourteenth century. Preparatory work on legal cases was by then being carried out by persons known as attorneys, who were officers of the court. The actual presentation and argument before the court was carried out by barristers, who were organised, like medieval guilds, in associations known as Inns of Court. Practising barristers had to be a member of one of these Inns of Court, four of which survive today. Solicitors did not appear until the next century, and initially undertook preparatory work on Chancery cases. Originally their status was below that of attorneys, but much of the work of solicitors was similar to that of attorneys, and by the seventeenth century it was often undertaken by the same persons. The distinction between solicitors and attorneys gradually became insignificant and the office of attorney was eventually abolished by the Judicature Act 1873.

The division between solicitors and barristers survived. Indeed, it was rigorously maintained by the Inns of Court, who refused to allow solicitors to undertake work comparable to that of the barristers. Judges were meanwhile appointed exclusively from amongst the ranks of barristers, a practice which continued until modern times. It was not until 1971 that solicitors could become even part-time judges (or recorders) of the Crown Court, and even today the vast majority of senior judges are former barristers.

Solicitors were driven to form their own professional organisation, 'The Society of Gentlemen Practitioners in the Courts of Law and Equity'. This eventually became the Law Society. Like the Inns of Court, the Law Society regulates the activities of its members and defends their interests, vigorously protecting such interests from outside attack or depredation.

The distinction between the work of the two professions thus continued for many more years, but in recent years it has become less rigid than of old. Solicitors are still primarily concerned with preparatory work (preparing cases that are eventually entrusted to barristers for presentation in court) and with non-contentious work such as conveyancing and probate (wills and estates) or the drafting of commercial agreements. Most barristers meanwhile continue to specialise in the actual presentation of contested cases. Solicitors, however, have increasingly obtained rights of audience (i.e., the right to appear as advocates in court) and, as we shall see below, this development has been significantly extended by the Courts and Legal Services Act 1990.

Modern changes within the legal profession

Before looking in detail at the work of barristers and solicitors, it will be necessary to take account of the fact that much of this work has changed significantly over recent years, as a result of major legislative changes in the law: changes which have abolished many of the monopolistic rights formerly held by the professions, and which have relaxed many of the old distinctions between the two halves of the legal profession.

Whilst opinions are divided as to the merits of the legislative changes, the enactment of such legislation in the face of determined opposition from the professions was in itself a remarkable achievement. Lawyers are well represented in government. Many barristers, for example, combine private practice with a Parliamentary career. For many years, this made it almost impossible for significant changes to be made to established legal practices, particularly where this threatened lucrative monopolies, such as the monopoly of conveyancing practice held by solicitors or the barristers' exclusive rights of audience in higher courts. There were many influential supporters of these monopolies. In 1979, a Royal Commission on Legal Services published a report (the Benson Report) which not only recommended the preservation of the Bar's exclusive rights of audience in the higher courts, but also recommended *extending* the conveyancing monopoly held by solicitors.

During the 1980s, however, Britain had a government which (rightly or wrongly) believed strongly in 'free market' principles, and was instinctively hostile to 'closed shops' or restrictive practices, wherever they were to be found. Once it had won its long and bitter battle with the trade unions, it turned its attention to reforming the provision of legal services. The government took the view that the way to provide the best possible access to legal services was to dismantle the various monopolies which the legal professions had developed. The Administration of Justice Act 1985, for example, included provisions which led to the establishment of a professional body of licensed conveyancers. This made a relatively minor dent in the conveyancing monopoly, but more drastic changes were still to come. After a period of fierce argument and consultation, the Courts and Legal Services Act 1990 (CALSA) was enacted, leading to some of the most far-reaching changes ever imposed upon the legal professions.

Section 17 of CALSA 1990 stated one of the principal aims of that Act, namely:

> ... the development of legal services in England and Wales (and in particular the development of advocacy, litigation, conveyancing and probate services) by making the provision for new or better ways of providing such services and a wider choice of persons providing them, while maintaining the proper and efficient administration of justice.

CALSA 1990 accordingly changed many of the rules governing rights of audience (i.e., the right to argue cases in court) and many of the rules governing the right to conduct litigation, probate work and conveyancing. Banks and building societies were enabled to compete with solicitors for both conveyancing and probate work. In return, some new opportunities were offered to the beleaguered professions. Under s. 66 of the 1990 Act, solicitors were enabled (subject to the Law Society's own regulations) to form 'multi-disciplinary partnerships' with accountants, surveyors, etc., or multi-national partnerships with foreign law firms, and ss. 27 to 33 of the 1990 Act laid the ground for changes which would eventually enable solicitors to seek special advocacy qualifications, under which they could at last begin to challenge the Bar's monopoly of audience rights in the higher courts. Changes were also made to the rules governing judicial appointments and the Act established a Legal Services Ombudsman, together with an Advisory Committee on Education and Conduct.

SOLICITORS

Qualifications needed to become a solicitor

The usual method of qualification for a would-be solicitor is to obtain a 'qualifying law degree' from a university (covering a range of subjects approved by the Law Society) and then proceed to a one year vocational course known as the 'Legal Practice Course' (LPC) at one of a number of universities or other institutions (such as the College of Law) which are authorised to teach such a course. This must then be followed by a two year period understudying a solicitor in practice, which is called a training contract (or 'Articles' as this contract is still sometimes known). It is possible to combine a part-time LPC course with a three year training contract. Would-be solicitors who do not have qualifying law degrees (mostly arts or science graduates) must first complete a special one year conversion course leading to the 'Common Professional Examination' (CPE) before attempting the Legal Practice Course. This remains a fairly common way into the profession, although this course provides a much narrower legal education than a qualifying law degree.

A training contract is intended to give trainees first-hand experience of the nature of the work carried out by a solicitor. Trainees must be properly paid during their training contracts, and in some of the larger firms they are handsomely paid, which is just as well because most trainees are saddled with the repayment of loans taken out to meet the substantial fees (typically £5,000 plus) charged by providers of the Legal Practice Course.

Upon successful completion of his training contract, a trainee may then apply to be admitted as a fully fledged solicitor. The Master of the Rolls will then add his name to the roll of Solicitors of the Supreme Court. Before he can practise he must obtain a practising certificate issued by the Law Society and take out compulsory insurance against possible claims for professional negligence.

After qualifying, newly enrolled solicitors must continue with their legal education. Further compulsory courses must be attended and solicitors who wish to undertake advocacy work in the higher courts must attend further courses and pass further examinations.

The work of solicitors

There are currently more than 60,000 solicitors practising throughout England and Wales. Although they can work alone, or be employed by companies, local government or public bodies such as the Crown Prosecution Service, the majority form partnerships with other solicitors, and/or employ other solicitors to work for them. As previously noted, CALSA 1990 also permits solicitors to form partnerships with other professions, such as accountants; but the Law Society has been slow to endorse that permission, and until it does so, no such partnerships can be formed.

The matters dealt with by a firm of solicitors may be extremely varied, and the larger firms will have separate specialist departments to deal with a range of different legal subjects. Firms may also specialise in particular areas. The largest city firms usually concentrate on lucrative banking, company and commercial work, leaving areas such as criminal law and family law to the smaller firms. The clients of these large firms are primarily public limited companies or other corporations. Although often thought of as 'general practitioners', many solicitors are nothing of the kind. A city solicitor may deal more or less exclusively with one narrow area of law, such as insurance or shipping contracts, and may indeed be far more specialised than many barristers.

Repercussions following the abolition of monopolies

Outside the big commercial firms, conveyancing and probate work for private clients has traditionally formed a substantial part of many solicitors' incomes, but as previously explained, the various monopolies once enjoyed by solicitors were abolished in a series of legislative reforms between 1985 and 1990. Today, conveyancing and probate work remains an important source of revenue for many solicitors, but can also be provided by any of a number of appropriately qualified persons or bodies, and solicitors now have to ensure that their own conveyancing charges are competitive *vis-à-vis* these potential competitors.

In response to the loss of these monopolies, the solicitors' profession began to make use of the new era of competition established by the government. In 1984, solicitors were for the first time permitted to advertise their services, subject to regulation by the Law Society. More significantly, the loss of their own monopolies led to a sustained attack by the Law Society on the Bar's monopolistic control over rights of audience in the superior courts. The Marre Committee of 1986, whose remit was to examine legal education, the legal profession and legal services, concluded that solicitors ought to have rights of audience in courts that had hitherto been closed to them. The government's free market approach to the supply of legal services, which had cost solicitors their own monopolies, now worked in their favour, and CALSA 1990 accordingly contains provisions which significantly extend the rights of suitably qualified solicitors to act as advocates in the higher course. (For further information on this, see the section on barristers, below.)

Solicitors have now also lost their monopoly over the right to conduct litigation (the power to issue writs, instruct barristers, etc.). Section 28 of CALSA 1990 states that any person is entitled to conduct litigation where a right to do so has been conferred by an appropriate body. The Law Society is of course an 'appropriate body', but other professional organisations may qualify as well. Despite this, however, the vast majority of such work is still undertaken by solicitors.

BARRISTERS

Qualifications needed to become a barrister

In order to become a barrister, a student must first obtain a qualifying law degree or pass the CPE examination, just as if he were aiming to become a solicitor. Thereafter, the paths of professional training diverge. A would-be barrister must become a member of one of the four surviving Inns of Court.

These are Gray's Inn, Middle Temple, Inner Temple and Lincoln's Inn. The Inns of Court are situated close to the Royal Courts of Justice in London. Once accepted at an Inn, the would-be barrister must undergo an intensive one year course, known as the Bar Vocational Course (BVC). This can be undertaken at the Inns of Court School of Law in London, or at one of the universities which now offer accredited BVC courses. If the student successfully completes this course (and keeps terms at his Inn by attending the requisite number of formal dinners), he may then be 'called to the Bar'. In order to practise as a barrister, however, he must then undertake pupillage. This involves apprenticeship to an established barrister for a 12 month period. The biggest hurdle, however, will often be that of finding a 'tenancy' in a set of chambers after completing pupillage. Competition for such tenancies is intense (see below).

Work of a barrister

There are still far fewer barristers than solicitors, although the number of practising barristers has risen sharply in recent years. There are now just over 8,500 practising barristers. The majority of these work in London, but there are also sets of chambers in a number of the larger provincial cities, such as Manchester and Cardiff. An established barrister will often specialise in a certain area of law, such as taxation or patent law, but newly qualified barristers may have less opportunity to specialise. Those starting out in general 'common law' practice may have to undertake a broad mix of crime, contract, tort and family matters.

Much of the work of a barrister involves giving written advice on difficult or complicated areas of law. Such advice is known as 'counsel's opinion'. Solicitors obtain such opinions for their clients in much the same way as a general medical practitioner might refer his patient to a consultant, although counsel will ordinarily depend quite heavily on the quality of the instructions provided by instructing solicitors. Solicitors will also 'instruct counsel' where a case is set to go to court, unless it is a case that the solicitor in question can handle as an advocate. Here again, the quality of the instructions provided (and evidence gathered) by the solicitors is often crucial to the success of the case. Not all barristers practise regularly as advocates in the courts, but for many it is the most important part of their work. Solicitors will often seek the services of a particular barrister who has done good work for them in the past and whose area of expertise matches the subject matter of the case in question.

Barristers are usually independent (or self-employed) and cannot practise as partnerships or companies. They may, however, be employed by commercial organisations or solicitors firms, or by local or national government. The Crown Prosecution Service is a major employer of barristers. Barristers employed in this way cannot, however, act as advocates in the higher courts and their work is largely comparable with that of solicitors in similar employment.

Independent barristers usually work together in groups known as chambers. By forming chambers, the barristers can share the cost of the premises and library facilities. They also share the services of specialist clerks, who are responsible for finding and dividing work amongst the barristers.

As previously explained, finding a permanent place (a tenancy) in chambers can be extremely difficult for a newly qualified barrister and the Bar has therefore recently relaxed the traditional requirement that barristers must work from chambers. They may, for example, be allowed to work from home instead, although this is subject to regulations laid down by the Bar Council.

Rules of conduct for barristers

Barristers have a number of antiquated rules which govern the way in which they practise: for example, a barrister cannot ordinarily be approached directly by a client, but only through a solicitor. This restriction, however, has been mitigated somewhat by the 1990 Code of Conduct, which allows members of certain recognised professional bodies to have direct access to a barrister. Some of the first recognised bodies to be allowed such direct access include accountants, surveyors, members of the government legal service, patent agents, arbitrators and licenced conveyancers. Unless the client approaches the barrister directly under one of these limited exceptions, there will be no contractual relationship between the barrister and his client, and he cannot sue the client for his fees (the client's contract is with his solicitor). Instead the barrister will have to rely upon the professional etiquette of the solicitor for his remuneration. For many years, certain solicitors took unfair advantage of barristers' inability to sue for fees, and took months or even years to pay barristers. As a result of protests from the Bar, the Law Society has moved to outlaw this practice. Solicitors who fail to pay fees to barristers after receiving payment from the client will now be liable to a charge of professional misconduct. The Legal Aid Board, however, remains a notoriously slow payer and barristers suffer even more than solicitors from this slowness.

Another custom, which is commonly referred to as the 'cab rank' rule, is that a barrister must accept any brief which he is offered at a proper fee and which he is competent to undertake. There are some exceptions to this rule, as for example where the barrister, because of other commitments, would have insufficient time to prepare for the case itself. The justification for this rule is that it 'secures for the public a right of representation in the court which is a pillar of British liberty'. The importance of this rule can be seen in some criminal cases where barristers might otherwise seek to avoid defending unpopular defendants. The level of fees set for a legally aided case may be well below the level of fees that a top barrister could obtain from privately funded work (and will usually be paid only after a long delay), but the cab rank principle deems the legal aid fee to be a proper one. Barristers ought not therefore (but sometimes contrive to) decline a case on that basis.

Junior barristers and Queen's Counsel (QCs)

Another distinguishing feature of the Bar is that it has two divisions. There are barristers who are 'Queen's Counsel' and those who are 'Junior' barristers. There are fewer than a thousand practising Queen's Counsel. A QC is appointed by the Queen on the advice of the Lord Chancellor from the ranks of junior barristers with ten or more years' experience. A QC mainly works on serious or complicated cases, either in an advisory capacity or as an advocate, and may be able to command hefty fees. On the other hand, a QC cannot ordinarily undertake some of the more widely available work which may be offered to junior counsel. Most senior judicial appointments are made from QCs (see below).

A QC may appear in court on his own, but will usually have a 'junior' to assist him. The junior barrister will then receive a fee appropriate to the case involved. It must be emphasised that junior barristers need not be young, inexperienced or unsuccessful. Some wealthy and successful barristers never apply to become QCs because they enjoy or do well out of the kind of work that QCs cannot undertake. The technical term to become a QC is to 'take silk', a term which derives from the fact that a QC's gown was made of silk, whilst a junior barrister's gown was made of a woollen cloth.

It is now possible, in theory, for solicitor advocates to become QCs, but none has been appointed as of the time of writing, and indeed none has yet been in practice as advocates in the higher courts for the minimum ten year period.

Changes to the legal profession: the effect upon barristers

As we have seen, the Bar's monopoly over the rights of audience in the superior courts was undermined by CALSA 1990. As a result, rights of audience now depend upon appropriate qualifications and not simply upon whether the advocate is a barrister or a solicitor. Section 27 of CALSA 1990 states that existing rights of audience for barristers and solicitors are preserved, but that rights of audience may also be extended e.g., so as to enable a solicitor to act as an advocate in the Crown Court or High Court. A solicitor seeking such rights must obtain the requisite qualification by attending courses and passing further examinations. Only a small minority of solicitors have done so and barristers still constitute the vast majority of advocates in the higher courts.

Crown prosecutors (lawyers employed by the CPS) whether barristers or solicitors, are still barred in most circumstances from acting as advocates in the Crown Court, Divisional Court, Court of Appeal or House of Lords. This is very much a bone of contention within the legal profession. Many crown prosecutors would be well qualified to act as advocates at Crown Court level, but it appears (despite denials) that such rights are denied to them in order to preserve the work of independent barristers.

The Bar has relaxed a number of its practice rules in an attempt to make barristers more competitive. Some of these changes have already been noted such as permitting barristers, under limited conditions, direct access to their clients. Sets of chambers have become involved, to a limited degree, with advertising, even listing their members in national newspapers.

Complaints against solicitors

Despite some changes introduced by CALSA 1990, the Law Society retains primary responsibility for the regulation of the activities of solicitors, and handles complaints of professional misconduct or inadequate professional services. The latter are defined as 'the provision by solicitors of services which are not of the quality which it is reasonable to expect of them'. Where serious complaints are proved against solicitors (e.g., misuse of clients' money), the Law Society has the power to suspend offenders or strike them off the roll of Solicitors of the Supreme Court.

Solicitors are not immune from actions for professional negligence, save in respect of the conduct of litigation, where they enjoy immunity on the same basis as barristers. There are many ways in which liability may be incurred, and insurance against such claims is mandatory. In *Ross* v *Caunters* [1980] Ch 297, for example, it was held that a solicitor could be liable to the disappointed beneficiary of a bequest in a will that had been rendered invalid as a result of his negligence. They may also be penalised by a 'wasted costs' order (in effect a fine) if their misconduct or inefficiency has caused delays and expense to the parties and/or the court.

Complaints against barristers

The conduct of barristers is primarily regulated by the profession itself. Barristers must comply with the Code of Conduct of the Bar of England and Wales. The Code's purpose is to 'provide the standards of conduct on the part of barristers which are appropriate in the interests of justice'. An example of a provision of the Code is the rule that barristers must not engage in conduct which is 'dishonest or which may otherwise bring the profession of a barrister into disrepute or which is prejudicial to the administration of justice'. If any barrister fails to comply with the Code of Conduct, this may be deemed to constitute professional misconduct and he will be made subject to disciplinary proceedings. The ultimate sanction in serious cases is that the offender may be 'disbarred'. This is equivalent to being struck off the roll of solicitors. Lesser sanctions include fines and reprimands.

A barrister cannot be sued for negligence when acting as an advocate. This rule supposedly exists so that a barrister can be free in court to act independently without fear of an action for negligence (*Rondel* v *Worsley* [1967] 3 All ER 993). This immunity also extends to matters intimately connected with the conduct of the case in court, such as advice concerning the settlement of a case which is already being tried, and in which the court must assent to the terms of settlement (*Kelly* v *Corston* [1997] 4 All ER 466). A barrister may, however, be sued for negligence in certain other situations, as for example where he provides a negligently inaccurate or misleading written opinion, or he may be subjected to a 'wasted costs' order (in effect a financial penalty) if his conduct results in unnecessary delay or expense to the parties.

The Legal Services Ombudsman

An office known as the Legal Services Ombudsman was created by CALSA 1990. The Ombudsman may investigate allegations relating to the manner in which complaints about professional misconduct have been dealt with by the Law Society or Bar Council. This would include, for example, allegations that no action has been taken in respect of a justified complaint against a solicitor or barrister, or that the investigation of such a complaint has been unsatisfactory. The Ombudsman may then recommend that some form of action be taken, such as the payment of compensation. His recommendations are not strictly binding, but it is unlikely that they would be ignored.

FUSION OF THE PROFESSIONS?

There have for many years been calls for the fusion of the solicitors' and barristers' professions. This might or might not involve abandonment of existing titles, but it would involve the introduction of common training and qualifications for lawyers, and (more importantly from the client's viewpoint) an end to the need for 'double manning' in the preparation and presentation of contested cases. Most other countries, even within the 'common law' world, have now fused their legal professions.

There is much to be said for reforming the present system of education and training, which forces young lawyers to make more or less irrevocable career decisions right at the start of their professional training; but as far as the 'double manning' argument is concerned, much of the heat has now been taken out of it by the CALSA 1990 reforms, which do indeed enable a single lawyer (if properly qualified) to retain a case right through from initial instruction to advocacy at a High Court or Crown Court trial. In practice, it appears that few lawyers choose to do so, at least in really complex cases. There will always be a need for specialisation in many areas of law, and it may be that the present system permits a satisfactory blend of specialism and flexibility.

JUDGES AND MAGISTRATES

In some countries, young law graduates may elect to train for and enter the judiciary instead of going into general legal practice. They may then work their way up, through minor judicial or magisterial posts, to senior positions equivalent to that of an English Law Lord or Lord Justice of Appeal.

Our system is very different. With the notable exception of the lay magistracy (or justices of the peace) the judiciary in England and Wales is selected exclusively from the ranks of experienced practising lawyers. Some appointments are full time and some may be combined, on a part-time basis, with private legal practice. Experience of part-time judicial work may enable a lawyer to decide whether he wishes to give up his private practice and become a full-time judge, but many are happy to continue on such a basis, without ever seeking a full-time position.

Justices of the peace

Justices of the peace (or lay magistrates) are almost all laymen, rather than trained lawyers (although possession of a professional legal qualification need not disqualify an individual from becoming one). They are appointed (and may be removed) by the Lord Chancellor. The Lord Chancellor chooses such persons after consultation with Local Advisory Committees, which are found in each county. In many cases these Advisory Committees will advertise for applicants who are willing to serve, but in other cases suggested names are put forward by local bodies such as chambers of commerce. The details of appropriate candidates are then passed on to the Lord Chancellor.

Lay magistrates are unpaid, although they are entitled to reasonable expenses for such things as travelling. No initial knowledge of the law is required to become a lay magistrate, although upon appointment a new magistrate is required to attend a training programme which covers, for example, basic criminal procedure and sentencing. Lay magistrates often rely for legal advice on the court clerk, who will not always be a qualified solicitor or barrister, but will hold a legal qualification of some kind. In difficult cases, a court clerk may be able to seek advice from the clerk to the justices, or his deputy. These are always qualified solicitors or barristers of several years' standing. The clerk to the justices, however, has become primarily a court administrator, and rarely has time to act as a court clerk himself.

In many cases, legal technicalities go unnoticed in magistrates' courts or are misunderstood by all concerned. Evidence may, for example, be excluded as hearsay when it is not really hearsay at all. Of course, even the most experienced professional judges make mistakes, but the lay element in the magistrates' courts does often lead to a rough and ready type of justice. In reply to such criticism, it might be said (a) that common sense may be worth more than legal correctness in some cases, and (b) that there is no way in which some 25,000 lay justices could all be replaced by sufficient professional magistrates — not without shattering current budgetary limits.

There have been allegations that lay magistrates have, in the past at least, been selected from predominantly male, white, middle-class backgrounds.

Indeed, this is hardly surprising, given that the office of justice of the peace was once the exclusive preserve of the landowning gentry. In recent years, there have been concerted attempts to redress this imbalance by recruiting more women and more people from other ethnic groups, but such changes only ever happen slowly. One of the biggest problems is that those who have to work standard nine-to-five shifts find it difficult to sit for the 35 days each year which would be expected of them. They must be allowed time off by their employer, but may not be paid during that time. This means that middle-class professionals, who often enjoy more flexible working hours, may be better represented on the bench. The unemployed might be able to find the time, but seem not to apply in significant numbers.

Stipendiary magistrates

These is a full-time, salaried judicial position. They are, in effect, professional magistrates, and deal mostly with the same types of cases as lay magistrates, the main difference being that they sit alone, rather than in benches of three. They sit in London (where there are over 60 of them) and in other major cities where the courts are busiest. Chief metropolitan stipendiaries also deal with extradition hearings at the Bow Street magistrates' court in London. This is a highly specialised area of law and often one of international sensitivity, although the rulings of the magistrate can be reviewed or appealed against in the High Court.

District judges

Formerly known as registrars, these deal with administrative business in the county courts, and have jurisdiction to deal with some of the smaller claims in that court. They regularly act as arbitrators in cases where the special small claims procedure is used. (As to the nature of this procedure, see Chapter 2, above.)

Recorders

These are part-time appointments and recorders serve primarily in the Crown Court. Recorders are practising barristers or solicitors who have jurisdiction to act as judges in some of the less serious cases in that Court. (They may try burglary cases, for example, but not cases of rape, murder or manslaughter.) Experience as a recorder is often a step on the road to a full-time judicial appointment.

Circuit judges

These judges are the workhorses of the Crown Court and county courts, and may be appointed from barristers or solicitors who hold an appropriate court qualification. Many will have previously gained experience as recorders. In some cases, a district judge or coroner can become a circuit judge. Circuit judges have the title 'His Honour, Judge Smith', or 'Her Honour, Judge Evans, QC'. They may sometimes be found sitting as temporary judges of the High Court, when pressures on that court require extra judges to be found.

High Court judges

A High Court judgeship is always a full-time appointment, and is regarded as a great honour. Appointees are usually QCs of considerable experience and distinction. There are nearly 100 of them, and they may, but need not, have previously served as circuit judges or recorders. Suitably qualified solicitors may now become High Court judges, but the vast majority of High Court judges are still selected from the ranks of successful barristers. Although well paid (with an annual salary of £116,000), High Court judges do not earn anything like as much as the most successful barristers, and some potential judges are therefore dissuaded from accepting office because of the loss of income that would be involved. The award of a knighthood on appointment helps sweeten the pill, however, as does the job security and the prospect (if successful) of eventual elevation to the peerage as a Law Lord.

Appointment has in the past been by invitation only, but the new Lord Chancellor (Lord Irvine) has instituted a new procedure, and the first ever advertisement inviting applications for High Court judgeships appeared early in 1998.

High Court judges hold the title 'Mr (or Mrs) Justice Smith' (which is usually printed as 'Smith J' in books or reports). Although they primarily sit in the High Court, judges of the Queen's Bench and Family divisions spend some time 'on circuit' where they sit in the Crown Court (e.g., hearing murder trials). Each Crown Court circuit is led by two such judges. High Court judges of the QBD also assist in the work of the criminal division of the Court of Appeal, and are occasionally seconded to other duties: one usually acts as Chairman of the Law Commission, whose task it is to formulate and develop proposals for law reform in various areas, others may be asked to chair major public enquiries or investigate and report on major public scandals, as may Lords Justices of Appeal. (See for example Sir Richard Scott's recent investigation into the 'Arms for Iraq' affair.) Their political independence is greatly valued here.

Lords Justices of Appeal

There are around 30 of these, who are invariably appointed from the ranks of successful High Court judges. They sit in both the civil and criminal divisions of the Court of Appeal, and regardless of their sex they hold the title 'Lord Justice Smith' (or 'Smith LJ'). As yet, very few are women, but as the numbers of women barristers and judges continue to rise, this will undoubtedly change in time.

Lords of Appeal in Ordinary

Lords of Appeal in Ordinary (or law lords) are in practice selected from amongst the more experienced and highly regarded Lords Justices of Appeal. There is a progression, in other words, from the High Court to the Court of Appeal, and thence to the House of Lords, but of course only the most successful make it to the top. As life peers, law lords may also take part in Parliamentary debates, although they always sit on the cross-benches as political neutrals.

Special judicial offices

The Vice-Chancellor and the President of the Family Division
The Vice-Chancellor (V-C) is in practice the head of the Chancery Division of the High Court. In theory, the Lord Chancellor holds that position, but the Vice-Chancellor actually manages and presides over the work of that division, and hears many of the most important cases himself. The President (P), as one would expect, serves a similar role in the Family Division. Both may sit, from time to time, in the Court of Appeal.

The Master of the Rolls
The signature of the Master of the Rolls (or of one of his predecessors) appears on the enrolment certificate of every qualified solicitor. The real significance of the office, however, is that it carries with it the presidency of the civil division of the Court of Appeal. Given that the Court of Appeal hears many more cases than the House of Lords, and that the Master of the Rolls determines the composition of his courts (i.e., which judges hear which cases in that division), his influence on the development of the law can be enormous. Lord Denning MR, who held that post for many years, was almost certainly the most important and influential judge in living memory. Significantly, he had recently been elevated to the House of Lords when the position of Master of the Rolls became vacant, but saw that returning to the Court of Appeal would give him greater influence over the development of the law, and readily accepted the appointment when it was offered to him. The present Master of the Rolls, Lord Woolf MR, has followed Lord Denning's example by giving up his post as a Law Lord in order to take charge of the Court of Appeal.

The Lord Chief Justice
Whereas the Master of the Rolls presides over the civil division of the Court of Appeal, the Lord Chief Justice presides over the criminal division and over the Queen's Bench Division of the High Court. It is the highest non-political judicial appointment in the land, although in some respects its status is more or less equal to that of the Master of the Rolls. The current holder of this office, Lord Bingham CJ, was formerly Master of the Rolls, but is unusual in that

respect. The Lord Chief Justice holds a life peerage, and as a peer who holds high judicial office, he may sit in the appellate committee of the House of Lords. In October 1995, for example, the Lord Chief Justice of the day, Lord Taylor, delivered the leading speech of the House of Lords in the case of *Derby Magistrates' Court, ex parte B* [1995] 3 WLR 681. The Lord Chief Justice may also preside over the Divisional Court of the Queen's Bench Division, but rarely does so.

The Lord Chancellor

The office of Lord Chancellor was originally that of the king's chief minister. Cardinal Wolsey, for example, was Chancellor to King Henry VIII, until replaced by a professional lawyer, Sir Thomas More. It remains very much a political post. The Chancellor is, in a sense, the British minister of justice. He is both a cabinet minister and the head of the judiciary. The holder at the time of writing is Lord Irvine, a Scottish lawyer. He succeeded another Scottish lawyer, Lord Mackay, who has become known as the most revolutionary Chancellor of recent years. It may be that only an 'outsider' could ever have been able to shake up and reform so thoroughly the established legal professions and their sometimes archaic working practices. Despite his political and governmental duties, Lord Mackay, like his predecessor, Lord Hailsham, became notable for the frequency with which he found time to preside over appeals in the appellate committee of the House of Lords. It remains to be seen whether Lord Irvine will do likewise.

The independence of the judiciary

It is important that judges can give objective, independent decisions free from political bias in cases. The judges must be free from any outside factors which could influence their decisions. The judiciary in particular must be protected from executive (i.e., government) or legislative pressure when applying the law. In any good constitutional system, these three functions must be independent from each other. It is difficult to have complete separation of power, but there are rules and conventions which have been developed in the United Kingdom which establish the independence of the judiciary from the legislature and the executive.

Separation of powers

The concept of separation of powers can mean at least three different things. First, that the same persons should not form more than one of the three organs of government. Thus, for example, a sitting judge could not also be a Member of Parliament. The only exception to this rule is that of the Lord Chancellor who is not only the head of the judiciary but is also a cabinet minister. Secondly, one organ of government should not exercise control over, or interfere with the work of another such as the judiciary. Thirdly, one organ of government should not exercise the functions of another.

Although the Lord Chancellor (and in some cases the Prime Minister) appoints or advises on the appointment of the judges, their independence once appointed is assured through law and through constitutional convention. Since the Act of Settlement in 1700, judges are entitled to hold their position during good behaviour and not at the whim of the executive. They do not have to stand for election, as do many judges in the United States. This is clearly desirable, because one of the functions of a judge is to protect the individual citizen against government encroachment and judges should not have to curry favour with the electorate (e.g., by tough sentencing) in order to secure reappointment.

The legal profession

Where a person has a qualifying law degree, or another degree plus the Common Professional Examination qualification, that person may go on to qualify as a solicitor or barrister.

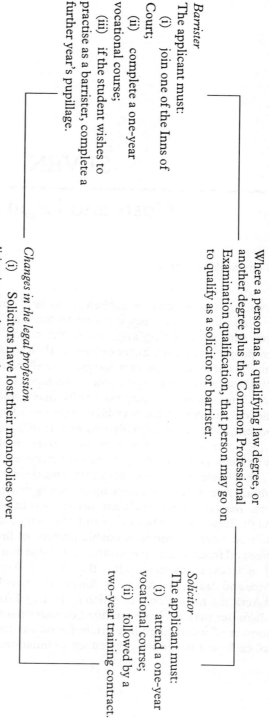

Barrister

The applicant must:

(i)   join one of the Inns of Court;

(ii)   complete a one-year vocational course;

(iii)   if the student wishes to practise as a barrister, complete a further year's pupillage.

Solicitor

The applicant must:

(i)   attend a one-year vocational course;

(ii)   followed by a two-year training contract.

Changes in the legal profession

(i)   Solicitors have lost their monopolies over litigation, probate and conveyancing.

(ii)   Barristers have lost their monopoly on rights of audience in the higher courts. These rights are now based on appropriate qualifications recognised by authorised bodies.

(iii)   Relaxation of rules of conduct by both professions in response to these changes.

SEVEN

Costs and Legal Aid

The costs of litigation

It is said that everyone is equal before the law, but this statement can be true only if all persons have equal access to the law. The cost of obtaining legal advice and of contesting litigation in the courts can prohibit or discourage many people from pursuing or defending their legal rights. This has sometimes led to the accusation that only the rich can afford to protect those rights.

Paradoxically, the persons who have most to fear from the cost of legal proceedings are not the very poor (who may get legal aid), but those who are moderately wealthy. A litigant who is unsuccessful may have to pay the costs of his opponent, as well as those of his own lawyers (which in High Court cases could be £10,000 or more, and far more in some cases). Although in some cases lawyers may now charge on a contingent, or 'no win, no fee' basis, that still does not avoid the risk of having to pay costs to the other parties involved. It is possible, however, to obtain relatively inexpensive insurance against the risk of that happening, at least in personal accident claims, where most litigants are successful anyway.

As the legal costs of both civil and criminal proceedings can be so great, the state now provides funds to enable persons of limited means to receive legal advice and representation in court. The first serious attempt to provide legal aid and assistance was made after the Second World War, through the Legal Advice and Assistance Act 1949. Since then there have been a number of Legal Aid Acts, the most recent of which is the Legal Aid Act 1988, and regulations made under that Act have modified or restricted the availability of legal aid in a number of ways. Eligibility limits for means-tested benefits are adjusted in April each year to allow for the effects of inflation.

Today, the administration of legal aid may be divided into two main categories: (i) legal advice and assistance; and (ii) civil and criminal legal aid. The former is primarily concerned with the provision of cheap and effective legal advice, whereas the latter deals with representation for the purpose of court proceedings. The annual cost of providing legal aid is huge. Over the last ten years alone, the amount of public expenditure on legal aid has spiralled. In 1985 the net cost was £306 million, but by 1996 it had risen to over £1,600 million. As a reaction to these escalating costs, successive Lord Chancellors have been forced to deal with the problem through the imposition of new regulations which have had the effect of reducing the number of potential legal aid recipients. In particular, it has been decided that personal injury (negligence) actions will largely cease to qualify for legal aid during the course of 1998. Most persons suing for personal injury will instead be expected to proceed by way of conditional (no win, no fee) agreements with their lawyers (as to which, see p. 101). It is anticipated that legal aid will also be withdrawn from other actions for damages in the relatively near future.

The Legal Aid Act 1988

Section 1 states that the purpose of this Act is:

> to establish a framework for the provision ... of advice, assistance and representation which is publicly funded with a view to helping persons who might otherwise be unable to obtain advice, assistance, representation on account of their means.

Although s. 1 lays down the general framework of the Act, the Lord Chancellor has been given wide powers to make any regulations which he thinks necessary for giving effect to the Act, or to prevent abuse of the system. He has already made a number of important regulations in this field.

Section 3 of the Act establishes the Legal Aid Board (LAB) which has responsibility for the day-to-day administration of the legal aid scheme. This function was formerly carried out by the Law Society, but the government's 'Efficiency Scrutiny Report' of 1986 declared that it was undesirable for the Law Society to control the purse strings, as such a large proportion of the legal aid budget is expended in solicitor's fees.

Section 4 of the Act deals with the LAB's powers and duties. The Board's main function is to ensure that advice, assistance and representation are made available in accordance with the provisions of the 1988 Act. This may include, with the concurrence of the Lord Chancellor, the securing of advice or assistance by contracting with certain persons and bodies for the provision of legal services. For example, the Board may reach franchise agreements with individual firms of solicitors. Firms without such franchises may find themselves largely excluded from legal aid work.

The LAB also has responsibility to publish information and reports and to advise the Lord Chancellor on legal services policy.

Legal advice and assistance: the green form scheme

The green form scheme is the system whereby advice and assistance is given cheaply and effectively to persons who cannot otherwise afford it. Such advice and assistance is usually given by solicitors in private practice. A solicitor may give either oral or written advice on any matter of English law, and may advise and assist the applicant on any steps which it may be appropriate for him to take. The solicitor may, if necessary, seek the advice of a barrister, although this will seldom be feasible, given the financial constraints imposed under the scheme.

The range of services which the solicitor can provide under this part of the legal aid scheme are relatively wide-ranging and include giving general advice, letter writing, negotiating settlements and filling out forms for claiming 'full' legal aid. The green form scheme initially was limited to the giving of advice and assistance and did not extend to actual representation in court. In 1979, however, it was extended, to a limited degree, to assistance by way of legal representation (ABWOR) in certain types of proceedings for which civil legal aid is not available (see below). In some areas, a modified scheme known as 'claim 10' has replaced the green form scheme on a trial or pilot basis, but it is similar in most important respects.

The means test
An applicant under the green form scheme is subject to a means test, which is carried out by the solicitor at the consultation. If the applicant satisfies the means test then he will be entitled to two hours' worth of work from the solicitor (or three hours if it is a matrimonial dispute). One advantage of the green form scheme is that it is administered directly by the solicitor, and this facilitates the provision of quick and cheap legal advice. If, however, the applicant requires more than two hours' worth of work (or three if matrimonial), the solicitor will have to obtain authorisation to proceed from the area director responsible for the provision of legal aid services in the vicinity. If the extension is urgent, permission may be granted by the director over the telephone. He will then stipulate the level of extension thought appropriate for the case.

Means testing by the solicitor includes looking at the applicant's disposable income and disposable capital. Disposable income is based upon what is left of a person's weekly income after specified deductions are made for income tax, national insurance contributions and prescribed allowances for the applicant's spouse/cohabitee, children or other dependants. Disposable capital, on the other hand, includes an assessment of the applicant's savings, anything of substantial value, such as jewellery, antiques, etc. (but does not include the normal furniture and clothes which the applicant possesses, or the tools of the applicant's trade). The applicant's main home cannot be taken into account, but any other dwelling, such as a holiday home, must be. The applicant's disposable capital is the total remaining after subtracting prescribed allowances for spouses, cohabitees, children or other dependants.

The relevant limits vary from time to time, but in 1998 applicants became entitled to advice and assistance under the scheme if their disposable capital was £1,000 or less *and* their disposable income (after deductions) was £80 per week or less. Persons in receipt of income support, family credit, or disability allowance qualify automatically as far as the income test is concerned, but will still become ineligible if their disposable capital exceeds £1,000. These limits effectively disqualify many people on relatively modest salaries, or those with relatively modest savings. Spouses' or cohabitees' incomes and savings are taken into account for these purposes, unless the matter in question involves a dispute between them.

Restraints imposed upon the scheme

As mentioned earlier, successive Lord Chancellors have been concerned in recent years at the spiralling costs associated with the provision of legal aid. As a result they have, by a series of regulations, narrowed the types of claims which can be dealt with under the scheme. For example, it can no longer ordinarily be used in connection with the giving of advice or assistance on conveyancing matters, nor may it ordinarily be used in connection with the drafting of wills. (There are some exceptions to this rule, e.g., for disabled persons.)

Limitations of the scheme

(a)   The advice and assistance scheme was never intended to supplant civil legal aid, which may be needed if serious litigation is to be undertaken. It was only ever intended to be about the provision of initial advice and simple assistance. The scope of the scheme has nevertheless been modified in various ways. Some forms of advice and assistance have been taken out of the scheme (see above), but on the other hand the ABWOR scheme (see below) now extends the original concept to include the provision of representation in certain tribunal hearings.

(b)   The scheme covers advice or assistance given on English law only, and does not extend to advice given on foreign law.

(c)   The scheme covers advice given by a solicitor (or by a barrister if the solicitor seeks the barrister's opinion on a case). If the advice is given by a lay specialist, even if the latter is hired by the solicitor for his expertise, the fees charged by the specialist are not recoverable under the scheme.

Assistance by way of representation

One of the main limitations of the green form scheme as first introduced was that it could not provide funding to enable a solicitor to present a client's case before a court or tribunal; and yet civil legal aid is only rarely available for proceedings in tribunals. This left a significant gap in the provision of assistance to litigants in such tribunals. In 1979, however, the scheme was extended to cover assistance by way of representation (ABWOR) at certain designated proceedings. Initially, it was thought that this would extend to representation in all manner of courts and tribunals, but for financial reasons its ambit has been significantly curtailed by the Lord Chancellor, who is empowered to make any regulations which he sees fit in relation to this scheme. Currently, ABWOR is available for most civil proceedings in magistrates' courts, proceedings before mental health review tribunals and disciplinary charges before Boards of Prison Visitors.

In some categories of representation under ABWOR the solicitor may proceed directly with the claim, whereas in others he must first obtain the permission of the area director before proceeding.

Eligibility for ABWOR

The rules governing eligibility for ABWOR are not the same as those governing eligibility to initial advice under the green form or 'claim 10' schemes. Although both schemes are means tested, eligibility for ABWOR also depends in some cases upon a 'merits test'. The legal aid area director must be satisfied (in the more expensive cases requiring his approval) that public money is not being wasted in hopeless or misconceived litigation.

As far as the means test is concerned, persons applying for ABWOR must not have a disposable income in excess of £172 per week and will have to meet a proportion of their own costs if their disposable weekly income is between £72 and £172. The limit for disposable capital is also higher, at £3,000. It follows that some applicants will qualify for ABWOR even if they do not qualify for free advice under the green form scheme.

Legal aid in civil cases

Although some matters may be adequately dealt with by advice or assistance under the green form scheme or ABWOR, major litigation requires a different kind of funding. Legal aid is available to cover the cost of work done in civil proceedings leading up to and including representation by either a solicitor or barrister at the court hearing. The scope and availability of the legal aid scheme, however, is restricted in many respects.

Legal aid is potentially available in most types of civil proceedings in all civil courts. It is not, however, generally available for tribunal hearings, other than those before the Lands Tribunal, Employment Appeal Tribunal and the Commons Commissioners, each of which adopts a formal legal procedure that requires expert legal representation. Furthermore, civil legal aid does not extend to coroner's courts, actions for defamation, county court arbitrations or undefended divorce actions and in 1998 will largely cease to be available in personal injury actions. The likelihood is that many other types of actions will cease to qualify for legal aid in future years.

Since the sums of public money that may be involved are likely to be very substantial, applications for civil legal aid cannot be determined by individual solicitors as under the green form scheme. They must instead be made to the area director. If the applicant disagrees with the director's decision then he may appeal to the area committee.

Eligibility for civil legal aid

The applicant for civil legal aid must satisfy both a means test and a merits test. Section 15(2) of the 1988 Act states that the applicant must satisfy the area director that he has reasonable grounds for taking, defending or being a party to the proceedings. The applicant, may, however, be refused civil legal aid for any one of a number of reasons laid down in the Act itself, e.g., where the area director believes that the client would obtain only a trivial advantage from the proceedings. If the applicant appears to have a hopeless case, public money will not be wasted in support of it. Even if the area director grants civil legal aid, the applicant's solicitor will be required by the LAB periodically to certify that he thinks it is reasonable for the client to go on receiving legal aid in respect of the action.

In a few cases, it might be decided that an applicant for legal aid could more sensibly proceed with a different form of action that would qualify for ABWOR; for example, in a case where a woman seeks an order against her violent husband, it may be unreasonable to expect civil legal aid for county court proceedings if the applicant would adequately be protected by seeking an exclusion or protection order from a (magistrates') family proceedings court. ABWOR would be available for the latter type of action, which would cost the taxpayer less money.

The applicant's means are tested by the Legal Aid Board. To be eligible for civil legal aid, an applicant must not ordinarily have disposable capital of more than £6,750, or a disposable income of more than £7,777 per annum. Even then, graded contributions may be required from applicants whose disposable incomes or savings exceed the 'lower' limits of £2,625 per annum or £3,000 capital, respectively, and if a legally-aided applicant is successful in recovering damages or property, he will find that the Legal Aid Board may seek to recover its expenses by means of the 'statutory charge' (below).

The statutory charge

The statutory charge enables the LAB to recover the cost of legal aid from any money or property recovered by the assisted person from the proceedings. It will exercise this right where the amount of costs awarded to the assisted person by the court, together with any financial contribution which the assisted person may have made, is insufficient to reimburse the legal aid fund. The statutory charge has been criticised by many, as damages or compensation which the assisted person receives may be at least partly swallowed up by the fund; but without it, the financial limits would no doubt have to be adjusted so that even fewer persons would qualify for legal aid in the first place.

Unfairness to unassisted parties
The 1988 Act regrettably maintains a procedure which penalises an unassisted party who successfully litigates against a legally-aided opponent. Costs may be awarded against a legally-aided party only if:

(a)   that party was the one who initiated the proceedings;
(b)   the court is satisfied that the unassisted party would otherwise suffer financial hardship; *and*
(c)   it would be just and equitable for the unassisted party to recover from public funds.

In the case of *Thew* v *Reeves* [1981] 3 WLR 190, Lord Denning MR referred to this rule as 'the ugly unacceptable face of British justice'.

Legal advice and assistance in criminal cases

The green form scheme described earlier in this chapter is equally applicable to consultation in connection with matters of criminal law. A person may thus visit a participating solicitor to seek written or oral advice and assistance in connection with actual or potential criminal proceedings against him. A means test applies, as in cases where advice is sought on civil matters.

The duty solicitor scheme

This scheme makes advice and assistance available in connection with certain criminal proceedings in the magistrates' courts and youth courts. ABWOR may be available in a limited range of circumstances to an accused who is otherwise unrepresented, especially if it is his first appearance in connection with the proceedings, or where he is in custody. These services are provided by solicitors designated by the LAB to attend at these courts. There is no merits test or means test.

Free advice and assistance is also provided for persons at police stations. From 1 January 1986, duty solicitor schemes were extended to cover persons arrested and detained at police stations and persons who were voluntarily at the station 'helping with enquiries'. These schemes allow a solicitor to give advice and assistance to such persons in those circumstances. This service is again free of any means test. Duty solicitors are remunerated out of the legal aid fund.

Legal aid in criminal cases

In contrast to legal aid in civil cases, legal aid in criminal cases is granted by the courts themselves. This helps to speed up the process. Legal aid in Crown

Court proceedings may be granted either by the Crown Court, or by the magistrates' court which sends the defendant for trial or sentence. The defendant may make an application for legal aid either to the justices' clerk (magistrates' court), or to the chief clerk (Crown Court). If the applicant is refused legal aid he must be told of the reason for the refusal, and this must be based either on the ground that it is not in the interests of justice to make such an order or on the ground that the applicant's disposable income or capital makes him ineligible.

If legal aid is refused, the applicant has a right to renew the application if it is a summary offence. If, on the other hand, the case involves either an indictable offence or one which is triable either way, the applicant may apply for a review to the area committee (or renew his application to the Crown Court if the offence is an indictable one).

Eligibility for legal aid in criminal cases
In certain circumstances, a financially eligible applicant *must* be granted criminal legal aid. Section 21 of the Legal Aid Act 1988 lists the situations in which this applies:

(a)   where the applicant is committed for trial for murder;
(b)   where his conviction has been quashed on appeal, but the prosecution are seeking to appeal to the House of Lords;
(c)   where he is likely to remain in custody and has no legal representation; or
(d)   where he has been found guilty and is to be held in custody for enquiries and reports to be made.

In all other cases, legal aid may be granted only where the applicant is financially eligible *and* it is 'desirable in the interests of justice'. Section 22 of the Act lays down criteria to help determine what is in the interests of justice. These are known as the 'Widgery criteria' after Lord Widgery CJ, who was the chairman of the 1966 Committee on Legal Aid in Criminal Proceedings where the guidelines were first put forward. These criteria include:

(a)   where the offence is grave, in the sense that the defendant, if convicted, will lose his livelihood or liberty, or suffer damage to his reputation;
(b)   where the case involves consideration of a substantial point of law;
(c)   where the defendant may be unable to follow the proceedings or to state his own case because of inadequate knowledge of English, mental illness or other mental or physical disability;
(d)   where the nature of the defence involves tracing and interviewing witnesses or expert cross-examination of a witness for the prosecution; or
(e)   where legal representation is desirable, such as in a case of alleged cruelty or sexual offences against children where it would be improper for the defendant to cross-examine the complainants in person.

These criteria are not exhaustive and the Lord Chancellor may amend them as he sees fit.

Means tests

The applicant will be required to pay a proportion of the costs if it appears to the court that he is able to afford it. A contribution will not be required if the applicant's disposable income is less than £50 per week and his disposable capital does not exceed £3,000. If the applicant's disposable income or capital exceeds this level, he will be required to make a contribution in accordance with a formula laid down by legal aid regulations.

Recovering costs of a successful defence

A defendant who is acquitted on a criminal charge and who has not received legal aid (or who has received insufficient to cover his necessary costs) may apply for his costs to be met from 'central funds' under the Prosecution of Offences Act 1985, s. 16; but it is recognised that in certain circumstances a full costs order may not be appropriate (as where a defendant is acquitted on some charges, but not others). It is also recognised that in some cases an order for costs may be refused altogether, as where the defendant was acquitted only on a mere technicality, or where his behaviour was such as to invite suspicion and prosecution (*Practice Direction (Crime: Costs)* [1991] 1 WLR 498).

Paying costs of the prosecution

Under the Prosecution of Offences Act 1985, s. 18, a convicted defendant who has the means and ability to pay a contribution to the costs of the prosecution may be required to do so. In practice, defendants may well feel that an order for costs amounts to an additional fine or penalty, and the costs factor may be instrumental in many decisions to plead guilty or accept summary trial, rather than seeking a full contested trial by jury, where the costs are likely to be highest.

The problems of legal aid

The provision of comprehensive legal aid, so as to make justice equally available to all, is at present an unattainable and unaffordable ideal. The very poor and the very rich are each, in their own way, free to contemplate expensive legal proceedings with some degree of security. The moderately poor and (even more so) the moderately rich have a great deal to fear. They will seldom qualify for any kind of legal aid (save for the free advice available at police stations, etc.) and may face financial ruin if they become involved in litigation which they eventually lose. They may feel particularly aggrieved when faced with litigation against a party who is legally aided. In some circumstances, they may even have to proceed in the knowledge that they will never recover their costs from such a party, even if they win. As Lord Denning MR rightly said in *Thew* v *Reeves* (above), this is unfair and morally unacceptable.

For the moderately poor and moderately wealthy, insurance policies and membership of associations or trade unions may provide some measure of protection or support. Motor insurance is compulsory for drivers, but policies are available that cover various kinds of other potential liability, including liability for costs. Accidents caused by pets, livestock, cycling or unsafe premises may all be protected, depending on the policy in question. Some household policies offer insurance against the cost of litigation and against the risk of winning a case but failing to recover costs or damages from an impecunious defendant.

Conditional and contingent fees

In some countries (notably in the USA) lawyers have for many years offered their potential clients the opportunity to litigate on a 'no win, no fee' basis. This is not, however, the simple solution to litigation costs that it might seem. American lawyers often do well by such systems, but they do so by claiming a contingent fee which is a proportion (and often a very substantial proportion) of any damages awarded. That system is sometimes blamed (perhaps unfairly) for some of the more unsavoury aspects of American justice, such as the 'win at all costs' approach to litigation, the excessive amount of litigation or the enormous damages often awarded by juries in civil actions. Juries, it is said, know that a large part of any damages awarded will be siphoned off by the plaintiff's lawyers, so they award increased damages, to ensure that the plaintiff still has enough.

In English law, 'percentage' contingent fee agreements of the American kind are still regarded as unlawful, but conditional fee agreements with lawyers have recently been approved as lawful, even at common law, as long as the lawyers in question do not seek to obtain more than their normal fee in the event of winning the case for the client. In *Thai Trading Company* v *Taylor* [1998] 3 All ER 65 the Court of Appeal overruled earlier authorities which had suggested that any kind of conditional agreement was unlawful and contrary to public policy. The way is now open to their further development, but because unsuccessful litigants under English law may have to pay the costs of their opponents (and of the court) conditional fee agreements must usually be backed by some kind of insurance policy, so as to ensure that the other side's legal expenses can be met if necessary.

Conditional fee agreements under the Courts and Legal Services Act 1990
A more radical kind of conditional fee agreements (or CFA) may be entered into in certain circumstances covered by s. 58 of the Courts and Legal Services Act 1990 and related statutory instruments. They are more radical because

they permit solicitors to charge *more* than their standard fees in the event of winning the case, although this is still not the same thing as a contingent percentage of whatever damages are recovered. The government sees CFAs as a way of largely replacing legal aid funding in civil cases, and they are thus likely to be used more widely in the future, but the first such instruments (made in 1995) confined these CFAs to personal injury cases, company insolvency and personal bankruptcy cases, and cases brought before the European Commission or before the Court of Human Rights. They lay down strict rules as to the form of such agreements, including a restriction 'capping' the maximum 'uplift' (i.e., the increase over normal litigation fees in the event of success) to 100 per cent of the normal fee. In other words, a solicitor who ordinarily charges £90 per hour may charge up to £180 per hour (conditional on success) under this kind of CFA. Successful actions thus finance the cost of unsuccessful actions. In practice, it seems that most solicitors charge an uplift of no more than 25 per cent, in line with Law Society recommendations. The uplift comes out of the damages awarded; the losing party does not have to pay the uplift element of the winning party's costs.

Standard insurance schemes, negotiated between the Law Society and leading insurance companies, are widely used by lawyers offering CFAs, and will become even more widely used when the right to legal aid is withdrawn from most personal injury actions during 1998. Insurers will not take on cases they consider to be more or less unwinnable, even if the solicitors are more optimistic, and of course they will only take part at all if their earnings from such policies consistently outweigh losses occasioned by payouts to successful opponents. Solicitors who lose more CFA cases than they win may find themselves unable to secure essential CFA insurance for their clients. That may be seen as a drawback, but some would see it as a form of quality control, reducing the amount of hopeless or misconceived litigation.

Insurance policies to cover simple injury cases may be quite cheap, because most such claims succeed, but complex medical negligence cases (which do not always succeed) will require more expensive policies. A £975 policy will currently buy insurance against liability for opponents' costs of up to £15,000, assuming that the insurers consider the case to be winnable.

Already widely used in personal injury cases, CFAs will eventually become widespread in other kinds of action for damages, as the availability of civil legal aid is gradually narrowed down. They are unlikely, however, to be extended to cases involving matrimonial breakdown or the welfare of children.

Legal aid

Civil

Advice and assistance
A quick and cheap method of obtaining advice. Available for non-litigious work. It can be obtained by making an application to a solicitor. Enables the applicant to receive 2 hours' worth of work (or 3 if matrimonial). An extension may be obtained by application to the Area Director of Legal Aid. Means tested.

ABWOR
Advice and assistance now extended to provide representation in certain designated proceedings. Means and merits tested.

Civil legal aid
Although many cases can be dealt with by advice and assistance or ABWOR, major litigation requires a different type of funding. Civil legal aid is available for the cost of work done in civil proceedings, leading up to and including representation in court. Means and merits tested. The trend is for civil legal aid to be replaced by insurance and CFAs in many areas.

Criminal

Advice and assistance
Available for matters connected with the criminal law. Means tested (but free advice and assistance may be provided at the police station under the duty solicitor scheme).

ABWOR
Available in a limited range of circumstances.

Criminal legal aid
In certain circumstances a financially eligible applicant *must* be granted legal aid. In other cases a financially eligible applicant will be given legal aid only if it is in the interests of justice.

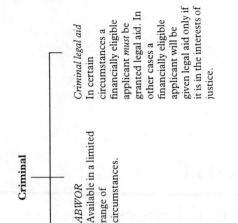
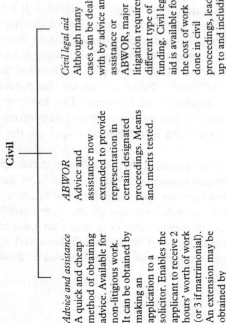

EIGHT

The Criminal Process

Prosecutions

Most prosecutions are instigated and conducted by public officials (the police, the Crown Prosecution Service (CPS), Customs and Excise, etc.), but a private individual or body may also bring a prosecution, and this right has been confirmed by s. 6 of the Prosecution of Offences Act 1985. This is referred to as a private prosecution, but it is still notionally brought on behalf of the Crown. Private prosecutors will have to pay their own costs, although these may be recovered from central funds if the prosecution is successful. If it fails, then the person who brought the action may have to pay part of the defence costs as well. Individuals do not have an unfettered right to bring or pursue a private prosecution, as the CPS may intervene at any time and either take over the case or stop it. Furthermore, some offences can be prosecuted only 'by or with the consent of' the Director of Public Prosecutions or the Attorney-General. Relatively few private prosecutions are brought. The majority are prosecutions for relatively minor assaults, but serious offences are sometimes prosecuted privately, usually where the CPS has declined to pursue the case itself.

The vast majority of prosecutions are initiated by the police and conducted by the CPS. The police are given greater powers than any private individual in relation to the investigation of crime and the apprehension of offenders. It is essential, however, that a balance is struck between giving them sufficient powers to perform this role and at the same time ensuring that people are allowed to go about their daily business without being unduly harassed by the police. In 1979, a Royal Commission on Criminal Procedure was established to look into the nature of police powers. The Commission reported in 1981, and the government responded by enacting the Police and Criminal Evidence Act (PACE) 1984. This gave the police greater powers of arrest and search than they had possessed before, but included many new safeguards for the suspect. It could be said that police powers before PACE 1984 were inadequate, but controls on the abuse of those powers were even more inadequate, with the result that the police resorted to unlawful actions in order to make arrests and obtain confessions or convictions. The next few sections will look at the powers which the police have today as regards powers of stop and search, arrest, detention and questioning.

Police powers to stop and search and question

At common law, the police had no power to stop or search or question citizens, save where they had already made an arrest. Citizens had no common law duty to permit such searches or to answer police questions. In *Rice v Connolly* [1966] 2 All ER 649, two police officers stopped Rice as he was walking at night through an area which had suffered a string of burglaries, and asked him where he was going. He refused to provide satisactory answers to their questions and he was therefore arrested and charged with 'obstructing a police officer in the execution of his duty'. His conviction for that offence was quashed on appeal. Giving judgment in the Divisional Court, Lord Parker CJ stated:

> ... the whole basis of the common law is the right of the individual to refuse to answer questions put to him by persons in authority, and to refuse to accompany those in authority to any particular place; short, of course, of arrest.

Extensive stop and search powers have subsequently been given to the police by various statutes, notably PACE 1984, the Firearms Act 1968, the Misuse of Drugs Act 1971, the Aviation Security Act 1982 and the Criminal Justice and Public Order Act 1994. Only the most important of these can be considered here.

Stop and search under PACE 1984

The main stop and search power is found in s.1 of PACE 1984. This is a lengthy section, which is supplemented by ss. 2 and 3 of the Act and by 'Code A' of the Codes of Practice drafted under the Act for the regulation of police officers in the exercise of their statutory powers. What follows is merely a brief summary of the main provisions.

A constable may detain a person or vehicle under s. 1 for the purpose of a search where he has reasonable grounds for believing that he will find stolen or prohibited articles. Prohibited articles are defined as including knives, offensive weapons (things designed, adapted or intended for causing injury) and articles which may be used in relation to offences under the Theft Acts. These might include skeleton keys, stolen credit cards, jemmies, tools for removing car radios, etc. The stop and search power may be exercised in a public place or a place to which some section of the public has access, but it cannot be exercised in a private dwelling, or in the grounds of a dwelling in which the person searched is known to reside.

Reasonable grounds for suspicion

Before the police officer can use his powers of stop and search under s. 1, he must have 'reasonable grounds' for believing that he will find stolen or prohibited articles on the person or vehicle to be searched. This must exist *before* the person or vehicle is stopped or searched. As Code A makes clear, 'there is no power to stop and detain a person against his will in order to find grounds for a search'. Once a suspect has been lawfully stopped, the officer may detain him in order to carry out the search, but for no longer, unless the officer then arrests him.

What constitutes reasonable grounds for suspicion?

Code A states that, 'Whether reasonable grounds for suspicion exist will depend on the circumstances in each case, but there must be some objective basis for it' (para. 1.6). A stop and search based upon a person's 'colour, age, hairstyle or manner of dress' is never enough, unless the officer has specific reasons to suspect a person matching such a description. Nor is it enough that the person searched is known to have a criminal record (para. 1.7). Furtive or suspicious behaviour may however suffice and it may also suffice that the police are acting on a tip-off or complaint.

Section 2 of the Act requires an officer to provide a person he has stopped with certain information if a search is to take place. If the constable is not in uniform, he must first show his warrant card. The purpose of the search must be explained. An officer must make a written record of any search he has carried out unless it is impracticable to do so (as for example where he is involved in dealing with a disturbance at the time). The *Notes for Guidance* appended to Code A warn officers that they must always act reasonably and may subsequently be required to justify their actions in court.

The search itself

Section 2(9) of the Act provides that, without an arrest, a police officer is only allowed to make the searched person remove certain items of clothing in public, namely an outer coat, jacket or gloves. An officer cannot require a person to remove his headgear if searched in public. This is for fear of causing offence to ethnic minorities, such as Sikhs, whose headgear forms a part of their culture or religion. If a more extensive search is required, it must be carried out by an officer of the same sex as the suspect and out of the public view.

Code A emphasises that officers should exercise their powers responsibly at all times and should if possible obtain the consent of the searched party before proceeding. If consent is not forthcoming, officers may use reasonable force to effect a search. An officer may detain a suspect for as long as it takes to carry out the search, but for no longer.

Further powers of stop and search are given to the police under s. 60 of the Criminal Justice and Public Order Act 1994, in cases (such as in or before major demonstrations) where senior officers fear serious violence may occur in the area.

Police powers of arrest

Nothing in PACE 1984 or in Code A seeks to prevent police officers talking to or questioning citizens in the ordinary course of their duties (i.e., without exercising any element of compulsion). It does not seek to discourage co-operation between police and public (*Notes for Guidance*, para. 1B), but if the police wish to detain a person for questioning as to his possible involvement in a crime, they must either obtain the voluntary co-operation of that person or arrest him. They cannot *require* him to 'accompany them to the police station'. He may agree to 'help them with their enquiries', but if he does not offer to do so they must either let him go or arrest him.

Most powers of arrest are statute-based. The only common law power of arrest without warrant is in relation to breach of the peace. This is often used by officers, because it covers a wide variety of situations and offences in which arrest may be called for. The police may also arrest under the authority of a warrant issued by a magistrate or by a judge of the Crown Court ('arrest under warrant'). Warrants are commonly issued where suspects have failed to attend court after being summonsed to do so, and may also be issued under the Extradition Act 1989, to authorise the arrest of alleged fugitive offenders who are wanted by the authorities in other countries.

Arrest without warrant

There are two categories of arrest powers under the Police and Criminal Evidence Act 1984. One relates to a power of arrest for 'arrestable offences' and the other gives the police a power of arrest in relation to *any* criminal offence, provided certain 'general arrest conditions' are satisfied. Other arrest powers exist under statutes such as the Public Order Act 1986, but the PACE 1984 provisions are the most important.

(1)   Arrestable offences   Section 24 of PACE 1984 permits an officer to arrest without a warrant:

(a)   anyone who is in the act of committing an arrestable offence;
(b)   anyone whom he has reasonable grounds for suspecting to be committing such an offence;

(c) anyone who is guilty of having committed such an offence;

(d) anyone whom he has reasonable grounds for suspecting to be guilty of having committed such an offence;

(e) anyone who is about to commit such an offence; or

(f) anyone whom he has reasonable grounds for suspecting to be about to commit such an offence.

The powers listed in (a), (b) and (c) may also be exercised by private citizens (in a 'citizen's arrest') but the power listed in (d) may only be lawfully exercised by a private citizen where such an offence has indeed been committed. A private citizen may therefore have a defence to an action for false imprisonment where he mistakenly arrests the wrong person, but *not* where he was mistaken in thinking that an arrestable offence had been committed in the first place. Powers (e) and (f) can be exercised only by the police.

These powers may only be relied upon where the offence in question is an arrestable one. An arrestable offence is defined in s. 24(1) as including any offence for which the sentence is fixed by law (i.e., murder or treason) and any offence which carries a maximum penalty of at least five years' imprisonment. A few offences which carry lesser sentences have also been added to this category, notably that of taking a conveyance without lawful authority or consent, contrary to s. 12 of the Theft Act 1968.

(2) Other statutory powers of arrest Many other statutory offences carry specific powers of arrest. These are usually exercisable only by a police officer, and sometimes only in specific circumstances (as where the offender is 'found committing' the offence in question). These are *not* 'arrestable offences' for the purpose of s. 24, above.

(3) General arrest conditions If a police officer witnesses or discovers the commission of an offence to which no special statutory power of arrest attaches, the offender (if found or identified) would ordinarily be proceeded against by means of a summons. In other words, for many less serious offences, such as minor motoring offences, there is ordinarily no need to make an arrest. It is enough for the suspect to be ordered to turn up at court to answer the charge against him. Section 25 of PACE 1984, however, recognises that, under certain circumstances, a 'report for summons' may not be effective. A constable may therefore arrest the suspect, if it appears to him that service of a summons would be impracticable because one or more of the 'general arrest conditions' are satisfied. These general arrest conditions are listed in s. 25(3). An officer may arrest the suspect if the latter's name cannot be readily ascertained; if the officer has reason to doubt the authenticity of the name he has been given; if no satisfactory address for the service of the summons has been given; if the officer believes an arrest is necessary to prevent the arrested person causing physical injury to himself or any other person, or causing loss or damage to property or

certain offences against public decency; if the arrested person is causing an obstruction of the highway; or if the officer reasonably believes that an arrest is necessary to protect a child or other vulnerable person.

Power of search upon arrest

The power to search a suspect who has just been arrested depends upon s. 32 of PACE 1984. Where the suspect has been arrested somewhere other than at a police station, the arresting officer may be able to search him on one of two grounds: (a) where the officer has reasonable grounds to believe that the suspect may try to injure himself or others; and (b) where the officer reasonably suspects the suspect may have anything which might be used by him to escape or which may be evidence in the case. The officer may search for evidence of *any* offence (not just that for which the arrest took place) if he has reasonable grounds for believing that such evidence may be concealed on the suspect's person; but as with stop and search powers, searches should not involve the removal of inner clothing or headgear in public. Whether the police may lawfully retain things found in the course of a search largely depends on whether they consider in good faith that the things in question may be needed in evidence.

Procedure following arrest

Following arrest, a suspect must ordinarily be taken to a police station as soon as reasonably practicable. The purpose of this rule is to ensure that he becomes subject to the safeguards of PACE 1984 as soon as possible. If, however, the arresting officer realises that he has made a mistake, he should at once release the arrested person. He need not take him to the police station before so doing.

Safeguards for persons in police custody

PACE 1984 has introduced stringent safeguards for the protection of persons in police custody, because this is the time when they may be most vulnerable in the criminal justice system. There have been several well-publicised cases over the last few years in which false confessions have been elicited from suspects while in police custody, or in which false confessions have been manufactured by the police and attributed to the suspect. (Most, it should be added, date from the time before the PACE 1984 safeguards were first introduced.) If a suspect confesses to a crime while in police custody, his chances of acquittal will be hugely reduced, even if he attempts to withdraw the confession at trial. In theory, the prosecution have always been required to prove to the judge that a confession was freely given, before the jury can be allowed to hear of it, but if the police insisted that no improper pressures were applied, and that the confession was genuinely that of the accused, the judges almost always tended to believe them. Indeed, if a defendant with a criminal record dares to allege that the police mistreated him or fabricated his confession, he can be cross-examined in front of the jury about his previous convictions. (This is known as the 'tit for tat' principle, and is derived from s. 1(f)(ii) of the Criminal Evidence Act 1898.)

The provisions set out in PACE 1984 and its Codes of Practice are geared to protect the detainee while in police custody, thereby decreasing the likelihood of a coerced or fabricated confession. These provisions deal with issues such as interviews, refreshments, and general treatment of the prisoner. A 'custody officer' is assigned the role of ensuring that these provisions are adhered to.

The custody officer must usually be of the rank of sergeant or above. One of the first responsibilities of the custody officer is to assess the evidence which the arresting officers wish to produce against the suspect. He must decide whether there is sufficient evidence to charge the suspect. If there is, the suspect must either be charged then and there, without further interrogation, or be released pending a decision as to whether the charge will actually be pressed. Once charged, the suspect may then be released (with or without bail) or detained in police custody pending his first appearance in court.

Where there appears to be insufficient evidence to charge the suspect, he must ordinarily be released. This does not mean that the case is closed. If the police consider that they need more time to gather evidence and/or to decide whether to proceed, the suspect may be released on police bail, and required to return to the police station at a future date (see s. 47(3) of PACE). He may subsequently be charged or cleared, or even bailed once again pending yet more enquiries.

Detention for questioning, etc.

In some cases the custody officer may be satisfied that the suspect's continued detention is necessary in order to obtain further evidence by questioning him, or to secure or preserve evidence relating to the offence for which the suspect is under arrest. In such circumstances, the custody officer may authorise the suspect's continued detention, although this will be subject to constant review (see below).

Upon the suspect's arrival at the station, the custody officer will open a custody record for him. This document will record everything that happens to him while in police custody. For example, it will include a record of refreshments given to the detainee, the times of interviews, etc. The suspect will be informed of certain legal rights on arrival at the station and will be asked to sign the custody record to indicate that he has been informed of these rights. The suspect must be told:

(a)   of his right to see a solicitor under s. 58 of PACE 1984 and that legal advice will be provided free of charge (see Chapter 7); and

(b)   that he has the right to have someone informed of his arrest (s. 56 of PACE 1984).

These rights can be denied to the suspect (and then only temporarily) only if the offence is a 'serious arrestable offence' (as defined under s. 116 of PACE 1984) and if an officer of the rank of superintendent or above believes that granting access to legal advice or allowing the suspect to inform another of his detention would be undesirable for one of the reasons specified in s. 56(5) of the Act (e.g., because it is feared that it would impede the course of justice or alert criminal associates etc.). These rights can be denied for a maximum 36-hour period only. After such time, the detainee must be given legal advice if he so wishes, or have someone informed of his whereabouts.

Certain categories of detainees, such as young persons or the mentally disabled, will be entitled to extra safeguards under the provisions of PACE 1984 and its Codes of Practice.

Questioning of suspects

PACE 1984 and its associated Codes of Practice have made substantial changes to the ways in which the police question (or 'interview') their suspects. Interviews of arrested suspects must ordinarily be conducted only in police stations, and must ordinarily be tape-recorded on special twin deck machines, which enables the suspect or his solicitor to keep a copy for their own reference. Although incriminating admissions may still be made elsewhere (e.g., in the back of a police car on the way to the station), the judges are increasingly reluctant to allow juries to hear of alleged admissions in such circumstances. Sections 76 and 78 of PACE 1984 may be invoked by the defence (or by the court) to exclude evidence that cannot be proved to have been properly or fairly obtained, or which might easily have been fabricated by the police.

On the other hand, the law now allows courts or juries to draw adverse inferences from a suspect's failure to provide answers to legitimate police questions. If, for example, the suspect fails to mention a particular defence (such as an alibi, or an innocent explanation for his behaviour), which he then raises a few months later at trial, the court may be invited to infer that the defence is a recent invention, which the suspect thought of only afterwards. The suspect must be warned that such inferences may be drawn, but is still not actually obliged to co-operate. In other words, it is not an offence to refuse to answer police questions, even after arrest. The relevant rules are set out in the Criminal Justice and Public Order Act 1994, ss. 34–38.

Period of time for which the detainee may be kept in police custody

If the custody officer has authorised the detention of the suspect without charge, the police have the power to detain him for up to 24 hours. If at the expiry of that period the police have insufficient evidence with which to charge the suspect then he must be released, either on bail or without bail. Under certain circumstances, however, the detainee may be kept beyond 24 hours, but this is subject to safeguards.

Procedure if suspect is to be detained beyond 24 hours without charge

(a)   A police officer of the rank of superintendent or above has the power to authorise the continued detention of the suspect for a further 12 hours (i.e., for 36 hours altogether). This can be done only where the offence for which the suspect was arrested is a serious arrestable offence *and* if the continued detention of the suspect is necessary to secure or preserve evidence relating to an offence for which he is under arrest, or to obtain such evidence by questioning him *and* the authorising officer believes that the investigation is being carried out diligently and expeditiously.

(b)   If the police need to keep the detainee for longer than 36 hours, they must apply to the magistrates' court for a warrant of further detention. The magistrates will apply the same criteria as the superintendent when considering this application, and may grant a warrant for further extension for a period not exceeding a further 36 hours (i.e., 72 hours in total).

(c)   If the police wish to keep the suspect for longer than 72 hours, they must return to the magistrates' court and ask for a further warrant of detention. The magistrates at this stage may grant the police a further 24 hours, taking total detention time up to 96 hours. After this the police must either charge the suspect or release him (with or without bail).

Throughout the time that the suspect is in police custody without charge, his detention will be checked by a review officer, who is a police officer of the rank of inspector or above who will regularly assess whether the grounds of continued detention still exist. If they do not, the suspect must be released with or without bail.

The decision to prosecute

The police have a discretion at the end of their enquiries whether to initiate criminal proceedings against the suspect. The police do not necessarily have to initiate such proceedings, but they must be able to defend their use of discretion, and may be found guilty of misconduct in public office or of perverting the course of public justice if they misuse it, for example by not charging an off-duty police officer with a drink-driving offence for which any other drunken driver would invariably be charged. In some cases, the police may issue an offender a formal caution. Cautions may be given to both juveniles and adults, and guidance as to when to issue a caution is to be found in Home Office Circulars. Although records are kept of cautions, they are not classed as convictions. Cautions given to juveniles are kept on record for three years or until the juvenile reaches 17. Cautions given to adults are kept for three years.

If a cautioned person is subsequently convicted of an offence, the caution may be used at the sentencing stage.

If the police decide to charge the suspect, PACE 1984 provides that he must be brought as soon as is practicable in front of a magistrates' court. The magistrates' court may decide to remand the defendant in custody until the trial (which it will do for those who are believed to be dangerous offenders or likely to abscond), or simply set a date on which the defendant is to attend to a specific magistrates' court. Alternatively the court may place the defendant on bail (as to which, see below).

The police gather the evidence, conduct the interviews and determine at the end of those investigations whether to initiate proceedings against the suspect. The Crown Prosecution Service (CPS) then step in and take over the conduct of prosecutions which have been initiated by the police. In many cases, the CPS then drop the charges, and decide to proceed no further. In deciding whether to proceed with a prosecution, CPS lawyers apply guidelines set out by the Director of Public Prosecutions (DPP), which include a consideration of the weight of evidence against the defendant and whether a prosecution would be in the public interest. If the CPS decide to proceed with the case, they must select the charges to bring against the defendant. If they feel that there is no case to answer, or that the evidence is unlikely to result in a conviction, they can discontinue or drop the case. Notoriously, the CPS often select 'lesser' charges which enable the case to be tried by magistrates or which may encourage the defendant to plead guilty, even if more serious charges might seem appropriate. Cases of wounding with intent to do grievous bodily harm (GBH) are charged as simple wounding or as assault; robbery is charged as simple theft, and so on. It is sometimes said (perhaps unfairly) that the CPS are more interested in saving money than in pursuing criminals through the courts!

Bail

The law relating to bail is extremely complicated. Only the barest outline can be provided here. It is commonly thought that the granting of bail necessarily involves the accused finding and depositing a sum of money by way of security for his promise not to abscond, or finding other persons ('sureties'), such as parents or friends, who undertake to forfeit such sums should the accused 'jump bail' and abscond. This is not so. Conditions such as these may sometimes be imposed, but only where there appears to be a risk that the accused would otherwise abscond. Other conditions (e.g., as to residence or travel) may be imposed where there is a fear of possible interference with witnesses or of the commission of further offences (Bail Act 1974, s. 3).

The presumption in most cases is that an accused person should get bail prior to trial (Bail Act 1974, s. 4). Imprisoning such persons 'on remand' is expensive, and may cause injustice, as where such a person is ultimately cleared by a jury after spending many months locked up on remand. In some cases, however, bail applications may be opposed and refused on specific grounds (as where there is a *substantial* risk of absconding or of interference with witnesses), and in others the granting of bail has been forbidden by s. 25 of the Criminal Justice and Public Order Act 1994. Persons charged with murder, manslaughter, rape or an attempt to commit murder or rape may not be granted bail if they have been convicted of any such offence in the past, or found 'not guilty by reason of insanity' or 'unfit to plead' when previously charged with such an offence. Such persons are presumed to be too dangerous for bail even to be considered. (There is an exception, namely, where a manslaughter conviction resulted in a non-custodial sentence.)

Appeals are possible in some cases. A person refused police bail may seek bail from a court, and a person refused bail on his first court appearance may make repeated applications on later occasions. An appeal may be made to the Crown Court or to a High Court judge 'in chambers' (i.e., not sitting in court, but in his own office). In limited circumstances, the prosecution may even appeal to have an award of bail by magistrates revoked by the Crown Court (Bail (Amendment) Act 1993).

Forms of trial

Which form of trial the accused will be subjected to depends in part on the seriousness of the offence. We saw in Chapter 2 that criminal offences are divided into three categories: (i) indictable offences; (ii) offences triable either way; and (iii) summary offences. Whichever form of trial the accused must submit to, if he requires legal representation and cannot afford it then the state will provide it (see Chapter 7 for further information).

Pre-trial disclosure

Great importance is attached to the pre-trial disclosure, to the accused or his lawyers, of the evidence on which the prosecution proposes to rely, *and* of any evidence in the prosecution's possession which may help the defence to challenge or undermine the prosecution case. Some of the worst miscarriages of justice in recent years have been attributable, in part at least, to failures of disclosure. In these cases, the prosecution or the police failed to inform the defence of 'secret' evidence which might, if disclosed, have enabled the defence to secure the accused's acquittal. In the case of *Stefan Kiszco*, for example, tests on a semen sample tended to prove the defendant's innocence of the murder charge he faced, but the evidence from that test was not even passed on to the prosecution's barristers, let alone to the defence, and Kiszco served several years in prison before his innocence was eventually established.

Striking the right balance between the interests of the prosecution and defence is not always easy, however. When the courts attempted to 'toughen up' the prosecution's duty of pre-trial disclosure, by insisting on the disclosure of any evidence in their hands that might possibly help the defence case, it was sometimes found that dozens of police and CPS employees ended up spending days or even weeks photocopying vast piles of documents for the defence, only to find that the defence lawyers eventually made no use of them at all. The Criminal Procedure and Investigations Act 1996 has therefore modified the rules. The prosecution's initial duty is to disclose only the evidence they intend to use at the trial and any other evidence in their possession which they feel may actually undermine their case. The defence are then expected to reply with some indication of their own case. They should disclose, for example, whether the accused admits being at the scene of the crime; and if so, whether he denies hitting the alleged victim, or whether he claims to have hit him by accident, or in lawful self-defence. Once the prosecution know how the trial will be contested, they must then disclose any other evidence in their possession which might have a bearing on that particular line of defence. In other words, the prosecution may sometimes 'hold back' on pre-trial disclosure until they know whether the evidence in question is likely to be relevant at the trial.

Evidence at trial

The rules of evidence in English criminal law are exceptionally (and some would say unnecessarily) complex. Only the briefest of outlines can be attempted here.

What has to be proved?

The substantive criminal law largely determines what facts have to be established in respect of any particular crime, but certain facts may be 'formally admitted' by the defence, and will not then need to be proved. The defence may, for example, concede that the defendant intentionally killed the alleged victim, and rely solely on a defence of self-defence. The court or jury will then have to decide whether the defendant was indeed acting in self-defence: that will then be the only 'fact in issue'. But they may have to consider many other matters that may be relevant to that issue. If, for example, it can be shown that the defendant had a strong financial motive for killing the alleged victim, his claim to have acted in self-defence may be left looking rather improbable; and if the defence can show that a key prosecution witness has a criminal record for offences of dishonesty, this may help to discredit any evidence which that witness may give.

The burden of proof

The general rule in criminal cases is that the prosecution must prove the guilt of the defendant 'beyond all reasonable doubt'. The defendant is therefore presumed 'innocent until proved guilty'. If the court or jury does not feel satisfied that he is indeed guilty, it is ordinarily their duty to acquit him, even if they think it more likely than not that he is guilty after all. This rule is often portrayed as the 'golden thread' which runs through the web of our criminal law. That term was used by Lord Sankey in the landmark case of *Woolmington* [1935] AC 462, in which it was held that a husband who had shot and killed his wife did not have to prove it was an accident in order to avoid conviction for murder, because it was the duty of the prosecution to prove it was *not* an accident. Nevertheless, the concept of proof beyond reasonable doubt is one which permits a court or jury to convict a defendant, even where not *absolutely* sure of his guilt. Few people would ever be convicted if absolute certainty was required.

Furthermore, in many circumstances, the burden of proof is reversed and placed on the defence. If a defendant wishes to plead insanity, he must prove it, by calling at least two medical experts. The jury should accept such evidence only if they are satisfied, on balance of probabilities, that it is true. There are also many statutory exceptions to the *Woolmington* principle. It is a defence, for example, on a charge of possessing or supplying a controlled drug, that the defendant did not realise or suspect or have reason to suspect, that it was such a drug; but he must prove that defence, on balance of probabilities, if he wishes to rely upon it (Misuse of Drugs Act 1971, s. 28). If a person is prosecuted for an offence of bribery or corruption, he may in certain circumstances have to prove that any payment or gift of money or other consideration alleged to have been made or received corruptly was not in fact so made or received. In other words, he may be presumed guilty unless proven to be innocent (Prevention of Corruption Act 1916, s. 2). It is even recognised that statutes may impose burdens of proof on defendants by implication, without expressly so providing (Magistrates' Courts Act 1980, s. 101; *Hunt* [1987] 1 All ER 1). There are scores of such exceptions, and together they leave Lord Sankey's 'golden thread' looking both frail and tarnished.

Even when the legal burden of proof clearly rests on the prosecution, a defendant who wishes to rely upon an affirmative defence (i.e., one which raises new issues, such as self-defence or provocation, rather than a plain denial of one or more of the basic elements of the offence alleged by the prosecution) may have an 'evidential' burden to discharge. This means that he must bring forward some credible evidence of the supposed provocation or self-defence. If he does not, the court cannot even consider that defence, and a trial judge will order the jury to ignore it. This is fair enough. The prosecution cannot be expected to disprove every possible defence which a defendant might or might not choose to run.

Admissibility and inadmissible evidence

What evidence can be used to prove a relevant fact? You might think that the answer must be 'anything that might logically tend to persuade the court or jury of that fact', but this is not how the English law of evidence operates. There are many 'exclusionary rules', designed in theory to ensure that only reliable forms of evidence are used. Many of these rules betray a lack of confidence in the rationality of jurors or magistrates, who seem not to be trusted to distinguish reliable forms of evidence from unreliable ones. As CP Harvey once said, our law of evidence is, 'founded on the propositions that all jurymen are deaf to reason, that all witnesses are presumptively liars and that all documents are presumptively forgeries ...'. Note in particular the following exclusionary rules.

Irrelevance

No evidence can be admissible unless it is relevant, but the layman's idea of relevance may differ from that of the judges. In *Kearley* [1992] 2 All ER 345, the defendant was charged with possessing drugs with intent to supply. Police officers testified that, after his arrest, large numbers of callers either telephoned his number or turned up on his doorstep, asking for him and seeking to buy drugs from him. The House of Lords held that this was not relevant evidence. It proved only that Kearley had a *reputation* as a drugs dealer, not that he actually was one!

The hearsay rule

The hearsay rule ought really to be called the rule against second-hand evidence. The essence of this rule is that a witness in criminal proceedings must ordinarily attend the trial to testify in person, and should testify only as to facts within his own first-hand knowledge. There are many good reasons for such a rule. One would not want to see persons convicted of crimes on the basis of written statements made by witnesses who cannot be bothered to attend the trial, or testimony given by witnesses who never really saw what happened, but merely heard about it from X, who heard about it from Y, who allegedly *did* see what happened. If the court wants to get to the heart of the evidence, it must if possible hear testimony from Y himself, and see how well his evidence holds up under cross-examination.

The hearsay rule is subject to a number of exceptions. Where, for example, a witness has died, or is ill, abroad or simply too scared to attend court, it may be possible for the court to fall back on his original written or tape recorded statement (Criminal Justice Act 1988, s. 23). Business records, such as bank statements, may also be used (s. 24); and if the defendant freely confesses to another person (perhaps to his wife, or to a police officer) that he committed the crime, that confession may be used in evidence against him (Police and Criminal Evidence Act 1984, s. 76(1)).

Opinion evidence

Witnesses must ordinarily confine their testimony to objective facts, and leave the drawing of inferences or the passing of judgments to the court. This rule is also subject to exceptions, notably where expert evidence is called for. Expert witnesses (who may be scientists, engineers, doctors, psychiatrists, fire or accident inspectors, pilots, etc.) may pass judgment on conduct ('this amounted in my opinion to serious professional negligence ...') or offer explanations as to the cause or effect of events ('the likely cause of the fire was ...'). The courts will not, however, listen to expert witnesses if they consider that the facts or events in question can be understood perfectly well without them. In *Turner* [1975] 1 All ER 70 the defendant killed his unfaithful girlfriend in a frenzied attack with a hammer. Afterwards, he felt very sorry for what he had done. His defence was provocation, and he sought to call a psychologist to explain how the news of his girlfriend's affair might have caused him to lose his temper. The trial judge and Court of Appeal both agreed that this evidence was not admissible. Juries, they said, understand such things perfectly well. Had the defence argued that Turner was mentally ill or abnormal, then expert evidence might have been relevant, in order to help the jury understand the effects of the illness or abnormality.

Character and 'similar fact' evidence

Various rules govern the use of character evidence. The best known are the rules restricting the use of evidence showing the bad character or criminal record of the defendant in a criminal case. As a general rule, a court or jury cannot be told that a defendant has committed similar crimes in the past, or even that he has a criminal record. This is because it is recognised that juries, in particular, are likely to be prejudiced against the defendant if they learn of this. Once again, however, there are important exceptions to this rule. If evidence of the defendant's involvement in other crimes would tend to prove, not just that he is a criminal, but that he *must* be guilty of the crime with which he is now charged, then the evidence of those other crimes may indeed be admitted. In the notorious case of *George Joseph Smith* (1915) 11 Cr App R 229 the defendant was charged with the murder of a young woman he had recently purported to marry. She had drowned in her bath shortly after her wedding (supposedly after suffering an epileptic fit), and Smith had profited financially from her death. The prosecution could prove that Smith (using false names) had 'married' two other women in the last few years; they too had drowned in their baths after supposedly suffering fits, and he had profited in each case. It would clearly have been absurd to have prevented the jury from learning that the same fate had befallen all three of his 'brides in the bath'. The evidence showed quite clearly that Smith was a serial killer, and it was held to be admissible on that basis. Without it, the jury might have believed that the death of just one bride was an unfortunate accident.

Illegally or improperly obtained evidence

Illegally obtained evidence is sometimes inadmissible (e.g., where confessions are obtained from suspects by oppression: PACE 1984, s. 76(2)) but there is no general rule forbidding courts from allowing the use of illegally or unfairly obtained evidence. The use of such evidence by the prosecution is, however, subject to the discretion of the court or judge, both at common law and under s.78(1) of PACE 1984, which provides:

> In any proceedings the court may refuse to allow evidence on which the prosecution proposes to rely to be given if it appears to the court that, having regard to all the circumstances, including the circumstances in which the evidence was obtained, the admission of the evidence would have such an adverse effect on the fairness of the proceedings that the court ought not to admit it.

In *Christou* [1992] 4 All ER 559 police officers posed as dishonest shopkeepers in order to trick thieves and burglars into betraying themselves by selling the officers stolen property. The Court of Appeal saw nothing wrong with this. Nor was the House of Lords in *Khan* [1996] 3 All ER 289 prepared to exclude evidence of drug smuggling obtained from hidden microphones which the police had illegally set up on private property; but s. 78 is often used to exclude evidence obtained from improper police interviews with suspects, and in the unreported case of *Stagg* (1995) the trial judge threw out a prosecution for murder in which the only evidence came from an undercover woman police officer, who had 'befriended' the defendant in order to trick him into making admissions. Ognall J condemned this tactic as 'a blatant attempt to incriminate a suspect by positive and deceptive conduct of the grossest kind'.

Is it right that the courts will sometimes permit the use of illegally obtained evidence? One school of thought would say that it is not, because it infringes civil rights and may encourage the police to break rules and 'cut corners' in order to obtain evidence. On the other hand, s. 78, by granting the courts an element of discretion, enables them to balance such considerations against the need to ensure that justice is done. Mandatory rules requiring the exclusion of improperly obtained evidence may result in the exclusion of important and reliable evidence of guilt, and in the acquittal of manifestly guilty defendants on the basis of mere technicalities. Indeed, this is what too often happens in drink-driving cases, where technical procedural irregularities in the gathering of evidential specimens necessarily result in the exclusion of the vital specimens. In *Murray* v *Director of Public Prosecutions* [1993] RTR 209, it was held that a positive specimen provided by a motorist was inadmissible to prove a charge of driving with excess alcohol, because the motorist concerned had not been warned that he would commit an offence if he *failed* to provide it. Such a warning should indeed have been given under s. 7 of the Road Traffic Act 1988, but the question of whether the warning was given was surely irrelevant, given that he was not being prosecuted for failing to provide a specimen, but for driving with excess alcohol in his bloodstream, an offence of which the specimen would have proved him to be guilty. This is the kind of absurdity that can result if the courts insist on the exclusion of all improperly obtained evidence.

Witnesses and the trial process

Apart from the exclusionary rules, evidence may be unavailable because the witness concerned claims 'privilege' in respect of the matter concerned or because its admission would be contrary to public policy (e.g., by betraying defence secrets). Furthermore, the evidence of some witnesses may be subject to special rules. An example is provided by *Turnbull* [1976] 3 All ER 549, in which the Court of Appeal laid down rules (the Turnbull guidelines) to govern the use of visual identification evidence in criminal trials. Juries must be warned of the dangers of mistaken identification (which has often caused miscarriages of justice in the past) and judges may in some cases have to stop trials in which the prosecution case depends too heavily on uncorroborated or unsatisfactory visual identification.

An important function of the law of evidence concerns the treatment of witnesses through examination (by the party calling them) and cross-examination. Cross-examination may be designed to discredit the witness or his testimony, and is usually carried out by the other side.

Special consideration must be given to the position of the defendant who chooses to testify at his own trial. He is ordinarily protected from the kind of 'bad character' attack to which other witnesses would be vulnerable. He cannot, for example, be cross-examined about his own criminal record, but this shield may be lost in certain ways. If the accused makes a false claim to respectability or good character then of course he deserves to have any past misdeeds used against him, but that is not the only way in which his 'shield' may be lost. It may also be lost if his defence involves the making of 'imputations' against prosecution witnesses or against the deceased victim of his alleged crime, or if his own evidence incriminates his co-defendant (Criminal Evidence Act 1898, s.1(f)(ii), (iii)).

Direct and circumstantial evidence

Direct evidence is evidence of a fact in issue (e.g., W saw X killing Y). Circumstantial evidence is evidence of some other fact, from which the fact(s) in issue may be inferred (e.g., W saw X disposing of the murder weapon; X had a motive to kill Y; X has lied about his movements, etc). There is nothing necessarily wrong with a case based on such evidence. Indeed, strong circumstantial evidence may be more reliable than weak or fleeting identification by an eye-witness to the crime, and may suffice to prove even the most serious offences. In *Onufrejczyk* [1955] 1 QB 388 the defendant was convicted of the murder of his partner, even though no corpse was ever found, and there was no direct evidence that his partner was even dead. There may nevertheless be some risk of the wrong inference being drawn in such cases. The more strands of circumstantial evidence, the less the risk of the inference being false.

Trial by jury

Trials on indictment are heard in the Crown Court before a judge and jury. (As to the types of offence which may or must be tried in this way, see Chapter 2.)

Juries have been used in criminal proceedings for centuries, but their role has changed significantly over that time. In the early days of the English legal system, the jury's role was a combination of police, witness and prosecutor. At that time, a local jury would often be responsible for accusing an offender and for bringing him in front of the court. Furthermore, the jury members would be used as prosecution witnesses by swearing to the accused's guilt. With the passage of time, however, the jury's role became one of uninvolved triers of fact. Nowadays, an essential feature of the jury system is that the 12 jurors and the accused are unknown to each other, so that jury can give the accused a fair and unbiased trial.

There is no jury in the magistrates' courts (or where the Crown Court hears appeals from magistrates' courts). Ninety-seven per cent of criminal cases are tried in the magistrates' courts, and only three per cent in the Crown Court. Furthermore, over 70 per cent of persons who are sent for trial to the Crown Court plead guilty and do not need a trial by jury. Beware, however, of misinterpreting such statistics. These figures may suggest that the use of the jury in criminal trials is rare, but the importance of trial by jury must not be underestimated, as it is used in all the most serious, complex and lengthy cases. A fraud or murder trial may last for weeks or months in the Crown Court, whereas a contested case in a magistrates' court may last for only an hour or less, and the proportion of guilty pleas in magistrates' courts is even higher than in the Crown Court.

Qualification for jury service and selection

Any person aged between 18 and 70 and who is registered as a Parliamentary or local government elector and who has been ordinarily resident in the United Kingdom for at least five years since the age of 13 and who is not either ineligible or disqualified may be called for jury service.

A person is *disqualified* from jury service who:

(a)   has at any time been sentenced (in the UK) to imprisonment for life, or to a term of imprisonment or youth custody of five years or more, or has been sentenced to be detained during Her Majesty's pleasure; or

(b)   has in the last ten years served any part of a sentence of imprisonment, youth custody or detention, or received a suspended sentence of imprisonment or order for detention or had a community service order made against him;

(c)   has in the last five years been placed on probation; or

(d)   is currently on bail in criminal proceedings.

Those who are rendered *ineligible* to sit on juries include those involved in the administration of justice, such as barristers, solicitors, police officers etc., those whose religious vocation makes it undesirable for them to sit (nuns, priests, etc.) and those who are mentally ill.

There is also another category of person who, though eligible, can be *excused* from having to sit. This would include persons whose occupations involve them in duties to the state, or in the relief of pain or suffering, such as members of the House of Commons, dentists, nurses, doctors, vets, chemists, full-time serving members of the armed forces etc. A person is also excused from serving on a jury if he has served on a jury in the last two years, or attended to serve on a jury in the last two years or been excused from jury service by any court for a period which has not yet expired. A person may also be excused on a discretionary basis, if he shows good reason, for example, illness, examinations or business commitments.

Summoning jurors

The supply of jurors for jury service is taken from names in the electoral register. Electoral lists are sent to designated officers of the court and the officers make a random list of those whom they wish to call for jury service on a particular occasion. Each selected person is then summoned to attend for jury service. The court officer concerned may at any time ask a potential juror such questions as he thinks fit in order to ascertain whether or not that person is suitable for jury service. The purpose of this questioning is to weed out those who may be disqualified or ineligible.

From those summoned, court officers prepare lists or panels of jurors for the various courts. A particular jury is then chosen by means of a ballot in open court, and each juror must be sworn in separately. The theory is that this ensures the provision of a random, and thus fair, selection of jurors. It is questionable whether it succeeds. In particular, the random selection is haphazard and often fails to provide a jury which properly reflects the racial or class divisions in the local area. The racial or ethnic composition of the jury may be quite a big issue in some trials, especially where the crime itself is alleged to involve racial issues or overtones. In the past, some judges have attempted to manipulate jury selections, so as to achieve a 'balanced' jury in a racially sensitive case before them. Such attempts typically involved 'standing by' (i.e., passing over) potential white jurors in order to ensure that two or three black or Asian jurors were selected from the panel available, or selecting a jury panel from a particular area known to contain large numbers of persons of a specific ethnic group. Such interference was doubtless well-intentioned and may have helped convince defendants that justice was being done, but it was not entirely satisfactory, and it was condemned and effectively ended by the decision of the Court of Appeal in *Ford* [1989] 1 QB 868. If such manipulation was desirable, said the Court, it should be provided for by properly thought-out legislation, rather than by judicial fudging. As the Court of Appeal recently re-iterated in *Tarrant, The Times*, 29 December 1997, a jury should be 'random, not average'.

In the USA, the art of jury selection is utterly different from the random British model. Days, or even weeks, may be taken up by the process of selecting the 'right' jury. Jurors have to fill out detailed forms, answer questions in court and so on. The process there seems to have become far too elaborate and time-consuming, to the extent that US lawyers regard the selection of a favourable jury as half the battle. English lawyers look at the American example and shudder. It may be that some kind of middle way could be found, but the American experience probably discourages anyone from looking. There are, however, certain ways in which the composition of a jury may be challenged, even in this country.

Challenging of jurors

Challenging of the jurors takes place as the jury is being sworn in, and either the prosecution or the defence may challenge the presence of a particular juror. If the challenge is successful the juror is removed. Before 1989 the defendant could challenge the presence of any juror without cause, but that right was abolished by the Criminal Justice Act 1988. Nowadays the defendant may challenge the presence of a juror 'for cause' only (e.g., on the basis that the juror is a relative of the alleged victim of the crime). The prosecution also have the right to challenge the presence of a juror for cause, or to 'stand by' any juror. Guidelines issued by the Attorney-General provide that the latter right should be exercised only in exceptional cases, as where a potential juror in a complex fraud case appears to be illiterate.

Jury vetting

A controversial development over the last few years has been the practice of random investigation of jurors, or jury vetting as it is commonly known (this should not be confused with challenging the jury). The concept of jury vetting is contrary to the idea that members of a jury are chosen at random from the appropriate panel and is considered by many to be unconstitutional. In a famous 1978 case known as the 'ABC official secrets trial', two journalists and a soldier were charged with collecting secret information. Lawyers for the defence discovered that some weeks before the trial the prosecution had received a list of potential jurors. The individuals named on the list had been vetted for their loyalty to the state. Upon discovery of such activity, a new trial was ordered and all three accused were eventually acquitted. As a result of this case, the Attorney-General published Guidelines on Jury Checks, and these have been revised and updated over the years. The guidelines basically reaffirm the principle that a jury should be randomly selected and that no one should be disqualified from sitting on a jury unless he falls within the exceptions laid down in the Juries Act 1974. But the guidelines then go on to provide that in exceptional cases, such as terrorist cases, vetting of a juror's political beliefs may indeed be appropriate. The vetting process usually consists of checking police and Special Branch records.

Death or discharge of jurors

If a juror dies, or is discharged because of illness or for any other reason, the trial may still continue, provided the number of jurors does not fall below nine.

Judge and jury

The general rule in criminal cases is that the judge decides any issues of law, and the jury decide any issues of fact with the help of the judge's 'summing up' of the evidence. The judge can nevertheless exercise considerable control over the jury's ability to determine the facts. To begin with, questions as to the admissibility of evidence are treated as questions of law. This means that the judge has some control over whether the jury ever hear certain items of evidence. If the judge actually has to hear evidence in order to make up his mind, he may hold a 'trial within a trial' in the absence of the jury.

Furthermore, the judge may sometimes withdraw an issue from the jury's consideration. He may rule, for example, that a special defence relied upon by the accused (such as insanity or provocation) is unsupported by any evidence, and that the jury cannot therefore even consider it. The judge may also rule that charges brought by the prosecution are unsupported by evidence, and direct (i.e., order) the jury to acquit the accused on those charges. The accused is then said to have 'No case to answer'. The judge may indicate to the jury that he considers a particular piece of evidence to be strong or weak. What the judge *cannot* do, however, is to order the jury to convict. If the defence offered appears not to be a defence at all, the judge can tell the jury so, but in some cases the jury may still acquit. In a recent case, the accused shot and injured a disqualified lorry driver who had killed the accused's child in a dreadful piece of drunken driving. The judge correctly told the jury that the accused had no excuse in law, but the jury still acquitted him on all charges. (See also *Ponting*, below.)

The verdict

Wherever possible the members of the jury must be unanimous as to their verdict, but in 1967 the concept of the majority verdict was introduced into English law and is now dealt with under s. 17 of the Juries Act 1974. A majority verdict is acceptable in the Crown Court if either there are not fewer than 11 jurors and ten of them agree, or there are only ten remaining jurors and nine of them agree. However, a judge must never be too hasty in accepting a majority verdict and should always do his best to encourage a jury to reach a unanimous verdict if they can.

Secrecy of jury deliberations

A jury's deliberations are totally secret and it is an offence under s. 8 of the Contempt of Court Act 1981 to obtain, disclose or solicit any particulars of statements made, votes cast or arguments put forward by the jury in the course of their deliberations. In *Young* [1995] 2 WLR 430, a case of murder, some of the jurors tried to 'contact' the deceased by using a ouija board while staying overnight at their hotel. The deceased's spirit apparently spelt out the message, 'Stephen Young done it'. The Court of Appeal heard of this and ordered a retrial, but *only* because the incident took place in the hotel, rather than in the jury room. It seems that the Court would otherwise have let the verdict stand, rather than allow jurors to inform on others and betray the secrecy of the jury room. As many critics point out, this elevates the sanctity of jury confidentiality to absurd heights.

Appeals against jury decisions

If the jury decide to acquit the accused, then no matter how unreasonable their decision may appear it cannot be challenged. In contrast, if the jury convict a person, then their decision may be overturned on appeal if (but only if) the conviction appears unsafe (Criminal Appeal Act 1968, s. 2(1), as amended by the Criminal Appeal Act 1995). The Court of Appeal has confirmed in *Chalkley* [1998] 2 All ER 155 that it can no longer quash a conviction merely because of irregularities at the trial. Such irregularities are only relevant if they cast doubt on the safety of the conviction. A retrial may be ordered (as in *Young*) if this seems appropriate, otherwise the successful appellant goes free.

Criticisms and defences of trial by jury

In *Bushell's Case* (1670), a jury went to prison rather than convict the Quaker, William Penn, of a crime he had not committed, but were eventually freed on the orders of the Lord Chief Justice. This case established the right of a jury to acquit, even where the judges wanted a conviction. Trial by jury thus came to be considered 'a bulwark of our liberties'. The jury system, however, has not been immune to criticism.

Supporters of trial by jury claim that the use of lay persons in the justice system creates greater public confidence in the legal system. Furthermore, the jury will be more likely to be guided by a sense of basic natural justice and thus will act as an antidote to the legalistic outlook of the professional lawyers and judges. It is also argued that the jury acts as a guardian against state encroachment on basic freedoms. An illustration of the jury performing such a role can be seen from the *Clive Ponting* case. The accused had been charged with an offence under the Official Secrets Act 1911, after he had leaked a government document to a national newspaper. Legally it was clear that Ponting was guilty of the offence, and the judge came as close as he could to saying so during his summing up. The jury, however, obviously sympathised with the accused, who had clearly acted in what he rightly or wrongly thought to be the public interest, and they returned a verdict of not guilty in the teeth of the evidence.

A criticism which is frequently levelled against juries is that they may be incapable of following the evidence in a long and complicated trial such as one involving commercial fraud. This has led many commentators to suggest that juries ought not to be used in this type of trial, and instead the issue should be resolved by a judge together with some independent experts in that particular field. Linked with the above point is the fear that juries are susceptible to the presence and rhetoric of clever lawyers and may thus react emotionally rather than rationally to arguments put forward in the courtroom. Juries may also be susceptible to coercion or to other factors unconnected with the reality of the trial. For this reason, jury trials for terrorist offences in Northern Ireland became impossible, and were replaced in such cases with trial by judge alone.

Miscarriages of justice

The image of the criminal justice system in England and Wales has been much damaged in recent years by a stream of high profile cases in which convictions have been quashed (often at a second or third appeal) only after long prison sentences have been served. Examples include the cases of Stefan Kiszco, the Birmingham Six, the Guildford Four and the Bridgewater Three. Even the cases of alleged murderers, wrongly hanged many years ago, continue to haunt us. How flawed then is our criminal justice system?

It must of course be conceded that no system of criminal justice is or can be perfect. The standard of proof is that of guilt 'beyond reasonable doubt', not absolute and incontrovertible proof of guilt, and this recognises and accepts the possibility of error. Adopting an 'absolute' standard would be unworkable, and would mean that most guilty persons would be acquitted. Even allowing for this, however, these miscarriages of justice mentioned above could not have happened but for serious faults within the system. In each of those cases, important evidence was concealed from the defence and from the court, and improper pressure was put on suspects by the police to induce them to make confessions. Police officers and Home Office forensic scientists seemed in some cases to forget that their duty was to establish the truth, not to secure convictions at all costs.

In the Birmingham Six case, basic mistakes were also made in obtaining and evaluating scientific evidence. A test that was claimed to be 99 per cent accurate in revealing recent contact with explosives was indeed 99 per cent likely to give a positive reading when applied to suspects who had recently handled such explosives, but it was nowhere near that accurate in recording *negative* results for persons who had *not* handled explosives. On the contrary, recent contact with soap or playing cards could easily trigger a false positive reading. All dogs have four legs, but it does not follow that an animal with four legs must be a dog.

The most notorious miscarriage of justice cases all date back to the period before PACE 1984 and its associated Codes of Practice were brought into force. Controls on police conduct were lax. There was no tape-recording of interviews with suspects, and it proved all too easy for improper pressure, amounting to oppression, to be applied in order to induce confessions. In some cases, it has been proved that officers actually fabricated non-existent confessions, or inserted 'extra' pages into written statements made by suspects. In all too many of these cases, senior judges presiding over the trial or over subsequent appeals were unwilling to believe that police officers could sink to such levels of deception. PACE 1984 cannot guarantee to eliminate all improper police practices, but it makes them more difficult.

The rules governing pre-trial disclosure are now much stricter than they were then (even after the modifications introduced by the Criminal Procedure and Investigations Act 1996) and the establishment of the Criminal Cases Review Commission (p. 27, above) has made it easier for problematic cases to be reinvestigated and if necessary sent back to the Court of Appeal.

On the other hand, some of the rights once afforded to suspects have been taken away. Judges or prosecutors may now invite courts or juries to draw adverse inferences from a defendant's failure to testify at his trial (Criminal Justice and Public Order Act 1994, s. 35), from failure to answer certain types of questions during police interviews (ss. 36, 37), or from failure to mention in an interview the defence he ultimately relies upon at his trial (s. 34). Many commentators fear that this new regime, coupled with the changes implemented under the Criminal Procedure and Investigations Act 1996, will produce a new flood of miscarriages of justice. Only time will tell whether these fears are justified. In defence of the new rules it might be argued that the innocent and vulnerable suspect could almost always be persuaded to answer questions during police interrogation, even under the old law. It takes great determination to remain silent under police questioning, and one may suspect that many of those who do so are 'tough nuts' with something to hide. Furthermore, if the defendant eventually comes out with a surprise (i.e., previously undisclosed) defence at his trial, why should the prosecution be prevented from commenting adversely on his failure to mention it when first questioned.

The criminal process

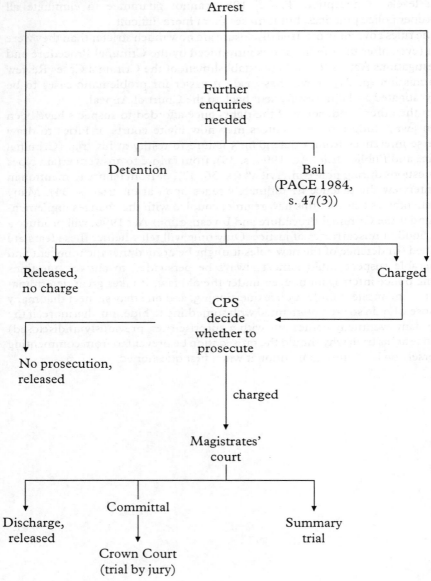

NINE

The Powers of the Criminal Courts

This chapter considers the powers which the criminal courts possess to deal with convicted persons, both adults and juvenile offenders. Their powers are not confined to the imposition of fines or sentences of imprisonment, disqualification, etc. They also extend to the making of compensation orders to victims and to the confiscation of the proceeds of criminal conduct.

Sentencing policy is a politically sensitive topic and is subject to frequent legislative changes. The most recent changes are those introduced by the Crime (Sentences) Act 1997 and the Sex Offenders Act 1997. Further proposals on sentencing law reform are to be found in the Crime and Disorder Act 1998.

The purpose of criminal sanctions

It would be wrong to suppose that there can only be one single purpose of justification behind the imposition of criminal sanctions. There are several, each of which may have some validity in a given context.

Retribution
The dominant purpose behind the imposition of criminal sanctions is to impose punishment upon the defendant because that is what he deserves in the light of his infringement of the law. In Stephen's *History of the Criminal Law of England*, it was stated that:

> The infliction of punishment by law gives definite expression and a solemn ratification and justification to the hatred which is excited by the commission

of the offence, and which constitutes the moral or popular as distinguished from the conscientious sanction of that part of morality which is also sanctioned by the criminal law. The criminal law thus proceeds upon the principle that it is morally right to hate criminals, and it confirms and justifies that sentiment by inflicting upon criminals punishments which express it.

This element of retribution may to some extent reflect society's instinctive desire for vengeance, but it should be stressed that the court's response must be both reasoned and reasonable and must not be a vindictive or emotional one. A further element, however, reflects society's abhorrence of the defendant's conduct, and emphasises this by visiting punishment on him. A crime which is never severely punished will inevitably cease to be regarded as serious.

Principles of retributive justice may sometimes operate so as to *oppose* the imposition of an excessively severe sentence on an offender. As Lord Taylor CJ stated in *Cunningham* [1993] 2 All ER 15, it is wrong to impose an unusually heavy sentence merely for the purpose of deterring others by 'making an example' of the offender. Deterrence is not inherently inconsistent with retribution or justice but, if carried to extreme lengths, it may be.

Deterrence
Deterrence may take either of two forms:

(a)   particular deterrence, which involves seeking to discourage the particular criminal from re-offending; and

(b)   general deterrence, which involves dissuading others from offending by making an example of those who are caught.

As already pointed out, however, the need to deter can never justify the imposition of a sentence which is significantly more severe than the gravity of the offence deserves. Surveys on the effects of sentencing seem to suggest that the probability of arrest and conviction has a greater deterrent effect upon would-be offenders than the nature of sentence which may be imposed, but this kind of thing is difficult to assess, and may vary according to the type of offence and offender. A combination of severe sentencing and vigorous high-profile policing may be very effective in some contexts. In respect of drink-driving, for example, many motorists are undoubtedly deterred from committing such offences by the knowledge that the law is vigorously enforced *and* that offenders are punished with mandatory disqualification.

Protection of the public (incapacitation)
Another purpose of criminal sanctions is that of protecting society from particular offenders. If the offender is imprisoned, the public are protected from further offences by him for so long as he is kept from society. There are

some dangerous and psychopathic offenders currently in custody, in prisons or secure hospitals, who may never be released during their lifetime.

It is an established sentencing principle that longer-than-usual prison sentences may be passed on certain violent offenders and sex offenders who appear to represent a serious danger to the public (a danger that they will cause death or serious physical or psychological injury). Protection of the public also appears to be the philosophy behind the controversial new rules introduced by the Crime (Sentences) Act 1997, under which minimum sentences (or in some cases mandatory life sentences) must ordinarily be passed on certain repeat or recidivist offenders (see below); and this is at least part of the rationale behind disqualification orders passed on delinquent motorists, etc.

Rehabilitation

At one time, it was felt that a major objective of punishment should be to reform and rehabilitate the offender, but imprisonment is widely considered to be ineffective or even counter-productive in this respect. Younger prisoners may sometimes be corrupted by older ones, rather than reformed by the efforts of the prison staff. Probation was introduced to give real effect to the idea of rehabilitation, and it is still widely used today. In recent years, however, the idea of rehabilitation as a sentencing objective seems to have fallen out of favour. Studies have indicated that there appears to be no great difference in reoffending rates as between those criminals who receive rehabilitative sentences and those who are given retributive sentences, such as fines.

The approach towards punishment today

As explained above, there are many aims associated with the imposition of criminal sanctions. A sentencing policy which managed to satisfy most or all of the above aims would no doubt be considered a successful one; and in a recent White Paper, entitled *Protecting the Public* (HMSO 1996), the previous government argued that, on the basis of such criteria, imprisonment is a highly effective sanction:

> First, by taking offenders out of circulation it prevents them from committing yet more crime. The majority of crimes are committed by a relatively small number of criminals. Research has shown that between three and 13 offences could be prevented for each burglar imprisoned for a year. Second, prison protects the public from dangerous criminals. Third, prison — and the threat of prison — acts as a deterrent to would-be criminals. Finally, time spent in prison can be used to rehabilitate criminals... Criminals sent to prison are no more likely to reoffend than those given community sentences — a recent survey based on a sample of 192 cases showed reconviction rates within two years of 51% for those released from prison, 55% for those who received a community sentence and 58% for those who received a probation order.

Whilst there is at least some truth in these assertions, not everyone would agree that 'prison works', and the claim that prison 'helps rehabilitation' is especially difficult to justify, given the high levels of crime (and, in particular, drug abuse) prevalent within our prisons.

Until relatively recently, there was no clear explanation as to which of the various aims of sentencing was to take priority in the event of conflict, but the Criminal Justice Act 1991 has made it clear that the main aim of sentencing is retribution and thus a sentence should be proportionate to the seriousness of the particular offence. There is therefore a recognised 'tariff' for most of the main criminal offences. For trials on indictment, a range of penalties is recommended by the Court of Appeal as appropriate for a given offence, and these can be looked up in one of the standard reference works for criminal lawyers and judges, such as *Blackstone's Criminal Practice*. 'Guideline judgments' indicate a starting point within the middle of that range, which may be increased by aggravating features, or decreased by mitigating factors. Rape, for example, merits a maximum sentence of life imprisonment, but the Court of Appeal has ruled that this must be reserved for grave cases involving dangerous psychopathic offenders (see below). The Court of Appeal has specified a 'starting point' for typical rapes of five years; with around eight years for cases aggravated by factors such as kidnapping of the victim. A guilty plea may help to reduce the sentence. Not all offences have been covered by guideline judgments, but the Crime and Disorder Act 1998 requires the Court of Appeal to lay down such judgments on a more regular and systematic basis. The Magistrates' Courts Association makes recommendations for the guidance of courts hearing summary cases. These are also reproduced in practitioners' texts.

Excessively severe sentences may be appealed against to the Court of Appeal. Until recently this was not true of allegedly lenient sentences, but the Attorney-General now has the power to appeal for an increase in a sentence he considers to be unduly lenient, and a number of lenient sentences have been increased following such appeals.

The accent is on justice in the form of just deserts. Rehabilitation as an aim has not been abandoned, but is apparently deemed less important than just retribution. The current climate of public and political opinion does not look favourably, for example, on the practice of sending juvenile offenders on expensive adventure holidays. Such holidays may be no more expensive than some forms of custody, and may actually do the offenders some good, but appear to condone or even reward criminal conduct, and this is not generally considered to be acceptable.

The 1991 Act nevertheless makes it clear that the imposition of a custodial sentence should only be used as a form of punishment as a last resort, encouraging the courts instead to employ community sentences, which are often far less expensive. The various forms of punishment available to the court will be looked at below.

Background information relevant to sentencing

The courts will often have a mass of information before them when deciding what sentence to impose upon a convicted defendant. They may be told by the police about the defendant's past criminal record. This is referred to as the defendant's antecedents. The antecedent report may also include a list of other offences which the defendant would like to have 'taken into consideration' at the sentencing stage. These are referred to as TICs for short. The advantage to the defendant of having offences taken into consideration is that if, for example, he goes to prison, he cannot be re-arrested for these offences once he comes out. The police also like this system because it helps them to claim better clear-up rates for crimes in their area.

In more serious or difficult cases, there will also be information on the defendant's family, work and domestic background, through pre-sentence reports (formerly referred to as social inquiry reports) carried out on the offender. These reports are compiled by probation officers or social workers and they contain more detailed information about the offender. There may also be medical or psychiatric reports on offenders, where these appear to be necessary. Sentencing may be adjourned for several days or weeks in order for such reports to be prepared.

Lastly, the defence will usually put forward a plea in mitigation, which may be supported by character witnesses or testimonials. This involves the defence putting forward reasons why the defendant ought not to be dealt with too severely. Armed with the above information, the courts will then decide which sentence would be the most appropriate for the particular case before them.

Imprisonment

Imprisonment is a severe but (at an annual cost of £30,000 per prisoner) costly sanction against crime. Attempts have been made to reduce the number of persons sent to prison, but the previous government believed strongly in the efficacy of imprisonment, and prison can undoubtedly achieve some things that other sanctions cannot. For some dangerous offenders, it may be the only sentence which could be considered. Nevertheless, a prison poulation which regularly exceeds 60,000 is a major cause for concern.

The Criminal Justice Act 1991 lays down statutory guidelines for determining whether a custodial sentence should be imposed in the first place and the appropriate length which that sentence should take. Section 1(2) (as amended by the CJA 1993) states that a custodial sentence ought not to be imposed on the offender unless the court is of the opinion:

(a)   that the offence, or the combination of the offence and one or more offences associated with it, was so serious that only such a sentence can be justified for the offence; or

(b)   where the offence is a violent or sexual offence, that only such a sentence would be adequate to protect the public from serious harm from him.

Section 2 then goes on to give guidance as to the criteria for determining the proper length of a custodial sentence. Priority is given to the principle that the length of the custodial sentence should reflect the seriousness of the offence and the court should take into account any aggravating or mitigating factors. An example of the former would include the commission of an offence by the defendant whilst on bail. The maximum sentence allowable by the statute creating the offence is only to be reserved for the gravest example of that particular type of crime. Furthermore, if the defendant pleads guilty to the offence with which he is charged, then the length of the prison sentence is normally (but not automatically) reduced. Encouraging guilty pleas helps minimise delays and expense in the criminal justice system, and may save victims from the ordeal of having to testify.

Life and death sentences
A conviction for murder requires a mandatory life sentence, which means that the offender remains in prison indefinitely, and can only ever be released (if at all) on licence or parole. In murder cases, judges may recommend a minimum term (sometimes 30 years or more) which should be served before any grant of parole. The judge who sentenced serial killer Rosemary West recommended that she should never be released. A mandatory death penalty still exists for high treason (and piracy with violence) but nobody has been hanged for treason since the Nazi collaborator William Joyce ('Lord Haw-Haw') in 1946.

Many offences carry a possible life sentence, but for crimes other than murder, life imprisonment can usually be justified only where the following three conditions are present:

(a)   the offence is grave enough to require a very long sentence;
(b)   it appears either from the offence or from the defendant's history, that he is a person of mental instability, who, if at large, would probably reoffend and present a grave danger to the public; and
(c)   he will remain unstable and a potential danger for a long period of time.

Automatic life sentences under the Crime (Sentences) Act 1997
Under the Crime (Sentences) Act 1997, courts may be obliged (in the absence of 'exceptional circumstances') to impose life sentences on persons who are convicted of certain specified 'serious offences' after having previously been convicted of other such offences. 'Serious offences' for this purpose are listed in s. 2(5) of the Act, and include attempting, conspiring, or inciting to murder; any form of manslaughter; wounding or causing GBH with intent; rape or attempted rape; unlawful sexual intercourse with a girl aged under 13; certain serious firearms offences; and robbery committed with a firearm or imitation

firearm. A past conviction in Scotland or Northern Ireland for an equivalent offence (e.g., culpable homicide in Scotland) may count as the first serious offence.

This may seem logical enough, if perhaps a little severe, but the new regime is very unpopular with senior judges and may give rise to some rather bizarre distinctions. For example, if D was convicted of wounding with intent 30 years ago, whilst only 16, and is now convicted of gross negligence manslaughter as a result of a road traffic accident, he will qualify for an automatic life sentence; whereas E, who has several convictions for indecent assault and is now convicted of a series of brutal knifepoint rapes, will not so qualify.

Exceptional circumstances, which may avoid the need for an automatic life sentence, are partially defined in s. 2(2), which makes it clear that they may relate to either the offences or to the offender himself. A body of case law will eventually grow up, illustrating the considerations which may properly be taken into account, but until then the concept remains a vague one.

Minimum sentences under the Crime (Sentences) Act 1997
Section 3 of the Act requires the imposition of a minimum sentence of at least seven years' imprisonment (or detention in a young offenders' institution) on an offender's third conviction for trafficking in specified 'Class A' hard drugs, such as cocaine or heroin, unless there are exceptional circumstances justifying a less serious penalty. Under s. 4 similar rules may eventually be imposed in respect of repeated convictions for domestic burglaries, but with a three year minimum term. This 'get tough' policy will be welcomed by many, but its effect on rates and terms of imprisonment (and thus on an already high prison population) may be serious.

Special rules for sex offenders
Under the Criminal Justice Act 1991, s. 44, a sex offender may be required, if released on licence from prison, to serve out the full term of his sentence under supervision in the community. The fear is that such offenders may remain a danger to the public. Under the Sex Offenders Act 1997, certain sex offenders may be required, after their release, to register their personal details and addresses with the police, so that their conduct may continue to be monitored. This may also lead to local residents being informed of the presence of a convicted sex offender in their midst. The period during which such notification remains necessary varies according to the circumstances of the case, but for 'lifers' released on licence, it will last indefinitely.

Suspended sentences
Section 22 of the Powers of Criminal Courts Act 1973 gives the courts the power to 'suspend' a prison sentence in certain circumstances. This means that the sentence will not have to be served, provided that the defendant avoids committing further imprisonable offences within a given period; but

subsequent amendments have restricted the use of this option by emphasising that the imposition of a suspended sentence must be regarded as exceptional. Despite the element of being 'let off with a warning', it must be reserved for cases which would otherwise be considered deserving of immediate imprisonment. If the offender does commit another offence punishable with imprisonment during the currency of the suspended sentence, the court may order that the original sentence take effect.

Detention and custody of young offenders

It is not usually considered desirable for young offenders to be given custodial sentences at all, particularly in the case of those under the age of 15, but in recent years well-documented cases of persistent offending by some such youngsters drew attention to the fact that the courts had become almost powerless to act against them, and a new form of custodial sentence, namely the 'secure training order', is being brought into force to deal with a hard core of persistent young offenders under that age. Secure training orders apply to persons under the age of 15, but above the age of 12, who are convicted of offences punishable by imprisonment. Section 1 of the Criminal Justice and Public Order Act 1994 states that,

> a secure training order is an order that the offender in respect of whom it is made shall be subject to a period of detention in a secure training centre followed by a period of supervision.

The first of four such centres (the Medway Secure Training Centre, in Kent) opened in April 1998, but the Crime and Disorder Bill (which at the time of writing was before Parliament) would replace secure training orders with 'detention and training orders', involving a mixture of custodial sentence and close supervision in the community. These may eventually be applied to persistent offenders who are no more than 10 years old.

Offenders aged between 15 and 21 years who are convicted of offences punishable with imprisonment may be sent to young offenders' institutions. In deciding whether to impose such a penalty, the courts should apply the same guidelines as when deciding on the possible imprisonment of an adult.

The most serious offences committed by dangerous young offenders may be dealt with by sentences of custody for life, or in cases of murder by those aged between 10 and 18, by 'detention during Her Majesty's pleasure' under s. 53 of the Children and Young Persons Act 1933. This is the equivalent of life imprisonment for adult offenders.

Community sentences

The term 'community sentence' (or 'community order') applies to a range of penalties falling in severity below imprisonment or other forms of custody, but above fines, binding over or any form of discharge. These include community service, probation, curfew, attendance centre or supervision orders, or any lawful combination thereof.

Community service orders

A community service order requires the offender to do unpaid work in the community. An order may be for anything between 40 and 240 hours work. It was originally possible to make such orders only where the offender consented to it, but this restriction has been abolished by the Crime (Sentences) Act 1997. The aim of a community service order is to make the offender pay for his crime and perhaps improve his attitude by doing useful work, but without locking him up in an expensive custodial institution.

A court must not ordinarily impose a community service order, unless it is of the opinion that the offence, or the combination of the offence and one or more offences associated with it, is 'serious enough to warrant such a sentence'. The idea is that community service orders come only just below custodial sentences in seriousness. They are not appropriate for dangerous offenders or for those who have proved themselves unwilling to co-operate on previous occasions.

The Crime (Sentences) Act 1997 does, however, permit courts to impose community service orders on fine defaulters or on persistent petty offenders who have proved themselves incapable of paying fines commensurate with the seriousness of their offences.

Probation orders and supervision orders

Probation orders may be imposed where the court is of the opinion that 'supervision of an offender by a probation officer is desirable in the interests of (a) securing his rehabilitation or (b) protecting the public from harm from him or preventing the commission of further offences'. A probation order may be for any period of between six months and three years, and involves the offender being under the supervision of a probation officer during that time. The probation officer should try to advise, befriend and assist the offender, and encourage him to mend his ways.

As with community service, probation is not regarded as appropriate for really minor offences. Probation is itself a type of community order, and must be justified in terms of the seriousness of the offences committed. Supervision orders may be made in respect of children or young persons: these serve a broadly similar function and are subject to broadly similar sentencing criteria.

Curfew orders and attendance centre orders

Section 12 of the Criminal Justice Act 1991 (as amended by the Crime (Sentences) Act 1997) gives the courts the power to impose curfew orders on adults or juveniles (and even on children as young as 10). A curfew order may also include provision for the electronic tagging of the offender's movements during the period specified in the curfew order (typically the night), so that the police can know where he is. Electronic tagging has not yet been widely used, nor has it proved an unqualified success so far.

An offender between the ages of 10 and 20 can be sentenced to an attendance centre order if he has been convicted of an offence punishable with imprisonment or if he has been in breach of a probation order, etc. This is designed to occupy the offender on a series of Saturday afternoons, typically attending courses run by the police.

Fines

Fines are one of the mainstays of the criminal justice system, and are the only form of traditional punitive sentence that makes a profit (but see also confiscation orders, below). Fines serve both punitive and deterrent purposes. In particular, they are the principal sanction behind hundreds of regulatory offences dealing with trading standards, health and safety, road traffic, etc.

The size of a fine should be determined both by the gravity of the offence and by the means of the offender. This means that a well-heeled first offender may sometimes be fined more than an impecunious repeat offender for the same kind of offence, but the government has wisely abandoned the ill-starred system of 'unit fines' first introduced in 1991. These unit fines required courts to fine offenders by a number of 'units' to match the seriousness of the offence. The offender's disposable income would then be assessed, and the size of the fine would be calculated by multiplying the value of the units according to that income. This resulted in well-off (and often respectable) offenders having to pay quite enormous fines for relatively trivial road traffic offences, and it accordingly caused enormous resentment.

Magistrates' courts are usually limited to a maximum fine of £5,000, but it may be higher where the legislation creating an offence so specifies. The Crown Court may impose enormous fines on wealthy individuals or companies (and especially on companies, which cannot be dealt with by imprisonment). Fines of £1 million are not unknown. An offender may be given a period of time (typically up to a year) in which to pay a fine by instalments (or have them deducted from his salary), and he may be sentenced to custody for wilful default in paying. Parents may have to pay fines imposed on their children. The Crime (Sentences) Act 1997 now enables community service or curfew orders to be imposed instead of fines on persistent offenders, in cases where the offender has proved himself incapable of paying such fines.

Absolute and conditional discharges

An absolute discharge indicates that no penalty at all is appropriate in the circumstances. It may sometimes indicate the court's feeling that the defendant, although guilty, should never have been prosecuted. A conditional discharge is a warning not to offend again during a specified period (not exceeding three years). Breach of the order may result in the court resentencing the offender for the original offence as well.

Disqualification and deportation

Following conviction for certain types of offences, motorists may be disqualified from driving, company directors disqualified from being involved in the management of a company, dog owners may be disqualified from keeping dogs, and so on. Conviction may also lead to disqualification from possession of a firearm. A new power introduced by the Crime (Sentences) Act 1997, ss. 39–40, is that of disqualifying an offender from driving even in cases where the offence was not itself a driving offence.

Foreigners who have no right of abode here may be recommended for deportation after serving any other sentence imposed. This is only a recommendation. The Home Secretary will decide whether to act upon it.

Confiscation, forfeiture and restitution orders

Forfeiture orders involve the confiscation of property used in connection with an offence, and may be made subject to rules laid down in the Powers of Criminal Courts Act 1973. Restitution orders require stolen property, etc., to be returned to the lawful owner. Confiscation orders were first introduced in respect of the proceeds of drug trafficking, and were designed to strip convicted traffickers of property in their possession which they cannot prove to have acquired without recourse to the proceeds of the trafficking. The power to make confiscation orders has now been extended to other crimes by the Proceeds of Crime Act 1995. This hard-hitting new legislation not only requires the confiscation of the proceeds of any profitable crime for which the defendant has been convicted, but in the case of a defendant who is convicted of more than one such offence within a period of six years, it may require the defendant to *prove* that any other money or property which he possesses has been legitimately acquired. Otherwise, this too will be presumed to represent the proceeds of crime and confiscated.

If the defendant appears to have spent sums of money that cannot be accounted for as legitimate earnings, etc. (as where money has been paid into a bank account and then withdrawn), any other property (such as a house inherited from his parents) may be seized in lieu. At present, magistrates' courts can exercise such powers only in respect of a handful of offences. Crown Court judges have much wider powers in this respect.

Compensation orders

As the Court of Appeal explained in *Inwood* (1974) 60 Cr App R 70, the purpose of compensation orders is *not* to allow offenders to buy their way out of the penalties that they deserve, but merely to save the victim of a crime from having to conduct his own civil litigation against the offender for any harm that he has done. In other words, such orders must be imposed in addition to, and not in place of, any other sentence that the offender's conduct deserves. It is recognised, however, that compensation should be paid in priority to any fine or confiscation order. As with fines, the amount of compensation ordered must bear some relationship to the means of the offender. The Home Office publishes guidelines for the courts on the amount of compensation that may be appropriate for a given type of injury.

TEN

Civil Procedure

Civil courts are a forum which may be used for the settlement of disputes between individuals, companies or other legal persons. The disputes may arise from alleged breaches of contract, from matrimonial or family proceedings, from alleged torts (such as personal injury claims) or from numerous other possible causes. The state and its organs sometimes play a part in civil proceedings, especially in actions for judicial review of administrative acts.

Proceedings in the civil courts are seldom cheap and, as explained in Chapter 5, there may be alternative methods of dispute resolution which might be pursued. Furthermore, a potential litigant must not only consider his own costs in bringing the action, but must also remember that, if unsuccessful, he may well have to pay the costs of the winning party. It is possible for some litigants to obtain legal aid, but it is only those of limited means who may apply for such funding (see Chapter 7). For private litigants, the support of insurers, trade unions or professional associations may sometimes make the pursuit or defence of an action possible where private funds would not. Insurance policies (even standard household policies) may provide cover against the risk of incurring certain legal costs, as well as against the risks of liability itself, but would not cover, for example, the costs of an unsuccessful libel claim.

Civil disputes may arise in a variety of different ways. The vast majority will be resolved outside the courts and a good proportion of them will be settled without either party seeking professional legal help. Even where professional legal advice is sought, the solicitors involved will often not be thinking of litigation at this stage in the process. Instead, they will probably attempt to reach an acceptable settlement through negotiating with (or threatening!) the other party to the dispute. In trying to reach an out-of-court settlement, legal representatives may well offer certain concessions which they would not be prepared to make in the courtroom. Consequently, negotiations between the parties at that stage are often called 'without prejudice' on the grounds that whatever is said at that stage cannot be used in any subsequent litigation. If all attempts at reaching an informal settlement fail, then the aggrieved party will have to decide whether it is worth pursuing the other in the courts.

The cost of pursuing a civil action in the courts depends upon a variety of factors, such as the nature of the dispute and the level of court at which the action is pursued. The following sections consider the procedure which must be followed in the county courts and in the High Court.

Pre-trial procedure

Initiating proceedings
Actions in the High Court can be commenced in one of four ways, although the more usual methods of commencing proceedings are through issue of an originating summons or by writ. The writ is the official document that must be served on the defendant in order to begin proceedings against him. Some types of action can be commenced only by writ. Actions for tort, claims based upon fraud and most other actions in the Queen's Bench Division are commenced in this way.

In contrast, proceedings in the county courts are commenced by means of a summons, which is essentially a simpler version of a High Court writ. There are two types of summons:

(a)   a default summons, which is used where a sum of money is being claimed against the other party; and
(b)   a fixed date summons, which is used where the plaintiff is seeking a remedy other than money.

The summons will then be submitted to the court, along with details of the particulars of the claim. The main difference between the two forms of summons is that the fixed date summons displays a date on which the hearing or pre-trial review will take place, whereas the default summons does not.

Cases destined for the High Court may be commenced in any District Registry or the Royal Courts of Justice in the Strand in London, as the plaintiff chooses. The court, does, however, have the right to transfer proceedings to another venue.

The writ or summons must be served upon the defendant and this may be done in a number of ways, such as handing it to the defendant or handing it to his solicitor, whereas a company may be served with a writ by sending it to the company's registered office.

Acknowledgement of service

Upon receipt of the High Court writ or county court summons, the defendant must return what is called an acknowledgement of service within 14 days, indicating that he intends to defend the action. If the defendant does not acknowledge receipt within this period, he loses without a fight and the judge may issue a 'judgment in default'. Such an order may also be given if the defendant indicates that he does not intend to fight the action. The plaintiff may also at this stage, if he feels that the defendant's reply discloses no defence to the action in law, apply for a 'summary judgment' under which an award will be made in the plaintiff's favour. This enables 'open and shut cases' to be disposed of without the need for a trial.

If the defendant intends to fight the action, he must take steps to file a defence or make a counterclaim against the plaintiff. A counterclaim may be made, for example, if the two parties blame each other for an accident in which they were both injured, or where one claims that the other has not paid what is owing on a contract and the other claims that the work was faulty and in breach of contract. Counterclaims may be tried at the same time as the original claim.

Pleadings

Pleadings are formal documents passed between the parties to the action after the writ or summons has been served. The purpose of pleadings is to identify the issues in the case as clearly as possible before the case goes to court. During the course of the pleadings, issues should be clarified, points of agreement acknowledged and relevant documents made available for inspection (this is known as 'discovery' and it may be ordered by the court where necessary).

Preliminary hearings

Preliminary hearings may be needed in some cases prior to the trial itself. The basic form of pre-trial hearing in the High Court is known as a 'summons for directions', and its purpose is procedural (what kind of trial is needed, is the evidence ready, what are the issues, how long should it last, etc.). Pre-trial reviews have also been introduced in the county courts, but have not been very popular with litigants who often seem to consider them an extra delay and expense.

Interim orders

In some cases, parties can obtain special orders from the court, prior to trial, in order to safeguard property or obtain evidence. The *Anton Piller* order may be obtained without the knowledge of the defendant, and allows the plaintiff or his agents to enter the defendant's premises in order to secure evidence (e.g., evidence of copyright or trade mark infringement, such as pirated goods) that might otherwise be destroyed. The power to make such orders is now set out in s. 7 of the Civil Procedure Act 1997. Such orders are not, however, made available to everyone who asks for one. Another such order is the *Mareva* injunction (which, like the *Anton Piller* order, was named after the first case to feature it). The *Mareva* injunction prevents the defendant transferring property abroad or otherwise disposing of it so as to ensure that he has nothing left for the plaintiff to seize should the plaintiff be successful in the case. The power to make such orders is now recognised in s. 37 of the Supreme Court Act 1981.

Settlement and payment into court

It is sometimes said that the main purpose of the often lengthy pre-trial proceedings is to ensure that most cases never come to court. Certainly, the vast majority are settled, compromised or abandoned before the trial begins. If they were not, English civil justice would quickly grind to a halt. Cases may be abandoned because the evidence or legal advice, when assembled, indicates that the defendant would win. They may be settled by the defendant when it becomes clear (i) that the plaintiff is not going to give up, and (ii) that the plaintiff would win. Why increase one's losses by going on with the trial? In many cases, however, the outcome is not certain. In particular, the plaintiff may know that he has a valid claim, but may not know what exactly it is worth: £10,000? £15,000? Here, compromise is often the order of the day. The plaintiff can be encouraged, if not coerced, into settling where the defendant (or the defendant's insurance company, acting on his behalf) makes a 'payment into court'. This is always a smaller sum than the plaintiff is claiming, but close enough to tempt him. If the plaintiff does not accept it, but eventually gets awarded the same amount or less by the judge, he has to pay the costs of the proceedings from the date of the offer he turned down. This may mean all the costs of the trial itself. If the plaintiff loses altogether, he pays everything. The judge does not know about the payment in, and may award a few pounds less, thereby landing the plaintiff with a huge bill for costs. Many plaintiffs therefore feel they have no choice but to 'play safe' and accept the payment into court.

Representative or class actions

In some cases where a large number of potential plaintiffs have a similar interest in suing the defendant over something which allegedly has harmed them all (as in the 'Opren' case, *Davies* v *Eli Lilly & Co.* [1987] 3 All ER 94, where some 1,500 persons alleged that they had suffered harm through use of a prescribed drug made by the defendants) some or all of those claimants may pool their resources in order to fight a few test cases. The result of these test cases is not strictly binding on the rest (as it would be in the USA), but in practice it determines whether their claims will be recognised, and if the test case fails other litigants would almost certainly give up.

The trial

Most civil trials are heard by a judge, sitting without a jury. He rules on the law and procedure, decides on the truth of the matters in dispute on the basis of the evidence heard, and decides on the remedy or compensation to be awarded to the plaintiff if successful. In a few cases, notably High Court actions for libel, the judge sits with a jury as in a criminal trial on indictment. The jury decide who is telling the truth and, more controversially, they decide on the amount of damages. As a result of the generosity of juries (or perhaps their dislike of tabloid newspapers) libel damages are often higher than damages for serious physical injury, which are carefully quantified by professional judges. (Jury trials are possible in actions for fraud or false imprisonment, but are commonly found only in libel cases.)

Most civil proceedings in British courts are 'adversarial'. This means that the court itself does not investigate the facts, but merely adjudicates on the basis of such evidence as the adversaries (plaintiff and defendant) manage to place before it. Judges, in other words, do not usually seek to discover the truth for themselves. There are some exceptions, notably proceedings involving the welfare of children, in which the court must be prepared to play a more active and assertive role. This is sometimes known as an inquisitorial procedure, but the adversarial approach is far more common.

The plaintiff calls his evidence first. Much of this evidence, as in a criminal trial, will be oral testimony from witnesses who were involved in or who saw what happened; but documentary evidence may dominate in some kinds of trial. The defendant or his lawyers may cross-examine the plaintiff's witnesses, and then, when the plaintiff closes his case, the defendant may call witnesses of his own. The parties may of course testify themselves. The burden of proof is usually on the plaintiff. If the plaintiff can produce enough evidence to satisfy the judge that his version of events is *probably* true, he will win. The plaintiff does *not* have to prove his case 'beyond all reasonable doubt' as in a criminal prosecution, neither can the plaintiff's damages be reduced on the basis that the judge is not 100 per cent certain; but if at the end of the trial the judge (or jury if there is one) either believes the defendant, or has *no idea* what happened or who to believe, then the defendant must win. There are some exceptions to this rule. In libel, for example, the plaintiff must prove that a damaging statement was published about him; but if the defendant wants to argue that the statement is true, it is up to the defendant to prove it. It is not for the plaintiff to prove that the statement is false.

Enforcement of judgments

One might think that, once the plaintiff gets the judgment sought (e.g., an order that the defendant pays damages of £15,000) then it is 'all over bar the shouting'. Sometimes it is. In some cases, however, the defendant may not be very co-operative in paying the damages or costs awarded, or may simply find it difficult to meet the award. Orders may therefore have to be obtained for 'execution' of the judgment through the seizure and sale of goods by court bailiffs, the attachment of earnings (where money is regularly deducted from the defendant's pay-packets at source) or the freezing of assets such as bank accounts (garnishee orders). Debtors who cannot pay are no longer liable to be thrown into prison, but those who deliberately defy the courts (e.g., by destroying or dissipating their own property to prevent the enforcement of the judgment) may sometimes be imprisoned for contempt of court.

Recommendations for reform of the civil justice system

The structure and organisation of the civil justice system have been the subject of a number of enquiries over the last few years. One of the more recent enquiries was the *Civil Justice Review*, which was instituted in 1985 by Lord Hailsham who was Lord Chancellor at the time. This review looked into how the civil courts' jurisdiction, procedure and administration could be improved and how costs, delays and complexities could be reduced. The report was published in 1988 and many of its recommendations were adopted and implemented by the Courts and Legal Services Act 1990 and by regulations made under that Act.

Investigation of the civil justice system did not end there. In 1993, a new Committee was established under the chairmanship of one of the law lords, Lord Woolf (now Master of the Rolls), to look into the operation of the civil system. The Committee published an interim report on its findings, entitled *Access to Justice*, in the summer of 1995. The full report was published in July 1996. Early on in the report, Lord Woolf states that serious flaws still remain within our system of civil justice and that civil litigation is in a state of crisis. He maintains that the main reasons for this state of affairs are 'cost, delay and complexity'. In 1993, for example, the *net* cost of civil proceedings, even excluding matrimonial cases, was £350 million. In addition, the report highlights the increasingly disproportionate costs involved in bringing civil actions compared to their outcomes. This problem was found to be most acute in smaller cases. Research carried out by the Supreme Court Training Office for the Woolf enquiry found that 50 per cent of such cases involved costs, for one or both parties, in excess of the cost of the claim itself. In other words, a claim for £5,000 in damages might easily involve additional legal costs of £6,000, and in some cases the costs can completely dwarf the value of the claim. Such costs often mean that 'those who are not eligible for legal aid, cannot afford legal assistance, even in relatively simple cases of modest value'.

In 1994, High Court cases took, on average, 163 weeks in London and 189 weeks (nearly four years!) elsewhere to progress from issue to trial. County court figures showed that, on average, progress from issue to trial was around 80 weeks.

The problem of complexity is attributable, the Woolf report argues, to a number of factors such as the rules of court, the existence of separate procedures in the county courts and High Court, the variety of ways of initiating proceedings, and other procedural matters.

Lord Woolf identified a number of possible areas of reform, advocating a 'new approach to litigation'. His report is a massive document, containing numerous recommendations for reform. A key proposal is that judges themselves should be responsible for managing the progress of cases. A judge should, Lord Woolf suggests, assume responsibility for the way in which a case proceeds through the system to actual trial, and indeed the form which the trial should take. This is referred to as 'case management'. Cases would be allocated to an 'appropriate track', of which there would be three to choose from, namely: (i) small claims track; (ii) fast track; and (iii) multi-track. Lord Woolf also proposed that small claims jurisdiction should be extended up to £3,000 for all cases other than those relating to personal injury. This recommendation has already been implemented and it is likely that the limit will be raised again (to £5,000) during 1998.

The fast track system is advocated for straightforward cases, including personal injury cases where the claim does not exceed £10,000 (or possibly £15,000). It is proposed that the fast track would quickly dispose of cases, and to that end court procedures would be strictly limited. For example, fast track cases would have a set timetable within which they should be heard. The figure provisionally suggested is one of between 20 and 30 weeks. The trial itself would be confined to three hours and there would be a system of fixed costs. Furthermore, the use of expert witnesses would be limited, with increased use instead of a neutral expert chosen by the court. The multi-track system would deal with larger and more complex cases involving sums in excess of £10,000 (or £15,000).

Lord Woolf makes a number of recommendations as far as rules of evidence and the presentation of cases are concerned. For example, the procedure of 'discovery' (under which documentary evidence in one party's possession must be revealed to the other side in advance of the trial) will be limited to discovery of documents which are readily available and which are of direct relevance to the case.

His lordship also argues that parties to a dispute should, wherever possible, be encouraged to pursue alternative options for the settlement of disputes. In particular he argues that ombudsman schemes offer a possible alternative form of dispute resolution and could be extended to deal with consumer complaints in the retail trade.

Needless to say, the report has stirred up a hornets' nest of criticism. Implementation of the more complex Woolf proposals must still be some way off (the most likely date for introduction of the multi-track system is April 1999) and much will depend on the willingness (and ability) of judges to act as case managers. If they (and their staff) cannot cope with such responsibilities on top of their existing duties, the progress of cases through the courts may actually be slowed under such a system.

Some changes have already been introduced as a result of the Woolf proposals. The Civil Procedure Act 1997 establishes a Civil Procedure Rule Committee and a Civil Justice Council, whose function is to review and advise on changes, 'so as to make the civil justice system more accessible, fair and efficient'.

PART TWO

Introduction to Criminal Law

The criminal law is a set of rules which regulate individual and corporate activity by prohibiting some forms of attention and (to a lesser extent) by requiring other acts to be performed on pain of a penalty or punishment that may be imposed by or on behalf of the state. Although the law permits some forms of private prosecution, the essence of the criminal law is that it exists for the protection of the state and of society as a whole, and prosecutions (even private ones) are ultimately brought on behalf of the state. Criminal cases tried on indictment are thus reported as *Regina* (i.e., the Queen) v *Smith* (which may be shortened to *Reg* v *Smith*, *R* v *Smith* or simply *Smith*).

Historically, the distinction between private wrongs (or torts) and crimes against the state or society was often confused. Whereas treason and witchcraft were clearly seen as public wrongs, theft, murder or assault were more of a private matter, which could be settled by payment of compensation to the victim. Indeed, even today the torts of assault and battery have a great deal in common with the crimes of the same name. It was eventually settled, however, that acts such as murder or theft had wider implications for society as a whole and created dangers which society as a whole (eventually, the state) had to take responsibility for dealing with. Today, there are literally thousands of criminal offences for which penalties may be imposed. Many of these are technical or 'regulatory' and are scarcely regarded as 'criminal' in the popular sense of the word, but they nevertheless fall into the legal definition of a crime, namely an act or omission that may lead to a penalty being imposed following conviction by a court of law. A crime, in other words, is anything which the law expressly or impliedly declares to be one.

This part of the book is concerned with what is called 'substantive' criminal law. This means that it deals with the definition of criminal conduct and with the essential ingredients of certain criminal offences and defences. It is not directly concerned with questions of evidence, procedure or sentencing, although such issues are considered in Chapters 8 to 9.

ELEVEN

The Essential Elements of a Crime

It is customary to break down the essential elements of any crime into two main components:

(a)   the prohibited actions, consequences or state of affairs, which are known as the *actus reus* (or guilty act); and

(b)   the criminal intent or other fault element (if any) required, which is known as the *mens rea* (or guilty mind).

In murder, for example, the actus reus is the unlawful killing of another person. The fatal blow is one part of that *actus reus*. So is the consequential death of the victim. So is the fact that the killing was unlawful. But not every unlawful killing is murder. A person charged with murder must be proved to have intended to kill, or at least to have intended grievous bodily harm (this is the *mens rea* for murder). Even for crimes of manslaughter, some degree of fault or *mens rea* must be proved against the defendant. This may be gross negligence, or it may be an intention to commit some other crime in circumstances where there is an obvious risk of injury to other persons; but a death caused by a tragic accident in which nobody was significantly to blame is not even manslaughter. Indeed, it would be classed as accidental death, rather than unlawful killing.

Must all crimes have both an *actus reus* and a *mens rea*? At common law, it is often said that there can be no guilty act without a guilty mind. This, however, is not entirely true. There are many crimes, particularly 'regulatory offences', for which proof of fault is not necessary. If, for example, a motorist drives through a red traffic light, or uses a vehicle with defective brakes or tyres, he will be guilty of a road traffic offence, regardless of blame or fault. Of course, such motorists will usually have been at least careless, but the prosecution does not have to prove this. It is enough that it happened. Such offences are known as 'strict liability offences' (see Chapter 12).

One can therefore have an *actus reus* without *mens rea*. The converse is not true, however. There can be no offence without an *actus reus*. Merely intending or hoping for harm cannot be a crime. Such an offence would amount to 'thought-crime', as in George Orwell's novel, *1984*. Having said that, it should be noted that a 'guilty mind' may turn what might otherwise have been an entirely innocent act into a guilty one (or *actus reus*). A witness who tells the court something that he believes to be a lie will, strictly speaking, be guilty of perjury, even if it turns out (to his astonishment) to be true after all. This is because the offence of perjury involves *either* giving evidence which you know to be false, *or* evidence which you do not believe to be true (Perjury Act 1911, s. 1). One can also be guilty of an attempt to commit a crime by doing entirely lawful things in the mistaken belief that you are doing something else, that would indeed have been criminal. Smuggling harmless vegetable powder through Customs is not an offence, but if you thought it was heroin or cocaine (having paid good money for it in Amsterdam) you may be guilty of attempting to import controlled drugs, contrary to the Criminal Attempts Act 1981 (*Shivpuri* [1987] 2 All ER 334). Perhaps we do have thought-crimes after all!

THE *ACTUS REUS*

The *actus reus* of an offence may take many different forms: it can take the shape of an act or omission, the causing of a prohibited consequence, or even the existence of a prohibited state of affairs. Smith and Hogan, in their classic textbook, *Criminal Law*, define the *actus reus* as including 'all elements of an offence which are not part of the accused's guilty mind or *mens rea*'. In other words, it represents the external manifestation of the offence. The following points should be noted regarding the *actus reus*.

Voluntary and involuntary conduct

If the *actus reus* of a given offence requires conduct on the defendant's part, this conduct must be willed or 'voluntary'. It is not enough that the defendant by his unconscious bodily movements brings about the prohibited act or prohibited consequences. Suppose for example that the defendant suffers a sudden blackout whilst driving a car, and the car careers through a red traffic light. In these circumstances, there will be no *actus reus* and no crime (even though it is otherwise a strict liability offence). Involuntary acts may also arise from external pressures, as for example where the defendant's car goes through a red light because it has been shunted over the line by a vehicle hitting it from behind.

If the conduct was involuntary because the defendant was in a state of unconsciousness when the act occurred, this is referred to as automatism, but automatism is not always a defence to a criminal charge. One of the main questions which must be considered is that of how the defendant got into that state in the first place. Was the automatism induced through the misuse of mind-altering drugs, such as LSD? If the defendant was in some way to blame for bringing on his automatism, he may still be liable for some kinds of crime. (For further information on this topic, see Chapter 18.)

Acts and omissions

Most criminal offences require the defendant to carry out some kind of positive act before liability can be imposed. Generally there is no liability for failure (or omission) to act, unless the law specifically imposes a duty to act upon a particular person. This principle can be illustrated by using the famous example cited by Stephen in his 1887 *Digest of the Criminal Law*:

> A sees B drowning and is able to save him by holding out his hand. A abstains from doing so in order that B may be drowned, and B is drowned. A has committed no offence.

In the above example, the person (if any) who pushed B into the water is the only one who has done a positive act to cause B's death. A may have failed to save B, but he did not do any positive act to cause B's death. Some countries (such as France and Germany) recognise that a person should always be under a duty to act in such a situation, as long as he does not have to put his own life in danger (the so-called 'Good Samaritan law'). Under English law, however, a duty to act only arises in certain specific situations.

Where statute imposes a duty to act
From time to time, legislation creates offences of *failing* to act. To give just one example, the Companies Act 1985 requires companies and their directors to do certain things at particular times, such as filing accounts and reports with the Registrar of Companies. If they fail to do so, they may be subject to substantial fines. This was recently pointed out in notices in the business pages of leading newspapers under the caption: 'Company directors: do you want to be fined for doing nothing?'

Close relationships
If persons are in a close or special relationship to one another, the law may impose on one a duty to act on behalf of the other. If, in the drowning example above, A was B's father then he would be under a legal obligation to try to help his child.

Duty arising from the assumption of care for another
If a person voluntarily undertakes to care for another person who is unable to care for himself as a result of age, illness or other infirmity, the law requires that this undertaking must be performed, at least until someone else can be found to discharge it. *Stone and Dobinson* [1977] 2 All ER 341 provides a harsh illustration of this rule. Stone and Dobinson were an unmarried couple of very limited intelligence. Stone's anorexic sister, Fanny, came to live with them. They were not obliged to take her in or look after her, but at first they did so. Fanny was not, at first, totally helpless. Gradually, however, her condition deteriorated, until she became bed-ridden. She needed medical help, but none was summoned. Neither of the defendants had any malice towards her, but neither of them seemed to have the wit or energy to do anything about it. Fanny eventually died in squalor, covered in bed sores and filth. The sores extended right into her bones and were infested with maggots. Stone and Dobinson were convicted of her manslaughter and the Court of Appeal upheld their convictions. The Court held that because they had taken Fanny into their home, they had assumed a duty of care for her and had been grossly negligent in the performance of that duty. It may well have been the case that Fanny was too ill for them to cope with her, but all they needed to do was to call for help, and in this they failed.

Doctor-patient relationships
A doctor is under a duty to treat his patients, but under certain circumstances that duty may be terminated, as for example where the patient refuses to undergo further medical treatment. If a patient has had a series of heart attacks he may perhaps inform his doctor that, if he were to suffer another, he is not to be given resuscitation. In this situation, the doctor would be under no duty to save him following the next heart attack. On the contrary, he would be guilty of unlawful battery if he did so. If an adult of sound mind gives clear instructions that he does not want to receive medical treatment, doctors must give effect to these wishes (*Re T (Adult: Refusal of Medical Treatment)* [1992] 4 All ER 649).

What if the patient is incapable of communicating his wishes? Ordinarily, the doctor's duty to his patient requires him to do everything that he reasonably can to keep the patient alive. Under certain circumstances, however, a doctor may be absolved of this duty, as can be seen in *Airedale National Health Service Trust* v *Bland* [1993] 1 All ER 821. The patient in this case was one of the victims of the Hillsborough Stadium disaster. He had not recovered consciousness since the tragedy, as he had suffered irreversible brain damage. He was breathing normally, but was in a 'persistent vegetative state', and was kept alive only by being fed through tubes. The NHS Trust sought a declaration from the courts that it might discontinue the life sustaining treatment and allow him to die with dignity and with minimum distress. The House of Lords held that in certain circumstances medical treatment could properly be removed. Lord Goff delivered the leading speech. He accepted that, even where the patient was not able to communicate his feelings on the issue of consent to treatment, there is not invariably an absolute obligation upon the doctor to prolong the patient's life. He must act in the best interests of the patient. In *Bland*, it was not in the best interests of the patient to be kept alive and he should instead be allowed to die with dignity. At the same time, the positive act of giving a lethal injection remains illegal (indeed, it is murder) however painful, distressing and hopeless the patient's condition may be:

> ... the law draws a crucial distinction between cases in which a doctor decides not to provide, or to continue to provide, for his patient treatment of care which could or might prolong his life, and those in which he decides, for example by administering a lethal drug, actively to bring his patient's life to an end.... The former may be lawful, either because the doctor is giving effect to his patient's wishes ... or even in certain circumstances in which the patient is incapacitated from stating whether or not he gives his consent. But it is not lawful for a doctor to administer a drug to his patient to bring about his death, even though that course is prompted by a humanitarian desire to end his suffering, however great that suffering may be: see *Cox* (unreported) September 18 1992 ... so to act is to cross the Rubicon which runs between on the one hand the care of his living patient and on the other hand euthanasia.

In the case of *Cox*, to which Lord Goff referred, a doctor was convicted of attempted murder when he administered a lethal injection to a long-term patient of his who was slowly dying in agony and whom he could no longer help with painkilling drugs. She had begged him to do it. Strictly speaking, his crime must have been murder, but the prosecution pretended that they could not prove whether the injection had killed her or whether she had (coincidentally) died of her illness just before the injection could take effect. That tactic saved the need for a mandatory life sentence, and Cox was (quite rightly) allowed to walk free after his conviction.

Other contractual and official obligations

Doctors are not the only persons who may incur criminal liability for failure to discharge their official duties or contractual obligations. In *Pittwood* (1902) 19 TLR 37, for example, P was employed to operate level-crossing gates on a railway, but omitted to close the gates when a train was signalled. A cart was crossing the railway through the open gates when the train struck it and killed one of the carters. P was convicted of manslaughter. In one sense, this was because his contractual duty required him to close the gates, but the victim was not, of course, a party to any such contract, and P's liability can more accurately be justified on the basis of his breach of his duty of care to users of the crossing, which his employers paid him to discharge, and on which the users of the crossing undoubtedly relied.

Neglect of duty by a police officer was examined by the Court of Appeal in *Dytham* [1979] 3 All ER 641. D, whilst on duty in uniform, stood aside and watched as a man was kicked and beaten to death outside a night-club. He then left the scene, without calling for assistance or even summoning an ambulance. For this he was convicted of the common law offence of wilful misconduct in public office. Lord Widgery CJ said:

> The allegation was ... one ... of deliberate failure and wilful neglect. This involves an element of culpability ... calculated to injure the public interest so as to call for condemnation and punishment.

D was not charged with manslaughter, probably because it was not clear that he could have saved the deceased, even if he had tried to do so.

Duty to avert a dangerous situation of one's own making
If a person creates a dangerous situation through his own fault, he may be under a duty to take reasonable steps to avert the danger. In *Miller* [1983] 1 All ER 978, the defendant was sleeping rough in a building, and fell asleep on his mattress while smoking a cigarette. When he awoke, he saw that his mattress was on fire, but instead of calling for help, he simply moved into another room, thereby allowing the fire to spread. He was convicted of arson, not for starting the fire, but for failing to do anything about it. Lord Diplock said:

> I see no rational ground for excluding from conduct capable of giving rise to criminal liability, conduct which consists of failing to take measures that lie within one's power to counteract a danger that one has oneself created, if at the time of such conduct one's state of mind is such as constitutes a necessary ingredient of the offence.

State-of-affairs offences

An *actus reus* usually requires some form of wrongful conduct or behaviour on the part of the defendant. Sometimes, however, the *actus reus* is defined in such a way that it takes the form of a proscribed state of affairs, for which the defendant may or may not be to blame. This can of course lead to some rather harsh decisions. In *Winzar* v *Chief Constable of Kent, The Times*, 28 March 1983, the police were called to a hospital to remove a drunk from the corridor. They took him to their police car which was parked on the highway. He was then convicted for being 'found drunk on a highway'. It was held that the manner in which he got on to the highway was irrelevant. This sounds very harsh, but it should be pointed out that the police had acted in good faith. They could not have left Winzar in the hospital, nor could they have left him lying drunk in the road. Had they dragged an innocent man out of his own house and then arrested him for being drunk on the highway, the courts would no doubt have refused to allow the prosecution to proceed, since that would have amounted to an 'abuse of process'. (See also *Larsonneur* (1933) 24 Cr App R 74.)

Causation

Problems relating to causation can only arise in relation to certain types of crime. On a charge of dangerous driving, for example, there is no need to prove that any consequence at all resulted from the driving in question; and on a charge of blackmail, it is not necessary to show that the victim even received the blackmailer's demands. Simply 'making' a blackmail demand is all that the offence of blackmail requires (see Chapter 15, below). If, however, the charge is one of causing death by dangerous driving, murder or obtaining property by deception, there may sometimes be problems in showing that a particular element of the crime was 'caused' by the accused's conduct.

Factual causation

Most causation problems arise in homicide cases. In order to establish whether the defendant's acts or omissions have brought about the prohibited consequences (in this case, death), one must first apply the factual causation test as a filter system to weed out non-relevant events. This is sometimes referred to as the 'but for' test: would the proscribed consequences have occurred, 'but for' the defendant's behaviour? It was this test that the prosecution failed in *White* [1910] 2 KB 124. The defendant put poison in his mother's bedtime drink, and was charged with her murder when she was found dead the next morning; but it turned out that he could not have been guilty of murder, because his mother had hardly drunk any of the poison. She had quite coincidentally died of natural causes that night. (White was, however, guilty of attempted murder.)

Imputable causation

The fact that the 'but for' test has been established does not necessarily mean that the defendant will be held responsible for the crime. If A suggests to B that he goes for a drive in his car, and B is killed in a traffic accident, that cannot mean that A has caused B's death. Applying the 'but for' test alone would suggest that he has, but the question to be decided is more subtle: was A's suggestion the *legal* cause of his friend's death? Is A to blame for his death? The answer must be 'No'. If, however, A had done something which created an obvious risk to B's life, then he might be held to blame for B's death, even if he did not cause it with his own hands. In *Pagett* (1983) 76 Cr App R 279, the defendant used his girlfriend as a human shield in a shoot-out with armed police officers. His girlfriend was hit by police bullets and died. He was held to be guilty of her manslaughter. He may not have fired the fatal bullet, but his actions still contributed to her death, because they created the dangerous situation in which she died.

Multiple causes and multiple blame

A defendant may be guilty of causing something to happen, even if his conduct was not the only cause of it. In *Hennigan* [1971] 3 All ER 133, the defendant argued that he was not guilty of causing death by dangerous driving, because another driver in the accident was more to blame than him. The Court of Appeal replied that this was not the point. As long as the defendant's contribution was significant, he could be held to blame.

In homicide cases, third parties', or even the victim's own conduct may contribute to death, but none of this will absolve the defendant, as long as his own contribution was a substantial one. In particular, the victim's failure to obtain, accept or receive proper medical treatment cannot be relied upon by the defendant. If it causes a minor injury inflicted by the defendant to get worse, the defendant may be liable for the more serious injury that results. If the victim dies, it may be murder or manslaughter (depending on the defendant's *mens rea* when he caused the original injury). In *Blaue* [1975] 3 All ER 446, the defendant stabbed a young woman. A blood transfusion would have saved her life, but she was a Jehovah's Witness and refused to accept one. She eventually died. The defendant was convicted of manslaughter (it would have been murder, but for his mental abnormality) and this verdict was upheld by the Court of Appeal. Lawton LJ said:

> It has long been the policy of the law that those who use violence on other people must take their victims as they find them. This in our judgment means the whole man, not just the physical man. It does not lie in the mouth of the assailant to say that the victim's religious beliefs which inhibited [her] from accepting certain kinds of treatment were unreasonable. The question for decision is what caused her death. The answer is the stab wound. The fact that the victim refused to stop this end coming about did not break the causal connection between the act and death.

The assailant will not necessarily be absolved of blame, even if the victim does things which positively aggravate his condition. In *Wall* (1802) 28 State Trials 51, W ordered the brutal and illegal flogging of a soldier. In order to ease his pain, the soldier subsequently drank a lot of alcohol and this aggravated his condition. Eventually he died, and W was convicted of his murder. This may be an old case, but more recently, in *Dear* [1996] Crim LR 595 a murder conviction was upheld, even though there was evidence that the victim had deliberately reopened the wounds inflicted by the defendant, from which he then bled to death.

Medical treatment

If the victim is injured by the defendant, it is foreseeable that he will require medical treatment. But what if the treatment he receives is improper or negligent? One such case where palpably wrong treatment was given to the victim was *Jordan* (1956) 40 Cr App R 152. The defendant stabbed the victim, who was taken to hospital, where he died. The defendant was convicted of murder, but on appeal new evidence was admitted. This showed that at the time of the victim's death the wound had almost totally healed and that the victim had died as a result of mistakenly being given antibiotics to which he had already proved highly allergic. His overall treatment was described by the Court of Appeal as 'palpably wrong' and they felt that if a jury had heard this evidence they would have concluded that it was the bad medical treatment which had caused the victim's death and not the stab wound. So the erroneous medical treatment had the effect of 'breaking the chain of causation'.

Jordan must, however, be contrasted with *Smith* [1959] 2 All ER 193. The defendant was a soldier who stabbed his victim with a bayonet during a brawl. Other soldiers carried the victim to the medical centre, but unfortunately dropped him twice on the way. The medical staff were under pressure because they had a lot of other fight victims to deal with. As a result they did not notice that one of the victim's lungs had been pierced and the treatment they gave was described at the trial as 'thoroughly bad ... it might well have affected his chances of recovery'. He died and the defendant was convicted of murder. On appeal it was argued that the treatment was abnormal and that (as in *Jordan*) the chain of causation had been broken. The appeal was nevertheless dismissed. The court stated:

> If at the time of death the original wound is still an operating cause and a substantial cause, then the death can properly be said to be the result of the wound, albeit that some other cause of death is also operating. Only if it can be said that the original wounding is merely the setting in which another cause operates can it be said that the death did not result from the wound. Putting it another way, only if the second cause is so overwhelming as to make the original wound merely part of the history can it be said that the death does not flow from the wound.

Smith was therefore a case of death by multiple causes, and the stab wound was still one of those causes. In contrast, the wound in *Jordan* had largely healed, and the hospital treatment was in effect the sole cause of death. Furthermore, the mistreatment was so bizarre as to be unforeseeable. It is foreseeable that sometimes medical treatment may, through error or through bad luck, kill the patient outright. Had Jordan's victim died as a result of the first routine dose of antibiotics, the murder conviction would almost certainly have been upheld. See, for example, the later case of *Cheshire* [1991] 3 All ER 670, where the defendant shot the victim, who later died as a result of unfortunate complications arising from the emergency surgery he had undergone. The gunshot wounds had actually healed at the time of death, but the Court of Appeal upheld the conviction on the grounds that the complications were a natural consequence of the defendant's acts. The Court made it clear that it would only be in the most extraordinary cases that the chain of causation would be broken as a result of medical negligence or improper treatment.

Death from fright or flight

If the victim dies or injures himself in a fall, etc., whilst attempting to escape from an attack by the defendant, it must be asked whether his behaviour in fleeing was understandable in those circumstances. If it was, then even if it was also unwise or foolhardy, the defendant may be guilty of causing the victim's injury or death. On the other hand, the defendant cannot be held responsible for behaviour which is 'so daft that it could not be foreseen'. In the case of *Roberts* (1971) 56 Cr App R 95 the defendant was convicted of an assault causing actual bodily harm to a young woman, who was injured jumping from his moving car after he had sexually assaulted her in the car. Jumping from the car may or may not have been a wise move on the part of the young woman, but it was certainly not 'so daft that it could not have been foreseen'. Liability may also arise for death or injury caused by shock or fright. A burglar who threatens an elderly victim may be liable for manslaughter if the victim collapses and dies of shock. In *Hayward* (1908) 21 Cox CC 692, the defendant chased his wife out of their house, uttering violent threats. She collapsed in the road and died. Medical evidence showed that she had been suffering from a condition which could be fatal if aggravated by physical assertion or any strong emotion such as fear. The judge told the jury that death from fright caused by an illegal act was sufficient for manslaughter, and the husband was duly convicted. (It would have been murder, had he actually intended to kill her or cause her really serious injury.)

MENS REA

Most crimes require the prosecution to prove a *mens rea* for every part of the *actus reus*, but some, as previously explained, do not. Apart from those regulatory (e.g., road traffic) offences which require no proof of *mens rea* at all, there are others, including some mainstream criminal offences, which require *mens rea* only as to some aspects of the *actus reus*. The crime of assault occasioning actual bodily harm, for example, requires an intention to commit an assault (or at least recklessness as to this), but does not require any *mens rea* as to the causing of the actual bodily harm; see *Savage* [1991] 4 All ER 698, which is discussed in Chapter 14.

  Mens rea can take many different forms. For example, a crime may require the prosecution to prove that the defendant intended to bring about the *actus reus*, or that he was reckless as to whether certain consequences would be brought about. In fact, most crimes can either be committed intentionally or recklessly. Other types of *mens rea* include knowledge, maliciousness, dishonesty and negligence. In the case of statutory offences, the provision creating the offence usually specifies the *mens rea* required. A combination of *mens rea* forms may be specified in the statute. Theft, for example, requires proof of dishonesty and of an intent to permanently deprive the owner of his property.

Intention or intent

The meaning of intent is a difficult concept to define. Cases of murder require proof of intent to kill or do GBH and murder cases will be used here as illustrations, but the same principles apply for any crime of intent.

Intention can be distinguished from motive or desire
Intention can usually be distinguished from motive. A paid assassin kills for money. The desire for money is the motive, and he may regret having to kill someone against whom he has no quarrel, but his intent is still to kill, and if he does so he is a murderer.

Purpose
If the defendant deliberately sets out to kill someone — if in other words his purpose is to kill — one would have no difficulty in saying that he intends to kill. Intent always includes purpose. It does not matter that the purpose in question is unlikely to be achieved. One can intend to commit a crime without really expecting to succeed. The more difficult question is whether a person can intend something even where it is not his purpose to achieve it.

Intention must be distinguished from foresight
A person does not, however, necessarily intend a result just because he knows it is a probable result of his actions. At one time it used to be held that a person was always 'deemed' to intend the natural consequences of his acts, but this rule was abolished by s.8 of the Criminal Justice Act 1967. A person who merely foresees that his act may kill someone, and who has not set out to cause death or serious injury, might be considered reckless or grossly negligent, and he may be guilty of manslaughter if death does indeed result, but he would not be guilty of murder. The House of Lords so decided in *Moloney* [1985] 1 All ER 1025 and more recently reiterated that point in *Woollin* (1998) *The Times*, 23 July. The defendant in that case had lost his temper with his baby son and thrown him against a hard surface. The baby died of the injuries inflicted. At his trial for murder, the trial judge told the jury that they could treat this as a case of intentional serious injury (and thus as murder) 'if the defendant had appreciated that there was a substantial risk of causing such injury'. Quashing his conviction for murder, and substituting a conviction for manslaughter, the House of Lords held that,

> By using the phrase, 'substantial risk' [the trial judge] had blurred the line between intention and recklessness, and hence between murder and manslaughter.

Oblique intent

Oblique intent is a controversial subject which arguably bridges the gap between intention and foresight. The idea behind the concept of oblique intent is that defendant should be regarded as intending any side effects of his actions that he knows to be inevitable. The most often used example to illustrate the idea of oblique intent is that of a defendant who places a bomb on an airliner, intending that it should explode in mid-air. He is not a terrorist, and his purpose in planting the bomb is not to kill people, but he aims to destroy the aircraft and its cargo of freight in order to claim on an insurance policy relating to that cargo. The bomber is nevertheless perfectly well aware that he *will* kill many people if the bomb explodes as intended. On such facts, it must be possible to argue that the bomber intended to kill the crew and passengers. He must have known that, if his bomb worked he intended, he *would* (not just might) kill the passengers and crew in the process. The only question was how many would die.

Do the courts agree? It was for many years difficult to answer this question, because the case law was so confused. The judges usually dealt with the issue (for example in *Nedrick* [1986] 3 All ER 1) by saying that, if the defendant knew he would kill people, that was *evidence* to suggest it may have been his intent to kill. The defendant in *Nedrick* had deliberately set fire to a woman's house, and one of the woman's children had died in the fire, but he denied having intended to kill anyone. His purpose, he said, had only been to frighten the woman and damage her house. Lord Lane CJ held that, in such cases (by which he presumably meant cases in which causing death is not the direct aim or purpose of the defendant) a jury could be permitted to 'infer' that the defendant intended to kill if (but only if) he realised at the time that death or really serious injury was virtually certain to result from his action. This was all very puzzling. The *Nedrick* approach unfortunately confused two issues, namely: (1) what do we mean by intention (a matter of definition); and (2) how do we prove what the defendant intended (a matter of evidence and inference). It offered an answer to (2) as if it were the answer to (1), which quite clearly it was not. What the Court of Appeal should have said (as the Lord Chief Justice frankly admitted a few years later) was that a person intends to kill *either* if that it is his purpose or if he knows that killing will be an inevitable side effect of his actions. But the judges felt unable to say this at the time, because they were obliged to follow precedents set by the House of Lords in *Hancock*. To make matters worse, *Nedrick* quickly became accepted by the courts as a definitive statement of the law governing intent, and convictions for murder were quashed in a number of cases where judges attempted to define intent any differently. One example was *Scalley* [1995] Crim LR 504, which provoked Professor Sir John Smith to write,

> Of course the judge and the Court of Appeal are obliged to follow precedent. But it is an unedifying process which requires the jury to be given a meaningless direction [on the meaning of intent] . . .

Some clarification has at last been offered by the House of Lords in *Woollin* (above). Whilst broadly approving of the ruling in *Nedrick*, Lord Steyn acknowledged in *Woollin* that the effect of *Nedrick* was that, 'a result foreseen as virtually certain was an intended result'. He added that judges should no longer speak of intention being 'inferred' in such cases: a further recognition of the fact that the problem is one of legal definition, rather than one of inference and proof.

Proving intent
Sometimes an offender admits (or confesses) to having intended to commit his crime; but if he denies it, how does the prosecution prove he is lying? Generally speaking, it will seek to do so by inviting the jury to draw inferences from the evidence. A man is known to hate his mother. There is evidence that he stands to inherit a lot of money on her death. He is seen to push her out of a third floor window. This evidence all points to his actions being deliberate murder. In particular, why should anyone push another person out of a third floor window, unless he intends to kill him? (See *Walker* (1990) 90 Cr App R 226, where the victim survived the fall, but the defendants were convicted of attempting to murder him.) Remember, however, that this is a question of drawing inferences. It is not a rule of law. The court or jury must take account of all relevant evidence. In *Moloney*, for example, the defendant had loaded a shotgun and blown his stepfather's head apart at close range. One would normally conclude that this must have been deliberate murder, but there was evidence that a stupid drunken game had gone horribly wrong, and the House of Lords held that a murder conviction could not safely be upheld.

Maliciousness

This is an old-fashioned term, but it is found in several statutes, notably in the Offences Against the Person Act 1861, where it is used many times. Maliciousness can mean one of two things: intent to do harm or recklessness as to whether harm might result. The harm intended for this purpose may have been something far less than the harm actually committed. If, for example, the defendant intended minor harm to the victim, but inadvertently caused him grievous bodily harm, he will have 'maliciously inflicted grievous bodily harm' under s. 20 of the Offences Against the Person Act 1861. As to the second meaning, the term 'recklessness' is used in what is known as the 'Cunningham' or 'subjective' sense. The facts of *Cunningham* [1957] 2 All ER 412, were that C removed a gas meter from an unoccupied house so that he could steal the money contained in it. The pipe was fractured and gas seeped into the neighbouring house where the victim inhaled it. C was charged with maliciously administering a noxious substance (the gas) so as to endanger life, contrary to s. 23 of the Offences Against the Person Act 1861, but it was held that he could not be adjudged malicious unless he had foreseen or been aware of the risk. It was not clear that C had been aware of it at all, so he was not guilty of the offence.

Recklessness

This is almost as troublesome a concept as intent, because its meaning manages to be both complex and variable. As explained above, offences requiring proof of maliciousness require at least deliberate risk taking or 'Cunningham' recklessness. The same is true of a number of crimes that do not use the word 'maliciously' at all. A man cannot be guilty of rape, for example, unless he at least suspected that his victim was not consenting to sex; but there are some crimes which can be committed on the basis of a lesser kind of recklessness. This is known as 'Caldwell' recklessness, after the case of Caldwell [1981] 1 All ER 961. In that case C got drunk and set fire to a hotel in pursuance of a grievance he had against the owner. There were guests in the hotel at the time of the fire, but the fire was discovered and extinguished before any serious harm was done. C was charged under s. 1(1) and (3) of the Criminal Damage Act 1971 with intentionally damaging by fire property belonging to another. He was also charged with the aggravated version of this offence, under s. 1(2) of the Criminal Damage Act 1971, namely with damaging such property *being reckless as to whether life would be endangered*. He admitted the lesser offence, but denied the aggravated one. He claimed not to have realised how dangerous his behaviour had been.

The House of Lords held that a person must be deemed to be reckless as to causing damage or endangering life, not only where he knowingly takes the risk of doing so, but also where he does an act which creates an obvious risk and fails to give any thought to the possibility of there being any such risk. This was a major extension of the concept of recklessness and was very controversial.

It was subsequently held in Elliott v C [1983] 2 All ER 1005, that it is irrelevant that the risk might not have been obvious to the particular defendant even if he had tried to think of it. The defendant may, for example, be mentally backward and unable to appreciate the risk. The sole question is whether the risk would have been obvious to the ordinary and reasonable adult man or woman. In Elliott v C itself, a 14-year-old entered a shed, found some white spirit and started a fire. The whole shed was destroyed. The girl maintained that she never thought that the fire would get out of control. She was backward and because of this fact the magistrates thought the risk of the shed being destroyed was not one which would be obvious to her and that therefore she had not been reckless. On appeal by the prosecution, the Divisional Court held that the risk had only to be obvious to a reasonable adult. It did not have to be a risk which could have been obvious to the defendant herself, even if she had given thought to it.

Which kind of recklessness applies?

For a while, it looked as though the *Caldwell* test of recklessness would become the one to apply in all situations. Nevertheless, the *Cunningham* test has eventually come out on top, and the *Caldwell* test has largely been confined to cases of arson and criminal damage, whence it first originated. In particular, most sexual offences or offences against the person that do not require proof of intent require at least proof of *Cunningham* style recklessness instead.

Negligence

Negligence is a common element in certain forms of civil liability, but it is a much less important feature of criminal liability. It does, however, feature in some important road traffic offences. For example, careless driving requires a slight degree of negligence or fault; dangerous driving and causing death by dangerous driving require a standard of driving that falls way below what would be expected of a competent and careful driver (Road Traffic Act 1988, s. 2A). There is also the very important offence of gross negligence manslaughter which is considered in Chapter 13.

What constitutes negligence?

This may mean carelessness in the usual sense of the word, but it can also encompass those who are simply incompetent or clumsy, because inexperience or ignorance is no defence. It has been held, for example, that a learner driver who is striving with every ounce of concentration to do his incompetent best may still be guilty of careless driving (*McCrone* v *Riding* [1938] 1 All ER 157). As to negligence in unlawful homicides, see Chapter 13.

Coincidence of *actus reus* and *mens rea*

If the crime is of a type which requires a *mens rea*, this *mens rea* is needed at the time when the defendant commits the *actus reus* of the offence. Suppose, however, that the defendant shoots his victim and then disposes of what he believes to be the victim's body; but the victim is still alive at the time, so the defendant in fact kills him 'inadvertently' by burying him alive. Is the defendant guilty of murder? When the defendant actually killed the victim by burying him, he may argue that he did not have the necessary *mens rea*. Why? Because he thought he was burying a corpse and you cannot intend to kill someone who is already dead! Not surprisingly (and quite rightly) the courts have found a way around this argument. The courts will treat the shooting and the burial or disposal of the body not as two incidents, but as different parts of the same incident, and if the defendant had the intention to kill at any point during this single incident, that will suffice for liability. The leading case is that of *Thabo Meli* [1954] 1 All ER 373. The defendants attacked their victim with the intention of killing him, and thinking him dead, they then disposed of his 'body' by rolling it over a cliff. In fact, the victim died from exposure at the bottom of the cliff, and not from the original attack, but the defendants were still held guilty of his murder. It was held by the Privy Council that:

> It is impossible to divide up what was really one series of acts in this way. There is no doubt that the accused set out to do all these acts in order to achieve their plan; and it was too refined a ground of judgment to say that, because they were under a misapprehension at one stage and thought that their guilty purpose had been achieved before in fact it was achieved, therefore they are to escape the penalties of the law.

In the case of *Church* [1965] 2 All ER 72, the Court of Appeal extended the decision in *Thabo Meli* to a case where there was no antecedent plan. In *Church* there was a fight and during the course of it the defendant struck the victim and attempted to strangle her. She fell unconscious and the defendant, believing her to be dead, threw her into the river, where she drowned. It was held that a conviction was justified if the conduct was part of 'a series of acts which culminated in her death'.

Furthermore, the defendant's *mens rea* need not last beyond the moment at which he causes the *actus reus* to occur. After inflicting a fatal injury on V with murderous intent, D may for example repent of his actions and may even do his utmost to save V's life; but if V dies he will be guilty of murder. In *Jakeman* (1983) 76 Cr App R 223, J booked suitcases containing drugs onto a series of flights terminating in London. She abandoned them in Paris, supposedly because she no longer intended to import them, but the cases were sent on to London, where the drugs were discovered, and the Court of Appeal held that J's supposed loss of *mens rea* came too late to prevent her being guilty of an importation offence.

Transferred malice

If the defendant intends to kill Sid, and deliberately kills a man he thinks is Sid, only to find out that it is Sid's brother Fred, this is still murder, and it is not necessary to rely upon any special doctrine to say so. It is nothing more than a case of mistaken identity. But what if the defendant misses Fred and the stray bullet hits Eric? The answer is that the defendant is guilty of wounding Eric, and of murdering him if he dies. The doctrine of 'transferred malice' (or transferred *mens rea*) applies. In *Mitchell* [1983] 2 All ER 427, M struck an old man in a post office queue. The old man fell into an old woman, who broke her hip and died. This was held to be manslaughter, even though M never intended to hurt her.

The same principle applies to crimes such as criminal damage. Under s. 1 of the Criminal Damage Act 1971, a person who destroys or damages property belonging to another, with intent to destroy or damage *any* such property, or being reckless as to whether *any* such property might be destroyed or damaged, will be guilty of an offence. It is not necessary that the defendant intended to damage the property which actually was damaged.

On the other hand, *mens rea* can only be transferred as between the same type of offence. A person who intends to smash a window by throwing a stone through it, but accidentally hits a police officer instead, cannot be convicted of assaulting or injuring the police officer on the basis of malice transferred from his intent to break the window. If he was reckless as to the likelihood of someone being hurt, he might be guilty on that basis, but that would be a different matter.

In *Attorney-General's Reference (No. 3 of 1994)* [1997] 3 All ER 936 the House of Lords refused to apply the doctrine of transferred malice to a case in which A stabbed B, a pregnant woman, causing her to give birth to a premature child, C, who then died. Their lordships emphasised that C had not even been born at the time of the stabbing, and so there was no living person to whom A's malice could be transferred. It could only be manslaughter (on the basis that the stabbing was an unlawful and dangerous act which eventually killed C).

The speeches delivered in *Attorney-General's Reference (No. 3 of 1994)* reveal a fundamental distaste for the 'fiction' behind the doctrine of transferred malice, which they were therefore unwilling to extend. This is puzzling, because it is hard to see what is unjust about it. A sets out to kill B. He kills C instead. Why should that make him any less a murderer?

Elements of a crime

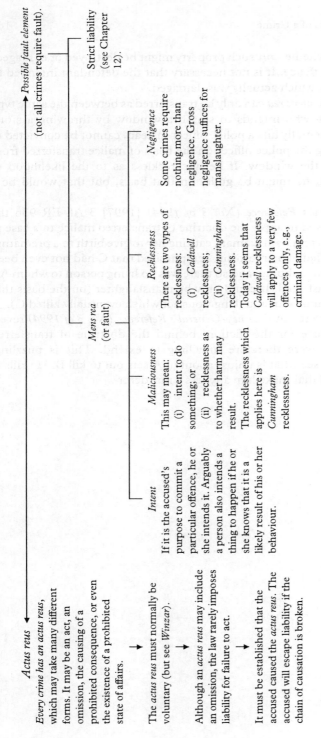

Actus reus →

Every crime has an actus reus, which may take many different forms. It may be an act, an omission, the causing of a prohibited consequence, or even the existence of a prohibited state of affairs.

The *actus reus* must normally be voluntary (but see *Winzar*).

Although an *actus reus* may include an omission, the law rarely imposes liability for failure to act.

It must be established that the accused caused the *actus reus*. The accused will escape liability if the chain of causation is broken.

Mens rea (or fault)

Intent

If it is the accused's purpose to commit a particular offence, he or she intends it. Arguably a person also intends a thing to happen if he or she knows that it is a likely result of his or her behaviour.

Maliciousness

This may mean:
(i) intent to do something; or
(ii) recklessness as to whether harm may result.
The recklessness which applies here is *Cunningham* recklessness.

Recklessness

There are two types of recklessness:
(i) *Caldwell* recklessness;
(ii) *Cunningham* recklessness.
Today it seems that *Caldwell* recklessness will apply to a very few offences only, e.g., criminal damage.

Negligence

Some crimes require nothing more than negligence. Gross negligence suffices for manslaughter.

Possible fault element (not all crimes require fault).

Strict liability (see Chapter 12).

TWELVE

Strict Liability Offences

Most criminal offences require proof of fault or *mens rea* before the accused can be convicted. There are some crimes, however, where one or more elements of the *actus reus* do *not* require any such fault. These are known as strict liability or 'no-fault' offences.

It is possible to divide strict liability offences into two main categories:

(a)   those which effectively do not require any *mens rea* at all (e.g., using a road vehicle with defective brakes, contrary to the Road Traffic Act 1988); and

(b)   those which require some *mens rea* (or fault), but which do not require it for every element of the *actus reus*.

An example of a 'partially strict' offence is that of assaulting a police officer in the execution of his duty, contrary to s. 89 of the Police Act 1996. With this particular offence, the accused must be shown to have intended the assault itself (it would not suffice that he tripped and bumped into the officer as he fell), but need not have realised or even suspected that the person assaulted was a police officer. In *Albert* v *Lavin* [1982] AC 546, Albert struck what he thought to be an interfering civilian, who tried to prevent him pushing his way to the front of a bus queue. The man he hit was in fact Constable Lavin, who was out of uniform but who was quite properly acting to keep order at the bus stop. The House of Lords held that Albert was guilty of assaulting a police officer. Even if Lavin had not been a police officer, Albert would have committed an unlawful assault. The fact that Lavin was a police officer was a matter of strict liability.

This chapter will consider how to identify strict liability offences and the arguments for and against their existence.

The process of identifying strict liability offences

Most strict liability offences are created by statute. Strict liability is almost unknown in common law offences, although examples include public nuisance, blasphemous libel and (to a limited extent) contempt of court. As most strict liability offences are statutory, one might think that Parliament would always make this fact clear somewhere in the body of the legislation. This, however, is not the case. The courts have to try to interpret legislation in order to see whether strict liability was intended to apply.

Partial mens rea

When interpreting a statute to see whether fault or *mens rea* must be proved, the first task for the courts is to look for words that import *mens rea*: words such as 'knowingly' or 'maliciously'. If such words are used, then clearly *some* fault has to be proved. That is not the end of the matter, however, because in some cases the fault element concerned may apply to (or govern) only one aspect of the offence. It may still, in other words, be an offence of partially strict liability.

Many of these partial or 'hybrid' offences are serious crimes, which carry substantial penalties. An example is the offence of maliciously administering a poisonous or noxious substance so as to endanger life or inflict GBH, contrary to s. 23 of the Offences Against the Person Act 1861. In *Cato* [1976] 1 All ER 260, the accused was charged under s. 23 after injecting his friend with heroin (a noxious substance) which caused the friend's death. (Cato was also charged with manslaughter.) The Court held that the specified fault element (maliciousness) governed only the actual administration of the substance concerned. In other words, this had to be proved to have been deliberate or reckless. No *mens rea* was required as to the (clearly unintended) consequences which then followed. In other words, since Cato clearly intended to administer the heroin, he was liable for the consequent endangerment of life, irrespective of whether he even suspected what might happen. Had the offence been one of 'maliciously inflicting injury by administering poison', the prosecution would have had to prove that Cato was at least reckless as to the infliction of such injury.

Regulatory offences and true crimes

Strict liability offences which require no proof of fault or *mens rea* at all are usually of a regulatory nature. An offence is said to be regulatory where it deals not with overtly criminal conduct, such as murder, rape, theft or arson, but with areas of social danger or concern that have to be regulated in the interests of public welfare or safety. Examples would include legislation on food hygiene, road safety, pollution etc. A person who is convicted of such an offence is not usually regarded as a real criminal. A conviction for using a defective road vehicle may carry a substantial fine (and penalty points on a licence), but it does not carry the stigma of an offence of theft or assault.

This does not mean that all regulatory offences carry strict liability. It is still a matter of statutory construction. What can be said, however, is that the courts are usually far more ready to interpret an offence as a strict liability one if it is regulatory, rather than one which bears the stigma of 'true criminality'. As far as 'true crimes' are concerned, the presumption is very much against strict liability. This was emphasised by the House of Lords in *Sweet* v *Parsley* [1969] 1 All ER 347, where the House refused to uphold the conviction of a schoolteacher (Miss Sweet) for being concerned in the management of premises used for smoking cannabis. It appears that some of her student tenants had smoked cannabis in a house she let out to them. There was no evidence that she knew of it or condoned it. The statute concerned (the Dangerous Drugs Act 1965, since repealed) did not use any words such as 'knowingly' when defining the offence, and the lower courts all concluded that, since no *mens rea* words were used, no *mens rea* was required. Quashing Miss Sweet's conviction, Lord Reid said:

> There has for centuries been a presumption that Parliament did not intend to make criminals of persons who were in no way blameworthy in what they did. That means that, whenever a section is silent as to *mens rea*, there is a presumption that, in order to give effect to the will of Parliament, we must read in words appropriate to require *mens rea* ... If a penal provision is capable of two interpretations, that most favourable to the accused must be adopted.

This presumption can, however, be rebutted:

(a)   if the offence is merely regulatory; *and*

(b)   if insistence on proof of *mens rea* would make it difficult to enforce the law, obtain convictions or maintain the standards of safety, etc. which it is designed to achieve.

For example, many road traffic offences would be almost impossible to prosecute if it were necessary to prove *mens rea* every time. If a person was charged with using a vehicle with defective brakes, it would be all too easy for that person to say; 'Sorry, I did not know that the brakes were faulty'. Such excuses cannot be used if the offence is one of strict liability. If the brakes are faulty the user of the car is guilty.

It could be said that the *Sweet* v *Parsley* principle simply does not apply in such cases. In *Gammon (Hong Kong) Ltd* v *Attorney-General of Hong Kong* [1984] 2 All ER 503, a case involving a prosecution for a breach of local building regulations, Lord Scarman said:

> The only situation in which the presumption of *mens rea* can be displaced is where the statute is concerned with an issue of social concern; public safety

is such an issue. Even then ... the presumption stands unless it can also be shown that the creation of strict liability will be effective to promote the objects of the statute by encouraging greater vigilance to prevent the commission of the prohibited act.

Aids to interpretation

Guidance may also be obtained from contrasting language in other sections of the statute in question. If *mens rea* words are used in other provisions of an Act, but not in the provision to be construed, this may suggest that the provision in question must be intended to create an offence of strict liability. An illustration of this principle can be seen from the case of *Cundy* v *Le Cocq* (1884) 13 QBD 207. The accused was a publican, who was charged with selling intoxicating liquor to a person who was drunk, contrary to s. 13 of the Licensing Act 1872. The accused did not know that the person was drunk and there was no evidence of negligence on his part. The accused's conviction was upheld because other sections of the Licensing Act contained the word 'knowingly' while s. 13 did not. This indicated, in the Court's opinion, that s. 13 created a strict liability offence. A similar approach was later taken in *Pharmaceutical Society of Great Britain* v *Storkwain* [1986] 2 All ER 635, where the court was concerned with the construction of s. 58 of the Medicines Act 1968. That section provides:

> Subject to the following provisions of this section — (a) no person shall sell by retail, or supply in circumstances corresponding to retail sale, a medicinal product of a description, or falling within a class, specified in an order under this section except in accordance with a prescription given by an appropriate practitioner ...

The House of Lords adopted the view that, whereas other offence-creating provisions in the Act expressly stipulated a *mens rea*, s. 58(2)(a) did not and must, therefore, create a strict liability offence. Pharmacists who had supplied drugs under forged prescriptions which they honestly believed to be genuine, were accordingly liable under s. 58(2)(a).

One case that adopts a contrary view, however, is *Sherras* v *De Rutzen* [1895] 1 QB 918. The provision under consideration was s. 16(2) of the Licensing Act 1872 (re-enacted in the Licensing Act 1964) which prohibits the supply of alcoholic liquor to a constable who is on duty. The accused in this case reasonably believed the officer to be off duty when he supplied him with liquor, because the officer had removed his duty armlet, thereby deliberately giving the impression that he was off duty. The Divisional Court held that the accused could not be guilty of an offence under s. 16(2) unless he knew that the officer was on duty. The court came to this conclusion even though s. 16(1) of the Act specifically used the word 'knowingly' while s. 16(2) did not (which would, according to the above cases, indicate a crime of strict liability.) The court thought that the absence of a reference to *mens rea* in s. 16(2) simply meant that the burden of proof was placed upon the accused, i.e., it was for the accused to prove that he did not know the officer was on duty. In light of the decision in *Storkwain*, the authority of this case (which was always somewhat suspect) must now be in great doubt, although it has never specifically been overruled.

Certain words have acquired distinct associations with strict liability. If the statute creates an offence of 'using', then the case law suggests that the judges will almost inevitably interpret this word as indicating that the offence is one of strict liability for example, using a vehicle with defective brakes. If an employee uses the employer's vehicle on business, and the vehicle is found to be defective, employee and employer may *both* be guilty of 'using' a defective vehicle. The offence imports vicarious liability as well (see Chapter 16). In contrast, offences of 'causing', 'permitting' or 'allowing' unlawful use by another person usually mean that some *mens rea* must be proved. Whereas the use of a defective vehicle is always a matter of strict liability, a prosecution for permitting such use requires proof of knowledge:

(a)   that the vehicle was being used; and
(b)   that it was defective.

In *James & Son Ltd* v *Smee* [1954] 3 All ER 273, the defendant company was charged with permitting the unlawful use of a trailer with defective brakes. It was acquitted because, although the company's lorry driver and mate had failed to connect the trailer brakes correctly after loading up, this was not something of which the company could have been aware. It could not have permitted something it did not even know was happening. The court observed, however, that a charge of 'using' would inevitably have resulted in conviction.

The presence of no-fault defence clauses

The presence of a clause in the statute enabling the accused to escape conviction if he can prove that he was not in any way at fault, paradoxically indicates that the offence concerned *must* basically be one of strict liability. If it were not a strict liability offence, it would be for the prosecution to prove *mens rea*, *not* for the defence to prove the absence of it. An example of such a clause can be found in s. 28 of the Misuse of Drugs Act 1971. If the prosecution can prove that the accused was in possession of a controlled drug, that is enough for conviction. They do not have to prove that the accused knew it was a drug. It is therefore an offence of strict liability. But the accused can escape conviction if the defence can positively prove that he 'neither knew, nor suspected, nor had reason to suspect' that the thing in his possession was a drug.

Arguments for and against strict liability offences

One advantage of strict liability offences, from the utilitarian or law enforcement viewpoint, is that they ensure the quick and cheap conviction of offenders in circumstances where fault-based convictions might often be difficult to establish. Without strict liability, some laws would become almost unenforceable, either because they would be unprovable, or because the magistrates' courts would be buried in an avalanche of contested cases (especially in areas such as road traffic law, where strict liability currently leads to huge numbers of guilty pleas).

Another argument which is commonly put forward in support of strict liability offences is that they encourage greater safety and improve standards of prevention, thereby offering the public better protection from accidental (but avoidable) harm. The distinguished social scientist Baroness Wootton has argued for the extension of strict liability to cover all or most crimes. In *Crime and the Criminal Law* she writes:

> If, however, the primary function of the courts is conceived as the prevention of forbidden acts, there is little cause to be disturbed by the multiplication of offences of strict liability. If the law says that certain things are not to be done, it is illogical to confine this prohibition to occasions on which they are done from malice aforethought; or at least the material consequences of an action, and the reasons for prohibiting it are the same whether it is the result of sinister malicious plotting, of negligence or of sheer accident.

It is respectfully submitted that Wootton overstates her case. There may be much to be said in favour of strict liability offences in some regulatory areas, but as far as most mainstream crimes are concerned, abolition of *mens rea* requirements would do little if anything to help with the enforcement of the law (how many muggers ever claim that the robbery they committed was an accident?) and might even bring the law into disrepute. To take an extreme example, any death caused on the roads is a tragedy, which the law should try to prevent, but if the law failed to distinguish between 'mere accident' and culpable negligence, or between negligence and deliberate murder (using the vehicle as a weapon) then the law would lose the respect of the people it is supposed to protect.

The argument that the imposition of strict liability leads to a higher standard of care has not gone unquestioned. In the Canadian case of *City of Saulte Ste Marie* (1978) 85 DLR (3d) 161, Dickson J stated:

> There is no evidence that a higher standard of care results from imposition of [strict] liability. If a person is already taking every reasonable precautionary measure, is he likely to take additional measures, knowing that however much care he takes, it will not serve as a defence in the event of a breach? If he has exercised care and skill, will conviction have a deterrent effect upon him?

Is that true? A person is far less likely to be convicted of a strict liability offence if he is careful than if he is not. As Lord Simon said in *Alphacell* v *Woodward* [1972] 2 All ER 475, strict liability for river pollution may encourage potential polluters 'not only to take reasonable steps to prevent pollution but to do everything possible to ensure that they do not cause it'.

In order to have this deterrent effect, strict liability offences often carry very substantial fines, especially in areas such as those concerning pollution or nuclear safety. A £1 million fine was imposed on an oil company for polluting the river Mersey. It must not appear cheaper for a large business to pay the occasional fine rather than spend money eradicating possible risks of pollution. Neither, as far as the motorist is concerned, should it make economic sense to drive around on worn out tyres and take the risk of a small fine. There is little perceived shame or disgrace in a conviction for using defective tyres, so the fines must be able to 'bite hard' in order to deter.

A half-way house?

Some academic writers (notably *Smith* and *Hogan*) have advocated what might be described as a 'half-way house' or compromise approach to the problem of strict liability. One such possible compromise would be to enable offenders to be convicted without proof of *mens rea* by the prosecution, but to entitle them to an acquittal if they should prove on a balance of probabilities that they lacked *mens rea* and were not at fault, i.e., that they had an honest and reasonable belief in a state of facts which, had it existed, would have made their act innocent. Alternatively, offenders might be required to put forward credible evidence of an honest and reasonable belief in a state of facts which, had it existed, would have made their act innocent, in which case the prosecution would then have to prove beyond reasonable doubt that the offender had no such honest and reasonable belief.

Both approaches are used occasionally in English law. There are many statutory defences which have to be proved by the accused if he is to rely on them, and some of them do indeed take the form of 'no fault' defences to strict liability crimes (see, for example, s. 28 of the Misuse of Drugs Act 1971, above). In some countries, such as Australia, the courts have adopted such defences on a more general basis, but this has not happened in England and Wales. It is important to remember that 'no fault' defences in English law apply *only* where legislation specifically provides for them.

Strict liability is a somewhat crude device, which tolerates the risk of imposing criminal liability on persons who are not really at fault. The reason for imposing such liability is not to punish the faultless, but to deter infringements, tighten up standards of care and punish (or weed out) the lazy and inefficient, particularly in areas where dangerous activities are carried on. It has to be accepted, however, that some blameless offenders will get caught in the net, and that this is unfortunate for them. Strict liability can mean rough justice; but no system of justice has ever been perfect. If fault had to be proved in even the most minor traffic case, many more of those offenders who now plead guilty by post would probably start to contest their cases, and the courts could not cope with that.

Strict liability offences

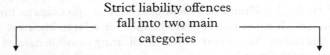

Strict liability offences fall into two main categories

1. Those which require no *mens rea* at all, e.g., driving a car with defective brakes.

2. Those which require some *mens rea*, but which do not require it for every element of the *actus reus*, e.g., assaulting a police officer in the execution of his duty.

(a)   The courts start with a presumption that, where a statute is silent as to *mens rea*, Parliament simply forgot to include it; therefore the courts will read *mens rea* into the statute (*Sweet* v *Parsley*).

(b)   This is only a presumption, however, and may be rebutted if one or more of the following factors are present:

(i)   the offence is of a regulatory nature;

(ii)   insistence on proof of *mens rea* would make the law difficult to enforce, e.g., standards of safety;

(c)   guidance may be obtained from the language used in other sections of the statute in question;

(d)   certain words are distinctly associated with the imposition of strict liability, e.g., 'using';

(e)   the presence of 'no fault' defence clauses indicates that the offence is (in all other respects) one of strict liability.

THIRTEEN

Unlawful Homicide and Related Offences

There are several varieties of unlawful homicide, namely murder, man-slaughter, infanticide, causing death by dangerous driving, and causing death by careless driving while under the influence of drink or drugs. Although these are all illustrations of unlawful homicide, the main distinguishing feature between them is the mens rea which each of them requires (see below). Issues of causation, on the other hand, are largely the same for any homicide, and reference should be made to Chapter 11 on this point. Do not fall into the trap of asserting that the defendant is only guilty of manslaughter, rather than murder, in cases where the chain of causation has been broken. If the chain has been severed, the defendant cannot be guilty of homicide at all, although it may sometimes be possible to charge him with an attempt, or with an offence under the Offences Against the Person Act 1861 (see Chapter 14). As far as sentencing is concerned, murder carries a mandatory life sentence, whereas in cases of manslaughter the judge has a discretion as to what penalty to impose. Penalties for the latter can range from life imprisonment down to a conditional or even an absolute discharge. The road traffic offences carry a maximum sentence of ten years' imprisonment (plus disqualification from driving) but the typical sentence imposed will be much shorter in all but the gravest cases.

The year and a day rule

At common law, a person could not be guilty of unlawful homicide if his victim survived for more than a year and a day after the attack or incident which allegedly caused death. Writing in the seventeenth century, Sir Edward Coke stated:

... for if he die after that time it cannot be discerned, as the law presumes whether he dies of the stroke or poison etc., or by a natural death.

The medical justification for this rule, as explained by Coke, disappeared long ago; but its repeal was by no means a simple or obvious matter. There were policy considerations favouring its survival. Many lawyers considered it inappropriate for a possible murder or manslaughter charge to be left hanging over an accused for an indefinite period of time. Take the case of a doctor or surgeon whose alleged negligence caused serious injury to a patient. Medical science may make it possible to prove, 20 years later, when the patient dies, that the injuries allegedly suffered at the doctor's hands shortened the patient's life by several years. Should the doctor then face a charge of manslaughter? If D attacks V and serves five years for causing grievous bodily harm with intent to do so (Offences Against the Person Act 1861, s. 18 (Chapter 14, below)), is it right that he should face a further charge of murder in the event that his victim dies thereafter?

A compromise approach was eventually adopted in the Law Reform (Year and a Day Rule) Act 1996, which has largely (but not entirely) abolished that rule in respect of deaths caused by injuries, etc., inflicted on or after 17 June 1996. In respect of injuries inflicted before that date, the old rule survives unchanged, and even where injuries are inflicted on or after that date, a prosecution for homicide will be barred after three years, unless the Attorney-General expressly gives leave for it to proceed. The consent of the Attorney-General will also be required in cases where the accused has already been convicted of a lesser offence connected with the original injury, such a wounding or dangerous driving.

Murder

The law on murder has effectively been covered in the chapters on *mens rea* and causation. It must suffice to remind you here that murder is 'unlawful killing with malice aforethought'. That does not mean it has to be premeditated, but only that it must be committed with an intent to kill or an intent to do grievous bodily harm.

Infanticide

This offence is of relatively limited importance today. Section 1 of the Infanticide Act 1938 in effect provides that a mother who kills her infant child (under the age of six months) whilst suffering from post-natal depression, may be charged with infanticide instead of murder, or convicted of infanticide if initially charged with murder. Infanticide is an offence comparable to manslaughter by reason of diminished responsibility. The latter, which was introduced in 1957, would in practice provide depressed mothers with similar protection from a murder conviction, and it is questionable whether any specific offence of infanticide need be retained today.

The different varieties of manslaughter

Manslaughter may take several forms, as illustrated in the diagram at the end of this chapter. At common law, manslaughter was originally defined as 'unlawful killing without malice aforethought'. This remains a correct definition as far as the two varieties of *involuntary* (or unintentional) manslaughter are concerned, but the common law and the Homicide Act 1957 have between them added three varieties of *voluntary* manslaughter (killing under provocation, diminished responsibility and suicide pacts) which are in effect forms of mitigated murder. In such cases, malice aforethought can be proved, but the mitigating circumstances enable the accused to avoid conviction for murder.

An important distinction between the voluntary and involuntary forms of manslaughter is that the latter can either be charged as an offence in its own right (i.e., the accused is charged that on the date in question he 'unlawfully killed' the deceased) or returned as an alternative verdict by a jury which is required to consider a charge of murder ('we find the accused not guilty of murder, but guilty of manslaughter'). In contrast, the accused can never be charged with any variety of voluntary manslaughter. These are only ever raised as partial defences to charges of murder.

Constructive manslaughter

If a person inadvertently kills another as a result of an intentional, criminal and dangerous act (such as arson, battery or robbery), there is no need for the prosecution to prove that he was grossly negligent as to the risk of death or serious injury. The defendant will automatically be guilty of manslaughter, even if the only obvious danger was one of some minor injury, and if the death was a horrible fluke. It is only necessary to prove recklessness or negligence if the defendant's conduct falls outside the parameters of constructive manslaughter. An example of how constructive manslaughter operates can be seen from the case of *Director of Public Prosecutions* v *Newbury* [1976] 2 All ER 365. The defendants in this case dropped a paving stone from a bridge into the path of an oncoming train, killing one of the train's crew. The defendants had not meant to kill anyone, nor had they even foreseen that death could result from their actions. This, however, was irrelevant, as they had committed a deliberate and dangerous criminal act, merely by dropping the paving stone onto the train, and they were therefore guilty of constructive manslaughter. Another example is provided by *Mitchell* [1983] 2 All ER 427. The defendant unlawfully struck an old man, who fell against an even older woman, who broke her hip and died a few weeks later. This was held to be manslaughter. The old woman's death was a ghastly fluke, but hitting another person is always dangerous (in the sense of being likely to cause *some* injury) and the defendant therefore had no defence to the charge.

To be classed as unlawful for this purpose, conduct must be *inherently* criminal. Acts which only become unlawful when performed negligently (e.g., dangerous driving), cannot be the basis of a conviction for constructive manslaughter.

Mens rea

The defendant himself does not have to appreciate that the act could result in any harm to the victim so long as a reasonable person could recognise the risk of some harm. Liability is, in that sense, based on an objective test. But the act which causes death must itself be deliberate. If, for example, the defendant starts a fatal fire carelessly or recklessly, rather than intentionally, he cannot be guilty of constructive manslaughter. He might however be guilty of gross negligence manslaughter (below).

Acts and omissions

As far as liability for constructive manslaughter is concerned, the act which causes death must be a positive one. A failure to act will not suffice for liability to arise in this context. Gross negligence manslaughter would be the better charge in cases of omission.

Gross negligence manslaughter

Unfortunately, there has been a great deal of inconsistency and confusion regarding this area of law. Gross negligence manslaughter has been recognised for years, and as a concept it is relatively easy to understand. As we saw earlier, negligence on a general level involves falling below the standard of care expected of the reasonable man. As far as gross negligence manslaughter is concerned, however, the criminal law is concerned to punish only those whose level of negligence can be classed as totally irresponsible. This can best be summarised by the test laid down in the case of *Bateman* (1925) 94 LJKB 791:

> ... in order to establish criminal liability, the facts must be such that, in the opinion of the jury, the negligence of the accused went beyond a mere matter of compensation between subjects, and showed such disregard for the life and safety of others as to amount to a crime against the state and conduct deserving of punishment.

This test received wide support from the judiciary, and was subsequently followed by the House of Lords in *Andrews* v *Director of Public Prosecutions* [1937] 2 All ER 552. It nevertheless fell into disfavour during the 1980s, and was doubted or disapproved in a number of cases, including that of *Seymour* [1983] 2 All ER 1058, where it was said that juries should be directed to apply a test based on *Caldwell* recklessness to manslaughter cases, rather than apply any test of gross negligence; but the *Bateman* test has recently been approved once again by the House of Lords in *Adomako* [1994] 3 All ER 79. Adomako acted as the anaesthetist during a routine eye operation on a patient. In the course of the operation, the tube from the ventilator supplying the patient with oxygen became disconnected. He failed to notice this for some six minutes, and the patient died. Adomako was charged with gross negligence manslaughter and his conviction was upheld on appeal to the House of Lords. It was held in *Adomako* that, in a case of gross negligence manslaughter, the jury would have to consider the following points:

(a)   did the defendant owe the victim a duty of care? Where a negligent act is alleged the existence of a duty of care is unlikely to cause a problem, because everyone is under a duty not to do acts which unnecessarily endanger the lives of others;

(b)   was the defendant in breach of this duty of care? A number of factors must be considered at this stage. His conduct must have fallen far below that expected of a reasonable man in the circumstances of the case. A person carrying out a specialised trade or profession (surgeon, scaffolder, airline pilot, bus driver, etc.) would be expected to achieve a standard of competence appropriate to that activity;

(c)   did the conduct involve a risk of death; and was it so bad in all the circumstances as in the opinion of the jury to amount to a crime?

If (but only if) all these points are proved, the defendant can be convicted of gross negligence manslaughter.

Manslaughter under provocation

The defence of provocation is only available in cases where the defendant is charged with murder. If the defence is accepted by the jury, the charge is reduced from murder to manslaughter. The defence of provocation cannot be used in any other context, not even on a charge of attempted murder.

Definition

A partial definition of provocation can be found in s. 3 of the Homicide Act 1957, which provides:

> Where on a charge of murder there is evidence on which the jury can find that the person charged was provoked (whether by things said or done or by both together) to lose his self control, the question whether the provocation was enough to make a reasonable man do as he did shall be left to be determined by the jury; and in determining that question the jury shall take into account

everything both done and said according to the effect which, in their opinion, it would have on a reasonable man.

If there is *any* evidence of acts of provocation resulting in loss of self-control, the burden of proof is on the prosecution to prove beyond all reasonable doubt that the defendant was not in fact provoked, or that he never lost his self-control, or that his reaction was excessive in relation to what might have been expected from a reasonable man in that situation. The defendant must get the benefit of any reasonable doubt.

When looking at the defence of provocation, it is important to distinguish between the two basic issues. First, was the accused in fact provoked into losing his self-control? Secondly, if he was, would a reasonable man have lost his self-control in such a way? As one can see, this approach involves both subjective and objective elements.

What can amount to provocation?
At common law, the defence of provocation was tightly controlled by the judges, who ruled that words alone could never constitute provocation. Defences of provocation had to be supported by evidence of something more. This might be evidence of violence used by the deceased against the accused, or it might be the discovery by a husband of his wife in the act of adultery or the discovery by a father of someone committing sodomy on his son. An admission of previous adultery by his wife would not suffice.

The Homicide Act 1957 removed these restrictions. If there is any evidence that the accused's actions were provoked by words or deeds (or by a combination of the two) causing loss of self-control, the defence must be put to the jury, so that they can determine the issue. In the case of *Doughty* (1986) 83 Cr App R 319, the Court of Appeal said that the provocation need not be illegal or wrongful and may even be something as natural as a baby crying, although it is most unlikely that any jury would consider this to be sufficient provocation.

The provocation may come from or be directed towards a third party. In *Pearson* [1992] Crim LR 193, two brothers, A and B, killed their father, who had mistreated A for several years. The Court of Appeal held that the jury should have been invited to take the mistreatment of A into account, even when considering the provocation defence put forward by B.

Loss of self-control
If the defendant was not really provoked into killing the deceased, but used the supposed provocation as an excuse or pretext for a cold-blooded killing, then the defence of provocation must fail, even though other men would indeed have been provoked by the incident. By the same token, even prolonged and vicious provocation will not be a defence, if the defendant has taken a calculated decision to revenge himself on his tormentor.

It follows that, where there is evidence that the defendant took steps to arm himself before killing the person who provoked him, it may be hard to resist the argument that the killing was premeditated rather than a result of a momentary loss of self-control. This can be illustrated by *Ibrams* (1982) 74 Cr App R 154, where it was confirmed that 'there must be a sudden and temporary loss of self control'. The Court of Appeal in this case approved Lord Devlin's *dictum* from the earlier case of *Duffy* [1949] 1 All ER 932:

> Circumstances which induce a desire for revenge are inconsistent with provocation, since the conscious formulation of a desire for revenge means that a person has had time to think, to reflect, and that would negative a sudden and temporary loss of self control, which is the essence of provocation.

The fact that the provocative behaviour has continued over a period of time does not by any means prevent the use of the defence, provided that the fatal act was still the result of a sudden and temporary loss of self-control. On the contrary, the courts now recognise that a history of abuse may mean that one more, relatively minor, piece of provocation may come to represent the 'last straw which breaks the camel's back' (*Humphreys* [1995] 4 All ER 1008). The courts have even recognised that some may suffer a 'slow burning' loss of control when provoked. Calculated revenge, however, is not the same thing, however understandable it may be. In *Ibrams*, the defendants had suffered prolonged and extreme provocation from a young thug called Monk. They decided to get rid of him for good, and a carefully planned murder was ruthlessly executed a week or so after Monk's last act of provocation. One defendant got Monk helplessly drunk, and then signalled to the others, who entered the room and hacked him to death with machetes. The trial judge stated that there was no evidence of any loss of self-control by the defendants, and so the issue of provocation was not put to the jury. The Court of Appeal asked the Home Secretary to consider releasing the defendants on licence (parole) as soon as possible, but would not interfere with the murder convictions.

Another noteworthy case is that of *Dryden* [1995] 4 All ER 987. The defendant, an eccentric old man, had built a bungalow without planning permission, and then ignored repeated demands to have it removed. He eventually found himself faced with council officials, who had arrived with bulldozers to demolish it. The defendant produced a revolver, and repeatedly shot a council officer in full view of the television cameras that had come to film the demolition. He was convicted of murder. Although the Court of Appeal were critical of some of the trial judge's directions to the jury, it was quite clear that there had been no loss of self-control on the part of the accused. On the contrary, he had merely done what he had always threatened to do in such circumstances, and his conviction was therefore upheld. In *Pearson* (above), there was nevertheless held to be evidence of provocation, even though the defendants had armed themselves in advance with weapons. The difference may lie in the fact that the defendants had still suffered very recent provocation.

The reasonable man

Once the jury is satisfied that the defendant killed the deceased as a result of a sudden and temporary loss of self-control, they must satisfy themselves that a reasonable man with the defendant's characteristics would react in the same way. At one time, the judges defined the reasonable man as an ordinary adult (see *Bedder* v *Director of Public Prosecutions* [1954] 2 All ER 801), but the courts have now learnt to make allowances for age, sex and special characteristics which might be a source of sensitivity to provocation. Suppose, for example, that a 15-year-old homosexual is tormented over his sexuality and kills the man who provokes him. The jury would have to consider the effect of such taunts on a reasonable 15-year-old homosexual. The defendant's background and experiences may have to be taken into account. In a domestic killing, where a wife has killed her violent (or allegedly violent) husband, juries may thus be asked to assess the likely effect of the husband's provocation on a woman who has suffered a history of abuse similar to that of the defendant (see *Humphreys*, above).

Not all the defendant's characteristics can be taken into account, however. As Lord Taylor CJ pointed out in *Dryden* (above), the reasonable man would otherwise be reincarnated as the defendant. Juries would then have to ask themselves absurd questions, such as 'How would a "reasonable" short-tempered psychopath (such as the defendant) react to such provocation?' (To which the answer would no doubt have to be, 'Just as the defendant did'.) Bad temper or drunkenness, for example, are not characteristics for which allowance can or should be made.

Alcoholism or drug dependency still needs careful consideration. If the defendant is provoked by criticism of his drug addiction or alcoholism, the jury must consider the likely effect of such provocation on a person who suffers from (and may be sensitive about) such a problem, but they cannot make allowance for the fact that the defendant is actually drunk, or in a foul temper because he is desperate for another fix of drugs. He may be sensitive about his condition, but must still be expected to retain reasonable control over his temper (*Morhall* [1995] 3 All ER 659). Juries cannot ask themselves how the reasonable man might be expected to behave when drunk or bad tempered, because the reasonable man would never be either of those things.

The leading case of *Camplin* [1978] AC 705, can be used to illustrate the points just made. V, a man in his fifties, forcibly buggered C, a boy aged 15 and then laughed at him. C, lost his temper and hit V over the head with a chapati pan killing him. At his trial, the judge wrongly told the jury to ignore C's age and to consider whether a reasonable adult would have been provoked to act as the accused had done. The House of Lords held that the reasonable man must be taken to mean a person of the same age and sex as the defendant who is not exceptionally excitable or pugnacious. Lord Diplock said:

> a proper direction to the jury should state that the reasonable man referred to in the question is a person having the power of self control to be expected of an ordinary person of the age and sex of the accused, but in other respects sharing such of the accused's characteristics as they think would affect the gravity of the provocation to him; the question is not merely whether such a person would in like circumstances be provoked to lose his self control but also whether he would react ... as the accused did.

In *Morhall* (above) the House of Lords confirmed the validity of the approach adopted in *Camplin*. One issue, however, has not been clarified. To what extent can allowance be made for any mental abnormality which may reduce the defendant's ability to control his behaviour? One view (and we would say, the better view) is that the proper defence in any such case ought to be one of diminished responsibility. This was indeed the view of the Privy Council in *Luc Thiet Thuan* [1996] 2 All ER 1033, in which Lord Goff (who had delivered the leading judgment in *Morhall*) explained that any abormal mental condition which restricts the accused's ability to control his temper will be inconsistent with the concept of reasonableness which lies at the heart of the provocation defence. The Court of Appeal has taken a different view, however. In cases such as *Dryden*, *Humphreys* and more recently *Campbell* [1997] 1 Cr App R 199 the Court of Appeal has repeatedly held that conditions such as obsessiveness, eccentricity, immaturity, attention-seeking and so on must after all be taken into account. So how *would* the 'reasonable' eccentric, immature and obsessive man behave when provoked? The Court of Appeal's view on this point is not only bizarre, but also (surely) a misinterpretation of what had been decided by the House of Lords in *Morhall*. Until the House of Lords has a chance to clarify the position, however, trial judges are bound to follow the Court of Appeal's interpretation — as Lord Bingham CJ was careful to remind them in *Campbell*.

Manslaughter under diminished responsibility

See Chapter 18, in which this partial defence to a charge of murder is considered alongside the general defences of insanity and automatism, to which it is closely related.

Suicide pacts

Killing in the course of a joint (and consensual) suicide pact is manslaughter, rather than murder, as long as the defendant can prove that he really intended to die along with the person he killed, and that the latter really had agreed to the joint suicide plan.

Causing death by dangerous driving, or by careless driving when intoxicated

Detailed coverage of these specialised road traffic offences cannot be attempted in a work such as this. It must suffice to note that, whereas liability for the offence of causing death by dangerous driving depends on proof that the defendant's standard of driving fell far below that required of a competent driver (ss. 1 and 2A of the Road Traffic Act 1988), the slightest error of judgment by a drunken or drug-affected motorist may give rise to liability for the offence of causing death by careless driving whilst intoxicated, if a fatal accident results. Even a driver who was stone-cold sober may be found guilty of this offence, if he is foolish enough to refuse to provide a breath or blood sample for analysis when required to do so by the police.

Killing the unborn foetus

Killing an unborn child or foetus cannot ordinarily be classed as homicide. It may amount to the offence of child destruction, under the Infant Life (Preservation) Act 1929, if the foetus was sufficiently developed to be capable of being born alive at the time. This is presumed to be the case (in the absence of evidence to the contrary) after 28 weeks from conception. It must be proved, however, that the act was not done in good faith in order to save the mother's life.

Before 28 weeks, the destruction of an unborn foetus is usually termed abortion. Under the Offences Against the Person Act 1861, s. 58, it is an offence for a pregnant woman or for anyone else to use instruments or poisons or 'other means' with intent to procure a miscarriage (or abortion). Note that it is the use of the instruments or poison that constitutes the offence, not the abortion itself. Providing or procuring poisons, etc., for that purpose is an offence under s. 59.

Since the enactment of the Abortion Act 1967, however, it is usually possible to obtain a lawful abortion from a medical practitioner, wherever this would involve less risk to the woman's life or health than a continuation of the pregnancy. Account may also be taken of her mental health and of the health of any existing children. It is a medically proven fact that abortion is less dangerous than childbirth, and the Act thus effectively offers abortion on demand. There is, however, a time limit of 24 weeks, after which an abortion can only be carried out on more limited grounds, such as to preserve the mother's life or health, or where there is a substantial risk that the child would be seriously handicapped.

Homicide from pre-natal injury

In *Attorney-General's Reference (No. 3 of 1994)* [1997] 3 All ER 936, the House of Lords accepted that it may be manslaughter if a person stabs (or shoots or beats or poisons) a pregnant woman, who then gives birth to a premature or injured child, which lives for a short time and then dies of the injury or premature birth caused by the stabbing or shooting etc. Even if the offender did not mean to hurt the child itself, the shooting, stabbing or beating of the mother is an unlawful and dangerous act, which kills. A murder conviction is more difficult. Any malice aimed at the mother cannot, according to their lordships, be transferred to the child (see Chapter 11), but it would suffice if the accused was trying to destroy the unborn child (e.g., by stabbing at it in the womb). It may seem odd that a homicide offence can be based on the fact that the infant was born and lived for just a few minutes before dying of an earlier injury, but such is the law. It would seem to follow that an illegal abortion resulting in the premature birth of a foetus which lives for a while and then dies as a result of being premature must also amount to manslaughter.

Murder and high treason

The murder of certain persons (notably the Queen or the heir to the throne) could be charged as high treason under the Treason Acts of 1351 and 1795. Indeed, even an unsuccessful attempt or conspiracy might amount to that offence. Treason remains a capital offence, the sentence for which is death by hanging. In practice, this would probably be commuted to life imprisonment.

Unlawful homicide

Types of homicide

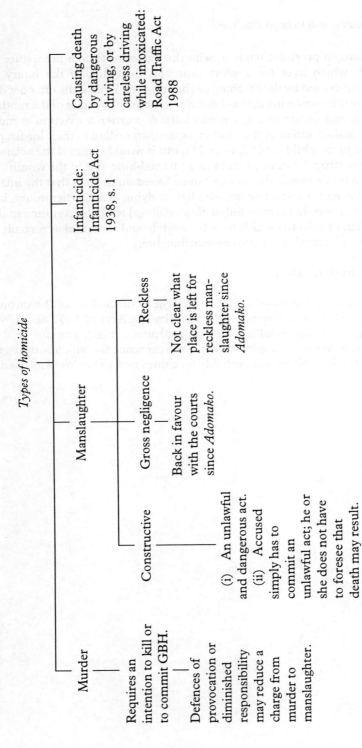

Murder

Requires an intention to kill or to commit GBH.

Defences of provocation or diminished responsibility may reduce a charge from murder to manslaughter.

Manslaughter

Constructive

(i) An unlawful and dangerous act.
(ii) Accused simply has to commit an unlawful act; he or she does not have to foresee that death may result.

Gross negligence

Back in favour with the courts since *Adomako*.

Reckless

Not clear what place is left for reckless manslaughter since *Adomako*.

Infanticide: Infanticide Act 1938, s. 1

Causing death by dangerous driving, or by careless driving while intoxicated: Road Traffic Act 1988

FOURTEEN

Non-fatal Offences Against the Person

The purpose of this chapter is to examine the principal offences involving non-fatal violence against the person. There are a number of different offences to be considered, most of which are to be found in the Offences Against the Person Act (OAPA) 1861. This Act, however, is far from perfect. It was a clumsy piece of 'consolidating legislation', drawing together a mixed bag of offences originally created by a variety of older statutes, without making any attempt to establish a logical, graded set of related offences, or even a common terminology. The Law Commission has put forward a series of proposals for reform in this area of law (Offences Against the Person and General Defences (Law Com No. 218)). These proposals, if implemented, would provide the courts with a logically graded set of offences. Lawyers have been waiting a long time for this to happen, but it is now expected that new legislation will at last be introduced for this purpose within the next year or so.

Assault and battery

Assault and battery were originally common law offences, but are now contained within the Criminal Justice Act 1988, s. 39. They are separate and distinct crimes (see *Lynsey* [1995] 3 All ER 654) but lawyers, judges and Parliamentary draftsmen often use the single term 'assault' to include both assault and battery, which can make things very confusing. An example can be found in s. 47 of the 1861 Act, which creates the offence of 'assault occasioning actual bodily harm'. A true assault can sometimes cause such harm (as for example where the victim is injured whilst attempting to escape from the threat of violence) but the vast majority of cases brought under s. 47 are really about *battery*, rather than assault. In this chapter, the terms 'assault' and 'battery' will be used in their proper legal senses.

Assault: inducing the apprehension of imminent violence

An assault is committed when the defendant intentionally or recklessly causes another person to apprehend that immediate and unlawful violence will (or may) be used against him. The victim does not necessarily have to be frightened; but he does have to be aware of the threat. If D throws a stone at P, who sees it and ducks out of the way, that is an assault; but if P does the stone as it hurtles harmlessly past him, there is no assault.

Actions and words

Generally, an assault requires some act or gesture by the defendant, such as the raising of a fist or the pointing of a gun. An imitation gun will do, as long as the victim does not know it is an imitation. It was once thought that words alone could never amount to an assault, but this view has now been rejected by the House of Lords in *Ireland* [1997] 4 All ER 225. As Lord Steyn said in that case:

> The proposition that a gesture may amount to an assault, but that words can never suffice, is unrealistic and indefensible. A thing said is also a thing done. There is no reason why a thing said should be incapable of causing an apprehension of immediate personal violence. . . I would therefore reject the proposition that an assault can never be committed by words. . .

The defendant in *Ireland* made sinister 'silent' telephone calls to a number of women, and it was held that such conduct could involve an assault (but not a battery) if it caused the victims to fear that physical violence would or might be used against them in the immediate future. This apparently means any time within the next few minutes. As Lord Steyn said:

> . . . there is no reason why a telephone caller who says to a woman in a menacing way, 'I will be at your door in a minute or two' may not be guilty of an assault . . .

A 'conditional' threat may still amount to an assault, even if the victim is assured that compliance will save him from violence (e.g., 'Your money or your life!'). In the civil case of *Read v Coker* (1853) 13 CB 850, R successfully sued C and his servants for the tort of assault when they surrounded him, rolling up their sleeves and threatening that they would break his neck unless he left the premises. The crime of assault is governed by the same principles.

In contrast, it is clear that words may defuse actions which might otherwise be classified as assaults. An example of this can be found in an even older tort case, *Tuberville v Savage* (1669) 1 Mod Rep 3, where T placed his hand on his sword and said to S, 'If it were not assize-time, I would not take such language from you.' It was held that this was not an assault. T had made it clear he would not use force on S, because the assize courts were sitting in the town at the time. S therefore had no excuse for wounding him in reply!

Battery: the application of unlawful force

The *actus reus* of a battery is the actual infliction of unlawful personal violence upon the victim. A battery often follows on from an assault, but this is not always the case. There is no assault, for example, if the defendant hits (or batters) his victim without warning, from behind. Even the slightest unlawful personal violence is sufficient to constitute a battery. The courts have recognised that some forms of physical contact are inevitable in everyday life and that such contacts cannot be classed as unlawful, but drawing the line between acceptable and unacceptable forms of day-to-day contact is not always easy. In *Collins* v *Wilcock* [1984] 3 All ER 374, Goff LJ said it was a question of fact in each case as to whether the particular form of contact was acceptable or not. He then went on to provide examples of the type of conduct which he considered to be acceptable:

> . . . nobody can complain of the jostling which is inevitable from his presence in, for example, a supermarket, an underground station, or a busy street; nor can a person who attends a party complain if his hand is seized in friendship, or even if his back is slapped. . . [Another] form of conduct long held to be acceptable is touching a person for the purpose of engaging his attention, though of course using no greater degree of physical contact than is reasonably necessary in the circumstances for that purpose.

A police officer may therefore tap a person on the shoulder to gain his attention, but may not ordinarily restrain him, unless making a lawful arrest or preventing a disturbance: see s. 89 of the Police Act 1996 (p. 196, below).

A battery must involve a physical attack on the victim, and an assault must involve the threat of one. Injuring someone through the setting of a trap, such as a trip wire across the top of some stairs, cannot therefore be treated as a battery (although it may amount to an offence under s. 20 of the 1861 Act, below). Authority for this can be found in statements made by the House of Lords in *Wilson* [1983] 3 All ER 448, and subsequently approved in *Ireland*, but the lower courts have sometimes been confused on this point. In *Director of Public Prosecutions* v *Khan* [1990] 1 WLR 1067, K, a schoolboy, poured acid into the hot air drier in his school toilets, and the next boy to use the drier was sprayed with acid when he turned it on. It was assumed (without considering *Wilson*) that this was a battery. Khan, however, has been held to be wrong on several other issues, and should not be relied upon.

Battery by omission?

Most batteries involve the commission of a positive act, but can a battery be committed by a mere omission? The case law suggests that an omission is not enough; but if the defendant inadvertently applies force to the victim and then refuses to withdraw it, this may be treated as an ongoing battery. In *Fagan* [1968] 3 All ER 442, F inadvertently (!) parked his car on a police officer's foot. When the officer asked him to move it, he refused. He was convicted of 'assaulting' (i.e. battering) a police officer in the execution of his duty. The Divisional Court refused to view this as an omission at all, and held that a battery was continued as long as F knowingly allowed his vehicle to rest on the officer's foot; but the judges conceded that they could not have upheld his conviction had it really been a case of pure omission.

Mens rea of assault or battery

An assault or battery must be committed either intentionally or recklessly. The recklessness required in this context is deliberate and unreasonable risk taking, or '*Cunningham*' recklessness (p. 163, above). The House of Lords so held in *Savage* [1991] 4 All ER 698 (below), thereby resolving a series of conflicting decisions in lower courts, some of which had suggested that the wider, *Caldwell*, variant of recklessness would suffice.

Valid and invalid consent

The essence of an assault or battery is that it is done without the consent of the victim. The burden of proving lack of consent rests upon the prosecution. It was at one time thought that an individual could consent to anything short of maiming (disablement) or death. The present position, however, seems to be that a person can only validly consent to what would otherwise be an assault or battery if no real harm is intended or caused, or if the public interest justifies its exemption from the usual rules (as in boxing or other 'contact sports'). In *Attorney-General's Reference (No. 6 of 1980)* [1981] 2 All ER 1057, the Court of Appeal held that a fist-fight between two young men could not be rendered lawful just because the parties consented to it:

> It is not in the public interest that people should try to cause or should cause each other actual bodily harm for no good reason ... [but] ... nothing which we have said is intended to cast doubt on the accepted legality of properly conducted games and sports, lawful chastisement or correction, reasonable surgical interference, dangerous exhibitions etc.

If a football player receives an injury in the course of a match, it would not be treated as a crime unless it was caused by a deliberate foul. Players of properly conducted sports consent to such force being used in the game as the rules permit. The risk of injury through honest but clumsy tackles must also be accepted, but if a rugby player or boxer bites an opponent's ear or a soccer player hacks down an opponent without even attempting to play the ball, that would be a criminal offence.

Sado-masochistic games

One area which has caused the courts problems over the years involves activities such as spanking or sado-masochistic games played in private between consenting adults. The fact that such games are carried out in private between consenting adults does not necessarily mean they are lawful. In *Donovan* [1934] 2 KB 498, the defendant was charged with caning a 17-year-old girl in a sado-masochistic game. The question in front of the court was the issue of the victim's consent. The Court of Appeal said that the girl's consent was irrelevant if the blows were intended or likely to cause bodily harm. This was confirmed by the House of Lords in the later case of *Brown* [1992] 2 All ER 552, where members of a sado-masochistic group were imprisoned after a videotape of their horrifically violent 'torture games' fell into the hands of the police. Lord Templeman said:

> The violence of sado-masochistic encounters involves the indulgence of cruelty by sadists and the degradation of victims. Such violence is injurious to the participants and unpredictably dangerous. I am not prepared to invent a defence of consent for sado-masochistic encounters which breed and glorify cruelty and result in [actual bodily harm].

The defendants in *Brown* sought redress from the European Court of Human Rights (*Laskey* v *United Kingdom* Case No. 109/1995) but the Court ruled that state interference in this aspect of their private lives could be justified on the basis of 'protection of health'.

Rough horseplay

A number of further qualifications to the basic rule have been identified. One concerns 'rough and undisciplined horseplay'. In *Jones* (1986) 83 Cr App R 375, a group of youths tossed other youths into the air and let them fall to the ground. They claimed that the victims had consented to this, but one of the victims suffered a ruptured spleen and another suffered a broken arm. The trial judge refused to allow the issue of consent to be raised, owing to the serious nature of the injuries, but the Court of Appeal held that the defence should have been left to the jury. One doubts whether any jury could really have believed that the victims consented to such bullying, but the problem in this case was that the jury were never asked to decide that question, so the convictions were quashed.

Tattooing, piercing and personal adornment

An adult (over 18) may consent to being tattooed, and reasonable body piercing (for earrings etc.) may also be lawful if the subject is old enough to understand what it involves. In *Wilson* [1996] 2 Cr App R 241, the Court of Appeal held that nothing said by the House of Lords in Brown prevented a wife from consenting to her husband branding his initials on her bottom. The branding was said to be more akin to tattooing for personal adornment than to an act of sado-masochism (whereas sado-masochistic branding was one of the acts declared criminal in *Brown*). Fair enough, but what if there had been a sado-masochistic element as well? The judges did not expressly decide that point, but their general view was that:

> Consensual activity between husband and wife in the privacy of the matrimonial home is not, in our judgment, normally a proper matter for criminal investigation, let alone criminal prosecution.

So what if the parties had not been married? There is still plenty of uncertainty in the law relating to consent.

Lawful correction or chastisement

At common law, a parent (or any other adult who is put in charge of children) may use reasonable force to control the behaviour of children in their care. This may in *some* cases extend to the infliction of reasonable corporal punishment. The limits of what may be considered reasonable appear to have narrowed in recent years. Hard caning, for example, is no longer likely to be considered reasonable, although individual courts and juries are likely to have varying views on what 'reasonable punishment' may involve.

The law governing the infliction of punishment in schools can now be found in the Education Act 1996. This largely prohibits the corporal punishment of pupils at public sector schools (or of publicly funded pupils at independent schools) and very few independent schools still practise it in any form.

Assault occasioning actual bodily harm

Assault occasioning actual bodily harm is an offence under s. 47 of the OAPA 1861. If a person is charged with a s. 47 offence, the prosecution must prove that an assault or battery has taken place and that some injury (not necessarily serious) has resulted.

Actual bodily harm was defined in the case of *Miller* [1954] 2 All ER 534 as 'any hurt or injury calculated (i.e. likely) to interfere with the health or comfort of the victim'. Mere grazes or mild bruising might in theory be sufficient for a s. 47 charge, but the agreed policy of the police and Crown Prosecution Service is that they will not charge this offence unless there is some injury serious enough to require medical or dental treatment. Psychiatric illness caused by nervous shock may suffice, although any such injury (and its causes) must be proved by expert medical evidence (see *Ireland*, above).

The *mens rea* for assault occasioning actual bodily harm is no different from that required in cases of common assault or battery. The defendant does not have to intend to cause bodily harm, nor does he even have to be reckless as to that possibility. This was confirmed by the House of Lords in *Savage* [1991] 4

All ER 698. Mrs Savage attempted to throw the contents of a glass of beer over another woman, with whom she had previously fallen out. The beer glass flew from her hand, apparently by accident, and injured the other woman. Savage had not intended any such injury, nor had she even foreseen it, but the House of Lords held that she could still be guilty of assault occasioning actual bodily harm. She had intended to assault the other woman, and no further *mens rea* was required.

Malicious wounding and inflicting grievous bodily harm

Section 20 of the Offences Against the Person Act 1861 provides:

> Whosoever shall unlawfully and maliciously wound or inflict any grievous bodily harm upon any other persons, either with or without any weapon or instrument, shall be ... liable ... to imprisonment for not more than five years.

The nature of the injury

The *actus reus* of this offence consists of *either* unlawful wounding *or* the unlawful infliction of grievous bodily harm. The meaning of 'wound' was defined in *JCC (a minor)* v *Eisenhower* [1983] Crim LR 567, as requiring penetration of the skin and not just broken blood vessels. To constitute a wound, both layers of skin (dermis and epidermis) must be broken. A bad graze, which does not break the inner layer of skin, would not be classed as a wound. A trivial pinprick can in theory be a wound, as long as it is deep enough, but in practice the agreed policy of the police and the CPS is that they will not charge a suspect with such a serious offence unless there is evidence of serious injury to the victim.

Grievous bodily harm was defined in *Director of Public Prosecutions* v *Smith* [1960] 3 All ER 161, as meaning 'really serious harm'. There is no legally binding list of injuries that may be grievous or of injuries that may not be, although the police and CPS do have a short list of examples in their booklet of agreed charging standards. These include, 'broken or displaced limbs or bones', 'permanent visible disfigurement' and 'injuries causing substantial loss of blood, usually necessitating a transfusion'. Severe psychiatric trauma may also qualify (a rule confirmed by the House of Lords in *Ireland*), but these are only examples. It is for a jury to decide whether a particular injury is grievous or not. A judge may sometimes direct a jury that an injury is not really serious, but he can never direct them that an injury *is* sufficiently serious, unless the defence have conceded that it is.

We saw above that a battery must involve a direct physical attack. Section 20, however, is wider. Injuries caused by the setting of a trap or tripwire could give rise to a s. 20 offence, provided they are serious enough. In *Martin* (1881) 8 QBD 54, the accused was held to be guilty of a s. 20 offence when he bolted the exits to a theatre and turned out the lights, thereby creating a panic which led to a number of serious injuries. It may seem odd that a trap which inflicts serious injuries is covered by s. 20, whilst one which causes only minor injuries is not covered by s. 47, but such is the illogical structure of the 1861 Act!

Mens rea

The mens rea for a s. 20 offence is maliciousness. The defendant must either intend or foresee that his attack would inflict some harm on the victim. If the harm suffered by the victim turns out to be more serious than the defendant intended, he will still be liable for it: *Mowatt* [1967] 3 All ER 47. In *Savage* (above) the defendant was guilty of a s. 47 offence when her deliberate assault caused accidental injury; but she was not guilty of the more serious s. 20 offence, because she had not intended any injury at all.

Wounding or causing grievous bodily harm with intent

Section 18 of the OAPA 1861 provides:

> Whosoever shall unlawfully and maliciously by any means whatsoever wound or cause any grievous bodily harm to any person with intent to do grievous bodily harm to any person, or with intent to resist or prevent the lawful apprehension or detainer of any person, shall be guilty of an offence and shall be liable to imprisonment for life.

Upon careful reading of s. 18 it is clear that there are four variants of the offence:

(a) wounding with intent to do grievous bodily harm;
(b) causing grievous bodily harm with intent to do so;
(c) wounding with intent to resist lawful arrest, etc.; and
(d) causing grievous bodily harm with intent to resist lawful arrest, etc.

There are many similarities between s. 18 and s. 20. The injuries that must be caused or inflicted are the same in each case. The *mens rea*, however, is different. If D realises that his unlawful conduct might possibly cause someone some kind of injury, that is sufficient *mens rea* under s. 20, but nothing less than a specific intent to cause really serious injury (or alternatively, intent to resist or prevent lawful arrest or detention) will suffice under s. 18. Note that an intent to cause grievous bodily harm suffices for a murder conviction, should the victim die of his injuries.

Assaulting a constable acting in the execution of his duty

Section 89 of the Police Act 1996 (which is effectively identical to s. 51 of the (now repealed) Police Act 1964) states that it is an offence to assault a constable in the execution of his duty. This offence protects not only police officers but also anyone assisting such officers. The defendant need not know that his victim is a police officer, nor does he need to know that the officer is acting in the course of his duty. The defendant must, however, have the *mens rea* for common assault or battery. If he hits an officer in the mistaken belief that the officer is just an interfering busybody, he is guilty of a s. 89 offence (see *Albert v Lavin* [1981] 3 All ER 878); but if he mistakes the officer for a criminal and acts in mistaken self-defence, he would not be guilty of any assault at all (see *Kenlin* v *Gardiner* [1966] 3 All ER 931, where a group of boys apparently thought the police officers were kidnappers!).

The police officer must have been acting in the course of his duty at the time of the assault. An officer who is trespassing or who is making an illegal arrest will not be deemed to be acting in the course of his duty (*Kenlin* v *Gardiner*, above). If an officer is assaulted in such circumstances, the accused could not be charged with this particular offence, although he might be charged with battery or with a s. 47 offence if the force he used in response was excessive.

Malicious administration of poisonous, destructive or noxious substances

These particular offences are to be found under ss. 23, 24 of the OAPA 1861. Section 23 is the more serious offence, requiring the actual (but not necessarily the intentional) infliction of grievous bodily harm or the endangerment of life. In contrast, s. 24 requires only an intent to injure or annoy. No actual injury or annoyance need even be caused, as long as it was intended.

Other offences involving violence or threats

There are several further offences which might be committed where physical violence is used or threatened. Robbery and blackmail are considered in Chapter 15. Detailed consideration of other offences will not be attempted here, but some general awareness of them is desirable.

The Public Order Act 1986 creates a series of offences dealing with violence, threats and disorder (not necessarily *public* violence or disorder). The most serious of these are riot (s. 1), violent disorder (s. 2) and affray (s. 3). Less serious offences include using threatening, abusive or insulting behaviour (s. 4) and causing harassment, alarm or distress (s. 5).

'Stalking' has been much in the news in recent years. Serious incidents of stalking, which result in psychological injury to the victims, may sometimes be dealt with under ss. 20 or 47 of the Offences Against the Person Act 1861 (see *Ireland*, above), but other cases may more appropriately be dealt with under s. 5 of the Public Order Act 1986 or under s. 2 of the Protection from Harassment Act 1997, under which it is an offence for a person to pursue a course of conduct which he knows, or ought to know, amounts to harassment of another.

Where the victim is put in fear of violence by such harassment, the stalker may face more serious charges under s. 4 of the 1997 Act. Victims of stalking may also seek injunctions against their stalkers in the civil courts. Breach of such an injunction may amount to an indictable offence under s. 5 of the 1997 Act.

Indecent assault and rape

Rape and indecent assault are examples of what is sometimes called 'sexual violence'. Men, women and children can all be the victims of such offences, which are often combined with ordinary forms of physical violence, or even murder.

The actus reus of rape

Rape is defined in s. 1 of the Sexual Offences Act 1956, as amended by the Criminal Justice and Public Order Act 1994. It can be committed where a man or boy has sexual intercourse (anal or vaginal) with a man or woman who does not at the time consent to it. It need not involve any struggle or the use of force: the victim may for example be drugged or even asleep. Although rape will usually be committed at the very moment of penetration, it is possible that the other party will withdraw consent at some later stage (e.g., because she is experiencing pain). The Privy Council in *Kaitamaki* [1984] 2 All ER 435 held that rape may be committed where the act of intercourse is deliberately persisted in or prolonged after the perpetrator has become aware that his partner is no longer consenting.

What exactly is consent?

What if the victim (or complainant) was too drunk to know what (s)he was consenting to? Or too naïve to understand what sexual intercourse is? In such cases, there is no real consent. In *Williams* [1923] 1 KB 340 an unscrupulous singing teacher was convicted of rape after persuading a very naïve 16-year-old girl that he was doing something to help improve her voice; but it would have been different if she knew what sexual intercourse was, and was tricked into thinking that 'having sex would improve her voice', or if she consented to sex only because he promised to marry her, when he never meant it. Using false pretences to procure a woman to have sex is a crime under s. 2 of the Sexual Offences Act 1956, but it can only be rape if the victim (typically a child) has no real idea what she is consenting to. Similarly, the complainant's drunkenness only nullifies her consent if she is too drunk to know what is going on. If she is merely tipsy and uninhibited, her consent is valid (*Lang* (1975) 62 Cr App R 50).

Recklessness, knowledge and mistaken belief

A man who honestly believes the complainant to be consenting cannot be guilty of rape, even if his mistake is an unreasonable one. This rule was established by the House of Lords in *Director of Public Prosecutions* v *Morgan* [1975] 2 All ER 347. Despite ferocious criticism, it was effectively codified by the Sexual Offences (Amendment) Act 1976 and is now restated in the 1994 revision of the 1956 Act. A rapist must either know the complainant is not consenting, or be reckless as to the possible absence of consent. Recklessness here means the conscious or *Cunningham* variety. Failing to consider the possibility that the complainant is not consenting (i.e., *Caldwell* recklessness) is not sufficient: see *Satnam Singh* (1984) 78 Cr App R 149.

Rape is nevertheless a crime of 'basic intent' for the purpose of the *Majewski* rule (Chapter 18). This means that self-induced drunkenness or intoxication that prevents a man from realising that the woman is not consenting cannot be a defence. Since drunkenness may prevent the complainant from giving valid consent (even though she offers no resistance) this is a recipe for disaster in cases where two very drunk people fall into bed together. She may be too drunk to give consent or to resist. He may be too drunk to realise that she is too drunk to consent. He may therefore be guilty of raping her, if sexual intercourse takes place in such circumstances.

Marital rape

Even at common law, husbands could be convicted as accessories to rape if they aided or procured the rape of their wives by other men. But could husbands be convicted as actual perpetrators? Sir Matthew Hale declared in his classic text, *Historia Placitorum Coronae* (1736) that such rape in marriage was impossible, because the wife '... hath given herself up in this kinde unto her husband, which she cannot retract'. This effectively represented the law of England for over 250 years, although it was recognised that an injunction or a separation agreement with a non-cohabitation clause would terminate that consent. The old rule was eventually deposed by the House of Lords in a case known simply as *R* [1991] 4 All ER 481. The judges rightly condemned marital rape as unacceptable in a modern society. Indeed so, but the change should surely have been effected by non-retroactive legislation, rather than by imprisoning a man from doing what the judges had previously said was his lawful right.

Indecent assault and unlawful sexual activity

Indecent assault typically involves unwanted sexual touching or groping, and is an offence under the Sexual Offences Act 1956, s. 14 (assault on a female) and s. 15 (assault on a male). Consent usually negatives assault, but boys or girls aged under 16 cannot give valid consent to any form of indecent sexual touching. Offences may be committed by persons of either sex. It is the only charge that can be brought against women who seduce underage boys. Men who seduce and have intercourse with underage girls can also be charged with 'unlawful sexual intercourse' or even (where the girl is too young to understand) with rape.

FIFTEEN

Offences Against Property

This chapter will look at offences involving damage to property or to pecuniary or financial interests. Rights to property can be interfered with or usurped in many different ways, and a correspondingly wide range of criminal offences have been developed in response. The basic property offences are theft, contrary to s. 1 of the Theft Act 1968, and criminal damage, contrary to s. 1 of the Criminal Damage Act 1971, but these basic provisions are reinforced by a number of other important offences, dealing with aggravated variants of the basic offences or with analogous forms of dishonesty or fraud. Where, for example, force or violence is used against other persons in order to commit theft, this turns the basic theft into the more serious offence of robbery; where buildings are broken into or unlawfully entered for the purpose of stealing, this is burglary; and where criminal damage is caused by means of fire, it will be charged as arson.

The Theft Acts of 1968 and 1978 (as amended by the Theft (Amendment) Act 1996) also contain a number of offences which are quite distinct from theft itself. These have been developed to deal with various other ways in which property can be misappropriated or interfered with. Examples include blackmail, taking a conveyance without the owner's consent (or 'joy-riding'), dishonest abstraction of electricity, handling stolen goods and obtaining services, money transfers or pecuniary advantages by deception. Other legislation deals with forgery of documents, counterfeiting of currency and falsification of trade marks; but such offences lie beyond the scope of this book.

Although property offences are almost all statutory, over the years the courts have added a considerable gloss to the statutory provisions and it is now quite impossible to understand many of these offences without taking account of the case law on the relevant topic.

. THEFT

Section 1 of the Theft Act 1968 provides that:

> A person is guilty of theft if he dishonestly appropriates property belonging to another with the intention of permanently depriving the other of it, and 'thief' and 'steal' shall be construed accordingly.

It can be seen from this provision that, before a person can be convicted of theft, five elements must be proved. The *actus reus* of theft requires (1) an appropriation (2) of property (3) belonging to another. The *mens rea* of theft requires two further elements, namely (4) dishonesty and (5) an intention to permanently deprive the other person of the property concerned. These elements are defined and explained in ss. 2 to 6 of the 1968 Act, and must be considered in some detail.

Property

For the purposes of the Theft Acts the word 'property' has been given a special meaning by virtue of s. 4(1) of the Theft Act 1968. This defines property so as to include 'money and all other property, real or personal, including things in action and other intangible property'. This is a wide-ranging provision, but it is subject to certain limitations which we will look at in due course. The effect of the width of s. 4(1) is that almost all tangible property is capable of being stolen. Money (in the form of notes or coins) is itself a form of tangible property.

Section 4(1) also makes it clear that intangible property and things (or 'choses') in action are capable of being stolen. Choses in action are rights which can only be enforced through the taking of legal action. The classic example of a chose in action is the right to enforce a debt. If, for example, Bloggs has saved £1,000 in his account at the High Street Bank, he does not really have any 'money in the bank' (any notes or coins in the bank belong to the bank itself). What he does own is a chose in action: the legally enforceable right to withdraw or recover £1,000 (plus any interest) from the bank. This is a form of intangible property, and can itself be stolen.

Intangible property also includes patents and copyrights, although it is difficult, in practice, to steal these (an infringement of copyright may be unlawful, but is not the same thing as theft of the right to enforce it).

One thing which is *not* classed as property for the purposes of the Theft Acts is electricity, but there is a separate offence of dishonestly abstracting electricity (s. 13 of the 1968 Act). Confidential information, such as the questions on an examination paper, is not classed as property either, although one could in some cases be charged with theft of the paper upon which the questions are written. In *Oxford v Moss* (1978) 68 Cr App R 183, a dishonest student 'borrowed' an examination paper and photocopied the questions before the exam. He could not be guilty of theft of confidential information as this did not amount to property under s. 4(1); nor could he be guilty of the theft of the paper, as he had simply borrowed and returned it, and did not intend to permanently deprive the owner of the paper. Similarly, trade secrets are incapable of being stolen, because they are not classed as property under s. 4(1). This is considered to be a major loophole in the law, and consideration is being given to possible means of closing that loophole.

Land and wild plants

Although land, buildings and fixtures are undoubtedly forms of property ('real property') they are not ordinarily capable of being stolen. Indeed, a landowner who cheekily fences in a piece of ground adjacent to his own may eventually acquire title or ownership rights over it. Land and fixtures can, however, be stolen in certain circumstances, notably where a trustee or executor steals land which he holds on trust for others, or where tenants or strangers dishonestly remove fixtures (e.g., doors, aerials, roofing materials or shrubs, etc.) from the land or building in question.

Cultivated plants are property, and picking or uprooting them can be theft; but the picking of wild flowers, plants, berries, etc. cannot be theft, unless it is done for reward or for sale or other commercial purpose (s. 4(3)). Even then, it will not be theft unless it is done dishonestly; and very few blackberry pickers would be considered dishonest, even if they do sell the occasional jar of blackberry jam at the village fete!

Wild creatures

Section 4(4) deals with wild creatures. If a creature (such as a circus elephant) is tamed or kept in captivity then the animal may be stolen. But other wild animals, such as wild birds or rabbits, are not owned by anyone and cannot be stolen, unless they have previously been caught by someone else, in which case they can be stolen from him. (Poaching game is a different offence, and outside the scope of this book.)

Belonging to another

Property cannot be stolen unless it belongs to another person at the time when it is appropriated. The purpose of the Theft Acts is to protect, not only rights of ownership, but also other interests in property, such as possession or control, and this is reflected in s. 5(1), which gives a wide definition to 'belonging' for the purposes of the theft. It provides:

> Property shall be regarded as belonging to any person having possession or control of it, or having in it any proprietary right or interest (not being an equitable interest arising only from an agreement to transfer or grant an interest).

Property can thus be stolen from a person who simply has control or possession over it, even if he does not enjoy legal ownership. If, for example, X is charged with stealing a car belonging to Y, it is no defence for him to argue that Y himself had previously stolen the car from Z or from some person unknown! In exceptional cases, a person can even be liable for theft of his own property, if he dishonestly takes it from someone who has possession or control over it at the time. A case on this point is *Turner* [1971] 2 All ER 441. The defendant left his car at a garage for repair. When the repairs were completed, he used a spare set of keys, and drove off without paying for the repairs. He was convicted of the theft of his own vehicle, because the garage owners had sufficient control over the car to bring it within the phrase 'belonging to another'. They also had a proprietary right to retain it until the repairs were paid for (a 'repairer's lien') but surprisingly this does not seem to have been relied upon in that case.

If the property in question has been abandoned, there cannot ordinarily be any theft of it, as it does not belong to anyone. If A throws away an old pair of shoes and B takes them, B cannot be guilty of theft. Property, however, will only be considered to be abandoned where the owner does not care what becomes of it. If A arranges for B to dispose of some dangerous or sensitive material, it could quite conceivably be stolen before B arrives to collect it; and if B is charged with the duty of destroying or disposing of it, he could commit theft by dishonestly keeping some of it for himself. Employees of the Royal Mint were recently convicted of stealing old banknotes which they had been instructed to incinerate. It was no defence to argue that their employers no longer required the notes.

Special cases

Although s. 5(1) takes a wide approach to 'property belonging to another', s. 5(3) and (4) give a further extended meaning to the phrase, in order to extend the application of the law of theft. Section 5(3) provides:

> Where a person receives property from or on account of another, and is under an obligation to the other to retain and deal with that property or its proceeds in a particular way, the property or proceeds shall be regarded (as against him) as belonging to the other.

If, for example, an employee is given money in order to buy materials for his employer, but spends it himself, that could be theft under s. 5(3). It must be proved, however, that the money was given to him for that specific purpose. It is not customary, for example, for a travel agent to use the deposit received for each holiday he books for the purpose of obtaining the travel tickets required by that particular customer. In the absence of specific agreement to the contrary, any deposit received is simply absorbed into his business account. Section 5(3) does not therefore apply, even if he ultimately fails to provided the travel tickets promised.

This is what happened in *Hall* [1972] 2 All ER 1009. The defendant received payments from clients who had booked holidays in America. The defendant paid the money into his firm's general trading account, but never actually arranged the trips, and was subsequently unable to repay the money to the clients. He was not guilty of theft, however, because it was not proved that he was under any obligation to retain and deal with the money in a particular way. Had he been an estate agent or solicitor receiving a deposit on a house purchase, the position would have been different, because it is clearly understood in such cases that deposits for clients must not be absorbed into the general trading account or expended in any other way (*Mainwaring* (1981) 74 Cr App R 99). Section 5(3) also covers situations in which the defendant collects money on another person's behalf, as where he acts as an agent to collect rent.

Section 5(4) deals with property acquired by another's mistake. It covers, amongst other things, cases in which persons are mistakenly overpaid for work done, or have large sums wrongly credited to their bank accounts. If they recognise the mistake and realise that they are legally obliged to repay the money or the bank credit, but nevertheless dishonestly spend, keep or dispose of it, they may be guilty of theft, because under s. 5(4) the money or credit is 'deemed' to belong to the person entitled to restitution of it.

Appropriation

In order to be stolen, property belonging to another must be dishonestly 'appropriated'. Appropriation is thus the crucial act in the crime of theft. One might suppose that the word 'appropriates' would be clear in meaning, but it is not. Furthermore, not every appropriation will amount to a theft, as the appropriation must be accompanied with the requisite *mens rea* (see below). The Theft Act 1968 attempts to provide a definition of appropriation, but as we shall see in the forthcoming section, the courts have placed an elaborate gloss on this definition, and the extensive case law on this topic will have to be analysed very carefully.

Assumption of the rights of an owner
Section 3(1) provides,

> Any assumption by a person of the rights of an owner amounts to an appropriation, and this includes, where he has come by the property (innocently or not) without stealing it, any later assumption of a right to it by keeping or dealing with it as owner.

The rights of an owner over goods include those of using, possessing, selling, hiring, destroying, lending or consuming them. If a person tries to usurp *any* of these rights, this may constitute an appropriation of the goods. An appropriation will typically involve an outright taking of the property concerned, as for example where a mugger grabs and runs off with the victim's handbag, or where the chairman of a charitable organisation illicitly withdraws funds from the organisation's bank account, in order to spend those funds on himself (*Hilton* [1997] Crim LR 761). Embezzlement (as such conduct used to be called) is now treated as a form of theft.

Nevertheless, the House of Lords in *Morris* [1983] 3 All ER 288, decided that it was not necessary for all the rights of an owner to be usurped in order for there to be an appropriation. It was sufficient if any *one* right of the owner was interfered with. The case involved two appeals heard together. Each involved dishonest shoppers who had switched the price labels on goods with the intention of buying the goods at a lower price. In one case, the culprit was arrested after paying for the goods at the lower price, whilst in the other, the culprit was arrested before reaching the checkout. The former could have been charged with obtaining property by deception, contrary to s. 15 of the Theft Act 1968, and the latter could perhaps have been charged with an attempt to commit that offence. However, the prosecution pursued a charge of theft against each defendant and the principal question was whether they had ever appropriated the property in question. Clearly, the labelling or pricing of goods is something which only the owner of the goods (or his staff) has the right to do. Their lordships accordingly held that the label-switching constituted an appropriation, and that the appropriation amounted to theft. This seems a bizarre conclusion, because the defendants were still acknowledging the shop as being the lawful owner of the goods, and by presenting them at the checkout were offering to buy the goods which they had supposedly already stolen! This is, with respect, an inept and disastrous decision, and one which ignores the wording of the Act. Section 3 refers to an assumption of the *rights* of the owner. How can a label-switcher be said to have assumed those rights when he is still willing to offer the shop money (albeit the wrong amount) in payment for the goods?

The relevance of consent to appropriation
One major question in respect of what constitutes an appropriation is whether an appropriation can take place with the consent of the owner. If P lets D drive off in P's car, after being duped into accepting a dud cheque in payment for it, has D stolen the car? It was assumed for many years that the answer was 'no'. D would no doubt be guilty of obtaining property by deception (which now carries a maximum penalty of ten years, rather than the maximum of seven for theft) but he would not be guilty of theft. This was sometimes important for insurance purposes: policies which insured against theft did not always protect against loss through deception.

The House of Lords in *Morris* (above) assumed that there could not be an appropriation where the owner had consented to the act in question. The dishonest shopper could not, on that view, commit theft merely by picking up the item that he intends to steal. He must first do something that is wrong, forbidden or unauthorised. Slipping the item into a hidden pocket would suffice; so too would label-switching (although it is questionable whether label-switching alone should ever be regarded as theft, because it cannot, in itself, be the cause of the owner being deprived of his goods).

However, in the later case of *Gomez* [1993] 1 All ER 1, the House of Lords took a completely different view and said that there can indeed be an appropriation, even where the alleged act has taken place with the owner's full consent. The decision in *Gomez* followed the approach taken by the House of Lords in the much earlier case of *Lawrence* [1971] 2 All ER 1253, which after *Morris* had been thought to be wrong.

Gomez was the assistant manager of an electrical goods shop. A dishonest friend approached him in an attempt to acquire goods from the shop in exchange for two building society cheques which he had stolen. Gomez asked the manager for authorisation for two sales totalling £16,950. The manager told him to confirm with the bank that the cheques were acceptable. Gomez later told the manager that he had done so. This was a lie, but the manager was deceived and the goods were sold in reliance on it. A few days later, the two cheques were returned marked, 'Orders not to pay — stolen cheques'. Gomez was charged, not with enabling his friend to obtain property by deception (the obvious charge on those facts), but with theft, and the House of Lords eventually upheld his conviction.

In *Lawrence*, the defendant was a taxi driver and was convicted of theft when he told the plaintiff, an Italian passenger, that the money which he had offered for the fare was not enough. The passenger then opened up his wallet indicating to the taxi driver to take the appropriate amount. The defendant took a total of £7, when the correct fare for the journey was only just over 50p. He was convicted of theft, but appealed on the grounds that the passenger had consented to him taking the money and that there could be no theft if the owner had consented to the act. The House of Lords rejected this argument and held that, even if the owner permits or consents to the property being taken there may nevertheless be an appropriation of it. Whether this constitutes theft hinges solely upon the presence of the requisite *mens rea*.

Of course, both Gomez and Lawrence were villains who deserved to be convicted of something. But were they convicted of the right offence, or did the House of Lords distort the law in an attempt to cover up for the prosecution's ineptitude in selecting the wrong charges in the first place? A consequence of the decision in *Gomez* is that theft has now become little more than a thought-crime. In *Gomez*, Lord Keith was even prepared to hold that the act of removing goods from supermarket shelves and putting them in the trolley or basket provided would amount to an appropriation. So why are all shoppers not thieves? The answer is that most shoppers are not dishonest and intend to pay the correct price for the goods when they put the items in the receptacle provided. If, on the other hand, a shopper puts goods in the basket, intending not to pay for them, or intending to pay with a stolen credit card, then he may be guilty of theft even at that stage, and will remain so even if he loses his nerve and pays the full price in cash; even though, in other words, he has done nothing objectively wrong. Liability for theft is now almost entirely dependent on the issue of the defendant's motives or honesty. Every shopper in a self-service store or supermarket routinely commits the full *actus reus* of theft each time he selects an item from the shelves. This, with respect, is absurd, and, as Lord Lowry demonstrated in a powerful dissenting speech in *Gomez*, it does considerable violence to the intended meaning of the Theft Act 1968.

Where the defendant was merely the recipient of a valid gift, it would seem that he cannot be said to have appropriated it (*Mazo* [1996] Crim LR 435) but if A is incapable of managing his affairs (through senility or mental illness, etc.) B may be guilty of theft if he dishonestly induces A to sign documents or instruments purporting to make gifts to B or to B's friends (*Hopkins* [1997] Crim LR 359).

The *mens rea* of theft

As we have already seen the *mens rea* of theft is made up of two elements, namely dishonesty and an intention to permanently deprive the owner. There is no requirement that the defendant must steal for gain, as is made clear by s. 1(2) of the Theft Act 1968.

Dishonesty

Dishonesty is only partially defined in the Theft Act 1968. Section 2(1) of the Act gives three examples in which the defendant's appropriation is *not* to be regarded as dishonest, whilst section 2(2) provides one example of conduct that *may* be classed as dishonesty. Section 2 does not purport to be exhaustive on this issue, and the courts have inevitably attempted to fill in the gaps. Section 2 provides:

(1) A person's appropriation of property belonging to another is not to be regarded as dishonest—

(a) if he appropriates the property in the belief that he has in law the right to deprive the other of it, on behalf of himself or of a third person; or

(b) if he appropriates the property in the belief that he would have the other's consent if the other knew of the appropriation and the circumstances of it; or

(c) (except where the property came to him as trustee or personal representative) if he appropriates the property in the belief that the person to whom the property belongs cannot be discovered by taking reasonable steps.

(2) A person's appropriation of property belonging to another may be dishonest notwithstanding that he is willing to pay for the property.

Under s. 2(1), it is clear that the test of dishonesty is a subjective one. It does not, in theory, matter whether the defendant had any reasonable grounds for his belief, or whether the owner would in fact have consented, or whether the owner could in fact have been found by taking reasonable steps. What matters is whether the defendant really believed it. If so, he cannot be guilty of theft. If, however, his supposed belief is preposterous ('I thought the boss would consent to me taking £10,000 from the cash till . . .') then no court will ever believe him. To that extent, it helps if the belief was a reasonable one.

Section 2(2) makes it clear that an appropriation can be dishonest even where the defendant is prepared to pay for the property. This does not mean that willingness to pay is irrelevant. D is far less likely to be considered dishonest if he offers to pay than if he does not. It is clear, however, that willingness to pay cannot give a wealthy collector *carte blanche* to help himself to property which the owners do not want to sell.

It is clear from the foregoing sections that s. 2 is not an exhaustive treatise of what constitutes dishonesty. The mere fact that the defendant cannot bring himself within one of the three exceptions laid out in s. 2(1) does not mean that he *is* dishonest. If the defendant relies on any other defence then it will be for the jury to adjudicate upon this fact under a more general test of dishonesty. The question as to what constitutes dishonesty in these circumstances is not one of law but rather one of fact for the jury to determine. The general test to be applied by the jury in these circumstances was laid down in *Ghosh* [1982] 2 All ER 689. It is a two-part test. The first part requires the court to consider whether what was done was dishonest according to the ordinary standards of reasonable and honest people. If the answer to that question is 'yes', then the jury must go on to consider whether the defendant realised that what he was doing was by those standards dishonest. In other words, did he realise that what he was doing would be considered dishonest by ordinary, right-thinking people?

Leaving decisions as to what is dishonest to the determination of the jury may lead to inconsistencies, in that views as to what may constitute dishonesty may vary from one set of jurors to another and from one part of the country to the other. On the other hand, fixed legal rules as to what is to be regarded as dishonest may become sources of hardship and injustice. How could rigid rules distinguish between X, who 'borrows' £1 from his employer's cashbox before lunch, knowing that he can and will replace an identical amount after going to the bank at lunchtime; and Y, who borrows £500, hoping to be able to repay it at the end of the next week, provided he wins some money on the horses? Flexible common sense can sometimes be better than rigid certainty in such cases.

Intent to permanently deprive
Unlawful borrowing is not theft, even if it is dishonest. The unlawful borrowing of a conveyance, such as a car that is taken for joy-riding, is however an offence

under s. 12 of the Theft Act (and there may even be theft of the petrol used when driving it).

If, however, the borrowing amounts in practice to the equivalent of an outright taking, as where D takes batteries or season tickets from E and returns them only when they are exhausted or expired, this may be treated as involving an intent to permanently deprive him of them, and may therefore be theft (see s. 6 of the 1968 Act).

Another form of 'borrowing' which will be treated as permanent taking is the borrowing of money. The reason for this is that any notes or coins returned by the borrower will in practice be different notes or coins from those originally taken. The best defence of the person who has committed illicit 'borrowing' of money is that, in view of his intent to repay, he was not dishonest.

ROBBERY AND ASSAULT WITH INTENT TO ROB

Robbery

Section 8 of the Theft Act 1968 states:

(1)   A person is guilty of robbery if he steals, and immediately before or at the time of doing so, and in order to do so, he uses force on any person or puts or seeks to put any person in fear of being then and there subjected to force.

(2)   A person guilty of robbery, or an assault with intent to rob, shall on conviction on indictment be liable to imprisonment for life.

Section 8 creates two offences: that of robbery (s. 8(1)) and assault with intent to rob (s. 8(2)) which is distinct from the offence of robbery itself. Robbery is an aggravated form of theft and therefore, in order that a successful charge of robbery can be brought against the defendant, the prosecution will have to establish all the elements of theft. It will have to be shown that there was a dishonest appropriation and an intention to permanently deprive. Thus, if a person takes money to which he honestly believes he is legally entitled, there will be no theft because of the absence of dishonesty. In the case of *Robinson* [1977] Crim LR 173, the accused demanded that the victim repay a debt owed by the victim's wife to him. He held a knife to reinforce his demand. The Court held that this did not amount to robbery because the accused genuinely believed that he was legally entitled to the money (such conduct may still amount to blackmail, however).

Force and threats of force

As well as proving the elements of theft, the prosecution will have to prove that force or threats of force were used 'immediately before or at the time of' the theft. The force or threats must be used in order to steal. If force is used after the theft is complete, this will not be sufficient to convert the theft into robbery. This principle can be seen from the case of *Donaghy* [1981] Crim LR 644. The defendant ordered a taxi driver to take him from Newmarket to London and made threats to his life. Once in London, he stole £22 from the driver. He was held not guilty of robbery because the threats were not made in order to take the money but simply to drive the defendant to his desired destination (London). Similarly if a participant in a fight knocks another to the floor and only then decides to take his wallet, he will not be guilty of robbery as the force was not used to enable him to steal. One must be careful, however, as theft is often treated by the courts as continuing for some time after the initial appropriation. In *Hale* (1978) Cr App 415, Eveleigh LJ said:

> The act of appropriation does not suddenly cease. It is a continuous act, and it is a matter for the jury to decide whether or not the appropriation has finished.

Consequently, if force is used to effect a 'getaway' from the scene of a theft, that would be treated as turning the crime into robbery. The word 'force' in this context can include a fairly slight degree of force, such as a nudge to push someone off balance. In marginal cases, however, it will be a question of fact for the jury to decide whether the defendant's conduct amounted to force.

Mens rea
As robbery is an aggravated form of theft, the defendant must have the *mens rea* for theft but in addition it is necessary to prove that the defendant intentionally or recklessly used or threatened to use force.

Assault with intent to rob

This is a distinct offence from robbery, and can sometimes be charged as an alternative to attempted robbery. The intended theft need not have succeeded, but in order to bring a successful prosecution for this alternative offence it is necessary to prove that someone was assaulted. Assault for these purposes has the same meaning as in s. 47 of the Offences Against the Person Act 1861 (see Chapter 14) although no actual bodily harm need result from it.

BLACKMAIL

Section 21 of the Theft Act 1968 provides:

> (1) A person is guilty of blackmail if, with a view to gain for himself or another or with intent to cause loss to another, he makes any unwarranted demand with menaces, and for this purpose a demand with menaces is unwarranted unless the person making it does so in the belief—
>   (a) that he has reasonable grounds for making the demand; and

(b)   that the use of the menaces is a proper means of reinforcing the demand.

(2)   The nature of the act or omission is immaterial, and it is also immaterial whether the menaces relate to action to be taken by the person making the demand.

(3)   A person guilty of blackmail shall on conviction on indictment be liable to imprisonment for a term not exceeding ten years.

The making of a demand

The essence of the offence of blackmail is the making of an unwarranted demand. It is not necessary for the blackmailer either to have intimidated his victim or to have obtained anything from the victim. For example, if a blackmailer makes an unwarranted demand with menaces to a person whose hearing is impaired or who cannot understand him, the offence of blackmail may still have taken place, because the unwarranted demand can be made, even if it has not been effective or has not been understood. In *Treacy v Director of Public Prosecutions* [1971] 1 All ER 110, the House of Lords went so far as to obviate even the need for the successful communication of the demand. In that case, the defendant committed the offence by posting a blackmail letter addressed to a woman in Germany. Blackmail committed in a foreign country is not ordinarily punishable under English law, but it was held that the offence was completed by the act of posting the letter in England, so the fact that the victim received it abroad did not matter.

The demand must be made with menaces

For these purposes, the menaces need not involve threats of violence, but the threats must be of such 'a nature and extent that the mind of an ordinary person might be influenced ... so as to accede unwillingly to the demand' (*Clear* [1968] 1 All ER 74). Trivial threats, therefore, are not menaces as can be seen from the case of *Harry* [1974] Crim LR 32. In this case, a student offered shopkeepers 'immunity from rag week activities' in return for donations to charity but this thinly veiled threat was held not to constitute menaces for the purposes of the Act. A similar kind of 'offer' from the Mafia would of course have been a very different proposition.

The demand must be an unwarranted demand

If the defendant genuinely believes that he has reasonable grounds for making the demand *and* that the menaces which he uses are a proper means of enforcing the demand, then he cannot be guilty of blackmail as the demand would not be 'unwarranted'. The requirement of belief is subjective: did this particular defendant believe that his demand was justified *and* that his threats were proper and reasonable in the circumstances? If he knows that the menaces which he is threatening are improper (e.g., because they involve threats of illegal violence) then he may be guilty of blackmail, even though he is demanding something to which he is legally entitled.

With a view to gain or intent to cause loss
Section 34(2)(a) of the Theft Act 1968 defines the terms gain and loss only in terms of money or other property. Procuring sexual favours by threats cannot amount to blackmail, but may constitute an offence under the Sexual Offences Act 1956. In some cases, the threats may cause the victim to submit to intercourse without really consenting to it: that would be rape.

BURGLARY AND AGGRAVATED BURGLARY

Burglary

Section 9 of the Theft Act 1968 provides:

(1) A person may be guilty of burglary if—
   (a)   he enters building or part of a building as a trespasser and with intent to commit any such offence as is mentioned in sub-section 2 below; or
   (b)   having entered any building or any part of a building as a trespasser he steals or attempts to steal anything in the building or part of it or inflicts or attempts to inflict on any person therein any grievous bodily harm.
   (2)   The offences referred to in subs. (1) above are offences of stealing anything in the building or part of a building in question, of inflicting on any person therein any grievous bodily harm or raping any woman therein, and of doing unlawful criminal damage to the building or anything therein.

As can be seen from s. 9, there are two principal ways in which the offence of burglary can be committed:

(a)   under s. 9(1)(a), where D enters a building, or part of it, as a trespasser with the intention *at the time of entering* of committing theft, rape, criminal damage or grievous bodily harm; or
(b)   under s. (1)(b), where *having already entered* the building, or part of it, as a trespasser, he steals or inflicts grievous bodily harm, or attempts to do so. Note that rape and criminal damage are not relevant for the purposes of s. 9(1)(b).

Enters
An entry may be effected without stepping into the building. Putting an arm or a hand through a window in order to steal may constitute an 'entry' for the purposes of an offence of burglary. Climbing onto an outside window ledge would not be sufficient for a burglary (*Collins* [1972] 2 All ER 1105), but it may constitute an attempt to commit that offence.

Buildings and parts of buildings
The Theft Act does not define a building, except in so far as s. 9(3) states that buildings include inhabited vehicles or vessels such as (inhabited) caravans, houseboats or ships on which the crew or passengers live or sleep. Case law,

however, provides some guidance on this point and sheds and coldstores etc. have been classed as buildings. Buildings (other than vehicles or vessels) *need not* be inhabited in order to be the subject of a burglary, but burglary of a dwelling carries a heavier penalty than 'non domestic' burglary (a maximum of 14 years rather than 10).

There will be many situations where the defendant will be entitled to enter a building without any question of trespass but where he would become a trespasser if he entered some other part of the building, as where a hotel guest enters another guest's room looking for money to steal, or a where a shopper goes behind a counter in a store, looking for money (*Walkington* [1979] 2 All ER 71).

As a trespasser

The defendant must either know or at least be reckless to the fact that he is trespassing. Whether the defendant is actually a trespasser is a question of law. There will be many occasions where it will be obvious that the defendant is a trespasser, but one area of difficulty revolves around the situation where the accused has had the owner's permission to enter the building. If the defendant has had permission to enter he may nevertheless be a trespasser and burglar if he enters for some unauthorised and dishonest purpose of his own. In *Jones* [1976] 3 All ER 54, the occupier's son had permission to enter the house, but he did *not* have permission to come with a friend to steal his father's two televisions! On that occasion, he became a trespasser.

Mens rea

The defendant must either know or be reckless as to the fact that he is a trespasser at the moment of entry. This is seldom a problem. The more significant *mens rea* as far as s. 9(1)(a) is concerned is the 'ulterior intent'. He must, at the moment of entry, intend to steal or rape, etc., once he is inside the building. If so, he will be guilty of burglary, even if he never actually finds anything to steal, or is caught before he does so.

Aggravated burglary

Section 10 of the Theft Act 1968 states:

(1) A person is guilty of aggravated burglary if he commits any burglary and at that time has with him any firearm or imitation firearm, any weapon of offence, or any explosive; and for this purpose—
(a) 'Firearm' includes an airgun or air pistol, and 'imitation firearm' means anything which has the appearance of being a firearm, whether capable of being discharged or not; and
(b) 'Weapon of offence' means any article made or adapted for use for causing injury to or incapacitating a person or intended by the person having it with him for such use . . .

(2) A person guilty of aggravated burglary shall on conviction on indictment be liable to imprisonment for life.

Section 10 states that a person can be guilty of aggravated burglary if he commits any burglary *and at the time* has with him a weapon, etc. The phrase 'at the time' indicates that for burglary under s. 9(1)(a) the defendant must have the weapon, at the time of entry; whereas under s. 9(1)(b) he must have the weapon, etc., at the moment of stealing or of inflicting grievous bodily harm. If the burglar arms himself with a knife from the kitchen after entering the house with intent to steal, and subsequently stabs the householder in the chest when disturbed by her, the s. 9(1)(a) burglary is not aggravated, but the s. 9(1)(b) variant is.

TAKING CONVEYANCES

Unlawfully 'borrowing' or joy-riding in cars or other conveyances is not theft (although it may involve theft of any petrol consumed in the process). If abandoned afterwards, the vehicle will almost always be recovered by the police, and it is therefore impossible to prove any intent to permanently deprive the owner. Car *thieves* (or their accomplices) must in practice disguise the cars they steal with false registration plates and documents, or break them up for spares.

'Twocking' (TWOC = taking without owner's consent) and subsequent joy-riding is nevertheless a serious problem, and s. 12 of the Theft Act 1968 accordingly creates offences:

(a) of unlawfully taking a conveyance without the consent of the owner; and

(b) of knowingly driving or riding in a conveyance that has been so taken.

These are purely summary offences, usually punished with a fine or a sentence of community service; but a new s. 12A was later inserted into the Theft Act 1968. This provides far more serious penalties for cases in which the taking of a motor vehicle is followed by dangerous driving or damage to the vehicle or in which an accident occurs that causes personal injury or damage. A prison sentence is likely in such a case, and the offence can be tried on indictment, before a judge and jury.

DECEPTION OFFENCES

A number of 'deception' offences were created by the Theft Acts of 1968 and 1978. The Theft (Amendment) Act 1996 has recently added one more, which was inserted into the 1968 Act as s. 15A in order to cover loopholes in the old law.

Lies and deception

Deception has the same meaning in all deception offences, under both the 1968 Act and the 1978 Act. Under s. 15(4) of the Theft Act 1968, it is (partially) defined as:

> ... any deception (whether deliberate or reckless) by words or conduct as to fact or as to law, including a deception as to the present intentions of the person using the deception or any other person.

Lies, as such, are not required, and even where lies are told, they may not succeed in deceiving anyone. Deception occurs only when someone is induced to believe something which is not true. This, however, can be achieved by the telling of misleading half-truths, or by misleading conduct, as well as by lies. The deception must also relate to *existing* circumstances. A promise as to the future events will not suffice, unless it can be inferred that the victim is being deceived as to present facts as well. If, for example, D passes V a worthless cheque, the prosecution cannot obtain a conviction for a deception offence on the basis that 'D promised the cheque would be honoured when presented'. They may, however, obtain a conviction if they can prove a different kind of deception. If they can prove that D knew, even as he passed the cheque, that it was worthless and had no chance of being honoured (e.g., because he had already closed his bank account), then they may be able to prove a deception as to a *present* fact (*Gilmartin* [1983] 1 All ER 829). As s. 15(4) makes clear, the accused's intentions as to his future conduct may also be a present fact. If D promises to do something he has no intention of doing, that may be a deception, not as to the future, but as to his present state of mind.

In any deception offence, the prosecution must be able to prove a causal link between deception and the obtaining or procuring alleged. If, for example, D stays in a hotel for a week, and then impulsively practises a deception in order to escape without paying, this deception cannot be a case of obtaining property (food/drink) or services by deception, because these had *already* been obtained before the deception was practised. It would be different if it could be shown that there was an ongoing deception as to D's intent to pay. (D may in any case be guilty of making off without payment or of evading an existing liability by deception.)

Obtaining property by deception

Obtaining property by deception, contrary to s. 15 of the 1968 Act, is analogous in many ways to theft. It involves similar concepts of 'dishonesty' (*Ghosh* was in fact a s. 15 case), 'property belonging to another' and 'intent to permanently deprive'. The main difference is that the property must be obtained by deception rather than simply being 'appropriated'. The lawyers who drafted the Theft Act 1968 clearly intended that s. 15 would apply where victims were induced to part with their property by the use of trickery or deception, whilst theft would be charged where property was simply taken without consent. As we have seen, however, the decision of the House of Lords in *Gomez* effectively means that theft can now be charged, even where the victim is tricked into willingly handing over his property. Charges of obtaining property by deception can still be brought in such cases (and sometimes still are), but the prosecution will usually find it easier to bring a charge of theft, whether trickery was used or not. That way, they are spared the necessity of proving that the victim was in fact deceived or that he parted with the property because of that deception. An interesting side effect of the decision in *Gomez* is that many insurance policies, which used to provide cover against loss by theft (but not against loss by deception), now exclude cases of 'theft involving deception'!

The value of s. 15 as a weapon in the prosecution's armoury received a further setback when the House of Lords ruled in *Preddy* [1996] 3 All ER 481 that no s. 15 offences were committed by persons who had dishonestly tricked banks or building societies into advancing them substantial mortgage loans by lying as to the value of the properties against which the mortgage advances were secured, or by lying as to the creditworthiness or other personal circumstances of the borrowers. These deceptions had undoubtedly led to the obtaining of property, namely the loans which were credited to the defendants' bank accounts. In some cases the loans were credited to the accounts by electronic transfer; in other cases, by cheque or banker's draft. The problem was that no actual money changed hands, and the credit balances added to the defendants' accounts were not 'property belonging to another'. They were newly created for the benefit of the defendants and had never belonged to anyone else. They could not therefore be obtained by deception within the meaning of s. 15.

Obtaining a money transfer by deception

A flood of cases decided shortly after *Preddy* established that alternative charges could often be pressed against mortgage or loan fraudsters. Such charges included procuring the execution (i.e., the drawing or signing) of cheques by deception (Theft Act 1968, s. 20) and conspiracy to defraud. It was clear, however, that a new offence was needed to cover such frauds, and the Theft (Amendment) Act 1996 was passed to add a new s. 15A to the Theft Act 1968. This makes it an offence dishonestly and by deception to obtain a money transfer for oneself from another. A money transfer is defined as occurring wherever one bank or building society account is debited and another is credited in return. It makes no difference whether this transfer of funds is effected by cheque or by electronic means, and the penalties are the same as for offences under s. 15.

Obtaining services by deception

Where deception is used to obtain services, such as holidays, travel, professional advice, repairs to property or private medical care, charges of theft or of obtaining property by deception are rarely possible or apposite (although it may sometimes be possible to charge theft of travel tickets, etc.) Section 1 of the Theft Act 1978 therefore creates an offence of dishonestly obtaining services by deception. This is defined as deceiving another person into conferring a benefit by doing some act (e.g., repairing a car, or allowing someone to travel on a train) on the understanding that the service in question has been or will be paid for. Usually the victim is deceived into thinking that he has been or will be paid when the defendant has no intention of paying at all, but the offence may also be committed where the victim is deceived into thinking that the defendant (or the defendant's child, friend, etc.) is qualified to receive the service or that the defendant, etc., is entitled to a special discount. A person who travels on a train for half price by claiming to be the holder of a discount railcard would thus be guilty of this offence.

A charge under this section was for many years precluded in mortgage fraud cases by the case of *Halai* [1983] Crim LR 624, in which the Court of Appeal held that the provision of a mortgage advance was not a 'service' for the purposes of the Theft Act 1978, s. 1. *Halai* was widely condemned, but it was not expressly overruled in *Preddy*. Nevertheless the Court of Appeal has subsequently declared it to have been decided *per incuriam* (*Graham* [1997] Crim LR 340). In respect of offences committed on or after 18 December 1996, a new subsection (3) (inserted by the Theft (Amendment) Act 1996) makes it clear beyond argument that the obtaining of a loan is indeed an obtaining of services.

Evading a liability by deception

Section 2 of the 1978 Act covers various situations in which a deception is used in order dishonestly to evade some legally enforceable liability to make a payment. There are in fact three distinct offences, which to some extent overlap with each other. Section 2(1)(a) creates an offence of dishonestly securing the remission of all or part of an existing liability to make payment. Remission means release. If D purports to pay for petrol already supplied to him by tendering a stolen credit card, so that the supplier wrongly looks to the credit card company for payment, D may be guilty of this offence (*Jackson* [1983] Crim LR 617]. Of course, if he intended to do this when actually taking the petrol, he might also be guilty of theft or of obtaining property by deception.

Where D tells a false 'hard luck' story in order to induce his creditor V to forgo payment of an existing debt, he may be guilty of an offence under s. 2(1)(b); but that offence can also be committed where D dishonestly deceives V to defer (or wait for) repayment. In the latter case, however, it must be proved that D ultimately intended to avoid having to pay V at all. Telling a lie in order to gain a few more days before paying is not an offence under s. 2.

The third possible variant of the offence (the s. 2(1)(c) offence) may be committed where D tricks V into granting him exemption from liability to pay in the first place. In *Sibartie* [1983] Crim LR 470 D was convicted of this offence after 'flashing' an invalid season ticket at a London Transport ticket inspector (in the hope that he would not notice it was invalid). The Court of Appeal were untroubled by the suggestion that D's conduct might better have been described as falling under s. 2(1)(b). If the offences overlapped, the existence of an alternative charge was 'neither here nor there'.

MAKING OFF WITHOUT PAYMENT

Where a person knows that he is required to pay 'on the spot' for goods or services, but dishonestly makes off without so doing, it may not always be possible to prove that he is guilty of theft or of obtaining property or services by deception. If, for example, he originally intended to pay for a meal in a restaurant, and only decided not to once he had finished eating it, then he can hardly be guilty of stealing the food that is already in his stomach! Even if the court suspects that he never intended to pay, proving it may be another matter. The Theft Act 1978, s. 3, accordingly creates an offence of dishonestly making off without payment. An intent to avoid (not merely delay) payment must be proved in such cases. The offence covers both those who sneak away and those who push their way out or 'run for it'; but note that if you find you have lost your money or accidentally left your credit card at home, and cannot pay for the food you have already eaten or the petrol already in your car, this does not entitle the restaurateur or garage owner to have you arrested. As long as you do nothing dishonest (such as making off without paying) the only claim against you is a civil claim for debt, which you can offer to settle later. Nor can you be arrested for refusing to pay for food or drink that you did not order, or food that proved inedible. A genuine dispute over such matters is once again a civil matter, and the police will usually decline to become involved.

HANDLING STOLEN GOODS

The offence of handling stolen property is found in s. 22 of the Theft Act 1968. It can be committed in many different ways, but usually involves receiving stolen property, either directly from the thief, or indirectly, as where the thief sells or gives the stolen goods to X, who then sells or gives them to Y. In such a case, both X and Y may be guilty of handling. They will only be guilty, however, if they know or believe the property to be stolen, and receive it dishonestly.

The offence of handling can be committed, not only in respect of property which has been stolen (e.g., in a burglary or robbery) but also in respect of property obtained by blackmail or deception, or even in respect of the proceeds of the sale or disposal of the property originally stolen. If D steals gold bullion and sells it to E for £1,000,000, and F then 'launders' the £1,000,000 for D by disguising it as the profits of business at his casino, E and F are both guilty of handling. The cash is deemed to be stolen goods as soon as it is exchanged for the stolen gold. Money laundering and disposing of criminal proceeds may also involve offences under the Criminal Justice Act 1988.

A point that is often overlooked is that a dishonest receiver of property that has been stolen will almost invariably 'appropriate' property which still belongs to the original owner. In other words, he will also commit theft. If the police find D to be in possession of property stolen in a burglary a few weeks before, but cannot establish whether he was the burglar or a subsequent receiver, the answer is to charge him with theft (*Stapylton* v *O'Callaghan* [1973] 2 All ER 782).

Other forms of handling

Apart from cases of receiving, the offence of handling can sometimes be committed by disposing of or assisting in the disposal or realisation of the stolen goods. This typically means moving the property from one place to another or converting it from one form into another (*Forsyth* [1997] 2 Cr App R 299). It must be done for or on behalf of another person.

The goods must be proved to have been stolen

If there was no theft (or blackmail etc.) then there can be no offence of handling of the proceeds. In *Walters* v *Lunt* [1951] 2 All ER 645 a small boy came home with a tricycle he had taken from another child. His parents knew what he had done, but allowed him to keep it, and helped by hiding it in their house. They were charged with receiving stolen goods, but were acquitted because their son was too young to have committed theft (he was below the age of criminal responsibility). On the other hand the acquittal of the alleged thief does not necessarily prove that he was innocent or that the goods were never stolen, and it does not guarantee acquittal of an alleged handler.

Wrongful bank credits and stolen goods

Where a thief (A) pays stolen money (or its proceeds) into his bank account, a subsequent transfer of funds from that account to an account held by another person (B) cannot be classed as stolen goods. This is because no stolen money is actually transferred in such cases. A new credit balance may thereby be created in B's account, but in law this is an entirely different thing from the credit balance which previously represented the stolen money in A's account. It may represent the proceeds of A's original crime, but it has never done so in A's own hands, and cannot be classified as stolen goods.

A new section, s. 24A has therefore been added to the Theft Act 1968 by the Theft (Amendment) Act 1996. This creates an offence of dishonestly retaining a bank or building society credit which is derived from the proceeds of theft, blackmail, a s. 15A offence or stolen goods. If A pays stolen money into his account, and transfers the funds from that account to an account owned by B, the latter will commit a s. 24A offence if he dishonestly retains it, knowing or believing it to be derived from one or other of those offences.

CRIMINAL DAMAGE

One might imagine criminal damage and theft to be totally different offences involving totally different kinds of criminal behaviour. There is, however, some potential overlap between the two offences, as we shall see.

The basic offence of criminal damage, contrary to s. 1(1) of the Criminal Damage Act 1971, involves the intentional or reckless damage or destruction of property belonging to another person, without lawful excuse. Recklessness, in this context, still means *Caldwell* recklessness; and a person may therefore be guilty of criminal damage, even if it never occurred to him that such damage might result. If there is an obvious danger of any such property being damaged, failure to stop and consider that danger amounts to recklessness under *Caldwell*.

Minor cases of criminal damage are usually triable only summarily, but if damage is caused by fire, it is called arson and is punishable (in theory) by life imprisonment. In practice, however, a really heavy prison sentence would be reserved for cases of criminal damage or arson in which the offender intended to endanger life or was reckless as to the endangerment of life contrary to s. 1(2). Apart from carrying more severe penalties (including a real risk of a life sentence), criminal damage involving intent or recklessness as to the endangering of life differs from the basic offence in that it may be committed even against the defendant's own property. If, for example, you are so fed up with your rusty old car that you deliberately smash it to pieces, that is up to you; but if you decide to set fire to it, without even thinking about the danger that may be caused to others by exploding petrol tanks, etc., you may be guilty of a very serious offence, even if you are lucky and nobody is in fact injured or endangered after all. If deliberate criminal damage leads to the death of another person, that is likely to be charged as constructive manslaughter: as in *Goodfellow* (1986) 83 Cr App R 23, where the defendant hoped to get his family rehoused in a better council house by burning down the old one. Unfortunately, some of his family died in the fire, and he was convicted of manslaughter.

The link between theft and criminal damage is this: if criminal damage is committed dishonestly, with intent to *destroy* property belonging to another (as for example where joy-riders deliberately set fire to a car they have taken) this may amount to a dishonest appropriation of the car, with intent to permanently deprive the owner. Theft need not be committed for gain, and an act of criminal damage may therefore amount to theft as well.

Offences against property

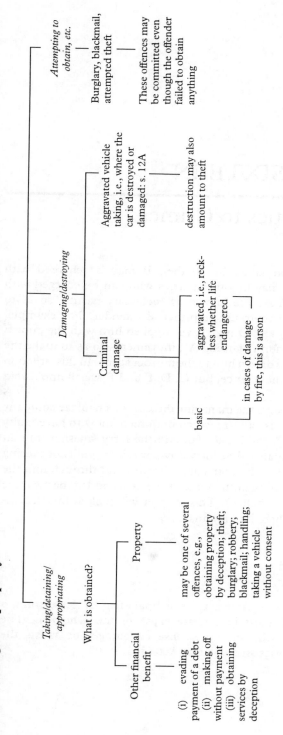

SIXTEEN

Parties to Crimes

If A is deliberately shot and killed by B, then B may be charged with A's murder. However, there may be other parties who can be charged with the murder as well as B. These are known as secondary parties, so as to distinguish them from the perpetrator or principal offender. For example, C may have encouraged B to kill; D may have supplied him with the gun; E may have given him information regarding A's movements so as to make the murder easier; and F may have driven him to the murder scene. In this situation B alone is the perpetrator of the offence, but C, D, E and F are all implicated in A's murder.

Another example might involve the managing director of a haulage company ordering one of his drivers to use a lorry which both men know to have faulty brakes. While on the journey, the brakes fail and the lorry smashes into an oncoming car, killing its occupants. The lorry driver would be guilty of causing death by dangerous driving, but the managing director, and through him the company itself, may well be guilty of the same crime as secondary parties (see *Robert Millar (Contractors) Ltd*, below). This chapter will look at the circumstances in which this kind of liability may arise.

Principals and accessories

The person who perpetrates the crime is the principal offender. A person is a perpetrator if his act is the most immediate cause of the *actus reus*. The secondary party is the one who in some sense encourages or assists the principal. Under the Accessories and Abettors Act 1861, s. 8:

Whosoever shall aid, abet, counsel or procure the commission of an indictable offence shall be liable to be tried and indicted as a principal offender.

This provision deals with the liability of accessories as far as indictable offences are concerned. There is a similar provision for summary offences, which can be found in the Magistrates' Courts Act 1980. As can be seen from s. 8 of the 1861 Act, secondary participation in a crime can take any one of the following forms, namely aiding, abetting, counselling or procuring the offence. The Act provides little by way of definitions of these words and it is therefore necessary to look at the case law on this subject.

Background to the law on secondary parties

Traditionally it was said that the words 'aiding' and 'abetting' covered situations in which the defendant was actually present at the scene, rendering assistance or encouragement. Such defendants used to be known as 'principals in the second degree'. Those who provided assistance but who were not actually present at the scene were referred to as 'accessories before the fact'. Persons who had rendered assistance to the offender after the crime had been committed were known as 'accessories after the fact'. The Criminal Law Act 1967 abolished these various categories, and the position today is that principals in the second degree and accessories before the fact are now classed together as secondary parties and may be jointly liable with the perpetrator of the crime. Those who would have been called accessories after the fact can now be charged with specific statutory offences of 'assisting offenders' (Criminal Law Act 1967, s. 4), or of 'concealing an arrestable offence' (s. 5). They are *not*, however, regarded as parties to the original offence, and will not be discussed further here.

The current position regarding secondary parties

According to the case of *Attorney-General's Reference (No. 1 of 1975)* [1975] 2 All ER 684, the words, 'aid, abet, counsel or procure' are all taken to have distinct meanings. However, the judges do not usually bother to differentiate between them. Indictments or charges may be framed in general terms. A defendant may be charged with aiding, abetting, counselling *and* procuring the offence, although he can hardly have done all four of those things! The prosecution do not have to establish the exact manner in which the defendant participated in the crime. It is enough for them to prove that the defendant was involved in the commission of the crime in some way. They do not have to establish exactly what the secondary party did, but merely prove that he was involved in its commission in some way. Indeed, the prosecution may sometimes be unable to prove which of two offenders was the perpetrator and which the secondary party. This does not matter, because s. 8 of the 1861 Act allows both to be charged as principal offenders. Both are, in any case, liable to exactly the same maximum punishment if convicted, and it is by no means unknown for secondary parties to receive heavier sentences than the perpetrator, especially if the latter is young and has been led astray by his more experienced accomplice.

Even though the courts do not seem to bother distinguishing between the various terms themselves, it is nevertheless worth noting what the general difference between them is supposed to be. 'Aiding' covers the situation where the secondary party provides some form of practical assistance, such as holding the victim while the principal offender stabs him. 'Abetting' seems to cover the situation where the secondary party encourages or instigates the commission of the offence. 'Counselling' is where the secondary party is not actually present at the scene, but advises on its commission or knowingly encourages the perpetrator. The word 'procuring', on the other hand, refers to acts which actually bring about or facilitate the commission of the offence. The essential thing which must be shown by the prosecution in a case of procurement is that the secondary party actually caused or brought about the commission of the offence. For example, A may procure B's offence of driving with excess alcohol by secretly lacing B's drinks with extra shots of vodka.

Mere inactivity or passive presence

Mere presence at the scene of the offence does not necessarily mean that a person will be an accessory. The established authority for this proposition is the case of *Coney* (1881) 8 QBD 534. The court in that case held that persons who simply stood and watched an illegal prize fight were not automatically abetting it. Hawkins J said that 'some active steps must be taken by word or action'. Thus in *Coney*, clapping encouragement or shouting for one of the parties could have been classed as abetting the illegal fight. A more modern example is *Bland* [1988] Crim LR 41, where the defendant was found not guilty as an accessory to the crime of unlawfully possessing drugs merely by continuing to share a room with the principal offender after he found out about the drugs. Furthermore, a secret resolve to help a friend in a crime (such as an illegal fight) if it went against him, would not be sufficient (*Allan* [1963] 2 All ER 897).

Joint principals

What if D and E both shoot the victim? The answer is that both can be charged as joint principals in wounding or (if the victim dies) murder. As previously explained, the prosecution would not have to prove who fired the fatal shot.

Joint enterprise

Another head of liability which must be looked at on the subject of secondary parties is that of the joint enterprise. A joint enterprise is where two or more persons agree to carry out a common purpose, and consequently share liability for crimes committed in the course of it. The same principles as apply to aiding and abetting apply to joint enterprise liability. When the parties carry out their common agreement, each encourages the other to commit the crime. An example of a joint enterprise would be where A and B agree to carry out an armed robbery, and during the course of that robbery A shoots dead a security guard. Here, A may be charged with murder as a principal offender. In addition, B may be charged as a secondary party to that murder, on the ground that A and B had agreed to carry out a joint criminal venture, and consequently B will be made liable for crimes committed during the execution of that agreement. B need not have shouted 'Kill him' or provided the gun with which the guard was shot. Mere agreement to take part in the robbery, knowing that loaded guns are being carried and may be used, provides sufficient evidence of support or encouragement for their use.

Will the secondary party be liable for all crimes committed on the venture?
A secondary party will not be liable for all crimes committed during a joint venture. His liability for crimes committed during it will arise only:

(a)   if the principal's act was within the scope of their agreement; or
(b)   if it was within the scope of what the secondary party envisaged *might* happen.

Some examples may help to illustrate this point. Let us assume that two parties set out to burgle a house, and that one of them kills the occupier. The other party will clearly be guilty of murder if it was part of their agreement to kill (or even to kill 'if necessary'). Even if there was no express agreement to kill, however, the secondary party may still be guilty of murder if he foresaw or envisaged that the killing *might* be a realistic possibility (*Chan Wing-siu* [1984] 3 All ER 877; *Hyde* [1990] 3 All ER 892; *Powell* [1997] 4 All ER 545). For example, if the perpetrator is 'Mad Rick', a man who likes violence and whom his accomplice knows is carrying a gun, then if Rick kills with it, his accomplice will be guilty too. Even if Rick had promised not to use the gun, that would not absolve the accomplice from liability if he knew only too well that Rick could not be trusted to keep his word. In the notorious case of *Craig and Bentley* (unreported, 1952), Derek Bentley was controversially hanged for the shooting of a police officer. The shot was fired by his young accomplice, Craig, when they were caught committing a burglary; but Bentley knew that Craig had a loaded gun, and he was possibly guilty on the basis of joint enterprise, whether or not he shouted (as was alleged) 'Let him have it, Chris!' But did he ever realise that Craig might do such a thing? His conviction was quashed as 'unsafe' in 1998, 45 years after his death.

Care may have to be taken in working out the liability of the secondary party. For example, suppose A and B agree to carry out a bank raid and agree to take along a loaded gun simply for the purpose of frightening people and for shooting out the security cameras. While in the bank, A nervously waves the gun at the cashier to make her hand over the money, and accidentally pulls the trigger, killing the cashier. A would be guilty of constructive manslaughter; and B would also be guilty of that offence, because it was part of their agreement to take a loaded gun with them on the job, and carrying a loaded gun on a robbery is an unlawful and dangerous act (see Chapter 15). If, however, A deliberately *and unexpectedly* turns to the cashier and shoots her, then B would not be liable for the death at all, because this deliberate killing was neither agreed to nor foreseen by B, neither did it result (as in the previous example) from the mere carrying of the gun. The perpetrator has *deliberately* gone beyond what was agreed and has acted on a frolic of his own. In *Davies* v *Director of Public Prosecutions* [1954] AC 378, Lord Simmonds LC illustrated this type of problem with the following example:

> I can see no reason why, if half a dozen boys fight another crowd, and one of them produces a knife and stabs one of the opponents to death, all the rest of his group should be treated as accomplices in the use of a knife and the infliction of mortal injury by that means, unless there is evidence that the rest intended or at least contemplated an attack with a knife by one of the number . . .

This rule was recently applied in *Perman* [1996] 1 Cr App R 24. A man was shot dead during a robbery. The robber who shot him was convicted of murder. His accomplice was at first convicted of manslaughter, after the judge had told the jury that they could convict him of that lesser offence on the basis that he had agreed to the carrying of a gun, *even if he did not know the gun would be loaded*. The Court of Appeal disagreed. The accomplice should not have been found guilty of homicide at all unless it was proved that he knew (or at least suspected) that his accomplice's gun was real and loaded. If, on the other hand, he knew the gunman might use a loaded gun to kill with, both would be guilty of murder.

In *Powell* [1997] 4 All ER 545, the House of Lords confirmed that a secondary party cannot ordinarily be guilty of murder if his accomplice used a different and more deadly form of attack than anything contemplated by the secondary party, but they added (*obiter*) that use by the accomplice of an unexpected *but no less deadly* form of attack would *not* absolve the secondary party. A more deadly form of attack will usually involve the use of a more lethal weapon, but not necessarily. It depends in part on how the weapons are to be used. Using a gun to carry out a 'kneecapping' is a less deadly form of assault than the use of a knife to cut the victim's throat, even though in other circumstances a gun might be considered the more lethal weapon. If A was only expecting to take part in a kneecapping, he will not be guilty of murder if, to his complete surprise, his accomplice B executes the victim by slitting his throat with a knife or shooting him in the head.

Accessories who cannot be principal offenders

A person may be convicted of encouraging or assisting in the commission of a crime which he could not commit as a principal offender. For example, a woman cannot be convicted of rape as a principal offender, but she can be convicted as an accessory to that crime if she helps to lure or restrain victims who are raped by her male companion.

Can a secondary party be convicted of a more serious offence than the perpetrator?

The perpetrator of an offence may possess a different *mens rea* from that of the secondary party. For example, the perpetrator may inflict grievous bodily harm (GBH) on his victim without intending to do anything more than cause slight injury, whereas the accomplice, who urges the perpetrator on, may fully intend that GBH should be caused. In other words, the accomplice may be the only one to possess the *mens rea* for the more serious offence of causing GBH with intent. If the victim later dies, the accomplice may likewise be the only one to possess the *mens rea* for murder, rather than manslaughter. Can the accomplice in either case be convicted of a more serious offence than the perpetrator? The answer is to be found in the House of Lords case of *Howe* [1987] 1 All ER 771, where Lord Mackay LC stated, in relation to a homicide offence:

> ... where a person has been killed and that result is the result intended by another participant, the mere fact that the actual killer may be convicted only of the reduced charge of manslaughter for some reason special to himself does not, in my opinion in any way, result in a compulsory reduction for the other participant.

The same principle must equally apply to GBH. Note also that s. 2 of the Homicide Act 1957 specifically provides that the successful use by one accused of a defence of diminished responsibility under that Act has no effect on the liability of other parties implicated in the relevant killing, who may accordingly remain guilty of murder. (The defence of diminished responsibility is discussed in Chapter 18.)

Withdrawal

A secondary party may seek to deny liability for an offence by claiming that he withdrew from the enterprise before the offence took place. Whether such a withdrawal will be effective will vary with the circumstances of the case. In *Becerra* (1975) 62 Cr App R 212, the appellant and some other men agreed to commit a burglary (and to use a knife on anyone who interrupted them). When they were in fact disturbed by the deceased during the burglary, the appellant said, 'There's a bloke coming. Let's go' and jumped out of the window. His friends stayed to confront the deceased and stabbed him to death. The Court of Appeal held that the appellant (who had earlier provided the knife) had not carried out an effective withdrawal and he was therefore convicted as an accessory to the murder. It would appear that the only effective withdrawal in those circumstances would be a physical intervention by the secondary party to stop the principal offender. In *Perman* [1996] 1 Cr App R 24, the Court of Appeal stated that 'It is questionable whether once the criminal activity contemplated in a joint enterprise has commenced, it is possible for a party to a joint enterprise to withdraw'.

In contrast, two cases which were particularly favourable to the secondary party on the issue of withdrawal were *Grundy* [1977] Crim LR 543 and *Whitefield* (1983) 79 Cr App R 36. In both these cases, the secondary party gave information to the principal offenders which would make burglary of particular premises much easier. In both cases the secondary parties had a change of heart and withdrew some time before the burglaries took place. The courts in these cases held that this was evidence of an effective withdrawal and there was no need for the secondary party to have notified the authorities or taken any other steps to try to prevent the offences taking place. It is questionable whether the courts would adopt such a lenient approach today, although it should be noted that in each case the secondary party withdrew before the criminal enterprise was put into effect.

Mens rea in relation to accessories and joint enterprises

A secondary party must intend to encourage, advise or assist the perpetrator of the offence before he can be liable. Agreement to take part in a joint enterprise may be construed as encouragement, but the accidental provision of assistance will not suffice.

As with other crimes, the defendant's motive in assisting, advising or encouraging is irrelevant. This principle can be seen in *National Coal Board* v *Gamble* [1958] 3 All ER 203. In this case, an employee of the NCB was a weighbridge operator. He told a driver that his lorry was overloaded. Driving an overloaded vehicle is an offence. The driver said that he was prepared to take the risk of being caught, and the operator gave him a weighbridge ticket without which the driver could not have left the pit. The question was whether the operator was a secondary party to the principal offence of driving an overloaded lorry. Devlin J said:

> ... an indifference to the result of the crime does not of itself negative abetting. If one man deliberately sells to another a gun to be used for murdering a third, he may be indifferent about whether the third man lives or dies and interested only in the cash profit to be made out of the sale, but he can still be an aider and abettor. To hold otherwise would be to negative the rule that *mens rea* is a matter of intent only and does not depend on desire or motive.

Knowledge of the circumstances constituting the offence
It was said in the case of *Johnson* v *Youden* [1950] 1 All ER 300 that:

> Before a person can be convicted of aiding and abetting the commission of an offence he must at least know the essential matters which constitute that offence. He need not actually know that an offence has been committed, because he may not know that the facts constitute an offence and ignorance of the law is not a defence.

It follows that a person cannot be liable as a secondary party if he is unaware of the circumstances which constitute the offence. This can be seen from the case of *Ferguson* v *Weaving* [1951] 1 KB 814, where the licensee of a pub was charged with aiding and abetting customers to commit the offence of consuming intoxicating liquor on licensed premises after permitted hours. She did not know, however, that this was happening. The court held that the licensee could not be convicted if she was unaware that customers were committing the principal offence.

Where, however, A sells B a gun, and is not sure whether it is for use in a robbery or for a killing, how can A be said to have the requisite *mens rea* for either? The law gets around this problem by ruling that A may be guilty of any offence committed with his help (i.e., in this case with the gun) as long as it is one of those types of offences that A contemplated B might commit (*Maxwell* v *Director of Public Prosecutions for Northern Ireland* (1979) 68 Cr App R 128). If, however, B commits a less obvious crime that A never considered at all (e.g., by hijacking an aircraft), A may escape liability for that unforeseen offence.

Vicarious liability

In the law of tort, employers are routinely held liable for the negligence of their employees. If, for example, a lorry driver's negligence causes damage to my car, I would be more likely to sue the haulage firm that employs him, rather than the driver himself, if only because the employers usually arrange for insurance against such eventualities.

In criminal law, the general rule is that employers are *not* liable for the acts of their employees. If, for example, the lorry driver was guilty of careless or dangerous driving under the Road Traffic Act 1988, it would not follow that his employers would be guilty of that offence. The concept of vicarious liability (liability for the act of another person) was largely rejected from criminal law following the case of *Huggins* (1730) 2 Strange 883, where the warden of the old Fleet Prison was held not to be liable for a murder committed by one of the jailers without his knowledge. Lord Raymond CJ said:

> In criminal cases the principal is not to be answerable for the act of the deputy, as he is in civil cases; they must each answer for their own acts and stand or fall by their own behaviour . . .

It is clear, however, that Huggins would have been guilty on normal principles of secondary liability, if he had helped or encouraged the acts of his subordinate. (See *Robert Millar (Contractors) Ltd*, below.)

Vicarious criminal liability does exist, but depends on the crime being one in which it can be said that one person's act is also that of another. The classic example of this can be seen in crimes of 'using', 'selling' and 'supplying'. When a driver uses a defective, overloaded, unlicensed or uninsured vehicle on the employer's business, the employer is regarded, through the driver, as using it too. (Note that these are 'using' offences, not 'driving ones'.) Both may be guilty of an offence under the Road Traffic Act 1988 (*Green* v *Burnett* [1955] 1 QB 78). When a shop assistant sells falsely-described goods, the shop owner, through the assistant, sells those goods. Both may therefore be guilty of an offence under the Trade Descriptions Act 1968 (cf. *Coppen* v *Moore* [1898] 2 QB 306, in which a shop assistant sold American ham as 'Scotch ham', thereby making his employer guilty of an offence under a predecessor of the 1968 Act).

Mens rea and delegation
The principle that certain acts of an employee are also attributed to the employer is sufficient to secure the conviction of the employer where (as in the examples above) the offence is one of strict liability. But what if it requires *mens rea*? The answer, generally, is that if *mens rea* is required and the employer has no idea what the employee has done, then the employer cannot be vicariously liable. In licensing cases, however, the courts have developed a 'delegation principle'. If the holder of a justices' licence (a drinks licence, gaming licence, etc.) chooses not to attend to the business he has been entrusted to perform, and leaves it in the hands of a manager or delegate, then if the manager knowingly commits a licensing offence in the course of his job, the licensee will be deemed to know of it too, and may accordingly be convicted of it. In *Allen* v *Whitehead* [1930] 1 KB 211, the licensee allowed a manager to run his premises, and the manager knowingly permitted prostitutes to meet and tout for business there. The licensee was accordingly held to be guilty of 'knowingly

permitting' that practice. He did not really know of it, but his manager did, and the delegation principle therefore applied.

The liability of companies

Registered companies are regarded in law as artificial legal persons. They can own property, hire employees and make contracts. They act, of course, through human agents. They are managed by directors and other senior executives, who represent the mind or brains of the company. And their employees sell goods, drive lorries, etc. If those employees commit 'using' or 'selling' offences, for which an individual employer would incur strict and vicarious liability, the corporate employer can incur strict and vicarious liability in exactly the same way. But what of mainstream *mens rea* offences such as fraud or manslaughter? Can a company ever commit that kind of offence? How could it ever be said to possess the *mens rea* required?

The answer is that a company can act through its human agents, and possess whatever *mens rea* its human directors possess. In *Robert Millar (Contractors) Ltd* [1970] 2 QB 74, the defendant company and its managing director, Millar, were each convicted of counselling and procuring the crime of causing death by dangerous driving. Millar had ordered one of the company's drivers to drive a lorry which they both knew to be a death-trap. Six people died in a horrific motorway crash as a result. The driver pleaded guilty; Millar was sent to prison as a secondary party and the company (to which Millar's guilty mind was imputed) was held to be a secondary party as well. It was punished by a large fine. Similarly, in *OLL Ltd* (unreported, 8 December 1994), a company and its managing director were each convicted of manslaughter following the deaths of six teenagers in the Lyme Bay canoe disaster. As in *Millar*, the company was heavily fined and the managing director imprisoned. Convictions of companies appear to be more easily secured where there is just one managing director who is clearly the culprit and who clearly represents the mind of the company. Where large companies are implicated in disasters of this kind (e.g., P&O Ferries, in the Zeebrugge disaster) it often seems to be almost impossible to find where within the organisation the blame really lies, and everyone (including the company itself) escapes liability as a result.

Parties to a crime: principal and secondary offenders

A perpetrator or *principal* offender is a person whose act is the most immediate cause of the *actus reus*. There may be two or more joint perpetrators.

A *secondary* party is one who in some sense encourages or assists the principal. See the Accessories and Abettors Act 1861, s. 8. Secondary parties may be divided into four types, although for prosecution purposes the precise distinction does not have to be made.

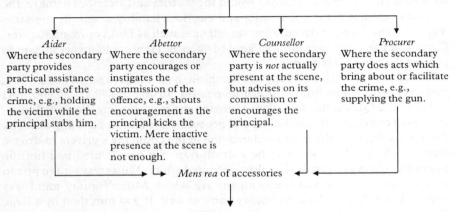

Aider
Where the secondary party provides practical assistance at the scene of the crime, e.g., holding the victim while the principal stabs him.

Abettor
Where the secondary party encourages or instigates the commission of the offence, e.g., shouts encouragement as the principal kicks the victim. Mere inactive presence at the scene is not enough.

Counsellor
Where the secondary party is *not* actually present at the scene, but advises on its commission or encourages the principal.

Procurer
Where the secondary party does acts which bring about or facilitate the crime, e.g., supplying the gun.

Mens rea of accessories

(i)   a secondary party must intend to encourage, advise, or assist the perpetrator of the offence; but

(ii)   need not know exactly which offence will be committed (see *Maxwell* v *DPP*).

Parties to a crime: joint enterprises

A joint enterprise occurs where two or more persons agree to carry out a *common purpose* and consequently share liability for crimes committed in the course of it, e.g., A and B agree to carry out an armed robbery and A shoots dead a security guard.

↓

A *secondary* party in a joint venture will not automatically be held liable for all crimes committed during the course of it. He will be liable for crimes committed during the joint venture only if

or

the principal's act was within the scope of their agreement, e.g., if A and B agree to burgle a house and A kills the occupier, B will also be guilty of murder if it was part of their agreement to kill.

it was within the scope of what the secondary party envisaged might happen, e.g., if A and B agree to burgle a house and A kills the occupier, B may be guilty of the murder even if there was no express agreement, *provided* B foresaw that such a killing was a realistic probability.

SEVENTEEN

Incitement, Conspiracy and Attempt

The criminal law deals not only with persons who actually commit substantive offences, but also with those who attempt to commit such offences, incite others to commit them or conspire with others to commit them. For example, if A tries to persuade B to murder C, this constitutes incitement to murder. If they agree and proceed to plan the commission of the murder, then they may be guilty of conspiracy to murder. If they then try to kill C, but fail, they may be guilty of attempted murder. The following chapter will look at the elements which must be proved before the offences of incitement, conspiracy or attempt can be said to have been committed. They are referred to as 'inchoate' (i.e. incomplete) offences.

Incitement

Incitement is primarily a common law offence. Statutory provisions relating to incitement can be found in s. 4 of the Offences Against the Persons Act 1861, which deals with incitement to murder, and in s. 19 of the Misuse of Drugs Act 1971, which deals with incitement to commit offences under that Act, but these provisions are based on the same principles as the common law offence, and in practice they add nothing to the common law.

The offence of incitement is one of soliciting, persuading, or encouraging another to commit a crime. It can take place by means of words or acts. It does not have to be directed towards a particular person, but can be directed towards people in general. It need not be successful. The offence of incitement may be committed, even if the person incited ignores every word, or goes straight to the police. Indeed, if that person goes ahead and commits the crime, the inciter will himself be guilty of the substantive offence as a secondary party (see Chapter 16), and would therefore be charged with that offence, rather than with mere incitement.

A person cannot, however, be guilty of incitement to commit a crime where the circumstances are such that the offence was impossible to commit. For example, there would be no offence of incitement where A encourages B to steal a non-existent work of art. Similarly, A could not be convicted of inciting B to handle stolen goods where the goods concerned have never in fact been stolen. Furthermore, the person incited by the offender must be viewed by the defendant as a potential criminal and not merely as an innocent agent. If, for example, the defendant tries to trick a delivery driver into unwittingly delivering a parcel bomb, he cannot be said to be inciting the latter to commit a crime.

Mens rea

The defendant must intend that, as a result of his persuasion, another person would commit an act amounting to a criminal offence. Because this is only a *mens rea* element, it does not matter if the other person refuses to be persuaded.

Conspiracy

There are common law offences of conspiracy and also a statutory offence of conspiracy, which was created by s. 1 of the Criminal Law Act 1977. Statutory conspiracy requires an agreement between two or more persons to carry out a course of action that will necessarily involve the commission of a crime. The original idea behind the drafting of that provision was that it would supersede all existing common law variants of conspiracy. In the end, however, uncertainty as to the possible limitations of the new statutory offence resulted in the 'temporary' retention of some common law variants alongside it. Twenty years later, they still co-exist alongside each other.

Common law conspiracy

A conspiracy at common law was originally defined as an agreement between two or more persons to perform an unlawful act *or* to commit a lawful act by unlawful means. Conspiracy at common law was not confined to agreements to commit crimes. For example, if two persons agreed to trespass on another's private property then they could be charged with conspiracy to trespass, even though trespassing on private property is nothing more than a tort. Conspiracy charges were even used to prevent the formation of trade unions, lest these encouraged the unlawful breaking of contracts of employment.

New forms of common law conspiracy were recognised, even in modern times. In *Shaw* v *Director of Public Prosecutions* [1961] 2 All ER 446, the House of Lords established the offence of 'conspiracy to corrupt public morals' and the later case of *Knuller* v *Director of Public Prosecutions* [1972] 2 All ER 898 added the offence of 'conspiracy to outrage public decency'. Shaw, for example, was convicted as a result of the publication of a book called the '*Ladies Directory*' which listed the names and addresses of prostitutes and the services they could provide. Defendants could be charged with such conspiracies if they entered into agreements with other persons, even though commission of the activity agreed upon would not necessarily have been a crime in itself. Offences of conspiracy to corrupt public morals or outrage public decency still exist today, but no such charges have been brought in the last 20 years, and it is now fairly clear that any such conspiracies would have to be charged as statutory conspiracies under the Criminal Law Act 1977 rather than as conspiracies at common law.

Conspiracy to defraud remains an important common law offence. This offence remains useful in the fight against crime, as it may cover a number of situations in which agreements to carry out fraudulent activities would not have involved the commission of specific criminal offences. In particular, it may be used to deal with financial swindles which jeopardise other people's financial interests (as for example by depriving them of future profits) but without actually stealing any of their property. In *Scott* v *Metropolitan Police Commissioner* [1974] 3 All ER 1032, the defendant agreed with the employees of certain cinemas to 'borrow' films for a short period of time and make copies of them without the consent or knowledge of the copyright owners. The copies were then sold privately resulting in a profit for the conspirators at the expense of profits which might otherwise have been secured by the copyright owners. Scott and his friends could not be charged with theft or with conspiracy to steal, because there had been no intention to permanently deprive the cinema owners of the films; nor had the films been obtained by means of a deception against the cinema owner; and yet the scam had cost the owners a great deal of money. The defendants were therefore charged with conspiracy to defraud. Viscount Dilhorne explained:

> An agreement by two or more persons by dishonesty to deprive a person of something which is his or to which he is or would or might be entitled or an agreement by two or more to injure some proprietary right of his, suffices to constitute the offence of conspiracy to defraud.

Statutory conspiracy
Section 1 of the Criminal Law Act 1977 established a new offence of statutory conspiracy and swept away all variants of common law conspiracy except for conspiracy to defraud (and just possibly conspiracy to corrupt public morals or outrage public decency). The judges had given the law of conspiracy a breadth of interpretation which alarmed many people, notably by turning some torts into criminal offences of conspiracy wherever two or more parties had agreed to commit them. Consequently, the 1977 Act attempted to confine the law of conspiracy within fixed and certain limits.

As a result of the Act, the vast majority of conspiracies must now be charged as statutory conspiracies under s. 1 of the Act. The conspirators must agree that a course of action will be pursued that will, if carried out, involve the commission of a substantive (i.e. complete) criminal offence by at least one of the conspirators. Mere negotiations are not sufficient; but once agreement has been reached, the conspiracy has been committed, even if it is never put into operation. For that reason, it is a popular charge against terrorists or robbers who have been arrested before getting the chance to carry out their plans. The charges in such cases may typically be 'conspiracy to cause explosions' or 'conspiracy to rob'.

Conspiracy to defraud and statutory conspiracy

There is a considerable overlap between statutory conspiracy and conspiracy to defraud and the question arises as to which charge to use and when. There are three possibilities.

(a) If the parties have agreed to commit a specific criminal offence, such as theft or rape, then the defendants may be charged with statutory conspiracy.

(b) It may be that the parties have conspired to commit a criminal offence, but it may nevertheless be unclear which specific criminal offence is involved. An example is provided by the practice of mortgage frauds, e.g., where a false valuation figure is put on a house or property against which the fraudsters are seeking to borrow money on a mortgage. Such a practice is obviously fraudulent, but which specific criminal offence would be involved? There are several options. Is it obtaining a money transfer by deception? Obtaining services by deception? Theft? When using statutory conspiracy, the prosecution have to specify which substantive offence was being planned. They would have to choose from any one of the above three possible charges and hope that the court agrees with their choice. If the court were to disagree, the prosecution for statutory conspiracy would have to fail. In such cases it may therefore be much safer for the prosecution to charge common law conspiracy to defraud. Whatever other offence might have been involved, the plan clearly involved defrauding the bank or building society into lending more money than they would otherwise have done.

(c) Another situation in which charges of common law conspiracy to defraud may be useful is where there has undoubtedly been an agreement to defraud someone, but where it is unclear whether the action was a substantive criminal offence at all. For example, suppose that waiters in a restaurant sell their own food or drink to the customers, who no doubt assume it is being sold to them by the restaurant owners. In those circumstances, the owners have been defrauded of the profits they might otherwise have made but have the waiters committed any substantive criminal offence? They have not stolen any of the employers' property, after all. If they have not committed any specific criminal offence, they cannot be charged with statutory conspiracy. In contrast, a charge of common law conspiracy to defraud may still be appropriate.

Attempt

The law on attempts is governed by the Criminal Attempts Act 1981. As far as this Act is concerned, only indictable offences can be the object of a criminal attempt. One cannot, for example, have an offence of attempting to assault a constable acting in the execution of his duty, because this particular type of assault is triable summarily only.

Actus reus

To commit a crime of attempt, the defendant must do an act which is 'more than merely preparatory' to the commission of the offence. If the defence dispute this, it becomes a question of fact for the jury to decide upon. This can be a tricky task and judges have tried to convey the idea by the use of phrases such as 'was the accused on the job?' or 'had he embarked on the job proper?' The principle can be illustrated by the cases of *Jones* [1990] 3 All ER 886 and *Campbell* [1991] Crim LR 268. Jones was convicted of the attempted murder of another man (F) who had taken up with Jones's former girlfriend. Jones acquired a shotgun, sawed off the end of the barrel, disguised himself and waited in ambush at the place where F regularly dropped off his daughter for school. He jumped into the rear seat of F's car and pointed the gun at F; but F managed to grab it and escape with it from the car. The prosecution failed to establish whether Jones had his finger on the trigger of the gun when he pointed it at F, but the Court of Appeal held that the jury had still been entitled to convict him of attempted murder. Lord Taylor CJ stated:

> The question for the judge in the present case was whether there was evidence from which a reasonable jury, properly directed, could conclude that the appellant had done acts which were more than merely preparatory. Clearly his actions in obtaining the gun, in shortening it, in loading it, in putting on his disguise and going to the school could only be regarded as preparatory acts. But, in our judgment, once he had got into the car, taken out the loaded gun and pointed it at the victim with the intention of killing him, there was sufficient evidence for the consideration of the jury on the charge of attempted murder. It was a matter for them to decide whether they were sure those acts were more than merely preparatory. In our judgment, the judge was right to allow the case to go to the jury.

In contrast, the defendant in *Campbell* armed and disguised himself with a view to committing a robbery in a post office, but ultimately did nothing more than skulk around outside it. He never drew his weapon, entered the post office or demanded any money. His conviction for attempted robbery was therefore quashed on appeal. It was held that the trial judge ought to have directed the jury to acquit him, because there was no evidence of anything going beyond mere preparation.

Impossibility

It is now possible to be guilty of attempting (or indeed of conspiring) to commit crimes which are, in the circumstances, impossible to commit, provided that the defendant believes in facts which, if true, would make the crime possible. If X puts poison in Y's drink, intending to kill her, and only later discovers that she has died already, X can still be guilty of attempted murder. The defendant must be judged on the facts as he believed them to be. If, for example, he is caught trying to smuggle what he clearly believes to have been heroin through customs control, and it turns out that his suppliers have tricked him into buying a harmless vegetable powder, he cannot be guilty of importing heroin, but he can be guilty of attempting to do so (cf. *Shivpuri* [1986] 2 All ER 334). Convictions in such cases are possible because of s. 1(2) of the Criminal Attempts Act 1981. Prior to that legislation, it was a defence to any charge of attempt or conspiracy to show that the crime attempted or conspired at could never have been committed.

Mens rea

Intent is the essence of any crime of attempt. It must always be a specific intent to commit the crime attempted. Thus, although murder may be committed by someone who only intended to cause GBH, attempted murder requires proof of nothing less than an intent to kill. In *Whybrow* (1951) 35 Cr App R 141, the defendant connected a mains electric current to the metal soap dish on his wife's bath. She was electrocuted, but not killed. The Court of Criminal Appeal held that the trial judge had been mistaken in telling the jury that they could convict the defendant of attempted murder if he had intended only GBH. At the same time, they upheld his conviction on the basis that he must have intended to kill her.

Recklessness will not ordinarily suffice in crimes of attempt, but it may suffice in respect of background circumstances. A man who tries to have sexual intercourse with a woman, being reckless whether she is consenting to it, may be guilty of attempted rape. If he had succeeded, it would have been rape (*Khan* [1990] 2 All ER 783).

Inchoate offences

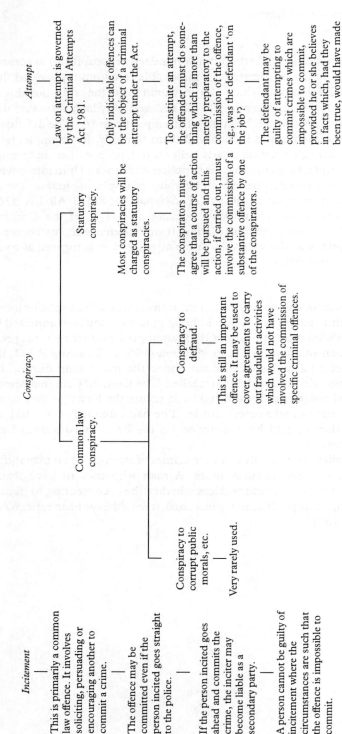

Incitement

This is primarily a common law offence. It involves soliciting, persuading or encouraging another to commit a crime.

The offence may be committed even if the person incited goes straight to the police.

If the person incited goes ahead and commits the crime, the inciter may become liable as a secondary party.

A person cannot be guilty of incitement where the circumstances are such that the offence is impossible to commit.

Conspiracy

Common law conspiracy.

Conspiracy to corrupt public morals, etc.

Very rarely used.

Conspiracy to defraud.

This is still an important offence. It may be used to cover agreements to carry out fraudulent activities which would not have involved the commission of specific criminal offences.

Statutory conspiracy.

Most conspiracies will be charged as statutory conspiracies.

The conspirators must agree that a course of action will be pursued and this action, if carried out, must involve the commission of a substantive offence by one of the conspirators.

Attempt

Law on attempt is governed by the Criminal Attempts Act 1981.

Only indictable offences can be the object of a criminal attempt under the Act.

To constitute an attempt, the offender must do something which is more than merely preparatory to the commission of the offence, e.g., was the defendant 'on the job'?

The defendant may be guilty of attempting to commit crimes which are impossible to commit, provided he or she believes in facts which, had they been true, would have made the crime possible.

EIGHTEEN

Incapacity and Defences

The subject of general defences to criminal charges is wide-ranging and includes both 'choice of evils' defences and defences based on incapacity. The principal defences are:

- intoxication;
- mistake;
- self-defence and crime-prevention;
- duress;
- necessity (or duress of circumstances);
- infancy;
- insanity and automatism.

The partial defence of diminished responsibility, which reduces murder to manslaughter, is also considered here, because of its relationship with insanity. (Other partial defences to homicide, such as provocation, are covered in Chapter 13.)

These are all defences of 'confession and avoidance'. In other words, the defendant says, 'Yes I did it, *but . . .*'. Some of these defences, such as the use of force to prevent crime, might be described as being based on justification. The defendant claims that he was right to have acted as he did. Others, such as duress, might be characterised as being based on excuse. The defendant regrets what he did, but claims that, in the circumstances, he should be excused for it. A third type of defence (including insanity) involves lack of capacity or awareness.

We are not concerned here with total denials of involvement, such as alibi defences or defences of mistaken identity. If the defendant had nothing to do with the crime, then he is, of course, innocent; but in such cases the defendant does not need to establish any special legal defence in order to secure an acquittal.

Intoxication

Intoxication may be caused either by alcohol or by drugs. The taking of alcohol or drugs may have a number of different effects upon a person. Alcohol is itself a drug, which can suppress a person's normal inhibitions. It can also impair judgment, and thus affect the degree to which a person can foresee the consequences of his actions. Lastly, it can affect the ability to do things safely (such as driving). The abuse of alcohol and drugs leads to the commission of a high proportion of crime in Britain, and the courts are understandably reluctant to allow defendants to get off, merely because they were intoxicated at the time.

Basic legal principles

(a)   In some cases intoxication may be the actual basis of liability, as, for example, in crimes of drink-driving or of being drunk and disorderly.

(b)   Evidence of intoxication may be an aggravating factor in other offences. If, for example, a person is charged with racing a car on the highway, and there is evidence that he was also drunk at the time, this may be viewed as an aggravating feature for sentencing purposes, because it makes that person's behaviour even more dangerous to other road users.

(c)   Intoxication is never *in itself* a defence to a criminal charge. In *Kingston* [1994] Crim LR 846, the House of Lords made it clear that even if intoxication is 'involuntary' (i.e., brought about by consumption of a drink that someone else has laced with drugs, or by an unfortunate reaction to prescribed medicines) it is not enough for the accused simply to deny that he would have committed the crime if sober. If the accused knew what he was doing and still *deliberately* committed the offence because the drink or drugs had relaxed his usual inhibitions, then he is guilty of that offence. The fact that someone else laced (or 'spiked') the accused's drink may be a matter of mitigation when it comes to sentencing, but that is all.

(d)   Evidence of intoxication in defence of a criminal charge may, however, be useful if the accused denies that he ever meant to commit the crime. In other words, it may enable the defence to show an absence of *mens rea*. In *Lipman* [1970] 1 QB 152, the accused experienced a 'bad trip' after taking LSD, and while hallucinating he mistakenly killed his girlfriend, believing her to be a monstrous snake. In *Moloney* [1985] 1 AC 905, the accused blew off his step-father's head during a drunken competition involving the loading of shotguns. In each of these cases, the killings would inevitably have been construed as deliberate murder but for the evidence of intoxication which made the accuseds' explanations plausible or credible. They were mistakes which a sober person could not have made, but which an intoxicated or drunken one could. Neither accused intended to kill or do serious injury, and so neither was guilty of murder.

Limitations on the use of intoxication evidence

Lipman and Moloney (above) were each convicted, ultimately, of manslaughter rather than murder. This tells us something about the limitations of self-induced intoxication as a defence to a criminal charge. It could work as a defence to a charge of murder, but could not prevent a conviction for manslaughter. Why not?

Murder is one of those offences for which guilt depends on proof of a 'specific intent'. The accused cannot be guilty of murder unless he intended to kill or cause GBH. A drunken person may still intend to kill another (in which case he is guilty of murder), but if that person is so drunk that (like Moloney) he scarcely knows what he is doing, evidence of that drunkenness can obviously help to show that it was not murder but an accident. In contrast, playing with loaded shotguns is stupid at the best of times, and even more stupid when you have been drinking. What better example of gross criminal negligence could there be, than a drunken game involving the high-speed loading and firing of shotguns?

In fact, there is another reason why Moloney could not escape a conviction for manslaughter. As a matter of policy, the courts never allow self-induced intoxication to be used as a defence to *any* offence which does not depend on proof of 'specific intent'. In respect of crimes involving recklessness, negligence or maliciousness (which are confusingly referred to as crimes of 'basic intent') judges must tell juries to ignore any defence based on evidence of self-induced intoxication. This is known as the *Majewski* rule, after the case of *Director of Public Prosecutions* v *Majewski* [1977] AC 443, in which a man who was high on a cocktail of drink and drugs committed a series of assaults on police officers who tried to restrain him. He claimed that he was too drunk to know what he was doing, but the House of Lords held that since the assault charges depended on recklessness rather than on any specific intent, his intoxication was no defence to any of them. This rule was later confirmed in *Caldwell* [1982] AC 341, where it was held that the defendant's drunkenness did not prevent him from being reckless as to whether lives might be endangered by his act of starting a fire in a hotel.

Basic intent and specific intent

Crimes of specific intent include murder, robbery, burglary, wounding or causing GBH with intent to do GBH, and any crime of attempt. Some form of intent must be proved in every case. Burglary, for example, requires a specific intent to steal.

Basic intent crimes include rape, manslaughter, criminal damage, malicious wounding, and assault or battery. In none of these cases need any specific intent be proved. Recklessness, negligence or maliciousness will be sufficient. In rape, for example, it suffices that the man is reckless as to whether his victim consents to sexual intercourse.

Voluntary and involuntary intoxication

Generally speaking, involuntary intoxication may result either from a bad reaction to prescribed medication, or from the spiking of one's drink (as where a 'friend' slips a drug into your coffee). A person who takes too many of his medicinal tablets, without realising that they may affect his behaviour, is also likely to be adjudged 'involuntarily' intoxicated, even if he has been rather careless (*Hardie* [1985] 1 WLR 64). But the defendant who claims not to have realised how strong his beer was cannot hope to be considered anything other than voluntarily intoxicated (*Allen* [1988] Crim LR 698).

Note, however, that the distinction between voluntary and involuntary intoxication matters only where the alleged offence is one of recklessness, negligence or maliciousness. If the crime is one of specific intent (like murder) it does not matter whether the intoxication is self-induced or not. The only question is, 'Did the accused intend to do it; or was he too drunk to realise?'

Drunken mistake

In *O'Grady* [1987] 3 WLR 321, the accused, while drunk, killed another man, supposedly in the belief that this other man was trying to kill him. Not surprisingly, the Court of Appeal held that this drunken mistake was no defence to a charge of manslaughter. More controversially, however, they added that it would not even have been a defence to murder, had that been the charge. This last remark was not necessary for the actual decision in that case, and was therefore an *obiter dictum*. As explained in Chapter 3, an *obiter dictum* is not binding on other courts. Most commentators take the view that this particular *obiter dictum* was seriously wrong, because murder is a crime of specific intent, and evidence of intoxication should always be relevant in such cases.

Self-defence, lawful arrest and the prevention of crime

Any person is permitted to use such force as is reasonable in the circumstances:

   (a)   to protect himself or other persons from attack;
   (b)   to prevent the commission of a criminal offence; or
   (c)   to arrest or prevent the escape of an offender, suspected offender or escaped prisoner.

Reasonable force may sometimes mean lethal force, if that is what is needed in the circumstances. To take an extreme example, the SAS used a battery of heavy machine guns in an ambush at Loughgall in 1987, in which eight heavily armed IRA terrorists died in a hail of bullets. This was considered to be 'reasonable force' against terrorists who were themselves armed with automatic weapons. In contrast, the use of lethal force to stop a teenage joy-rider was categorised as murder in *Clegg* [1995] Crim LR 418.

Self-defence (or the defence of others) remains governed by common law principles. The use of force to prevent crime or effect arrest, etc., is governed by s. 3 of the Criminal Law Act 1967. In practice, however, the principles applicable are broadly similar in each type of case. There will be some cases in which the defendant will raise both kinds of defence together. If, for example, a policeman is attacked by a suspect he is attempting to arrest, and injures that suspect in an attempt to restrain him, he may argue that the force used was necessary both to defend himself and to effect a lawful arrest.

In any event, the force used must be reasonable in the circumstances, or at least in the light of the circumstances that the defendant *believes* to exist. If, for example, the defendant beats up an elderly woman whom he suspects of attempting to steal from his shop, he cannot be allowed to plead a defence under s. 3 (*Owino* [1995] Crim LR 743). Neither would a police officer who shoots and kills an unarmed suspect ordinarily have any defence (cf. *Clegg*, above). If, however, the officer honestly believed that the suspect was threatening him with a gun, it would be different. Even if the officer was wrong (e.g., because the gun was a replica or toy) he would be judged on the facts as he honestly believed them to be (*Williams* (1984) 78 Cr App R 276). In *Williams*, the accused tried to save another man from what he took to be an unlawful attack. He misunderstood the situation, however, and ended up assaulting an innocent man who had just lawfully arrested a robber. Given that Williams's mistake was a genuine one, he was not guilty of any offence. It did not matter that his mistake was arguably a foolish one.

Although the force used must be reasonable, the courts do not expect a person who has been attacked to 'weigh to a nicety the exact measure of his necessary action' (*Shannon* (1980) 71 Cr App R 192). Allowance must be made, in other words, both for mistakes and for some measure of understand-able over-reaction in the heat of the moment.

Duress and necessity

Duress
Necessity and duress are very closely related. As far as duress is concerned, D argues that he committed the alleged crime only because someone threatened him (or another person) with death or serious injury if he did not commit it. The argument is that committing the crime was the lesser of two evils. For most purposes, this is a complete defence. The bank clerk who fills a sack with notes

and passes it to the robber who is menacing her with a shotgun would never in practice be charged with aiding the robber, but if charged would certainly be able to plead duress as a defence. The only major limitations are:

(a)   It is not possible to plead duress as a defence to a charge of murder (*Howe* [1987] 1 All ER 771) or attempted murder (*Gotts* [1992] 1 All ER 832). It was once thought that a secondary party might be able to raise a defence of duress on a charge of murder, whilst a principal offender would not (*Director of Public Prosecutions for Northern Ireland* v *Lynch* [1975] 1 All ER 913) but this distinction was rejected by the House of Lords in *Howe*. The refusal of the law to allow such a defence to be advanced in a murder case, even where (as in *Lynch*) the accused has merely acted as a driver for the getaway car, seems quite unreasonably harsh. It does not even allow the concession of a manslaughter verdict. The person threatened may choose a hero's death or risk life imprisonment as a murderer, but it seems there is no middle way.

(b)   Such heroism is not required where other offences are involved, but the defendant is nevertheless expected to display reasonable courage and resolve. It is not enough that he gave in to unrealistic or absurd threats because he is a fool and/or a coward (*Graham* [1982] 1 All ER 801).

(c)   The defendant cannot plead duress if he has knowingly and willingly become involved with a violent criminal gang or terrorist organisation which exercises such duress over any of its members who step out of line (*Sharp* [1987] 3 All ER 103). If the law were otherwise, IRA terrorists might escape conviction for bomb outrages by claiming that they were obeying orders from their commanders.

(d)   It is usually said that the defendant can only rely on duress if he had no opportunity to escape and/or seek police protection. This assumes, however, that the police would be able to protect him. In *Hudson* [1971] 2 All ER 244, two young women were called as witnesses at a criminal trial, but changed their initial stories and failed to give the evidence expected of them. It appears that they had been intimidated by threats from 'friends' of the accused, one of whom unnerved them by watching the trial from the public gallery. The women were then charged with perjury, and the trial judge refused to let them plead duress because they could easily have sought police protection. Quashing their convictions, the Court of Appeal held that the duress issue should have been properly explored. If the police could not guarantee to protect the women after the trial, the defence of duress was still open to them.

If the defence of duress is raised by the defendant, and supported by evidence, it is for the prosecution to prove that defence is untrue. If the court or jury is left in doubt, the defendant should be given the benefit of that doubt.

What if the defendant wrongly believes that his life is being threatened? Such a scenario is more likely to occur in cases of alleged necessity than in one of duress, but the principles are essentially the same. Most authorities on this point, including *Howe* and *Graham*, appear to require that the mistake must be a reasonable one, in order to support either kind of defence, but in the recent case of *Director of Public Prosecutions* v *Rogers* [1998] Crim LR 202, the Divisional Court has confused matters by stating that a genuine but foolish mistake will suffice. Most commentators regard *Rogers* to be incorrect on this point, but it is not a binding precedent in any event, because that ruling was strictly *obiter* in light of the court's ultimate ruling on the facts of the case, namely, that the defendant's story of mistaken duress was one which no reasonable magistrates could have believed.

Necessity

With necessity on the other hand, the defendant claims to have acted so as to avoid a greater evil posed by dangers arising from the circumstances in which he or another is placed. The defendant is threatened by circumstances, rather than by another person. Hence the alternative title, 'duress of circumstances'. During the Zeebruge ferry disaster in 1987, survivors were making their way to safety from within the vessel when one of them froze with fear on the escape ladder, thereby preventing those behind him from escaping. The water was rapidly rising behind them, and the man who froze on the ladder was eventually pushed off it, thereby giving the others the chance of survival. No charges were ever brought. The question, however, is this: assuming the man who was pushed off the ladder then died, would those who pushed him have been able to rely on a defence of necessity to a charge of murder?

The question of whether a general defence of necessity exists under English law has been the subject of heated debate. For many years, the judges seemed to deny that any such general defence existed. For example, Lord Denning MR stated in the case of *Buckoke* v *GLC* [1971] 2 All ER 254:

> A driver of a fire engine with ladders approaches the traffic lights. He sees 200 yards down the road a blazing house with a man at an upstairs window in extreme peril. The road is clear in all directions. At that moment the lights turn red. Is the driver to wait for 60 seconds, or more, for the lights to turn to green? If the driver waits for that time, the man's life will be lost. I suggested to both counsel that the driver might be excused in crossing the lights to save the man. He might have the defence of necessity. Both counsel denied it. They would not allow him any defence in law. The circumstances went to mitigation, they said, and did not take away his guilt. If counsel are correct — and I accept that they are — nevertheless such a man should not be prosecuted. He should be congratulated.

This can hardly be regarded as a satisfactory approach. Indeed, regulations were subsequently passed specifically permitting emergency vehicles to cross red lights where necessary. More recent authority clearly recognises a limited defence of necessity, albeit one that goes under the title 'duress of circumstances'.

In *Martin* [1989] 1 All ER 652, Simon Brown J summarised what he understood to be the relevant principles:

... first, English law does, in extreme circumstances, recognise a defence of necessity. Most commonly this defence arises as duress, that is pressure on the accused's will from the wrongful threats or violence of another. Equally however it can arise from objective dangers threatening the accused or others. Arising thus it is conveniently called 'duress of circumstances'.

Duress of circumstances would therefore appear to be subject to the same limiting factors as govern the defence of duress. If so, it cannot be available on a charge of murder or attempted murder. However, there are many who would strongly argue that, under certain circumstances, the killing of an innocent man may be necessary and even commendable. Professor J. C. Smith in *Justification and Excuse in the Criminal Law* illustrates this point by reference to the incident from the Zeebruge ferry disaster (above). Assuming that pushing off the man who froze to the ladder ultimately saved the lives of many others, could it not be said that the man who pushed him off did absolutely the right thing? Should not the law promote the net saving of human life? As Professor Smith argues: 'The law has lost touch with reality if it condemns as murder conduct which right thinking people regard as praiseworthy.'

A much older maritime necessity case is that of *Dudley and Stephens* (1884) 14 QBD 273, in which the survivors of a sunken vessel found themselves adrift on the ocean. Since they were starving, the captain and the mate killed and ate the cabin boy. Rejecting what was in effect a plea of necessity, the court held that they were guilty of murder. Since necessity is no defence to murder, this is consistent with modern views on the law, but another reason given was that there was no reason why the boy should have died, rather than one of the men, except that he was weak and defenceless. No lots had been drawn. Even if necessity had been recognised as a defence to murder, it is doubtful whether Dudley and Stephens could have relied upon it.

Mistake

Little need be said here about mistake as a defence. If a person's mistake or misunderstanding prevents him having the *mens rea* required for a particular offence, it is a defence. In the notorious case of *Director of Public Prosecutions* v *Morgan* [1976] AC 182, the House of Lords held that since the offence of raping a woman can only be committed by a man who either knows that the woman does not consent to sexual intercourse, or who is reckless whether she consents or not, a man who mistakenly assumes a woman to be consenting cannot be guilty of rape. They added, however, that a jury are unlikely to believe a defence of mistake if that supposed mistake was so unreasonable as to be implausible.

In some cases, even a mistake of law may be relevant. If the defendant takes property to which he genuinely believes he is legally entitled, he cannot be guilty of theft, even if the defendant's understanding of the law is wrong and he is not entitled to it at all. This is because theft requires dishonesty, and s. 2 of the Theft Act 1968 states that a taking of property cannot be considered dishonest if the person taking it does so in the belief that he is legally entitled to it.

(As for mistaken self-defence, see p. 245 above.)

Infancy

A child under the age of ten years is deemed incapable of committing a criminal offence. This is a statutory rule, contained in s. 50 of the Children and Young Persons Act 1933. This means not only that a child under this age cannot be charged with or convicted of an offence, but also that an adult cannot be guilty of aiding and abetting the child's 'offence', or of dishonestly handling goods allegedly stolen by the child. In *Walters* v *Lunt* [1951] 2 All ER 645, little Richard Lunt took another child's tricycle. His parents decided that he should be allowed to keep it. The prosecutor realised that he could not charge the child, but assumed that he would have no difficulty in securing the conviction of the parents for handling. He was wrong. The child was too young to commit theft, so the trike was not stolen by him. The parents could probably have been convicted on a charge of theft (or larceny as it was then called), but they were never charged with that offence.

A child aged between ten and 14 years can be found guilty of an offence, but only if the prosecution can prove that the child knew that what he was doing was seriously wrong (not just naughty). This moral awareness is sometimes called 'mischievous discretion' or '*doli capax*'. One might think that any normal ten-year-old should know that burglary or criminal damage is seriously wrong, but the House of Lords has confirmed, in *Curry* v *Director of Public Prosecutions* [1995] Crim LR 801, that this cannot be assumed. Moral awareness must be proved, for example by evidence of cunning attempts to evade detection, or by evidence of previous warnings from the police or courts. The Crime and Disorder Act 1998 contains provisions abolishing the need for proof of mischievous discretion.

A child who cannot be convicted of a crime, but who is clearly out of parental control, may be placed in local authority care under the Children Act 1989, although experience shows that this does not necessarily prevent the child repeating his delinquent behaviour.

Insanity, automatism and unfitness to plead

Insanity
At common law, according to rules laid down in the case of *M'Naghten* (1843) 10 Cl & F 200, a person may be considered to have a defence of insanity if it is

proved by medical evidence that, at the time of the alleged offence, he suffered from a 'disease of the mind' producing such a 'defect of reason' as to prevent him from knowing the 'nature and quality of his act'. In other words, such a person would be considered insane if he suffered from an illness that:

(a)   disturbed his mind to such an extent that he did not know what he was doing; or
(b)   prevented him from realising that what he was doing was wrong.

This is not a test of insanity in any medical sense: it is more a test of criminal responsibility. Some 'madmen', such as the 'Yorkshire Ripper' (*Sutcliffe* (unreported, 1982)), are not considered to be legally insane. Sutcliffe, for example, 'heard voices' and believed he had a divine mission to kill prostitutes; but he knew exactly what he was doing when he killed his victims, *and* he knew that it was illegal. That precluded any defence of insanity as a matter of law. In contrast, an epileptic who injures another person while suffering a fit *would* be regarded as insane under the *M'Naghten* rules. *Sullivan* [1984] AC 156 was such a case, although the defendant eventually chose to plead guilty to assault, rather than rely upon a defence of insanity.

Unconscious or uncontrolled behaviour can give rise to a defence of insanity only if it is caused by some kind of illness or disease. This may be a kind of psychosis (such as paranoia). It may alternatively be a physical illness affecting the mind (such as a brain tumour), or it may be brain damage following an accident or injury. The behaviour may even be caused by epilepsy, as in *Sullivan* (above); or by hyperglycaemia (high blood-sugar levels arising from diabetes) as in *Hennessy* [1989] 2 All ER 9. Sleep-walking would not ordinarily be regarded as insanity, but a person who attacks others while sleepwalking may be very disturbed, and may be regarded as insane (*Burgess* [1991] QB 92).

Non-insane automatism
In contrast, if a person causes damage or injury while concussed, or while suffering from some externally induced illness, such as hypoglycaemia (*low* blood-sugar levels caused, *not* by diabetes, but by a reaction to an incorrectly taken dose of insulin), he will not be regarded as insane at the time. The correct defence would be one of automatism (*Quick* [1973] QB 910). An unexpected stroke or heart attack, leading to a road accident, would by the same token provide the affected driver with a defence of automatism, rather than one of insanity. Note, however, that under the *Majewski* rule (above), automatism caused by drug or alcohol abuse can only be a defence to a crime which requires proof of specific intent.

Importance of the distinction between insanity and automatism
The distinction between insanity and non-insane automatism is very important. Both may be defences to criminal charges, but whereas automatism leads

to outright acquittal, insanity leads to a special verdict of 'not guilty by reason of insanity'. This verdict used to require the judge to commit the 'acquitted' defendant to an indefinite period of detention in a secure mental hospital, such as Broadmoor. Faced with this, many defendants who might otherwise have pleaded insanity pleaded guilty instead. (Only a total madman, it was said, would ever choose to rely on a defence of insanity!) Under the Criminal Procedure (Insanity and Unfitness to Plead) Act 1991, however, the courts now have far more discretion in disposing of such cases. If the defendant is not a menace to society (and was not charged with murder) a supervision and treatment order (or even an absolute discharge) might suffice. If the charge was murder, the killer must still be sent to a secure hospital.

Unfitness to plead
A successful defence of insanity must be distinguished from a case in which the defendant is found incapable of understanding or answering the charges against him (although the end result may be broadly the same). If a jury find that D did the act alleged, but there is expert medical evidence proving that he is incapable of instructing his lawyers or explaining his defence, he may be dealt with as if he had been found not guilty by reason of insanity.

Do not assume that the person who is found unfit to plead must equally have been insane at the time of committing the offence. If, for example, A kills B in a robbery, and is later shot in the head by a police marksman, suffering severe brain damage, it may be clear that he was perfectly sane at the time of the robbery, but it may equally be clear that he is now unfit to stand trial. If the defendant merely claims to be suffering from amnesia, and says that he cannot remember the incident which gave rise to the prosecution, that does not mean that he is unfit to stand trial. The question is whether the defendant understands, not whether he remembers. In *Podola* [1960] 1 QB 325 the accused was charged with the murder of a policeman. He claimed to remember nothing, but he was found fit to plead, convicted and hanged.

Diminished responsibility

Given the difficulty of establishing a defence of insanity, a need was felt for a defence that would make some allowance for lesser degrees of mental impairment. This was especially true in cases of alleged murder, where the prescribed penalty was formerly death by hanging. The statutory defence of diminished responsibility was accordingly introduced by s. 2 of the Homicide Act 1957. It is not a complete defence, but if successful it reduces murder to manslaughter. Unlike insanity, it has no application to any other crimes, and in contrast to insanity, it requires proof only of impaired (or diminished) responsibility, not a total absence of responsibility. The accused may, for example, know what he is doing and know it is illegal; but if the accused suffers from some mental disorder that makes it hard for him to resist his homicidal urges, he may be able to plead the s. 2 defence. In *Byrne* [1960] 2 QB 396, the accused attacked and mutilated his victim as a result of perverted and psychopathic sexual urges which he found almost irresistible. This was held to be a proper basis for a defence of diminished responsibility.

There must be proof of some abnormality of mind, and it must be caused by disease, injury, arrested or retarded development or some other inherent cause. A mentally abnormal person who kills, not because of the mental abnormality, but because of a loss of temper brought on by alcohol or drug abuse, cannot plead diminished responsibility (*Egan* [1993] Crim LR 131). On the other hand, severe depression may suffice.

There is an element of value-judgment in cases of diminished responsibility. Medical experts may tell the jury whether the accused is or is not mentally abnormal; but unless the evidence of abnormality is quite overwhelming, it is for the jury to decide whether any abnormality of mind that is proved was sufficient to have 'substantially impaired his mental responsibility for his acts' as required by s. 2(1). In *Sutcliffe*, for example, there was clear and uncontradicted evidence of the accused's abnormality, but only the jury could decide whether this was enough substantially to impair his responsibility for the many terrible killings he had committed. The jury convicted him of murder: a harsh verdict, but a valid one in the circumstances.

If a killer is found to be guilty of manslaughter by reason of diminished responsibility, he may be sentenced to imprisonment (sometimes for life) or the judge may make a hospital order, or the killer may even, in some cases, be freed with some lenient non-custodial sentence.

Mentally disordered offenders generally

If a person is charged with something other than murder, and is not proved to have been insane at the time, then he can have no defence based on mental disorder. Many convicted criminals are mentally disordered. The disorder may be a valid basis for making a hospital or supervision order, rather than sending the offender to prison, but sentencing considerations of this kind lie outside the scope of this book.

General Defences

Intoxication through drink or drugs	Insanity and automatism	Diminished responsibility	Mistake	Prevention of crime or self-defence	Duress and necessity
Intoxication is not in itself a defence to any offence.	Under the *M'Naghten* rules, a defendant may be adjudged insane if he suffers from a disease of the mind (which may mean anything from a psychosis to a condition such as epilepsy) which at the time of the offence either (a) disturbed his mind to such an extent that he did not know what he was doing; or (b) prevented him from realising that it was wrong. It leads to a special insanity verdict, not outright acquittal.	This is not a complete defence. It applies only to a charge of murder. If accepted, it reduces a charge from murder to manslaughter.	If a person's mistake prevents him from forming the requisite *mens rea*, it is a defence.	Any person is permitted to use such force as is reasonable (a) to protect himself or others from attack; (b) to prevent the commission of a criminal offence; (c) to arrest or prevent the escape of an offender.	Duress can be used by the defendant where he commits a crime because he or another was threatened with death or serious injury by a third party.
Evidence of intoxication may, however, suggest that the defendant did not intend or foresee the consequences of his act. It may suggest that he had no *mens rea*.		Unlike insanity, which requires a total absence of responsibility, diminished responsibility requires only proof of impaired responsibility. For example, the defendant knows what he is doing is illegal but his mental disorder makes it hard for him to resist his homicidal urges.	Drunken mistake: *O'Grady* suggests that a drunken mistake would not be a defence to murder, i.e., a specific intent crime. This is contrary to the general rules on intoxication. *O'Grady* is generally thought by commentators to be wrong.	Category (a) is governed by common law principles. Categories (b) and (c) are governed by s. 3 of the Criminal Law Act 1967. There is little difference between the common law and s. 3. in practice.	Necessity (or duress of circumstances) can be used by the defendant where he has committed a crime so as to avoid the greater evils or dangers arising from the circumstances in which he or another is placed.
The courts will not always allow a defence based on evidence of intoxication. If the crime does not require any 'specific intent' on the part of the defendant, and he was intoxicated through his own choice or fault, the court will not make any allowance for the fact that he was drunk.	Unconscious behaviour resulting from temporary conditions, such as concussion, may give rise to a defence of non-insane automatism. This entitles the defendant to a complete defence, assuming he was not to blame for getting into such condition (e.g., through drug abuse).	In order for this defence to succeed, the defendant must (a) prove abnormality of mind and (b) it must be caused by injury, disease or retarded development. For example, severe clinical depression might suffice.			Neither duress nor necessity can be defences to murder or attempted murder.

PART THREE

Introduction to the Law of Contract

Contracts may be defined as voluntary agreements or bargains which give rise to legally enforceable obligations on those individuals or corporations who are party to them. The law of contract identifies and governs such agreements. Not all agreements give rise to legally enforceable obligations, but it is the function of contract law to determine which agreements are legally enforceable and which are not. The law also regulates the making, content and performance of legally binding agreements and determines what remedies may be available when contractual obligations are broken.

The same basic principles underlie all contracts, from simple everyday bargains which may be agreed informally by word of mouth, to formal written contracts which may be signed and exchanged in the presence of the parties' lawyers. Some types of contract, such as those for the sale or leasing of houses or land, involve additional rules and formalities, which may be of crucial importance to their operation and enforceability. Additional rules are also found in the law governing employment contracts, loan or credit agreements and contracts for the sale of goods; but it must be emphasised that these rules are built onto, and presuppose the existence of, the basic principles of contract. A general knowledge of these basic principles is thus essential to anyone who is seeking to understand more advanced forms of commercial law or conveyancing.

The law of contract has primarily developed through case law, and many of today's contractual principles were first expounded in cases dating from the eighteenth and nineteenth centuries. The predominant prevailing view at that time was that parties should be freely able to enter into agreements with each other as equals, and that such agreements should be subject to as little judicial interference as possible. This was known as the principle of 'freedom of contract'. The courts at that time were not unduly concerned if one party agreed to harsh or unfair terms within a contract. They took the view that parties to contracts were free agents and should be left to look after their own interests. One illustration of that philosophy can be seen in the old maxim, '*caveat emptor*' (let the buyer beware). This, however, was often an unrealistic approach, because in many cases the parties are not equals. Consumers or tenants, for example, may not be in any position to bargain as equals with major retailers or powerful landlords, and may not even know how to look after their own best interests. As a result, the twentieth century has witnessed the decline of the doctrine of freedom of contract, and has instead seen increased statutory intervention to regulate specific areas of contract law. An example is provided by the Unfair Contract Terms Act 1977, which may in certain circumstances invalidate express contractual terms. The courts themselves have also become more concerned with the genuineness of agreements reached between parties of unequal status, and are more ready to intervene in cases where it appears that parties have been coerced into unfairly prejudicial bargains (see Chapter 25).

Chapters 19 to 31 of this book will look at the general rules governing the law of contract and these will be followed in Chapters 32 to 35 with a look at some of the statutory encroachments made into the law of contract in order to protect weaker parties, one of whom is the individual consumer. It will be seen, for example, that many inroads have been made into the principle of *caveat emptor*. The unwary buyer (particularly where he is a consumer) may well have a remedy in the courts if the goods or services he pays for turn out to be shoddy or substandard.

NINETEEN

The Formation of a Contract

The essential elements of a contract

There are three elements which must always be present before a contract can be said to have been concluded. These are:

(a) agreement;
(b) consideration; and
(c) an intention to create legal relations.

The need for agreement clearly lies right at the heart of the concept of a contract. How indeed could a bargain be struck between two or more parties, if they never agree as to what this supposed bargain may be? Consideration is a less obvious element; but it is important to understand that the law of contract is concerned with enforcing bargains, rather than gratuitous promises, and the essence of any bargain is that something is given or promised in exchange for something else. As for the need for an intention to create legal relations, this means that bargains are not legally enforceable, unless the parties at least appear to have intended that they should be. The mother who tells her son that he can watch *Match of the Day* if he tidies his bedroom may indeed be striking a bargain with him, but would surely not intend it to be a legally enforceable contract.

Formal and informal contracts

Formal written contracts are not ordinarily essential. Some types of contract do indeed require a written or printed agreement, signed by the parties. This is true, for example, of contracts for the sale or disposal of interests in land (Law of Property (Miscellaneous Provisions) Act 1989, s. 2) and of certain types of consumer credit agreement, which are governed by the Consumer Credit Act 1974. Most contracts, however, require no such formalities. If very large sums of money are involved, it is likely that the parties will instruct lawyers and prepare formal documentation, if only to ensure that there is no room for subsequent argument as to what exactly was agreed; but there may still be no legal requirement for such formality. As far as the law is concerned, a £10m contract can be agreed by the parties in a brief telephone call, without formalities or independent witnesses.

This chapter will consider the meaning of agreement in contracts. Consideration and intention to create legal relations are discussed in Chapters 20 and 21.

AGREEMENT

Before a legally binding contract can come into existence, the contracting parties must at least appear to reach an agreement or meeting of minds (or a *consensus ad idem*, as it is sometimes known). When determining whether there has been such an agreement, however, the court is not actually concerned with what was in the minds of the parties at the time of contracting; instead, it adopts an objective approach. In other words, it studies the words and actions of the parties to the contract, and asks whether it would appear, looking at all that was said and done, that the parties reached an agreement. As Lord Denning MR stated in *Storer* v *Manchester City Council* [1974] 3 All ER 824, 'In contracts, you do not look into the actual intent in a man's mind. You look at what he said and did. A contract is formed when there is, to all outward appearances, a contract.'

This was emphaised more recently by the Court of Appeal in *G Percy Trentham Ltd* v *Archital Luxfer* [1993] 1 Lloyds Rep 25. It would be unfair on other parties, said the Court, if a party's 'subjective expectations and unexpressed mental reservations' should be allowed to prevail over his actual words and deeds. The relevant yardstick must be the 'reasonable expectations of sensible businessmen'.

Offer and acceptance

One might think that the task of determining whether parties have reached an agreement would be a relatively straightforward one, but this is not always the case. Even in relatively simple contracts, it can sometimes be difficult to determine whether a real agreement has been concluded between the parties and (if so) what exactly they have agreed to. The traditional approach taken by the courts is to examine all the circumstances of the case and categorise the parties' conduct into stages to see:

(a)   whether one of the parties has made an offer; and if so,
(b)   whether that offer has been accepted by the other party.

This is almost always a sound method for ascertaining the formation of an agreement, and it is widely adopted by the judges, but according to the Court of Appeal in *Trentham* v *Archital Luxfer*, there may be cases in which contracts come into existence 'during performance' even if they cannot be precisely analysed in terms of offer and acceptance.

OFFER AND INVITATIONS TO TREAT

An offer can be defined as a promise to enter into a contract on a particular set of terms, with the intention (or at least the apparent intention) that it shall become binding as soon as it is accepted by the person to whom it is addressed (*Treitel's Law of Contract*). The essential ingredient of an offer is the intention with which the promise is apparently made. The maker (or offeror) must at least appear to intend that he should be bound by his promise as soon as it is accepted by the other party (the offeree). There must be no need for further bargaining in order to resolve the terms of the agreement. 'I will sell you my car' cannot be an offer, because no price has yet been mentioned. In contrast, 'I will sell you my car for £1,000, cash' may be a valid offer. An offer can be made either orally or in writing, and it can be made to an individual, to a group of people or even to the entire world, as in *Carlill* v *Carbolic Smoke Ball Company* [1893] 1 QB 256 (below).

An offer must always be distinguished from what is classed as an 'invitation to treat'. An invitation to treat is simply one stage in the bargaining process; it is a statement made with the intention of encouraging or moving towards a contractual agreement. 'Make me an offer' is the classic form of invitation to treat. It invites other parties to make an offer, but does not guarantee that any such offer will be accepted.

During the negotiating process, much discussion may take place, and it may sometimes be hard to determine whether a particular statement was intended as an offer or merely as an invitation to treat. One must consider whether the statement suggested a willingness to be bound as soon as the other party accepted. Two closely related cases are traditionally cited as illustrations of the difficulties of distinguishing between an offer and an invitation to treat. They are *Gibson* v *Manchester City Council* [1979] 1 All ER 972 and *Storer* v *Manchester City Council* [1974] 3 All ER 824.

Both cases arose out of the same series of events. During 1970 and early 1971, Manchester City Council adopted a policy of selling council houses to tenants. This policy was reversed when political control of the Council changed hands in May 1971, and a number of individual sales to tenants were caught up in the change of policy. The question in each case was whether it was too late for the planned sale to be stopped, and that depended on whether matters had gone beyond mere negotiations; it depended in other words on whether an offer had been accepted and an agreement concluded.

In *Gibson*, the Council's Treasurer wrote to the plaintiff in February 1971, stating that, 'the Council may be prepared to sell [your] house to you at the purchase price of . . . £2,180 (freehold)'. The letter then invited him to make a formal application, which he did. Before matters could proceed any further, control of the Council changed hands in the elections of May 1971, and the policy of selling council houses was reversed. The question was whether an offer had already been made by the Council and accepted by the plaintiff, or whether the statement made by the Council had merely been an invitation to treat, in which case the plaintiff's offer to buy his house had never been accepted by the Council. The difficulty of distinguishing between an offer and an invitation to treat can be seen from the fact that the Court of Appeal and the House of Lords came to different conclusions. The Court of Appeal agreed with the trial judge that there had been an agreement and accordingly ordered the Council to complete the transaction. The House of Lords, however, took the view that there had been no agreement at all. The language used in the Treasurer's original letter included phrases such as, 'we *may be* prepared to sell'; 'this letter is not to be regarded as a firm offer of a mortgage', and 'if you would like to make a formal application to buy your council house, please complete the enclosed application form'. These indicated, in their Lordships' view, that there was no intention on the part of the Council to be bound at that stage. The letter from the Treasurer was merely an invitation to plaintiff to make the Council an offer.

This case must be contrasted with that of *Storer*, in which the Council's officer sent the plaintiff a letter which stated, 'I understand you wish to purchase your council house and enclose the Agreement for Sale. If you sign the agreement and return it to me I will send you the Agreement signed on behalf of the Corporation.' The plaintiff signed and returned the Council's standard-form 'Agreement for Sale' before control of the Council changed. The Court of Appeal decided that there was a binding contract here, despite the fact that the Council had not signed the agreement.

The obvious distinction between *Storer* and *Gibson* is that the letter from the Council to Storer was capable of being interpreted as a firm offer to sell. The Council sent Storer an official form, the Agreement for Sale, which indicated a promise to complete the transaction as soon as the form was correctly filled in and returned. In contrast, the language contained in the form sent by the Council to Gibson ('. . . we *may* be prepared to sell . . .') was far more tentative. However, there were other factors in *Storer* which make the distinction seem less convincing. The Council never signed the Agreement for Sale, and the letter containing the initial offer left certain important details unresolved. There was, for example, no mention of the date on which payment of the mortgage was to start, and there was no clear indication of when the current tenancy was to end.

Examples of offers and invitations to treat

As can be seen from the cases above, it may be difficult to distinguish between an offer and an invitation to treat. The courts have therefore tried to make the position clearer by classifying some things as necessarily being offers and others as necessarily being invitations to treat.

Advertisements

The general rule is that advertisements are not offers, but mere invitations to treat. This rule was applied in *Partridge* v *Crittenden* [1968] 2 All ER 421. The appellant was charged with the criminal offence of 'offering' wild birds for sale, contrary to the Protection of Birds Act 1954. He had placed an entry in the classified advertisements section of a magazine, which read, 'Bramblefinch cocks and hens, 25 shillings each.' The question for the criminal court was one of contract law, namely whether he had actually *offered* wild birds for sale. The Court held that he had not, because the advert was merely an invitation to treat. He was not therefore guilty of that offence. Statutes prohibiting the sale or supply of banned goods are now worded so as to make it an offence merely to advertise or display such goods with a view to sale, thereby closing the loophole which was exposed in *Partridge* v *Crittenden*.

For practical reasons, it makes sense that advertisements are not treated as offers, because sellers of goods need to be able to supply information about their goods (i.e., to advertise) in order to be competitive. If an advert were classified as an offer it would mean that a seller would become contractually bound to supply his goods to anyone who placed an order. If the seller then failed to supply the goods (e.g., because he had already sold out) he could be sued for breach of contract. This rule might appear to suggest that unscrupulous traders could advertise goods at a temptingly low price, and then, having attracted potential buyers, decline to sell unless a higher price is agreed to. In practice, however, misleading price indications of that kind could lead to criminal prosecution under the Consumer Protection Act 1987, s. 20.

Although advertisements are normally classed as invitations to treat, there are nevertheless situations in which an advert only makes sense if construed as an offer. A common example is that of adverts offering rewards for information or for the return of lost property. Suppose that an advert is placed in a local newspaper stating 'Lost: Scottish Terrier; answers to the name of Blackie; £500 will be paid upon her safe return.' It is clear that this must be an offer. As soon as the dog is found and returned, the owner will be obliged to pay the promised £500, and can be sued for it if necessary.

Adverts for rewards are known as 'unilateral contracts', because only one of the parties is actually obliged to do anything. The only person so obliged is the one making the offer of the reward. He promises to pay £500 if the dog is found and returned to him. There is no obligation upon anyone to go and actually look for the dog. The most famous example of a unilateral contract can be seen in the landmark case of *Carlill* v *Carbolic Smoke Ball Company* [1893] 1 QB 256. During the height of an influenza epidemic, the defendant company placed an advertisement in a newspaper offering £100 to anyone who contracted influenza after purchasing and using one of its patent carbolic smoke balls. To show its 'sincerity in the matter', the company deposited £1,000 with its bank. Relying upon this advert, Mrs Carlill purchased a smoke ball, used it as directed, but still (not surprisingly) caught influenza. She then sued the defendant company for £100 and won.

Displays in shops and shop windows
Displays of goods in shops or shop windows will also be treated as mere invitations to treat. A customer who selects goods from the display does not therefore accept an offer to sell the goods but instead he makes an offer to buy them. One of the leading cases in this area is *Pharmaceutical Society of Great Britain* v *Boots Cash Chemists (Southern) Ltd* [1953] 1 All ER 482. The case involved a prosecution under s. 18(1) of the Pharmacy and Poisons Act 1933, which stated that '... it shall not be lawful for a person to sell a listed poison, unless ... the sale is effected by or under the supervision of a registered pharmacist'. Boots used a self-service system, and customers therefore selected items from the shelves before paying for them at the cash desk. Near the cashdesk was a registered pharmacist who was authorised, if required, to stop a customer from removing any drug from the shop. The court had to decide whether Boots had violated s. 18. As the pharmacist was standing by the cash desk, the court held that the customer's 'offer' to buy the drugs would only be accepted if the transaction was approved by the pharmacist himself. There would accordingly be no breach of s. 18. Lord Goddard CJ said:

> The transaction is in no way different from the normal transaction in a shop in which there is no self service scheme. I am quite satisfied it would be wrong to say that the shopkeeper is making an offer to sell every article in the shop to any person who might come in and that person can insist on buying any article by saying 'I accept your offer'. I agree with the illustration put forward during the case of a person who might go into a shop where books are displayed. In most book shops, customers are invited to go in and pick up books and look at them, even if they do not actually buy them. There is no contract by the shopkeeper to sell until the customer has taken the book to the shopkeeper or his assistant and said: 'I want to buy this book' and the shopkeeper says 'Yes'. That would not prevent the shopkeeper, seeing the book picked up and saying: 'I am sorry I cannot let you have that book; it is the only copy I have got and I have already promised it to another customer.' Therefore, in my opinion, the mere fact that a customer picks up a bottle of medicine from the shelves in this case does not amount to an acceptance of an offer to sell. It is an offer by the customer to buy, and there is no sale effected until the buyer's offer to buy is accepted by the acceptance of the price.

Auctions

The general rule is that, at an auction sale, an offer is made by the bidder and accepted by the auctioneer when he indicates his acceptance in the customary manner, e.g., by bringing down his hammer (Sale of Goods Act 1979, s. 57). If, on the other hand, the property is put up for auction, subject to a reserve price, then there will be no contract if the auctioneer mistakenly accepts a bid which is lower than the reserve price.

Vending machines

Goods or tickets displayed in automatic vending machines require special consideration. The display must be construed as an offer to sell the goods or tickets in question, because once the customer places his money in the machine and presses the requisite buttons, there is no room for further bargaining. The offer is accepted and the purchaser becomes entitled to the goods or the ticket. As Lord Denning MR said in *Thornton* v *Shoe Lane Parking* [1971] 1 All ER 686:

> The customer pays his money and gets a ticket. He cannot refuse it . . . he was committed at the very moment when he put his money into the machine. It can be translated into offer and acceptance in this way; the offer is made when the proprietor of the machine holds it out as being ready to receive the money. The acceptance takes place when the customer puts his money into the slot.

ACCEPTANCE

Once satisfied that an offer has been made, the next step is to determine whether that offer has been accepted. There are two essential requirements which must usually be satisfied before a reply can be classed as a valid acceptance:

(a) the acceptance must be a final and unqualified expression of assent to the terms of an offer; and
(b) the acceptance must be communicated to the offeror.

To accept an offer, the offeree must accept the terms of the offer completely. If he tries to alter the terms of the offer, this is likely to be regarded as a counter-offer, rather than an acceptance. The original offeror can then either accept or reject the terms of that counter-offer. Furthermore, a counter-offer is taken by the courts to constitute a rejection of the original offer. Having thus rejected it, the offeree cannot subsequently purport to accept it after all. In *Hyde* v *Wrench* (1840) 3 Beav 334, the defendant offered to sell his farm to the plaintiff for £1,000, but the plaintiff replied that he would give only £950 for it. The defendant refused to sell at £950, but a few days later the plaintiff purported to 'accept' the original £1,000 offer after all. The defendant now refused to sell, even at this price, and the court upheld his right to do so. There was still no contract, because the plaintiff's counter-offer had constituted a rejection of the defendant's original offer, bringing it to an end. His belated 'acceptance' at £1,000 could only be a new offer, which the defendant was entitled to accept or reject, as he chose.

One must be careful, however, to distinguish between situations in which the offeree attempts to vary the terms of the offer and those in which the offeree is merely making a request for further information or seeking clarification about the terms of the offer. If it is simply an enquiry or a request for clarification, this does not amount to a counter-offer or a rejection of the original offer. In such circumstances, the offer is still open and the offeree may accept it. This principle can be seen in *Stevenson, Jacques & Co.* v *McLean* (1880) 5 QB 346. The defendant offered the plaintiffs a consignment of iron at '40 shillings (£2) per ton, cash'. He promised that the offer would be kept open until the following Monday. Early on that day, the plaintiffs sent the defendant a telegram which said, 'Please wire whether you would accept 40 for delivery over two months, or if not, longest limit you would give.' The defendant did not immediately reply, but treated this as a rejection of his original offer and promptly sold the consignment to another party. As the plaintiffs received no reply, they sent the defendant another telegram later that same day accepting the offer to sell at 40 shillings cash. Since the defendant could no longer supply the iron, the plaintiffs then sued for breach of contract, and won. As Lush J said, this was not a counter-proposal, 'but a mere enquiry, which should have been answered and not treated as a rejection of the offer'.

The battle of the forms

Almost all major trading companies (and many smaller firms) now use printed standard-form contracts, which set out the terms on which they do business. Ordinary consumers who wish to deal with these companies usually have no option but to accede to these terms or look elsewhere. (As to the validity of unfair terms or exclusion clauses inserted within the small print of such contracts, see Chapters 32 to 34.)

Problems may arise, however, if two such companies each try to impose their own sets of conditions on the other. Suppose that A & Co. make an offer to sell goods using their standard-form printed terms, and B & Co. 'accept' it by sending A & Co. their own standard form, containing a different set of printed terms. It may be that neither party is giving much thought to what is happening, or it may be that each of them is trying to exploit the process of offer and acceptance in an attempt to contract on their own terms; but in either event, difficulties may arise in identifying which terms have been agreed to.

The reality of such situations may be that the parties have not reached an agreement at all. If they have not yet started to perform the supposed contract, the court may be tempted to hold there is no contract between them; but if the parties have already performed a substantial part of it (as will often be the case) the court will almost always feel obliged to decide whose terms should prevail (*G Percy Trentham Ltd* v *Archital Luxfer* [1993] 1 Lloyds Rep 25).

The general rule appers to be that the party who gets in his terms last, without the other party objecting, gets to contract on his own standard terms. This is known as 'the last shot doctrine'. Such an approach was adopted in *Butler Machine Tool Company Ltd* v *Ex-Cell-O Corporation (England) Ltd* [1979] 1 All ER 965. The contract concerned an order for machinery. The plaintiffs offered to supply this machinery within 10 months for £75,535, subject to their standard price variation clause, which would entitle them to raise the price in certain circumstances, where their own costs would be increased. The defendants returned an order form, incorporating their own terms, under which the price was fixed at £75,535. This was effectively a counter-offer. The plaintiffs signed and returned the 'acknowledgement slip' from this form, thereby in effect accepting the counter-offer. They also enclosed a covering letter referring once again to their own standard terms, but this was never acknowledged by the defendants, and was therefore ineffective. The Court of Appeal held that the parties had agreed on a fixed-price contract, and when the plaintiffs tried to claim an extra £2,892 to cover their increased costs, they failed.

These 'battle of the forms' cases show how the traditional principles of offer and acceptance may become strained. There is, however, no simple solution to these types of cases. Each one needs to be decided upon its own particular facts.

Communication of acceptance

The general rule is that any acceptance must be communicated to the offeror before it can have legal effect (*Entores* v *Miles Far East Corporation* [1955] 2 All ER 493). Communication in this context means that the acceptance must actually be brought to the offeror's attention. The reason for this rule is that the law requires the offeree to take active steps, by words or by conduct, which can be viewed objectively as evidence of assent. A mere silent resolution to accept the offer cannot constitute a valid acceptance. In *Felthouse* v *Bindley* (1862) 11 CB (NS) 869, the plaintiff wrote to his nephew, John, offering to buy a certain horse from him. The letter stated, 'If I hear no more about him, I consider the horse to be mine at £30 15s.' John did not reply to the letter, but apparently intended to accept it, because he instructed his auctioneer (the defendant) to withdraw the horse from a forthcoming sale of his farm stock. The defendant, unfortunately, forgot this instruction and sold the horse to another person. The plaintiff then sued the defendant for the tort of conversion, on the ground that the horse already belonged to him. The court held that this action must fail, because there had been no communication of John's decision to sell to the plaintiff and thus the horse had never become his property. Had John sued the defendant, he would presumably have succeeded.

Unsolicited goods and services

The law as stated in *Felthouse* v *Bindley* did not prevent certain sharp operators from developing a practice known as 'inertia selling', under which unsuspecting members of the public would be sent goods or offered services which they were told would be considered sold to them (usually at an excessive price) if not immediately returned or rejected. This was no more than a bluff, but many people paid up because they knew no better, and legislation was eventually passed (in the shape of the Unsolicited Goods and Services Act 1971) to outlaw the practice. Any person demanding payment or threatening court proceedings in respect of unsolicited goods now risks criminal prosecution under s. 2 of that Act.

Estoppel

If the offeror fails to receive an acceptance due to his own fault, and the offeree understandably thinks that his message has been received, the offeror may be prevented (or 'estopped') from denying that he has received it. As Denning LJ pointed out in *Entores* v *Miles Far East Corporation*:

> This may happen if the listener on the telephone does not catch the words of acceptance, but nevertheless does not take the trouble to ask for them to be repeated; or if the ink on the teleprinter fails at the receiving end, but the clerk does not ask for the message to be repeated; so that the man who sends an acceptance reasonably believes that his message has been received. The offeror in such circumstances is clearly bound, because he will be estopped from saying that he did not receive the message of acceptance. It is his own fault that he did not get it.

Acceptance by post: the postal rule

The general rule is that an acceptance is only effective when it is actually received by the offeror. A postal acceptance, however, will ordinarily take effect when the letter containing it is posted, and not when it is actually received. This rule originated from the case of *Adams* v *Linsell* (1818) 1 B & Ald 681. The defendants wrote to the plaintiffs offering to sell a consignment of woollen fleeces, and requested a reply by return of post. The defendants sent their offer to the wrong address, and it took an extra two days to reach the plaintiff. On receiving the offer, the plaintiffs posted their letter of acceptance straightaway, but before it arrived, the defendants sold the fleeces to a third party, having heard no reply from the plaintiffs.

It was held that a contract was concluded as soon as the letter of acceptance was posted by the plaintiffs. This is known as the postal rule, and it applies even where the letter of acceptance is lost or delayed in the post, unless it is misdirected as a result of a mistake by the offeree himself. Note that the same rule does *not* apply to offers, counter-offers or revocations, which must be communicated in order to have any legal effect.

Limitations on the scope of the postal rule
Before the postal rule can be relied upon, certain conditions must be satisfied. First, it must be reasonable to use the post as a means of communicating an acceptance. If an offer is made by post, then it is usually reasonable to accept it by post as well; and if the parties live some distance away, it may also be reasonable to post an acceptance, even where the original offer was an oral one. It is *not* usually reasonable, however, to send a letter of acceptance if the offer is made by fax or telex or e-mail, or if it is known that the postal service is subject to disruption (e.g., where there is a strike by postal workers).

Secondly, it is always open to the offeror expressly or impliedly to indicate the mode which any acceptance is to take. The offeror may stipulate in his offer that any reply should be made by fax or telephone. This would make it clear that acceptance by post would not be sufficient. Alternatively, the offeror may request a written reply, but at the same time may make it clear that the acceptance must actually be communicated or received by him, before the contract is concluded. In *Holwell Securities v Hughes* [1974] 1 All ER 161, the defendant offered the plaintiffs an option to purchase some property, exercisable 'by notice in writing to the vendor' at any time within six months. Within this period, the plaintiffs' solicitors wrote to the defendant (the vendor), purporting to notify him of their acceptance of the offer. The letter never arrived, even though it was properly stamped and addressed. The six-month period duly expired. The plaintiffs claimed that the contract was completed when their solicitors posted the letter, but it was held that, since the terms of the offer had stipulated that acceptance had to be 'notified to the vendor', mere posting was insufficient.

Acceptance and unilateral contracts

Communication of acceptance is not required in a unilateral contract. As far as unilateral contracts are concerned, acceptance is complete upon the performance of the act or acts stipulated in the offer. An example can be seen in *Carlill v Carbolic Smoke Ball Company*, where the offer stipulated that money would be paid to anyone who caught influenza after using their patent smoke ball. The Court of Appeal held that the need to notify the offeror of acceptance had impliedly been dispensed with. Using the smoke ball and catching influenza sufficed. Similarly, in reward cases, the offer is accepted as soon as the act demanded in the reward is completed. As Bowen LJ said in *Carlill*:

> If I advertise to the world that my dog is lost, and that anybody who brings the dog to a particular place will be paid some money, are all the police or

other persons whose business it is to find the dog to be expected to sit down and write me a note saying that they had accepted my proposal? Why of course, they at once look [for] the dog, and as soon as they have found the dog they have performed the condition. The essence of the transaction is that the dog should be found, and it is not necessary under such circumstances, as it seems to me, that in order to make the contract binding there should be a notification of acceptance. It follows from the nature of the thing that the performance of the condition is sufficient acceptance without the notification of it . . .

Stipulated modes of acceptance

The offeror may always stipulate, in the terms of the offer, the precise form which the acceptance must take. An example of the offeror laying down a prescribed form of acceptance was seen in *Holwell Securities* v *Hughes* (above). In those circumstances, the offeree must usually comply completely with those terms for there to be an effective acceptance. But where the offeror merely demands a particular form of acceptance in order to achieve a particular result, such as a speedy reply, then if the offeree uses a different, but equally efficient, form of acceptance, that may sometimes suffice.

Knowledge of the offer

Can a contract arise where a person fulfils the terms of the offer in ignorance of the fact that the offer exists at all? If, for example, a person supplies information to the police which leads to the conviction of a robber, unaware of the fact that there is a reward for such information, can he then claim the reward? In *Gibbons* v *Proctor* (1891) 64 LT 594, the court held that they could. This case, however, has been widely criticised, and the Australian case of *R* v *Clarke* (1927) 40 CLR 227 reached a different conclusion. Clarke gave information upon certain murderers, but at the time of so doing he was unaware of the existence of a £1,000 reward for such information. Clarke then claimed the reward, but the court held that he could not, because a person cannot be deemed to 'accept' an offer of which he is not aware at the relevant time.

Withdrawal or revocation of offers

If it appears that there has been a valid acceptance of an offer, the next question to determine is whether the offer was still open at the time of the purported acceptance. The general rule is that an offer may be withdrawn any time before the acceptance has taken place. Once an acceptance has taken place, the offer can no longer be withdrawn. In the absence of such acceptance, however, an offer may generally be withdrawn, even if it was originally promised that the offer would be held open for a specific period of time. (A promise of this kind is unenforceable in the absence of consideration, but see 'Options' (p. 271 below).)

In *Routledge* v *Grant* (1828) 130 ER 920, the defendant offered to take a lease of property belonging to the plaintiff and told the plaintiff that the offer would remain open for six weeks. After three weeks, however, the defendant withdrew his offer. The plaintiff then purported to accept the original offer within the six-week period, and sued on that basis. He failed. The court held that the defendant had been under no obligation to keep the offer open and was free to withdraw it any time, provided of course that it had not already been accepted. His original promise to keep it open was gratuitous and unenforceable. The position would, however, have been different if the plaintiff had purchased from the defendant an option to buy the property within a given period (see below).

Before any withdrawal of an offer can be effective, however, the withdrawal must actually be communicated to the offeree. This is true even of a postal withdrawal. As already explained, the postal rule does not apply to withdrawals, and a postal withdrawal will only be effective when received by the offeree. In *Byrne* v *Van Tienhoven* (1880) 5 CPD 344, the defendants wrote from Britain to the plaintiffs in America, offering to sell them a consignment of tinplate. Before this letter arrived, the defendants changed their minds and posted a second letter withdrawing the offer. The original letter naturally arrived first, and the plaintiffs promptly accepted by means of a telegram. The letter of withdrawal did not reach the plaintiffs much later. The court held that the plaintiff's acceptance of the original letter concluded a contract with the defendants, and the purported 'withdrawal' of the offer had come too late to affect this.

The case of *Dickinson* v *Dodds* (1876) 2 Ch D 463 suggests that communication of the withdrawal of an offer does not always have to be made by the offeror himself, but can be made by any reliable source. The plaintiff in that case was invited to buy some houses from the defendant for £800. The defendant promised to keep the offer open until 9.00 a.m. on 12th June. On 11th June, however, he sold the houses to another person. The plaintiff learnt of this sale by pure chance from a third party some time later on the 11th. He then purported to accept the offer at 7.00 a.m. on the 12th. The question was whether this was a valid acceptance. The court held that it was not, because the offer had already been effectively withdrawn before this purported acceptance. As James LJ stated, '... the plaintiff knew that Dodds was no longer minded to sell the property to him as plainly and clearly as if Dodds had told him in so many words, "I withdraw the offer" ...'.

The defendant had nevertheless behaved very rashly in selling the houses to a third party before warning the plaintiff that his offer was withdrawn. It was only by chance that the plaintiff had learnt of this on the 11th. Had he not done so, the defendant might well have found himself in breach of contract.

Withdrawal and unilateral contracts

One problem with unilateral contracts is that it may be difficult to indicate precisely when a binding acceptance has occurred. It may accordingly be difficult to determine the stage at which the offer can safely be withdrawn. Once, for example, the Carbolic Smoke Ball Co. Ltd had woken up to the fact that its products did not work, could it then have revoked its much publicised offer *vis-à-vis* customers who had already purchased their smoke balls, but who had not as yet contracted influenza? Similarly, if the owner of the lost terrier learns that someone has found it, can she withdraw or reduce the offer of the £500 reward before the dog is actually returned to her? There is relatively little direct authority on this point, but it is generally agreed that an offer cannot be withdrawn in such circumstances. Some writers argue that the offeror must be deemed to make two offers. The first is the express offer itself (i.e., the promise to pay in the event of) and the second is an unspoken collateral one, whereby the offeror impliedly promises not to withdraw the principal offer once the offeree has started performance of the required acts.

One case which provides solid support for this view is *Errington v Errington* [1952] 1 All ER 149. A father purchased a house for his son and daughter-in-law to live in. The house was conveyed into his own name, but he promised his son and daughter-in-law that, if they remained in the house and paid all the mortgage instalments, he would eventually transfer the property to them. Until the father's death nine years later, the young couple occupied the house and paid the mortgage as agreed. On his death, however, all his property (including the house in question) was left to his widow, and she brought an action to recover the house. She failed. In the Court of Appeal, Denning LJ said:

> The father's promise was a unilateral contract — a promise of the house in return for their act of paying the instalments. It could not be revoked by him once the couple entered on performance of the act, but it would cease to bind him if they left it incomplete and unperformed, which they have not done.

It thus appears that a unilateral offer can only be accepted by performance of the required act or acts, but once the offeree has started to perform the act, the offer can no longer be withdrawn and the offeree must be given the opportunity to complete. There may sometimes be difficulties in distinguishing between commencement of performance and mere preparation to perform. It is likely that a reward offered for the return of lost property could be withdrawn after somebody had spent time looking for it but without any success; but once the property has been found and the finder is in the process of returning it to the offeror, the offer can no longer be withdrawn.

Other forms of termination

Rejection

Once an offer has been rejected by the offeree, he cannot subsequently accept it, unless it has been renewed by the offeror. He may, however, make a new offer of his own, in the hope that it will be accepted by the other parties (see 'Counter-offers', above).

Death

Whether the death of the offeror terminates the offer depends on the nature of the offer itself. If the offer is one of personal services, such as employment, then the offer will usually come to an end upon the death of the offeror. In some other circumstances, it is possible for the offer to continue after the offeror's death, as the contract may sometimes be taken on by the deceased's executors or personal representatives.

Conditional offers

Where an offer is made subject to the occurrence of some particular condition, then if that condition does not occur, the offer will come to an end.

Lapse of time

If the offeror stipulates that the offer must be accepted within a particular period of time and it is not accepted within that period, it will come to an end. If no time period is stipulated, the offeree must accept within a reasonable period of time. What amounts to a reasonable period of time will depend upon the facts of the case. Some offers (such as offers involving perishable goods) must, by their nature, lapse more quickly than others.

Withdrawal after acceptance

At common law, neither party may withdraw once an offer has been accepted. There are some types of contract, however, in which the common law rule is qualified by legislation. These are primarily 'consumer contracts' involving credit terms, in which the consumer is given a statutory 'cooling-off' (or second thoughts) period, during which he can change his mind and withdraw from the conract he has agreed to. Notable examples are provided by the Consumer Credit Act 1974 and the Timeshare Act 1992.

Options

An offer, which may be withdrawn before it is accepted, must be distinguished from an option which has actually been purchased by the other party. An option is itself an enforceable contract. If, for example, X pays Y £500 for an option to purchase Y's land for £50,000 within the next three months, Y is then obliged to keep the option open, and would be in breach of contract if he sold the land to anyone else during that period. If X fails to 'exercise his option', Y then keeps the £500. If, however, the value of the land rises during the three-month period, X might do very well by choosing to exercise his option.

Agreement to form a contract

Invitation to treat? *or* **Offer?**

Further negotiation expected. Adverts, displays in stores and in shop windows are normally invitations to treat.

Sometimes adverts may constitute offers where their wording indicates an intention to be bound as soon as the offer is accepted. The most common examples are unilateral contracts.

To be classed as an offer the statement must indicate a clear intention on the part of the offeror to be bound as soon as the offer is accepted.

→ **Has the offer been accepted?**

Acceptance requires

Communication to the offeror. *and* Unequivocal acceptance of the terms of the offer by the offeree.

Acceptance must usually be received by the offeror. Exceptions include (i) unilateral contracts, (ii) acceptance by post.

Consider, is there a counter-offer? If so, the original offer is rejected. Counter-offers must be distinguished from requests for further information.

Consider whether the offer was still open at the time of the purported acceptance. In particular:

(i) whether the offer has lapsed (expiry of a specified acceptance period, death of offeror, rejection); or
(ii) whether the offer has been revoked.

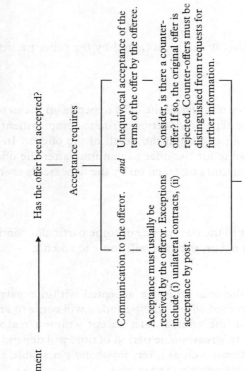
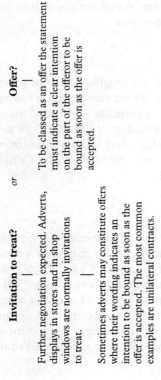

TWENTY

Consideration

As previously explained, not all agreements will be deemed to be legally enforceable contracts. The law of contract is primarily concerned with the enforcement of bargains, and the concept of consideration is central to that of any bargain. The law will not therefore enforce gratuitous promises of gifts or favours. For example, the promise of a birthday present, or even of a donation to a charity, will not generally be enforceable, because the person to whom the promise is made (the promisee) will not have done or offered anything in return for it.

One exception to this rule is that if a gift is promised, not just in writing, but 'by deed' (using a special form of document, marked with a special stamp or seal) then it need not be supported by consideration. Deeds promising gifts, however, are rare and are of limited practical importance.

The concept of consideration requires that something of value must be given or promised by each party, i.e., something must be offered in return for something else. A bargain thus involves reciprocal obligations upon each party to the contract.

Consideration defined

Many attempts have been made by the courts to provide a definition of the concept of consideration, but few if any of them have been entirely satisfactory. One of the better known definitions comes from the case of *Currie* v *Misa* (1878) LR 10 Ex 153, in which Lush LJ stated:

> A valuable consideration ... may consist either in some right, interest, profit or benefit accruing to the one party or some forbearance, detriment, loss or responsibility given, suffered or undertaken by the other.

In other words, each party must *either* offer something of benefit or value to the other *or* (alternatively) agree to forgo some benefit or suffer some detriment on behalf of the other. In most cases, a benefit to one party is simultaneously a detriment to the other, as for example where A agrees to sell B his car and B agrees to pay A £3,000 in return. Each party benefits in some way from such a transaction and each suffers a matching detriment (one gains a car, the other loses it; one gains £3,000 and the other loses that sum) but this balancing of benefit and detriment is not necessary in every case.

Analysis of consideration in terms of benefit and detriment can still occasionally be seen in modern case law (as for example in *Williams* v *Roffey Bros & Nicholls (Contractors) Ltd* [1990] 1 All ER 512, but it is often criticised by commentators, because it is misleading to suggest that consideration must either be of value to one party or of detriment to the other. The courts do not in practice insist that consideration should have any significant value at all. Purely nominal payment, such as one penny or even (to use an old historical example) one peppercorn will always suffice as valid consideration, even in exchange for something of considerable value, such as a lease of land. As Professor J. C. Smith observes (*The Law of Contract* (2nd edition) at p. 70):

> If O makes a promise to A in consideration of A supplying him with three quite useless chocolate wrappers, which O will instantly throw away, there is a perfectly good contract, provided that the promise was seriously intended. O has got what he asked for, and that is sufficient benefit. A has parted with something he might have kept, he has done something which he did not have to do, and that is a sufficient detriment. It is immaterial that the wrappers are of no value and that A is glad to be rid of them.

The case which inspired this comment was *Chappell & Co.* v *Nestlé Co. Ltd* [1959] 2 All ER 701, in which Nestlé offered recordings of a popular song for just 1s 6d (the price of three chocolate bars) to anyone who sent them three wrappers taken from bars of Nestlé chocolate. Chappell & Co., as holders of the copyright in the song, were offered royalties based on a percentage of the selling price of 1s 6d, but they objected that the records were not merely being sold for cash, because the wrappers (although worthless) were part of the consideration required for the sale. The House of Lords agreed. Quite apart from the fact that Nestle would expect to benefit from extra sales of chocolate, the worthlessness of the wrappers was irrelevant. As Lord Reid said, 'A contracting party can stipulate for what consideration he chooses'. Chappell & Co. were awarded an injunction against Nestlé, preventing further sales of the records until more satisfactory royalty terms could be agreed.

Consideration may take the form of an act, a forbearance (such as the giving up of some right) or a promise. It may also be classed as either 'executory' or 'executed'. In most bilateral contracts, the consideration will be executory, in the sense that a promise is given in exchange for another promise (e.g., A promises to paint B's house and B promises to pay A £500 when the job is finished). When the contract is concluded, the consideration consists of promises which are yet to be performed. In contrast consideration is described as executed when an act is performed in exchange for a promise. If A promises to pay £100 to anyone who finds and returns her dog, nobody undertakes to find the dog in return. There is no reciprocal promise and at that stage there is no contract. But if B does find the dog and returns it to A, he can be said to have provided 'executed' consideration. This completes the contract and B can therefore demand the £100 promised by A.

Rules relating to consideration

The essence of consideration is that something must be promised or given in return for something else, and this concept is reinforced by two particular rules, namely:

    (a)   consideration must not be 'past'; and
    (b)   consideration must 'move from the promisee'.

Consideration must not be past
If A hires B to paint his house for £1,000, B's undertaking to paint the house will be good consideration for A's promise of payment. However, a promise which is made only *after* an act has already been performed is generally unenforceable, because 'past consideration is no consideration'. Past consideration could not have been performed as part of any later bargain struck between the parties, and it cannot therefore be relied upon in order to enforce any later bargain. For example, if B were to decorate or repair A's house *without* any prior request from A, and if A later promised B payment for the job, B would not be able to enforce A's promise.

This principle can be illustrated by the old case of *Roscorla* v *Thomas* (1842) 3 QB 234. Roscorla bought a horse from Thomas for £30. *After* the sale, Thomas promised that the horse was 'sound and free from vice'. When the horse turned out to be vicious, Roscorla sued for breach of contract. It was held that, since the promise was made after the sale and was not supported by any fresh consideration, no contract could possibly be based upon it.

The rule that past consideration is not generally good consideration is basically a sound one, but it can sometimes cause injustice and it has, to a very limited extent, been modified by the creation of certain exceptions to the general rule. Lord Scarman, in *Pao On* v *Lau Yiu Long* [1979] 3 All ER 65, offered this summary of the circumstances under which the courts will enforce past consideration:

    An act done before the giving of a promise to make payment or to confer some other benefit can sometimes be consideration for the promise. The act must have been done at the promisor's request, the parties must have understood that the act was to be remunerated either by a payment or the conferment of some other benefit, and payment, or the conferment of a benefit, must have been legally enforceable had it been promised in advance ...

The first requirement for past consideration to be good consideration is that the act performed must have been requested by the promisor. An illustration of this rule is provided by the old case of *Lampleigh* v *Braithwait* (1615) Hob 105. Braithwait had killed a man, and asked Lampleigh to seek a pardon for him from the King. Lampleigh did so, at considerable personal expense, and he duly obtained the pardon. Afterwards, Braithwait promised to pay him £100 for his troubles, but this payment was never made, and Lampleigh eventually sued him for the promised sum. The Court upheld this claim, on the ground that Lampleigh had performed the services at Braithwait's request and the latter's subsequent promise to him was clearly related to the earlier request for help. 'Although it followed the promise, yet it was not naked [i.e., gratuitous] but coupled itself with the suit before.'

The second requirement is that there must have been an expressed or implied understanding between the parties that the act would be remunerated. This factor was presumably present in *Lampleigh* v *Braithwait* but was highlighted in the later case of *Re Casey's Patents*; *Stewart* v *Casey* [1892] 1 Ch 104. Stewart and Charlton were the joint owners of certain patent rights (i.e., the right to exploit an invention). They promised to transfer a one-third share in these rights to Casey, in return for his past services as their manager; but when Stewart died, his executors argued that Casey was not legally entitled to this share. They argued that the only consideration for the original promise was past consideration and that the contract was therefore unenforceable. The Court of Appeal rejected this argument and held that there had been an implied understanding between the parties at the time, to the effect that Casey's services would be remunerated at some point. The later promise of a one-third share of the patents simply fixed the precise amount of remuneration involved. In cases where payment was always expected, but the precise amount remains unclear, a subsequent promise of a specified amount acceptable to both parties merely fills a lacuna in the original agreement. Indeed, in the absence of any later agreement as to the quantification of such remuneration, the courts will sometimes determine the level of remuneration themselves, on the basis of *quantum meruit* ('the amount deserved').

Consideration must move from the promisee

Before a person can enforce or sue on another's promise, he must himself have provided the consideration for it. In other words 'consideration must move from the promisee'. If A is promised some benefit by B, and the only consideration for B's promise is provided, not by A, but by C, then the promise will not be enforceable by A. This may be illustrated by the case of *Tweddle* v *Atkinson* (1861) 1 B & S 393. The plaintiff, Tweddle, was to be married to the daughter of one William Guy. Guy and the plaintiff's father each agreed to pay a sum of money to the young couple, but Guy died without ever having done so, and the plaintiff tried to enforce his late father-in-law's promise in an action brought against his executor, Atkinson. The action failed, as the plaintiff had not provided any consideration in return for Guy's promise. His father was the only one who could have sued, as it was he who had provided the consideration. It was held that:

> Consideration must move from the party entitled to sue upon the contract. It would be a monstrous proposition to say that a person was a party to the contract for the purpose of suing upon it for his own advantage, and not a party to it for the purpose of being sued . . .

This rule can sometimes cause hardship in cases where some other person provided the consideration on the beneficiary's behalf, but there may nevertheless be ways in which such a promise can still be enforced. For example the beneficiary may sometimes be able to persuade that other person to sue upon the promise.

Adequacy of consideration

The concept of freedom of contract demands that parties strike their own bargains and the courts do not seek to ensure that the bargain itself is a fair one. The courts merely ensure that something which they class as amounting to consideration is promised or exchanged. For example, if A agrees to sell his brand new car to B in exchange for a cup final ticket, that will generally be an enforceable agreement. It may seem strange that such a deal should be struck, still less enforced, and the courts must be watchful that such an agreement was not reached as a result of deception, duress, mental incapacity or undue influence; but if it is clear that it is a genuine agreement, then the courts will uphold it and will not interfere with that bargain. This is expressed in the rule that consideration need not be adequate. To put it another way, a bad or foolish bargain may still be an enforceable one.

Consideration must be sufficient

Although consideration need not appear to be of adequate value, it must nevertheless be something which the courts will recognise as capable of constituting consideration. It must in other words be 'sufficient'. In order to be sufficient it is sometimes said that the consideration must be of some economic value, but as previously explained, this is not really the case, because something of purely nominal value (such as 'peppercorn rent') may be treated as valid consideration. The real point is that, for various reasons, including in some cases considerations of public policy, the courts are unwilling to treat certain forms of consideration as valid at all.

In *White* v *Bluett* (1853) 23 LJ Ex 36, a father supposedly told his son that he would be excused from repaying a debt to him if he promised to stop complaining about being treated unfairly, but it was held that a promise to refrain from making complaints was incapable of being sufficient consideration for any contract. This rather narrow view must, however, be contrasted with the later case of *Ward* v *Byham* [1956] 2 All ER 318, in which the father of an illegitimate child promised the mother £1 a week if she ensured that the child was 'well looked after and happy'. The Court of Appeal held that this promise could be enforced, even though the plaintiff was already under a legal obligation to look after the child. She had agreed to go beyond that basic duty by promising the father that the child would be well looked after and happy.

The supposed distinctions between these cases are at best highly questionable. In reality, the *Byham* case is little different from that of *White* v *Bluett*. It may be that in the years since *White* v *Bluett* the courts have become more flexible in deciding what may constitute valid consideration.

Performance of a legal duty

Suppose that A is already under a legal duty to perform a particular duty, but subsequently enters into a contract with B whereby A promises to perform the same task in return for an additional payment from B. The question is whether A can enforce B's promise of payment. In other words, has A provided sufficient consideration for B's promise by performing a duty which A was already bound to perform by virtue of another contract?

There is no simple answer to this question. Instead, the answer varies according to the circumstances. There are three distinct situations under which the question can arise:

(a)   performance of a public duty;
(b)   performance of a duty already owed to the other party; and
(c)   performance of a duty already owed to a third party.

Public duty imposed by law   The general rule is that, if someone is already under a public legal duty to perform a particular act, then a promise to perform this act for a fee will not be enforceable. This rule is clearly based upon policy considerations. The courts will not, for example, allow public officials, such as police officers, to demand payment from members of the public before agreeing to carry out their existing public duties, nor can anyone demand payment for carrying out the public duties of an ordinary citizen. An application of this principle can be seen in the case of *Collins* v *Godefroy* (1831) 1 B & Ad 950. The plaintiff was summonsed to give evidence on the defendant's behalf at a trial in which the defendant was involved. The plaintiff claimed that the defendant had promised him a guinea per day for attending court. The question was whether the plaintiff could enforce this promise. Had the plaintiff provided consideration by turning up at the court and giving evidence? The court held that he had not, because he was in any case legally obliged to appear as a witness in court. He would have been in contempt of court had he refused to do so. (In contrast, it is legitimate and common practice for a potential 'expert witness' who is as yet uninvolved in a case to charge substantial fees before agreeing to become involved by undertaking experiments, writing reports, attending court, etc.)

This rule, however, no longer applies where the person demanding payment has agreed to go beyond the mere performance of an existing legal obligation. In *Glasbrook Bros Ltd* v *Glamorgan County Council* [1925] AC 270, some mine owners feared violence occurring during a miners' strike. The mine owners felt that the amount of protection afforded to them by the police was inadequate (even though the police themselves thought that the amount of protection which they were in fact providing was perfectly satisfactory). In the end, the company promised to pay £2,200 for extra police protection, but they later refused to make any payment on the grounds that the police were already under a legal duty to provide such protection. The House of Lords held that the police were in fact entitled to the money on the grounds that they agreed to provide more than the basic level of protection to which the mine owners were entitled. On this basis, it is now standard policy for police forces to charge football clubs substantial sums for the provision of a police presence inside the ground.

Performance of a duty owed to the promisor   Suppose A makes a promise to B in exchange for B's promise to do something which he is already obliged to do under an existing contract between them. If B does nothing more than he is already legally bound to do, it is difficult to see what consideration he can have provided for A's promise. Again policy reasons have played an important role in the development of this area of law. The courts felt at one time that it would be contrary to the public interest for someone who has already contracted to perform certain services to extort further remuneration from the other party merely for performing the same promised service. This principle can be traced back to the case of *Stilk* v *Myrick* (1809) 2 Camp 317. Two sailors from a British merchant ship deserted in the Baltic port of Kronstadt. The ship's master was unable to find replacements for them, but promised to divide their wages amongst the remaining crew members in exchange for their sailing the ship short-handed on the return journey. His promise was held to be unenforceable. The crew had not strictly speaking provided any consideration because they were already under an obligation to sail the ship home, short-handed or not.

The rule laid down in *Stilk* v *Myrick* is not, however, an inflexible one, and has been distinguished in a number of more recent cases. As in the 'public duty' cases, if it can be shown that the claimant agreed to act even slightly beyond his original contractual duty, this can be good consideration for a promise of extra payment. In *Hartley v Ponsonby* (1857) 7 El & Bl 872, a crew of 36 sailors was so badly depleted as a result of a series of desertions that only 19 were left. The captain promised the remaining crew extra money if they stayed on to sail the ship home, but this time they were able to hold him to his promise. This case was distinguished from *Stilk v Myrick* in that the captain's promise of extra payment to the remaining crew members was enforceable due to the exceptional set of circumstances under which they had been forced to work. The crew, by continuing with the voyage, were risking their lives and were undertaking a new set of obligations, rather than simply fulfilling existing ones. The crew were therefore entitled to make a fresh and enforceable bargain with the captain for extra payment on what was left of the voyage.

The rule in *Stilk v Myrick* was less convincingly distinguished by the Court of Appeal in *Williams v Roffey Bros & Nicholls (Contractors) Ltd* [1990] 1 All ER 512. The defendants were building contractors and were under a contractual duty to X to refurbish a block of 27 flats. They sub-contracted the carpentry work to the plaintiff for £20,000, but this sum was clearly too low to cover his costs and it soon became apparent that he would not be able to complete the work in time. Anxious to avoid losing money under a penalty clause in their main contract with X, the defendants promised the plaintiff an extra £575 per flat, but although he was then able to finish the work on time, they failed to pay the extra money. They argued that no consideration had been provided to them in return for the promise of extra payment, because the plaintiff was simply doing what he was already legally obliged to do under his sub-contract. The Court of Appeal disagreed. They held that the plaintiff was entitled to the extra payment. He had not used economic duress (as to which see Chapter 25) and the defendants obtained a practical benefit from their extra promise (because the work was finished on time, and they therefore avoided liability to X under the penalty clause in the main contract).

Although *Williams v Roffey Bros* does not purport to overrule *Stilk v Myrick*, but merely to 'refine and limit the application of that principle' (as Glidewell LJ preferred to put it), it appears in practice to allow parties to carry out reasonable commercial renegotiation of the rate of remuneration under an existing contract, which is precisely what *Stilk v Myrick* seems to prohibit. The defendants in *Williams v Roffey Bros* may indeed have obtained a practical benefit by enabling the plaintiff to finish the work on time, but the same must have been true for the ship's master in *Stilk v Myrick*. As Professor J. C. Smith observes (*The Law of Contract*, p. 80), 'Surely it was a great benefit ... to the master in that case to have the crew sail the ship home rather than abandon him and it in a foreign port.'

Overall, the status and extent of the rule in *Stilk v Myrick* has become far from clear. In *Re Selectmove* [1995] 2 All ER 531, however, the court held that the principle laid down in *Williams v Roffey Bros* could not be applied to a promise by a debtor to accept part payment of a debt from his creditor in satisfaction for the whole amount. The rule in *Pinnel's Case* (below, p. 282) still applies to this situation.

Performance of a duty already owed to a third party   In contrast to the rules considered above, the courts are generally willing to enforce a contract under which A promises B that he will do something he is already obliged to do under a contract with C. The probable reason for this different approach is that the courts perceive no strong policy considerations against allowing the enforcement of such promises. The old case of *Shadwell* v *Shadwell* (1860) 9 CB (NS) 159, is sometimes offered as an illustration of this principle, but it is a troublesome case in several respects.

Lancey Shadwell, the plaintiff, was starting up a career as a barrister and was engaged to be married to his fiancée, Ellen. In those days, a man who broke off an engagement could be sued by his fiancée for 'breach of promise of marriage', but there was no suggestion that Lancey ever contemplated any such breach. He received a letter from his uncle, Charles Shadwell, who expressed pleasure at the forthcoming marriage and stated: '. . . as I promised to assist you at starting . . . I will pay to you £150 yearly during my life . . .'. Lancey duly married Ellen, but Charles died leaving several of the promised payments unmade. Lancey sued his uncle's executors for the arrears. They replied that Lancey had provided no consideration for his uncle's promise (an argument accepted by Byles J in his dissenting judgment) but a majority of the Court of Appeal took the view that Charles had indeed received consideration, in so far as the plaintiff had ultimately married Ellen, to Charles's evident pleasure.

The majority view has been much criticised, but *not* because Lancey was already committed to marrying Ellen. There is indeed no reason why that should have prevented him from entering into a further contract with his uncle, thereby increasing his potential liability in the event of him calling off the marriage. The real objection to the majority ruling is surely that Lancey and his uncle never struck any bargain. Charles never said, '*if* you marry Ellen, I will pay you £150 per month', nor did Lancey ever promise his uncle that he would marry her. Charles merely offered Lancey a very generous wedding present.

The rule that a promise made can be good consideration, even where the promisor is already obliged so to act under a contract with a third party, has more recently been supported by the Privy Council in *The Eurymedon* [1974] 1 All ER 1015.

Part payment of a debt
Despite the apparent relaxation of the rule in *Stilk* v *Myrick* in cases such as *Williams* v *Roffey Bros*, the law remains adamant that, if A owes B money (say £100) and B promises to accept part payment of the debt (say £75) in exchange for releasing A from the rest of it, that promise will be unenforceable. A has given no valid consideration in exchange for B's promise because B was already obliged to pay the £100. The policy considerations behind this rule are

little different from those behind the rule in *Stilk* v *Myrick*, but there is a very genuine fear that, without such a rule, debtors might be encouraged to delay paying for an unreasonable amount of time in the hope of coercing their creditors into accepting something less than full payment of the debt. Small firms with cash-flow problems could be particularly susceptible to such coercion. As it is, many debtors, whether large companies or private individuals, often delay unreasonably in paying their debts and one would hardly wish to offer them any further encouragement in that direction.

The origins of the rule concerning part payment can be found in *Pinnel's Case* (1602) 5 Co Rep 117a, where it was stated that part payment of a debt can never be satisfaction for the whole sum. If, however, the debtor provides something different from what was originally agreed between himself and the creditor ('a hawk, a horse or a robe'), or if the debtor agrees to pay a lesser sum *before* the date on which the original debt was due, then the debtor will indeed have provided good consideration.

The rule in *Pinnel's* case was later affirmed by the House of Lords in *Foakes* v *Beer* (1884) 9 App Cas 605, but it still has its critics. One frequently heard objection to the rule is that, where a creditor promises to accept part payment of a debt in settlement of the full amount, the debtor may rely upon this promise and alter his position in some detrimental way. It may sometimes be unjust to allow the creditor to go back on his promise in such a situation, especially if the creditor has benefited from the transaction. For example, in the business world a creditor may prefer that the debtor pays a lesser sum promptly rather than having to resort to the strict letter of the law to enforce payment of the entire sum. The harshness of the rule has, however, been mitigated somewhat through the equitable concept of promissory estoppel.

The concept of promissory estoppel

Shortly after the Second World War, *Central London Property Trust Ltd* v *High Trees House Ltd* [1947] KB 130 (popularly referred to as the 'High Trees' case) laid the foundations of what was later to become a means of mitigating the common law rules on part payment of debts. The plaintiffs let a block of flats to the defendants in September 1937, at a rent of £2,500 per year. By 1940, due to wartime conditions, many of the flats were empty. The plaintiffs therefore agreed to reduce the defendants' rent to £1,250. When the war ended in 1945, the flats were fully occupied and the plaintiffs wanted to claim full rent from the defendants once again. The plaintiffs claimed the full rent for the last two quarters of 1945. They did not claim any arrears of rent for any preceding period. Denning J (as he then was) held in favour of the plaintiffs on the ground that the agreement to accept the lower rent was intended to cover only the period when many of the flats were empty during the war years. They had been fully let since mid-1945, and consequently the plaintiffs were entitled to resume charging the defendants the full rent that had originally been agreed between the parties.

The principal significance of the *High Trees* case is, however, to be found not in the decision itself, but in an *obiter dictum*. Denning J stated that, if any attempt *had* been made by the plaintiffs to recover the full rent for the period 1940–45, they would not have succeeded. In other words, the plaintiffs would not have been allowed to go back on the promise made by them to the defendants to accept a lesser rent for the period from 1940 up to the last two quarters of 1945 (i.e., during the wartime conditions). They would be bound by their initial promise to accept a lesser sum from the defendants. This was a direct challenge to the principle laid down in *Pinnel's Case*. Denning J based his decision upon the principle of estoppel, which seemed to originate from the earlier case of *Hughes* v *Metropolitan Railway Co.* (1877) 2 App Cas 439, where it was said:

> ... it is the first principle upon which all Courts of Equity proceed, that if parties who have entered into definite and distinct terms involving certain legal results — certain penalties or legal forfeiture — afterwards by their own act or with their own consent enter upon a course of negotiation which has the effect of leading one of the parties to suppose that the strict rights arising under the contract will not be enforced, or will be kept in suspense, or held in abeyance, the person who otherwise might have enforced those rights will not be allowed to enforce them where it would be inequitable having regard to the dealings which have thus taken place between the parties.

Over the years the doctrine has been added to and limitations imposed upon its operation, and these are discussed below. There are now important modern limitations upon the operation of promissory estoppel.

The doctrine does not create a cause of action

Promissory estoppel does not create a cause of action, but merely operates to prevent a person from insisting on his strict legal rights when it would be unjust to allow them in light of the dealings which have taken place between the parties. Consequently, the doctrine of promissory estoppel is frequently described as 'a shield and not a sword'. This was made quite clear in *Combe* v *Combe* [1951] 2 KB 215, where a husband had agreed to pay his wife £100 a year at the time of their divorce. He failed to make any payment and she sued him for £600 arrears, i.e., for six years' arrears. The trial judge applied the doctrine of promissory estoppel and consequently the husband's promise was enforceable. The husband appealed and the Court of Appeal allowed his appeal on the ground that the wife was using the doctrine of promissory estoppel as a cause of action against her husband, and not as a defence to any action brought by him.

There must be evidence of clear agreement between the parties

In order for the doctrine to operate there must be a promise, either by words or by conduct, which must be clear and unequivocal.

Reliance
In order to be able to rely upon the doctrine of promissory estoppel it must be shown that there has been reliance upon the promise. The balance of authority seems to suggest that the reliance does not have to be a detrimental one. It merely has to be shown that as a result of the promise the other party was led to act differently from the way he would otherwise have done.

It must be inequitable to go back on the promise
As the doctrine of promissory estoppel is a creation of equity, this means that the equitable maxims apply such as 'He who comes to equity must come with clean hands'. An example of the courts applying one of these maxims can be seen in the case of *D & C Builders* v *Rees* [1966] 2 QB 617, where the defendant took advantage of the financial hardship of the plaintiffs in order to force them to accept a lesser sum in full settlement of the debt that he owed them. The court held that the plaintiffs were entitled to go back on their promise and demand the full sum originally agreed, because it would not be inequitable for them to go back on the original promise bearing in mind the unfair pressure which had been exerted on them in the first place.

Are rights extinguished or merely suspended?
If promissory estoppel is established, the effect of the estoppel upon the parties' rights must be carefully considered. The case law suggests that its effect is normally to suspend rather than to extinguish legal rights. These rights may, therefore, be revived by the giving of reasonable notice unless it is impossible for the promisee ever to resume his original position having relied on the promise (*Ajayi* v *R. T. Briscoe Ltd* [1964] 3 All ER 556). Such restriction on the operation of the doctrine of promissory estoppel causes less offence to the common law principle laid down in *Pinnel's Case* and thus is an attempt to allow the two doctrines to co-exist side by side.

In conclusion, therefore, the doctrine of promissory estoppel has been used as a device to mitigate the harshness of the old common law rule laid down in *Pinnel's Case* and confirmed by *Foakes* v *Beer*. Where, however, the common law rule does not lead to any unfairness then the equitable doctrine does not need to be applied.

Consideration

An agreement must be supported by consideration

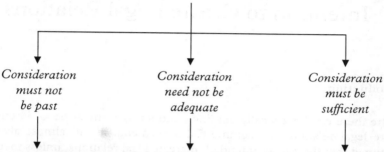

Consideration represents the idea of reciprocal obligations (i.e., something in return for something else)

The doctrine of consideration is made up of a series of rules:

Consideration must not be past	*Consideration need not be adequate*	*Consideration must be sufficient*
(i) A promise which is made *after* an act has been performed is generally not enforceable. This is known as past consideration. (ii) In limited circumstances, however, past consideration can be good consideration.	The courts are not concerned with whether 'adequate' value has been given in exchange for a promise. If, for example, A agrees to sell a car to B for £1, the court will not ask whether that was a proper price.	Although consideration need not be adequate it must be sufficient. This usually means that the consideration must be of some economic value.

TWENTY ONE

Intention to Create Legal Relations

Introduction

Before there can be a legally binding contract there must be an intention to create legal relations. In commercial agreements it will almost always be presumed that the parties intended to create legal relations, unless there is an express provision to the contrary. In social and domestic agreements, on the other hand, it will normally be presumed that the parties did *not* intend such consequences.

Social and domestic agreements

Each day, hundreds of domestic or social agreements are made. Parents agree to give their children pocket money in return for them carrying out household or garden chores. A wife agrees to do the shopping if her husband promises to clean the gutters and cut the lawn. Friends promise to bring food or wine to a party. In each of these examples, agreement and consideration is provided, but did the parties intend any legal consequences to arise from their agreement?

In the majority of social or domestic agreements (especially within a family), it is probably accurate to say that the parties did not intend to create legal relations. The law takes an objective approach to such agreements, and consequently the question becomes: would the reasonable man assume that the parties intended to create legal relations? An illustration of a domestic agreement between a husband and wife which was not enforceable due to a lack of intention to create legal relations can be seen in *Balfour v Balfour* [1919] 2

KB 571. The defendant worked as a civil servant stationed abroad and left his wife (the plaintiff) at home. Before leaving, he said that he would pay the plaintiff an allowance of £30 per month whilst they were apart. The defendant did not keep up the payments and she sued him for breach of contract. The trial judge found in her favour, but the Court of Appeal reversed this decision and held that the contract was unenforceable as there had been no intention to create legal relations. Lord Atkin stated:

> . . . there are agreements between parties which do not result in contracts within the meaning of that term in our law . . . and one of the most usual forms of agreement which does not constitute a contract appears to me to be the arrangements which are made between husband and wife . . . and they do not result in contracts even though there may be what as between other parties would constitute consideration for the agreement. . . The courts would have to be multiplied one hundred fold if these arrangements were held to result in legal obligations . . .

This part of Lord Atkin's speech suggests that even though the outward justification for the decision was a lack of intention to create legal relations between the parties, the true reason was one of policy, namely, the fear that the floodgates would open if such claims were allowed.

Nevertheless, the courts are unlikely to reach such a conclusion where the couples are separated or are about to separate. *Balfour* must in this respect be contrasted with *Merritt* v *Merritt* [1970] 2 All ER 260. The husband left his wife and moved out of the home which they jointly owned, in order to move in with another woman. The parties agreed that the husband would pay the wife £40 a month and that she was to pay the mortgage out of this sum. The wife insisted that this was put into a written agreement which stipulated:

> In consideration of the fact that you will pay all charges in connection with the house . . . until such time as the mortgage repayment has been completed . . . I will agree to transfer the property into your sole ownership.

The Court of Appeal held that this was an enforceable contract between the parties and that, once the wife had cleared the mortgage, she was entitled to be registered as the sole owner of the house. The decision in *Balfour* did not apply to couples who had ceased to be on friendly terms and were about to separate or who had indeed separated. Indeed, the wife's insistence on a written agreement was the strongest possible evidence of her specific intent to make it legally enforceable.

Domestic arrangements can also occur between other members of the family and again the same question arises as to whether there was an intention to create legal relations between the parties. In *Jones* v *Padavatton* [1969] 2 All ER 616, a mother had promised her daughter that she would give her an allowance if she moved to London to qualify as a barrister. In place of the allowance, she later bought a house in London for her daughter to live in. After several years, the mother and daughter quarrelled and the mother claimed possession of the house, although the daughter had still not passed her Bar exams. The Court of Appeal held that there had been no intention to create legal relations and that the mother (as owner) was entitled to possession. The Court was of the opinion that disputes of this nature should never be brought to court.

Commercial agreements

Commercial agreements will generally be presumed to have been made with an intention to create legal relations, and this presumption is not easily displaced. In *Esso Petroleum* v *Commissioners of Customs and Excise* [1976] 1 All ER 117, the House of Lords refused to abandon that presumption where a petrol company offered promotional 'World Cup Coins' to customers buying petrol at their service stations. Their Lordships held (by a narrow majority) that the offer to supply such coins to customers in return for qualifying petrol purchases was enforceable under the law of contract. This in turn meant that Esso were liable to pay 'purchase tax' (a tax since replaced by VAT) on the coins.

Non-binding agreements

The presumption can, however, be rebutted. In *Rose and Frank Co.* v *Crompton Bros Ltd* [1924] All ER 245 an agreement for the supply of trial samples of tissue paper was held to be unenforceable on the ground that it was expressly stated to be nothing more than an 'honourable pledge' which was not to be 'subject to legal jurisdiction'. Nevertheless, orders subsequently placed for the commercial supply of such paper were held to be enforceable contracts. The House of Lords was naturally (and quite rightly) unwilling to construe the initial 'honourable pledge' as extending to later transactions between the parties.

In respect of the sale of land or houses, it is common practice to stipulate that the initial agreement is 'subject to contract'. Such agreements are not intended to have any binding legal effect, and either party can withdraw at any time until formal written contracts have been exchanged. Any deposit may be reclaimed. As many house buyers and sellers have learnt to their cost, these 'subject to contract' agreements can, and often do, fall through. A disappointing survey or valuation, or a failure to sell or buy other properties, may lead to one or other party withdrawing, and if house prices are rising rapidly, the seller may even practise the despised art of 'gazumping' — accepting or threatening to accept a higher offer from a third party. Once contracts are signed and exchanged, however, the deal is binding, and either party can be sued to enforce performance of their obligations under it. The seller may be forced to execute a conveyance to the buyer, and the buyer who is unable to raise the necessary funds by the appointed completion day must expect (at the least) to forfeit his deposit.

Mere puffs and serious promises

Where manufacturers make boastful claims about their products in advertisements, the courts will not necessarily regard these as creating binding obligations. Many such statements are regarded as 'mere puffs' which do not have any legal effect. A litigious consumer who complains that Persil does not really 'wash whiter' than other powders cannot seriously expect to succeed in a lawsuit against the manufacturer. Some adverts, however, may be expressed in such a way as to suggest that an intention to create legal relations was indeed present. An example of this can be seen in the famous case of *Carlill v Carbolic Smoke Ball Co.*, the facts of which appear in Chapter 19. Because the defendants claimed to have deposited £1,000 with a bank 'to show their sincerity in the matter', the Court of Appeal concluded that their promise to pay £100 to anyone who caught influenza after using their products was no mere puff. It was intended to be taken seriously, and was legally enforceable.

Intention to create legal relations

Before there can be a legally binding contract there must be an intention to create legal relations.

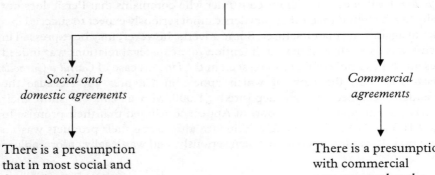

Social and domestic agreements

There is a presumption that in most social and domestic agreements there is no intention to create legal relations: *Balfour* v *Balfour*; *Jones* v *Padavatton*

This presumption may be rebutted where there is clear evidence that the parties did intend legal consequences to follow on from their agreement: see *Merritt* v *Merritt*.

Commercial agreements

There is a presumption with commercial agreements that the parties did intend to create legal relations

In some cases, however, the parties may deliberately make it clear that there is no intention to create legal relations, such as in provisional agreements for the sale of land or houses (i.e., those described as 'subject to contract') which are not intended to be binding.

TWENTY TWO

Express and Implied Terms

Introduction

The previous chapters dealt with the formalities which must be satisfied before a legally binding contract can come into existence. Here we are concerned with the actual terms of a contract. The terms of a contract define the content and the scope of the parties' rights and obligations. For example, in a contract for the sale of goods, matters such as the price of the goods, the quantity to be supplied and the standard or specification which the goods must satisfy are all likely to be contractual terms. A breach of any of these terms will therefore amount to a breach of contract.

It may nevertheless be difficult to ascertain the precise terms of some contracts. There may be months of negotiations leading up to the final conclusion of a contract, during which time many statements or promises may be made. It does not by any means follow that these will become terms of the contract. Some may be inconsequential; others may be regarded as 'mere representations'. The problem is complicated by the fact that, quite apart from those terms expressly agreed between the parties, the contract may also be deemed to contain certain other 'implied' terms. In some cases these are supposed to represent the presumed (but unexpressed) intentions of the parties. In others, the additional terms are in fact imposed by law, regardless of the parties' actual or presumed intentions.

Written contracts usually provide greater precision and certainty than oral ones, because there will be a document in which the terms are set out, but problems may arise where one party insists that certain other matters, not included in the written contract, were nevertheless agreed by the parties and intended to be terms of the contract. Can it ever be permissible for a party to argue that the written contract should be qualified, supplemented or contradicted by inclusion of these other, unwritten, terms? This requires consideration of the 'parol evidence rule', as to which, see p. 295, below.

Once the terms of the contract have been ascertained, the next step is to assess the relative importance of each of the terms. Not all terms of a contract are of equal importance, and it is necessary to distinguish between them because the remedy available for breach of contract varies according to this classification. The first part of this chapter will look at how the terms of a contract are ascertained and this will be followed by a consideration of how the relative importance of terms within a contract is determined.

Ascertainment of the express terms of a contract

Oral statements made by the parties before or at the time of contracting may, if significant at all, be one of two things:

(a)   they may be terms of the contract; or
(b)   they may be mere representations.

If a statement is classified as a term of the contract, but turns out to be untrue or is not satisfied, the injured party may sue for breach of contract. If, on the other hand, a statement is merely classed as an untrue representation, the injured party will be confined to an action for misrepresentation (see Chapter 23). Why does it matter whether the injured party sues for breach of contract or for misrepresentation? The difference may be significant for a number of reasons, but primarily because different kinds of remedies may be available, and any damages awarded by way of compensation will be assessed on a different basis. To put it crudely, a plaintiff may sometimes recover higher damages for breach of contract than he could have recovered for misrepresentation. In some of the older cases considered below, the distinction was even more important, because at one time *no* damages could be obtained for an innocent misrepresentation unless it had been incorporated as a contractual term. This changed with the enactment of the Misrepresentation Act 1967, as a result of which it is now far more likely that misrepresentation will provide a plaintiff with an adequate remedy (see Chapter 31).

The incorporation of written statements into contracts will be dealt with in Chapter 32 (Exclusion Clauses), as it is in respect of such clauses that the issue most frequently arises.

The basic test

The basic test for determining whether a statement is a contractual term or merely a representation is one of apparent intention. This was acknowledged in the case of *Heilbut, Symons & Co.* v *Buckleton* [1913] AC 30. In other words, do the parties appear to intend the statement to be a term of the contract? An objective approach is taken when determining the parties' intention, as was made clear by Denning LJ in the case of *Oscar Chess Ltd* v *Williams* [1957] 1 All ER 325:

> It is sometimes supposed that the tribunal must look into the minds of the parties to see what they themselves intended. That is a mistake... The question of whether a warranty (a type of term) was intended depends on the conduct of the parties, on their words and behaviour, rather than on their thoughts. If an intelligent bystander would reasonably infer that a warranty was intended, that will suffice.

One must therefore ascertain what a reasonable man would have inferred from the parties' behaviour. Looking at their actions, would he have thought the parties intended the statement to be a term or a representation?

Guides to classification

It can be difficult, even using an objective test, to ascertain the parties' apparent intentions. The courts have therefore developed a series of indicators which they can apply in order to help them in this task. Note, however, that these represent nothing more than starting points for the courts in working out the parties' intentions. There is no single decisive test. The final outcome will depend upon all the facts and circumstances of the case.

Importance of the statement
If one or more parties to a contract make it clear that a particular factor is crucial to his or her decision to enter into a contract, any statement dealing with that factor is likely to be classed as a term of that contract. In *Bannerman* v *White* (1861) 10 CBNS 844, Bannerman offered to sell hops to White, who sought an assurance that they had not been treated with sulphur when growing. White made it clear that he would not buy the hops if they had been. Unfortunately, however, it was eventually discovered that some of the hops had indeed been contaminated by sulphur. The court held that this amounted to a breach of a term of the contract.

Reliance
If one of the parties to the contract makes it clear that the statement he makes need not be checked, this may indicate that the statement was intended to become a term of the contract. The seller of goods may, for example, tell the buyer 'to take his word for it' that the goods are in sound condition. In *Schawel* v *Reade* [1913] 2 IR 64, the plaintiff visited the defendant's farm in order to purchase a stallion for stud purposes. Whilst the plaintiff was inspecting a

stallion called 'Mallow Man', the defendant said, 'You need not look for anything; the horse is perfectly sound. If there was anything the matter with the horse I would tell you.' As a result of that statement, the plaintiff stopped his examination of the horse and bought it. It transpired, however, that 'Mallow Man' suffered from a congenital eye defect which completely ruined his suitability as a stud horse.

The House of Lords held that the statement over the soundness of the horse was a term of the contract. It was clear that the defendant had indicated to the plaintiff that he could rely upon his statement. As Lord Moulton said:

> ... The essence of such warranty is that it becomes plain by the words, and the action, of the parties that it is intended that in the purchase the responsibility of the soundness shall rest upon the vendor; and how ... could a vendor more clearly indicate that he is prepared and intends to take upon himself the responsibility of the soundness than by saying: 'You need not look at that horse because it is perfectly sound', and sees that the purchaser thereupon desists from his immediate independent examination?

Schawel v *Reade* may be contrasted with *Ecay* v *Godfrey* (1947) 80 Lloyd's Rep 286. Godfrey sold Ecay a boat which he said was sound. He nevertheless advised Ecay to obtain a survey on the boat, and that negatived any suggestion that he intended to make soundness a contractual term.

Special knowledge of the representor

When deciding whether a statement is intended to be a term or a mere representation, one must consider whether one of the parties was more knowledgeable than the other. Was it reasonable for the other party to rely upon the statement? The court will be more likely to classify a statement as a term if it was made by the person who was in a better position to have discovered its truth. The cases of *Oscar Chess Ltd* v *Williams* [1957] 1 All ER 325 and *Dick Bentley Productions Ltd* v *Harold Smith (Motors) Ltd* [1965] 2 All ER 65 illustrate this point.

In *Oscar Chess Ltd* v *Williams*, the defendant sold an elderly Morris car to the plaintiffs, who were car dealers. The car's log book indicated that it was a 1948 model but, unknown to either party, this had been falsified at some time before the defendant acquired it. The car was in fact a 1939 model. There was no obvious difference in appearance between a 1939 model and a 1948 model, because no significant modifications had been incorporated during the war years, but a 1939 car was obviously much older and therefore worth much less. Had the plaintiffs been aware of the true age of the car, they would have paid £115 less for it (a lot of money in those days). When the true facts were discovered, the plaintiffs sued for recovery of this £115, but the Court of Appeal held that, despite its obvious importance, the statement as to age could not have been intended to be a term of the contract, because the defendant was clearly in no position to guarantee the age of the car. The plaintiffs, being in the business of buying and selling cars, were in a much better position to establish the true age of the car and it was unreasonable for them to rely upon the statement made by the defendant. Had they asked the defendant to verify the age of the car, he would probably have replied (as Denning LJ put it), 'I cannot do that. I have only the log book to go by, the same as you.' He might even have added, 'Well, you are the experts, not me!'

In contrast, the defendants in *Dick Bentley Productions Ltd v Harold Smith (Motors) Ltd* offered to sell the plaintiff a used Bentley which they assured him had been fitted with a new engine and gearbox and had covered only 20,000 miles since then. The odometer seemed to confirm this. The plaintiff purchased the car, but it turned out that the statement and odometer reading were false. The plaintiff sued for breach of contract, and won. Distinguishing *Oscar Chess Ltd v Williams*, the Court of Appeal held that these were terms of the contract. Not only were they important to the plaintiff, but in addition it was clear that the plaintiff had relied on the expertise of the defendants who ought to have verified the accuracy of such matters.

Has the contract been reduced to writing?

If the contract between the parties is put into writing, any precontractual statement not included in the written contract is likely to be construed as a mere representation. It may indeed be difficult for anyone to argue otherwise (see the 'parol evidence rule', below).

Interval between the making of the statement and conclusion of the contract

The longer the interval between the making of the statement and the conclusion of the contract, the more likely it is that the courts will infer that the precontractual statement was simply a representation.

The final three indicators of intention, described immediately above, can all be discerned in *Routledge v McKay* [1954] 1 All ER 855. The contract concerned the sale of a motorcycle and sidecar combination. The defendant wrongly told the plaintiff that it was a 1942 model, but he made it clear that he had no personal knowledge of this, and had merely obtained the information from the registration book. A week later, the contract between the parties was reduced into writing, but no mention of the age of the cycle was made in this written contract. It turned out to be a 1930 model, but the Court of Appeal held that the age of the cycle could not be a term of the contract.

Written contracts and the parol evidence rule

Where the terms of a contract appear to be set out in a written or printed document, this provides a degree of certainty often missing from oral contracts. If a particular matter (such as the colour of the goods to be supplied or the date of delivery) is not specified in the written contract, the presumption must be that it is not intended to be a term of that contract (see *Routledge* v *McKay*, above). This does not necessarily provide an absolute guarantee of certainty, however. Cases may still arise in which one of the parties insists that something else was agreed, which for some reason failed to be included in the written contract. Is it permissible for extra, unwritten, terms to be incorporated, or should the courts insist on the 'sanctity' of the written terms? Why, after all, bother with a written contract if the parties can still argue over the existence of other, unwritten, terms?

The 'parol evidence rule' restricts the extent to which oral evidence may be admitted to vary, alter or contradict a written contract or deed. It was at one time very strictly applied. Thus, in *Angell* v *Duke* (1875) 32 LT 320, there was a written contract for the letting of a house, together with the furniture it contained. The plaintiff then tried to argue that the defendant had previously agreed to provide additional furniture not mentioned in the written contract, but the court refused even to admit (i.e., would not even listen to) his evidence on that point. He was not permitted to contradict the terms of the written contract which he himself had signed.

More recent cases, however, show that the parol evidence rule has become subject to many exceptions, which undermine its status as a rule. For example, parol or extrinsic evidence may be received to show that the written contract contains errors, and does not really record the parties' true agreement. If the parties agree on a price of £4,000, but sign a contract which had been mistyped so as to read £40,000, this error can be rectified, as long as there is cogent evidence that the document is erroneous. Furthermore, the courts will sometimes hold that a written contract does not include the whole of the agreement between the parties. In *J. Evans & Son (Portsmouth) Ltd* v *Andrea Merzario Ltd* [1976] 2 All ER 930, the plaintiffs had for many years used the defendants' ships to transport their lorry trailers, and agreed to the service being 'containerised' provided that the containers were stored below decks, as their trailers always had been. They received an oral assurance to that effect, but this was not incorporated in the written contract. The Court of Appeal nevertheless held that there was a valid agreement to store the containers safely below deck. The contract, they said, was only partly reduced to writing. Part of it was oral and a further part was implied from past relations between the parties.

Collateral contracts

Even where there does appear to be a complete written contract, the courts sometimes deem a statement which is not incorporated within that contract to be part of another connected or 'collateral' contract. An action for breach of contract may then be brought on the collateral contract. Lord Moulton in *Heilbut Symons & Co.* v *Buckleton* [1913] AC 30 offered this example:

It is evident, both on principle and on authority, that there may be a contract the consideration for which is the making of some other contract. 'If you will make such and such a contract I will give you one hundred pounds.' It is in every sense of the word a complete legal contract. It is collateral to the main contract, but each has an independent existence, and they do not differ in respect of their possessing to the full the character and status of a contract.

IMPLIED TERMS

So far, we have looked at terms agreed to by the parties themselves or, in other words, express terms. Terms, however, may also be *implied* into a contract. When parties enter into a contract, they often fail to deal specifically with every problem which could arise under it. They may have overlooked the possibility of some eventuality arising or they may have considered something too obvious to state. If a problem arises which has not been dealt with by the express terms of the contract, then an appropriate term may, in some circumstances, be implied into the contract, notwithstanding the supposed restrictions of the parol evidence rule. There are various ways in which terms may be implied into a contract, namely:

(a)   terms implied as fact;
(b)   terms implied in law (whether by statute or by the courts); and
(c)   terms implied by custom.

Terms implied as fact

When the courts imply terms 'as fact' into a contract, the theory is that they are merely giving effect to the unexpressed intentions of the parties. The court will not simply rewrite the contract so as to impose its own solution on the parties, and will only imply a term in this way if it is 'necessary to give the transaction such business efficacy as the parties must have intended' (*The Moorcock* (1889) 14 PD 64, per Bowen LJ) or alternatively if it is obvious that both parties must have intended it to be part of the contract. This is known as the 'officious bystander' test and was invoked in *Shirlaw* v *Southern Foundries (1926) Ltd* [1939] 2 All ER 113, where Mackinnon LJ said:

> Prima facie, that which in any contract is left to be implied and need not be expressed is something so obvious that it goes without saying; so that, if while the parties were making their bargain, an officious bystander were to suggest some express provision for it in the agreement, they would testily suppress him with a common 'Oh, of course'.

Terms implied 'in law'

Terms implied as fact can, provided the above criteria are satisfied, be implied into any type of contract. In contrast, terms are only implied in law in respect of contracts of a defined type, such as contracts for the sale of goods, or tenancy agreements. In many cases, terms are implied by legislation, as for example under the Sale of Goods Act 1979. In the absence of such legislation, the courts may still imply terms in circumstances where this is necessary to give efficacy to contracts of the type concerned.

An example of this process at work can be seen in *Liverpool City Council* v *Irwin* [1976] 2 All ER 39. Certain tenants of a tower block containing council flats became dissatisfied with its poor state of repair. The lifts and rubbish chutes were regularly out of order, and the stairs were often unlit and dangerous. The tenants refused to pay their rent, arguing that the council was in breach of an implied term of the tenancy agreement to repair and maintain the common parts of the block. The council blamed the tenants and local vandals, and sued to regain possession of the flats.

The House of Lords held that there was an implied term in the tenancy agreement under which the Council was required to take reasonable care to maintain the common parts of the building. Someone had to be responsible for their maintenance, and it could only be the Council, because it controlled the areas and services in question. Their Lordships did not rely on any supposed unexpressed intention of the parties (as where terms are implied as fact) but took account of the type of contract involved and the relationship between the parties, and interfered with it by adding new terms in so far as this was necessary in order to make the contract workable. Tenants could not be expected to live in high rise flats without working lifts or lighted staircases. The tenants nevertheless failed to prove that the Council was in breach of its duty, because the Council had made reasonable efforts to maintain the facilities in the face of persistent vandalism and unco-operative tenants, and could not be required to guarantee working facilities at all times.

Legislation increasingly dictates that certain terms should be implied into contracts, thereby seeking to maintain minimum standards of performance. For example, the Sale of Goods Act 1979 (as amended) implies certain terms into contracts for the sale of goods. Goods sold in the course of business must, for example, be of satisfactory quality and be fit for their purpose. If a customer buys a kettle that is incapable of boiling water, that kettle will neither be of satisfactory quality nor fit for its purpose, and the dissatisfied customer can (at least) demand his money back. See further Chapter 35.

Terms implied by custom

There may be contractual terms which are customary in a particular trade, profession or locality. In the absence of any express term to the contrary, these customary terms will be implied into a contract, because it is assumed that this is what the parties would reasonably have expected. In *Hutton* v *Warren* (1836) 1 M & W 466 the court implied a term into an agricultural tenancy agreement to the effect that the tenant farmer given notice to quit should receive some allowance for seeds and labour already expended, because this was customary in that industry. If, however, the written agreement had not just failed to mention such a term, but had expressly contradicted it, there would no longer have been room for any such implication.

CONDITIONS, WARRANTIES AND INNOMINATE TERMS

The terms of a contract define both the content and scope of the parties' rights and obligations. Not all terms contained within the contract, however, will be of the same importance, and this is reflected in the different remedies given for breach.

There are three types of terms, namely, conditions, warranties and 'innominate' terms. These terms are distinguishable from each other by the legal consequences which flow from the breach of any of them. A breach of any contractual term entitles the injured party to claim damages for breach of contract, but damages will not always be an adequate remedy, and the aggrieved party may also wish to terminate the contract. Whether termination is possible depends upon what type of term has been broken. The following rules apply:

(a)   if a term is classified as a *condition* and it turns out to be untrue or is not fulfilled, then the injured party can sue for damages and /or treat the contract as terminated, no matter how minor the breach;

(b)   if a term is classed as a *warranty*, the only remedy for the injured party if that term is broken is that of damages. Termination of the contract is not available as a remedy for breach of a warranty;

(c)   in the case of *Hong Kong Fir Shipping Co. Ltd* v *Kawasaki Kisen Kaisha Ltd* [1962] 1 All ER 474, the Court of Appeal recognised the existence of a third type, the innominate term. The remedy available for the breach of an innominate term depends upon the factual consequences which flow from its breach. The aggrieved party may terminate the contract (as for breach of a condition) if the breach is such as to deprive him of most or all of the benefit which he was intended to derive from the contract. If on the other hand the breach is relatively minor, the only remedy will be that of damages, as for breach of a warranty.

This classification of terms and the remedies available for breach will be discussed in further detail below.

How are terms classified?

The most obvious method of ascertaining what type of term is involved is to look at the contract itself, to see if the parties themselves have expressly classified it. If they have not, the next step is to ascertain (objectively) the apparent intention of the parties *at the time of contracting*, so as to see whether a reasonable man would have intended the term to be a condition, a warranty or an innominate term. When classifying the term, the courts do not look at the parties' intention at the time of the breach, but note that the *nature* of the breach itself becomes relevant where the term has been classed as an innominate one.

Practical consequences of classification

Breach of a condition

If a term is classified as a condition then as soon as that term is broken the injured party may, if he so elects, treat the contract as terminated, irrespective of the seriousness of the breach. An illustration can be found in a sale of goods case, *Re Moore & Co. Ltd and Landauer & Co. Ltd* [1921] 2 KB 519. This involved a contract for the sale of canned fruit. It was expressly stated in the contract that the tins were to be packed in cases containing 35 tins each, but when they arrived there were only 24 tins in each case. The court held it to be a condition of the contract that the goods would correspond with their description (i.e., that the tins were to be packed 35 per case) and as this had not been complied with, the other party was entitled to terminate the contract. (A minor discrepancy such as this in a commercial contract would no longer be assumed to be a breach of a condition: see now s. 15A of the Sale of Goods Act 1979, p. 406, below.)

The ability to terminate a contract for a breach of condition, even where the harm suffered from the breach is minor, can enable a party who has simply made a bad bargain to escape his contractual obligations, which may be very harsh on the other party. On the other hand, the advantage of classifying a term in this way is that it brings certainty to the contract, and this may be vital in certain commercial situations. The injured party knows as soon as a condition is broken that he can terminate the contract, and this may, for example, enable him to find an alternative source of supply as quickly as possible. For this reason, time or date clauses in commercial contracts are often specified as conditions, or interpreted as such by the courts.

The right of an injured party to terminate a contract for breach of a condition is not one which he is obliged to exercise. He may instead choose to continue with (or 'affirm') the contract, contenting himself with damages for the breach. His decision, once made, is irrevocable, and if he does not terminate it, both parties remain obliged to perform any remaining obligations they may have under the contract. If the injured party does not expressly communicate his decision to the offending one, a court or arbitrator may need to examine his subsequent conduct, in light of the particular circumstances of the case, in order to determine whether it implies a termination of the contract (*Vitol SA* v *Norelf Ltd* [1996] 3 All ER 193).

Breach of an innominate term

One of the major advantages associated with the innominate term is that of flexibility. The remedy which the injured party will receive when an innominate term is broken will be proportionate to the damage which he has suffered. For example, the more extreme remedy of termination will only be awarded if the breach has the effect of depriving the injured party of substantially all of the benefit which he was supposed to receive under the contract. In contrast, if the breach is minor, the injured party's remedy will be restricted to that of damages.

This classification is particularly appropriate where the term in question is of a type which can be breached in many different ways, ranging from something relatively minor to something crucial. The *Hong Kong Fir* case is a good example of the application of an innominate term. The defendants chartered a cargo ship, the '*Hong Kong Fir*' from the plaintiff shipowners for a period of two years. The ship was supposedly 'fitted in every way for ordinary cargo service', but on her first voyage under the charter, her elderly engines broke down and took five weeks to be repaired. The engine room crew were inexperienced and had to be replaced and it was another 15 weeks before the ship was ready for sea again. By this stage, she was fully seaworthy, but the charterers had lost patience, and purported to terminate the contract on the ground that seaworthiness was a condition of the contract. The shipowners, on the other hand, denied this, and sued the charterers for wrongfully terminating the contract.

The Court of Appeal held that there are some contractual undertakings which are too complicated to be classified simply as conditions or warranties. Undertakings as to the seaworthiness of vessels came into that category. A ship could be classed as unseaworthy if it merely lacked an anchor, but it might also be unseaworthy because of fundamental problems, such as a leaking hull or corroded bulkheads. By classifying terms as to seaworthiness as 'innominate', the courts can provide a remedy which is proportionate to the injury suffered by the aggrieved party. Damages may suffice for lesser breaches, whilst termination should be reserved for cases in which the consequences of the breach are such as to deprive the injured party of 'substantially all of the benefit' they are entitled to receive under the contract. In *Hong Kong Fir*, the problems with the engines had been fixed, and the charter still had some 20 months to run. Damages were therefore an adequate remedy.

The disadvantage of classifying a term as innominate is that of uncertainty. The parties cannot always know whether they can terminate, but may have to wait to see the effect of the breach on their contract, and this uncertainty may cause difficulties in some cases.

Breach of a warranty

The discussion so far has concentrated on conditions and innominate terms. This is because these are more important today. With the development of the innominate term, the warranty has greatly decreased in importance. In most cases, the courts will tend to construe terms as innominate. This gives greater flexibility in the award of remedies.

Terms of a contract

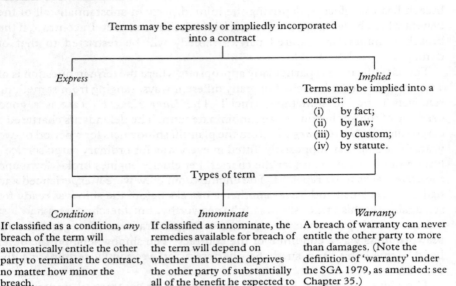

Terms may be expressly or impliedly incorporated
into a contract

Express

Implied
Terms may be implied into a
contract:
   (i)   by fact;
   (ii)   by law;
   (iii) by custom;
   (iv) by statute.

Types of term

Condition
If classified as a condition, *any* breach of the term will automatically entitle the other party to terminate the contract, no matter how minor the breach.

Innominate
If classified as innominate, the remedies available for breach of the term will depend on whether that breach deprives the other party of substantially all of the benefit he expected to receive under the contract.

Warranty
A breach of warranty can never entitle the other party to more than damages. (Note the definition of 'warranty' under the SGA 1979, as amended: see Chapter 35.)

TWENTY THREE
Misrepresentation

During precontractual negotiations, a person may make a number of statements or promises in an attempt to induce other parties to enter into the contract. A person trying to sell a used car may, for example, tell a prospective customer that the car has recently had a new engine, or that it has been undersealed to protect it from rust. We saw in the preceding chapter that, if such a precontractual statement is later incorporated as a term of the contract and turns out to be false, the buyer can sue for breach of contract; but even if it cannot be shown to have been incorporated as a term, the buyer may nevertheless attempt to rescind the contract and/or claim damages under the law of misrepresentation.

To succeed in an action for misrepresentation, a party must prove that he has been induced to enter into the contract on the basis of a false statement of past or present fact. He may be able to show that this false statement was fraudulent or that it was made negligently, but even if he cannot show either of these, he may still be able to seek rescission or damages on the basis of an 'innocent' misrepresentation.

It must be emphasised that there are certain practical differences between the various types of claims, and any damages awarded for misrepresentation will be calculated quite differently from damages awarded for breach of contract (as to which, see Chapter 31). Whereas damages for breach of contract are intended to put the plaintiff in the financial position he would expect to be in if the contract had properly been performed (compensating him for loss of anticipated profits or 'expectation loss'), damages for misrepresentation are merely intended to compensate for any actual (or out-of-pocket) loss he may have suffered through agreeing to the contract.

If a plaintiff is unsure whether he can succeed in showing that a misrepresentation made to him has been incorporated as one of the terms of his contract, there is nothing to prevent him raising both claims in the alternative. He may therefore claim:

(a)   that the false statement has become incorporated as a contractual term, so that the maker is in breach of contract; and

(b)   that the statement is, alternatively, an actionable misrepresentation.

ELEMENTS OF AN ACTIONABLE MISREPRESENTATION

An actionable or 'operative' misrepresentation can be defined as 'a false statement of existing or past fact, made by one party to the contract to the other, before or at the time of contracting, which induces the other party to contract' (Koffman & Macdonald, *The Law of Contract*, 2nd ed., at p. 240). As Koffman & Macdonald point out, however, a statement of this kind may sometimes be implied by silence or may be based on physical appearances. It does not always have to be stated expressly.

There are at least three things which must be proved by the plaintiff (or conceded by the defendant) if an action for misrepresentation is to succeed. These are:

(a)   that a representation of past or present fact was made by the defendant (or his agent) to the plaintiff (or his agent) at or before the time of contracting;

(b)   that the representation was or became false or misleading in some material respect; and

(c)   that the plaintiff was induced to contract on the basis of that misrepresentation.

Representations of fact

The first requirement is that a misrepresentation must be a false statement as to an existing or past fact. Statements of opinion, future intentions or law will not ordinarily qualify as statements of fact. Care must, however, be taken in interpreting and applying this rule, because it is not always easy to distinguish a statement of opinion or law from one of fact, or a statement as to the future from one as to the present; nor indeed is it always easy to distinguish between a statement and an act.

Fact and opinion

As a general rule, statements of opinion cannot constitute actionable misrepresentations. This is illustrated by the case of *Bisset* v *Wilkinson* [1927] AC 177. Bisset offered to sell Wilkinson two parcels of land in New Zealand. Wilkinson wanted to use the land to graze sheep and he asked Bisset how many sheep the land would support. Bisset replied that he thought it could accommodate 2,000 sheep, but this was merely a guess, because (as both parties well knew) the land in question had never been used to graze sheep before. Wilkinson bought the land, and found that it could not support anywhere near 2,000 sheep, but the Privy Council nevertheless rejected his action for misrepresentation. The land in question had never previously been used for sheep farming, and so Bisset's statement could only be one of opinion rather than fact.

The position may, however, be different where the party making the representation (the representor) does not truly hold the opinion he expresses. When a person expresses an opinion or belief, he impliedly represents that he genuinely holds it. If it transpires that he did not genuinely hold that belief at all, then he has misrepresented a matter of fact, namely his state of mind (cf. *Edgington* v *Fitzmaurice* (below)).

Furthermore, where the party making the representation has a particular expertise, or is in a better position to know the facts than is the other party, the courts may be reluctant to construe his statements as mere matters of opinion, as can be seen from the case of *Smith* v *Land and House Property Corporation* (1884) 28 Ch D 7. The plaintiff sold a hotel to the defendants. The particulars on the sale documents stated that it was 'let to Mr Frederick Fleck (a most desirable tenant), at a rental of £400 per annum, for an unexpired term of 27 and a half years'. In fact, Fleck's rent was seriously in arrears, and had been so for a considerable time. When they discovered this, the defendants sought to rescind the contract, and the Court of Appeal found in their favour. The assertion made by the plaintiff regarding Fleck's desirability as a tenant was more than a mere statement of opinion. It was calculated to mislead the defendants as to the underlying facts. Nobody could regard a tenant as 'most desirable' if he cannot even pay his rent! As Bowen LJ said:

> ... if the facts are not equally known to both sides, then a statement of opinion by the one who knows the facts best involves very often a statement of a material fact, for he impliedly states that he knows facts which justify his opinion.

Statements of intention and future events

A statement concerning something that is supposed to happen in the future cannot be classed as a misrepresentation, merely because that thing never happens, because a misrepresentation must concern present or past facts. If, for example, A promises to obtain spare parts for the car he is selling to B, but subsequently forgets to do so, his forgetfulness does not make his initial promise a misrepresentation. A statement of this kind *may*, however, amount to a misrepresentation as to the maker's *present* intentions. If A makes such a promise to B, without ever really intending to do any such thing, then he has misrepresented his own state of mind. An example of this rule can be seen in the case of *Edgington* v *Fitzmaurice* (1885) 29 Ch D 459. The directors of the 'Army & Navy Provision Market Ltd' published a prospectus in an attempt to raise money from investors through the issue of debentures (securities issued by companies in return for loans). The prospectus stipulated that the directors intended to use the money to make improvements to company buildings and to acquire the company's own horse-drawn transport. However, the real intention of the directors, from the very beginning, was to use the new money to pay off existing debts. It was held that the prospectus was a fraudulent misrepresentation. In a famous passage from his judgment in the Court of Appeal, Bowen LJ said:

> The state of a man's mind is as much a fact as the state of his digestion. It is true that it is very difficult to prove what the state of a man's mind at a particular time is, but if it can be ascertained it is as much a fact as anything else. A misrepresentation as to the state of a man's mind is, therefore, a misstatement of fact.

Statements of law

A statement of law cannot ordinarily constitute a misrepresentation, even if it is clearly wrong, but a false statement as to one's *view* of the law can be classed as a statement of fact under the same principles as govern statements of intention (above).

Silent misrepresentation

The general rule is that silence cannot constitute a misrepresentation. There are, however, certain situations where silence can lead to an implied misrepresentation.

Contracts 'uberrimae fidei'

Contracts *uberrimae fidei* are contracts which are held to require 'the utmost good faith'. In such contracts, there is a duty to disclose all material facts. The most important examples are contracts of insurance, under which the assured is under a duty to disclose to his insurers all material facts within his knowledge which might influence the judgment of a prudent insurer in fixing the premium or determining whether he will take the risk. If something is not disclosed which should have been, as where a motorist fails to mention a previous speeding conviction when applying for motor insurance, then the contract may be avoided by the insurance company, who may elect to return any premiums whilst refusing to pay any claim being made on the policy. In such cases, however, the insurance company must show that the non-disclosure actually influenced them in accepting the contract or in setting the premium (*Pan Atlantic Insurance Co. Ltd* v *Pine Top Insurance Co. Ltd* [1994] 3 All ER 581).

Fiduciary relationships

Where there is a fiduciary relationship, there will be a duty on the part of the fiduciary to disclose all material facts. Examples of fiduciary relationships would include a solicitor and his client, a bank manager and a customer or a director and his company.

Changes in circumstances

If a statement of fact, although true at the time it was made, becomes false before the contract is concluded, then if the representor becomes aware of this change, he must inform the other party of it. Failure to do so may cause it to be regarded as a misrepresentation. In *With* v *O'Flannagan* [1936] Ch 575, Dr O'Flannagan offered to sell his medical practice to Dr With. In January, he told With that the practice was worth £2,000 a year. At that time, this was quite true. Unfortunately, O'Flannagan had become too ill to practise, and by the time that the contract was signed in May, almost all his patients had left him. The practice had become practically worthless, with takings of less than £5 per week. O'Flannagan never informed With of this, and the court held that the original statement became a misrepresentation.

Half truths and falsity

A person who tells only part of the truth about something may mislead others by reason of the facts which he has omitted to mention. Misleading half truths may therefore amount to misrepresentations (*Dimmock* v *Hallett* (1866) LR 2 Ch App 21). In *Inner London Justices, ex p Wandsworth Borough Council* [1983] RTR 1012, a case brought under the Trade Descriptions Act 1968, a dealer was convicted of falsely describing a car as having had just one owner, even though that was strictly speaking correct. What he omitted to point out was that the 'one previous owner' was a car leasing company, and the car must have been used by dozens of different drivers! Anyone who bought the car on the basis of this 'one owner' label would clearly have had a remedy for misrepresentation.

Misrepresentation by conduct

Misrepresentations must be statements of fact, but it is recognised that facts may sometimes be stated by implication, and an implication may arise from conduct as well as from words. If A induces B to contract with him by dressing as a bishop, admiral or police officer, that may amount to a misrepresentation, even though he never actually says that he is such a person.

Another example of misrepresentation by conduct might be the concealment of rust damage on a car with paint and filler (but as to the need to prove reliance, see *Horsfall* v *Thomas*, below).

The effect on the other party

To be actionable, a misrepresentation must not only have been intended to influence the other party: it must actually have induced that party to enter into the contract. It follows, therefore, that there can be no action for misrepresentation if the representation had not even come to the other party's notice or if the party to whom it was made decided not to rely upon it, but relied instead upon his own knowledge or on the advice of his own expert valuer. Nor can it be actionable if the other party knew it to be false, and decided to overlook or ignore it when entering into the contract.

Thus, in *Horsfall* v *Thomas* (1862) 1 H & C 90, the vendor of a gun went to the trouble of concealing a dangerous fault in the barrel before offering it to the purchaser. The latter, however, did not even give the gun a cursory inspection before buying it, so he could not subsequently claim that the concealment of the fault had misled him.

In *Attwood* v *Small* (1838) 6 Cl & F 232, the vendor of a mine misrepresented its capacity to the prospective purchaser, but the latter very properly insisted on obtaining his own expert valuation before buying it. The mine unfortunately proved incapable of producing as much ore as either the vendor or the expert valuer had suggested. Worse still, the vendor's statement had not been relied upon by the purchaser, so he could not claim it was an actionable misrepresentation.

On the other hand, it is no defence to an action for misrepresentation that the other party could have obtained or conducted an independent valuation if he or she had wished to do so. In *Redgrave* v *Hurd* (1881) 20 Ch D 1, the purchaser of a legal practice was told that it was worth up to £400 a year, and he relied upon this. If he had checked the accounts for himself, he might have seen that the practice was worth little more than half of that, but he did not, so the misrepresentation was an actionable one and he was able to rescind the contract.

REMEDIES FOR MISREPRESENTATION

Once an actionable misrepresentation has been established, the court must determine what type of misrepresentation is involved. As mentioned earlier, there are several types of misrepresentation, and slightly different rules apply to each.

Fraudulent misrepresentation

The classic definition of fraudulent misrepresentation can be found in *Derry* v *Peek* (1889) 14 App Cas 337, where Lord Herschell said, '. . . fraud is proved when it is shown that a false misrepresentation has been made (1) knowingly, (2) without belief in its truth, or (3) recklessly, careless whether it be true or false'. More recently, Jacob J stated that fraud requires a dishonest disregard for the truth (*Thomas Witter Ltd* v *TBP Industries Ltd* [1996] 2 All ER 573 at p. 587). The person making the representation must lack belief in the truth of his statement, or at least not care whether it is true or not; but he does not have to know for certain that it is false. The representor must also have intended that his statement would influence the other party. If he genuinely but foolishly believed in the truth of his statement, he cannot of course have been fraudulent.

Remedies for fraudulent misrepresentation

The principal remedy for any misrepresentation is rescission of the contract. This involves each party returning any property or money that has changed hands, so as to put each party back to the position they would have been in had the contract never been made. As explained below, however, full rescission may not always be possible, and damages may therefore be claimed instead. There may also be consequential losses or expenses to be compensated for, even where rescission is available.

An action for a fraudulent misrepresentation is brought under the tort of deceit, rather than under the law of contract. Any award of damages is therefore calculated so as to compensate the plaintiff for any actual loss he has suffered by entering into the contract in reliance on the misrepresentation. It is not designed to compensate him for profits he might have expected to make if the statement had been true. If the plaintiff seeks damages on that latter basis, he must sue for breach of contract and prove that the misrepresentation has been incorporated as a contractual term.

There may be significant advantages in proving fraud when suing for misrepresentation. The amount of damages which an injured party may recover is usually limited by some kind of objective test. In cases of negligent misrepresentation, for example, the plaintiff may only recover damages for loss if that loss was a reasonably foreseeable consequence of the defendant's actions. The tort of deceit is different, however. The plaintiff may recover for any damage which stemmed or 'flowed on' from the fraudulent misrepresentation, *whether that damage was foreseeable or not*. In *Smith New Court Securities Ltd v Scrimgeour Vickers (Asset Management) Ltd* [1996] 4 All ER 769, the plaintiff was deceived by the defendant into buying shares in a company. The shares concerned could not easily or quickly be resold. Unknown to either party, a third person then practised a monumental fraud on the company in question, wiping no less than £11m. off the value of the shares acquired by the plaintiff. The House of Lords held that the plaintiff could recover his entire loss from the defendants, even though neither of them could have foreseen that loss.

It is sometimes said that the burden of proving fraud is much higher than that of proving mere negligence. In some respects, this is true. No such allegation will succeed unless there is clear and credible evidence to support it. It is wrong, however, to suggest that the burden of proof is as high as that in criminal cases (i.e., proof beyond reasonable doubt). Proof on balance of probabilities will suffice in any civil action.

Negligent misrepresentations

At one time, the law failed to provide adequate remedies for victims of negligent misrepresentations. Rescission of the contract might be possible, as for any other kind of misrepresentation, but that remedy could only be claimed if the circumstances permitted it, and not, for example, where the parties could no longer be restored to their original positions (see below). In 1964, however, the House of Lords in *Hedley Byrne Ltd* v *Heller & Partners* [1963] 2 All ER 575 established a basis of liability for certain negligent statements under the law of tort. Shortly afterwards, Parliament enacted a statutory remedy for negligent misrepresentations in contracts. This is contained in s. 2(1) of the Misrepresentation Act 1967.

Negligent misstatement under the law of tort

Before a plaintiff can succeed in an action for tort relating to negligent misstatement under the principle established in *Hedley Byrne Ltd* v *Heller & Partners*, he must establish that the defendant owed him a duty of care, that the defendant was in breach of that duty of care and that the plaintiff's reliance on that statement caused him loss or harm. A contractual relationship need not be established, but the plaintiff must prove that a 'special relationship' existed between himself and the defendant. For further discussion of this rule, see Chapter 37.

Negligent misrepresentation under s. 2(1) of the Misrepresentation Act 1967

Section 2(1) states:

> Where a person has entered into a contract after a misrepresentation has been made to him by another party thereto and as a result thereof he has suffered loss, then, if the person making the misrepresentation would be liable to damages in respect thereof had the misrepresentation been made fraudulently, that person shall be so liable notwithstanding that the misrepresentation was not made fraudulently, unless he proves that he had reasonable grounds to believe and did believe up to the time the contract was made that the facts represented were true.

This covers the situation where a party enters into a contract in reliance upon a false statement made by the other party, who cannot establish that he had reasonable grounds for believing it to be true.

There are certain advantages to bringing an action under s. 2(1), rather than under the *Hedley Byrne* principle or the tort of deceit. In the first place, it is easier to bring such an action because s. 2(1) reverses the usual burden of proof. A plaintiff claiming under it only has to show that he relied upon the misrepresentation and thereby suffered a loss. The burden then shifts to the defendant to prove that he had reasonable grounds for believing what he said to be true. If he cannot prove this, he will be liable under s. 2(1).

Furthermore, a plaintiff suing under s. 2(1) need not prove that the maker of the statement owed him any duty of care. It is enough merely to show that the misrepresentation led to a contract between them.

Damages awarded under s. 2(1) are quantified on the usual principles used to assess damages in tort cases (i.e., they should reflect actual loss suffered through reliance on the misrepresentation, rather than lost expectations of future profits under the contract). In *Royscott Trust Ltd* v *Rogerson* [1991] 3 All E R 294, the Court of Appeal held that damages under s. 2(1) can be recovered for *any* damage or loss which is caused by reliance upon the misrepresentation, whether it was foreseeable or not. This would suggest that there is no difference in practice between damages awarded under s. 2(1) and damages awarded under the tort of deceit, but in *Smith New Court Securities* v *Scrimgeour Vickers* (above) Lord Steyn and Lord Browne-Wilkinson each suggested that *Royscott Trust* v *Rogerson* was wrongly decided. According to Lord Steyn, liability for negligence should not extend to cover unforeseeable loss, although this was strictly speaking *obiter* on the facts of the case before him.

Innocent misrepresentation

Innocent misrepresentations are those not covered by any of the above categories (i.e., they are neither fraudulent nor negligent). Prior to the 1967 Act, the only possible remedy for an innocent misrepresentation was that of rescission, and, as explained below, this is a remedy that is all too easily lost through delay or through circumstances which make it impossible to restore the parties to their precontractual positions.

Damages in lieu of rescission (Misrepresentation Act 1967, s. 2(2))
Under s. 2(2) of the 1967 Act, the court has a *discretion* to award damages in lieu of rescission. Damages may be a more appropriate remedy where the effect of the misrepresentation was small, and it appears that the courts can award damages under s. 2(2), even where the original right of rescission has been lost.

The power to award damages in lieu of a *lost* right to rescission is by no means obvious from the literal wording of s. 2(2), which refers to the situations in which the plaintiff, '. . . would be entitled, by reason of the misrepresentation, to rescind the contract . . .'. In *Thomas Witter Ltd* v *TBP Industries Ltd* [1996] 2 All ER 573, however, Jacob J was referred to a passage in *Hansard* which showed that the Solicitor-General had presented the provision to Parliament as one designed to provide a remedy where the right to rescission had been lost. This satisfied him that, 'the power to award damages under s. 2(2) does not depend upon an extant right to rescission — it depends only upon a right having existed in the past'. (As to the use of *Hansard* to resolve ambiguities in legislation, see further Chapter 3.)

Rescission

A misrepresentation renders a contract voidable which means that the injured party is entitled, but not obliged, to rescind the contract. The right to rescind is available as a remedy for all types of misrepresentation. The purpose of rescission is to restore the parties to their precontractual position. If this cannot be achieved, as for example, where the goods have been sold on to another person, consumed or destroyed, then the courts cannot grant the remedy of rescission. This and other 'bars to rescission' are discussed below.

How does rescission take place?
The effect of a contract being voidable is that the contract continues in existence until and unless the injured party elects to have it rescinded or set aside. To rescind, the injured party must ordinarily inform the other of his decision or (alternatively) do something from which an inference to rescind may be inferred. In *Car and Universal Finance Ltd* v *Caldwell* [1964] 1 All ER 290, Caldwell sold his car to a man called Norris, who 'paid' for it with what proved to be a dud cheque. Caldwell then sought to rescind the contract, but of course Norris had already disappeared with the car. Caldwell promptly informed the police and the Automobile Association of the deception and asked them to trace the car. Norris meanwhile sold the car to a dealer, who subsequently sold it on to the defendants before it was traced to them.

The question for the court to decide was, 'who now owned the car?'. Was it the original owner, (Caldwell), or was it the defendants, who had acted in good faith throughout? The answer to that question depended upon whether Caldwell had rescinded the contract *before* the car was acquired by the defendants. If he had not done so, the defendants would have acquired a good title to the car, because the original contract with Norris was only voidable, not void. The Court of Appeal held that, by informing the police and the AA, which was all that he reasonably could have done, Caldwell had clearly indicated his intention to rescind. Norris had deliberately avoided communication of this rescission and must have realised that Caldwell would have wanted rescission. Consequently Caldwell remained the owner of the car as he had effectively rescinded the contract between himself and Norris before the car had been sold to the innocent defendants.

The ruling was tough luck on the defendants, who would have had no means of knowing what had happened to the car before they bought it. The necessary legal documentation (which we now call the vehicle registration document) would have been completed and handed over when Caldwell sold the car to Norris, and the defendants (being a finance company) would certainly not have acquired the car without that documentation. It may be that the case turns largely on its own unusual facts, and it may therefore be dangerous to rely upon it as a precedent unless the facts are largely indistinguishable.

Bars to rescission

The right to rescind was historically an equitable remedy, and may be barred by affirmation, by lapse of time, by the impossibility of returning parties to their original position, or by innocent third parties having acquired rights over the subject matter of the contract.

Affirmation

As soon as a party becomes aware that he is the victim of an actionable misrepresentation, he must choose either to affirm the contract or to rescind it. Once he has affirmed the contract, any right to rescind is lost. He may either notify the representor that he has decided not to rescind the contract or his affirmation may be implied from his conduct. Affirmation may be implied where he does an act that is inconsistent with any intention to rescind, such as claiming rights due to him under the contract.

Lapse of time

Where a substantial period of time has passed since the misrepresentation was made, any right to rescind may lapse. In *Leaf* v *International Galleries Ltd* [1950] 1 All ER 693, the defendants represented to Leaf that a painting which they were selling was by Constable, and he subsequently bought it for the princely sum of £85. Five years later, when he tried to sell the picture, he discovered that it was not by Constable at all. He then tried to rescind the original contract, but the Court of Appeal held that rescission was no longer possible after such a lapse of time. Jenkins LJ said: 'Contracts such as this cannot be kept open and subject to the possibility of recession indefinitely ... it behoves the purchaser either to verify or, as the case may be, to disprove the representation within a reasonable time.'

Impossibility of returning parties to their original position

Rescission is intended to restore all parties to their original position and this will not be possible if the subject matter of the contract has been radically altered, consumed, sold on or destroyed. Some flexibility is necessary, however, because exact restitution is seldom possible. As Lord Blackburn said in *Erlanger* v *New Sombrero Phosphate Co.* (1873) 3 App Cas 1218, a court may 'take account of profits and make allowances for deterioration ... and do what is practically just, though it cannot restore the parties precisely to the position they were in before the contract'.

Third party rights

As we have seen, the effect of a misrepresentation on a contract is to make it voidable and not void, and any right of rescission is lost where the subject matter of the contract has already been sold on to an innocent (or *bona fide*) third party. It may also be lost if a third party has acquired some other proprietary right over the subject matter, such as a mortgage.

Exclusion clauses and misrepresentations

Exclusion clauses are examined in Chapters 32 to 34, but for present purposes it must suffice to note that an exclusion clause which attempts to exclude or restrict liability in relation to any type of misrepresentation will be ineffective unless it satisfies the reasonableness test laid down in s. 11(1) of the Unfair Contract Terms Act 1977, which has been incorporated in s. 3 of the Misrepresentation Act 1967.

Misrepresentation

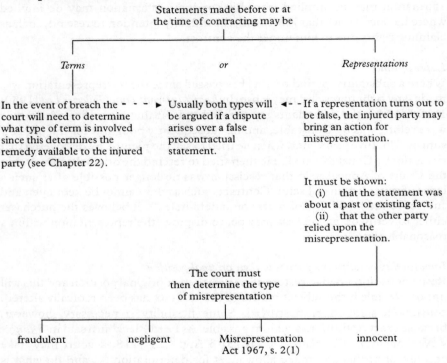

Statements made before or at the time of contracting may be

Terms or *Representations*

In the event of breach the court will need to determine what type of term is involved since this determines the remedy available to the injured party (see Chapter 22).

Usually both types will be argued if a dispute arises over a false precontractual statement.

If a representation turns out to be false, the injured party may bring an action for misrepresentation.

It must be shown:
  (i)   that the statement was about a past or existing fact;
  (ii) that the other party relied upon the misrepresentation.

The court must then determine the type of misrepresentation

fraudulent   negligent   Misrepresentation   innocent
                                   Act 1967, s. 2(1)

The remedies available depend on the type of misrepresentation made.

TWENTY FOUR
Mistake

The law on mistake covers a wide range of situations for which the common law and equity have each developed separate solutions. One might think that if one or both parties to a contract have made a mistake, then the contract ought to be dissolved, but this is not always the case because such an approach is not always feasible. The reason for this is that the courts have to consider two competing interests when deciding upon questions of mistake. In every case, the interest of the party who has acted under the misapprehension must be balanced against the general principle of upholding contracts in order to promote commercial certainty.

At common law, the only remedy for an operative mistake is to render the contract void *ab initio*, that is, to treat the contract as completely ineffective from the start. This is a severe remedy, and for that reason the courts will rarely deem a mistake to be grave enough to render a contract void. To hold a contract to be void conflicts with the principle of commercial certainty. Furthermore, a drastic effect of a contract being held to be void is that the parties to it will lose any rights which they might otherwise have acquired under the contract, including any title to goods which may already have come into their possession. Consequently, an innocent third party who has purchased the goods from such a person may find that he has no legal title to them, even though they were bought and sold in good faith.

Where the courts are not prepared to hold a contract void at common law, equity may provide a remedy, however, by deeming the contract to be voidable. The effect of this is that although the contract itself is set aside, the rights of individuals already acquired during the validity of the contract are still protected.

This chapter will look at the different types of mistake and the different of approaches taken by common law and equity.

TYPES OF MISTAKE

'Mistake' can cover a wide range of situations and there are many ways of describing the various types of mistake. There are, however, two broad divisions which may be made relating to the cases on mistake and they are:

(a)   mistakes which relate to the performability of the contract; and
(b)   agreement mistakes.

These two broad categories may then be broken down into further sub-divisions. (It may help you at this stage to refer to the summary diagram at the end of this chapter.)

Agreement mistake

With agreement mistake, it can be said that the mistake is such that the parties have never truly reached an agreement or a meeting of minds. Agreement mistake would include:

(a)   *Mutual mistake.* In mutual mistake, the parties misunderstand each other and are at cross-purposes, either as to the terms of the contract, or as to the subject-matter. For example, A and B enter into a contract for the sale of a Ford Escort. A believes that the contract relates to a top-range model with sunroof, but B believes he is selling a basic model, with no sunroof.

(b)   *Unilateral mistake.* In the above example, both parties are under some misapprehension, but it may happen that only one of those parties makes a mistake. This is known as a unilateral mistake. It takes place where one of the parties enters into a contract under some misapprehension and the other party is fully aware of the mistake. For example, suppose Albert intends to make a contract with Boris Becker, the famous tennis player, under which Becker is to be paid several thousand pounds for promoting sportswear, but instead he makes a contract with Fritz Hoffel, a Boris Becker lookalike, who specialises in defrauding people into believing that he is Becker. In that situation, the mistake is unilateral, as Hoffel knows that Albert has made a mistake as to his identity.

Mistake as to performability: common mistake

In common mistake, both parties to the contract labour under the same misapprehension as to some particular fact. Both parties make the same mistake. For example, they may have entered into a contract of sale for a car which, unknown to either of them, was destroyed before the contract was made. Here the parties are not arguing that they have not reached an agreement with each other, but rather that they have made a mistake about some underlying quality of the contract. In other words, they have made a mistake as to its performability.

AGREEMENT MISTAKE

Unilateral mistake as to identity

Mistake as to identity occurs where A believes he is contracting with B, when he is in fact contracting with C. In most cases, such mistakes are of no consequence, but it may be different if A has been tricked by C into selling him goods in return for a forged cheque which he has stolen from the real B. C may then have sold the goods to D, an innocent third party who purchased them in good faith. The main difficulty with such cases is deciding who is the true legal owner of these goods. Are they still the property of A, or do they now belong to the innocent third party? The answer depends upon the legal status of the initial contract between A and C. If it was totally void (a complete nullity) A remains the owner; but D may argue that there *was* a contract of sorts — one that was merely voidable as a result of the fraudulent misrepresentation (see Chapter 23). If this argument is accepted, C will have acquired a voidable title to the goods and will be able to pass a good legal title in them to the third party, D, provided two conditions are satisfied:

(a)   D, must have been a *bona fide* purchaser for value without notice. In other words, he must have given something of value for the goods *and* must not have been aware of the fraud or have been involved in the fraud in any way.

(b)   A must not have rescinded the original contract with C before the goods were sold to D.

Is the contract void for mistake as to identity?
In order to establish that the contract with C was wholly void, A must prove:

(a)   that he intended to deal with some person other than the one with whom he was apparently dealing;

(b)   that the latter was aware of the mistake;

(c)   that at the time of negotiating the contract, the identity of the other party was seen as crucial; and

(d)   that all reasonable steps were taken to verify the identity of the other party.

Two features in particular which must be distinguished in these types of cases are those of identity and attribute. The mistake must relate to the *identity* of the other person and not to that person's attributes. It can be difficult to distinguish between the two, as a person's attributes are often an integral part of his identity. (Note, however, that a mistake over someone's creditworthiness alone can never be classed as a case of mistaken identity; it is simply an attribute on which a seller takes a deliberate risk when parting with goods.)

One case which may be used to illustrate the difficulties associated with trying to distinguish attributes and identity is *Cundy v Lindsay & Co.* (1878) 3 App Cas 459. The plaintiffs, Lindsay & Co., were tricked by a rogue called Blenkarn into supplying him with a large consignment of handkerchiefs. Blenkarn had deliberately set up his business in the same street as a reputable company with a very similar name to his own (Blenkiron & Co.) and the plaintiffs assumed it was the latter with whom they were dealing. Before the fraud was discovered Blenkarn had sold 250 dozen handkerchiefs to Cundy (the defendant) who was an innocent purchaser. The plaintiffs sued the defendant for the return of the goods. In order to succeed, they had to prove that there was no contract between themselves and the rogue, Blenkarn. If there was no contract at that stage, then no legal title had been passed to Blenkarn and therefore none could be acquired by Cundy. The House of Lords upheld the plaintiffs' claim. They had not intended to deal with Blenkarn *at all*, but only with the respectable firm of Blenkiron & Co. The identity of the person they were dealing with was crucial to the plaintiffs, and since they were mistaken as to this there was no contract. This decision obviously protected the original owners, but was most unfortunate for Cundy, the innocent third party.

Cundy v *Lindsay & Co.* must, however, be contrasted with the later case of *King's Norton Metal Co.* v *Edridge, Merrett & Co.* (1897) 14 TLR 98. In this case, the plaintiffs had dealt on a number of occasions with a customer known to them as 'Hallam & Co.' of Sheffield. 'Hallam & Co.' purported to be a large company with a factory and three overseas depots, and had paid for goods on previous occasions. When they received another, larger, order from 'Hallam & Co.' the plaintiffs had no hesitation in providing the goods on credit. This time no payment arrived and, on further investigation, it was found (a) that 'Hallam & Co.' was a mere alias for a rogue called Wallis; (b) it had no overseas depots or factories; and (c) that Wallis had already sold the goods to an innocent third party, Edridge, Merrett & Co., who became the defendants. The plaintiffs sued them for the tort of conversion (see Chapter 39) in an attempt to recover damages for the loss of their property. The issue was exactly the same as in *Cundy* v *Lindsay*. In order for the plaintiffs to succeed, they had to establish that there was no contract between themselves and the rogue, Wallis, so that no title could have been passed by him to Edridge Merrett & Co. On the particular facts of the case, however, the plaintiffs failed. The Court of Appeal held that the contract between the plaintiffs and Wallis was not void for mistaken identity but was merely *voidable* for fraud. A voidable title had passed to Wallis and the defendants had bought the goods from him in good faith before the plaintiffs had rescinded the contract. The reason given by the Court for this decision was that Wallis and Hallam & Co. were one and the same person, and therefore the plaintiffs could not have been mistaken as to the identity of the person they were dealing with. They had simply made a mistake as to the creditworthiness of the person they were dealing with. It was, in other words, a mere mistake as to the buyer's attributes.

The distinction is at best a subtle one, but in *Cundy* v *Lindsay & Co.* there was at least an actual firm called Blenkiron & Co. which the plaintiffs had heard of and with which they thought they were dealing. In the *King's Norton* case, however, there was no such firm as Hallam & Co. This was nothing more than a fictitious name made up by the rogue, Wallis. It was Wallis in another guise. Had there actually been a Hallam & Co. of which the plaintiffs had been aware, the outcome would presumably have been different.

Parties dealing face-to-face and the issue of mistaken identity
The cases on mistaken identity considered so far have involved situations where the parties did not deal with each other face-to-face, but instead communicated their orders for goods, etc., by means of letters. In that type of situation, it is easy to see how a case of mistaken identity could arise. Here we deal with cases of mistake as to identity where the parties have dealt with each other face-to-face.

In *Phillips* v *Brooks Ltd* [1919] 2 KB 243, a well-dressed man called North, who purported to be Sir George Bullough of St James' Square, tricked the plaintiff into selling him a ring worth £450. The plaintiff took the precaution of checking Bullough's address in a local directory before letting the man he thought was Bullough take the ring away. The cheque with which North paid for the ring was of course a forgery, but by the time the plaintiff had discovered this North had pledged the ring with the defendants who were a firm of pawnbrokers. The plaintiff traced the ring and sued the defendants for its return (or for damages in lieu). He argued that there had been no contract between himself and North, because he had intended to deal with Sir George Bullough and not with the man who came into the shop. On the face of it, it must have seemed a good argument; the facts seemed analogous to *Cundy* v *Lindsay*. The court nevertheless held that the contract between the plaintiff and the rogue was not void for mistaken identity, but was merely voidable for fraud. North had duly acquired a voidable title to the ring which enabled the defendants to acquire a good legal title from him. They had bought it in good faith and the plaintiff had not managed to avoid the contract before the defendants had purchased the goods. The reasoning given by Horridge J was:

> ... although [the plaintiff] believed the person to whom he was handing the ring was Sir George Bullough, he in fact contracted to sell and deliver it to the person who came into his shop ... his intention was to sell to the person present, and identified by sight and hearing ...

The plaintiff's mistake, therefore, was not one of identity but merely one of attribute; that is, he thought that the person he was dealing with was richer and more trustworthy than he actually was. Clearly, therefore, when parties deal face-to-face, there must be a strong presumption that the seller intends to deal with the person who is physically present in front of him. It is not an absolute rule — the presumption may in some cases be rebutted as where, for example, the rogue disguises himself as another person whom he physically resembles, but given the importance that the plaintiff in *Phillips* v *Brooks Ltd* attached to proof of identity, it would seem that the presumption cannot be an easy one to rebut.

One case in which the presumption was apparently rebutted, however, is that of *Ingram* v *Little* [1960] 3 All ER 332. It is not a very satisfactory decision and is difficult to reconcile with the others. The plaintiffs were joint owners of a car which they advertised for sale. A man who called himself Hutchinson came to look at the car. He offered to pay £717 for it. The plaintiffs, after some discussion, agreed to accept the cheque after verifying Hutchinson's address in the telephone directory. But of course he was not the true Hutchinson and the cheque was a worthless forgery. By the time the fraud had been discovered, the car had been sold to an innocent third party, namely, the defendant. The plaintiffs tried to recover the car from the defendant.

The trial judge held that the contract between the plaintiffs and the rogue was completely void on the basis of mistaken identity. The car was therefore still the legal property of the plaintiffs and they were entitled to recover it from the defendant. The Court of Appeal (Devlin LJ dissenting) upheld the trial judge's decision.

On the face of it, there is no material difference between *Phillips* v *Brooks* and *Ingram* v *Little*. Indeed, Devlin LJ could see none, but the majority of the Court of Appeal held that the question whether the plaintiffs intended to deal with the real Hutchinson or the rogue in front of them was one of fact rather than law and that it was open to the trial judge to reach the decision he did.

The subsequent case of *Lewis* v *Averay* [1973] 2 All ER 229, supports the decision taken in *Phillips* v *Brooks Ltd*, and it is likely that this is the approach which would be taken by the courts today. The plaintiff offered his car for sale. A man purporting to be Richard Greene, star of the long-running television series, *Robin Hood*, offered to buy it, produced fake identification and paid for the car by means of a forged cheque, before reselling it to the defendant, Averay. On discovering the deception, the plaintiff traced the car to Averay and sued for its return. Despite the obvious similarities with *Ingram* v *Little*, the Court of Appeal declined to follow that precedent, on the basis that it was irreconcilable with *Phillips* v *Brooks*, which they preferred. The plaintiff's contract with 'Richard Greene' had therefore been voidable, rather than void, and Averay acquired a good title to the car before the plaintiff could rescind that contract.

It is all very unsatisfactory. In the absence of any real judicial consistency (the worst inconsistency being the decision in *Ingram* v *Little*) it cannot be easy for lawyers to advise their clients as to how the courts will decide such cases in future. These cases usually involve two innocent persons, each of whom has become a victim of the fraudster. The courts have to decide which of the parties is to lose out. Ought it to be the original seller of the goods, or the innocent third party? It has been argued that the law should permit a division of the loss between the parties in such proportions as is reasonable in all the circumstances of the case. The Law Reform Committee of 1966, however, rejected this argument. Consequently, the courts must choose who is to bear the loss. The courts apparently feel that it ought to be the original seller of the goods who should bear the consequences of the fraud. The original seller is in the better position to protect himself against such fraud in the sense that he always has the option to demand cash rather than a cheque; and even if he accepts the latter as a form of payment, he can always hold on to the goods until the cheque is cleared. The innocent third party, on the other hand, is in a far worse position to guard against the fraud, as it is extremely difficult to discover the history of goods. On that basis, the Law Reform Committee of 1966 recommended that, 'where goods are sold under a mistake as to the buyer's identity, the contract should, so far as third parties are concerned, be voidable and not void'.

Mutual mistake as to terms or subject-matter

If the parties to a supposed contract misunderstand each other, then it can be argued that there is no agreement (and thus no contract) between them. As previously explained, however, the courts must judge such cases objectively. If there is no real ambiguity in the apparent agreement, then the agreement will be valid and enforceable, even if one or other party has completely misunderstood it. An example of a real ambiguity, sufficient to prevent even the objective appearance of agreement, is provided by the case of *Raffles* v *Wichelhaus* (1864) 2 H & C 906. The defendants agreed to buy from the plaintiffs a cargo of cotton which was to be shipped on a vessel named the 'Peerless', sailing from Bombay. By an unfortunate coincidence there were two ships called 'Peerless', both sailing from Bombay with cargoes of cotton at about that time. The defendants meant the *Peerless* which sailed in October whilst the plaintiffs assumed they meant the *Peerless* which sailed in December. When the plaintiffs attempted to sue the defendants for the price of the cargo loaded on the December sailing, the court held that the defendants were not liable. There was no real agreement between the parties on which a contract could be based.

Agreement mistake in equity

Equity interferes less in this area of mistake than in any other. If there is no real agreement (as in *Raffles* v *Wichelhaus*) there is no contract at common law, and that is that. If there is an agreement, equity will not strike it out as invalid. Equitable remedies, however, are always discretionary, and in some cases the courts may consider that it would be unduly harsh to award an equitable remedy such as specific performance (see Chapter 31) against a party who has entered into a contract on the basis of an unfortunate mistake. Thus, in *Malins* v *Freeman* (1837) 2 Keen 25, the court refused to order specific performance against a defendant who had arrived late at an auction and mistakenly bid for (and acquired) the wrong property. The court took the view that the plaintiff already had a remedy against him in damages, and did not think it right to let him take advantage of the defendant's mistake by making a possibly ruinous order for specific performance instead.

In contrast, however, the defendant in *Tamplin* v *James* (1879) 15 Ch D 215 purchased the right property at an auction, but got a poorer bargain than he anticipated because he had not studied the plans, which showed that certain gardens adjoining the property were not included in the sale. The Court of Appeal seems to have had little sympathy for him, and awarded specific performance against him. In other words, it forced him to go ahead with the purchase.

MISTAKE AS TO THE PERFORMABILITY OF THE CONTRACT: COMMON MISTAKE

The cases which we have looked at so far have dealt with mistakes which have prevented the parties from reaching true agreement. This section deals with cases where the parties do not dispute that they have reached an agreement, but have made a mistake as to some underlying assumption relating to the contract. In other words, they have made a mistake about the performability of the contract. This type of mistake is often referred to as 'common mistake', as both parties are acting under the same misapprehension about some underlying fact which makes the contract impossible to perform. It may be that the property has already been destroyed, or it may be that both parties have made a serious mistake as to its character. They may believe that a painting which is to be sold under the contract is a Rembrandt, when it is in fact a picture by a 'lesser' artist of the same period. What is the legal position in this type of situation? Is the contract void? Would the party who agreed to buy the picture still have to go ahead with the purchase? Such mistakes are rare but they can happen, and we need to look at how the law deals with the problems they create.

Absence of subject-matter

The parties may enter into a contract when, unknown to them, the subject-matter has already ceased to exist. The leading case on the topic is *Couturier* v *Hastie* (1856) 5 HL Cas 673. This involved a contract for the sale of a shipload of corn which was thought to be *en route* between Salonika and London, but unknown to either party the corn had become overheated (so it would not have kept) and it had quite sensibly been sold by the master of the ship at Tunis even before the contract was made.

On the face of it, one might think that nothing could be more simple: the cargo no longer existed; the whole agreement was fatally flawed and could surely not be enforceable. Nevertheless, the seller still tried to argue that the buyer was liable to pay for the cargo. This was not as silly as it might seem. The argument was that the buyer had not simply purchased the cargo of corn, but had bought 'an interest in a maritime adventure', *including all the risks*, as shown by the shipping documents and insurance. The buyer, on the other hand, argued that he had simply bought the cargo, which no longer existed. Lord Cranworth said: 'Looking to the contract itself, it appears to me that what the parties contemplated ... was that there was something to be sold and bought. The contract plainly imports that there was something to be sold at the time of the contract, and something to be purchased.' On that basis, the contract was void. Lord Cranworth's speech makes it clear, however, that if the subject-matter of a contract has ceased to exist before the contract is entered into, then the effect upon the contract itself will be a matter of construction. It may sometimes be possible to infer from the construction of the contract that one of the parties accepts the risk of the goods having ceased to exist. If that is the case, the contract will be valid and the party who accepted the responsibility will be liable for failing to deliver his part of the bargain. A case to illustrate the point is that of *McRae* v *Commonwealth Disposals Commission* (1951) 84 CLR 377. The defendants (the Commission) invited tenders for the salvage rights to a wrecked oil tanker supposedly lying at a place called Jourmand Reef, off Papua New Guinea, 100 miles north of Samarai. The plaintiffs then purchased the salvage rights from the defendants. The plaintiffs went to great expense in preparing a salvage expedition, only to discover that there was no wrecked tanker anywhere near that location. The High Court of Australia had to consider what effect the non-existence of the tanker had upon the contract. The Court held that even though the goods were not in existence at the time the contract was entered into, the contract was not void for mistake. On a true construction of the contract, it was clear that the defendants impliedly promised that there was indeed such a wreck to be salvaged at that particular location. They were therefore in breach of contract to the plaintiff and had to pay damages to the plaintiff for failing to keep their side of the bargain.

In respect of contracts for the sale of goods, s. 6 of the Sale of Goods Act 1979 now provides that:

> Where there is a contract for the sale of specific goods, and the goods without the knowledge of the seller have perished at the time when the contract was made, the contract is void.

The effect of s. 6 (or rather of its identical predecessor under the old 1893 Act) may be seen in *Barrow, Lane & Ballard* v *Phillips & Co. Ltd* [1929] 1 KB 574. Here the plaintiffs sold 700 bags of nuts to the defendants, but at the time the contract was made there were only 591 bags remaining. The plaintiffs claimed the price of 591 bags. The judge rejected the plaintiffs' claim and held that the Sale of Goods Act made the contract void because the consignment of 700 bags had ceased to exist at the time the contract was made: 'A contract for a parcel of 700 bags is something different from a contract for 591 bags, and the position appears to me to be no different from what it would have been if the whole 700 bags had ceased to exist.'

Mistake as to quality

What happens where both parties are mistaken about a fundamental fact or quality of the subject-matter of the contract? For example, what if an individual buys a painting believing it to be a Picasso, but it transpires that it is a painting by one of his pupils: will the contract be void, or will it be a case of let the buyer beware (*caveat emptor*)? The case law on this is diverse, but it appears that the common law will rarely treat a contract as void merely because the parties made a mistake about a fundamental quality of the subject-matter. In contrast, as will be seen below, equity is far more flexible on this matter.

The leading case at common law is *Bell* v *Lever Bros* [1932] AC 161. Lever Bros employed the appellants on five-year service contracts as executive directors of one of their subsidiaries, but subsequently wanted to terminate their contracts before the end of that period. Lever Bros contracted to pay the appellants a total of £50,000 in compensation for premature termination of their contracts. After paying this compensation, Lever Bros discovered that the appellants had committed serious breaches of duty which would have justified their instant dismissal without any compensation. (The appellants had forgotten about their breaches of duty, so this was a question of common mistake.) Lever Bros tried to recover the £50,000 on the ground that the compensation agreements were void for mistake. The House of Lords nevertheless held that the agreements were valid. Lord Atkin said:

> I have come to the conclusion that it would be wrong to decide that an agreement to terminate a definite specified contract is void if it turns out that the agreement has already been broken and could have been terminated otherwise. The contract released is the identical contract in both cases, and the party paying for release gets exactly what he bargains for. It seems immaterial that he could have got the same result in another way, or that if he had known the true facts he would not have entered into the bargain...

The general tenor of their Lordships' speeches in *Bell* v *Lever Bros* clearly indicated that it would only be in the most exceptional cases that a contract could be made void at common law for mistake as to quality. Lord Atkin stated later in his speech that a mistake as to quality would not make a contract void even if a man bought a filling station on a road which was about to be starved of all traffic by the construction of a by-pass. He also gave the following example, where again he thought the mistake as to quality would not be sufficient to render the contract void:

> A buys a picture from B; both A and B believe it to be the work of an old master, and a high price is paid. It turns out to be a modern copy. A has no remedy in the absence of [mis]representation or warranty.

From this speech it is difficult to imagine any cases in which the courts would render a contract void for mistake as to quality. Lord Atkin's approach was reaffirmed in the later case of *Leaf* v *International Galleries* (above).

The position in equity

If the mistake does not come within the strict definition of common law mistake, then the courts may consider the issue of mistake in equity. Mistake in equity is a far more flexible concept. An example of how equity can operate in this area may be seen in *Solle* v *Butcher* [1950] 1 KB 671. The defendant owned a building containing several flats, and the plaintiff agreed to lease one of these flats for seven years at an annual rent of £250. Neither party realised that the flat was subject to rent control, which limited the rent that could be charged to the pre-war figure of £140 a year, even though a lot of work had been done on it since then. Indeed, the plaintiff, who was a surveyor, had assured the defendant (apparently in good faith) that the flat was *not* subject to rent restriction. After two years, the plaintiff discovered the mistake and sought to take advantage of the rent restriction. The only way for the defendant to increase the rent was for a 'notice of intention to increase' to be served, but this could not be done during the currency of an existing lease, and the plaintiff had a seven year lease, which was clearly valid in law. Nevertheless, the Court of Appeal exercised its equitable jurisdiction to order rescission of that lease, so that the defendant could serve notice of his intention to raise the rent to £250 a year.

The defence of *non est factum*

The normal rule is that a person who signs a contractual document will be bound by its contents, unless the signature was obtained by fraud or by misrepresentation. If a fraud or misrepresentation has taken place, the contract will be voidable and the signer may rescind it. From the signer's viewpoint, however, it would be preferable to classify the original contract as void, because with voidable contracts third parties may acquire an interest under the contract. In order to establish that the contract was void, the signer would have to establish the defence of *non est factum* , or in other words prove that 'his mind did not accompany the signing of the document'.

The defence of *non est factum* is an old one which originally developed at a time when much of the population was illiterate. It was designed to protect those persons who signed a document which had been incorrectly read to them. See *Thoroughgood's Case* (1852) 2 Co Rep 9a. As a successful plea of *non est factum* will make the contract void because of lack of intent on the part of the signer, this means that the plea will be strictly limited in application for fear of compromising the principle of commercial certainty. A modern case on *non est factum* which shows the narrow limits of the defence is *Saunders* v *Anglia Building Society*; *Gallie* v *Lee* [1971] AC 1004. The plaintiff, Mrs Gallie, was an elderly widow who handed the deeds of her house to her nephew and his unscrupulous business partner, Lee. She knew that they were to use the deeds to raise money for their business and signed a document, which Lee wrongly told her was a deed of gift to the nephew. The document actually transferred the house to Lee who mortgaged it to the Anglia Building Society. When he failed to pay the interest due on the mortgage, the Anglia claimed possession of the house. The plaintiff raised the defence of *non est factum* because she had broken her glasses and was unable to read when she signed the form. She had relied on what Lee had told her concerning the effect of the document. The House of Lords held that her defence could not succeed. This may seem surprising, but in fact Mrs Gallie had at least known that she was letting the men use her house as a security, to enable them to raise the money they needed. Had she been told that she was signing a totally different kind of document, the defence of *non est factum* might have succeeded.

There would still have been a further obstacle in Mrs Gallie's way, however. A person cannot rely on the plea where he has been careless, and the House of Lords took the view that Mrs Gallie had been careless. She could easily have waited until her glasses had been fixed, or perhaps have asked some third person to confirm Lee's explanation of the document's effect.

Mistake

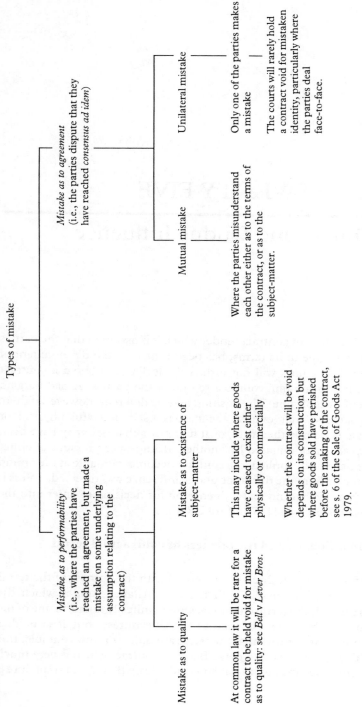

Types of mistake

Mistake as to performability (i.e., where the parties have reached an agreement, but made a mistake on some underlying assumption relating to the contract)

Mistake as to quality

At common law it will be rare for a contract to be held void for mistake as to quality: see *Bell v Lever Bros.*

Mistake as to existence of subject-matter

This may include where goods have ceased to exist either physically or commercially

Whether the contract will be void depends on its construction but where goods sold have perished before the making of the contract, see s. 6 of the Sale of Goods Act 1979.

Mistake as to agreement (i.e., the parties dispute that they have reached *consensus ad idem*)

Mutual mistake

Where the parties misunderstand each other either as to the terms of the contract, or as to the subject-matter.

Unilateral mistake

Only one of the parties makes a mistake

The courts will rarely hold a contract void for mistaken identity, particularly where the parties deal face-to-face.

Note in the above that the common law will rarely hold a contract void for mistake. Equity, however, may provide more flexible remedies.

TWENTY FIVE

Duress and Undue Influence

Introduction

The doctrine of freedom of contract, under which it is assumed that the parties to a contract freely agree to its terms, has been central to the development of the modern law. The courts will not ordinarily decline to uphold a contract merely because it appears unfavourable to one of the parties. A bad bargain may still be an enforceable one. The position may be different, however, if there is evidence to suggest that one of the parties used unlawful physical or economic threats to coerce the other, or if it appears that one may have been 'unduly influenced' or dominated by another. If improper pressure of either kind is found to have been applied, the contract becomes voidable at the option of the party against whom the duress or undue influence was directed, unless it can be shown that this had no real influence on his decision to enter into the contract (*Barton* v *Armstrong* [1975] 2 All ER 465).

Duress, undue influence and the fairness of contractual terms

The concept of duress is not directly concerned with the fairness of the terms of the contract itself, but merely with the circumstances under which the contract was created. If the terms themselves are manifestly unfair to one of the parties, this may perhaps be evidence of possible duress, but it is neither necessary nor sufficient to prove that the terms are unfair or unfavourable. If A threatens B with a gun in order to make B sign a contract which is very much in B's own best interests, the contract is still voidable by B on grounds of duress

(*Barton* v *Armstrong*, above). The same is ordinarily true of undue influence. As Lord Browne-Wilkinson said in *CIBC Mortgages plc* v *Pitt* [1993] 4 All ER 433:

> like any other victim of fraud, a person who has been induced by undue influence to carry out a transaction which he did not freely and knowingly enter into is entitled to have that transaction set aside as of right.

There is, however, a special category of cases involving 'presumed undue influence' (i.e., where undue influence may be presumed from the nature of the relationship between the parties, even where there is no positive evidence that such influence was exerted). It appears that this presumption can only be relied upon where the contract was of 'manifest disadvantage' to the party in question (*National Westminster Bank plc* v *Morgan* [1985] 1 All ER 821) although some doubts have been expressed as to this rule, notably by Lord Browne-Wilkinson in *CIBC Mortgages plc* v *Pitt*. 'Manifest disadvantage' is involved only where it should have been obvious to any reasonable person *at the time of contracting* that the terms were disadvantageous to the party in question.

DURESS

Physical threats made to a person in order to make him to enter into a contract have always been accepted by the courts as duress, as, for example, where a gun is held to the party's head (see *Barton* v *Armstrong* [1975] 2 All ER 465). In practice, however, allegations of 'economic duress' are far more common. The case of *Atlas Express* v *Kafco (Importers and Distributors) Ltd* [1989] 1 All ER 641 gives a good indication of the type of situation in which the plea of economic duress is now most commonly raised. Kafco made a contract with FW Woolworth & Co. to supply them with basketware, and also contracted with Atlas, who were to act as carriers for their products. Atlas belatedly discovered that they had made a serious mistake over the carriage rates they had specified, which would leave them significantly out of pocket on the deal. They did not discuss this with Kafco. Instead, when Atlas's delivery driver arrived to collect the next shipment, he bluntly informed Kafco that he would not load his vehicle unless they signed a document agreeing to a much higher rate of charges. Kafco was heavily dependent on the contract with Woolworths, and it was impossible for them to find any other carrier in time to meet their delivery deadlines. They had little alternative but to sign the document agreeing to Atlas's new demands. They nevertheless made it clear that they considered themselves to be acting under duress, and it was eventually decided that they could not be forced to pay the increased charges. They could refuse to pay for two reasons: first, Atlas offered them no valid consideration for the increased charges (see Chapter 20); secondly, Atlas had been guilty of using unlawful economic duress.

The test for the existence of economic duress

The case law suggests that there are two factors which must be established before a contract becomes voidable for economic duress. In *The Olib* [1991] 2 Lloyd's Rep 108, it was stated:

    (a)   that the threat must be illegitimate or unlawful; and

    (b)   that the party threatened must have had no reasonable alternative but to give way to it.

The threat must be illegitimate

Further authority for the first of these propositions can be found in the case of *The Universe Sentinel* [1982] 2 All ER 67, in which it was held that money paid to a trade union by the *Universe Sentinel's* owners in order to extract it from a port in which it had been 'blacked' was money paid under economic duress, and was therefore recoverable. In this context, illegality includes not only criminal acts, but also civil wrong such as breaches of contract or torts. It has more recently been suggested (*obiter*) by the Court of Appeal in *CTN Cash and Carry Ltd* v *Gallagher* [1994] 4 All ER 714, that duress might, in very limited circumstances, arise from lawful economic pressure, but it is difficult to envisage any likely scenario in which this might be the case.

Lack of reasonable alternatives

If the alleged economic duress did not involve any threat of criminal acts, one must also consider whether the party threatened had any reasonable alternative but to agree to the contract in question. In *The Universe Sentinel*, Lord Scarman encapsulated the essence of economic duress:

> There must be pressure, the practical effect of which is compulsion or the absence of choice... The classic case of duress is, however, ... the victim's intentional submission arising from the realisation that there is no practical choice open to him.

The cornerstone of the doctrine of economic duress is the absence of an effective choice. It is not essential that the victim's will was completely overborne; it is enough if he accepted the oppressor's terms, on the basis that there was no reasonable alternative open to him. If the consequences of a threat of breach of contract were to be serious, such as the consequential loss of another important contract, then the oppressed party may well have had no reasonable alternative but to submit to it (see *Atlas Express* v *Kafco*, above).

UNDUE INFLUENCE

As noted above, the common law definition of duress was initially confined solely to physical threats. As a reaction to this rigidity, the law of equity responded by developing the separate doctrine of undue influence. There are two main forms of undue influence, which have been awarded identifying 'class numbers' by the courts (see *Barclays Bank plc* v *O'Brien* [1993] 4 All ER 417). 'Class 1' requires actual proof of the exercise of undue influence by one party over another. 'Class 2' involves a presumption of undue influence arising from the nature of the relationship between one party and another. Class 2 is further divided into sub-classes 2A and 2B, according to the nature of the relationship (see below). If any of these forms of undue influence is found to exist, the contract will be held voidable at the option of the party who was unduly influenced.

Actual undue influence (class 1)

Actual undue influence does not depend on any particular form of relationship, nor does it require proof that the contract involves terms that are unfair or disadvantageous to the party complaining of it. The party seeking to avoid the contract must, however, clearly and specifically prove that, as a result of improper pressure by the other party, he felt compelled to enter into the contract.

An example of actual undue influence is provided by *Bank of Credit and Commerce International SA* v *Aboody* [1990] 1 QB 923. This case involved an Iraqi-born couple, where the husband clearly exercised control or mental domination over the wife, and ensured that she signed any document which he required her to sign. A charge over the family business signed by her in favour of the bank was held to have been procured by undue influence.

Presumed undue influence (class 2)

Presumed undue influence arises from the nature of a relationship between the parties. There are certain types of relationships which automatically give rise to a presumption of undue influence (class 2A) and other specific relationships where undue influence may sometimes be presumed (class 2B), assuming in each case that the contract was 'manifestly disadvantageous' to the party allegedly subjected to this undue influence.

Presumed undue influence from the type of relationship between the parties (class 2A)
Only a few specific relationships fall into this category, notably those of parent and child, doctor and patient, and solicitor and client. The husband and wife relationship does *not* fall into this category, but may in some cases fall into class 2B (below), or there may be proof of actual undue influence, as in the *Aboody* case (above). Where a class 2A relationship is involved, a presumption of undue influence will *automatically* arise, wherever the transaction was manifestly disadvantageous to the influenced party. The presumption is, however, rebuttable, if it can be shown that this party entered into the transaction after full, free and informed consideration.

Presumed undue influence from the nature of a specific relationship (class 2B)
We are concerned here with relationships which *may* give rise to a presumption of undue influence, but do not automatically do so. In a case involving husband and wife, for example, there is no automatic presumption of undue influence, but such a presumption may arise in a given case if there is evidence that one of the spouses is habitually dependent in all financial matters on the other and has regularly done as the other required. It may then be presumed that undue influence was exerted in respect of the particular transaction in question (*Barclays Bank plc* v *O'Brien* [1993] 4 All ER 417).

Such relationships need not involve marriage, but must be ones in which one party habitually relied upon and trusted in the advice of the other. The banker-customer relationship may sometimes involve such trust and reliance. An example can be seen in the case of *Lloyds Bank* v *Bundy* [1974] 3 All ER 757. Bundy was an elderly farmer. He was not very knowledgeable about financial dealings and always relied on his bank for advice. When his son got into financial difficulties he was persuaded by his bank to mortgage his home for more than its total value in order to help the son's overdraft. He charged his own home to guarantee his son's debts to the bank. The bank's assistant manager took the necessary documents round to Bundy's house in order for him to sign them. He looked to the assistant manager for advice on the matter and they discussed the charge and the position of his son's company. The bank later claimed possession of his home when his son defaulted on payments of the money he owed the bank.

Bundy argued that the charge should be set aside for undue influence because he had looked to the assistant manager for impartial advice. The latter frankly conceded he had not warned Bundy to seek independent advice on the matter. The Court of Appeal held that Bundy's reliance upon the bank's advice raised the presumption of undue influence. This presumption could, however, have been rebutted had the bank advised him to obtain independent financial advice.

Lloyds Bank v *Bundy* must be contrasted with the decision of the House of Lords in *National Westminster Bank plc* v *Morgan* [1985] 1 All ER 821. A husband and wife had mortgaged their home to a building society which was seeking possession for non-payment of the mortgage. The bank agreed to provide a bridging loan for a few weeks until the husband could obtain money from another source. The bank, in the meantime, required a charge on the house for the loan. The bank manager called at the couple's home and acquired the wife's signature on the mortgage. Unfortunately, the husband then died and the bank sought possession of the house. The wife claimed that the bank had used undue influence in obtaining her signature to the charge, but she had no actual evidence of this (such as would bring the matter within class 1) and the House of Lords held that the relationship between the parties did not raise the presumption of undue influence. The manager had explained the nature of the charge to her, but she had not relied on him for advice over the wisdom of the transaction. Furthermore, the transaction was not 'manifestly disadvantageous' to her at the time.

Third party rights

Since economic duress or undue influence only renders contracts voidable, the general rule is that any rights acquired by innocent third parties cannot subsequently be impugned. This rule must, however, be qualified in certain respects. If, for example, a husband exerts undue influence on his wife in order to persuade her to agree to the mortgaging of their jointly-owned home as security for his business debts, the rights of the mortgagee bank may be compromised, as against the wife, by that undue influence. If it was aware of, or merely *should have been* aware of, a risk that undue influence has been exerted, it may not be able to prevent rescission of the contract by the wife. It may be necessary for the bank to ensure that the wife has obtained independent legal advice before safely relying on her agreement to a mortgage which may not be in her own best interests.

It is not enough for the bank merely to advise the wife in such a case to obtain legal advice (*Credit Lyonnaise* v *Burch* [1997] 1 All ER 144). In recent years, the usual procedure has been for the bank to require a certificate issued by a solicitor, to the effect that the contents and effect of any such mortgage have indeed been explained to and consented to by the spouse or other affected party; but in *Royal Bank of Scotland* v *Etridge* [1997] 3 All ER 628 the Court of Appeal held that it might still be open to a spouse to argue that the certificate is incorrect and that proper advice has not in fact been given — at least where the solicitor has been appointed by the bank itself, making him the bank's agent.

Improper pressure

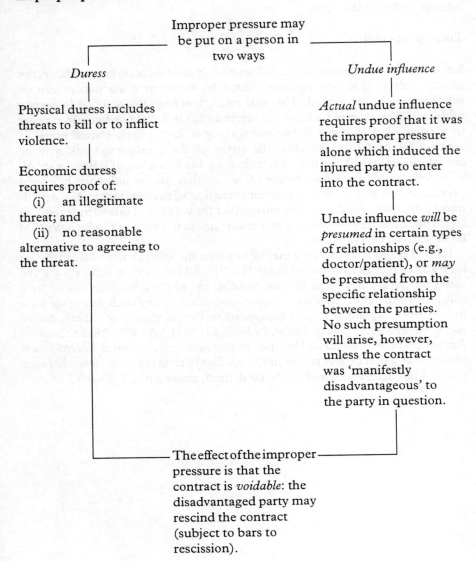

Improper pressure may
be put on a person in
two ways

Duress

Physical duress includes
threats to kill or to inflict
violence.

Economic duress
requires proof of:
   (i)   an illegitimate
threat; and
   (ii)   no reasonable
alternative to agreeing to
the threat.

Undue influence

Actual undue influence
requires proof that it was
the improper pressure
alone which induced the
injured party to enter
into the contract.

Undue influence *will* be
presumed in certain types
of relationships (e.g.,
doctor/patient), or *may*
be presumed from the
specific relationship
between the parties.
No such presumption
will arise, however,
unless the contract
was 'manifestly
disadvantageous' to
the party in question.

The effect of the improper
pressure is that the
contract is *voidable*: the
disadvantaged party may
rescind the contract
(subject to bars to
rescission).

TWENTY SIX

Void and Illegal Contracts

A contract will naturally be struck down and declared void by the courts if it is illegal, in the sense that it contravenes (or requires the parties to contravene) some specific legal rule. A criminal conspiracy involves an agreement, but it can never be an enforceable contract.

Less obviously, a contract may be declared void and unenforceable by the courts where, although not illegal in the above sense, it is perceived to be 'contrary to public policy'. Agreements in restraint of trade (as for example where A promises not to compete with B's business) may sometimes fall into that category, as may agreements which tend to undermine the status of marriage.

A third type of contract, although not illegal, is void and unenforceable in the courts, because legislation expressly so provides. Gaming or wagering (i.e. betting) contracts are caught by such a rule, even though there is no law against placing a bet. As there are many and various reasons for legal intervention on the basis of illegality or public policy, which are often difficult to classify within any coherent pattern, this chapter can only attempt to give a very brief and basic overview of the subject.

ILLEGAL CONTRACTS

Contracts to commit crimes or other unlawful acts

Any agreement to commit a crime, fraud, tort or breach of contract against another party is void for illegality. If A agrees to pay B £10,000 in return for B's promise to smuggle controlled drugs for him, to beat up C, or to publish defamatory lies about D, then obviously neither party can sue the other for failing to honour the contract.

Less obvious cases may be caught up in that rule. In *Re Mahmoud and Ispahani* [1921] 2 KB 716, the plaintiff agreed to sell linseed oil to the defendant, who assured him that he had a licence to buy the oil under laws which at that time made it illegal to buy oil without one. The defendant then backed out of the contract on the basis that he did not, after all, hold a licence, and the court held that the plaintiff could not sue him for breach of contract, because in the absence of that licence, the contract was void for illegality.

Contracts promoting sexual immorality

An agreement to promote sexual immorality may be held to be illegal at common law. Some of the old cases on this subject must now be considered obsolete, because views on sexual morality have changed since Victorian times, but contracts which promote or encourage prostitution may still be open to attack on this basis. In *Pearce* v *Brooks* (1866) LR 1 Ex 213, the plaintiff agreed to hire a horse and carriage to a prostitute, knowing that these items would be used by her in order to ply her trade. The court held that the plaintiff could not recover the hire charge from the defendant when she refused to pay. In contrast, a contract to sell her something largely unconnected with her business would not have been open to attack.

Contracts contrary to the administration of justice

It was said in the case of *Egerton* v *Brownlow* (1853) 4 HL Cas 1 that, 'any contract or engagement having a tendency, however slight, to affect the administration of justice, is illegal and void.' Agreements to interfere with or suppress a prosecution may thus be void for illegality. Indeed, a witness, even if he is the alleged victim of a crime, may not legally accept payment in return for withdrawing or changing his evidence. Such an agreement may very well amount to a conspiracy to pervert the course of public justice, which is a serious offence at common law. A victim may, however, agree to accept reasonable compensation in return for not pressing ahead with a private prosecution for a minor offence, such as common assault or battery.

Further consequences of illegality

It has already been explained that neither party to an illegal agreement can enforce the agreement against the other, even where (as in *Re Mahmoud and Ispahani*) the party seeking to enforce it has acted in good faith throughout. There may, however, be further consequences where a contract is declared to be illegal.

Money or property transferred under the contract is not recoverable
If money or property has already been transferred under an illegal contract, it will not normally be recoverable. In *Parkinson* v *College of Ambulance Ltd* [1925] 2 KB 1, the plaintiff donated money to the defendant charity, supposedly on the basis of a promise that it would obtain a knighthood for him. No such knighthood was forthcoming, and the plaintiff tried to recover his money. His claim failed, because an agreement to procure honours by bribery is void for illegality.

Where, however, an innocent party has given money or property to the other, without realising the other's illegal purpose, he may be able to recover it. This would presumably have been the case if the plaintiff in *Re Mahmoud and Ispahani* had delivered the oil but had never been paid for it.

Related transactions
Any subsequent agreement which is based upon the illegal transaction will also be affected by the initial illegality and will also be unenforceable. A cheque or bill of exchange given in payment will be tainted by this illegality, and will not ordinarily be enforceable, unless it has subsequently been negotiated (i.e. signed over) to a bona fide purchaser who has no knowledge of the illegal contract and no reason to suspect it.

Lawful contracts performed in an illegal manner

If the contract itself was not unlawful but one of the parties performs it in an illegal manner, without the other party's knowledge, this does not prejudice the rights of the other party. In *Archbold's (Freightage) Ltd* v *Spanglett Ltd* [1961] 1 All ER 417 the defendants were contracted to carry a consignment of whisky. The whisky was stolen due to the negligence of their driver. The defendants nevertheless argued (on the basis of *Re Mahmoud and Ispahani*) that they were not liable for the loss because their lorry was not properly licensed to carry that freight. The court rightly rejected this argument. The plaintiffs had no knowledge of this 'illegality' but it was in any case nothing to do with them. The contract itself (unlike that in *Mahmoud*) was perfectly legal. It was up to the defendants to provide a vehicle which was properly licensed.

VOID CONTRACTS

Gambling (gaming or wagering) contracts

Section 18 of the Gaming Act 1845 provides:

All contracts or agreements, whether [oral] or in writing, by way of gaming or wagering, shall be null and void; and no suit shall be brought or maintained in any court of law or equity for recovering any sum of money or valuable thing alleged to be won upon any wager, or which shall have been deposited in the hands of any person to abide the event on which any wager shall have been made.

A wagering contract is a bet between two parties on some existing fact or as to the outcome of a future event. A gaming contract involves betting on the outcome of a game or race. There are some differences between them, but we need not explore these here. It must suffice to note that, although gambling is not in itself illegal, no rights can be conferred upon either party to such a contract. Furthermore, a cheque given in payment for a gambling debt is unenforceable by the payee. In other words, if the drawer's bank dishonour it, either because the drawer has insufficient funds in his account, or because he has 'stopped' it (ordered them not to pay it) the payee cannot sue the drawer. It should be noted, however, that a cheque given to a casino in order to purchase gaming chips is fully enforceable.

The moral for any would-be gambler is that he should never take on a bet with someone unless that person can be trusted to pay up if he loses. Would-be cheats should note that it may be a criminal offence under s. 16 of the Theft Act 1968 dishonestly to deceive another person into accepting a bet which you have no intention of honouring if you lose.

Contracts in restraint of trade

Agreements involving price-fixing cartels (where firms in a given area of business agree to keep their prices artificially high and not undercut each other) may be unlawful under the Competition Act 1980 and its associated regulations. Other contracts in restraint of trade are primarily governed by common law principles. A contract in restraint of trade is one under which one party agrees to accept constraints upon his freedom to trade or carry on a profession in the future. The constraints may be geographical and /or cover a specific period of time. An employee who is leaving his old firm may for example agree (as part of a severance package) not to carry on a competing business within a seven miles radius of a certain town for the next ten years. Similarly, if X buys Y's thriving plumbing business, he may make it a condition of the contract that Y does not then open a rival business in the same area and win back many of his old customers. Such agreements are not automatically void, but the overall approach taken by the judiciary has been to treat them as such unless they can be justified as being reasonable between the parties and not contrary to the public interest.

In *Nordenfelt* v *Maxim Nordenfelt Guns and Ammunition Co. Ltd* [1894] AC 535, Lord MacNaghten explained the basic approach to be taken in restraint of trade cases:

The public have an interest in every person's carrying on his trade freely: so has the individual. All interference with individual liberty of action in trading, and all restraints of trade of themselves, if there is nothing more, are contrary to public policy, and therefore void. That is the general rule. But there are exceptions; restraints of trade and interference with individual liberty of action may be justified by special circumstances of a particular case. It is a sufficient justification, and indeed it is the only justification, if the restriction is reasonable: reasonable, that is, in reference to the interests of the parties concerned and reasonable in reference to the interests of the public. . .

If reasonable in that sense, such agreements may therefore be valid and enforceable.

Contracts which oust the jurisdiction of the court

Contracts which attempt to limit a person's right of access to the courts are likely to be viewed critically by the courts. This does not mean that they will necessarily be struck down as void. Many commercial contracts provide for disputes to be referred to arbitration. This is not merely tolerated by the courts, but regarded as perfectly sound practice, given the expense of resorting to litigation in the courts. The arbitrator makes a final adjudication upon the facts (e.g., were the goods of satisfactory quality and fit for their purpose?), but if the contract tries to make the arbitrator the final voice *on matters of law*, that part of the agreement will be void.

Contracts undermining the status of marriage

Contracts which attempt to restrict a person's right to marry or agreements for reward for the procurement of marriage are void, because they tend to undermine the status and sanctity of marriage.

The effects of a contract being held to be void

If the contract has been made void by a legislative provision then it will be necessary to scrutinise the relevant statute in order to assess the full effect of the impropriety. In contracts deemed void at common law, it may be possible to separate the offending part of the agreement from the rest. For example, in *Goldsoll* v *Goldman* [1915] 1 Ch 292, the vendor of an imitation jewellery business in New Bond Street contracted with the buyer that he would not deal in real or imitation jewellery for two years in Britain or abroad. The court held that it was an unreasonable restraint of trade to prevent him from dealing in real jewellery in Britain or from dealing in any kind of jewellery abroad, but that his undertaking not to deal in imitation jewellery in Britain remained valid.

Void and illegal contracts

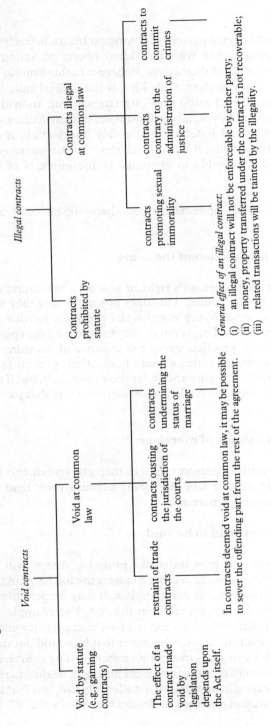

Void contracts

Void by statute (e.g., gaming contracts)

The effect of a contract made void by legislation depends upon the Act itself.

Void at common law

restraint of trade contracts

contracts ousting the jurisdiction of the courts

contracts undermining the status of marriage

In contracts deemed void at common law, it may be possible to sever the offending part from the rest of the agreement.

Illegal contracts

Contracts prohibited by statute

Contracts illegal at common law

contracts promoting sexual immorality

contracts contrary to the administration of justice

contracts to commit crimes

General effect of an illegal contract:
(i) an illegal contract will not be enforceable by either party;
(ii) money, property transferred under the contract is not recoverable;
(iii) related transactions will be tainted by the illegality.

TWENTY SEVEN

Capacity

Not everyone has the capacity to enter into a legally binding contract. Minors and persons of unsound mind may lack such capacity. It is also necessary to look at the capacity of companies to enter into contracts, and this will form a small section at the end of this chapter.

Minors

A minor is anyone under the age of 18. The general rule is that minors may make and enforce such contracts as they wish, but others may not be able to enforce certain types of contracts against them. In other words, the minor is not generally bound by any contract he makes but the party contracting with the minor will be.

There are some contracts which will bind the minor, by way of exception to the above rule. These are contracts relating to the supply of 'necessaries' to the minor, contracts of employment and certain analogous contracts. Contracts made by minors may thus be divided for current purposes into two categories:

(a)   contracts for necessaries and contracts of employment, which may be enforced by either party; and

(b)   other contracts which are voidable at the minor's option.

What is meant by 'necessaries'?
A minor is under a legal obligation to pay a reasonable price for necessaries which are sold and delivered to him. Necessaries include both goods and services and obviously include food, drink and clothing. In relation to the sale

of goods, s. 3(3) of the Sale of Goods Act 1979 states that necessaries are goods 'suitable to the condition in life of the minor . . . and to his actual requirements at the time of the sale and delivery'. It is clear from this provision that the question of whether something will be classed as a necessary will depend upon the minor's needs at the time of contracting. Thus if the minor already has an adequate supply of a particular item, the contract will not be classed as one for the supply of necessaries. The minor does not, even then, have to pay the agreed contract price for the necessaries; he merely has to pay a reasonable price for them.

As far as contracts of employment are concerned, the courts recognise that these (and certain analogous contracts, e.g., apprenticeships) are enforceable against a minor, provided the contract as a whole is beneficial to him.

Voidable contracts
All other classes of contract entered into by the minor are voidable at the minor's option. Any of these contracts may be repudiated by the minor provided he does so before the age of 18 or within a reasonable time thereafter. Once a minor attains the age of 18, he may ratify such contracts, either expressly or by implication from his conduct (e.g., by continuing to claim any benefits accruing under them). If the minor wishes to repudiate the contract, he may be required to return any property acquired by him under that contract.

How do these rules affect the rights of minors?
At first sight, it might seem that minors do very well out of the law of contract. They can enforce contracts, but can rarely have them enforced against them. If they foolishly agree to pay an excessive price, even for necessaries, they cannot be held to that agreement. They can at most be required to pay a reasonable price. The reality, of course, is very different. The rules mean that minors must almost always 'pay cash'. They cannot ordinarily obtain loans, order goods on credit, or even operate ordinary bank accounts, because businessmen and companies simply will not give credit to parties who cannot be sued for what they owe. Alternatively, they may insist that an adult, such as a parent, guarantees the contract.

Persons of unsound mind

Some individuals are certified under the Mental Health Act 1983 as being unfit to deal with their property. Consequently their property comes under the control of the courts. On the other hand, there are persons of unsound mind who have not been certified under the above Act. In such cases, the position is that any contracts entered into by them will be considered binding unless the person claiming incapacity (or more probably a relative, etc., acting on his behalf) can prove that the other contracting party knew of the disorder and that the disorder was such that the person affected was unaware of the effect of the contract.

Persons who are drunk

If a person is so drunk as to be incapable of understanding the contract and the other party is aware of this, then the drunken party may, on regaining his faculties, apply to the court to have the contract set aside.

Companies

When a company is created, its memorandum of association must state what its 'objects' (or purposes) are. If the company acts outside these objects, the company will be said to have acted *ultra vires* and at common law the contract would be void. However, the Companies Acts of 1985 and 1989 have largely abolished the doctrine of *ultra vires* (which was deemed to be inconsistent with European Community law) and it will now be only in exceptional circumstances that contracts may be invalidated on this basis. Even then, such contracts are likely to be voidable rather than void.

Pre-incorporation contracts

Businessmen who are forming a new company sometimes make the mistake of purporting to contract on behalf of that company before the process of incorporation has been completed (i.e., before the company has come into existence). At common law, such contracts were usually deemed to be void, because if the company did not yet exist, it could not be a party to a contract. Section 36C of the Companies Act 1985 now provides that such contracts are binding, not on the company, but on the person who claimed to act on the company's behalf.

Capacity

Most adults of sound mind are able to enter into legally binding contracts. Certain persons, however, are said to lack the capacity to contract.

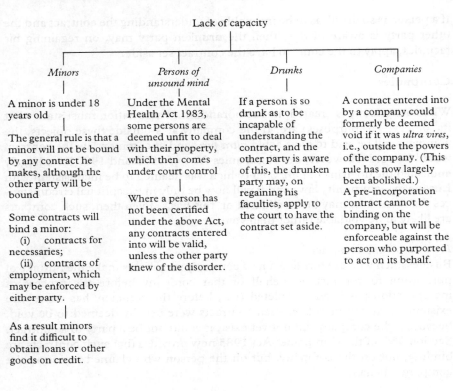

Lack of capacity

Minors

A minor is under 18 years old

The general rule is that a minor will not be bound by any contract he makes, although the other party will be bound

Some contracts will bind a minor:
   (i) contracts for necessaries;
   (ii) contracts of employment, which may be enforced by either party.

As a result minors find it difficult to obtain loans or other goods on credit.

Persons of unsound mind

Under the Mental Health Act 1983, some persons are deemed unfit to deal with their property, which then comes under court control

Where a person has not been certified under the above Act, any contracts entered into will be valid, unless the other party knew of the disorder.

Drunks

If a person is so drunk as to be incapable of understanding the contract, and the other party is aware of this, the drunken party may, on regaining his faculties, apply to the court to have the contract set aside.

Companies

A contract entered into by a company could formerly be deemed void if it was *ultra vires*, i.e., outside the powers of the company. (This rule has now largely been abolished.)
A pre-incorporation contract cannot be binding on the company, but will be enforceable against the person who purported to act on its behalf.

TWENTY EIGHT
Privity of Contract

The general rule at common law is that only a party to a contract can enforce rights or have duties enforced against him under that contract. A party to a contract is one of those between whom the agreement is made. Under the doctrine of consideration (Chapter 20), such a person must have given or promised some benefit to the other parties, in return for their promises.

It is easy to see why the rule of privity of contract exists. It would be wrong, for example, to allow X and Y to conclude a contract between them, placing obligations upon Z. It would be most unfair if Z could have unwanted obligations forced upon him in that way. The negative side of the rule, however, is that if X and Y have made a contract which confers a benefit upon Z as a third party, he cannot enforce that promise.

The privity rule is neatly illustrated by the case of *Tweddle* v *Atkinson* (1861) 1 B & S 393, the facts of which are set out in Chapter 20. Apart from the fact that the plaintiff in that case had provided no consideration for the agreement under which he was to be paid a sum of money on his marriage, he was not even a party to that agreement, notwithstanding that it was made for his benefit. Persons who are not parties to a contract cannot even rely on provisions in the contract which purport to protect them from any liability they might incur to one of the parties. In *Scruttons Ltd* v *Midland Silicones Ltd* [1962] AC 446, a shipping contract limited the liability of the carriers for loss or damage to the cargo to just $500. Part of the cargo was damaged, not by the carriers, but by stevedores hired by the carriers to unload it. The House of Lords held that the stevedores could be sued for the full cost of the damage.

The doctrine of privity of contract has not escaped criticism. The Law Revision Committee in 1937 and the Law Commission in 1991 each recommended that a third party should be able to enforce a contractual promise received by another for his benefit (as in *Tweddle* v *Atkinson*). Although it would be objectionable for a third party to have obligations imposed on him through someone else's agreement, neither body could see any compelling reason why a stranger to a contract should not be allowed to benefit from it, if that was what the parties to the contract agreed. Nevertheless, the doctrine of privity is now so well entrenched in the case law that it would clearly take legislation to displace it.

Enforcement by a contracting party

Where there is a contract which purports to confer some benefit on a third party, it may be possible for one of the contracting parties to obtain an order of specific performance from the other party, to ensure that the benefit is provided. This would force the latter to perform his part of the bargain and the third party would obtain the promised benefit. In *Beswick* v *Beswick* [1967] 2 All ER 1197 the defendant purchased a coal business from his uncle, the plaintiff's husband, and contracted that he would pay the plaintiff an annuity after his uncle's death. When the uncle died, the defendant failed to make the payments. The House of Lords held that, as a mere beneficiary of the deal, the plaintiff had no right to enforce it. Fortunately, however, she was also the administrator of the uncle's estate, and in that capacity she could enforce the contract 'on his behalf'.

Note, however, that there are restrictions on the award of specific performance, so this remedy will not be available in all cases (see Chapter 31). A further consideration to bear in mind is that few people would be prepared to launch expensive legal proceedings on someone else's behalf, unless their legal costs are paid or underwritten by that other person, or unless they have previously contracted to protect that other person's interests.

Damages awarded on behalf of third parties

If an order for specific performance cannot be obtained, the only remedy will be that of damages, assuming once again that one of the parties to the contract is prepared (or obliged) to litigate on the third party's behalf; but to what extent can a party to a contract seek damages for someone else's loss? In *Jackson* v *Horizon Holidays Ltd* [1975] 3 All ER 92, the plaintiff booked a £1,200 holiday in Sri Lanka for himself and his family of four. The holiday was a shambles. Neither the food nor the accommodation was of the standard that he had booked. The plaintiff therefore brought an action for breach of contract against the defendant travel company, claiming damages to cover both his own disappointment and that of his family. The defendants did not dispute that they were liable to the plaintiff, but disputed his right to claim damages on behalf of the family, who were not parties to the contract. The Court of Appeal upheld an award of £1,100 damages reflecting the total value of the family holiday. Lord Denning MR said:

> In this case it was a husband making a contract for the benefit of himself, his wife and his children. Other cases readily come to mind. A host makes a contract with a restaurant for a dinner for himself and his friends. It would be a fiction to say that the contract was made by all the family, or all the guests... The real truth is that in each instance, the father, the host, was making a contract himself for the benefit of the whole party. In short, a contract for the benefit of third persons.

In contrast, James LJ upheld the award of extra damages, not on the basis that the plaintiff could claim on the others' behalf, but on the basis that he had contracted for a family holiday, and had not received one. His approach appeared to avoid any conflict with the concept of privity of contract, and seems to have been preferred by the House of Lords in the later case of *Woodar Investment Development Ltd* v *Wimpey Construction UK Ltd* [1980] 1 All ER 571. Their Lordships criticised Lord Denning's approach in *Jackson*, although they did not overrule it.

There are certainly some circumstances in which one party to a contract can obtain damages from another party on the basis of loss suffered by a third party. In *St Martin's Property Corp. Ltd* v *Sir Robert McAlpine & Sons Ltd* [1993] 3 All ER 417, the House of Lords held that McAlpine's were liable to pay substantial damages to St Martin's for faulty building work they had undertaken for them, even though St Martin's had sold the building concerned to a third party before the fault became apparent. Lord Browne-Wilkinson stated that it was foreseeable in a contract of that kind that the property in question would be sold to a third party and that any damage caused by a breach of contract on the part of the builders would cause loss to a later owner, rather than to the original contracting party.

Exceptions to the general rule

The privity rule can sometimes be a harsh one, and a number of devices have evolved over the years in an attempt to circumvent the rule.

Statutory intervention

Where the doctrine of privity of contract has caused particularly acute problems, Parliament has sometimes intervened so as to create special statutory exceptions to the general rule. An example may be found in the area of insurance contracts, where various statutes have conferred specific contractual rights on third parties. A car owner may obtain insurance cover not only for his own use of the car, but also for its use by other people who use the car with the owner's consent. The doctrine of privity of contract would ordinarily prevent third parties claiming on such a policy, but it would be most inconvenient if all possible drivers had to be parties to the contract, and legislation therefore allows third parties to claim the benefit of such contracts, assuming of course that the policy does indeed extend to them (e.g., it is possible for a car owner to take out a 'named driver only' policy which would not cover other users).

Assignment of choses in action

If X owes Y £2,000, X is known as the debtor and Y as the creditor. It is possible for Y to assign or transfer the debt to Z (a third party) who will then be able to enforce the debt against X directly. A debt is a species of intangible property. You cannot see or touch it, but it gives rise to rights that can be enforced in the courts, and it is therefore known as a 'chose in action' or 'thing in action' (as opposed to a tangible object, which can be physically possessed, and is accordingly known as a chose (or thing) in possession).

The rules governing assignment of choses in action represent a significant exception to the privity of contract rule. Assignment of choses in action is quite common. Examples of rights which can be assigned in this way include copyrights, patents, shares in a company, rights under insurance policies, or benefits under a trust.

Cheques and bills of exchange

Cheques and bills of exchange are a special case. The payee of a cheque or bill may assign or 'negotiate' his right to payment to a third person, who may then enforce that right against the drawer (the person who wrote it). If the drawer's bank refuses to pay (e.g., because the drawer has insufficient funds in his account) the drawer may be sued by the present holder, who may not necessarily be the original payee. It may be someone of whom the drawer has never heard before, or someone with whom he would never choose to do business. Furthermore, even if the cheque or bill was originally handed to the payee as a gift, it might still be enforceable by a subsequent holder to whom it was traded or 'negotiated' by the payee. If, for example, A gives his nephew, B, a cheque for his birthday, and B (who has no bank account) sells it to his father, C, in return for cash, C could now demand that A honours the cheque, even though there is no privity of contract and no consideration passed between A and C. The issue would arise, of course, only if A's bank refused to pay out on the cheque: if, in other words, it 'bounced'. Most cheques are now printed with 'a/c payee' crossings. This makes them very difficult to negotiate to third parties, but does not necessarily prevent that practice altogether.

Agency

Another important limit on the privity of contract rule is provided by the law of agency. When an agent makes a contract with a third party (Z) on behalf of his principal (P), the law treats this transaction as if the principal had made the contract. Therefore, P and Z may sue and be sued by each other on the contract.

Privity of contract

The privity of contract rule states that only a party to a contract may sue or be sued on it.

The negative side of the rule is that if X and Y have made a contract which confers a benefit on Z, Z as a third party cannot enforce that contract.

Where a contract confers a benefit on a third party, it may be possible for one of the contracting parties to obtain an order for *specific performance* of the contract to ensure that the third party receives the benefit.

If an order for specific performance cannot be obtained, the only remedy will be damages (assuming that one of the parties to the contract is prepared to sue on the third party's behalf). Note the decision in *Jackson v Horizon Holidays*.

Due to the harshness of the privity of contract rule in contracts which confer benefits on third parties, a number of devices have evolved to circumvent it.

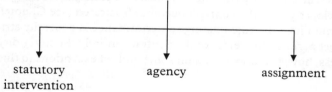

statutory intervention   agency   assignment

TWENTY NINE

Discharge

This chapter considers the various ways in which a contract may come to an end or be discharged. The most common way for a contract to be discharged is by the parties performing their obligations under it, but contracts may also be discharged by agreement, breach or frustration.

Discharge by performance

If the parties perform their respective obligations under the contract, this is known as discharge by performance. The degree of performance required from the parties will depend upon the terms of the contract. Failure to perform these obligations will ordinarily constitute a breach of contract, but may sometimes be excusable, as where the contract becomes frustrated (see Chapter 30).

At common law, the rule relating to performance is generally strict and the parties must perform the terms of the contract entirely. Such rigidity may lead to harshness, however, and as a result some limited exceptions to this rule have evolved.

Substantial performance
Under certain circumstances, where one party has substantially (but not entirely) performed his part of the contract, he may still recover the contract price from the other, subject to any appropriate deductions made for any shortcomings on his part. Whether or not substantial performance has taken place will depend upon the circumstances of the case. In this context, distinctions between conditions, warranties and innominate terms may be important, because performance of some terms will be more important than

others (see Chapter 22). The principle of substantial performance is well illustrated by *Hoenig v Isaacs* [1952] 2 All ER 176, in which Hoenig hired Isaacs to redecorate and furnish his flat, the agreement being that Isaacs would be paid £400 on account and the balance of £350 on completion of the work. Hoenig refused to pay any of this balance on completion, because he said that the work was faulty. Had the work been fundamentally flawed, this refusal would have been justified, but the Court of Appeal found only a few minor defects in a bookcase and wardrobe, which could be rectified for less than £56. Hoenig was therefore obliged to pay a balance of some £294.

Acceptance of part-performance

Even where A has fallen well short of his obligations to B under their contract, so that 'substantial performance' cannot be claimed, A may still be entitled to claim some payment from B if the latter has chosen to accept the benefit of such part of the contract as A has indeed performed. If A promises B 1,000 widgets, but can only produce 500, B must pay A for the 500 widgets if he wants them to keep them.

If, however, B has been left with no option but to keep and make use of what A has provided, this rule no longer applies. An obvious example would be faulty or unfinished work carried out on B's home. In *Bolton v Mahadeva* [1972] 2 All ER 1322, the plaintiff had contracted to install a heating system in the defendant's home for £560, but the system did not work properly and the plaintiff repeatedly failed to correct serious faults in that system. As a result, he was held to be in breach of contract and was unable to recover one penny of the £560. It was not a case of substantial performance, nor had the plaintiff chosen to adopt the benefit of the work that had been done.

Prevention of performance

If one of the parties prevents the other from carrying out his obligations under the contract, the innocent party may not thus be deprived of the fruits of his labour. He may claim damages for breach of contract, or receive compensation for the work already done.

Divisible contracts

Many contracts may be described as consisting of severable obligations, i.e., the contract is performed in stages and each party performs its respective obligations before moving on to the next part. Such contracts are common in the building trade. For example, X and Y may have an agreement to build a house which is to be paid for in stages. If X defaults after completing the first stage and does no further work, he will still be entitled to be paid the sum agreed for completion of the first stage. This is in contrast to entire contracts, where complete performance is ordinarily required.

Discharge by agreement

As a contract is made by agreement, it may also be discharged by agreement. An agreement to discharge an existing contract is itself a binding contract, provided it is either made by deed (under seal) or supported by consideration. If the contractual obligations have not yet been performed, consideration will not be a problem, because each party can agree to release his rights under the contract in return for a similar release by the other party. The situation is different where one of the parties to the contract performs his side of the bargain and charitably releases the other from providing anything in return. An example would be that of a seller supplying the goods requested by the buyer under the contract and then discharging the buyer from having to pay for them. This 'unilateral discharge' will not be binding on the seller (who may later change his mind) unless the promise to discharge is made under seal, or unless the buyer provides some alternative consideration. The extra element of consideration that may have to be provided is normally referred to as the provision of 'accord and satisfaction'. The accord is the agreement to discharge the original contract, and the satisfaction is the consideration which must be provided by the party who has not performed his part of the bargain.

Discharge by breach

Any breach of contract enables the injured party to sue for damages. Where certain breaches occur, however, the injured party has a choice whether to terminate the contract.

Actual breach

The right to terminate for an actual breach arises where the term breached is either a condition or, where it is a sufficiently serious breach, if the term itself is an innominate one. A breach will be deemed to be sufficiently serious where it deprives the injured party of 'substantially all' of the benefit he was supposed to receive under the contract (in other words, if the breach goes to the root of the contract).

Anticipatory breach

An anticipatory breach occurs where A and B have entered into a contract, but before the time for performance arrives B states that he cannot or will not perform. In *Freeth* v *Burr* (1874) LR 9 CP 208, Lord Coleridge stated that an anticipatory breach occurs where one of the parties to a contract gives 'an intimation to abandon and altogether to refuse performance of the contract'. Where this happens, the other party can treat the contract as broken. He can freely enter into an alternative contract with a third party. In *Hochester* v *De La Tour* (1853) 2 E & B 678, the defendant asked the plaintiff in April to act as a courier for him from 1 June, and the plaintiff agreed to do so. In May, however, the defendant told the plaintiff that his services were no longer wanted. Later that same month, the plaintiff brought an action for breach of contract against the defendant. The defendant claimed that he was not in breach of contract and that an action could not be brought against him until 1 June. The court rejected this argument and held that the plaintiff could sue him, even before the date originally set for performance.

What if A waits until the performance date and then sues for breach of contract? In most cases he will be able to recover damages as before; but there is a risk that the contract may be overtaken by events, as *Avery* v *Bowden* (1856) 6 E & B 953 shows. The defendants in that case had chartered the plaintiff's ship, the *Lebanon,* to load a cargo at the Russian port of Odessa 'within 45 days'. The *Lebanon* was ready to load, but long before the 45 days were up, the defendants told the ship's master that there was no cargo for him to load and he was advised to sail away. This arguably amounted to a repudiation of the contract. The master nevertheless kept the contract alive, in the hope that the defendants would eventually find a cargo and perform their part of the contract. The *Lebanon* therefore remained at Odessa, but before the 45 days were up, the Crimean War broke out between Russia and Britain and it became illegal to load cargo at what was now an enemy port. The contract thus became frustrated and it followed that the plaintiff could no longer hope to recover damages. The plaintiff (acting through the ship's master) had not accepted the initial repudiation. The plaintiff had kept the contract open and the war had broken out before the date for it to be completed.

(As to the doctrine of frustration, see Chapter 30.)

Problems may arise if A mistakenly construes B's behaviour as amounting to anticipatory breach of contract, when B has perhaps merely made a statement which indicates a misunderstanding of the contract's terms. If A 'over-reacts' by announcing that he regards the contract as repudiated, he may find that he himself is the one who is guilty of anticipatory breach. As a general rule, it would seem that a party who purports (albeit mistakenly) to exercise a right supposedly granted to him under the contract, should not be regarded as repudiating that contract, and should not therefore be regarded as committing an anticipatory breach. As Lord Wilberforce said in *Woodar Investment Development Ltd* v *Wimpey Construction (UK) Ltd* [1980] 1 All ER 571, 'repudiation is a drastic conclusion which should only be held to arise in clear cases of a refusal, in a matter going to the root of the contract, to perform contractual obligations'.

Discharge

Contracts may be discharged in any one of four ways

By performance	*By agreement*	*By breach*	*Frustration* see Chapter 30

This occurs where both parties perform their respective obligations under the contract. The common law rule relating to performance is strict and so a number of exceptions to this rule have evolved:

   (i)   Substantial performance.

   (ii)   Acceptance of part-performance.

   (iii)   Prevention of performance.

   (iv)   Divisible contracts.

An agreement to discharge an existing contract is itself a binding contract, provided it is either made under seal, or supported by consideration.

Distinguish between an actual breach and an anticipatory breach.

A party can terminate for an actual breach where the term breached is a condition or an innominate term which deprives the injured party of substantially all of the benefit he expected to receive under the contract.

An anticipatory breach occurs where one of the parties gives 'an intimation to abandon and altogether to refuse performance of the contract'. The other party can treat the contract as terminated.

THIRTY

Frustration

Frustration refers to a supervening event which occurs after a contract has been concluded, and which could not reasonably have been contemplated by the parties. This event must either radically alter the foundation or object of the contract itself, or render it physically or legally impossible to perform. In such cases, the contract may properly be said to have become frustrated. An example of an event making a contract physically impossible to perform would be a fire which destroys a holiday cottage, a day after a contract has been completed for its hire the following week. Such an event, assuming it is a mere accident, would be said to frustrate the contract. The hirer would no longer be obliged to pay for the cottage's hire, and the owner would not be liable for any breach of contract through failure to provide the promised accommodation.

A more difficult issue may arise where the contract, although not rendered physically impossible to perform, has been so drastically affected by some unforeseen event that it no longer bears any relation to what the parties originally intended. At what point can a contract be said to have become frustrated? As we shall see, mere inconvenience or increased financial hardship is not enough; there must be clear evidence of a fundamental change in the nature of the parties' obligations as a result of the frustrating event.

In considering whether a contract has become frustrated, it may be necessary to identify the 'object' of the contract. In this context, the 'object' must be divorced from the parties' motives in entering into that contract. It is only where the object of the contract has been destroyed or radically altered that the contract can be said to have become frustrated. For example, X may purchase a return rail ticket to Wembley in order to see Radiohead in concert, only for the concert to be cancelled due to Thom Yorke having lost his voice. In these circumstances, although the train journey may now seem pointless to him as his *motive* for the journey no longer exists, the *object* of the contract with the railway company is still performable, i.e., to take him to Wembley and back. The railway company would not even have known what the traveller's motive was.

The following sections will look at the development of the doctrine of frustration and the parameters within which the doctrine operates.

Development of the doctrine of frustration

The traditional common law approach, both to contracts which had become impossible to perform and to those whose obligations had become radically different from those originally intended, was very harsh. Once a party had entered into a contract, he was obliged to fulfil his obligations under that contract, regardless of the fact that he could derive no benefit from it. If hired property was destroyed by fire one day after the contract for hire had been completed, the hirer would still be liable to pay rent for it.

The courts took the view that the parties could always have made provision for such eventualities in the contract itself, and if they did not then the loss was to lie where it fell. An example of this approach may be seen in the old case of *Paradine* v *Jane* (1647) Aleyn 26. The plaintiff brought an action for rent on a lease against the defendant. The defendant, however, argued that he had been dispossessed of the land by force and had lost the profits from it. He therefore denied that he was liable for the rent. The court rejected this argument and held that he was still bound to pay. No doctrine of frustration appears to have been recognised at this time.

Taylor v *Caldwell* (1863) 3 B & S 826 is generally credited with being the case which first marked the recognition of the doctrine of frustration. The plaintiff entered into a contract with the defendant for the hire of the Surrey Gardens and its music hall on four separate days in June, July and August. The plaintiff was to use the premises for four 'grand' concerts, with 'day and night' fetes on the dates in question, but before the date of the first concert, the music hall was gutted by fire. Neither party was to blame for the fire, but it obviously made it impossible for the plaintiff to hold his concerts. No express provision for this eventuality was included in the contract and the plaintiff therefore claimed damages from the defendant for the money he had wasted in advertising the concerts. The court held that his claim could not succeed. Blackburn J stated:

> ... where, from the nature of the contract, it appears that the parties must from the beginning have known that it could not be fulfilled unless when the time for fulfilment of the contract arrived some particular specified thing continued to exist, so that, when entering into the contract, they must have contemplated such continuing existence as the foundation of what was to be

done; there, in the absence of any express or implied warranty that the thing shall exist, the contract is not to be construed as a positive contract, but as subject to an implied condition that the parties shall be excused in case, before breach, the performance becomes impossible from the perishing of the thing without default of the contractor.

It can be seen from this case that where a contract has been frustrated by some supervening event, the doctrine of frustration operates so as to absolve both parties from any further obligations under it.

Justification for the doctrine

There are two theories put forward for the justification of the doctrine of frustration. They are:

(a)   the 'implied term' theory; and
(b)   the 'radical change in obligation' theory.

The implied term theory
This theory was adopted by Blackburn J in *Taylor v Caldwell*, but has now been abandoned by the courts. This approach was based upon the artificial pretext that a term could be implied into the contract to the effect that if certain facts did not continue, or if some supervening fact occurred, then the parties could be released from their contractual obligations. The weakness in this theory is that although implication of such a term is supposedly based on the parties' intentions, they had probably never envisaged the situation which that implied term was invented to resolve.

The radical change in obligation theory
This is currently the favoured approach, and was adopted by the House of Lords in *Davis Contractors Ltd v Fareham UDC* [1956] AC 696 (for the facts of this case see below). The essence of this approach is that, before a contract can be said to be frustrated, the court must be satisfied that the whole purpose of the obligation must have changed as a result of the supervening event, and that it is not simply the surrounding circumstances which have altered. In the *Davis Contractors* case, Lord Radcliffe argued:

... perhaps it would be simpler to say at the outset that frustration occurs whenever the law recognises that without default of either party a contractual obligation has become incapable of being performed because the circumstances in which performance is called for would render it a thing radically different from that which was undertaken by the contract...

Whether this approach is adopted or the implied term theory, the doctrine nevertheless operates within narrow confines. The following section looks at the limitations which exist upon the operation of the doctrine of frustration.

Limitations on the operation of the doctrine

The supervening event must not have been foreseeable
The doctrine of frustration will not generally apply to situations in which the supervening event was foreseeable. In such circumstances, the eventuality should have been provided for within the body of the contract itself. An example of this can be seen in *Davis Contractors Ltd v Fareham UDC* (above). The appellants agreed to build 78 houses for the council within eight months. Due to various difficulties with the supply of both men and materials, the work took 22 months to complete and cost far more than had originally been estimated. The appellants tried to argue that the contract had become frustrated due to delays which were not the fault of either party. The House of Lords held that the contract had not been frustrated, as these were foreseeable events which ought to have been provided for in the body of the contract itself. Lord Radcliffe said:

> Two things seem to me to prevent the application of the principle of frustration to this case. One is that the cause of the delay was not any new state of things which the parties could not reasonably be thought to have foreseen. On the contrary, the possibility of enough labour and materials not being available was before their eyes and could have been the subject of special contractual stipulation. It was not so made.

Self-induced frustration
The frustrating event must not be the fault of either party. The supervening event must have been beyond the control of the parties. In other words, the frustration should be caused by some extraneous change or event. Consequently, a deliberate act by one of the parties will not be treated as frustrating the contract. An example of this principle may be seen in *The Eugenia* [1964] 1 All ER 161. The *Eugenia* was chartered in 1956 to travel from Genoa to the Black Sea to load cargo, and thereafter to India. The route which the ship took to India was *via* the Suez Canal. This route was in breach of contract, which contained a 'war clause' prohibiting the charterers from sailing the ship into a dangerous war zone (which Suez then was) without the owner's consent. After the ship entered the Suez Canal it became trapped, due to the Canal's closure. The charterers tried to argue that the contract was frustrated, but the Court of Appeal held that it was not, as it was the charterers' fault that the ship gone into the Canal. The charterers were therefore liable to pay for the charter throughout the period during whch the *Eugenia* lay trapped in the canal.

The position may be different, however, if the fault of the party can be classed as minor. It will then be a matter of degree as to whether what has occured will be classed as self-induced frustration.

Where the purpose of the contract has been drastically affected
A difficult issue arises where physical performance of the contract itself is still possible but the *purpose* of the contract has been drastically affected by some supervening event. A good example of this problem may be seen from the famous case of *Krell* v *Henry* [1903] 2 KB 740. The defendant, Henry, agreed to hire a flat in Pall Mall from the plaintiff, Krell, for the days of 26 June and 27 June 1902. Krell had specifically advertised his flat as being suitable for viewing the coronation processions scheduled to take place on those days, and the windows in the flat provided excellent views of the procession route. The defendant agreed on 20 June to pay £75 for the exclusive use of the flat on those two days. The contract, however, made no express reference to the coronation procession. The defendant paid a deposit of £25 at the time of contracting, and the balance of £50 was to be submitted the day before the coronation. Unfortunately, the King fell ill and the processions did not take place on the scheduled dates. Krell claimed the remaining £50 from Henry, who counter-claimed for the return of his deposit. The Court of Appeal held that the contract had been frustrated, and found in favour of Henry. The defendant would not have hired the flat on such a high daily rate had it not been in a prime position to view the coronation procession and both parties must have been aware of this fact. Thus, when the coronation procession was cancelled, the foundation of the contract had been radically altered. Without the procession there was no purpose to the contract.

That case, however, may be contrasted with *Herne Bay Steamboat Co.* v *Hutton* [1903] 2 KB 683. The defendant agreed to hire a steam launch from the plaintiffs for 28 and 29 June 1902 at a cost of £250. The boat was hired 'for the purpose of viewing the naval review and for a day's cruise round the fleet'. The naval review was part of the coronation celebrations and was cancelled upon the King's illness, but the fleet itself was still anchored at Spithead on 28 June and could have been viewed by the defendant if he had wished. The defendant nevertheless chose not to use the boat and pleaded frustration when the plaintiffs sued for the outstanding charge. The Court of Appeal held that the contract had not been frustrated. This case is distinguishable from *Krell* v *Henry*, in that the naval review was not the sole basis of the contract. The defendant could still use the boat which he had hired to at least view the huge fleet of ships at anchor on the 28th.

Later cases indicate that the courts take a very strict approach towards contracts where supervening events have merely made contractual obligations more onerous. An example of this strict approach may be seen in *Tsakiroglou & Co. Ltd* v *Noblee Thorl GmbH* [1961] 2 All ER 179. The appellants had contracted to sell a cargo of groundnuts to the respondents at £50 per ton. This price was to cover carriage by sea from Port Sudan, in East Africa, to Hamburg. The obvious sea route was via the Suez Canal and the Mediterranean, and the price had been worked out on that assumption; but when the Suez Canal was suddenly closed as a result of the 1956 war, the appellants found that the only other option open to them was to ship the groundnuts all the way around the Cape of Good Hope. This would more than double the cost of carriage and they could not even cover their own costs at £50 per ton. They therefore claimed that the contract had been frustrated. Had it specified carriage via Suez, then it would have been, but it did not, and carriage via the Cape was not impossible, but merely expensive. The House of Lords accordingly ruled that the contract was not frustrated. The appellants would simply have to bear the extra costs involved.

Examples of the doctrine of frustration

The most common factor in frustration cases is that the contract has become impossible to perform; but not every impossibility will frustrate a contract.

Destruction of the subject-matter of the contract

Taylor v *Caldwell* (above) provides a clear example of frustration of a contract through the destruction of the subject-matter of the contract. Also note that s. 7 of the Sale of Goods Act 1979 provides:

> Where there is an agreement to sell specific goods, and subsequently the goods without any fault on the part of the seller or buyer, perish before the risk passes to the buyer, the agreement is avoided.

Death or illness

If a contract requires performance of a personal service by a particular person, then if that person dies or becomes incapacitated, it can be said that performance of the contract has become impossible. For example in *Whincup* v *Hughes* (1871) LR 6 CP 78, the plaintiff's son was apprenticed to a watchmaker for a six-year period, but the watchmaker died soon afterwards. Since the contract was for a personal and skilled service it was held to have been frustrated.

Unavailability

Non-availability of the subject-matter of a contract may sometimes be only temporary, but if the contract crucially requires performance by a particular date then if the subject-matter is unavailable the contract will be frustrated. A particular problem in this context is where the contract extends over a lengthy period of time and supervening events, such as a strike, cover only part of that period. In those circumstances the delay will frustrate the contract only if it defeats the commercial object of the contract, which can be a difficult question for the courts to resolve. The court will obviously have to consider the length of the contract and the degree of the interference.

Illegality

A contract will be frustrated where the performance of the contract would be contrary to a law which is created after the contract is made. In *Gamerco SA* v *ICM Fair Warning (Agency) Ltd* [1995] 1 WLR 1226 a Guns 'n' Roses concert had to be cancelled when the necessary licence was suddenly withdrawn because of previously unsuspected safety problems at the venue. The concert could not lawfully proceed without this licence, so the contract to provide the concert was held to have been frustrated. This will apply even if the change in the law does not make the contract physically impossible to perform. Trading with an enemy country after the outbreak of war would fall into this category. By the same token, the imposition of an import or export ban on certain goods, or on trade with certain countries, would frustrate any relevant contracts previously entered into but not yet performed.

Consequences of frustration

Where a contract is held to have become frustrated, it automatically comes to an end from the time of the frustrating event. The practical effect of this is that the contract remains valid up to the frustrating event and any rights or obligations incurred up to that point remain valid. Only rights and obligations still to be performed after the frustrating event will be cancelled.

Prior to 1943, the common law was extremely harsh in that no compensation was awarded for any pre-frustration expense incurred by either party. Instead, any such losses had to lie where they fell.

The harshness of the common law was reduced by the introduction of the Law Reform (Frustrated Contracts) Act 1943. In outline the Act provides that:

(a) Any advance sum of money paid to either party under a contract before that contract was frustrated, will be recoverable from that party.

(b) Any sums which were payable to either party under the contract before the contract was frustrated will cease to be payable.

(c) If either party had already obtained some benefit under the contract before it was frustrated, the court has a discretion under s. 1(3) of the Act to require some payment to be made for that benefit, having regard to various matters, including in particular any expenses already incurred by the other party. This principle was applied by the courts in *BP Exploration Co. (Libya) Ltd* v *Hunt (No. 2)* [1982] 1 All ER 925, in which BP were able to recover some of the expenses they had incurred in developing a Libyan oil field under an agreement with Hunt, whereby they would finance and develop Hunt's oil concession in return for a share of future profits. The oil field was developed, but the deal was frustrated a few years later when Colonel Gaddafi expropriated the concession on behalf of his new revolutionary government. In the meantime, Hunt had already profited from the deal, but BP had not been fully compensated for their initial development expenses. They were duly allowed to recover from Hunt a sum which the courts considered to be fair or just in the circumstances.

The relationship between mistake and frustration

Many writers argue that there are similarities between the doctrine of frustration and the rules under which contracts may be held to be void *ab initio* for mistake. The problem of whether the parties can be excused from continued contractual obligations arises in both. Furthermore, the dividing line between the two branches of law can be a very fine one. It can boil down to a matter of timing. This may be illustrated by the case of *Amalgamated Investment & Property Co. Ltd* v *John Walker & Sons Ltd* [1976] 3 All ER 509. The plaintiffs sought to buy a large commercial property from the defendants in order to redevelop it. Planning permission would be required for any such development, and in the course of pre-contractual enquiries the plaintiffs therefore asked the defendants whether the property was a listed building. The defendants replied on 14 August that it was not. This was correct at the time. Unknown to either party, however, officials at the Department of the Environment had already decided to list the building. On 25 September the parties exchanged contracts. The very next day, the Department of Environment wrote to the defendants to inform them that the building had now been listed. Without redevelopment potential, the building was worth a mere fraction of the agreed contract price, and so the plaintiffs claimed to rescind the contract.

Unfortunately, there was no basis on which they could do so. They could not claim common mistake, as the property had been listed the day *after* the contract had been concluded. Their alternative argument was that the contract had become frustrated, but this also failed. The plaintiffs had simply been unlucky that the building had been listed so soon after purchase, but this was a risk which the plaintiffs had to bear.

Frustration

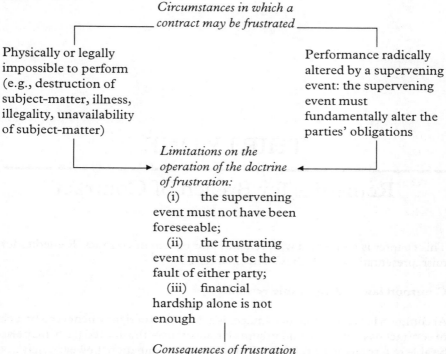

Circumstances in which a contract may be frustrated

Physically or legally impossible to perform (e.g., destruction of subject-matter, illness, illegality, unavailability of subject-matter)

Performance radically altered by a supervening event: the supervening event must fundamentally alter the parties' obligations

Limitations on the operation of the doctrine of frustration:
(i)   the supervening event must not have been foreseeable;
(ii)   the frustrating event must not be the fault of either party;
(iii)   financial hardship alone is not enough

Consequences of frustration

At common law the effect of the frustrating event is to terminate the contract automatically at the time of the event. This means that the contract will be held to be valid up to the time of the frustrating event, and only rights and obligations to be performed after the frustrating event will be cancelled. The common law provided no compensation for pre-frustration expense. The harshness of the common law has been modified by the Law Reform (Frustrated Contracts) Act 1943.

THIRTY ONE

Remedies for Breach of Contract

This chapter is concerned with remedies for breach of contract. Remedies for misrepresentation are dealt with in Chapter 23.

Common law and equitable remedies

At common law, an action for damages is available as of right whenever a breach of contract has occurred, and in some circumstances the injured party may also be able to terminate the contract. Damages and termination, however, may not always be entirely satisfactory remedies. If, for example, A has contracted to sell B his house, but has persistently refused to execute a conveyance of that house to B, it may be that what B wants is not damages, still less termination. He probably wants the house conveyed to him in accordance with the contract. Consequently, the law of equity has, over the years, supplemented the common law with a number of alternative remedies, such as specific performance, injunctions and orders for restitution. As these are equitable remedies, they are not available as of right (as are damages) but are awarded only at the discretion of the court.

This chapter will look at the general principles governing the computation of damages for breach of contract and at some of the equitable remedies which may be available.

DAMAGES

General principles governing the award of damages

A successful plaintiff is always entitled to damages in the event of a breach of contract. If, however, the plaintiff has suffered no real loss, he will only be able to recover 'nominal damages', as a simple acknowledgement that his legal rights have been broken. In most cases, however, the plaintiff will claim damages for substantial loss. Loss in these circumstances can include compensation for personal injury, damage to property or, under limited circumstances, injury to feelings or distress, but most commonly the plaintiff's claim will be for compensation for damage to his economic position (i.e., compensation for harm suffered to his economic position as a result of the contract not being properly performed).

The principal purpose of an award of contractual damages is to put the plaintiff, financially, into the position he would have been in had the contract been properly performed; or in other words to compensate him for his expectation loss. It is not the aim of contractual damages to punish the defendant, nor will the plaintiff be compensated for losses which cannot be attributed to the defendant's breach of contract. Assume, for example, that the plaintiff loses £25,000 in respect of a business venture: £10,000 of this loss is attributable to the defendant's failure to deliver goods or provide services to the plaintiff by the date specified in a contract between them; but the remaining £15,000 loss can be attributed to the plaintiff's own misjudgment of the market, or to a downturn in market conditions which could not have been avoided even by prompt performance of the defendant's obligations. On such facts, the defendant can only be liable for the £10,000 loss suffered as a result of his failure to deliver on time.

Types of loss for which damages may be awarded

There are various ways in which the plaintiff can be compensated for his loss and the plaintiff may choose whichever type of compensation he feels is more appropriate to his case. Sometimes more than one form of claim may be possible (e.g., for lost profits and consequential loss) and the plaintiff may also combine claims where he is not sure which offers the best chance of success, but he cannot recover for the same loss twice over.

Expectation loss
This is the usual aim of contractual damages, namely, to put the plaintiff in the position, financially, that he would have been in had the contract been performed. Damages assessed on that basis can cover the profit which the injured party would have received had the contract been properly performed. If, for example, A books a room for the night at B's hotel, but cancels or simply fails to show up, B may charge him (and if necessary sue him) for that booking. It does not ordinarily matter whether B could have let the room to anyone else. His claim will be based on the profit he would have made if A had honoured his booking. On the other hand, if this was B's last room, and B was able to let it to C on learning of A's cancellation, B will have lost nothing, even on an 'expectation basis', and could therefore obtain only nominal damages from A.

Damages can also be assessed, in appropriate cases, by reference to the cost of putting right things that have not been done or which have been done badly. Nevertheless, there may be cases in which the courts decide that the cost of rectification would be disproportionate to the breach of contract, and thus decline to award damages on that basis. This is what happened in *Ruxley Electronics and Constructions Ltd* v *Forsyth* [1995] 3 All ER 268. The plaintiffs were hired to construct a swimming pool for the defendant. The pool they built was an excellent one — except that it was not quite as deep as the defendant had specified. This was a disappointment to the defendant (who was refusing to pay for it) but it scarcely affected its market value. In contrast, the only way of deepening the pool would be to dig it up and rebuild it at a cost of no less than £21,650. The House of Lords held that damages of that order would not be appropriate, and the defendant was required to pay for the pool, subject to a deduction of just £2,500 for his disappointment or 'loss of amenity'.

Reliance loss
An alternative to claiming expectation loss is to claim reliance loss, much as in actions brought in respect of alleged torts (see Chapter 43). Damages may be claimed on a reliance basis where the plaintiff would find it difficult to establish what profit, if any, he would have derived from the contract. In those circumstances, the plaintiff may instead claim compensation for expenses incurred in reliance on the contract. An example of a plaintiff making a claim for reliance loss can be seen in *Anglia Television* v *Reed* [1971] 3 All ER 690. Reed broke a contract with Anglia under which he was to appear in a film. His breach meant that the film could not be made. Anglia sued him for damages, but they could not claim for lost profits because they could not establish what the profit would have been if Reed had performed as agreed. There may not have been any. Anglia therefore sued only for their wasted expenditure and in this they were successful.

Damages for incidental and consequential loss
Damages may also be claimed for incidental or consequential loss suffered by the plaintiff as a result of a breach of contract. Damages for incidental loss involve recovering compensation for expenditure suffered by the plaintiff after the breach has come to his attention, and would include such things as recovery of the cost of sending back faulty goods and the cost of hiring substitute goods in the meantime. Consequential losses, on the other hand, could include compensation for losses suffered as a result of the breach, such as personal injury or damage to other property, as where A sells B a faulty hi-fi amplifier which short-circuits and damages B's loudspeakers. (For damage caused by defective products, see also Chapter 38.)

Damages for mental distress, disappointment or other non-pecuniary loss
In some cases, the plaintiff may recover damages for non-pecuniary loss, such as disappointment (see *Ruxley Electronics and Constructions Ltd* v *Forsyth*, above)

or mental distress; but such damages will only be recoverable under contracts whose objects or purposes include the provision of comfort or pleasure or peace of mind. Contracts to provide holidays or wedding photographs may come into that category, but in *Hayes v James & Charles Dodd* [1990] 2 All ER 815 the Court of Appeal emphasised that such considerations will not feature in ordinary commercial contracts.

In *Jarvis v Swan Tour Operators Ltd* [1973] 1 All ER 71, damages were awarded for lost enjoyment in relation to a contract for a holiday. The plaintiff booked a winter sports holiday with Swan Tours. The company's brochure promised that clients would form a 'houseparty'. There would be afternoon tea and cakes, skiing equipment would be provided, a yodeller would provide evening entertainment, and so on. The plaintiff was disappointed in almost every respect. No proper teas were provided. Full-sized skis were only available for two days. The yodeller turned out to be a local man in ordinary work clothes who would turn up at the hotel after work and sing a few songs. Worst of all, the plaintiff found that for half the holiday he was the only member of the supposed 'house party'. He claimed damages on the grounds that the holiday was not as described in the brochure. The Court of Appeal awarded him damages to cover the difference in value between what he paid for and what he got, but they also awarded further substantial damages to compensate him for his disappointment.

Damages for mental distress can also be awarded in cases where mental anxiety is suffered as a result of physical inconvenience caused by the breach. In *Perry v Sidney Phillips & Son* [1982] 3 All ER 705, the plaintiff bought a house on the basis of a survey carried out by the defendants, which stated that the house was in good order. Unfortunately, this was not the case; amongst other problems, the septic tank was insanitary and the roof leaked when it rained. These defects caused the plaintiff a lot of worry and his financial position was such that he could not afford to have them fixed. He was awarded damages, not only for the reduced value of the house, but also for the mental distress he had suffered.

Causation and remoteness of damage

The courts will not necessarily compensate a plaintiff for everything that may occur to him following a breach of contract. The law imposes a limit upon the damage for which the party in breach can be held responsible. As already explained, damages cannot be awarded as compensation for loss or damage which would have happened even without the defendant's breach of contract, and even where a causal link *can* be proved, damages will not be awarded in respect of loss or damage which is said to be 'too remote from the breach' to be compensatable. This is known as the 'remoteness of damage' test.

The test for remoteness of damage
The rule regarding remoteness of damage was first stated in *Hadley v Baxendale* (1854) 9 Ex 341. The plaintiffs' mill was rendered inoperative by the collapse

of the crank shaft of their steam engine. The plaintiffs arranged for the defendants to take the old shaft to engineers in Greenwich, who would use the old shaft as a model to make a new one. The defendants, however, failed to deliver the broken shaft promptly, and this obviously delayed construction of the replacement. The plaintiffs claimed damages for the profits which they had lost due to this delay. The defendants argued that they were not liable for the lost profits as they were too remote from the breach of contract. Baron Alderson set out the test for remoteness:

> Where two parties have made a contract which one of them has broken the damages which the other party ought to receive in respect of such a breach of contract should be such as may fairly and reasonably be considered as either arising naturally, i.e., according to the usual course of things, from such breach of the contract itself, or such as may reasonably be supposed to have been in the contemplation of both parties at the time they made the contract as the probable result of the breach of it . . .

The defendant, therefore, will be liable for any loss arising in the normal course of events as a result of his breach, but will be liable for any unusual consequences only if he had special knowledge of them at the time of contracting.

In *Hadley v Baxendale* the extra time for which the mill was closed, and the loss of profits therefrom, was not viewed as a loss naturally arising from the defendants' breach, because in the majority of cases the absence of a mill shaft would not have caused such a stoppage. Most millers would have had a spare shaft available. Furthermore, the defendants were not proved to have had knowledge of the circumstances, so as to bring them within the second limb of the test.

The later case of *Victoria Laundry (Windsor) v Newman Industries, Coulson & Co. Ltd* [1945] 2 KB 528 was decided on the basis of the rules laid down in *Hadley v Baxendale*. Victoria Laundry wanted to expand their business and to that end ordered a larger boiler from Newman Industries. Delivery of the boiler was supposed to take place upon 5 June, but the boiler was found to be damaged and was not made fit for delivery until 8 November. Victoria Laundry claimed: (1) for the profit they would have earned between the dates of 5 June and 8 November, including the loss of extra laundry business they could have expected to have taken on with their new boiler during that time; and (2) for the loss of a number of lucrative dyeing contracts offered to them by the Ministry of Supply during that period. The Court of Appeal allowed the laundry to recover damages for loss suffered under head (1) but not for head (2). Newmans knew the nature of Victoria Laundry's business and would (or at least should) have foreseen that they would lose such business if delivery of the boiler was delayed. On the other hand, Newmans had no knowledge of the dyeing contracts from the Ministry of Supply and could not have foreseen the plaintiffs' loss in that particular respect.

The rules laid down in *Hadley* v *Baxendale* were further examined by the House of Lords in the case of the *Heron II* [1967] 3 All ER 686. This case involved a cargo ship which was nine days late in delivering its cargo of sugar at Basra, because of unauthorised deviations from its agreed route. The market price of sugar had fallen heavily in that period, and the ship's charterers were held liable for the consequential loss of profit, on the basis that the loss was one which the contracting parties could reasonably have contemplated at the time of contracting as 'not unlikely' to result from such a breach. In other words, it was not necessary to prove that the loss was probable (in the sense of being more likely to happen than not) but it was necessary to show that it was foreseeable as a significant, rather than a remote, kind of risk.

Quantification of damages

If the damage is not too remote a consequence of the breach, the next step is to decide how much compensation the injured party should receive. If the plaintiff has suffered no damage as a result of the breach then he will be awarded only nominal damages. The general aim, however, is that the plaintiff should be put into the financial position he would have been in had the contract been performed properly. What this amount will be will depend upon the contract itself. There are, however, many situations in which general principles have been established which may be followed, such as in contracts for the sale of goods.

Where the contract relates to the sale of goods, the amount of damages can be quantified by reference to the market price of the goods. For example, if a seller fails to deliver the goods, the buyer will be entitled to damages for the difference between the contract price and the greater amount which he would have to pay for the goods on the open market. Conversely, if it is the buyer who refuses to accept delivery of the items, the seller will be entitled to compensation for the difference between the contract price of the goods and any lesser amount which he gets for the goods by selling them (at the best price he can manage) elsewhere.

Mitigation of loss

The injured party is under a duty to take all reasonable steps to reduce (mitigate) the loss consequent upon the breach. Three things follow on from this:

(a)   if the injured party fails to take these reasonable steps, the damages awarded to him will be limited to what he would have lost had he acted reasonably;

(b)   the injured party will be able to recover compensation for any costs incurred in the taking of reasonable steps to mitigate the loss; and

(c) if the injured party takes action which in fact reduces his loss, the compensation paid will be reduced accordingly, as he cannot recover for a loss which has been avoided. If, for example, the plaintiff resold his goods at a *higher* price, following the defendant's failure to pay for them, and covered all losses and expenses thereby, he would be left with only a nominal claim for damages against the defendant, which would not be worth pursuing.

Liquidated damages and penalty clauses

It is a feature of many commercial contracts, such as building contracts, to have a clause incorporated into the contract setting out what damages are to be paid in the event of a breach. These are known as 'liquidated damages' clauses. In the event of a breach, the plaintiff will be able to claim damages only to the amount laid down in the clause, even if the damage actually suffered exceeds that amount. A liquidated damages clause must, however, be a genuine assessment of the appropriate level of compensation to be awarded. Sometimes, however, the amount laid down may be very high in an attempt to threaten the other party not to breach the contract. These clauses are referred to as 'penalty clauses'. The courts will strike down such clauses, and they must accordingly be distinguished from liquidated damages clauses.

How to distinguish a penalty clause from a liquidated damages clause
Express labelling of the clause itself by the parties is not conclusive, as they may not have used the labels in their correct technical sense. Therefore it is a matter of construction for the court to determine what is the true status of the clause. In *Dunlop Pneumatic Tyre Co. Ltd* v *New Garage and Motor Company* [1915] AC 79, Lord Dunedin laid down four tests to help solve the problem. He stated:

(a) It will be held to be a penalty if the sum stipulated for is extravagant and unconscionable in amount in comparison with the greatest loss that could conceivably be proved to have followed from the breach.

(b) It will be held to be a penalty if the breach consists only in not paying a sum of money, and the sum stipulated is a sum greater than the sum which ought to have been paid [e.g., if a debtor is made to pay £2,000 if he does not pay a debt of £200 by the deadline date] . . .

(c) There is a presumption (but no more) that it is a penalty when 'a single lump sum is made payable by way of compensation, on the occurrence of one or more or all of several events, some of which may occasion serious and others but trifling damage'. . .

(d) It is no obstacle to the sum stipulated being a genuine pre-estimate of damages, that the consequences of the breach are such as to make precise pre-estimation almost an impossibility. On the contrary, that is just the situation when it is probable that pre-estimated damage was the true bargain between the parties. . .

EQUITABLE REMEDIES

Monetary compensation may not always compensate the plaintiff properly, and he may therefore seek a more appropriate equitable remedy. As the plaintiff does not have an automatic right to an equitable remedy, he has to establish why damages alone are not a sufficient remedy. The courts then have a discretion whether to award an equitable remedy.

Specific performance

A decree of specific performance is an order from the court compelling the defendant to fulfil his obligations under the contract. An application for specific performance may be made where, for example, the plaintiff is unable to obtain a satisfactory substitute (e.g., a rare antique, or a particular house or plot of land). Specific performance is generally available in respect of contracts for land or houses, because no two pieces of land can ever be quite the same.

When deciding whether to award a decree of specific performance the court will pay attention to the following factors:

(a) A decree will not be granted if damages would be a satisfactory remedy.

(b) A decree will be ordered only if, were the parties' roles to be reversed, the same order could be made against the plaintiff. This is known as the principle of mutuality.

(c) If the plaintiff has acted unfairly or dishonestly he will be refused a decree, because 'He who comes to equity must come with clean hands'.

(d) The courts will rarely grant specific performance of a contract that would need constant supervision. A contract involving an undertaking or covenant to carry on a business will not, for that reason, be specifically enforceable, as the House of Lords recently confirmed in *Co-operative Insurance Society Ltd* v *Argyll Stores Ltd* [1997] 2 WLR 898.

(e) The courts will not normally grant an order of specific performance in relation to contracts for personal services.

Injunctions

An injunction is a court order restraining the defendant from committing a particular act, such as a breach of contract. If, for example, the plaintiff learns that the defendant is proposing to sell the property in question to a third person, in breach of their existing contract, he may obtain a court injunction forbidding it. Breach of an injunction amounts to a civil contempt of court (as does refusal to comply with an order for specific performance) and the defendant could be fined or committed to prison for such contempt.

Restitution

The basis of such an action is that the defendant has been unjustly enriched at the plaintiff's expense. In a claim for restitution, the plaintiff is not actually seeking damages but is seeking to deprive the defendant of any benefit which he may have received under the contract. Restitution may be sought, for example, where a seller of goods has been paid in advance but then fails to deliver the goods. Under an action for restitution, the seller would be bound to restore the price to the buyer, with the result that the parties are effectively put back into the position they were in before the contract was made.

Remedies

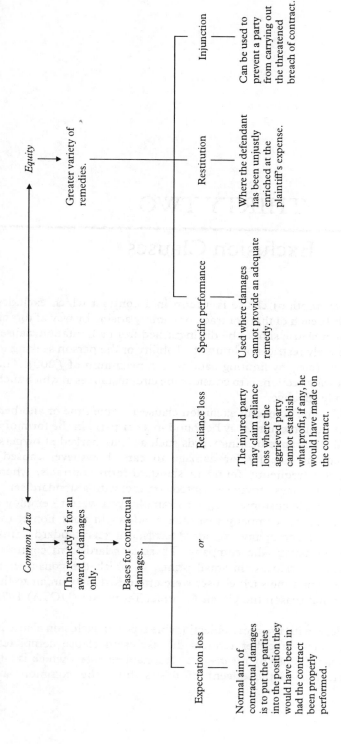

Common Law → **Equity**

The remedy is for an award of damages only.

Greater variety of remedies.

Bases for contractual damages.

Expectation loss *or* **Reliance loss**

Expectation loss

Normal aim of contractual damages is to put the parties into the position they would have been in had the contract been properly performed.

Reliance loss

The injured party may claim reliance loss where the aggrieved party cannot establish what profit, if any, he would have made on the contract.

Specific performance

Used where damages cannot provide an adequate remedy.

Restitution

Where the defendant has been unjustly enriched at the plaintiff's expense.

Injunction

Can be used to prevent a party from carrying out the threatened breach of contract.

THIRTY TWO

Exclusion Clauses

An exclusion (or exemption) clause is a term in a contract which excludes liability for possible breach of that contract, or liability arising by way of tort or statute. An exclusion clause should be distinguished from a limitation clause, in that the latter merely restricts or limits the liability of the person seeking to rely upon the clause (e.g., by limiting liability to a maximum of £200). The purpose of the following sections is to consider the circumstances in which such clauses will be legally effective.

Most people will come across an exclusion clause at some time or another. For example, an exclusion clause may be found in a car park, in the form of a sign displayed at the entrance bearing words such as 'cars parked at owners' risk', or 'we accept no liability for damage to cars, howsoever caused'. Exclusion clauses are frequently found in standard-form contracts, where suppliers of goods or services provide a printed contract with a standard set of terms for almost all their customers. If, for example, you were to employ a nationwide double-glazing company to install windows in your home, the contract would be on the company's standard terms, using its standard forms, and would inevitably favour the company. These standard-form contracts often contain exclusion clauses (in small print), of which the consumer is usually unaware. At one time such clauses were often extremely unfair to the consumer, and for that reason the Unfair Contract Terms Act (UCTA) 1977 was introduced.

The 1977 Act deals with the more objectionable types of exclusion clause in one of two main ways. It either renders the exclusion clause completely ineffective, or restricts its use by means of a reasonableness test which is laid down in the Act. Before the advent of this statute, the common law endeavoured to curb the worst excesses of the exclusion clause through the use of rules relating to the incorporation and construction of exclusion clauses. The use of such techniques is no longer as important, because of UCTA 1977, but they nevertheless still need to be studied. There are two main reasons for this: first, UCTA 1977 does not cover every type of exclusion clause; secondly, even if a clause satisfies the reasonableness test under the Act, it may nevertheless fall foul of the common law and thus be devoid of any legal effect. For example, the clause may be reasonable under UCTA 1977 but may not have been brought to the other party's attention before the contract was concluded.

Exclusion clauses may also be affected by the Unfair Terms in Consumer Contracts Regulations 1994, which implement a European Community Directive and are dealt with in Chapter 34. This chapter will concentrate on the common law rules of incorporation and construction, while Chapter 33 will consider the provisions of UCTA 1977.

When considering the validity of an exclusion clause, there are three questions which should be considered: first, whether the exclusion clause has been incorporated into the contract; secondly, whether the wording of the exclusion clause is wide enough to cover the damage which has actually occurred; and thirdly, whether the clause is affected by the Unfair Contract Terms Act 1977 or by the Unfair Terms in Consumer Contracts Regulations 1994.

INCORPORATION

There are three basic ways in which an exclusion clause may be incorporated into a contract, namely, by signature, by notice, or by a consistent course of dealing.

Incorporation by signature

As a general rule, an exclusion clause will necessarily be incorporated into a contract if it is contained in a contractual document which has been signed by the party against whom it is to take effect. This principle can been seen in the unfortunate case of *L'Estrange* v *Graucob Ltd* [1934] 2 KB 394. The plaintiff, a café owner, purchased a vending machine from the defendants, but unwittingly signed an order form containing a clause that exempted the defendants from any obligation to supply a machine that actually worked. Her signature on the order form had the effect (at that time) of making her bound by this exclusion clause, even though she had not read the 'regrettably small print' in which it was contained. Graucob Ltd were not therefore in breach of contract, even though the vending machine was manifestly defective and unfit for its purpose. Scrutton LJ said:

> In cases in which the contract is contained in a railway ticket or other unsigned document, it is necessary to prove that [the affected party] was

aware, or ought to have been aware, of its terms and conditions. These cases
have no application where the document has been signed ... In the absence
of fraud or ... misrepresentation, the party signing it is bound, and it is
wholly immaterial whether he has read the document or not ...

If such facts arose again today, the result would be different, because the
obligation to supply goods which are of satisfactory quality and fit for their
purpose can no longer so easily be negated (see the Unfair Contract Terms Act
1977, s. 6, in Chapter 33); but the case remains a valid illustration of the
principle that a signature on a document ordinarily prevents the party signing
it from denying that it has been incorporated into the contract.

Nevertheless, Scrutton LJ did refer in that case to certain circumstances in
which the general rule would cease to apply. Where the party seeking to rely on
the exclusion clause has misrepresented its meaning or effect (fraudulently or
otherwise) then, even if the document containing that clause has been signed
by the other party, it will not be effective. This can be illustrated by the case of
Curtis v *Chemical Cleaning and Dyeing Co.* [1951] 1 All ER 631. The plaintiff
took her wedding dress to the defendant dry cleaners. She was asked to sign a
document headed 'receipt', and was told that it excluded the defendants from
any liability for damage to the beads and sequins on her dress. The receipt,
however, contained a clause which purported to do much more than this. It
stated, 'This article ... is accepted on condition that the company is not liable
for any damage however arising.' As a result of the negligence of the
defendants, the wedding dress was badly stained, but they were not permitted
to rely upon their exclusion clause. Although its wording was wide enough to
cover the staining of the dress, and although the plaintiff had signed the receipt,
it was held that the contents of the clause had been misrepresented to her.

Incorporation by notice

An *unsigned* document or notice can sometimes become incorporated into a
contract, but the party seeking to rely on it will have to prove that it was brought
to the attention of the party against whom it is to be used, at or before the
moment of contracting. This may often be difficult to prove. There are two
potential issues here, namely:

(a)   was the clause or term brought to the other party's attention at all; and
(b)   if so, was it brought to his attention in time to become a term of the
contract?

Sufficiency of notice
Unless actual knowledge of the clause is proved against, or admitted by the
other party, a clause contained on a sign or in an unsigned document will only
be deemed to have been incorporated into a contract if reasonably sufficient

notice of it has been given to him. This rule was established in the old case of *Parker* v *South Eastern Railway Co.* [1877] 2 CPD 416. What notice is reasonably sufficient is largely a question of fact, and depends upon all the circumstances of the case. In *Parker* v *South Eastern Railway Co.*, for example, the defendant railway company sought to rely upon a clause on the back of a left-luggage ticket, limiting their liability for any loss of luggage to a maximum of £10 per item. The plaintiff's bag (which was worth more than £10) was lost by the company, and he claimed to have been unaware of the limitation clause on the ticket. The trial judge failed to ask the jury whether they were satisfied that the defendants had given the plaintiff proper notice of this clause, and the Court of Appeal therefore ordered a new trial. Mellish LJ said:

> We cannot lay down as a matter of law, either that the plaintiff was bound or that he was not bound by the limitations on the ticket... The railway company ... must be entitled to make some assumptions respecting the person who deposits the luggage with them; I think they are entitled to assume that he can read, that he understands the English language and that he pays such attention to what he is about as may reasonably be expected from a person in such a transaction as that of depositing luggage in a cloakroom... But if what the railway company do is not sufficient to convey to the minds of people in general that the ticket contains conditions, then they have received goods on deposit without obtaining the consent of the person depositing them to the conditions limiting their liability.

The type of document involved may be an important consideration. It was arguable that a reasonably well-informed traveller would know that left luggage tickets contain contractual terms, but if the relevant document is not of a type in which one would expect to find such terms, the other party cannot properly be deemed to have been aware of them. *Chapelton* v *Barry Urban District Council* [1940] 1 All ER 356, illustrates this point. The plaintiff decided to hire a deck chair on the beach at Barry. A notice told customers to acquire a ticket from the attendant and to retain the ticket for inspection. The plaintiff selected a chair and obtained a ticket which he placed in his pocket, without reading it. When he sat down on the chair, however, it collapsed and injured him. The defendants sought to rely upon an exclusion clause printed on the ticket, which purported to exclude liability for personal injury. It was held, however, that the clause was invalid, as it was not part of the contract. The ticket was not a document on which anyone would expect to find a term of that kind. It appeared merely to be a receipt for payment.

Reference to the terms It is not always necessary for a document or notice to contain the relevant exclusion or limitation clause. Terms may be incorporated into the contract if a notice or document simply refers the party to where those terms may be found. In *Thompson* v *LMS Railway Co.* [1930] 1 KB 41, the plaintiff purchased a half-price excursion ticket. On the back of the ticket, she was referred to the current LMS timetable in order to discover the conditions under which it was issued. Had she consulted this timetable (which was unlikely, since she could not even read) she might have found (at page 552!) a clause excluding the liability for negligent injury to excursion passengers, such as her. The plaintiff was injured whilst alighting from her train, but it was held that she had no cause of action against the LMS. The court held that the clause had been incorporated into the contract, despite the fact that she would have had to purchase the timetable in order to find the clause; and as Mellish LJ had previously stated in *Parker*, the fact that this particular plaintiff could not read was irrelevant.

(This is yet another situation in which an exclusion clause would no longer be effective today. Since this particular clause purported to exclude liability for personal injury, it would now be invalidated by s. 2(1) of UCTA 1977 (see Chapter 33) without it even being necessary to show that it was unreasonable.)

The 'red hand' rule   At one time, sellers or suppliers would commonly try to incorporate unreasonable terms into their contracts by using small notices or 'small print' at the bottom or on the back of standard forms. *L'Estrange* v *Graucob Ltd* (above) was an example. Even before the passing of the Unfair Contract Terms Act 1977, the courts threatened to limit such practices by adapting the common law rules on incorporation so as to make it more difficult for such clauses to be effective. In the case of *Spurling* v *Bradshaw* [1956] 2 All ER 121, a typically colourful *obiter dictum* from Denning LJ gave birth to what became known as the 'red hand' rule:

> The more unreasonable a clause is, the greater the notice which must be given of it. Some clauses which I have seen would need to be printed in red ink on the face of the document with a red hand pointing to them, before the notice could be held to be sufficient.

Since the enactment of UCTA 1977, it will no longer be necessary for the courts to use this device in order to attack objectionable exclusion clauses, but the principle remains valid, and may still be invoked in cases involving unfair contract terms which are not exclusion clauses and which do not fall within the ambit of UCTA 1977 or of the 1994 Regulations governing consumer contracts. The case of *Interfoto Picture Library* v *Stiletto Visual Programmes* [1988] 1 All ER 348 provides an example. Stiletto, an advertising agency, hired a set of 47 photographic transparencies from another agency, Interfoto. The hire period was to be 14 days, but if Stiletto had studied the delivery note carefully, they would have seen that Interfoto purported to charge a whopping £5 (plus VAT) per transparency per day if the items were not returned within the 14-day-period. The usual holding fee within the advertising business was no more than one tenth of this (or £3.50 *per week*). As a result, Stiletto found themselves faced with a holding charge of £3,783. They refused to pay, and the Court of Appeal agreed that it was not part of the contract. Stiletto had not signed the delivery note, and not enough had been done to draw the objectionable clause to their attention. Interfoto were therefore allowed only one tenth of what they claimed, on the basis of a *quantum meruit*.

The timing of the notice
Clauses found on signs or within unsigned documents cannot be incorporated into a contract unless they have been brought to the other party's attention, either before or at the time of contracting. It will not suffice to show the other party an exclusion clause (or any other supposed contractual term) *after* the contract has already been entered into. In *Olley* v *Marlborough Court Hotel* [1949] 1 KB 532 the plaintiffs went to stay at the defendant hotel and checked in at reception when they arrived. They were then shown to their room. There was a sign in the room which purported to exclude the hotel's liability for the theft of guests' property, unless this property was deposited with the manager-ess for safe-keeping. Valuable furs were stolen from their room, but the hotel tried to rely upon the exclusion clause to exclude any liability for the loss. The Court of Appeal held that the notice could not have formed any part of the contract between the plaintiffs and the hotel. The contract had already been made at the reception desk when they arrived. The hotel was therefore liable for the loss of the furs. See also (to similar effect) *Thornton* v *Shoe Lane Parking* [1971] 1 All ER 686, in which a notice excluding liability for personal injury to persons using a car park was held to be invalid because it could have been seen by customers only *after* they had purchased a ticket and thereby entered into a contract with the operators.

Incorporation by a consistent course of dealing

Incorporation may sometimes be based upon a previous course of dealings between the parties. *Henry Kendall & Sons* v *Lillico & Sons Ltd* [1968] 2 All ER 444 provides an illustration of this principle. The defendants sold groundnut extract to the plaintiffs, on a regular basis. All contracts were initially concluded orally by the telephone, but they were always followed up by a contract document in which the defendants set out their standard terms, including a clause exempting them from any liability for latent defects. The parties traded for several years, until a defective consignment poisoned the poultry to which it was fed. The question was whether the defendants were liable for this, or whether they were protected by the exclusion clause. The House of Lords held that, although the document had arrived after this particular transaction had been agreed, the clause was nevertheless incorporated on the basis of the parties' previous dealings. In other words, the plaintiffs knew perfectly well that those were the terms on which their business was transacted.

Whether there has been a consistent course of dealing is a question of fact. In each case where this issue arises, the court must look at what was included in the previous dealings and at what has been said and done in the current transaction. If a reasonable man would have assumed that the parties would contract in this particular transaction as they had done on previous occasions then it is likely that the clause will be included. If, on the other hand, there was something significantly different about this particular transaction, it is unlikely that such a clause could be incorporated (*McCutcheon* v *David MacBrayne Ltd* [1964] 1 All ER 430).

Construction of exclusion clauses

Once it has been established that the exclusion clause has been incorporated into the contract then the next step is to construe the wording of the exclusion clause to see if it covers the damage which has actually occurred. Prior to the passing of UCTA 1977, the courts would construe any ambiguity in the wording of the exclusion clause against the person trying to rely upon it, so as to protect the weaker party (normally the consumer). With the advent of UCTA 1977, however, such devices are rarely necessary, and older case law should be viewed in this light. Here we look at the approach taken by the courts towards the construction of exclusion clauses.

The contra proferentem rule
The basic approach taken by the courts when interpreting exclusion clauses has been to construe any ambiguity in the wording of the clause against the party seeking to rely upon it. This is known as the *contra proferentem* rule. Consequently, the words used must clearly cover the damage which has actually occurred. In *Andrew Bros (Bournemouth) Ltd* v *Singer & Co. Ltd* [1934] 1 KB 17, the defendants had contracted to sell Andrew Bros 'new Singer cars'. A dispute arose over one car, which had previously been driven and demonstrated to another customer and was not, therefore, strictly speaking a new car. The defendants sought to rely upon clause 5 of the contract which stated, 'all conditions, warranties and liabilities implied by statute, common law or otherwise are excluded'. The Court of Appeal held that this clause did not protect them. The clause referred only to implied terms and it was an *express* term that the car should be 'new'.

Exclusion of liability for negligence
Most exclusion clauses dealing with negligence are now covered by the UCTA 1977, but prior to that the courts adopted an artificially narrow test when construing such clauses. If there was any way at all in which an exclusion clause could be read so as to fall short of excluding liability for damage or injury caused by negligence, that is how the courts would construe it. If the party in breach could be liable on some other ground, the courts would normally infer

that the clause was effective in excluding liability for the non-negligent head of liability only. In *White* v *John Warwick & Co. Ltd* [1953] 2 All ER 1021, the plaintiff hired from the defendant a tradesman's tricycle. This proved defective and the plaintiff was injured when the saddle slipped as he was riding it. The contract of hire contained an exclusion clause stating 'nothing in this agreement shall render the owners liable for any injuries to the riders of the machine hired'. The plaintiff sued the defendants for damages for his injuries, alleging that the defendants were in breach of contract for failing to supply a cycle which was reasonably fit for its purpose, and that they were liable for negligently failing to see that the cycle was kept in good repair. The Court of Appeal held that the exclusion clause only covered the former kind of liability and not the liability for negligence.

Fundamental breach

The notion of fundamental breach was yet another device developed by the courts in an attempt to deal with the more objectionable kinds of exclusion clause and to protect those with inferior bargaining power. The courts developed the idea that an exclusion clause could never, as a matter of law, be applied to a fundamental breach (i.e., one that went to the root of the contract itself). This approach was adopted in *Karsales (Harrow) Ltd* v *Wallis* [1956] 1 WLR 936. Wallis wanted to buy a car from a man called Stinton. Karsales provided the hire purchase finance he needed. The car was eventually delivered to him, but it had been vandalised or wrecked before delivery. It was so badly damaged that it could no longer move under its own power. Despite the state of the car, Karsales tried to sue Wallis for the instalments due. In an attempt to recover the payments, the company relied upon a clause in the hire-purchase contract which stated: 'No condition or warranty that the vehicle is roadworthy, or as to its age, condition, or fitness for any purpose is given by the owner express or implied herein'. It was held that the company could not rely upon the exclusion clause because the wrecked car delivered to Wallis was not what he had contracted to buy, and as a matter of law no clause of that kind could exclude liability for such a fundamental breach.

In later cases, however, such as *Suisse Atlantique Société d'Armement Maritime SA* v *NV Rotterdamsche Kolen Centrale* [1967] 1 AC 361, the courts emphasised that the notion of fundamental breach was not a rule of law, but merely one of construction. Therefore, as long as the wording of the exclusion clause covered the breach, even a fundamental one, liability could be excluded. The reason for the change in approach was that the blanket rule as stated in the *Karsales* case was capable of invalidating exclusion clauses where the risk had been fairly allocated between parties of equal bargaining power and not just those (such as in *Karsales* itself) where parties of unequal status were involved and the weaker one needed protection.

Today the concept of fundamental breach can largely be ignored, because UCTA 1977 deals with such cases by other means (see Chapter 33).

Limitation clauses

Limitation clauses, as the name suggests, are clauses which limit liability as opposed to excluding it altogether. The courts have traditionally taken a less severe approach towards limitation clauses than they have to total exclusion clauses. Lord Wilberforce in *Ailsa Craig Fishing Co. Ltd* v *Malvern Fishing Co. and Securicor Ltd* [1983] 1 WLR 964, stated that limitation clauses were not to be treated with 'the same hostility as clauses of exclusion'. In this case, Securicor was under a contract to provide security for boats in Aberdeen harbour. One of the plaintiffs' boats sank in the harbour, and the plaintiffs claimed compensation of £55,000 from Securicor. Securicor admitted that they had been negligent and that they were in breach of contract, but relied upon a clause in the contract limiting liability to £1,000. The House of Lords held that Securicor could rely on such a clause.

The difficulty with this view is that limitation clauses may sometimes be so extreme that they may in practice be as effective as a complete exclusion clause. In view of the increased protection provided now by UCTA 1977, however, the problem of the unreasonable limitation clause can usually be dealt with under that Act (see Chapter 33).

Exclusion clauses

An exclusion clause is a term in a contract which excludes or restricts liability for breach, or liability arising by way of tort or statute. Three basic questions may need to be answered when assessing whether such a clause has any legal effect:

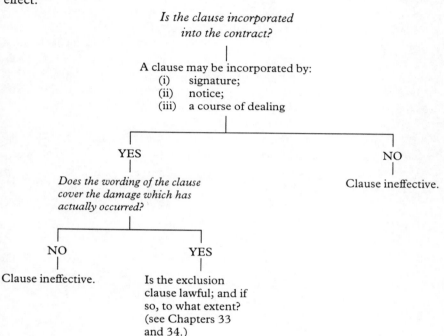

Is the clause incorporated into the contract?

A clause may be incorporated by:
- (i) signature;
- (ii) notice;
- (iii) a course of dealing

YES

Does the wording of the clause cover the damage which has actually occurred?

NO

Clause ineffective.

NO

Clause ineffective.

YES

Is the exclusion clause lawful; and if so, to what extent? (see Chapters 33 and 34.)

PART FOUR

Statutory Encroachments on Freedom of Contract

As we saw in the introduction to the law of contract, the twentieth century has witnessed increased statutory interference with the traditional doctrine of freedom of contract, in order to protect parties who may be inferior in bargaining power and who might otherwise be forced or induced to accept unfair or oppressive contractual terms when dealing with more powerful parties, such as banks, finance companies and commercial suppliers of goods or services. Here we examine some of the legislation which has been introduced to protect such parties, particularly individual consumers.

THIRTY THREE

The Unfair Contract Terms Act 1977

Where a dispute arises as to the validity or effect of an exclusion or limitation clause in a contract, it may be logical to consider, first of all, whether that clause has ever been incorporated within the contract. If not, it cannot be applicable. If it has been incorporated, its terms must then be construed. Any ambiguities must then be resolved against the party seeking to rely on it. The Unfair Contract Terms Act 1977 (or UCTA) then provides, in some cases, a third line of defence against unfair exclusion or limitation clauses. In practice, there is no particular order of priorities which must be followed when challenging such a clause. It may, for example, be difficult to determine whether a certain exclusion clause has been incorporated in a contract, and yet it may be quite obvious that the clause would, if thus incorporated, be struck down by UCTA 1977. Rather than waste time hearing extensive argument on the difficult (but in the circumstances merely academic) incorporation point, a judge might therefore quite legitimately turn straight to UCTA 1977 and rule accordingly.

The way in which UCTA 1977 deals with exclusion clauses is twofold. On the one hand, it renders certain types of exclusion clauses completely invalid; on the other, it may permit the use of certain clauses, provided they satisfy a 'reasonableness' test.

UCTA 1977 arguably interferes with the concept of freedom of contract (according to which parties should be allowed to agree their own contractual terms without external interference) but, as Lord Reid pointed out in the *Suisse Atlantique* case (see Chapter 32), freedom of contract is often a largely theoretical concept, especially for the individual consumer:

> Probably the most objectionable [kinds of exclusion clause] are found in the complex standard conditions which are now so common. In the ordinary way

the customer has no time to read them, and if he did read them then he probably would not understand them. And if he did understand and object to any of them, he would generally be told to take it or leave it. And if he then went to another supplier the result would be the same. Freedom to contract must surely imply some choice or room for bargaining.

General structure of the Act

When applying UCTA 1977, a court must consider:

(a)   whether the offending clause is covered by the Act at all; and
(b)   how the relevant provision of the Act deals with the clause, i.e., whether it disallows the clause completely, or merely subjects it to a reasonableness test.

The Act controls the use of exclusion clauses in three principal ways:

(a)   it restricts attempts to exclude liability for negligence;
(b)   it imposes controls on exclusion clauses which seek to exclude or restrict one party's liability for breach of contract; and
(c)   it imposes further controls over contract terms which purport to exclude or restrict liability for breach of terms implied by statutes such as the Sale of Goods Act 1979.

Clauses which purport to exclude or restrict liability for negligence

UCTA 1977 distinguishes between liability for negligence causing personal injury and liability for negligent damage to property. Section 2(1) of the Act *totally prohibits* the use of any contractual term *or* non-contractual notice which attempts either to exclude or limit liability for death or personal injury resulting from negligence. Any such term will be invalid. In contrast, s. 2(2) effectively permits a person to rely upon a contract term or non-contractual notice so as to exclude or restrict liability for negligent loss or damage to property, *provided that* the term or notice in question satisfies the requirement of reasonableness (as to which, see p. 392, below). Negligence is defined in s. 1(1) of the Act, and includes breach:

(a)   of any obligation arising from the express or implied terms of a contract to take reasonable care or exercise reasonable skill in the perform-ance of the contract;
(b)   of any common law duty to take reasonable care or exercise skill...; or
(c)   of the common duty of care imposed by the Occupiers' Liability Act 1957.

(See Chapters 36 and 41 for discussion of the tort of negligence and occupiers' liability.)

Note that, although the title to the Act refers only to 'contract terms', s. 2 in fact applies, not only to such terms, but also to notices which attempt to exclude non-contractual liability for negligence under the law of tort. For example, s. 2(1) would invalidate a notice at a fun fair which attempted to exclude tortious liability to bystanders for any personal injuries caused by the negligence of the operators. Even where the injured person was fully aware of the notice, this cannot of itself indicate that he voluntarily accepted the risk of injury (s. 2(3); and see p. 488, below).

Clauses which seek to exclude or restrict liability for breach of contract

In contrast to s. 2, s. 3 of the Act deals only with clauses which attempt to exclude or restrict liability for breach of contract. Furthermore, it deals with such clauses only in contracts where one party deals, either as a 'consumer', or on the other's 'written standard terms of business'. In many cases, written standard terms of business are imposed on consumers by suppliers, thus falling within both limbs of s. 3; but consumer contracts may fall within s. 3 even without there being any written standard terms, and s. 3 may also apply where written standard terms are imposed in contracts between companies or businessmen who are not consumers.

Section 3(2) provides that a party imposing such a term cannot rely upon it so as to exclude or restrict his own liability for breach of contract; nor may he claim to be entitled to render a substantially different performance from that which would reasonably be expected under the contract; nor indeed may he claim to be excused from rendering any performance at all, *except* in so far as that term satisfies the test of reasonableness.

To illustrate the effect of this provision: if a passenger enters into a contract with an airline on the latter's standard written terms, which purportedly permit the airline to fly him to a different destination from the one to which he has booked, this would involve a 'substantially different performance' from the one which he would reasonably expect. Such a term will therefore be valid only if, and in so far as it is reasonable. (It may indeed be reasonable to allow for the possibility of a diversion from a fog-bound or accident-blocked airport to a nearby working airport, but reasonableness is a question of fact in every case, and it is difficult to generalise about it.)

Excluding liability for breach of terms implied by statute

Section 6 of the Act deals with exclusion clauses which attempt to exclude the application of implied terms in contracts for the sale or hire-purchase of goods. Implied terms governing the sale of goods are contained in the Sale of Goods Act 1979 (SGA). Section 12 of the SGA 1979 provides that a seller of goods impliedly warrants that he has proper legal title to any goods he purports to sell. Section 13 implies a term that the goods will correspond with their description (if any) in the contract. Section 14 provides that any goods sold in the course of a business must be of satisfactory quality and must be fit for any known or stated purpose for which they are supplied. Finally, s. 15 provides that goods sold on the basis of samples shown to the purchaser must correspond with any such samples. (See Chapter 35 for further explanation of these terms.)

UCTA 1977 s. 6(1)(a) provides that a seller of goods can *never* exclude or restrict his liability for breach of terms implied by SGA 1979, s. 12. Even private sellers are thus prevented from excluding any liability that they might incur should the goods prove not to be theirs to sell.

Section 6(2)(a) and (3) of UCTA 1977 deal with attempts by sellers to exclude or restrict any liability under SGA 1979, ss. 13 to 15. Section 6(2)(a) totally invalidates any attempt by a seller to exclude the application of those provisions, but it applies only where the purchaser of the goods is acting as a consumer.

If the purchaser is *not* a consumer s. 6(3) applies. This permits the seller to exclude or restrict his liability for breach of terms implied by SGA 1979, ss. 13 to 15, provided that the exclusion or limitation clause concerned satisfies the reasonableness test.

Unreasonable indemnity clauses

Although UCTA 1977 is primarily concerned with exclusion clauses, it should be noted, in passing, that it also contains, in s. 4, a provision restricting the imposition on a consumer of an unfair or unreasonable obligation to indemnify the other party against any liability which the latter might incur to third parties. Suppose, for example, that A (a consumer) hires a JCB digger and driver from Plant Hire Ltd, on terms that A will indemnify Plant Hire Ltd if their driver should negligently injure a third party or cause damage to a third party's property whilst hired to A. Such a clause is not necessarily invalid, but it will be struck down if the court considers it to be unreasonable. A contract which is *not* a consumer contract is not subject to s. 4, however, and since such clauses are not exclusion clauses, they are not subject to s. 2. It will, in other words, be valid and enforceable (cf. *Thompson* v *T Lohan (Plant Hire) Ltd* [1987] 2 All ER 631).

Who is a consumer?

It is necessary in several of the above circumstances to understand what exactly is meant by the terms 'consumer' and 'acting in the course of a business'. Section 12 provides a definition:

A party to a contract 'deals as a consumer' in relation to another party if—

(a) he neither makes the contract in the course of a business, nor holds himself out as doing so; and

(b) the other party does make the contract in the course of a business; and

(c) in the case of a contract governed by the law of sale of goods or hire purchase ... the goods passing under or in pursuance of the contract are of a type ordinarily supplied for private use or consumption.

The first point to note is that, before a purchaser can be held to be dealing as a consumer, it must be shown that he did not make the contract in the course of a business or hold himself out as doing so. The question therefore arises as to what is meant by the phrase 'in the course of a business'? The Court of Appeal had to consider its meaning in *R&B Customs Brokers Co. Ltd* v *United Dominions Trust* [1988] 1 All ER 847. Dillon LJ stated:

... there are some transactions which are clearly integral parts of the business concerned, and these should be held to have been carried out in the course of those businesses; this would cover, apart from much else, the instance of a one-off adventure in the nature of trade where the transaction itself would constitute a trade or business. There are other transactions, however, such as the purchase of a car in the present case, which are at the highest only incidental to the carrying on of the relevant business; here a degree of regularity is required before it can be said that they are an integral part of the business carried on and so entered into in the course of that business.

It is therefore clear that there are two ways in which a transaction may be made in the course of a business:

(a) if the particular transaction can be said to be an integral part of the business itself; or

(b) if it is incidental to the business itself, but occurs with sufficient regularity to be classed as occurring in the course of that business.

A case which illustrates the problems associated with ascertaining whether a transaction was carried out in the course of a business is *Havering LBC* v *Stevenson* [1970] 3 All ER 609. This case is an authority on s. 1 of the Trade Descriptions Act 1968, rather than on UCTA 1977 itself, but the issue to be resolved was the same. The defendant operated a car-hire business. To keep his fleet modern, he always sold his cars once they were about two years old. The proceeds of the sales helped to finance the purchase of new cars, etc. A prosecution for applying a false trade description to goods was brought against him after he had sold a car the odometer on which showed a false mileage. This would be an offence under s. 1 of the Trade Descriptions Act 1968, but only if he had applied this false description 'in the course of a business'. Stevenson's actual line of business was the car-hire trade, but the sale and purchase of cars had become such an established part of his operation that it was therefore held that the sale in question was made in the course of business. Stevenson could thus be convicted of a criminal offence under the Act.

Havering LBC v *Stevenson* may be contrasted with *Davies* v *Sumner* [1984] 3 All ER 831. Davies was a self-employed courier and used his own car to transport films, videos and other material throughout Wales. After his first car had covered 100,000 miles, he traded it in to a garage in part exchange for a new one, but had apparently falsified the odometer beforehand so that it showed only 18,100 miles. On the face of it, this was a gross misdescription; but was it a false *trade* description? The sale of the car was only incidental to his business, and could be classed as being made in the 'course of a business' only if there was a sufficient regularity regarding such transactions. Davies had not, however, carried out any previous transactions of that kind, and he was thus deemed to be a consumer, rather than a businessman, for those purposes. As far as UCTA 1977 is concerned, the case indicates that persons who carry out a trade or business may still be 'consumers' for some purposes connected with their business (and thus entitled to the extra degree of protection which that Act provides for consumers), but this will depend on the particular circumstances of the transaction.

The second part of the definition in UCTA 1977, s. 12(1)(a) states that an individual will not be treated as a consumer if he holds himself out as acting in the course of a business (even if he is not really so acting at all). What might amount to such 'holding out' must to some extent be a question of fact, but an attempt to claim a 'trade discount' would presumably suffice.

Lastly, s. 12(3) stipulates that if the contract involves the sale or supply of goods then before the purchaser can be classified as dealing as a consumer, the goods must be of a type which are ordinarily supplied for private use or consumption. A solicitor buying a small personal computer for his home or office might thus be regarded as a consumer, but if he buys a computer network, he could not be dealing as a consumer , because computer networks (even small ones) are not ordinarily bought for private use.

REASONABLENESS

Central to many of the provisions of UCTA 1977 dealing with exclusion clauses is the requirement of reasonableness.

The time at which reasonableness is to be assessed

Section 11(1) of UCTA 1977 provides:

> In relation to a contract term, the requirement of reasonableness . . . is that the term shall have been a fair and reasonable one to be included having

regard to the circumstances which were, or ought reasonably to have been, known to or in the contemplation of the parties when the contract was made.

Section 11 thus indicates that the reasonableness of the clause is to be assessed on the basis of the circumstances which were known, or which should have been known, by the parties at the time of contracting and not on the circumstances at the time of the breach.

Guidelines as to what is reasonable

Schedule 2 of UCTA 1977 contains guidelines for determining what is meant by reasonableness. The schedule includes factors such as the inequality of bargaining power between the parties, the ability of parties to cover themselves by insurance, the availability of alternative forms of contract without such an exclusion clause, whether the party against whom the exclusion clause was being used had any knowledge of the existence of the clause, and so on. Such factors must all be taken into account and balanced against each other by the court when assessing the reasonableness of a given clause.

OTHER UNFAIR TERMS

The provisions we have looked at from UCTA 1977 have so far all been concerned with clauses which exclude or restrict liability, but the effects of the Act are not limited to clauses which expressly have such a purpose. Section 13(1) attempts to ensure that liability is not unfairly avoided by the insertion of more subtle terms, such as ones which impose unfair conditions on the other party's rights of enforcement. It states:

(1)   To the extent that this Part of this Act prevents the exclusion or restriction of any liability it also prevents—
(a)   making the liability or its enforcement subject to restrictive or onerous conditions;
(b)   excluding or restricting any right or remedy in respect of the liability, or subjecting a person to any prejudice in consequence of his pursuing any such right or remedy;
(c)   excluding or restricting rules of evidence or procedure;
and (to that extent) sections 2 and 5 to 7 also prevent excluding or restricting liability by reference to terms and notices which exclude or restrict the relevant obligation or duty.

Unfair Contract Terms Act 1977

The effect of UCTA 1977 is twofold, in that it allows certain types of exclusion clauses provided that they satisfy the reasonableness test, whereas others are rendered completely ineffective.

Clauses

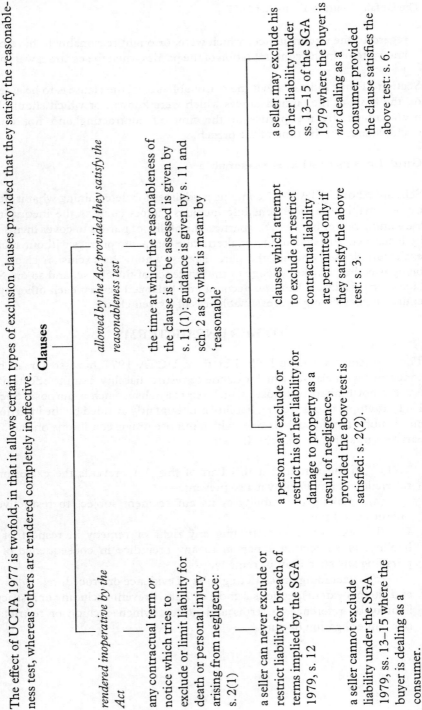

rendered inoperative by the Act

any contractual term *or* notice which tries to exclude or limit liability for death or personal injury arising from negligence: s. 2(1)

a seller can never exclude or restrict liability for breach of terms implied by the SGA 1979, s. 12

a seller cannot exclude liability under the SGA 1979, ss. 13–15 where the buyer is dealing as a consumer.

allowed by the Act provided they satisfy the reasonableness test

the time at which the reasonableness of the clause is to be assessed is given by s. 11(1): guidance is given by s. 11 and sch. 2 as to what is meant by 'reasonable'

a person may exclude or restrict his or her liability for damage to property as a result of negligence, provided the above test is satisfied: s. 2(2).

clauses which attempt to exclude or restrict contractual liability are permitted only if they satisfy the above test: s. 3.

a seller may exclude his or her liability under ss. 13–15 of the SGA 1979 where the buyer is *not* dealing as a consumer provided the clause satisfies the above test: s. 6.

THIRTY FOUR

Unfair Terms in Consumer Contracts

Background: the European Community Directive

In 1993, a European Community Directive was issued requiring the provision of a minimum level of consumer protection throughout all states in the Community. The impetus for this Directive was the Maastricht Treaty and the planned creation of a single internal market within the Community. The Directive lays down minimum standards to which member states must adhere, although it also allows them to provide more extensive protection through their national laws, should they so wish.

The Directive was implemented into United Kingdom law by the Unfair Terms in Consumer Contracts Regulations 1994 ('the Regulations'), which came into force on 1 July 1995. The provisions of the Regulations and UCTA 1977 must be read together. Between them, they provide a high level of protection to consumers against the imposition of unfair terms in contracts to which they are parties. The Regulations do not only apply to exclusion clauses, but to any unfair terms in a consumer contract. The following sections explain the Regulations in outline and examine their relationship with UCTA 1977.

The Unfair Terms in Consumer Contracts Regulations 1994

The basic scheme
The principal thrust of the Regulations can be found in reg. 3, which provides that a fairness test applies to certain terms within any contract between an individual consumer and a seller or supplier. The terms subject to this test are those which have not been individually negotiated and which neither define in

plain terms the subject matter of the contract nor deal in plain terms with the price or remuneration to be paid for goods or services supplied. In other words, the Regulations are primarily concerned with the fairness of imposed standard-form terms dealing with matters such as time-limits, remedies, complaint procedures and penalties for breach. Terms which are subject to, but fail to satisfy, this fairness will not be binding on a consumer (reg. 5); under reg. 8, the Director General of Fair Trading has been given powers to take action against sellers or suppliers who persist in using such terms in contracts with consumers.

Consumers

Regulation 2 defines a 'consumer' as a natural person who, in making a contract to which the Regulations apply, is acting for purposes which are outside his business. In this context, a business includes 'a trade or profession and the activities of any government department or local or public authority'. This differs from the definition of a consumer adopted under UCTA 1977. The Regulations limit the meaning of a 'consumer' to natural persons (individuals), whereas a company may in appropriate circumstances be classed as a consumer for the purposes of UCTA 1977.

Sellers or suppliers

Regulation 2 defines a 'seller or supplier' as one who sells goods or supplies services and who, in making a contract to which the Regulations apply, is acting for purposes relating to his business. A seller or supplier may be either a natural person or a corporation, but must be acting within the scope of a trade, business or profession.

'Not individually negotiated'

The Regulations will apply only to terms in contracts between consumers and sellers or suppliers which have not been individually negotiated. The phrase 'individually negotiated' is partially defined in reg. 3(3), which states:

A term shall always be regarded as not having been individually negotiated where it has been drafted in advance and the consumer has not been able to influence the substance of the term.

Unfair terms

Guidance as to what is meant by the term 'unfairness' is found in reg. 4(1):

In these regulations, subject to paragraphs (2) and (3) below, 'unfair term' means any term which contrary to the requirement of good faith causes a significant imbalance in the parties' rights and obligations under the contract to the detriment of the consumer.

As can be seen from the above definition, there are two essential requirements which have to be met before a term will fail the fairness test. The first is that the term creates a significant imbalance in the parties' rights and obligations to the detriment of the consumer. It must, in other words, significantly favour the supplier at the consumer's expense. The second requirement is that the term must be 'contrary to the requirement of good faith'. Schedule 2 to the Regulations provides some guidance as to what is meant by this phrase. It states:

In making an assessment of good faith, regard shall be had in particular to—
(a)   the strength of the bargaining position of the parties;
(b)   whether the consumer had an inducement to agree to the term;
(c)   whether the goods or services were sold or supplied to the special order of the consumer;
(d)   the extent to which the seller or supplier has dealt fairly and equitably with the consumer.

Many of the phrases used above should appear familiar, because they are similar to those used in Schedule 2 to UCTA 1977, in dealing with the concept of reasonableness (see Chapter 33).

List of terms which may be regarded as unfair
Schedule 3 to the Regulations provides a list of terms which may be classed as unfair. For example, terms which exclude or limit the liability of the supplier in the event of the death or personal injury of the consumer will be deemed to be unfair; any term requiring a consumer who fails to fulfil his obligation to pay a disproportionately high sum in compensation will also be deemed unfair. The list does not purport to provide anything more than general guidance as to the kind of term that might be deemed unfair.

Terms which are not subject to the fairness test
The fairness test does not apply to every type of term contained within a contract. Regulation 3(2) stipulates that 'core' terms will *not* be subject to the fairness test. So what is a core term? Regulation 3(2) states:

In so far as it is in plain intelligible language, no assessment shall be made of the fairness of any term which;
(a)   defines the main subject matter of the contract; or
(b)   concerns the adequacy of the price or remuneration as against the goods or services sold or supplied.

It can be seen from the above that the fairness test cannot be applied to any plainly worded term which defines the main subject-matter of the contract or which deals with the adequacy of the price. The Regulations are not concerned with whether the consumer has made a bad bargain or paid too high a price for the goods.

Regulation 3(2) nevertheless makes it clear that in order for any 'core' terms to be exempted from the fairness test, the words used must be in plain, intelligible language. If the words used are not in plain, intelligible language then a term may be classed as unfair, even though it is a core term.

Invoking the Regulations

The Regulations may be invoked by the consumer to challenge an unfair term in a contract between the consumer and the supplier or seller. (This is the form of remedy which aggrieved persons may take under UCTA 1977.) If the term is held by the courts to be unfair, the consumer will cease to be bound by that particular term. The contract itself can nevertheless remain in force, unless the unfair term is so significant that its cancellation undermines the entire contract.

The Director General of Fair Trading

An innovative aspect of the Regulations is the new enforcement role given by them to the Director General of Fair Trading. Regulation 8 provides that the Director General may consider any complaint made to him that a term 'drawn up for general use' is unfair. If he agrees with the complainant, then he may, if he thinks it appropriate, seek an injunction against 'any person appearing to him to be using or recommending the use of such a term in contracts concluded with consumers'. If an injunction is sought it may relate not only to the offending term, but also to any similar term.

The Director General does not have to implement injunction proceedings; he may, alternatively, seek an undertaking from the person concerned against the continued use of such terms. Furthermore, reg. 8 enables him to bring proceedings not only against the individual using the term, but also against any body 'recommending the use of such terms'.

These new enforcement powers are a significant amendment to the law of consumer protection, since they are capable of facilitating much broader attacks on unfair practices than any individual consumer could hope to launch.

Unfair Terms in Consumer Contracts Regulation 1994

These 1994 Regulations exist in addition to the protection offered by UCTA 1977.

The Regulations apply a fairness test to terms in contracts between consumers and sellers which have 'not been individually negotiated'.

The Regulations are not simply limited to exclusion clauses. Any 'standard form' may be subject to them.

If a term is deemed unfair, the consumer will not be bound by it.

Schedule 3 of the Regulations lists terms which may be regarded as unfair. This is not an exhaustive list.

The fairness test does not apply to every term contained within a contract. For example 'core' terms will not be subject to the fairness test.

The Director General of Fair Trading has been given a new enforcement role under the Regulations.

THIRTY FIVE

The Sale and Supply of Goods and Services

We saw in Chapter 22 that terms may be implied into contracts in any one of a variety of ways. This chapter explains how statute implies specific terms into contracts for the sale or supply of goods, or for the supply of services.

CONTRACTS FOR THE SALE OF GOODS

The law relating to the sale of goods derives from numerous sources and deals with many aspects of such contracts, but for present purposes we are concerned only with the terms relating to title (i.e. ownership), quality, description and fitness for purpose.

The original common law rule on the sale of goods was encapsulated in the phrase *caveat emptor* ('let the buyer beware'). In other words, buyers had to look after themselves. If a buyer bought defective goods (other than on the basis of a misrepresentation by the seller), that was the buyer's problem. In 1893, however, the first Sale of Goods Act was passed, and this substantially mitigated the harshness of the common law rule by imposing certain minimum standards in respect of quality and fitness of goods sold. This Act was amended over the years and was eventually replaced by the Sale of Goods Act (SGA) 1979.

The 1979 Act revised the old implied terms relating to quality, description and fitness for purpose. It stated that the goods had to fit their description, be of merchantable (i.e. satisfactory) quality and be fit for their purpose. This Act, however, provided for the implication of such terms only in relation to contracts for the sale of goods. In 1982, the Supply of Goods and Services Act was passed. This implies broadly similar terms as to quality and fitness in relation to the supply of goods and services which will be looked at in the second part of this chapter. More recently, as we shall see, the implied terms found in the 1979 Act have been amended by the Sale and Supply of Goods Act 1994. The 1979 Act, as amended, remains the principal legislation.

What is a contract for the sale of goods?

Section 21(1) of the SGA 1979 provides a basic definition of what constitutes a sale. It states that: 'A contract of sale of goods is a contract by which the seller transfers or agrees to transfer the property in goods to the buyer for a money consideration, called the price.'

From this definition it can be seen that a sale of goods contract has four essential elements:

(a)   there must be a contract;

(b)   goods must form the subject-matter of the contract (not land, company shares, investments or securities);

(c)   there must be a transfer of, or at least an agreement to transfer the property or legal ownership in the goods from the seller to the buyer; and

(d)   the buyer must provide money consideration for the goods.

There will rarely be any issue as to what is, or is not, properly to be called 'goods', but in *St Albans District Council v ICL* [1996] 4 All ER 481 the Court of Appeal had to consider the status of a computer programme which ICL had designed for the plaintiff authority to use in calculating, administering and collecting its council tax. The programme worked very poorly, and produced errors which cost the council thousands of pounds in lost revenue; but it had been downloaded by ICL onto the council's computers, rather than supplied to them on disk, and the Court of Appeal accordingly held that the programme could not be described as 'goods'. The council therefore had to seek a remedy at common law, rather than under the Sale of Goods Act 1979. (It succeeded by proving that there was an *express* term in the contract, to the effect that the programme would do the job required of it.) The case was an unusual one. If a computer software supplier markets disks or CD-roms containing faulty programmes, buyers of those disks would indeed be able to rely upon the Sale of Goods Act 1979.

Legal title must be passed to the buyer

Section 12(1) of the Act implies a term as to title into every contract for the sale of goods, namely that the seller has the right to sell the goods and will be able to pass on a good legal title to the buyer. If this term is breached, there will have been a total failure of consideration and the buyer will be able to recover the price of the goods, no matter how long he has been in possession of them (*Rowland v Divall* [1923] 1 All ER 270).

Goods must comply with their description

Section 13 of the SGA 1979 states:

(1)   Where there is a contract for the sale of goods by description, there is an implied term that the goods correspond with the description.

(2)   If the sale is by sample, as well as by description, it is not sufficient that the bulk of the goods correspond with the sample if the goods do not also correspond with the description.

(3)   A sale of goods is not prevented from being a sale by description by reason only that, being exposed for sale or hire, they are selected by the buyer.

In *Varley* v *Whipp* [1900] 1 QB 513, it was held that the concept of a sale by description 'must apply to cases where the purchaser has not seen the goods but is relying upon the description alone'. However, s. 13(3) now makes it clear that a sale by description can also include an ordinary sale in a shop, as in a supermarket, where the buyer selects the goods. In *Grant* v *Australian Knitting Mills Ltd* [1936] AC 85, Lord Wright said:

It may also be pointed out that there is a sale by description, even though the buyer is buying something displayed before him on the counter: a thing is sold by description though it is specific, so long as it is sold not merely as a specific thing, but as a thing corresponding to a description, e.g., woollen undergarments, a hot water bottle, a secondhand reaping machine, to select a few obvious examples.

Section 13 provides that goods must correspond with their description, but the case law suggests that not all terms describing the goods form part of the description for the purposes of s. 13. In *Ashington Piggeries* v *Christopher Hill* [1972] AC 441, for example, the House of Lords held that only words which identify the subject-matter of the contract should be treated as descriptive words for the purposes of s. 13. Lord Diplock said: 'The description by which goods are sold is . . . confined to those words in the contract which are intended by the parties to identify the kind of goods which were to be supplied.'

Whether the goods correspond with their description is a question of fact, but the courts take a very strict approach towards compliance with the descriptive term. An example of this may be seen in *Arcos* v *Ronnasen* [1933] AC 470, where the contract involved the sale of wooden staves half an inch thick to the buyers. A number of the staves, however, were not half an inch thick but varied between half an inch and nine-sixteenths of an inch thick. The House of Lords held that this constituted a breach of s. 13 and the buyers were entitled to reject the staves. This, however, meant that buyers could reject goods even for minor or trivial breaches. Lord Atkin said: 'If the . . . contract specifies conditions of weight, measurement and the like, those conditions must be complied with. A ton does not mean "about a ton", or a yard "about a yard".' Microscopic deviations from the description may be ignored, however and s. 15A of the Act now limits the circumstances in which goods may be rejected for minor or trivial blemishes. Note that s. 13 is not limited to sales conducted in 'the course of business' and can therefore apply to private sales as well.

Goods must be of satisfactory quality

Section 14 of the SGA 1979 (as substituted by the 1994 Act) provides:

(2)   Where the seller sells goods in the course of a business, there is an implied term that the goods supplied under the contract are of satisfactory quality.

(2A)   For the purposes of the Act, goods are of satisfactory quality if they meet the standard that a reasonable person would regard as satisfactory, taking account of any description of the goods, the price (if relevant) and all other relevant circumstances.

(2B)   For the purposes of this Act, the quality of goods includes their state and condition and the following (among other things) are in appropriate cases aspects of the quality of goods—

(a)   fitness for all the purposes for which goods of the kind in question are commonly supplied,

(b)   appearance and finish,

(c)   freedom from minor defects,

(d)   safety, and

(e)   durability.

(2C)   The term implied by subsection (2) does not extend to any matter making the quality of goods unsatisfactory—

(a)   which is specifically drawn to the buyer's attention before the contract is made,

(b)   where the buyer examines the goods before the contract is made, which that examination ought to reveal, or

(c)   in the case of a contract for the sale by sample, which would have been apparent on a reasonable examination of a sample.

Section 14 therefore implies into contracts for the sale of goods the term that goods sold must be of satisfactory quality. This replaces the old test of 'merchantable quality' formerly used in the 1979 Act. It seems unlikely, however, that anything of substance will turn on this new form of words. Cases decided on 'merchantability' under the old Act will continue to be relied upon as guides to the interpretation of the term 'satisfactory' in the new Act.

When does the obligation arise to provide goods of satisfactory quality?
When looking at s. 13, above, we saw that private and business sellers are both
under an obligation to provide goods which comply with their description. In
contrast, the implied term as to satisfactory quality applies only to goods sold
by a seller in the course of a business. Goods sold by a private seller do not fall
within s. 14.

Extent of the seller's obligation under s. 14(2)
The old case law established that the seller's obligations of fitness and
quality covered not only the goods actually bought by the buyer, but also
any packaging in which the goods were sold. In *Geddling* v *Marsh* [1920]
1 KB 668, for example, it was held that a seller of bottled mineral water
was responsible not only for quality of the water, but also for the fitness of
the bottles in which the water was stored. Nothing in the new provision appears
to change this rule.

What is meant by 'satisfactory'?
Section 14(2) of the SGA 1979 makes it clear that the overriding test for
assessing the fitness and quality of goods is that of satisfactory quality
(s. 14(2A)). Section 14(2B) lists a number of specific factors which may be
taken into account in applying the criterion of satisfactory quality. If, for
example, the product suffers from non-functional defects, such as scratches or
blemishes, then whether the goods will be deemed unsatisfactory in those
circumstances will depend upon whether a reasonable person would regard
such defects as rendering the article unsatisfactory.

It can also be seen from s. 14(2B) that the factors which the court will
consider in determining whether the goods are of satisfactory quality include
safety, durability and fitness for all the purposes for which goods of that type
are commonly supplied. Goods can often be used for a variety of purposes,
some of which are common purposes while others are not. Section 14(2B)
suggests that goods must be good enough to be used for any of those purposes
for which goods of that type are commonly bought. If goods are not suitable for
all such purposes, the seller should draw the buyer's attention to this in
accordance with s. 14(2C).

When terms relating to satisfactory quality may not be implied
Section 14(2C) of the 1979 Act provides that the implied term as to quality
does not extend to defects specifically drawn to the buyer's attention before the
contract is made; neither does it apply where the buyer examines the goods
before the contract is made, unless the defect is not one which such an
examination could be expected to reveal.

Goods must be fit for their purpose

Section 14(3) of the SGA 1979 states:

> Where the seller sells goods in the course of a business and the buyer, expressly or by implication, makes known—
>
> (a) to the seller [etc.] any particular purpose for which the goods are being bought, there is an implied condition that the goods supplied under the contract are reasonably fit for that purpose, whether or not that is a purpose for which goods of that type are commonly supplied, except where the circumstances show that the buyer does not rely, or that it is unreasonable for him to rely, on the skill or judgment of the seller . . .'.

This term will be implied only where the seller is acting in the course of a business, i.e., it does not extend to impose an obligation on the private seller. This section states that effectively the goods supplied must be reasonably fit for the purpose for which the buyer stipulates (either expressly or impliedly) the goods are being bought. For example, 'Bondo' glue may be widely used for sticking paper or card, but Paul may specifically ask a shopkeeper for a glue to mend broken china. If the shopkeeper then sells him 'Bondo' and it does not work for that purpose, Paul may have a good claim under s. 14(3), even though such glue is not usually bought for this purpose. The seller of goods ought to know about the product he is selling.

Terms implied in sales by sample

A sale by sample is defined in s. 15(1) of the SGA 1979: 'A contract of sale is a contract for sale by sample where there is an express or implied term to that effect in the contract.' Thus a sale by sample is not made simply where a sample is provided for the purchaser's inspection, but only where the parties intend that it should be such. If it is a sale by sample, then there are implied terms:

(a) that the bulk will correspond with the sample in quality;

(b) that the buyer will have a reasonable opportunity of comparing the bulk with the sample; and

(c) that the goods will be free from any defect which would make their quality unsatisfactory and which would not be apparent upon a reasonable examination of the sample.

Remedies for breach of ss. 13, 14 and 15

The SGA 1979 states that these implied terms are all conditions, and if they are breached the buyer ordinarily has the right to terminate the contract and/or recover damages. There has always been a fear that classifying these terms as conditions might lead buyers to repudiate contracts for minor breaches. Consequently, the 1994 Act inserts a new s. 15A into the 1979 Act. This states that a breach of the conditions in ss. 13 to 15 may in certain circumstances be treated as a mere breach of warranty, giving rise only to a remedy in damages. This applies only where the buyer does not deal as a consumer and where the breach is so small that it would be unreasonable to terminate the contract.

Exclusion of liability arising under ss. 13 to 15

UCTA 1977 prohibits a seller from excluding his liability for terms implied under ss. 13 to 15 of the SGA 1979 where the purchaser is dealing as a consumer. If the purchaser is not dealing as a consumer, the seller may exclude his liability provided the clause satisfies the reasonableness test. (See Chapter 33 for further information on this.)

CONTRACTS FOR THE SUPPLY OF GOODS AND SERVICES

The sale of goods legislation considered above deals only with goods which are sold for money consideration and thus does not cover dealings with goods other than by way of sale; neither does it deal with the provision of services. The Supply of Goods and Services Act 1982 deals specifically with these areas, and the rest of this chapter will concentrate upon the provisions of that Act.

Scope of the Supply of Goods and Services Act 1982

The 1982 Act deals with three areas of law, namely:

(a)   contracts for the transfer of property, other than by sale;
(b)   contracts for the hire of goods, such as the hire of a wedding suit or a car; and
(c)   contracts for the supply of services.

The supply of goods

Contracts for the transfer of property
The 1982 Act deals with contracts for the transfer of property in goods which are *not* contracts for the sale of goods or contracts of hire-purchase. Sections 2 to 5 imply terms to protect the transferee under such contracts in relation to matters of title, description, satisfactory quality, fitness for purpose and correspondence with any sample provided. These terms are similar to those implied under ss. 12 to 15 of the SGA 1979.

Such terms will be implied into contracts such as those of barter or exchange. Common barter contracts include promotions, in which wrappers or vouchers or tokens from cereal packets are exchanged for goods such as glassware or compact discs. The 1982 Act deals with the quality of the goods supplied. It would also apply to collateral contracts relating to the supply of goods (an example of which would include contracts where, upon the purchase of one item, the purchaser will be entitled to another 'free of charge'). Lastly, it may apply to contracts where, although the contract involves the supply of goods, the main basis of the contract is the provision of services. This would include contracts relating to the fitting of new parts to a car during a routine service, but if the complaint relates only to negligent workmanship (i.e. services), this must be dealt with under s. 13 of the 1982 Act. Sections 3 to 5 deal with complaints arising as a result of the newly supplied part or component proving unsatisfactory.

As far as such implied terms are concerned, s. 2 (which relates to title to goods) cannot, according to the UCTA 1977, be excluded by any term of any contract. Sections 3 to 5 of the 1982 Act cannot be excluded as against a person dealing as a consumer. If the person is not classified as a consumer, however, then liability may be excluded, provided that the clause satisfies the reasonableness test laid down in UCTA 1977 (as to which see Chapter 33).

Contracts for the hire of goods

Sections 7 to 10 of the 1982 Act imply terms relating to quality into contracts for the hire of goods. Section 6 of the Act defines a contract for the hire of goods as one under which 'one person bails or agrees to bail goods to another by way of hire'. This covers contracts under which the hirer obtains possession of the goods, but does not acquire legal title in them. For example, hiring a television set would be included under the 1982 Act, but contracts for hire-purchase (a credit arrangement under which the hirer acquires title to the goods at the end of the hire period) would not be.

The terms implied into hire contracts by the 1982 Act include terms relating to description, satisfactory quality, fitness for purpose and correspondence with any sample, together with an implied condition on the part of the bailor that he has a right to possession of the goods by way of hire for the duration of the bailment.

UCTA 1977 applies to contracts of hire, and the implied terms relating to description, quality, fitness for purpose and correspondence with any sample cannot be excluded if the person is dealing as a consumer. In other cases, they can be excluded subject to satisfaction of the reasonableness test. (Note the implied term relating to title can never be excluded.)

Contracts for the supply of services

The 1982 Act implies three terms into contracts for the supply of services (which include such diverse things as the servicing of cars, the provision of expert advice, the repair of broken dentures or the laying of a carpet).

Reasonable care and skill
Section 13 of the 1982 Act provides that:

> In a contract for the supply of a service where the supplier is acting in the
> course of a business, there is an implied term that the supplier will carry out
> the service with reasonable care and skill.

Whether reasonable care and skill have been used will depend on all the facts
and circumstances of the case. The supplier is expected at least to be
competent, and it is always open to the parties expressly to lay down stricter
terms in this area, but the Act does not make the supplier of services strictly
liable for any failure of inadequacy. In that respect, the buyer of defective goods
is in a much stronger position.

Time for performance
Section 14 provides:

> (1)   Where, under a contract for the supply of a service by a supplier
> acting in the course of a business, the time for the service to be carried out is
> not fixed by the contract, left to be fixed in a manner agreed between the
> parties or determined by the course of dealing between the parties, there is
> an implied term that the supplier will carry out the service within a
> reasonable time.
> (2)   What is a reasonable time is a question of fact.

Consideration for the service
Section 15 deals with situations where the parties have not fixed a price for the
service:

> (1)   Where, under a contract for the supply of a service, the consideration
> for the service is not determined by the contract, left to be determined in a
> manner agreed by the contract, or determined by the course of dealing
> between the parties, there is an implied term that the party contracting with
> the supplier will pay a reasonable charge.
> (2)   What is a reasonable charge is a question of fact.

Whether the parties have indeed agreed upon a price is also a question of fact.
If A asks B Ltd to service his car, and B Ltd display a price list on their premises,
it will be very difficult for A to challenge any bill presented to him, if it
corresponds with the price list displayed. The natural inference for any court to
draw must be that A has impliedly agreed to B Ltd's standard charges, even if
he has not bothered to check them for himself.

Exclusion of liability

Once again, these terms cannot easily be excluded. Any clause purporting to exclude them will be subject to a test of reasonableness if the person to whom the service was supplied is a consumer, or if the term is imposed on a standard-form contract (UCTA 1977, s. 3). A clause purporting to exclude liability for negligence leading to death or personal injury under s. 13 would be invalidated by UCTA 1977, s. 2.

PART FIVE

Introduction to the Law of Tort

The law of tort can broadly be defined as a system designed to provide compensation for individuals who have suffered a legal wrong. This definition, however, is not sufficiently specific because a breach of contract is also a legal wrong, as is a crime. The law of tort thus deals only with certain kinds of legal wrong, but it protects a variety of interests and this makes definition difficult. For example, it protects a person's reputation through the tort of defamation (libel or slander); and it protects a person's use and enjoyment of land by means of a variety of actions, such as trespass to land and nuisance. This has led some commentators to define the law of tort as dealing with any *civil* wrong not based upon a breach of contract or breach of trust.

The law of tort came to prominence in the nineteenth and twentieth centuries, with the onset of the Industrial Revolution in the former and the increased use of roads as a means of transport in the latter. The dominant principle which emerged in the nineteenth century was that nobody should ordinarily be liable for a tort without proof of fault. This is not to say that no form of strict liability existed under the law of tort at that time. Strict liability was recognised under the law of nuisance (below), but its role was a relatively limited one. As a general rule, liability in tort had to be based either on negligence, or on deliberate wrongdoing.

The burden of proving fault ordinarily rests upon the plaintiff, and this can sometimes be a difficult burden to discharge. Ordinarily this is surely fair enough: a person who is held liable for a tort (a tortfeasor) which has caused serious damage or injury may have to pay out hundreds of thousands of pounds in compensation; such a burden should not be imposed lightly without clear evidence of fault on the tortfeasor's part. Nevertheless, problems of proof are particularly apparent in the field of product liability. Where, for example, injuries or deformities are caused by prescribed drugs or medicines (as happened with the drug Thalidomide), negligence on the part of the manufacturers may be unduly hard to prove, if only because the vital evidence may be difficult to obtain. The law governing product liability has now been modified by the Consumer Protection Act 1987, which imposes strict liability upon producers (and certain others) for defective products which cause injury to others (see Chapter 38); but does the current (generally fault-based) system in the law of tort provide a good civil liability compensation procedure as regards accidents? What should be the aims of such a procedure?

Aims of tort law

The aims of a good civil compensation procedure should arguably be:

    (a)   to attempt to reduce the overall number of accidents and injuries;
    (b)   to provide compensation so as to minimise any disruption which injuries may have upon the victim's lifestyle and family; and
    (c)   to ensure the speedy and effective distribution of compensation.

The problem with the present tort system is that the emphasis upon the fault principle has 'led lawyers to concentrate upon legal rules rather than on these aims'. Research has shown low success rates for victims seeking compensation under the tort system. The reasons for this are the expense involved in pursuing such claims and the considerable hurdles to be faced in establishing the requisite level of fault — all for the possibility, rather than certainty, of an indeterminate amount of compensation at the end of the proceedings. A Royal Commission Report in 1978 (the Pearson Report) stated that only 6 per cent of victims successfully gain compensation under the tort system. This is not because most claims fail — on the contrary, around 90 per cent of personal injury claims that are pursued will succeed, and one must assume that a proportion of those that fail do not deserve to succeed — the real explanation for the small number of victims who recover is that most potential claims are not pursued in the first place. Nearly 20 years on, the figure of 6 per cent is not likely to have changed much. Even today, it is doubtful whether the system could cope if every valid claim was pursued through tort litigation.

    Fortunately, however, not all victims have to enter the civil compensation arena, because for many there are other avenues which may be explored in order to gain some recompense. Notable amongst these are insurance benefits or benefits from pension funds and schemes which pay compensation to victims, such as the Criminal Injuries Compensation Board and the Vaccine Damage Compensation Scheme. The most significant of these options is the social security system, which may provide income support, sickness benefit, etc. The social security system emphasises collective social responsibility for the victims of society's activities. This is in contrast to the tort system which pitches individual against individual. Atiyah, in *Accidents, Compensation and the Law*, suggested that the social security system should be remodelled so as to provide compensation for all injuries, disabilities and illnesses caused through work. In today's economic climate, however, such an idea would not be financially acceptable.

The New Zealand example

New Zealand has discarded the use of the tort system as a means of obtaining compensation for death or personal injury and has replaced it with a no-fault accident compensation system. The fund is financed by a tax on employers; a motor vehicle tax funds road accidents and state funds finance all other accident victims. Claims for compensation are made to the fund, which can pay better damages than the social security system. Many criticise the scheme, however, because they believe that the cost of accidents should be borne by those who cause them (or by their insurers) and not by the state.

THIRTY SIX
Negligence

In this section, the word 'negligence' refers specifically to the tort of negligence. The tort of negligence deals with persons whose careless or incompetent acts or omissions cause harm or damage to others, but not all forms of careless behaviour which lead to damage will be actionable. In order to bring a successful action in the tort of negligence, a plaintiff must establish:

(a) that the defendant owed him a duty of care. It must have been 'reasonably foreseeable' that the plaintiff could be harmed unless the defendant took care to prevent this, but this duty of care is not necessarily owed in *every* case where such harm is foreseeable;

(b) that the defendant breached that duty of care. It must be established that the defendant fell below the standard of care or competence which ought to have been exhibited in those circumstances;

(c) that the defendant's actions caused the plaintiff's harm and that the harm caused was not too 'remote' a consequence of those actions.

If the plaintiff succeeds in establishing these points, then the defendant may be liable to pay him damages under the tort of negligence.

DUTY OF CARE

A person can only be liable in negligence if he is in breach of a duty of care to the plaintiff. Establishing whether or when such a duty of care arises remains one of the most difficult problems in the law of tort, and remains so, despite (or perhaps because of) numerous judicial attempts to resolve it. The courts have flirted with, but ultimately rejected, the notion that there may be a single or universal test which can be used to determine the existence of such a duty in all cases. They now recognise that issues of law, fact and policy make it impossible for an almost infinitely wide range of different cases to be governed by any single, generalised, rule. As Lord Roskill stated in *Caparo Industries plc* v *Dickman* [1990] 1 All ER 568:

> It has now to be accepted that there is no simple formula or touchstone to which recourse can be had in order to provide in every case a ready answer to the questions whether, given certain facts, the law will or will not impose liability for negligence or, in cases where such liability can be shown to exist, determine the extent of liability. Phrases such as 'foreseeability', 'proximity', 'neighbourhood', 'just and reasonable', 'fairness', 'voluntary acceptance of risk', or 'voluntary assumption of responsibility' will be found used from time to time in the different cases. But ... such phrases are not precise definitions. At best they are but labels or phrases descriptive of the very different factual situations which can exist in particular cases and which must be carefully examined in each case before it can be pragmatically determined whether a duty of care exists and, if so, what is the scope and extent of that duty.

The search for a general principle

The law of negligence originally developed on what might be called a piecemeal basis. In certain situations, it became established that a duty of care was owed. Thus, it was established that persons using or driving vehicles on the highway owed a duty of care to other road users. By the end of the nineteenth century, the courts had recognised a number of particular categories of cases in which such a duty of care could be said to exist. These were gradually added to, on a case by case basis, but there was no general test by which the courts could determine whether a duty of care was owed, and the tort of negligence consequently lacked any identifiable structure. Various attempts were made to formulate a general principle, but none were significant until Lord Atkin formulated his famous 'neighbour test' in the landmark case of *Donoghue* v *Stevenson* [1932] AC 562.

Donoghue v *Stevenson*

This leading case on the law of negligence originated in Scotland. The plaintiff (or in Scots law, the 'pursuer'), Mrs Donoghue, went with a friend to a café in Paisley, where her friend bought her a bottle of Stevenson's ginger beer. The bottle was made of opaque glass which made examination of the contents impossible. The café owner poured some of this ginger beer over a portion of ice cream and the plaintiff consumed it, but as a second glass was poured out for her, the decomposed remains of a snail floated to the top. As a result of this experience, she claimed to have suffered shock and gastroenteritis. The question was whether she could recover damages for this harm.

One cause of action might seem to have been an action in contract against the café owner, but this was impossible in her case, because the ginger beer had been purchased by the plaintiff's friend, who had suffered no harm at all. There was therefore no privity of contract. It was not even clear that the plaintiff had any possible cause of action in tort. As the law stood at that time, the prevailing view was that liability for negligence of that kind could only arise where there had been some contract or other special relationship between the parties. The statutory imposition of liability on the producers of dangerous products (as to which, see Chapter 38) was still another 55 years away. Nevertheless, Mrs Donoghue brought an action in negligence against Stevenson, the brewer and bottler of the ginger beer.

Because of the novel nature of the claim, a preliminary legal ruling was sought as to whether such an action could be sustained at all, and this found its way, via the Scottish Court of Session, to the House of Lords. The question to be determined was whether, in the absence of contractual relationships, a manufacturer or producer could ever be under a legal duty of care to the ultimate consumer of his product. It was held that he could be. This 'narrow' aspect of the case is examined in Chapter 38; but *Donoghue* v *Stevenson* was much more than just a case on product liability because, in his leading speech, Lord Atkin attempted to lay down a more general principle, defining the essence of the duty of care in tort as a duty not to injure one's 'neighbour'. He said:

> You must take reasonable care to avoid acts or omissions which you can reasonably foresee would be likely to injure your neighbour. Who, then, in law is my neighbour? The answer seems to be — persons who are so closely and directly affected by my act that I ought reasonably to have them in contemplation as being so affected when I am directing my mind to the acts or omissions which are called in question.

According to this 'neighbour' test, a duty of care may be owed where the loss or injury to the plaintiff is reasonably foreseeable by the defendant. It should be noted, however, that this was not a test propounded by the House of Lords as a whole, and does not form part of the *ratio decidendi* of that case

The rise and fall of the 'neighbour' principle

The significance of Lord Atkin's 'neighbour test' in *Donoghue* v *Stevenson* was that it offered a general unifying principle to govern various situations in which liability for negligent conduct might be imposed. It also made it easier to argue that liability should be imposed for negligently inflicted damage in a whole range of new situations, not previously covered by the case law. Later cases appeared to take advantage of that principle, in order to extend the scope of the duty of care. By 1970 the position had been reached where Lord Reid in *Home Office* v *Dorset Yacht* [1970] 2 All ER 294 could say of Lord Atkin's neighbour test:

[It] . . . is not to be treated as if it were a statutory definition. It will require qualification in new circumstances. But I think the time has come when we can say and should say that it ought to apply unless there is some justification or valid explanation for its exclusion.

It was held in that case that the Home Office were liable for damage caused by borstal trainees (young offenders) who had escaped from a camp on an island off Poole harbour owing to the negligence of the staff in charge of them, and had attempted to make good their escape by seizing a yacht. There was no exact precedent for the imposition of such liability, but the 'neighbour' principle was held to be applicable. Lord Reid's sentiments were later adopted by Lord Wilberforce in *Anns* v *Merton London Borough Council* [1977] 2 All ER 492. He stated that the question of duty of care should be approached in two stages:

First, one has to ask whether, as between the alleged wrongdoer and the person who suffered the damage there is a sufficient relationship of proximity or neighbourhood such that, in the reasonable contemplation of the former, carelessness on his part may be likely to cause damage to the latter — in which case a prima facie duty of care arises. Secondly, if the first question is answered affirmatively, it is necessary to consider whether there are any considerations which ought to negative or reduce or limit the scope of the duty or the class of person to whom it is owed or the damages to which a breach of it may give rise.

Lord Wilberforce's approach in *Anns* appeared to suggest that the foreseeability test alone would be applied to determine whether a duty of care existed between the parties, unless there were any exceptional policy considerations that might impose some limitation on that duty. This two-stage test came close to establishing a principle of general applicability. Later cases, however, have witnessed a significant retreat from the *Anns* test. The Privy Council and House of Lords have each rejected it as being far too general in its scope. In *Peabody Donation Fund* v *Sir Lindsay Parkinson & Co. Ltd* [1984] 3 All ER 529, Lord Keith warned that the 'temptation to treat it as a definitive statement of the scope of the duty of care should be resisted'.

In its place, the courts have developed a more restrictive three-part test, which was applied by the House of Lords in *Caparo Industries plc* v *Dickman* [1990] 1 All ER 568, the facts of which are considered in Chapter 37. This test involves a consideration of the following conditions when considering whether a duty of care exists:

(a)   the damage must be foreseeable;

(b)   there must be a sufficiently proximate relationship between the plaintiff and the defendant; and

(c)   the court must be satisfied that it would be just and reasonable to impose a duty of care.

It should be noted, however, that the concepts of foreseeability, proximity, justice and reasonableness, are not really capable of any precise definition and thus are of little practical use as tests. They may even be categorised as merely 'facets of the same thing' (*Marc Rich & Co.* v *Bishop Rock Marine Co. Ltd* [1995] 3 All ER 307).

It therefore appears that the future development of the law of negligence will take place on a piecemeal basis, by analogy with cases in established categories. Lord Keith in *Murphy* v *Brentwood District Council* [1990] 2 All ER 908, cited and approved the following passage from the judgment of Brennan J in the Australian case of *Sutherland Shire Council* v *Heyman* (1985) 60 ALR 1:

It is preferable, in my view, that the law should develop novel categories incrementally and by analogy with established categories, rather than by a massive extension of a prima facie duty of care restrained only by identifiable considerations which ought to negative, or to reduce, or limit the scope of the duty or the class of person to whom it is owed.

In *Caparo Industries plc* v *Dickman* Lord Bridge stated:

I think the law has now moved in the direction of attaching greater significance to the more traditional categorisation of distinct and recognisable situations as guides to the existence, scope and the limits of the varied duties of care which the law imposes.

A number of more recent cases consider the question of when it may be 'just and reasonable' to impose a duty of care on a defendant for perfectly foreseeable damage. Policy issues figure very strongly here. Can it be just and reasonable to impose such a duty on a person or public body providing an emergency service, such as the coastguard or fire brigade? As a general rule, the answer here is, 'no'. If, for example, the fire brigade are slow in responding to a call, or fail to provide sufficient water to tackle a major blaze, it is foreseeable that damage may be suffered by the owner of the property affected, and that lives may be endangered, but there are good policy reasons for not imposing liability in such cases (*Capital & Counties plc* v *Hampshire County Council* [1997] 2 All ER 865). It may, however, be proper to impose on the emergency services a duty not to act in such a way as to *create* a new danger, or so as to cause damage that would not otherwise have occurred at all. In the *Capital & Counties* case, the Court of Appeal held that a local authority was accordingly liable for the act of a senior officer in its fire service who had, for some reason, switched off the plaintiff's sprinkler system, causing a fire to spread catastrophically out of control, totally destroying the plaintiff's business premises.

Another recent case in which public policy considerations loomed large was *X and others* v *Bedfordshire County Council* [1995] 3 All ER 353, in which it was held that it would be prejudicial to the proper operations of a social services authority to impose a duty of care on them in respect of their functions in protecting potentially 'at risk' children.

Such cases are not confined to those in which attempts are made to impose liability on public authorities. Much controversy surrounded a negligence action brought against a rugby referee in respect of his failure to prevent a schoolboy suffering serious injuries when a scrum collapsed (*Smolden* v *Whitworth, The Times*, 23 April 1996). One can see the force of the argument that an unpaid referee should not have to face (or insure against) the risk of liability in such a context. Nevertheless, it was held that, given the youth of the players, the referee did indeed owe them a duty of care. Had it been an adult match, the ruling would apparently have been different.

In Chapter 37 we will look more closely at two particular areas in which the concept of determining whether a duty of care exists has been especially problematical; namely cases involving injury caused by nervous shock and cases (such as *Caparo Industries* v *Dickman*) which involve claims for purely economic loss, rather than physical damage. Before getting too deeply into those issues, however, it is desirable that the student should consider the general principles governing breaches of the duty of care.

BREACH OF THE DUTY OF CARE

Once the plaintiff has established that the defendant owed him a duty of care, he must then go on to show that the defendant has breached that duty of care. In other words, the plaintiff must prove that the defendant was negligent.

There are two things which need to be considered in this context. First, a decision has to be made as to what standard of care ought to have been exercised, or in other words how strict a standard should be imposed. Secondly, it must be determined whether the defendant's behaviour fell below that standard. The former is a question of law and the latter is a question of fact.

The standard of care

The standard of care required is that which an ordinary reasonable man would exercise if placed in the circumstances of the defendant. This was made clear in *Blyth* v *Birmingham Waterworks Company* (1856) 11 Exch 781, where Alderson B said:

Negligence is the omission to do something which a reasonable man, guided upon those considerations which ordinarily regulate the conduct of human affairs, would do, or doing something which a prudent and reasonable man would not do.

Who is the reasonable man?

This is the ordinary man, the average man, or as is commonly stated 'the man on the Clapham omnibus'. The reasonable man is prudent and intelligent, but is not expected to be obsessively cautious or an infallible genius. The correct test is that of whether the defendant exercised reasonable care in the circumstances. The concept of reasonable care is a flexible one in that it can be manipulated by the courts to produce a range of standards from very low to very high, depending on the circumstances. One would not expect a reasonable man handling cartons of milk to exercise the same degree of care as one handling a priceless work of art or a phial containing dangerous micro-organisms.

The objective standard

The standard of care expected from the reasonable man is largely objective. Allowance must be made for the inexperience or rashness of childhood so that a child is expected only to display the prudence or foresight of an ordinary, sensible child of his own age (*Mullin* v *Richards* [1998] 1 All ER 921) but, with that exception, no allowance will be made for the defendant's personal weaknesses or incompetence. This can be seen in *Nettleship* v *Weston* [1971] 3 All ER 581. The defendant was a learner driver who crashed into a lamp post, injuring her instructor. She was not driving 'carelessly' in the normal sense of the word. On the contrary, she was doing her incompetent best to control the car. The Court of Appeal, however, held that the standard of care required of a learner driver is the same as that required of any other driver, namely that of a reasonably competent driver. The defendant's driving had fallen below that standard, and it was irrelevant that she was merely a learner driver.

The objective standard will vary in accordance with all the circumstances of the case. If, for example, a person is faced with an emergency and has to respond in an instant, he will not be held liable for understandable errors or oversights, merely because a different procedure may be seen, with hindsight and prolonged consideration, to have been more appropriate.

The circumstances of the case may also include a consideration of the defendant's profession. If, for example, the defendant is a surgeon, he will ordinarily be judged by the standard of care expected from a reasonably competent surgeon. It will not then be a defence for him to argue that he is short of experience in that role, any more than a learner driver can rely on her lack of driving experience, but nor on the other hand would it be fair to judge him against the standards of the very best surgeons in the land, or worse still, against new standards which have been set only *after* the alleged act of negligence giving rise to the action (*Sidaway* v *Governors of the Bethlehem Royal Hospital* [1985] 1 All ER 643). As McNair J said, directing the jury in *Bolam* v *Friern Hospital Management Committee* [1957] 2 All ER 118:

> The test is the standard of the ordinary skilled man exercising and professing to have that special skill. A man need not possess the highest expert skill at the risk of being found negligent . . . it is sufficient if he exercises the ordinary skill of an ordinary competent man exercising that particular art. . . You are considering whether it was negligent for certain actions to be taken in 1954 . . . you must not look with 1957 spectacles at what happened in 1954.

Another illustration of this principle can be found in *Roe* v *Minister of Health* [1954] 2 QB 66. The plaintiff entered hospital for a minor operation and was given an anaesthetic. During the course of the operation he was paralysed by the anaesthetic, which had become contaminated. Unknown to the hospital, the ampoule containing the anaesthetic had hairline cracks and a fluid in which it had been stored had entered the ampoule and contaminated it. At the time of the accident (in 1947) this risk was wholly unknown. The Court of Appeal held that the hospital authorities were not liable for negligence. If the same thing had happened in 1955 or 1997, the result would almost certainly have been different.

The likelihood of harm or injury

The law requires a degree of care which is commensurate with the risk. In *Bolton* v *Stone* [1951] 1 All ER 1078, the plaintiff was struck by a cricket ball which a batsman had hit out of the local cricket ground. From past experience it was rare for cricket balls to be hit out of this ground. It had only happened some six times in the last 30 years. The court held that the defendants were not liable for negligence because, whilst the incident itself was not entirely unforeseeable, the likelihood of it actually occurring was very small. The House of Lords therefore held that the defendants were not liable. This case, however, is not authority for the proposition that it is always reasonable to ignore remote or minor risks. The risk must always be measured against the defendant's purpose, the damage that could be done and the practicability of taking precautions.

  Bolton v *Stone* was distinguished on its facts in the later case of *Miller* v *Jackson* [1977] 3 All ER 338. Past experience in this case had shown that cricket balls were hit out of the (somewhat smaller) ground some eight or nine times per season. The Court of Appeal held that the risk of harm was such that the defendants were indeed negligent in failing to take precautions against it.

The seriousness of the risk

The greater the damage that may be done, the greater the degree of care that may be considered appropriate. Greater precautions must, for example, be expected at a laboratory handling the smallpox virus than at one handling the virus which causes the common cold. Similarly, if a school teacher knows that one of his pupils suffers from haemophilia, he may be expected to take special care to prevent that pupil from suffering cuts or bruises that would be accepted as an everyday playground hazard to most young children. This principle was applied in *Paris* v *Stepney Borough Council* [1951] 1 All ER 52. The plaintiff, a one-eyed man, was employed as a mechanic by the defendants and, whilst working on a car, he was struck in his one eye by a splinter and totally blinded. He was not wearing protective goggles at the time of the accident. The House of Lords held that, although the risk of eye injury had only been a slight one, the consequences of any injury to the plaintiff's one good eye were likely to be so serious that the defendants should have provided goggles for his use.

Practicality of taking precautions

Some risks can be eliminated or reduced with little effort and at little expense, whereas others can be reduced only at huge expense or great inconvenience. On a practical level, the cost of preventing the risk must be balanced against the danger of running it. A point may be reached, however, where the reasonable man may be justified in not taking extra precautions. The question is, at what stage does this occur? In *Latimer* v *AEC Ltd* [1953] AC 643, the defendants owned a factory at which channels in which oil flowed were cut into the floor. After an exceptionally heavy rainstorm the factory was flooded and the oil rose out of the channels and mixed with the water. After the water had subsided, the factory floor was covered with an oily film. The defendants (AEC) used sawdust to cover the floor, but did not have enough supplies to cover it all, and so some areas were left bare. The plaintiff, an employee, slipped on an untreated part of the floor and was injured. The question was whether AEC were liable for not taking enough precautions as far as the state of the floor and the safety of individuals on it were concerned. The Court held that AEC had done all that could reasonably be expected. They could have closed the workshop and sent the employees home, but this would have caused great financial loss and it would not have been reasonable to do so.

Although the shortage of sawdust was a factor in the *AEC* case, a defendant's lack of resources will not necessarily excuse a failure to take reasonable precautions. In particular, a defendant who lacks the resources to carry on a particular activity safely may be told that in such circumstances he is at fault for attempting to carry on that activity at all. If precautions are not practicable, the risks of continuing the activity have to be weighed against the disadvantages of stopping the activity altogether.

Accepted practice

The general practice of persons engaged in the same trade, profession or activity as the defendant may provide a strong indication as to whether he has been negligent, but is not necessarily decisive. If the defendant has followed a generally or widely accepted practice, he is most unlikely to be adjudged negligent, but the court may in some cases conclude that this generally accepted practice is indefensible. Conversely, if the defendant has departed from accepted practice, this may well be considered to be evidence of negligence, but the court must always examine the case as a whole. Unortho-dox procedures may sometimes be justifiable.

The importance of accepted practice is perhaps most clearly seen in cases involving allegations of medical negligence. Unfortunately, doctors do not always agree on the best way of treating medical conditions, and it is often impossible to find a universal consensus as to what is right. In *Bolam* v *Friern Hospital Management Committee* [1957] 2 All ER 118, McNair J said that a doctor:

> ... is not guilty of negligence if he has acted in accordance with a practice accepted as proper by a responsible body of medical men skilled in that particular art ... [even if] ... there is a body of opinion who would take the contrary view.

The *Bolam* principle was recently modified by the House of Lords in *Bolitho* v *City and Hackney Health Authority* [1997] 4 All ER 771. The infant plaintiff in that case suffered brain damage following a respiratory failure and cardiac arrest whilst in hospital. It was apparent, with the benefit of hindsight, that the brain damage could have been avoided if a doctor had attended the plaintiff before respiratory failure occurred, and had then intubated him, so as to ensure that an airway remained open into his lungs. The doctor's failure to attend when the first warning signs were reported was acknowledged to have been a breach of duty on her part, but this would not make the health authority liable for the brain damage unless it was clear that the doctor would, or at least *should,* have intubated the plaintiff on observing his symptoms. In other words, the question was whether a failure to intubate would have been categorised as medical negligence.

Expert medical evidence was called, but the experts were divided. A number considered that the need for intubation would have been obvious to any competent doctor, but others stated that it would not have been obvious at all. The *Bolam* test thus favoured the health authority, but the House of Lords held that it was not enough merely to show that many doctors would not have intubated a patient in such circumstances. It was necessary to consider *why* many doctors would not have intubated, and whether they would have had good reasons for not so doing. As Lord Browne-Wilkinson explained, 'The court has to be satisfied that the exponents of the body of opinion relied upon can demonstrate that such an opinion has a logical basis'. The House of Lords concluded that there was nothing illogical in either viewpoint, and on that basis the plaintiff's claim failed.

Necessity and social utility

In some cases, it may be justifiable to expose others to some risk of injury, notably where the social utility of one's actions justifies taking greater risks than would otherwise be the case. In *Watt v Hertfordshire County Council* [1954] 1 WLR 835, an accident occurred in which a woman was trapped under a car, and it was considered necessary to take a heavy lifting jack to the scene. The vehicle which was equipped to carry the jack was unavailable, and so the jack was taken on a normal lorry which had no means of securing the jack. Unfortunately, the jack slid forward and injured one of the firemen when the lorry had to brake suddenly. It was held that the fireman's employers were not liable for his injury. The risk taken had to be balanced against the end to be achieved. The Court of Appeal thought that the risk taken by the fire officer was not too great when balanced against the attempt to save the woman's life. This does not, however, mean that the purpose of saving a life justifies taking any risk. It depends on all the circumstances of the case. Fire or ambulance crews are permitted to treat red traffic lights as if they were only 'give way' signs, but would certainly be considered negligent if they drove through red lights at high speed without checking for other traffic. Similarly, police officers may sometimes be required to abandon high-speed car chases because of danger to other road users. The need to halt a bandit vehicle must be balanced against the risks of an accident. How dangerous are the bandits? How much danger is the chase creating?

Res ipsa loquitur

If the plaintiff proves that he suffered a loss or injury in circumstances in which accidents do not normally happen unless there has been negligence by someone, the court may draw an inference of negligence against the defendant without the plaintiff producing any further evidence. This is referred to as the doctrine of *res ipsa loquitur*, which may be translated as meaning, 'the fact speaks for itself'. It effectively puts the burden on the defendant to show that he was not negligent after all.

In *Scott v London & St Katherine Docks Co.* (1865) 3 H & C 596, the plaintiff was injured by bags of sugar which fell from a hoist on the upper floor of the defendant's warehouse. It was held that this gave rise to an inference of *res ipsa loquitur*. Erle CJ stated the basis of the doctrine in the following terms:

There must be reasonable evidence of negligence. But where the thing is shown to be under the management of the defendant or his servants, and the accident is such as in the ordinary course of things does not happen if those who have the management use proper care, it affords reasonable evidence in the absence of explanation by the defendants, that the accident arose from want of care. . .

The following criteria must be satisfied before the maxim can be applied:

(a) *The accident must be such as would not normally happen without negligence.* Bags of sugar do not tend to fall from upper windows of warehouses unless someone has been negligent. By the same token, the brakes on a lorry do not usually fail unless they have been negligently maintained (*Henderson* v *Henry Jenkins & Sons* [1970] AC 282).

(b) *The defendant must have had sole control of the thing which caused the accident.* If the event or thing was also under the control of someone else, then there will be insufficient evidence against the defendant.

(c) *The exact cause of the accident must be unknown.* Res ipsa loquitur is an evidential short-cut, designed to enable decisions to be made on the basis of an incomplete set of facts. 'On the basis of the known facts, it looks as if the defendant was probably negligent, because such accidents do not usually occur otherwise.' If all the facts are known, short-cuts are not needed, and the maxim does not apply. The issue is simply whether the defendant was in fact negligent.

The recent case of *Widdowson* v *Newgate Meat Corporation, The Times,* 4 December 1997, provides a good illustration of *res ipsa loquitur* in operation. It was clearly proved that the defendant's van had struck the plaintiff, who had been walking along a dark unlit road, but neither party could testify as to how exactly this had happened. Despite the lack of any such evidence, the Court of Appeal felt able to conclude, on the basis of *res ipsa loquitur,* that there must almost certainly have been some blame on each side. Such an accident was unlikely to have happened if either party had been exercising proper vigilance. The court therefore found for the plaintiff, but reduced his damages by 50 per cent on the basis of his contributory negligence.

CAUSATION AND REMOTENESS

In order to succeed in an action in tort, the plaintiff must prove that it was the defendant's conduct which caused him the damage or injury complained of. If the plaintiff is unable to establish this, then the defendant will not be liable, no matter how culpable his behaviour.

Factual causation: the 'but for' test

When considering questions of causation, one must first establish what is known as factual causation. In other words, one must ascertain whether the defendant's actions were in any real sense a factor leading to the plaintiff's loss. If harm to the plaintiff would not have occurred 'but for' the defendant's negligence, then it can generally be classed as a cause of the victim's harm (although there may well be other events from a causation point of view which may be relevant as well). Conversely, if the harm would have occurred in any event, then the defendant's conduct cannot ordinarily be said to be the cause of it. In cases of doubt, the burden of proof is on the plaintiff. This can be illustrated by the case of *Barnett* v *Chelsea & Kensington Hospital Management Committee* [1968] 1 All ER 1068. The plaintiff's husband and two of his colleagues attended the hospital, all complaining of persistent vomiting after sharing a pot of tea. The duty casualty officer, who was himself feeling unwell, refused to see them, but told them to go home and consult their own doctors. Later that day, the plaintiff's husband died of arsenic poisoning. The question was whether the duty casualty officer was liable for negligence.

It was held that the casualty officer was not liable for the death, even though he had clearly been in breach of his duty of care, because even if he had examined and treated the deceased, it would probably have been impossible to save him. The doctor could not have been expected immediately to have diagnosed arsenic poisoning in time to administer B.A.L., the only known antidote to the poison. The doctor's negligence did not therefore cause the man's death and the plaintiff's claim against the hospital therefore failed.

The 'but for' test nevertheless has its limitations, as it cannot resolve all problems of factual causation. For example, where there are two simultaneous wrongs to the plaintiff, each of which would be sufficient to cause the damage, then a crude application of the 'but for' test would arguably produce the bizarre result that neither wrong could be deemed to have caused the harm. To take an extreme example, assume A and B each negligently drop lighted cigarette ends inside C's haystack. Each sets off a huge fire, and the haystack is destroyed. The 'but for' test may seem inappropriate in such a situation, as each of the defendants could point to each other as a sufficient cause of the destruction. Would it have been destroyed but for each negligent act? Technically, yes, because in each case the other party's act was in itself a sufficient cause on its own; but this would be misleading, because the true position must surely be that A and B each caused the fire. In most cases, however, the basic test works well enough.

Causation in law

Once the courts have eliminated all logically irrelevant events, they may be left with several factual causes of the harm. The court must subsequently decide as a matter of law which can be said to be the effective cause(s) of the harm for the purpose of attributing legal responsibility. This is not always easy and the courts have adopted varying techniques in carrying out this selection process. This selection invariably involves the courts in making policy decisions and value judgments. As Lord Wright stated in *Liesbosch Dredger* v *SS Edison* [1933] AC 449: 'In the varied web of affairs, the law must abstract some consequences as relevant, not perhaps on the grounds of pure logic, but simply for practical reasons.' Common sense plays a role here. One must in practice look for some kind of abnormal and /or culpable behaviour. As Hart and Honore explain in *Causation in the Law* (2nd edn., 1985):

> The notion that a cause is essentially something which interferes with or intervenes in the course of events which would normally take place, is central to our common-sense concept of cause... In distinguishing between causes and conditions, two contrasts are of prime importance. These are the contrasts between what is abnormal and what is normal in relation to any given thing or subject-matter, and between a free deliberate human action and all other conditions...
>
> In the case of a building destroyed by fire, 'mere conditions' will be factors such as the oxygen in the air, the presence of combustible material or the dryness of the building ... which are present alike both ... where such accidents occur and ... where they do not... Such factors do not 'make the difference' between disaster and normal functioning, as ... the dropping of a lighted cigarette does...

The chain of causation

Causation is concerned with the physical connection between the defendant's act or omission and the damage suffered by the plaintiff. This is known as the 'chain of causation'. Sometimes, an event occurs between the original conduct and the eventual damage, which is not a natural or predictable consequence of that original conduct, and which can more directly be identified the immediate cause of the plaintiff's loss or damage. Such an event may 'break the chain of causation' and relieve the defendant from responsibility. An event which breaks the chain is usually known as a *novus actus interveniens*. As Lord Wright said in *The Oropesa* [1943] P 32:

> To break the chain of causation it must be shown that there is something which I will call ultroneous, something unwarrantable; a new cause which disturbs the sequence of events; something which can be described as either unreasonable or extraneous or extrinsic.

The intervening act may be a natural event or it may be committed by a third party, or even by the plaintiff himself.

Acts of the plaintiff
McKew v *Holland, Hannen & Cubitts* [1969] 3 All ER 1621 provides an example of a case in which the plaintiff himself provided the *novus actus*

interveniens. The plaintiff suffered an injury to his leg caused by the defendant's negligence. A few days later, the plaintiff went with his family to look at a flat. While he was descending the very steep stairs from this flat (which had no handrail) his injured leg gave way. He fractured his ankle as he fell. The House of Lords held that the chain of causation had been broken by the plaintiff unnecessarily placing himself in such a position, and therefore the defendants were not liable for the second accident. The plaintiff's conduct was unreasonable, and was therefore a *novus actus interveniens*. It would not have been fair to expect the defendant to pay for this further injury that was occasioned by the plaintiff's own error of judgment.

McKew must be contrasted with *Wieland* v *Cyril Lord Carpets Ltd* [1969] 3 All ER 1006. The plaintiff in this case wore a surgical collar as a result of a neck injury, which had been caused by the defendant's negligence. This restricted her ability to move her head and this in turn affected her ability to use her bifocal spectacles. As a result, the plaintiff fell down some stairs. The court held the defendants liable both for the initial injury and for the further injuries sustained by the plaintiff when she fell. It was entirely foreseeable that the initial injury would affect the plaintiff's ability to cope with basic activities such as descending stairs, and thereby lead to another injury. The plaintiff had not acted unreasonably, whilst in *McKew* the plaintiff had tackled some particularly dangerous stairs and brought his second injury upon himself.

Contributory negligence

In cases where plaintiffs negligently contribute to their own injuries, the defendant will usually claim the defence of contributory negligence. Contributory negligence requires the courts to apportion responsibility for what happens and reduce the amount of any damages payable accordingly. It is a less drastic argument than the claim that the chain of causation has been broken. An example of the use of contributory negligence may be found in the case of *Sayers* v *Harlow Urban District Council* [1958] 1 WLR 623. The plaintiff had become trapped in a public toilet as a result of a faulty lock on the cubicle. She decided to climb out of the cubicle when her cries for help were ignored. Unfortunately, she fell and injured herself when she unwisely placed her full weight on a toilet-roll holder which collapsed beneath her. It was held that it was reasonable for the plaintiff to have tried to escape, but she had nevertheless been foolish in the way in which she had attempted to do so. The plaintiff was consequently held to be contributorily negligent in respect of her injuries. Comments in recent cases suggest that where the plaintiff has negligently contributed to his own injuries, contributory negligence ordinarily provides a more appropriate defence than *novus actus interveniens*.

Intervention by third parties

Negligent acts by third parties may or may not break the chain of causation, depending on the circumstances. No clear answer can be given. An intentional intervening act is more likely to break the chain of causation than a mere mistake made by another when dealing with an emergency created by the defendant's acts, but an unreasonable mistake may suffice to break the chain. An example of deliberate intervention would be deliberate and extensive damage inflicted by squatters using the plaintiff's house after it has been temporarily left empty as a result of a small fire previously caused by the defendant. The courts would be most unlikely to impose liability on the defendant for the ensuing squatter damage, even though the defendant's fire had led to the house standing empty.

Remoteness of damage

If the plaintiff has shown that the defendant's act was a cause of the plaintiff's loss, the next question is whether the defendant will be liable for all the plaintiff's loss. The rule is that the plaintiff will be entitled to damages only if the damage suffered is, as a matter of law, not too remote from the original wrongful act. The test of remoteness adopted by the courts in the tort of negligence is that laid down by the Judicial Committee of the Privy Council in *Overseas Tankship (UK) Ltd v Morts Dock and Engineering Co. Ltd (The Wagon Mound (No. 1))* [1961] 1 AC 388. The SS *Wagon Mound* was moored in Sydney Harbour, when the defendant stevedores, whilst refuelling the ship, negligently spilt fuel oil into the harbour. Some hours later, the fuel had spread some 600 yards, towards the plaintiff's wharf, where welding operations were being carried out. The welding was not discountinued because it was believed that the fuel was non-inflammable in the open air. Unfortunately, some sparks from the welding operations ignited a piece of cotton waste which was floating on the oil. The plaintiff's wharf was destroyed in the ensuing fire. Were the defendants to be held liable for the plaintiff's loss? The Privy Council held that they were not, because it was not reasonably foreseeable that fuel oil floating on water would catch fire and destroy the plaintiff's wharf. Thus under the tort of negligence the defendant will only be liable for losses which are reasonably foreseeable. (The same test was later applied to a claim in nuisance (*The Wagon Mound (No. 2)* [1967] AC 617) and more recently to a claim based on the rule in *Rylands* v *Fletcher* (see the *Cambridge Water* case, discussed in Chapter 40).)

The type of harm
The next question is what exactly has to be foreseeable before the defendant will be liable for harm caused to the plaintiff? The answer is to ask whether the *type* of damage suffered by the plaintiff was reasonably foreseeable.

In order to give rise to liability, the plaintiff's damage must of the same type or kind as some harm that could reasonably have been foreseen. If it is not, it will be too remote. The decision whether the harm is foreseeable will depend upon the approach taken by the courts towards the categorisation of the type of harm. This may be illustrated by means of a few examples. In *Bradford* v

Robinson Rentals Ltd [1967] 1 All ER 267, the plaintiff was sent on a journey by his employers in an unheated van during very severe winter weather. He suffered frostbite as a result. The court held that frostbite was an injury of a type that was foreseeable as a consequence of exposure to extreme cold. This can be contrasted with the case of *Tremain* v *Pike* [1969] 3 All ER 1303, where the plaintiff, a farm employee, contracted a rare disease which was transmitted as a result of coming into contact with rat urine. The judge held that whereas injuries from rat bites or from food contaminated by rats was foreseeable, a disease from contact with rat urine was unforeseeable.

Extent of the harm

Once it has been established to the satisfaction of the court that the damage suffered by the plaintiff was of a type which was reasonably foreseeable, it is irrelevant that the actual physical extent of the damage suffered by the plaintiff was unforeseeable. This rule applies both to damage to property and to personal injuries. This principle was explained by Lord Reid in *Hughes* v *Lord Advocate* [1963] AC 837 as follows:

> No doubt it was not expected that the injuries would be as serious as those which the appellant in fact sustained. But a defender is liable, although the damage may be a good deal greater than was foreseeable. He can only escape liability if the damage can be regarded as differing in kind from what was foreseeable.

In *Vacwell Engineering Co. Ltd* v *BDH Chemicals Ltd* [1971] 1 QB 88, a chemical distributed by the defendants produced a toxic vapour when it came into contact with water. The fact that it would do so was widely known. Unfortunately, on one particular occasion, the chemical, on coming into contact with water, produced a violent explosion, completely out of proportion to anything which would normally be expected. It was held that the defendants were liable, because the type of harm was foreseeable and it was irrelevant that the degree of the explosion and resultant damage were unforeseeable.

'Eggshell skull' rule

The 'eggshell skull' rule takes the above rule one step further, at least in personal injury cases, in that the defendant 'must take his victim as he finds him'. If, for example, the plaintiff has a thin or brittle skull and suffers a more extensive head injury than would a normal person, the defendant will be liable for the full extent of the injury and not just for the damage which a normal person would have suffered. The rule therefore allows recovery for harm of a different type from that which is foreseeable. An example of this rule in operation may be seen in *Smith* v *Leech Brain & Co. Ltd* [1962] 2 QB 405. The plaintiff's husband was burned on the lip by a piece of molten metal. The burn triggered a pre-existing but hitherto dormant cancerous growth which ultimately killed him. The question was whether the defendants could be held responsible for her husband's death. This was answered in the affirmative. Lord Parker CJ stated:

> The test is not whether these [defendants] could reasonably have foreseen that a burn would cause cancer and that [Mr Smith] would die. The question is whether [the defendants] could reasonably foresee the type of injury he suffered, namely, the burn. What, in the particular case, is the amount of damage which he suffers as a result of that burn, depends upon the characteristics and constitution of the victim.

The decision is a harsh one, because the cause of death was not a burn, but a form of cancer. Nevertheless, a similarly harsh rule operates in criminal cases (see Chapter 11).

Causation and remoteness

Once it has been established that the defendant was in breach of his duty of care, it is necessary to prove that it was the defendant's actions which caused the damage:

1. Eliminate all irrelevant causes through the application of the 'but for' test.

2. Having eliminated all irrelevant causes, the court must establish the legal cause of the damage.

3. Sometimes an event occurs between the act/omission of the defendant which is complained of and the damage suffered by the plaintiff which breaks the chain of causation. This is known as a *novus actus interveniens*.

4. If the chain of causation has not been broken it must then be shown that the damage suffered by the plaintiff was not too remote a consequence of the defendant's actions.

5. The damage will not be too remote provided the harm suffered was a *type* which was reasonably foreseeable.

6. Once the court is satisfied that the damage suffered was of a type which was reasonably foreseeable, it is irrelevant that the actual physical extent of the harm suffered was unforeseeable.

Breach of duty of care

If it can be established that the defendant owed the plaintiff a duty of care, the next step is to determine whether the defendant was in breach of that duty. Two questions must be answered in this context:

What standard of care ought the defendant to have exercised?

The standard of care is that which the ordinary reasonable man would exercise if placed in the defendant's position.

Did the defendant's behaviour fall below that standard?

There are a number of factors which the courts may take into account in answering this question, bearing in mind that an objective approach is adopted throughout:

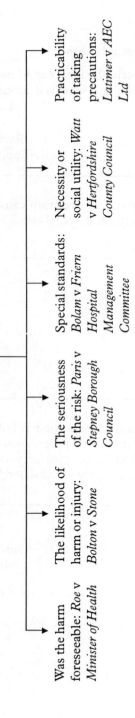

| Was the harm foreseeable: *Roe v Minister of Health* | The likelihood of harm or injury: *Bolton v Stone* | The seriousness of the risk: *Paris v Stepney Borough Council* | Special standards: *Bolam v Friern Hospital Management Committee* | Necessity or social utility: *Watt v Hertfordshire County Council* | Practicability of taking precautions: *Latimer v AEC Ltd* |

THIRTY SEVEN

Liability for Nervous Shock and Economic Loss

In Chapter 36 we examined the concept of a duty of care in the tort of negligence. There are two areas in which it is particularly difficult to determine whether a duty of care exists, and this chapter discusses these.

NERVOUS SHOCK

It is now possible, in limited circumstances, for a person who negligently injures or kills another to be liable for any nervous shock caused to a third person, as a result of the latter's perception of the incident. In order to bring an action for nervous shock, a plaintiff must establish that he has suffered a recognisable psychiatric illness or disorder, such as depression, personality change, neurosis, etc., and that this was as a result of witnessing events caused by the defendant's negligence. The courts do not accept claims for mere emotional distress or grief. It can sometimes be difficult, however, to distinguish between mere grief and a recognisable psychiatric illness, but the distinction remains important.

Initial reluctance to recognise liability for nervous shock

The courts have long been prepared to allow a plaintiff to recover damages for nervous shock suffered as a result of some personal physical injury inflicted upon him. They were reluctant, however, to allow recovery for nervous shock which was not connected with any physical injury to the claimant himself. This initial reluctance could be attributed to a number of factors, of which the most important was the fear of encouraging a flood of applications, some of which might be fraudulent. Slowly, however, the courts began to relax their guard, and further claims for nervous shock were recognised. The first development was to allow a plaintiff to recover for mental trauma suffered as a result of fully justified fears for his own safety, as for example where he narrowly escapes serious injury or death (as in *Dulieu* v *White* [1901] 2 KB 669). The next stage was to allow claims for nervous shock suffered as the result of a threat to the safety of a close relative, as where a mother suffered shock through fear for the safety of her child (see *Hambrook* v *Stokes* [1925] 1 KB 141).

Once the courts began to allow recovery in such cases, the next problem was one of determining how wide the scope of such liability should be. In determining this question, a distinction must now be drawn, according to *Page* v *Smith* [1995] 2 WLR 644, between primary victims and secondary victims. In this case, Smith carelessly collided with a car driven by Page. The accident was of a minor nature and no one was hurt, although Page's car had to be written off because it was too old to be worth repairing. A few hours after the accident, however, Page suffered a recurrence of post-viral fatigue syndrome, a condition from which he had suffered intermittently for some 20 years. At first instance, Page was awarded damages for the recurrence of this condition, but this award was overturned by the Court of Appeal on the grounds that Page had failed to establish that psychiatric injury was foreseeable and was of a type which would be suffered by the ordinary reasonable man. The case then went on to the House of Lords, who allowed the plaintiff's claim on the basis that he was a primary victim.

Primary victims

A primary victim (or participant) is someone who is injured or put in fear of physical injury in the accident or incident concerned. Such a primary victim will be able to claim damages for nervous shock, even if the defendant could have foreseen only that the plaintiff might suffer *physical* injury. Because of the principle that the defendant must take the plaintiff 'as he finds him', the defendant will be liable for any psychiatric injury that the plaintiff then suffers, even if such injury was not itself foreseeable and resulted only because the plaintiff's makeup left him particularly vulnerable to such injury. In other words, as far as the primary victim is concerned, there is no distinction between physical and psychiatric injury. The position in respect of secondary victims is more restrictive as we shall see.

Secondary victims

A secondary victim may be classed as one who foreseeably suffers nervous shock as a result of witnessing the predicament of someone else. The first recognition of a claim for nervous shock from a secondary victim involved a case where the plaintiff had feared for the imminent safety of another (see *Hambrook* v *Stokes* [1925] 1 KB 141). This was later extended to allow secondary parties to recover damages where they suffered a recognisable psychiatric injury as a result of witnessing a shocking event. The ambit of secondary party claims was then further extended in the case of *McLoughlin* v *O'Brian* [1982] 2 All ER 298, where a secondary victim was allowed to recover damages for nervous shock as a result of coming across the *aftermath* of a shocking event. In this case, the plaintiff's husband and her three children were involved in a road accident caused by the defendant's negligence. One of the children was killed and the husband and other two children were badly injured. The plaintiff did not actually witness the accident, neither did she come across her family immediately afterwards, but she went to the hospital some two hours after the accident having been informed of the event. When she arrived at the hospital, she was told about the death of one of her children and stumbled upon the rest of her family, still untreated and bloodstained, in a hospital corridor, as their injuries had not yet been treated. Mrs McLoughlin suffered shock. The House of Lords held that she could recover because she had come across the immediate aftermath of the accident. (Note the importance of the fact that her family had not yet been attended to by hospital staff when she saw them. If they had been attended to before her arrival, the plaintiff would not have recovered because she would not then have truly witnessed the immediate aftermath of the shocking event.)

The limits of liability for secondary victims
Although claims from secondary parties have been accepted by the courts, a more complex test must be applied when considering the claims of such parties in order to control the type of claims made. Application of the foresight (or foreseeability) test alone is not enough and a number of other strict criteria must be established. These rules were clarified in the case of *Alcock* v *Chief Constable of South Yorkshire* [1991] All ER 907.

This was a case which arose out of the Hillsborough disaster, in which the police negligently allowed a large number of football fans to pour uncontrolled into a stadium which was already nearly full. In the resulting crush, dozens of spectators were killed and hundreds were injured. The match was televised and consequently the disaster was shown live on television. All the plaintiffs in the case claimed to have suffered psychiatric damage, but the claimants fell into a number of different categories: some were present at the match; some identified bodies in the mortuary; some saw the disaster on television. The plaintiffs were relatives of people who were in the disaster area, but none of them were parents or spouses of the primary victims.

The plaintiffs argued that the police were liable for the shock which they had suffered, on the ground that reasonable foresight alone was sufficient to establish liability. The House of Lords rejected the plaintiffs' claims and stated that such 'witnessing' cases needed to satisfy the tests of 'familial, temporal and spatial proximity' and that application of the foresight test alone was insufficient. In other words, in any claim by a secondary victim for recovery for nervous shock, consideration must be taken of that person's physical proximity to the accident, his relationship with the primary victim of the accident and the means by which the shock was caused.

The relationship between the plaintiff and the primary victim

The nature of the relationship between the primary accident victim and the person who suffered shock is deemed to be important. A close family relationship between the victim and the secondary party who suffers the shock is much more likely to be accepted by the courts as falling within the scope of the duty of care owed by the defendant. The House of Lords said that while there was a rebuttable presumption that these ties would be present in a parent/child or husband/wife relationship, there was no reason why such ties may not also be present in more remote relationships. For example, an engaged couple may be closer in this sense than a couple who have been unhappily married for several years.

Due to the close relationship requirement between the victim and the secondary party who suffers the shock, it follows that a duty of care would not normally be owed by the defendant to a mere bystander. However, Lords Ackner, Keith and Oliver all stated (obiter) that, if an incident was exceptionally horrific, a bystander might possibly be able to claim. Lord Ackner gave as an example a petrol tanker careering out of control into a crowded school and bursting into flames.

This idea was rejected, however, in *McFarlane* v *EE Caledonia Ltd* [1994] 2 All ER 1. The plaintiff had been employed as a painter on an oil rig in the North Sea for seven years. The oil rig, Piper Alpha, was owned by the defendants. On the night of 6 July 1988, a terrible fire broke out, which resulted in the death of 164 people and many more seriously injured. At the time of the fire, the plaintiff was on board a vessel called *The Tharos*, which was designed to provide support for off-shore installations. *The Tharos* came close to the oil rig and one of the bases for the plaintiff's claim for damages for nervous shock was that the psychiatric injury he suffered was as a result of witnessing such horrific events. The Court of Appeal rejected the plaintiff's claim for nervous shock on all grounds, including the ground that he suffered it as a result of witnessing the terrible scene. Stuart-Smith LJ, with whom McGowan and Gibson LJJ agreed, stated:

> The whole basis of the decision in *Alcock* . . . is that where the shock is caused by fear to others as opposed to fear of injury to the participant, the test of proximity is not simply reasonable foreseeability. There must be a sufficiently close tie of love and affection between the plaintiff and the victim. To extend the duty to those who have no such connection, is to base the test purely on foreseeability.

Although the general basis for liability in the *Alcock* case was the presence of close ties of love and affection, it seems strange that the Court of Appeal should reject the bystander's claim on the ground of lack of such ties, when their Lordships themselves were prepared to allow such claims, albeit in limited circumstances.

One exception to the normal rule that unrelated bystanders cannot recover for nervous shock is 'rescuer' cases, such as *Chadwick v British Railway Board* [1967] 1 WLR 912. There the plaintiff became actively involved in a rescue operation, during the course of which he was exposed to horrific sights. It was held that such a rescuer may be a person to whom the defendant may owe a duty of care; and if despite being of reasonable fortitude he suffers mental trauma, causing injury, he may be able to recover damages. See also *Frost v Chief Constable of South Yorkshire* [1997] 1 All ER 540. This case involved claims by several police constables who were sent in to help at Hillsborough and who claimed to have suffered psychiatric injuries as a result of what they had witnessed. Those who took part in the rescue operation were able to succeed in their claims, but one who only became involved with victims outside the stadium could not.

The proximity of the plaintiff to the accident
In *Alcock v Chief Constable of South Yorkshire*, their Lordships held it to be necessary for the plaintiff to be close to the incident in both *time* and *space*. It is not necessary for him directly to hear or see the incident: it would be enough for him to come across the immediate aftermath of the incident, as in *McLoughlin v O'Brian*. Their Lordships in *Alcock* stated that in their opinion damages were not recoverable for nervous shock as a result of identifying victims in the mortuary soon after the tragedy, because this could not be described as falling within the immediate aftermath.

How the plaintiff learned of the accident
Lord Wilberforce said in *McLoughlin v O'Brian* that the plaintiff must either see or hear the incident, or come across its immediate aftermath (i.e., it is not enough simply to be told of the incident — the alleged sufferer of nervous shock must witness the incident himself). Consequently, nervous shock suffered as a result of witnessing a live disaster on television would not normally be recoverable. In *Alcock*, however, their Lordships left open the possibility that a plaintiff might be able to sue if he suffered shock from seeing live television pictures of *identifiable* victims.

ECONOMIC LOSS

Claims for damages in tort may sometimes be problematic where the plaintiff alleges that the defendant has caused him economic loss, rather than personal injury or physical damage to property. Generally speaking, the courts are willing to compensate for economic loss which is directly and/or intentionally caused, such as by the tort of deceit (i.e. fraud), or which is consequential to physical damage or personal injury, but they are less willing to award damages for 'pure' economic loss caused by negligence. This section primarily is concerned with those limited circumstances in which a plaintiff can indeed recover for such loss.

Economic loss consequential to physical damage or personal injury

One situation in which the courts are quite prepared to award damages for economic loss is that in which such loss is consequent upon personal injury or physical damage to property. For example, if the plaintiff is injured through the defendant's negligence and consequently suffers loss of earnings, he may be able to recover for those lost earnings. Similarly, if the plaintiff's property is damaged, he may be able to claim compensation for any profit lost while waiting for the property to be repaired or replaced. It is where claims are made for *pure* economic loss that the problems most commonly occur.

Pure economic loss

Pure economic loss arises where the plaintiff's loss is not connected with any physical damage to his own person or property. The distinction between physical damage, consequential economic loss and pure economic loss may be seen in *Spartan Steel & Alloys Ltd* v *Martin & Co.* [1973] QB 27. The defendant negligently damaged an electricity cable, which did *not* belong to the plaintiffs but which supplied power to their factory. The damage caused the power supply to be cut off for a number of hours. The plaintiffs manufactured stainless steel, and at the time of the failure there was a 'melt' in the process of being manufactured. This melt was damaged, because it had to be poured off prematurely to prevent it solidifying in the furnace, and the steel concerned was worth far less as a result. The plaintiffs were awarded compensation for the damage caused to this melt and for the consequential loss of profit from it, but they were unsuccessful in a further claim for loss of profit on four other melts which would have been carried out but for the power cut. This was a claim for pure economic loss. If, however, the damaged cable had belonged to the plaintiffs themselves, the loss of the further melts would have been consequential to damage to the plaintiffs' own property and they could have recovered for it.

Claims for pure economic loss may also arise as a result of the plaintiff relying upon a statement negligently made by the defendant, as, for example, where negligent investment advice is given. The problem in each case is largely the same: whether the defendant negligently interrupts a mains power supply, or whether he gives negligent investment advice, the range of potential claimants (and losses) may be enormous. This factor has weighed heavily upon the judiciary, and the inevitable question arises: if the courts start to allow recoverability for economic loss, where will it stop? The problem facing the courts is that of deciding how to frame a general rule which will avoid over-burdening the defendant with potential liability. Is it possible to frame such a rule?

Why do cases of economic loss cause difficulties?

Claims for economic loss are usually brought under the tort of negligence by plaintiffs who are unable to bring an action in contract against the defendant. The law of contract is the more usual route by which an injured party would try to obtain compensation for economic loss suffered as a result of the defendant's actions. Unfortunately, a plaintiff's ability to pursue a contractual claim may be hampered by a number of factors, especially where there has been no consideration or where the plaintiff is not deemed to be a party to the contract in question (see Chapter 28). Economic loss cases are thus frequently about determining the boundaries between the law of contract and the law of tort.

The following sections examine the limited exceptions under the tort of negligence where the plaintiff may recover for pure economic loss. The first inroad into the courts' traditional reluctance to allow claims for such loss was the case of *Hedley Byrne* v *Heller*.

The Hedley Byrne case
Hedley Byrne & Co. v *Heller and Partners* [1964] AC 465 was the first attempt by the House of Lords to establish a general principle which could be applied to recoverability for economic loss. The claim for economic loss in this case arose from reliance upon a negligent misstatement. Prior to *Hedley Byrne* v *Heller*, a person could be liable for a negligent misstatement or negligent advice only if he owed a contractual duty to the plaintiff, or if there was a fiduciary relationship between the parties, such as that which exists between a solicitor and his client. *Hedley Byrne* v *Heller* established the principle that in certain circumstances liability could be attached for a negligent misstatement, regardless of whether there was a contractual relationship, and that a plaintiff could receive compensation for loss suffered through reliance on that misstatement, even if his loss was purely economic in nature.

The facts of the case were as follows. The plaintiffs were advertising agents, who became concerned as to whether they could safely give credit to one of their customers, Easipower Ltd. Consequently, they asked their bankers to verify Easipower's financial standing. The plaintiffs' bankers wrote to the defendants (who were Easipower's bankers) asking whether they considered Easipower trustworthy to the extent of £100,000 per annum. The defendants replied, in a cautious letter headed 'without responsibility', that Easipower was a 'respectably constituted company, considered good for its ordinary business engagements'. The plaintiffs relied on this statement, and when Easipower later went into liquidation they suffered a loss of nearly £18,000. The plaintiffs sought to recover this loss from the defendants, on the basis that the defendants had been negligent in giving favourable references about Easipower. The House of Lords held that the defendants would ordinarily have been liable for negligent misstatement, but that in this case they could rely on the disclaimer of responsibility which they had very prudently inserted at the beginning of their letter.

Although the plaintiffs' claim thus failed, *Hedley Byrne* v *Heller* was nevertheless an important landmark, as it was the first case to acknowledge the possibility of an action for recovery of pure economic loss arising from reliance upon a negligent misstatement. The difficult issue, however, was to determine when exactly a duty of care would be owed in such circumstances. In addressing this question, their Lordships stressed the difference between negligent words and negligent acts. They held that while the foresight test (i.e., Lord Atkin's 'neighbour' test in *Donoghue* v *Stevenson*), was appropriate for determining a duty of care in respect of negligent acts, it would be going too far to allow recovery for negligent misstatements on the basis of the foresight test alone. Incorrect advice can easily be repeated, leading to numerous possible claims for damages. It was therefore held that a defendant could owe a duty of care in respect of a negligent misstatement only if there was a 'special relationship' between the parties involved. For such a relationship to exist, three things had to be established:

(a)   that the plaintiff relied upon the defendant's skill;

(b)   that the defendant knew or ought reasonably to have known, that the plaintiff was relying upon that skill; and

(c)   that it was reasonable for the plaintiff to rely upon the defendant under those circumstances.

Needless to say *Hedley Byrne* v *Heller* has given rise to many detailed discussions over the years and is still the subject of debate. The next section looks at some of the more significant cases in the last few years which have grappled with the concepts thrown up by that case.

Refinement of the Hedley Byrne principle

In *Caparo Industries plc* v *Dickman* [1990] 1 All ER 568, the House of Lords reconsidered the issue of when a duty of care would be owed for a negligent misstatement and took this opportunity to adopt a very narrow view of the matter. The plaintiffs sought damages from the defendants after making a successful take-over bid for a company whose accounts had been audited by the defendants. The plaintiffs alleged that the accounts had seriously overvalued the company, that they had made their take-over bid in reliance on those accounts, and that they had thereby suffered serious financial loss. The Court of Appeal had held that an auditor did not owe a potential take-over bidder any duty of care, as there was no sufficiently proximate relationship between them. The House of Lords went further. Their Lordships held that an auditor would not ordinarily owe any duty of care either to potential future investors, or even to existing shareholders of the company (as opposed to the company itself). It was held that an auditor would owe such a duty of care only if:

(a) he knows (or must be assumed to know) that his statement will be communicated to the plaintiff, either as an individual or as a member of an identifiable class, specifically in connection with a particular transaction or transactions; and

(b) if he knows that the plaintiff is likely to rely on it for the purpose of deciding whether or not to enter into the transaction.

Lord Oliver said:

The necessary relationship between the maker of a statement or giver of advice (the adviser) and the recipient who acts in reliance on it (the advisee) may typically be held to exist where (1) the advice is required for a purpose, whether particularly specified or generally described, which is made known, either actually or inferentially, to the adviser at the time when the advice is given, (2) the adviser knows, either actually or inferentially, that his advice will be communicated to the advisee, either specifically or as a member of an ascertainable class, in order that it should be used by the advisee for that purpose, (3) it is known, either actually or inferentially, that the advice so communicated is likely to be acted upon by the advisee for that purpose without independent enquiry, and (4) it is so acted on by the advisee to his detriment. That it is not, of course, to suggest that these conditions are either conclusive or exclusive, but merely that the actual decision in the case does not warrant any broader propositions.

It can be seen from the above extract that the emphasis is upon the defendant's knowledge of the specific transaction for which the plaintiff would be very likely to rely upon the defendant's advice. It was also clear from *Caparo* v *Dickman*, that their Lordships were not minded to formulate any test of more general application in order to determine whether a duty of care exists for a negligent misstatement.

More recently, in *Henderson* v *Merrett Syndicates Ltd* [1994] 3 All ER 506, Lord Goff, with whom a majority of the House of Lords concurred, attempted to identify the 'true underlying principle' established in *Hedley Byrne* v *Heller*, namely that a duty of care should be imposed where the defendant, exercising a special skill, 'assumes responsibility' for the plaintiff's economic welfare, or where the relationship between the parties is 'equivalent to contract' and the plaintiff relies upon the defendant to exercise his skill and in so doing suffers damage. Furthermore, he stated that the principle laid down in *Hedley Byrne* v

Heller should not be limited to cases of economic loss arising from negligent misstatements, but should also extend to any such loss arising from negligent acts.

The case arose out of the economic disaster that befell hundreds of Lloyd's names as a result of huge losses suffered by insurance underwriting syndicates of which they were members. The losses were allegedly suffered by these syndicates, in part at least, because of the negligence of the underwriting agents (the defendants) who actually ran the business of the syndicates. They had allegedly exposed the syndicates and their members to unwise, improper and eventually ruinous underwriting risks. Some of those agents had been in a direct contractual relationship with the members, whom they advised and recruited, some had managed the underwriting contracts, and some had done both.

The House of Lords held that both types of agent were potentially liable in tort, on the basis of the *Hedley Byrne* v *Heller* principle. (The question of whether the agents were indeed negligent was not decided at that stage: the point is that they were held to have owed a duty of care to the 'names' who invested in the syndicates.) The test preferred by their lordships in this case appears to be based on an 'assumption of responsibility'. Where economic loss is suffered, either as a result of negligent advice or statements, or as a result of negligent acts, liability will be imposed, at least upon professionals and quasi-professionals who are deemed to have assumed responsibility to the plaintiffs for their actions or advice. The underwriting agents satisfied this test, as it was clear that the 'names' depended on their actions and advice.

Following close on the heels of *Henderson* v *Merrett* came the House of Lords decision in *Spring* v *Guardian Assurance plc* [1994] 3 All ER 129, where Lord Goff once again pushed his new theory of 'assumption of responsibility'. The case concerned a plaintiff who sued his former employers for economic loss allegedly caused to him by a reference they had provided which was so unfavourable (and unfair) that it ruined his chances of securing another job. Lord Goff once again turned to the *Hedley Byrne* v *Heller* principle and concluded that the employers were liable for the loss suffered by the plaintiff, because they had assumed responsibility for the reference and because the plaintiff had relied on them to take reasonable care in so doing. Lord Goff and Lord Woolf, however, also approved of the 'equivalent to contract' test as a basis for *Hedley Byrne* v *Heller* liability.

Thus these two cases give the impression that pure economic loss is not recoverable except under the limited principle of *Hedley Byrne* v *Heller* where the parties are in a relationship almost 'equivalent to contract'. The later case of *White* v *Jones* [1995] 1 All ER 691 seems, however, to have extended this principle somewhat, as in that case the plaintiff and defendant were not in such a relationship. What, then, was the basis of the decision? This is not altogether clear. The defendant, a solicitor, had negligently omitted to re-draft a will when instructed to do so by his client. The discontented beneficiary was the plaintiff, who would have inherited under the will if it had been re-drafted as instructed. As the contract to draw up the will was between the solicitor and the testator (the person who made the will), the plaintiff could not hope to obtain a remedy in contract. She was not a party to any such contract (see Chapter 28). The plaintiff was therefore forced to pursue an action in tort. By a majority of three to two, their Lordships found in favour of the plaintiff. Lord Goff and Lord Browne-Wilkinson each conceded that the beneficiary was a foreseeable victim of the defendant's negligence and that it would therefore be fair to extend the solicitor's liability to that beneficiary; but the ways in which they found in favour of the plaintiff differed. Lord Browne-Wilkinson stated that it was of crucial importance to establish a sufficient degree of proximity between the parties, or a special relationship between them, before a duty of care could be imposed. The defendant solicitor was liable on that basis because he had assumed a responsibility for re-drafting the will. Lord Goff, on the other hand, seemed to be heavily influenced by the consideration that, if liability for negligence was rejected, a beneficiary thus denied her rightful share of the deceased's estate would have no recourse against the negligent solicitor.

Concurrent jurisdiction of tort and contract

Lord Goff also made it clear in *Henderson* v *Merrett* that where concurrent liability in tort and contract arose, the plaintiff could choose which course of action was the more advantageous to him. Thus just because the plaintiff could have brought an action in contract does not preclude him from pursuing a remedy in tort. The only circumstances where concurrent liability would not be permissible is where it would allow the plaintiff to avoid a contractual limitation of liability for the tortious act or omission.

Economic loss resulting from negligent acts

Recovery of damages for economic loss under this head remains rare. A common situation in which such claims might arise is where the plaintiff acquires property, only to discover that it is defective and that money has to be spent in order to replace or remedy it. If the plaintiff acquired such property from the defendant, the obvious basis of any claim would be in contract but, if the action has to be brought in tort (as where there was no contractual relationship between the parties), there may be difficulties. Money spent on property in either of the above ways is pure economic loss.

Many of the cases dealing with the recoverability of pure economic loss in tort have arisen out of claims in respect of defective buildings. One of the earliest cases in this area was that of *Dutton* v *Bognor Regis Urban District Council* [1972] 1 QB 373, in which the Court of Appeal held that a local authority was liable to the purchaser of a building in respect of the previous negligent inspection by their surveyor of the foundations when it was under construction. The foundations proved to be defective, and this led to damage to the building for which the local authority was required to pay compensation. This decision was later approved by the House of Lords in *Anns* v *Merton London Borough Council* [1978] AC 728. The facts were very similar to those of *Dutton* v *Bognor Regis UDC*, and their Lordships stated that a local authority owed a duty of care to the purchaser or later owner of a building, and would therefore be liable to him if its inspectors had been negligent and had failed to spot a defect creating a 'present or imminent danger' to the health or safety of the occupants of the building.

In *Dutton* v *Bognor Regis UDC*, Lord Denning MR held that the plaintiff's loss was physical rather than economic. Lord Wilberforce in *Anns* v *Merton LBC* said that the damage was 'material, physical damage' and that the plaintiff could therefore recover the cost of restoring the house to a condition in which it was no longer a danger to health or safety. But were the judges in these cases correct in treating the plaintiffs' claims as claims for physical damage? The reality of these situations was surely different. The plaintiffs were not claiming that the surveyors had damaged the buildings (not, at least, while the plaintiffs were the owners of them), or that the defective buildings had caused injury or damaged some other property. They were merely claiming that the property they had acquired was already defective. A claim for damages to remedy it should surely have been categorised as a claim for economic loss.

Later cases acknowledged this error, but nevertheless extended the principles laid down in *Anns* v *Merton LBC*. In *Junior Books* v *Veitchi Co. Ltd* [1983] 1 AC 520, the House of Lords held that damages could be recoverable for pure economic loss suffered as a result of the defendants' negligent conduct. The defendants were engaged as sub-contractors under a building contract between the plaintiffs and the main building contractors. They were hired to lay flooring in commercial premises. The plaintiffs claimed that the floor was defective and sued the defendants in tort for the cost of replacing it and for consequential financial loss. Normally the plaintiffs in such a case would have sued the main contractors for breach of contract, and the main contractors would then have sued the sub-contractors, again for breach of contract. The plaintiffs apparently resorted to a claim in tort because the main contractors had gone bankrupt and were no longer worth suing.

The House of Lords held that the defendants owed the plaintiffs a duty of care as the proximity of their relationship was 'almost as close a commercial relationship as it is possible to envisage short of privity of contract'. As a result, the plaintiffs were able to recover the cost of relaying the defective floor and their loss of profits while the building was closed for the work to be done.

The decision was not without practical difficulties. The possible implications were enormous. Would this mean that a manufacturer of a defective product could be made tortiously liable to the ultimate consumer of it for defects of quality of the product itself, even where no question of consequential damage or injury was involved? There may be good policy reasons for making manufacturers liable to consumers (as in *Donoghue* v *Stevenson*, see

Chapter 36) for damage or injury caused by defective products, but imposing tortious liability for products that simply fail to come up to standard is another matter.

The view taken by many commentators on *Junior Books* v *Veitchi* was that it was a 'one-off' case: one which turned on the existence of a special, near-contractual relationship between the parties. This alone enabled the court to reach the decision which it did. This was a case on the tort/contract boundary. Significantly, *Junior Books* v *Veitchi* has never been applied in subsequent cases, but has either been distinguished or ignored. The decision, however, has never been overruled, and the decisions in *Henderson*, *Spring* and *White* (above), suggest that it may now be explained as coming within the *Hedley Byrne* v *Heller* principle, i.e., where the relationship between the parties can be said to be equivalent to contract.

The leading case after *Junior Books* v *Veitchi* was *Murphy* v *Brentwood District Council* [1990] 2 All ER 908. In 1970, the plaintiff purchased a newly built house from a construction company. The house had been built on an in-filled site. A concrete raft foundation had been used to prevent damage from settlement. The plans had been approved by Brentwood District Council after advice from an independent consultant engineer. From the early 1980s, serious cracks appeared in the internal walls of the plaintiff's house, due to the distortion of the raft foundation which was defective. The plaintiff brought a negligence action against the council, which had approved the plans. He alleged that his family had suffered an imminent risk to their health and safety because of gas pipes which had broken and that there were further risks of breaks. The plaintiff naturally relied upon the *Anns* case, but the House of Lords overruled their previous decision. They held that the plaintiff could not recover, because if a dangerous defect in property is discovered *before* it causes personal injury or damage to property then the claimant is merely alleging that the property is defective in quality. That is a claim for pure economic loss, and is not therefore recoverable in tort. Lord Bridge also held that a manufacturer's liability in respect of products which are merely defective in quality arises *only* in contract. There was no liability, he continued, in tort to persons who merely suffer economic loss because of a quality defect. His Lordship gave the following example:

> If I buy a secondhand car and find it to be faulty, it can make no difference to the manufacturer's liability in tort whether the fault is in the brakes or in the engine, i.e., whether the car will not stop or will not start. In either case the car is useless until repaired. The manufacturer is no more liable in tort for the cost of repairs in the one case than in the other.

Therefore, in brief, the effect of the *Murphy* case was that economic loss arising from a defective product was generally not be recoverable in tort actions, and it was irrelevant whether the defect rendered the product dangerously defective or merely defective in quality. The defendant would become liable only if he was in breach of contract with the plaintiff, or if the defective product actually caused physical injury to another person or property.

Basic principles for claims for nervous shock

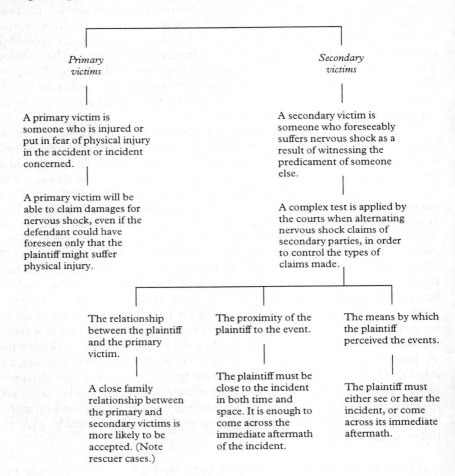

Primary victims

A primary victim is someone who is injured or put in fear of physical injury in the accident or incident concerned.

A primary victim will be able to claim damages for nervous shock, even if the defendant could have foreseen only that the plaintiff might suffer physical injury.

Secondary victims

A secondary victim is someone who foreseeably suffers nervous shock as a result of witnessing the predicament of someone else.

A complex test is applied by the courts when alternating nervous shock claims of secondary parties, in order to control the types of claims made.

The relationship between the plaintiff and the primary victim.

A close family relationship between the primary and secondary victims is more likely to be accepted. (Note rescuer cases.)

The proximity of the plaintiff to the event.

The plaintiff must be close to the incident in both time and space. It is enough to come across the immediate aftermath of the incident.

The means by which the plaintiff perceived the events.

The plaintiff must either see or hear the incident, or come across its immediate aftermath.

Recovery for economic loss under the tort of negligence

The courts are generally willing to compensate for economic loss which is directly and intentionally caused (e.g., tort of deceit), but are less willing to award damages for economic loss caused by negligence unless it is consequential to physical injury:

When will damages be awarded for pure economic loss suffered as a result of the defendant's negligence?

Compensation for economic loss may be recovered under what may be referred to as the *Hedley Byrne* v *Heller* principle'.

The case of *Henderson* v *Merrett* involves an attempt to identify the true principle laid down in *Hedley Byrne* v *Heller*. Lord Goff said liability under the *Hedley Byrne* v *Heller* exception was based upon the principle of assumption of responsibility, or equivalent to contract.

This approach was used again in *Spring* v *Guardian Assurance plc*; and *White* v *Jones* seems to have extended the principle further, although the reasoning in the latter case is far from clear.

THIRTY EIGHT

Liability for Defective Products

Introduction

A company or individual manufacturing, producing, importing or selling defective goods or products may incur liability under a number of possible heads, particularly where the defect in question causes damage to other goods or property and/or injury to the buyer or to other persons. One must distinguish in particular between contractually based liability, which is subject to the principles of privity of contract, and liability under the law of tort or under the Consumer Protection Act 1987, each of which can exist independently of any contractual relationships. If A purchases a used car from B, a dealer, and finds that it will not start in the mornings, he may be able to sue B under the Sale of Goods Act 1979 (Chapter 35) for breach of the statutorily implied contractual terms as to quality and fitness for purpose, but only A can sue on that basis, and he can only sue B, with whom his contract was made. In contrast, a car which crashes or bursts into flames because of design or manufacturing faults, causing death or injury to its occupants or other road users, may also give rise to tortious liability or to liability under the 1987 Act, and anyone thus injured may have a cause of action, even if they are not parties to any relevant contract. The damages involved may be very substantial, and manufacturers, importers and suppliers may all face potential liability in such circumstances.

This has not always been the case. Prior to the landmark ruling of the House of Lords in *Donoghue* v *Stevenson* [1932] AC 562 (see Chapter 36), the general rule had been that a supplier of a defective product could only be liable for injury to or damage suffered by the person to whom he had sold it, as if such liability depended on privity of contract. It was held in that case and in cases following it that a producer of goods owes a duty of care to the ultimate consumer or indeed to anyone else who might foreseeably be harmed by any defects in those goods. Liability in tort for defective products was at last seen as being wholly independent of contractual relationships.

The burden of proving negligence falls upon the plaintiff and may be far from easy to discharge. Consequently, legislation (in the form of the Consumer Protection Act 1987) was eventually introduced to impose strict liability (i.e., liability without proof of fault) on the producers and importers of defective products which cause injury.

Contractual liability

A purchaser of goods is given the protection of any express terms contained within his contract with the supplier, and also of the terms implied under the Sale of Goods Act 1979 (as amended by the Sale of Goods and Supply of Services Act 1994). Section 14 of the 1979 Act provides that goods sold in the course of a business must be of satisfactory quality and fit for their purpose. The plaintiff may thus recover damages for defects in quality in the goods (which may or may not be dangerous) under the law of contract. If no damage has been caused, he may be satisfied with returning the goods and getting his money back.

Claims for defects in quality are classed as claims for economic loss and are not recoverable under the law of tort (see Chapter 37). It is therefore important to use contract, not tort, as the basis of any claim of this kind. On the other hand, the purchaser of the goods alone may sue if the product is defective in quality and, in the absence of a producer's warranty, his only contractual remedy will be against his immediate supplier. The supplier's liability is strict in the sense that it does not have to be shown that the defect was foreseeable or that it was in any way his fault. He may be liable not only for the loss arising under the contract itself, but also for any consequential loss caused by the defective product, such as personal injury to the purchaser himself.

The retailer will normally have a contractual claim for indemnity against his own supplier (wholesaler, distributor, etc.) and this chain may continue up to the producer or manufacturer. The prudent retailer will in any case be insured against the risk of such claims being made against him.

Common law liability in tort

In *Donoghue* v *Stevenson*, it was held that a manufacturer of goods owes a duty of care under the tort of negligence to the ultimate consumer of the product, regardless of whether there was any contractual relationship between the parties. In that case, the plaintiff's friend bought her a bottle of Stevenson's ginger beer, which turned out to have been contaminated with the decomposed remains of a snail. The opaque glass concealed the presence of the snail, which must have crawled into the bottle before it was filled. The plaintiff drank some of the ginger beer (mixed with ice cream) before discovering the snail's remains. Afterwards, she fell ill, and sued the defendant, alleging negligence. In the House of Lords, Lord Atkin stated that the manufacturer of a product owes a duty of care to the ultimate consumer of his product, regardless of contractual relationships. He stated the duty in the following terms:

> A manufacturer of products which he sells in such a form as to show that he intends them to reach the ultimate consumer in the form in which they left him, with no reasonable possibility of intermediate examination, and with the knowledge that the absence of reasonable care in the preparation or putting up of the products will result in injury to the consumer's life or property, owes a duty to the consumer to take that reasonable care.

Although there is no reference here to the duties of intermediate suppliers or to the rights of injured bystanders, we shall see that some of the wider dicta in that case anticipated and encouraged the extension of tortious liability in those particular directions. Thus, in *Stennet* v *Hancock* [1939] 2 All ER 578, it was held that a bystander could sue a repairer under the *Donoghue* v *Stevenson* principle when struck by a wheel flange which had come loose from a passing lorry which the latter had negligently repaired; and in *Watson* v *Buckley* [1940] 1 All ER 174, a distributor of hair dye which proved harmful was successfully sued by a consumer who had been injured by that dye. It must be stressed, however, that such liability is not strict or automatic, but depends upon proof of negligence. In *Watson* v *Buckley* for example, the distributors of the hair dye had not dealt previously with the manufacturer (described by the judge as 'a gentleman who had emerged unexpectedly from Spain') nor had they tested the product themselves.

Proving liability in negligence
The plaintiff in a negligence action may face a considerable burden in trying to establish that the manufacturer or distributor has actually breached his duty of care. If suing the manufacturer or producer, he will have to prove that the defect was not caused by subsequent mishandling or misuse. In some cases it may appear obvious that the producer has breached his duty of care, because the facts will appear to speak for themselves, as for example where a broken razor blade is found in a cake or a dead mouse is found in a tin of baked beans. As Lord Wright said in *Grant* v *Australian Knitting Mills Ltd* [1936] AC 85 (a case in which the plaintiff had suffered dermatitis after wearing woollen underpants contaminated by sulphites):

> The danger of excess sulphites being left was recognised and was guarded against. If excess sulphites were left in the garment, that could only be

because someone was at fault. The [plaintiff] is not required to lay his hand on the exact person in all the chain who was responsible, or to specify what he did wrong. Negligence is found as a matter of inference from the existence of the defects in connection with all the known circumstances ...

See also *Carroll* v *Fearon*, *The Times*, 26 January 1998.

In other cases, however, proof of negligence will be more difficult, because there may be factors which make it difficult to establish whether the defendant could have known of or foreseen the defect, or indeed whether the defect existed at the time that the product left the manufacturer. Proof of causation, in other words, may also be a problem. An example can be seen in *Evans* v *Triplex Glass Co. Ltd* [1936] 1 All ER 283. The plaintiff bought a car fitted with a safety windscreen which had been manufactured by the defendants. One year later, for no apparent reason, the windscreen shattered, injuring the occupants of the car. The manufacturers were found not to be liable, as there was no evidence to prove that the windscreen had been badly designed or manufactured, or indeed that it was a defect in the windscreen which caused the accident. The accident could equally have been caused by incorrect fitting of the windscreen to the car. Furthermore, any defect in the windscreen as first manufactured should have been spotted by the persons who fitted it to the car. As Lord Atkin had conceded in *Donoghue* v *Stevenson*, where a defect was so obvious that any retailer or consumer could reasonably have been expected to discover it, then the manufacturer could not be held liable in negligence for any subsequent accident.

Type of loss
Recoverability of damages under the tort of negligence for liability arising from defective products applies to physical injuries to the person and physical damage to property, *other than to the product itself* (which can only be recovered in an action based on contract). It can, however, be difficult to distinguish between 'the product' and 'other property'. An illustration of this difficulty can be seen in *Aswan Engineering Company* v *Lupdine Ltd* [1987] 1 All ER 135. The plaintiffs purchased waterproofing compound from the first defendants. This was contained in plastic pails which were supplied by the second defendants. The compound was shipped to Kuwait, where the pails were left for several hours stacked on the quayside in blazing sunshine. The pails softened and collapsed in the intense heat, spilling their contents. One of the arguments put forward by the plaintiffs was that the pails were defective and had caused the loss of their contents, which they alleged constituted 'other property'. The Court of Appeal tended to agree with this argument, although they did not need to decide the point, because the action failed on the ground that the mishap had not been reasonably foreseeable.

The Consumer Protection Act 1987

The greatest difficulty facing a plaintiff injured by a defective product is usually that of proving negligence. This was brought home vividly in the long-drawn-out litigation following the 'Thalidomide' tragedy of the 1960s, in which hundreds of babies were born with deformed limbs as a result of an unknown side effect in a drug which had been widely prescribed for use by pregnant women. It was possible to prove the causal connection between the drug and the birth defects, but proof of liability depended on proof of negligence, which was difficult and this delayed the eventual settlement of the claims by many years.

Both the Law Commission and the Pearson Commission Report of 1978 recommended the introduction of strict liability for defective products. The most powerful stimulus for reform, however, came from the European Community Directive on Liability for Defective Products 1985. This required all member states to implement strict liability for defective products, and was put into effect within the United Kingdom by the Consumer Protection Act 1987. This came into force in March 1988 and applies to damage caused by products put into circulation after that date. Liability under the Act is subject to certain defences, and is thus strict, but not absolute.

The Consumer Protection Act 1987 (CPA) supplements, but has not replaced, the possible causes of action which existed at common law. Consequently, in cases where the Act itself does not apply, a plaintiff may sometimes be able to succeed in a claim based on negligence or on breach of contract.

Who can bring an action under the Act?
Section 2(1) of the CPA 1987 provides that:

> Subject to the following provisions of this Part [of the Act], where any damage is caused wholly or partly by a defect in a product, every person to whom subsection (2) below applies shall be liable for the damage.

There is no need to prove that the defendant was negligent or that it was foreseeable that the plaintiff would be affected by the product. It only has to be shown that the product was defective and that the defect caused damage to the plaintiff. Once these facts are established the burden will pass to the defendant to establish that he comes within the defences under the Act if he is to escape liability.

Who can be liable?
Section 2(2) provides that the following may be made liable to the provisions of the Act: first, the producer of the product; secondly, anyone who holds himself out as the producer; and thirdly, anyone who has imported the product

into any part of the European Community. The supplier of the goods can also be held liable under s. 2(3) if he fails or refuses to identify any of the above to the plaintiff when required to do so.

A producer for these purposes is defined in s. 1 as the manufacturer or (in the case of a product which is not manufactured) the person who won, abstracted or processed it. Agricultural products (processed by canning, packaging, freezing, etc.) are covered by the Act in this way. The manufacturer of an individual component may be jointly liable with the manufacturer of the final product if the damage caused by the finished product is due to a defect in that component.

Section 2(2)(b) extends liability to a person who holds himself out as a producer of the product by putting his name on the product or using a trade mark or other distinguishing mark in relation to the product. This may be done, for example, by placing an 'own brand name' on a product made by someone else, a common practice with large retail chains, whose own-branded goods are produced for them by a wide range of different suppliers.

Section (2)(c) provides that an importer of a product will be liable if he imported it from a place outside the European Community into a member state in the course of any business of his, to supply it to another. If a product is imported from outside the Community and then re-exported to another community country, only the original importer can be liable under this subsection.

What are 'products'?
The term 'product' includes goods or electricity and also includes products which are comprised in other products, whether as component parts or as raw material (s. 1(2)). Section 45 explains what is meant by the term 'goods' and includes 'substances, growing crops and things comprised in land by virtue of being attached to it, and any ship, aircraft or vehicle'. Section 46(3), however, specifically excludes buildings from this definition. Furthermore, the Act does not extend to agricultural produce or game unless it has undergone some industrial process. The Act does not explain what is meant by the phrase 'industrial process', but it must at least include canning or freezing produce for subsequent sale.

The plaintiff must show that the product was defective
In order to bring a successful claim under the Act, the plaintiff must establish that it was the defect in the product which caused the damage. Section 3(1) states that a product has a defect 'if the safety of the product is not such as persons generally are entitled to expect'. This involves questions of fact and will obviously depend upon all the circumstances of the case.

Section 3(2) states that all the circumstances must be taken into account when deciding what persons are generally entitled to expect, including the way in which the product has been marketed and any warnings or instructions.

Misuse of the product by the consumer may absolve the producer, etc., from liability. A product will not, however, be deemed to be defective merely because later versions of it have been improved so as to make them safer.

What is meant by 'damage' for the purposes of the Act?
The plaintiff must prove that he has suffered damage as a result of the defective product. Damage is defined in s. 5(1) as including 'death or personal injury or any loss of, or damage to any property (including land)'. Personal injury is defined in s. 45(1) so as to include 'any disease and any other impairment of a person's physical or mental condition'. As far as recovery for damage to property is concerned, the Act imposes a number of limitations upon its recovery (see below).

Limitations upon recovery of property damage under the Act
The Act does not allow recovery for pure economic loss and recovery for the following is excluded: (1) for damage to the product itself; (2) for damage to commercial property; and (3) claims for damage to property are limited to claims over £275.

Loss of, or damage to, the defective product itself is excluded by s. 5(2) of the Act, as is loss of or damage to a product 'which has been supplied with the product in question comprised in it'. Consequently, if a defective valve on a new washing machine fails, causing damage to the rest of the machine, this damage will not be recoverable under the Act. Damages may, however, be recoverable in contract or tort. The manufacturer of the defective part (and the manufacturer of the machine, if different) would, however, be liable under the Act for any personal injuries caused to the user of the machine or for any damage caused to other property, such as clothing ruined in the wash.

By virtue of s. 5(3), property claims are restricted to damage to property which is 'ordinarily intended for private use, occupation or consumption and intended by the person suffering the loss or damage mainly for his own private use or consumption'. Property used for business purposes is thus excluded from the ambit of the Act.

A further restriction upon recoverability for property damage is found in s. 5(4), which excludes claims for property damage under £275 from the ambit of the Act. The purpose of such a provision is to eliminate trivial claims. No such limitation is applied to claims relating to personal injury, or indeed to actions for breach of contract or under the tort of negligence at common law.

Defences
If the plaintiff establishes that a defective product produced or imported by the defendant has caused him loss or damage, the latter may still escape liability in certain circumstances. Liability under the Act cannot be avoided by use of exclusion clauses, but there are a number of defences available under s. 4 of the Act if the defendant can prove that they apply on the facts of the case. In

particular, it is a defence for a manufacturer, importer or producer to prove that the defect did not exist in the product when he supplied it. A producer should not, for example, be liable for mishandling by an intermediate supplier, if this causes the product to deteriorate. Note, however, that the burden of proof is on the defendant, and not, as in tort cases, on the plaintiff. A latent defect which only comes to light after some months of use may still be a defect which existed at the time of production, for which the producer may be liable. Certain products may be expected to withstand repeated use for years. If such a product fails after a few weeks then it may well be considered defective.

One of the more controversial defences under the CPA 1987 is the 'development risk' defence. Section 4(1)(e) states that it is a defence to establish that:

> the state of scientific and technical knowledge at the relevant time was not such that a producer of products of the same description as the product in question might be expected to have discovered the defect if it had existed in his products while they were under his control.

The effect of such a defence is that a producer or manufacturer can escape liability if the defect was unknown and unforeseeable when the product was in circulation. Neither the Law Commission nor the Pearson Commission recommended that such a defence should be made available, but a balance must be struck somewhere between the interests of the consumer and those of producers. Hindsight is a priceless commodity, but it may be very expensive for producers of new products to guard against largely unforeseeable risks.

There are various other defences, but they cannot all be considered here. Contributory negligence by the plaintiff may offer a partial defence, as in tort cases at common law.

Defective products

Contract	Negligence	CPA 1987

Contract

SGA 1979 (as amended), implies terms relating to quality into contracts for the sale of goods.

↓

Under s. 13 goods sold must correspond with their description. Under s. 14(2) they must be of satisfactory quality. Under s. 14(3) they must be fit for their purpose.

↓

The seller is strictly liable.

↓

The seller may also be made liable for any consequential loss caused by the defective product.

↓

Due to the doctrine of privity of contract, only the purchaser of the defective item may sue the seller of the product.

↓

Although the seller's liability to the purchaser is strict, he may nevertheless have a contractual remedy for indemnity against his own supplier.

Negligence

Donoghue v *Stevenson* established that a manufacturer could be liable to the ultimate consumer of negligently made products

↓

Claims for pure economic loss are generally not recoverable under the tort of negligence. Thus claims to remedy defective goods must be brought under the law of contract.

↓

In order to bring a successful claim for negligence, the plaintiff must establish three things:
  (i)   that the defendant owed him a duty of care;
  (ii)   breach of that duty; and
  (iii) that the damage suffered was not too remote.

↓

It can be difficult to establish a case of negligence against the defendant.

↓

This led to calls for no fault liability against producers of goods.

CPA 1987

Basically, the Act provides that any person who suffers damage which is caused by a defective product is entitled to sue the producer and certain others, without having to prove fault.

↓

The plaintiff must establish that he suffered damage as a result of the defective product. Damage includes death or personal injury, or any loss of or damage to any property.

↓

There are, however, limits to recoverability for property damage:
  (i)   claims are limited to claims over £275.
  (ii)   the Act does not allow recovery for pure economic loss;
  (iii) the Act does not allow recovery for damage to commercial property.

↓

Once the plaintiff has established that it was the defect which caused the damage, then the burden of proof passes to the defendant. There are a number of defences available to the defendant under s. 4 of the Act.

THIRTY NINE
Trespass

'Trespass' is usually thought of as meaning unauthorised entry or presence on another person's property. To the lawyer, however, it has a rather wider meaning. It may involve a wrongful interference with another person's land, goods or person. Entering another person's property without authority is just one kind of trespass.

Trespass to land

This involves unauthorised interference with another person's possession of land or premises. Trespass to land is one of the oldest common law actions and is actionable *per se*, which means that an action can be brought by the plaintiff even though he has suffered no real loss or harm. It is enough if the plaintiff establishes that the defendant has directly interfered with the plaintiff's possession of land. It may appear strange that a person should wish to pursue an action for trespass when he has suffered no harm, but there are a few circumstances in which this course of action would be followed. For example, one might sue for trespass as a means of protecting one's privacy or civil liberties. Under English law, an individual has no legal right to privacy. Consequently, if a newspaper reporter trespasses onto a film star's private property in order to acquire a picture, the star cannot obtain a remedy for breach of privacy, but may sue for trespass to land, either to obtain some kind of compensation, or to seek an injunction against further behaviour of that kind by the photographer or his paper. In such a case, any damages awarded for trespass may be only nominal, but the star may still feel the point is worth making.

Types of trespass
The most usual form of trespass involves entering onto the plaintiff's land; but trespass can take many different forms, such as placing unwanted objects on the

plaintiff's land. It can be committed only if the defendant's actions in entering onto, or otherwise interfering with, the plaintiff's land were voluntary. An involuntary act, as where the defendant is pushed onto the plaintiff's land, or crashes onto it when a tyre bursts on his car, is not actionable as a trespass.

Airspace and subsoil

A landowner's right in possession of his land extends both below the surface of the land and to the airspace above it. Consequently, either tunnelling or invasion of airspace may constitute a trespass, although rights of action in this context are limited. A person's rights to airspace are restricted to 'such height as is necessary for the ordinary use and enjoyment of his land and structures on it'. It would not, therefore, be a trespass for an aircraft to fly at a reasonable height above the land, so long as it did not interfere with a person's use or enjoyment of the land. The Civil Aviation Act 1982, s. 76(1), provides that:

> no action shall lie in respect of a trespass or nuisance by reason only of the flight of an aircraft over any property at a height which is reasonable having regard to the wind, weather and all the circumstances of the case.

In contrast, an invasion of airspace was held to constitute a trespass in *Kelsen* v *Imperial Tobacco Co. Ltd* [1957] 2 QB 334, where the defendants had erected an advertising sign which projected over the plaintiff's property. They were ordered by the court to remove it.

Highways

Highways were defined in *Lang* v *Hindhaugh* [1986] RTR 271 as:

> anywhere where the public has the right to pass and repass, whether on foot or with vehicles or animals, as the case may be . . . footpaths may be highways if the public has the right to use them for that purpose.

A waterway may also be a highway. A person has the right to pass and repass along the highway and to use the highway for purposes reasonably incidental to passage along it, even where the highway crosses private land (as many do). Stopping to look in a shop window or admire scenery from a public footpath would constitute a reasonable use of the highway. Processions along the highway will not usually constitute a trespass because the persons involved are simply exercising their right of passage. On the other hand, a static demonstration may be deemed a trespass.

Unlawfulness

There can be no action for trespass if the defendant can establish that his presence on the land was lawful. The following are examples of circumstances in which presence upon another's land may be lawful:

(a) *Licence* A licence involves permission being given for a person to be on the land, without which the presence would have been unlawful. The granting of a licence does not give a person a legal right in the land itself, but merely permission to be there to the extent permitted by the licence itself. A licence may, however, be revoked at any time; and if a person exceeds the authority of the licence, his presence will cease to be lawful and he will become a trespasser, but must then be allowed a reasonable amount of time to leave the land before any action may be taken against him.

(b) *Rights of entry* Rights of entry onto premises may be conferred either by common law or by statute. For example, police and other public officials have certain statutory powers of entry and there is a common law power of entry in order to 'abate a nuisance'. Rights of entry may also be justified in the exercise of an easement such as a private right of way. Where, for example, two or more houses stand close together, it is quite common for the occupiers of one to have rights of way over some part of the neighbouring land, and they may also have the right to run (and if necessary maintain) drainage pipes or cables under the soil of the other property.

Who can sue for the tort of trespass to land?

The only person who can sue for a trespass to land is the person who has possession of the land. Ownership of land without possession is insufficient. A landlord cannot sue for trespass to land while a lease is in force. This is because the tort of trespass to land is concerned with wrongs relating to *possession* of the land and not to ownership.

Remedies for trespass to land

A plaintiff may seek either damages and/or an injunction in an action for trespass to land. If the trespass was trivial, it is likely that the plaintiff will be awarded only nominal damages and an injunction may well be denied (although the plaintiff will usually be awarded an injunction to prevent a continuing trespass).

Where a person has been unlawfully dispossessed of his land, he may of course bring an action to recover it. Compensation may also be recovered for any losses suffered during the period that that person was dispossessed. A person who has been dispossessed of his land may also pursue a self-help remedy known as re-entry. He may in *some* circumstances use reasonable force in order to effect this, notably where he is (or acts on behalf of) a 'displaced residential occupier' who finds that squatters have taken over the house during the occupier's absence. In some other cases, the use of force to repossess land may itself amount to a crime (Criminal Law Act 1977).

Trespass and nuisance

The actions of trespass to land and private nuisance both have the common aim of protecting the use and enjoyment of land. Trespass is concerned with direct invasions onto land, whereas nuisance is concerned with indirect invasions such as smells, smoke, or diseases which drift onto the plaintiff's land. The law of private nuisance is designed to protect against 'injury to amenity'. It must be distinguished from a 'public nuisance' which must affect the comfort of a whole section of society. The main difference between trespass to land and private nuisance is that an actionable nuisance requires proof of damage, whereas a trespass does not. The tort of nuisance is examined in Chapter 40.

Trespass to the person

Trespass to the person consists of three separate and independent torts, namely, assault, battery, and false imprisonment. In proportion to the overall number of assaults and batteries, the number of victims who seek compensation under the law of tort is relatively small. One reason for this is that victims of these torts (which are also crimes) may more easily (and at no cost to themselves) obtain compensation orders from their assailants in the criminal courts (see Chapter 14).

Distinctive features of the tort of trespass to the person are:

(a)   that it is actionable *per se* (without proof of actual damage or injury) and
(b)   that the trespass must be a direct result of the defendant's act.

Consequently, if X were to throw a stone at Y, that might constitute a trespass to the person, but if X were simply to leave a wire deliberately in the middle of the pavement for Y to trip over, that would not be a trespass because Y's fall would be the result of an indirect act. In those circumstances the injured party's only hope would be to sue the defendant under the tort of negligence.

An assault

An assault is an act which causes another person to apprehend the direct infliction of immediate, unlawful force on his person. As to the meaning of these terms (which have the same meaning in both tort cases and criminal cases) see the discussion in Chapter 14. As in criminal cases, words alone must now be considered capable of amounting to an assault, and when combined with actions may well be relevant in deciding whether an assault was intended. This again is discussed in Chapter 14.

A battery

As in criminal cases, a battery requires a direct infliction of unlawful force upon another, but this is not limited to direct personal contact. For example, setting one's dog on another person may constitute a battery. A battery can only take place, however, where the defendant has done some form of positive act so that a form of passive obstruction could not be a battery. As with criminal cases, some physical contact may simply be an unavoidable part of living in a crowded society and may not then be actionable. Once again, see Chapter 14 for further discussion.

(a)   State of mind of the defendant   In *Fowler* v *Lanning* [1959] 1 QB 426 it was held that a battery requires the defendant 'intentionally and directly [to] apply unlawful force to the plaintiff'. It is not therefore enough for the plaintiff merely to allege or prove that the defendant hit or shot him. This requirement was reaffirmed in the later case of *Letang* v *Cooper* [1965] 1 QB 232. But what is meant by intent? Clearly, if it is the defendant's *purpose* to inflict harm on the plaintiff then he has the requisite intent. Furthermore, if direct contact was virtually a certain consequence of the defendant's actions, even though the defendant may not have desired such contact, that also may be classed as intent. Recklessness will also suffice, but it is doubtful whether negligence can be enough, even though authority on this point is divided. (See *Letang* v *Cooper* above and *Wilson* v *Pringle* [1986] 2 All ER 44.)

As in criminal cases, it is not necessary to establish that the defendant intended the harmful consequences which flowed from his battery. For example, D may have intended to strike P, but not to injure him; but if D causes injury, he will be liable for it (cf. *Savage* [1991] 4 All ER 698, which is discussed in Chapter 14).

(b)   Must the contact be hostile?   *Wilson* v *Pringle* (above) suggests that contact must be hostile in order to constitute a battery. In this case a schoolboy was carrying a bag over his shoulder when another schoolboy pulled at the bag, causing the first boy to fall and suffer an injury to his hip. The defendant admitted that he had pulled the bag off the plaintiff's shoulder, but that this had merely been horseplay. The Court of Appeal held that such horseplay, if that is what it was, would not automatically amount to a battery. Later cases have, however, cast doubt upon the requirement of hostility. In *Re F* [1990] 2 AC, Lord Goff stated that:

> the suggested qualification (i.e., hostility) is difficult to reconcile with the principle that any touching of another's body, is in the absence of lawful excuse, capable of amounting to a battery and a trespass.

On that basis, the horseplay in *Wilson* v *Pringle* must clearly have amounted to a battery.

False imprisonment

False imprisonment is another form of trespass to the person, and involves 'the unlawful imposition of constraint on another's freedom of movement from a particular place'. It does not require incarceration, or even the use of force; it may simply involve an unlawful, temporary restraint. A person may be falsely imprisoned in the street if his freedom of movement is unlawfully restrained. The circumstances in which a modern action for false imprisonment will usually arise are where the police carry out an unlawful arrest, or where a store detective carries out an unlawful arrest. (See *Collins* v *Wilcock* [1984] 3 All ER 374.)

Although false imprisonment may occasionally take place without the use of force, it will almost always be accompanied by a battery, such as a hand on the shoulder to suggest that a person's movement is restrained. The restraint of movement must, however, be complete. Thus if the plaintiff can leave, albeit not by the route of his choice, there will be no false imprisonment. In *Bird* v *Jones* (1845) 7 QB 742, the plaintiff demanded to use a section of the highway which had been cordoned off, and was prevented from doing so by the defendant. The plaintiff was told that he could go back the way that he had just come but could not proceed in the direction he was going. It was held that this did not amount to false imprisonment, because it was not a total restraint on the plaintiff's liberty. As Coleridge J stated:

> If, in the course of a night, both ends of a street were walled up, and there were no egress from the house but into the street, I should have no difficulty in saying that the inhabitants were thereby imprisoned, but if only one end were walled up, and an armed force stationed outside to prevent any scaling of the wall or passage that way, I should feel equally clear that there was no imprisonment. If there were, the street would obviously be a prison; and yet, as obviously, none would be confined to it.

It is permissible for any person to use reasonable force to prevent a crime, or to effect or assist in the lawful arrest of an offender or of an escaped prisoner (the Criminal Law Act 1967, s. 3, provides a defence to tort actions for assault or false imprisonment, as well as a defence to charges of criminal assault). In *Sunbolf* v *Alford* (1838) 3 M & W 248, however, an innkeeper was held liable for false imprisonment after locking up a customer for refusing to pay his bill. It does not seem that the customer was guilty of any crime. It was a civil dispute, and the innkeeper's only lawful remedy was a civil action against the customer. If a customer dishonestly tries to make off without paying for a meal, the position is different, because s. 3 of the Theft Act 1978 permits the arrest of such a person.

Trespass to goods

The law relating to trespass to goods is extremely technical and this section will deal with it only in outline. Trespass to goods involves a wrongful interference with them and can include things such as scratching the paint on a car or killing livestock, etc. Again this tort is actionable *per se*, without proof of actual damage. Before a person can bring an action for trespass to goods it must generally be shown that he was in possession of the goods at the time of the trespass (although there are limited exceptions to this rule). See generally the Torts (Interference with Goods) Act 1977.

Conversion

The tort of conversion may be committed by:

> ... wrongly taking possession of goods, by wrongfully disposing of them, by wrongfully damaging or destroying them or simply by wrongfully refusing to give them up when demanded, for in all these cases can be traced conduct by the defendant which amounts to a denial of the plaintiff's rights or the assertion of inconsistent rights. (*Winfield on Tort*)

For example, if a fraudster acquires property from the plaintiff and then sells the goods to a third party, the third party may not have acquired a good legal title to the goods and the plaintiff may bring an action of conversion against him. Thieves and dishonest receivers of stolen goods may of course be liable in tort for conversion (although the victim's usual remedy against them would be an application for a compensation order when they are convicted in the criminal courts), but it can be seen that honest people may also incur liability through unwittingly dealing with stolen or misapplied property. Some enjoy special protection from liability. Banks run the risk of dealing every day with cheques that, unknown to them, have been stolen. In recognition of this, legislation such as the Cheques Act 1957 provides banks with special protection. As long as they deal with cheques in good faith and in the normal course of business, they are largely protected from actions for conversion, even if the cheques turn out to have been stolen.

Trespass

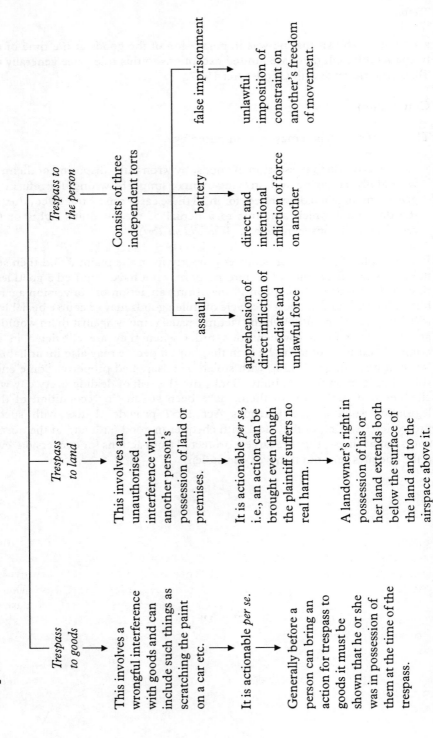

Trespass to goods

→ This involves a wrongful interference with goods and can include such things as scratching the paint on a car etc.

→ It is actionable *per se*.

→ Generally before a person can bring an action for trespass to goods it must be shown that he or she was in possession of them at the time of the trespass.

Trespass to land

→ This involves an unauthorised interference with another person's possession of land or premises.

→ It is actionable *per se*, i.e., an action can be brought even though the plaintiff suffers no real harm.

→ A landowner's right in possession of his or her land extends both below the surface of the land and to the airspace above it.

Trespass to the person

→ Consists of three independent torts

assault

→ apprehension of direct infliction of immediate and unlawful force

battery

→ direct and intentional infliction of force on another

false imprisonment

→ unlawful imposition of constraint on another's freedom of movement.

FORTY

Strict and Vicarious Liability

The general rule in tort, as in criminal law, is that before a defendant can be made liable, it must be shown that he was at fault. There are, however, certain torts where liability is imposed regardless of fault, and these are known as torts of strict liability. The significance of a tort being classed as one of strict liability is that the defendant may be held responsible even where he has taken all reasonable steps to avoid causing harm, and in some cases even for harm which was not reasonably foreseeable. Examples of such torts include liability for dangerous animals or for dogs which kill livestock (Animals Act 1971, s. 3) and liability for defective products (as to which see Chapter 38). To a limited extent, liability for nuisance, including that form of nuisance sometimes known as 'the rule in *Rylands* v *Fletcher*', may involve strict liability, but only in respect of foreseeable kinds of harm.

LIABIITY FOR NUISANCE

An occupier of land, or anyone else, who creates an unlawful interference with another occupier's enjoyment or use of his land, as for example by creating some form of environmental pollution, may be strictly liable for the resulting damage or interference. Fault or negligence need not be proved, provided that the damage or nuisance was not unforeseeable (*The Wagon Mound (No. 2)* [1967] 1 AC 617). As Lord Hope pointed out in the recent case of *Hunter* v *Canary Wharf Ltd* [1997] 2 All ER 426, 'nuisance is a tort of strict liability in the sense that it is no defence to say that the defendant took all reasonable care to prevent it'.

Generally speaking, a person may undertake any lawful activity he wishes on his own land. The law of nuisance qualifies this freedom in the interests of his neighbours, who are entitled to protection from unreasonable interference with their use or enjoyment of their own land. This may require a delicate balancing act by the courts, and the instrument which the courts use to achieve this balance is the concept of reasonableness.

There are three things which must be established before a plaintiff can bring an action for nuisance. First, the plaintiff must have a legally recognised interest in land affected by the alleged nuisance (as owner, tenant or licensee with sole possession). Nuisance is a tort protecting interests in land, in contrast to negligence, which can be used to protect personal interests or security. It is not therefore enough to show that a plaintiff is in occupation of the affected land as his home, etc. On this issue, the House of Lords in *Hunter* v *Canary Wharf Ltd* overruled an earlier decision of the Court of Appeal (*Khorasandjian* v *Bush* [1993] QB 727). According to Lords Lloyd and Hoffman in the *Canary Wharf* case, damages for personal injuries cannot be recovered by means of a nuisance action, even if suffered by a landowner as a result of his occupation of land affected by an actionable nuisance.

Secondly, there must be interference with the plaintiff's use or enjoyment of his land (as in *Bliss* v *Hall* (1838) 4 Bing NC 183, where fumes and smells from a candle maker's business wafted onto the plaintiff's land); or alternatively, actual damage to the land itself. 'Land' includes buildings, etc. In *St Helen's Smelting Co.* v *Tipping* (1865) 11 HL Cas 642, crops growing on the plaintiff's land were damaged by fumes from the defendant's smelting works. This was held to be an actionable nuisance, because the crops were in law a part of the land.

Thirdly, the interference must be unlawful, and it will only be unlawful if the defendant's conduct was reasonable in the circumstances. Factors relevant to the concept of reasonableness include the nature of the area in which the nuisance occurred. In *Sturges* v *Bridgman* (1879) 11 Ch D 852, it was said that 'what would be a nuisance in Belgrave Square would not be in Bermondsey'. For example, a person who lives in an area of heavy industry and in close proximity to power stations cannot expect to enjoy the quality of air he would expect in the countryside. Thus an activity which may be reasonable in one area may not be in another.

In *Hunter* v *Canary Wharf Ltd*, the House of Lords refused to allow any recovery to be made in nuisance for interference with local television signals, caused by the construction of the enormous steel-clad Canary Wharf tower in Docklands. Their Lordships were not entirely unanimous in their reasoning, but it appears that they were unwilling to allow a person's right to build on his own land (after obtaining necessary planning permission) to be restricted by the interests of neighbouring television watchers. This would be an excessive and unreasonable limitation on development.

The case law suggests that the activity complained of can usually only be classified as a nuisance if it has an element of continuity about it, although this is not always the case. For example, if the incident is an isolated one, but nevertheless causes sufficiently grave harm, it may be evidence from which to infer that there was a pre-existing dangerous state of affairs. In *Spicer* v *Smee* [1946] 1 All ER 489, the plaintiff's house was destroyed by fire caused by defective electrical wiring in the defendant's adjacent house. The judge found the defendant liable in nuisance, because the wiring in his house was classed as a pre-existing dangerous state of affairs. The rule in *Rylands* v *Fletcher* (below) is now best thought of as an extension of the tort of nuisance so as to cover cases of damage caused by isolated incidents involving the escape of dangerous things.

Because it involves strict liability, the presence or absence of malice is not usually relevant to an action for nuisance, but actions not normally classed as a nuisance may nevertheless become so classified if done for the purpose of annoying the plaintiff. In *Christie* v *Davey* [1893] 1 Ch 316, the defendant beat trays and blew whistles whilst the plaintiff attempted to give music lessons next door. It was held that this was an actionable nuisance because it was designed to be so. Similarly, in the *Canary Wharf* case, some at least of the Law Lords expressed the view (*obiter*) that a malicious interference with television signals could be an actionable nuisance.

THE RULE IN *RYLANDS* v *FLETCHER*

In *Rylands* v *Fletcher* (1886) LR 1 Ex 265, the defendant hired contractors to construct a reservoir on his land. The plaintiff owned a coal mine on the adjoining land. Under the reservoir site there were disused mine shafts which, unknown to the defendant, connected with the plaintiff's mines. These shafts appeared to be filled with earth and so the contractors did not properly block them up. When the reservoir was filled, however, the water burst through the old shafts and flooded the plaintiff's mines, causing extensive damage. It was held that the defendant had not been negligent, but he was nevertheless held liable on the basis of what has since become known as the rule in *Rylands* v *Fletcher*. Blackburn J said:

> We think that the true rule of law is, that the person who for his own purposes brings on his lands and collects and keeps there anything likely to do mischief if it escapes, must keep it at his peril, and, if he does not do so, is prima facie answerable for all the damage which is the natural consequence of its escape...

The House of Lords broadly approved of what Blackburn J had said, but qualified it with the proviso that the defendant's use of the land must be 'non-natural' before the rule would apply. Subsequent cases, notably *Cambridge Water Co. Ltd* v *Eastern Counties Leather plc* [1994] 1 All ER 53 have qualified the principle still further. It is now clear that liability under the *Rylands* v *Fletcher* principle is 'strict' only in the same limited sense as in other cases of nuisance.

'Anything likely to do mischief'

The rule in *Rylands* v *Fletcher* merely applies to 'anything likely to do mischief if it escapes'. The thing does not have to be likely to escape, but must be likely to cause damage if it should do so. The damage must not be wholly unforeseeable. In the *Cambridge Water* case, a company which used chemicals in the course of tanning leather goods caused contamination of a borehole sited over a mile away from its factory when traces of the chemical unforeseeably percolated all the way through to it. The damage was expensive (a new borehole had to be sunk elsewhere at a cost of £1 million), but it was unforeseeable and so the leather company was not liable for it.

Gas, fire, water, oil, chemicals and explosive substances have all been held to be within the rule, at least when stored in unusually large quantities. The list of potential dangers falling within this rule, however, is not closed.

Escape

There must be an 'escape from a place where the defendant has occupation or control over land to a place which is outside his occupation or control'. In *Read* v *J. Lyons & Co. Ltd* [1947] AC 156, the plaintiff failed to recover damages as a result of injuries sustained following an explosion in the defendant's factory, because the explosion was in the factory itself and had not 'escaped'. Had the explosion caused damage to neighbouring property or to persons on that property, it would have been different. Furthermore, the thing that 'escapes and causes damage' need not be the dangerous thing that was brought onto the land, provided the escape occurs because of that dangerous thing. For example, in *Miles* v *Forest Rock Granite Co.* (1918) 34 TLR 500, the plaintiff was injured by rocks thrown onto the highway as a result of blasting explosives on the defendants' land. The defendants were held liable because the rock was blown onto the highway by the dangerous thing, namely, the explosives.

Non-natural user

The rule will apply only where there has been a non-natural user of the land, that is something has been brought onto the defendant's land which was not there either naturally or usually. In *Rickards* v *Lothian* [1913] AC 263, Lord Moulton said that it 'must be some special use bringing with it increased danger to others and must not merely be the ordinary use of the land'. Thus, water in a large reservoir would be within the rule, but water in an ordinary household tank would not be. It is also worth noting a comment made by Lord Porter in *Read* v *J. Lyons & Co.* [1947] AC 156: 'All the circumstances of the time and place and the practices of mankind must be taken into consideration, so what might be regarded as dangerous or non-natural may vary according to those circumstances.' What may be deemed a non-natural use of the land can therefore alter as social conditions change. Whereas the petrol in a car's tank was once considered an 'unnatural' hazard, it could not be so considered today. The storage of large quantities of dangerous or poisonous chemicals may, however, be within the scope of the rule, even in areas of heavy industry where such storage is quite normal (*Cambridge Water Co. v Eastern Counties Leather*).

Accumulation

Rylands v *Fletcher* applies only to things which the defendant deliberately accumulates, that is brings onto his land and collects and keeps there. It does not apply to things naturally on the land or to natural accumulations. So, whereas the collapse of a coal slag heap would be covered by the rule, a 'natural' landslide would not be.

Damage

The plaintiff must prove that he has suffered damage. The rule in *Rylands* v *Fletcher* covers both personal injury and damage to property.

Defences to actions under the rule in *Rylands* v *Fletcher*

Although liability under *Rylands* v *Fletcher* does not depend on proof of negligence or other fault, there are a number of defences upon which a defendant may be able to rely. These include statutory authority for the storage of the material (although the Reservoirs Act 1975 expressly rejects any such defence in respect of reservoirs constructed after 1930). Certain other defences require a little more explanation.

Consent
There will be no liability under the rule in *Rylands* v *Fletcher* where the plaintiff has consented to the presence of the allegedly dangerous thing on the land. Consent will not be implied, however, simply because a person occupies a property which is situated closely to a known source of danger; neither would consent to its presence prevent the bringing of an action based on negligence, if that could be proved.

Plaintiff's act or default
There will be no liability where damage is caused entirely by the plaintiff's own conduct. If he is partly to blame, any damages recovered may be reduced, as in cases of contributory negligence.

Acts of God
It may be a defence to prove that the escape of the dangerous substance was caused by freakish forces of nature (or 'acts of God') which 'no human foresight

can provide against and of which human prudence is not bound to recognise'; but this must by definition be a difficult defence to prove, because it would be entirely reasonable to expect someone who stores highly dangerous materials on his land to guard against things such as freak winds, freak downpours or mild earthquakes, none of which are entirely unknown in this country.

Act of a stranger

The unforeseeable act of a stranger over whom the defendant has no control is a defence. Once again, however, this defence will often be difficult to establish, because the defendant must not have been negligent in failing to prevent the stranger's act. If, for example, the defendant stored hazardous material on his land and failed to take reasonable precautions against the foreseeable acts of vandalism which caused the escape of that hazardous material, this defence must fail. What would amount to reasonable precautions must be a question of fact. How hazardous was the material? How feasible would it have been to have prevented trespassers getting access to it?

Liability for damage caused by fire

Where damage is caused by fires which spread out of control, liability may sometimes arise under a rule which is very similar to that in *Rylands* v *Fletcher*. In *Mason* v *Levy Auto Parts of England Ltd* [1967] 2 QB 530, it was held that a defendant would be liable if:

(a)   he brought onto his land things likely to catch fire and kept them there in such conditions that, if they did ignite, the fire would be likely to spread to the plaintiff's land;

(b)   he did so in the course of some non-natural use of the land; and

(c)   the thing ignited and the fire did indeed spread.

In other cases, liability may be based on negligence, but strict liability will not ordinarily be imposed in respect of accidental fires which do not arise in the manner described above and spread through no fault of the defendant (Fires Prevention (Metropolis) Act 1774).

VICARIOUS LIABILITY

The term 'vicarious liability' imports the notion that someone will be held responsible for the acts of another. The most common type of relationship giving rise to vicarious liability is that of employer and employee. Employers, whether individuals or corporations (such as a registered company), can be held liable for the tortious (and sometimes even the criminal) acts of their employees even though the employers themselves are not at fault. Vicarious liability in criminal cases (which is of very restricted application) is dealt with in Chapter 16. In either case, liability is basically strict. It may sometimes be necessary to prove that the employee was negligent or culpable in some other sense, but it will not be necessary to prove that the employer itself was at a fault.

A number of policy considerations have been put forward in order to justify the application of vicarious liability in tort cases. Employers usually have greater resources and can more readily provide compensation. When the plaintiff is deciding who to sue, he will usually find that a wealthy employer makes a better target than a humble employee. Furthermore, the existence of vicarious liability encourages accident prevention, because it gives employers an economic interest in ensuring that their employees take all reasonable care. There is, however, a more principled argument in its favour, namely, that since it is the employer which profits from the activities of its employees, the employer should also bear responsibility for any losses or damage which those activities may inadvertently cause.

In order for vicarious liability to be placed upon an employer, it is necessary to show:

(a) that the tort was committed by its employee; and
(b) that it was committed within the course of employment.

Employees and independent contractors

It is easy enough to give individual examples of employees and independent contractors. Thus, a personal chauffeur would be an employee, whereas a taxi driver would be an independent contractor. It can nevertheless be difficult to identify or define the factors which distinguish them from each other.

The intention of the parties
The intention of the parties may be a relevant consideration. Did they intend their relationship to be one of employer and employee? This cannot always be a conclusive factor, however, and the courts will be vigilant against being deceived by agreements which appear designed only to avoid the usual consequences of an employer/employee relationship. In *Ferguson* v *Dawson Partners (Contractors) Ltd* [1976] 1 WLR 1213, a building worker was expressly classed as 'a labour only contractor', but he was nevertheless held to be an employee because in all other respects that is what he was.

The control test
In the past, one of the standard tests was that of control. An employer/employee relationship would be recognised where the former could control both what was by done by the latter and how it was done. Control is now recognised to be only one of the factors which may have to be taken into account. Many employers are in no position to control how their employees carry out specialised work, and yet in every other respect it may be obvious that the employer/employee relationship exists.

Integration and financial independence

A distinction must be drawn between what are known as contracts *of service* and contracts *for services*. In the latter, the person concerned will be an independent contractor, whereas in the former he will be an employee. For example, taxi drivers and self-employed electricians and freelance journalists are all employed on contracts *for services*; in contracts *of service*, the person who is employed will normally be an integral part of the employer's business and the employer will (if that test is applied) be vicariously liable for that person's acts. An independent contractor is in effect self-employed, and thus dependent on the profits or losses of his own business. Lord Wright in *Montreal v Montreal Locomotive Works Ltd* [1947] 1 DLR 161, accordingly suggested the following test to distinguish between employees and independent contractors: (i) control; (ii) ownership of tools; (iii) chance of profit; and (iv) risk of loss. Employees will ordinarily work for a wage and do not participate in the profit and loss side of the business (except perhaps under a subsidiary employee share-owning scheme). In *Market Investigations Ltd v Minister of Social Security* [1969] 2 QB 173, Cooke J added two more possible factors to the list given by Lord Wright, namely, whether the person hires his own helpers and the degree of independent responsibility he possesses.

In practice, there is no single test for identifying the employer/employee relationship. It may be necessary, as Lord Wright recognised, to weigh up a number of factors. Precedents and statutory provisions must of course be referred to where applicable. It is recognised, for example, that hospital authorities are vicariously liable for torts committed by their full-time members of staff; and the Police Act 1964 provides that a chief constable (meaning in effect the police authority of which he is the chief) will be liable for any torts committed by police officers when acting under his direction and control in the performance of their functions.

Whose employee?

Problems may arise where A is ordinarily employed by B, but is 'loaned' by B to another operator, C, for a particular length of time or for a particular purpose. This is a common procedure where specialised equipment, such as JCB excavators, is leased out by plant hire companies. A skilled operator (their employee) may be provided to work the machine, but the contract of hire may purport to assign responsibility for the operator's actions to the hirer. The question then arises as to whether this is effective to exclude the plant hire company's potential liability to third parties, should their operator commit a tort during the period he is on loan.

Such cases may largely turn on their own individual facts, but it is difficult for the general employer (such as the plant hire company) to shift responsibility to the temporary employer. In *Mersey Docks & Harbour Board v Coggins & Griffith (Liverpool) Ltd* [1947] AC 1, a crane driver and his crane were loaned by the Mersey Harbour Board to a firm of stevedores under a contract which provided that 'drivers so provided shall be the servants of the stevedores'. Whilst loading a ship, the crane driver negligently caused an accident in which a person was injured. Who, apart from the driver himself, was liable for this accident? The stevedores supervised the crane driver but they had no control over the way he handled the crane. Furthermore, the driver was paid by the Harbour Board, who alone had the power to dismiss him. On those facts, the House of Lords naturally held that the Harbour Board remained vicariously liable for his action. The driver was still employed by them and he was still operating their crane.

In many such cases, plant hire companies will seek to rely on a standard form contract term, requiring the hirer of their plant to indemnify them against any liability they (the plant hire company) might incur as a result of the actions of their driver. This is not an exclusion clause, and will therefore be valid, unless it is a consumer contract, in which case such a clause is subject to a 'reasonableness test' under the Unfair Contract Terms Act 1977, s. 4 (see Chapter 33). A person injured by the negligence of a JCB driver need not concern himself with any of this, however, since it does not affect his own right to sue the driver's employers.

The course of employment

The employer will be vicariously liable for the torts of the employee only if the wrongful act was committed within the employee's course of employment. It will usually be easy to see whether the employee was so acting, but difficult cases can arise, which the courts will treat as turning on questions of fact. (In other words, such cases tend not to establish legal principles or precedents.) Generally an act will be regarded as done in the course of employment if it is expressly or impliedly authorised by the employer, *or* if it is an unauthorised way of doing something which the employee was employed to do. If, on the other hand, the act in question was a complete departure from the employee's duties then the employer will not be liable. In *Bayley* v *Manchester Sheffield & Lincolnshire Rail Co.* (1873) LR 8 CP 148 a remarkably stupid railway porter somehow became convinced that the plaintiff, a passenger, had boarded the wrong train, even though the plaintiff said that he was going to Macclesfield and the train was indeed going there. As the train was moving out, he forcibly pulled the plaintiff off the train and pushed him onto a different one, which did not, of course, take him anywhere near Macclesfield. It was held that the defendants were liable to the plaintiff for his mistreatment, because the porter was trying, in his own rough and misguided way, to ensure that passengers were assisted onto the right trains. He was indeed acting as a railway porter. Had he caused an accident by improperly seizing the train controls, the result would surely have been different.

In *Century Insurance Co.* v *Northern Ireland Road Transport Board* [1942] AC 509, the driver of a petrol lorry was transferring petrol from his lorry to a storage tank at a garage. He foolishly lit a cigarette and threw the lighted match onto the floor. This ignited petrol vapour and caused a huge explosion. The employers were held liable for the employee's acts. His negligent behaviour took place while he was carrying out his duties. It did not take him outside the course of those duties.

Simply asking what the employee was employed to do will not always provide a conclusive answer, as sometimes he may perform an act which is different in kind from what he is generally employed to do but nevertheless may still be within the course of that employment. In *Polland v Parr & Sons* [1927] 1 KB 236, an off-duty employee mistakenly concluded that some boys were stealing sugar from one of his employer's wagons. He struck one of the boys, who fell in front of a moving wagon and was injured. The employer was held liable on the ground that the employee had implied authority to act to protect his employer's property. He was acting wrongfully only because he was mistaken.

Express prohibition

Even where an employer has expressly forbidden its employees to do a particular act, the employer may still be liable for the act if the employee goes ahead and does it. If it were otherwise, an employer could escape liability simply by an express prohibition, such as 'employees must not act unlawfully'. In order for an express prohibition to be effective, it must limit the scope of the employee's actions and not simply limit the method of performance. In *Limpus v London General Omnibus Company* (1862) 1 H & C 526, the driver of a horse-drawn bus was ordered not to race with or obstruct the buses of rival companies. The driver ignored the instruction and thereby caused a collision. The employers were held liable, as the driver was simply performing his duties in an improper way. But in *Iqbal v London Transport Executive* [1953] 1 WLR 997, a bus conductor was prohibited from driving the buses. This prohibition was effective because driving is not a method of performing the duties of a bus conductor, and his employers were not liable for injuries caused when he infringed this prohibition.

One area where the issue of prohibition has arisen quite frequently is that of employees giving unauthorised lifts to persons. In *Rose v Plenty* [1976] 1 WLR 141, a milkman ignored his employers' instructions and allowed a child of 13 to assist him and ride on the milk float. The child was injured, but the employers argued that the milkman alone was responsible because he had breached their clear instructions. The Court of Appeal nevertheless held the employers to be vicariously liable. The milkman had used the boy to help him in the course of his work. Had he been using his vehicle to give lifts to hitch-hikers, said Lord Denning MR, the outcome might have been different (cf. *Twine v Bean's Express Ltd* (1946) 62 TLR 458).

Vicarious liability not based on employment: motor vehicles

If the owner of a motor vehicle allows another person to use that vehicle, he will not ordinarily be liable for negligent driving by that other person (*Morgans* v *Launchbury* [1973] AC 127) but may incur liability:

(a) where that other person was acting as the owner's agent, e.g., by delivering the vehicle to another country on the owner's behalf (*Ormrod* v *Crossville Motor Services Ltd* [1953] 1 WLR 1120); or

(b) where the owner has permitted uninsured use of the vehicle, contrary to the Road Traffic Act 1988. Apart from amounting to a criminal offence, the grant of such permission may give rise to an action against the owner for breach of statutory duty in the event of an accident (*Monk* v *Warbey* [1935] 1 KB 75). It would not matter that the owner thought the driver was properly insured.

FORTY ONE

Dangerous Premises

This chapter discusses the special legal rules which govern the duty owed by an occupier of land, premises or structures to persons entering or coming upon them. This is known as occupier's liability and is usually concerned with personal injury caused to visitors and others on the occupier's premises. If, on the other hand, the damage occurs off the premises then the legal actions which may be pursued are those of nuisance or negligence.

The law on occupier's liability is now primarily governed by legislation. The liability of an occupier will depend upon whether the person injured is classed as a visitor or a non-visitor. The occupier's liability towards visitors is governed by the Occupiers' Liability Act 1957, whereas his liability to non-visitors is dealt with by the Occupiers' Liability Act 1984. (The liability of non-occupiers of premises for the safety of entrants is still largely governed by the law of negligence.)

Liability to visitors under the Occupiers' Liability Act 1957

Section 2(1) of the Occupiers' Liability Act 1957 provides that 'an occupier of premises owes a common duty of care to all his visitors'.

Who is an occupier?

One of the first things to consider is what is meant by an 'occupier' for the purposes of the 1957 Act. Unfortunately, the Act itself does not define the term, but instead stipulates that the common law rules should apply. The common law test uses the concept of occupational control to determine who is an occupier. It follows that a person may be deemed to have control over land or premises either by being present on those premises or by carrying out some activity thereon. He need not own the premises or have exclusive control over them. As Lord Denning stated in *Wheat* v *E Lacon & Co. Ltd* [1966] 1 All ER 582:

> Wherever a person has a sufficient degree of control over premises that he ought to realise that any failure on his part to use care may result in injury to a person lawfully coming there, then he is an 'occupier'.

In *Wheat* v *Lacon*, the defendant brewery company owned a public house which was run by a manager, to whom they had granted a licence to use the first floor as private accommodation. The licence gave the defendants the right to enter the flat to carry out repairs and the manager had permission to have paying guests (or lodgers) in the spare room. A lodger (Mr Wheat) fell down the back stairs of the flat and was killed. It was alleged that the handrail was faulty and that the light bulb was missing. The House of Lords concluded that the defendants were occupiers and thus owed Wheat a common duty of care, but prior to the fatal accident there had never been any indication or suggestion that the stairs had been dangerous, and the duty of care had therefore not been breached.

If it can be shown that a person has ownership or control over premises, then he may be deemed to be an occupier for the purposes of the Act, even if he has never taken physical control over them. In *Harris* v *Birkenhead Corporation* [1976] 1 All ER 341, a local authority made a compulsory purchase order over property which was in the middle of a slum clearance area. The local authority served notices of entry on the owner of the property and on her tenant, who then left the house without informing them. The house remained unoccupied and became derelict. The local authority should no doubt have boarded it up, but never did so, and a four-year-old child was injured after getting into the house and falling from an upstairs window. The court held that the local authority was an occupier, even though it had never taken possession of the property, because it had the power to control what state the premises were kept in.

There may be more than one occupier and each occupier may be made responsible for different aspects of the safety of the premises. In *Collier* v *Anglian Water Authority*, *The Times*, 26 March 1983, the plaintiff was injured after tripping over an uneven pavement on the promenade at Mablethorpe. The local authority owned the promenade and was responsible for keeping it clean, but it was not directly responsible for repair work, which was carried out by the water authority as part of its statutory duty to maintain Mablethorpe's sea defences, even though it did not have any proprietary interest in the promenade. The court held that both the local authority and the Water Authority owed duties of care as occupiers of the promenade.

What are premises?
Section 1(3) of the Act defines premises so as to include buildings, land and any fixed or moveable structures, such as vehicles, ships and aircraft.

Who is a visitor?
A visitor is anyone who has express or implied permission to enter the premises. Visitors may include guests, lodgers, postmen, milkmen, customers or clients, members of the public using parks, public toilets, etc. The term 'visitor' does not include trespassers or persons exercising a public or private right of way. This rule was confirmed in *McGeown* v *Northern Ireland Housing Executive* [1994] 3 All ER 53. The plaintiff tripped and broke her leg on a footpath which belonged to the defendant. The House of Lords held that those using public or private rights of way were neither visitors nor trespassers. Lord Keith stated:

> Rights of way pass over many different types of terrain, and it would place an impossible burden upon landowners if they not only had to submit to the passage over them of anyone who might choose to exercise them but also were under a duty to maintain them in a safe condition. Persons using rights of way do so not with the permission of the owner ... but in the exercise of a right.

As a result, the only duty owed to the plaintiff was the lesser duty of care specified by the Occupiers' Liability Act 1984 (see below).

The occupier may, however, set limits on the permission for entry granted to a visitor. For example, restrictions may be made as to where visitors may go once on the premises, or on the length of time for which a visitor may be on the premises. If the visitor disregards these restrictions he will cease to be classed as a visitor.

Section 2(6) of the 1957 Act further states that persons who enter premises for any purpose in the exercise of a right conferred by law will be treated as a visitor only for that specific purpose. For example, a postman is permitted by law to enter premises to deliver mail. If the postman goes beyond such purposes, as, for example, by looking into garden sheds or wandering around the premises, then in those circumstances he may be treated as a non-visitor.

The extent of the duty
Section 2(1) of the 1957 Act states that occupiers of premises owe a common duty of care to all their visitors. Section 2(2) then goes on to define the common duty of care as follows:

> ... a duty to take such care as in all the circumstances of the case is reasonable to see that the visitor will be reasonably safe in using the premises for the purposes for which he is invited or permitted by the occupier to be there.

A number of points may be made upon the extent of this duty:

(a)   An occupier is entitled to assume that any visitors will act reasonably once on the premises. As Scrutton LJ said in *The Calgarth* [1927] P 93 'when you invite a person into your house to use the staircase you do not invite him to slide down the banisters'.

(b)   Section 2(4)(a) states that warning visitors about possible dangers may suffice, rather than removing or fencing off the danger, provided the warning is clear enough to enable the visitor to be reasonably safe.

(c)   Section 2(3)(a) states that an occupier must be prepared to expect children to be less careful than adults, and thus it may be necessary to take extra precautions where children are involved. An occupier must take into account that children can be inquisitive and may be allured to objects or places which they have no right to go near. An example of this may be seen in the case of *Glasgow Corporation* v *Taylor* [1922] 1 AC 44. A seven-year-old boy died after eating poisonous berries which he picked from a shrub in a park owned by the corporation. The corporation knew that the berries were poisonous, but had not bothered to fence off the shrub or give a warning and was therefore liable. Technically the child in this case had been a trespasser, but because the berries were a temptation to children, the occupier ought to have taken precautions, such as by fencing off the shrub itself.

In the case of very young children, almost anything may constitute an allurement, and few occupiers can be expected to make their premises as safe as a nursery. Consequently, an occupier is entitled to assume that parents will behave in a prudent way and exercise proper care for the safety of such young children.

(d)   Section 2(3)(b) states that an occupier may expect that an adult who enters premises in the exercise of his particular trade will appreciate and guard against any special risks involved in that trade. In *Roles* v *Nathan* [1963] 1 WLR 1117, two chimney sweeps died from carbon monoxide poisoning while cleaning a flue of a boiler while the boiler was alight. It was held that the occupier was not liable. The sweeps had been warned of the danger and as specialists could reasonably have been expected to see to their own safety. It was entirely their own fault.

Acceptance of the risk

An occupier will not be liable if the visitor knows of the risk and willingly accepts it (s. 2(5) of the 1957 Act). In order to rely upon this defence, it has to be shown that the victim was aware of the specific risk that caused the injury, and it is arguable that it must also be shown that the plaintiff had effectively waived the legal rights that would normally have arisen from the defendant's conduct.

Independent contractors

In some cases, an injury caused to a visitor to premises may be attributed not to the negligence of the occupier, but to that of an independent contractor hired to build, repair, maintain or demolish things on the premises. The occupier is not vicariously liable for the negligence of the contractor (as he would be for the negligence of his own employees), but may be liable in his own right if he has 'countenanced the unsafe working methods of cowboy operators' (*Ferguson* v *Welsh* [1987] 3 All ER 777). How far an occupier can be expected to check on the skill and working practices of a contractor (or on the quality of that work) must vary according to the circumstances.

In some cases, a contractor may, for a time at least, qualify as an occupier of the premises; but in other cases, a contractor's liability is based on the common law duty of care, rather than on any special rules regarding premises. The contractor must, in other words, take reasonable care to avoid any risk of harming persons or property which he might reasonably expect to be affected by his operations (*A. C. Billings & Sons Ltd* v *Riden* [1958] AC 240).

Exclusion of occupier's liability

Section 2(1) of the 1957 Act states that the occupier of premises owes visitors a common duty of care 'except insofar as he is free to and does extend, restrict, modify or exclude his duty to any visitor or visitors by agreement or otherwise'. The basic effect of an exclusion clause of this type, where it is valid and effective, is that the plaintiff is deemed to have waived his right to sue for risks specified in the notice. The plaintiff need not have fully understood the risks involved, nor need he have properly read the notice.

(a) Business premises and unfair terms

Private occupiers may, as we shall see below, exclude their liability under the 1957 Act, 'by agreement or otherwise', but the ability of business occupiers to do this has been curtailed by UCTA 1977. UCTA 1977 applies only to business liability, namely, liability for breach of obligations arising 'from things done to or done by another person in the course of a business or from the occupation of premises used for business purposes of the occupier'. This includes premises used for carrying out a trade or profession, and also those used for the activities of a government or local or public authority, but does not include the granting of access for recreational or educational purposes, unless this falls within the business purposes of the occupier. The purpose of the last provision is to protect persons such as farmers who let people use their land, for example, to ride horses, but who wish to protect themselves from possible legal claims by excluding or restricting their liability by notice.

If the premises are deemed to be used for business purposes, s. 2(1) of UCTA 1977 states that an occupier cannot by any contract term or by any notice exclude or restrict his liability for death or personal injury resulting from negligence. The word 'negligence' in this context includes the common law duty of care and the occupier's duty under s. 2 of the 1957 Act (above). In the case of other loss or damage (e.g., damage to goods) liability for negligence can sometimes be excluded, but only insofar as the exclusion satisfies the reasonableness test (UCTA 1977, s. 2(2)). For further information on exclusion clauses, see Chapter 32.

(b) Private occupiers

An example of the principle that a private occupier may 'restrict, modify or exclude his duty to any visitor or visitors by agreement or otherwise' may be seen in operation in *White* v *Blackmore* [1972] 3 All ER 158. (The case actually involved business premises, but it pre-dated UCTA 1977, and so the principles applied in that case are now applicable to private premises only.) The plaintiff's husband was flung into the air and killed while watching a jalopy race. A notice at the entrance of the course and at other points in the field stated that the organisers were absolved from all liabilities arising out of accidents causing damage or personal injury, howsoever caused. It was held that this clause was effective in absolving the organisers. In other words, it was a complete defence.

It can be seen from *White* v *Blackmore* that the most common way for an occupier to exclude liability to visitors is through the display of notices on the premises. The visitor does not, however, have to have actual notice of these conditions, because it is enough if the occupier has simply taken reasonable steps to bring these conditions to the attention of any visitor. This is known as constructive notice. It is difficult to see how this principle can be applied to young child visitors, especially those who may be unable to read or comprehend the notice.

Liability to non-visitors

The common law position

At one time, an occupier owed no duty of care to trespassers, although he could be made liable if he either intentionally or recklessly inflicted harm on a trespasser who was known to be on the land. This rule was modified, however, in the case of *British Railways Board* v *Herrington* [1972] 1 All ER 749, in which British Rail were held liable for injuries caused to a child who had trespassed on an electrified railway line by climbing through a hole in the fence. It was known to British Rail that children were able to get onto the line at that point, but nothing had been done to repair the fence. The House of Lords declined to hold that an occupier could owe a normal duty of care to trespassers, but did hold that an occupier owed a duty of 'common humanity' to protect trespassers from known risks of harm if the presence of such trespassers was likely or foreseeable and the prevention of such harm was within the occupier's capacity or resources.

The *Herrington* rule has now been superseded by the Occupiers' Liability Act 1984. There are similarities between the new statutory duty and the old common law duty of humanity, and the case law after *BRB* v *Herrington* may still provide useful illustrations as to how the 1984 Act may be applied.

The Occupiers' Liability Act 1984

An occupier may owe a duty under the 1984 Act to 'persons other than his visitors' (or 'non-visitors'). Included in this category would be:

   (a) trespassers;

   (b) persons lawfully exercising public or private rights of way (see *McGeown* v *Northern Ireland Housing Executive*, above); and

   (c) persons who enter land in the exercise of rights conferred by an access agreement or under the National Parks and Access to the Countryside Act 1949.

When is a duty owed to non-visitors?

Section 1(3) of the 1984 Act states that an occupier will owe a non-visitor a duty under the Act if the following conditions are satisfied:

   (a) he is aware of the danger or has reasonable grounds to believe that it exists;

   (b) he knows or has reasonable grounds to believe that the non-visitor is in the vicinity of the danger concerned, or that the non-visitor may come into the vicinity of the danger; and

   (c) the risk is one against which, in all the circumstances of the case, he may reasonably be expected to offer the non-visitor some protection.

It can be seen that the occupier will not owe a statutory duty to every non-visitor. As far as (a) and (b) are concerned, the question arises as to what degree of knowledge the occupier must have before the duty under the 1984 arises. In *White* v *St Albans City & District Council*, *The Times*, 12 March 1990, the plaintiff was injured when he fell down a trench while taking a short-cut across the defendant council's land in order to get to a car park. The trench was on private land and the land was surrounded by a fence. There was no evidence that the land was regularly used as a short-cut to the car park. The Court of Appeal held that the fact that the council had fenced off its land did not necessarily mean that it had reason to believe that someone was likely to cross it. The question had to be determined by looking at the actual state of affairs when the injury occurred. Had there been a hole in the fence, which would have suggested that persons were regularly using it as a form of short-cut across the land, the council might have had reasonable grounds to suspect that someone might be in the vicinity.

The next question is whether the particular risk or danger is one against which the occupier ought reasonably to provide some protection for non-visitors. This will depend upon a number of different factors, such as the nature of the risk itself, the possibility and practicability of precautions and the type of entrant who may be expected to come across the danger, etc. A manifestly grave hazard on unfenced land next to a children's playground would more or less demand to be dealt with by the occupier of that land, especially if it would be 'attractive' to children, whereas the risk of an adult trespasser falling into a trench on fenced-off land which he has no business to be crossing might be seen to be a risk which a reasonable occupier could properly tolerate. If the court feel that the occupier did owe a statutory duty to a non-visitor under s. 1(3), they must then consider whether that duty has been broken.

Extent of the duty

Section 1(4) of the 1984 Act states that the occupier must take such care as is reasonable in all the circumstances of the case to see that the non-visitor does not suffer injury on the premises as a result of the danger concerned. What constitutes reasonable care will depend upon the nature of the risk and on the cost of precautions, etc., so to some extent there is an overlap between s. 1(3) and (4).

Warning

The occupier may be able to discharge his duty to non-visitors by warning of the danger concerned (s. 1(5)). Such notices will not in practice be effective as against very young children, but may sometimes be effective against older children or adults (and see s. 1(6) below).

Acceptance of the risk

Section 1(6) of the 1984 Act expressly preserves the defence of *volenti non fit injuria* (see further Chapter 42). It is therefore possible to argue that non-visitors who ignore signs warning of danger (or who know of the danger anyway) thereby accept the risk of injury, and cannot sue the occupier if such injuries are suffered by them.

Exclusion of liability

UCTA 1977 does not apply to the statutory duty laid down in the 1984 Act, because it refers only to the common law duty of care and the statutory duty of care under the 1957 Act. The question of exclusion of the statutory duty imposed under the 1984 Act is therefore an open one. It would, however, seem unlikely as a matter of policy that an occupier would be permitted to exclude a duty which is no more than the very minimum imposed by the law. If so, it is also arguable that private occupiers must be precluded from excluding their liability to visitors in respect of this statutory minimum, because that would put non-visitors in a better position than legitimate visitors.

Occupiers' liability

An occupier of land, premises or structures on them, may be liable to persons entering or coming on to the land, etc. The extent of the occupier's liability will depend on whether the person injured is classed as a visitor or non-visitor.

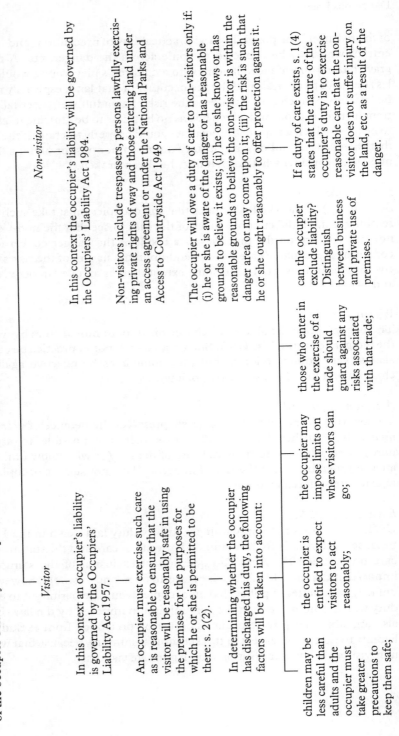

Visitor

In this context an occupier's liability is governed by the Occupiers' Liability Act 1957.

An occupier must exercise such care as is reasonable to ensure that the visitor will be reasonably safe in using the premises for the purposes for which he or she is permitted to be there: s. 2(2).

In determining whether the occupier has discharged his duty, the following factors will be taken into account:

- children may be less careful than adults and the occupier must take greater precautions to keep them safe;
- the occupier is entitled to expect visitors to act reasonably;
- the occupier may impose limits on where visitors can go;
- those who enter in the exercise of a trade should guard against any risks associated with that trade;
- can the occupier exclude liability? Distinguish between business and private use of premises.

Non-visitor

In this context the occupier's liability will be governed by the Occupiers' Liability Act 1984.

Non-visitors include trespassers, persons lawfully exercising private rights of way and those entering land under an access agreement or under the National Parks and Access to Countryside Act 1949.

The occupier will owe a duty of care to non-visitors only if: (i) he or she is aware of the danger or has reasonable grounds to believe it exists; (ii) he or she knows or has reasonable grounds to believe the non-visitor is within the danger area or may come upon it; (iii) the risk is such that he or she ought reasonably to offer protection against it.

If a duty of care exists, s. 1(4) states that the nature of the occupier's duty is to exercise reasonable care that the non-visitor does not suffer injury on the land, etc. as a result of the danger.

FORTY TWO

Defences in Tort

Defences, denials and burdens of proof

As in criminal law, the law of tort recognises a number of specific defences in addition to more general defences of outright or partial denial. The essential difference between general denials ('I didn't do it', or 'I wasn't negligent', etc.) and specific or 'affirmative' defences is evidential. The general rule in tort cases, as in contract, is that 'he who asserts must prove'. If the defendant merely denies the plaintiff's allegations, or pleads what is sometimes called 'inevitable accident', no burden of proof rests on him. It is not for the defendant to prove that he was *not* negligent; rather, it is for the plaintiff to prove that the defendant *was* negligent. If, however, the defendant alleges that the plaintiff's claim should fail because the plaintiff voluntarily took the risk of being injured (the defence of *volenti non fit injuria*), or that any damages the plaintiff gets should be reduced because he was partially to blame for the accident that injured him (the defence of contributory negligence), these are not just mere denials of the plaintiff's allegations: they introduce new issues for the court to consider, and it is for the defendant to prove what he alleges, assuming that the plaintiff can prove the defendant's own negligence in the first place. (Clearly, if the plaintiff cannot prove his case against the defendant, it will not matter if the defendant cannot prove his defences: the defendant will win without needing them.)

Some defences are restricted to particular torts, such as the defences of fair comment or justification in defamation cases (i.e., actions for libel or slander). These fall outside the scope of this book. This chapter will concentrate on defences to negligence actions and on defences which are of more general application.

Volenti non fit injuria

Volenti non fit injuria involves a voluntary but usually unspoken agreement under which one person agrees to absolve another from the legal consequences of an otherwise unreasonable risk of harm created by that other person. In an action for negligence, the defendant may allege that the plaintiff thus agreed both to accept the risk of such injury *and* not to blame the defendant for any such injury or seek compensation from him. It follows that if the defence succeeds, the plaintiff's action must fail completely.

This defence can succeed, however, only where the plaintiff has full knowledge of both the nature and the extent of the risk. Thus in order for the defence of *volenti* to apply, the following criteria must be satisfied:

(a) The plaintiff's agreement must be voluntary. In other words, there must be true consent. In *Bowater* v *Rowley Regis Corporation* [1944] KB 476, Scott LJ stated:

> A man cannot be said to be truly 'willing' unless he is in a position to choose freely, and freedom of choice predicates, not only full knowledge of the circumstances on which the exercise of choice is conditioned, so that he may be able to choose wisely, but the absence from his mind of any feeling of constraint so that nothing shall interfere with the freedom of his will.

It follows that where an employee feels forced to tolerate unsafe working practices, because he would otherwise lose his job, the defence of *volenti* will not be open to the employer if the employee is subsequently injured.

(b) The plaintiff must not only be aware of the risk, but must be fully aware of its nature and extent. A spectator watching a sporting event does not necessarily assume the risk of negligently inflicted injury simply by being there. In order to rely upon the defence of *volenti* in those circumstances, the defendant would have to prove not only that the plaintiff consented to a risk of injury, but that he consented 'to the lack of reasonable care that may produce the risk' (*Wooldridge* v *Sumner* [1963] 2 QB 43). In any event, attempts by organisers of dangerous spectator sports (such as motor racing) to exclude their own liability by notices deeming spectators voluntarily to have accepted the risk of suffering negligent injury would generally be invalidated under the UCTA 1977 (see Chapter 33).

A rare example of the successful use of a *volenti* defence is provided by the case of *Morris* v *Murray* [1990] 3 All ER 801. The plaintiff had been drinking whisky with the defendant all afternoon, before accepting the defendant's suggestion that they go for a flight in the defendant's light aircraft. Inevitably, the aircraft crashed. The defendant was killed and the plaintiff was lucky to escape with serious injuries. A negligence action by the plaintiff against the defendant's estate failed. Fox LJ said: 'The wild irresponsibility of the venture is such that the law should not intervene and award damages [but] should leave the loss where it falls ... flying with a drunken pilot is great folly.'

Note, however, that s. 149 of the Road Traffic Act 1988 precludes the use of this defence by a motorist who is required to hold compulsory insurance against third-party injuries or damage. The passenger who is injured after accepting a lift with a drunken motorist may be held to have been guilty of contributory negligence, but his claim cannot be defeated by a *volenti* defence (*Pitts* v *Hunt* [1990] 3 All ER 344).

Mistake

Mistake, whether as to fact or to law, is not generally a defence in its own right, but may be relevant in considering whether the plaintiff can prove his case. If the plaintiff's allegation is one of fraud or deceit, the defendant's 'defence' of mistake amounts to a general denial of the plaintiff's allegation, rather than an affirmative defence. It follows that the burden of proof remains with the plaintiff. The defendant does not have to prove that he was mistaken: instead, the plaintiff has to prove the defendant was fraudulent. If the plaintiff's claim is one of negligence, the question is whether the defendant's alleged mistake was a reasonable one or a negligent one.

Necessity and private defence

These defences may be relied upon where a tort (or what would otherwise be a tort) is committed so as to prevent damage to the public, a third party or the defendant, and where there is no reasonable alternative. If, for example, P's dog attacks D, who hits it on the head with his walking stick and kills it, D has a complete defence, assuming his actions were not unreasonable.

Act of God

An act of God may be pleaded in defence where damage is caused by unforeseeable natural causes, such as a major earthquake or a freak storm. Inevitably, such a defence is rarely relied upon. Persons who keep dangerous things on their land should in any event take reasonable precautions against natural events such as severe storms, that might cause such things to escape. See further, Chapter 40.

Contributory negligence

Sometimes, the defendant is not solely to blame for the plaintiff's loss or injury. In certain circumstances, the plaintiff's own negligence may have contributed to his loss or injury. Before 1945, if the plaintiff was shown to have contributed to the accident by his own negligence, no matter how slight, his action in negligence against the defendant would have to fail and the plaintiff would receive nothing. This rule was abolished by the Law Reform (Contributory Negligence) Act 1945, s. 1 of which states:

> Where any person suffers damage as a result partly of his own fault and partly of the fault of any other person or persons, a claim in respect of that damage shall not be defeated by reason of the fault of the person suffering the damage, but the damages recoverable in respect thereof shall be reduced to such extent as the court thinks just and equitable having regard to the claimant's share in the responsibility for the damage. . .

The plaintiff's negligence need not have contributed to the accident: it is enough that the plaintiff's negligence has contributed to the *damage* caused by the accident. In other words, if the plaintiff's injuries are made worse because he has failed to take care of his own health or safety, then the amount of damages the plaintiff will receive from the defendant will be reduced. In *Froom* v *Butcher* [1976] QB 286, the defendant negligently collided with the plaintiff's car. The plaintiff, however, had not been wearing a seat belt and was thrown through the windscreen. The plaintiff's damages were reduced by 15 per cent, because he was found to be contributorily negligent in not wearing a seat belt. Lord Denning MR stated: 'The *accident* is caused by bad driving. The *damage* is caused in part by the bad driving of the defendant, and in part by the failure of the plaintiff to wear a seat belt.'

We are considering here contributory negligence as a defence to a claim by the plaintiff. This does not depend in any sense on the plaintiff owing a duty of care to the defendant. A *counterclaim* against the plaintiff for loss, damage or injury suffered by the defendant in an incident which the defendant alleges was partly or wholly the fault of the plaintiff, would be another matter. For the defendant's counterclaim to succeed, the plaintiff must be proved to have been in breach of his own duty of care to the defendant.

Unlawful conduct as contributory negligence

In *Revill* v *Newberry* [1996] 1 All ER 291, the plaintiff was shot and injured by the defendant, an elderly man, whilst trying to break into and steal from the defendant's shed. Hearing the plaintiff's attempts to break into the shed, the defendant had fired blindly through the shed door. He was held to have used excessive force in the circumstances, and was thus in breach of his duty of care to the plaintiff (under the Occupier's Liability Act 1984 or at common law). Nevertheless the Court of Appeal held that the plaintiff's damages should be reduced by two-thirds, because of his own culpability, which was deemed to be 'contributory negligence'.

Contributory negligence and children
In *Gough* v *Thorne* [1966] 3 All ER 398, Lord Denning MR said:

> A very young child cannot be guilty of contributory negligence. An older child may be; but it depends on the circumstances. A judge should only find a child guilty of contributory negligence if he is of such an age as reasonably to be expected to take precautions for his own safety.

Defences in tort

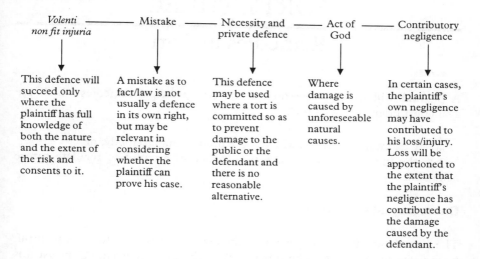

Volenti non fit injuria	Mistake	Necessity and private defence	Act of God	Contributory negligence
This defence will succeed only where the plaintiff has full knowledge of both the nature and the extent of the risk and consents to it.	A mistake as to fact/law is not usually a defence in its own right, but may be relevant in considering whether the plaintiff can prove his case.	This defence may be used where a tort is committed so as to prevent damage to the public or the defendant and there is no reasonable alternative.	Where damage is caused by unforeseeable natural causes.	In certain cases, the plaintiff's own negligence may have contributed to his loss/injury. Loss will be apportioned to the extent that the plaintiff's negligence has contributed to the damage caused by the defendant.

FORTY THREE
Remedies in Tort

A plaintiff will usually seek one of the two principal remedies which are available under the law of tort:

(a) a claim for damages, which is the predominant remedy; or

(b) the injunction, which can be used in an attempt to regulate future behaviour.

Damages and settlements

The aim of awarding damages under the law of tort is to restore the plaintiff, financially, to the position he was in before the tort occurred. (Contrast this with the purpose of damages in respect of expectation loss under the law of contract: see Chapter 31.) Making an award for property damage is relatively straightforward, but it is considerably more difficult when personal injuries are involved. Providing compensation for personal injuries can be problematic, because assessment has to be made of the plaintiff's future needs and the courts do not have psychic abilities. For example, the plaintiff's condition may become worse than was originally anticipated at the trial and he may ultimately be undercompensated for the injuries.

Sometimes, the courts will award extra compensation to the plaintiff in order to inflict punishment on the defendant because of his conduct. This occurs only in relation to certain torts such as defamation, wrongful imprisonment and trespass, and only in limited circumstances, because it is not ordinarily a function of the law of tort to punish the defendant. An example of a libel case in which such punitive or exemplary damages might be awarded is one in which the defendant appears to have calculated that his profits from publication of an unfairly defamatory work would exceed any normal sum of damages that might be awarded against him in an action for libel (see *Broome* v *Cassell & Co.* [1972] AC 1027).

In other circumstances, the court may sometimes only award nominal damages, namely where it wishes to acknowledge that the plaintiff's legal rights have been infringed, but where it is not apparent that he has suffered any real detriment as a result of that infringement.

Parties to litigation may sometimes be able to agree on more elaborate settlement terms than any which could be imposed on them by the courts without their consent (e.g., 'structured settlements', involving the purchase by the defendants of an annuity, in place of lump sum damages, for the benefit of the plaintiff). The enforceability of such settlements is recognised by the Damages Act 1996.

Lump sum awards and periodical payments

A plaintiff who has been the victim of a tort may not ordinarily bring more than one action in respect of that particular tort. Consequently, if the damage turns out to be more extensive than originally thought, he cannot ordinarily bring a second action on the same facts (although there are some exceptions to this rule). Damages are thus assessed on a once and for all basis and the plaintiff will ordinarily be awarded a single lump sum. Periodical payments can be awarded in personal injury cases, but only with the consent of the parties concerned (Damages Act 1996, s. 2). It may be difficult to assess the appropriate level of lump sum compensation in personal injury cases. In particular, it may be difficult to predict what real effect the injuries incurred in an accident may have upon the plaintiff in the future. There may be a possibility, but no certainty, that the original injury will heal in time, or a possibility that it will continue to deteriorate. It may be almost impossible to predict how long the plaintiff will live.

There is a relatively new procedure applicable in personal injury cases where there is a possibility that the plaintiff will develop further incapacity or that his injury will deteriorate etc. A lump sum may be awarded 'provisionally' calculated on the assumption that the original injury will not deteriorate or lead to further incapacity, but if it does so, the plaintiff may make a further application for damages to cover it. A provisional award of damages does not preclude the bringing of a further claim under the Fatal Accidents Act 1976 (p. 495 below), in the event of the victim's subsequent death as a result of his injuries (Damages Act 1996, s. 3).

Calculating damages in personal injury cases

An award of damages for personal injuries will be calculated to take into account various matters, as follows.

(a) *Pecuniary loss* Pecuniary loss is harm which is capable of being calculated in money terms, such as loss of earnings, medical expenses, travelling expenses etc.

(b) Non-pecuniary loss   Non-pecuniary loss covers harm which is not easy to convert into monetary terms, such as pain and suffering (see below). The courts as a result adopt a tariff for specific types of injury, and this at least brings some consistency to decisions. Such tariffs may be looked up in practitioners' textbooks, in which the relevant precedents may be found, setting out the 'going rate' for loss of a leg, eye, or finger, for broken bones and crippled backs.

(c) Medical and associated expenses   The plaintiff can recover damages for his medical and other associated expenses. He may recover expenses for private medical treatment, even though he could have obtained the same treatment under the National Health Service. If the plaintiff saves any living expenses due to being hospitalised, however, this saving will be set off against any income lost by him as a result of the injuries. If the plaintiff needs specialised nursing help, or to have his home adapted to cater for his needs then these costs may be recovered provided that they are reasonable in the circumstances.

(d) Pain and suffering   The plaintiff is entitled to compensation for the pain and suffering he experiences as a result of his injuries. This may also include compensation for nervous shock, but not simply for sorrow or grief. If the plaintiff is permanently unconscious and incapable of actually experiencing pain, he will not recover under this head.

(e) Loss of faculties and amenities   Loss of amenities covers matters such as inability to engage in leisure activities, sports or hobbies as a result of the injury. Loss of faculties, on the other hand, covers losses arising out of the injury itself, such as an arm or a leg. As noted earlier, the courts adopt a form of tariff system when awarding damages in this context, and this figure includes compensation for loss of both faculties and amenities.

(f) Loss of earnings   The plaintiff can accurately be compensated for any loss of actual earnings between the date of injury and date of assessment. This figure is usually easy to calculate as it is based upon the plaintiff's net (overall) loss during that period. The more difficult issue is the assessment of future earnings. The starting point in trying to arrive at such a figure is to discover the plaintiff's net annual loss of earnings. This figure is then adjusted slightly to take account of the promotion chances which may have been available to the plaintiff, and multiplied by the number of years for which the loss is likely to continue. For example, if a person was injured at age 50 and was expected to work until age 65 then the number of years the loss of income would be likely to continue would be 15. Where the plaintiff receives compensation in the form of a lump sum, the courts take into account the fact that the capital will be invested and the plaintiff will receive interest from it. See the Damages Act 1996, s. 1.

(g) Loss of life expectancy If the plaintiff's life expectancy has been reduced by the injury, he may claim compensation for the earnings which he might have expected to receive during his normal working life had it not been for the injuries resulting from the accident. It does not matter whether the plaintiff has dependants. This was accepted as correct by the House of Lords in *Pickett* v *British Rail Engineering Ltd* [1980] AC 136. There will, however, be a deduction for the amount which the plaintiff would have spent on his own living expenses during that period.

(h) What can be deducted from the amount of damages the plaintiff receives? There are a number of other sources from which the plaintiff may receive damages, as well as from the defendant. They may include social security payments, pensions and private insurance. Such other sources of finance may be deducted from the award of damages which the plaintiff will receive.

As far as social security payments are concerned, the position before 1988 was that they would be deducted from the amount awarded to the plaintiff in damages against the defendant. In 1989, however, there was a change in policy and the Social Security Act of that year (now incorporated in the Social Security Administration Act 1992) provided that the state could recoup certain prescribed social security benefits from tortfeasors. The Act applies to any tort compensation payments made after 3 September 1990 in respect of an accident or injury occurring on or after 1 January 1989. The Act allows recoupment only of certain forms of social security benefits, such as unemployment benefit, and sickness benefit for a period of usually no more than five years. As far as other social security payments are concerned, the pre-1988 rules still apply.

(i) Death A plaintiff clearly cannot claim damages in respect of his own death. In some cases, however, the plaintiff's dependants may claim for his loss under the Fatal Accidents Act 1976. They will succeed only if the deceased could have succeeded had he lived, and the amount of any claim may be reduced if contributory negligence on the part of the deceased can be proved. Claims may include damages to cover the cost of funeral expenses and loss of dependency (financial or domestic support). A bereaved spouse or the parents of an unmarried child may also be able to claim a fixed sum of £7,500 as damages for bereavement, without proof of financial loss.

Damage to property
The aim of damages under this head is again to put the plaintiff into the position he was in before the tort took place. If, for example, the property has been completely destroyed, the damages will be assessed as the market value of the property at the time it was destroyed. If it has been damaged, the amount claimed may reflect the cost of repairing it.

Mitigation
The plaintiff is under a duty to mitigate any damage which results from the defendant's tort. In other words, if the plaintiff is forced to give up one job, he should attempt to obtain another one. Equally, the plaintiff must seek reasonable medical treatment for injuries, failing which any damages he might have obtained may be reduced. The plaintiff is not entitled to be extravagant at the defendant's expense (*Darbyshire* v *Warran* [1963] 1 WLR 1067).

Injunctions

A detailed discussion of injunctions is beyond the scope of this book, and a brief outline only is given here.

The injunction may be used by the court in order to prevent the defendant engaging in conduct which is likely to inflict unlawful harm or annoyance on the plaintiff in the future. Injunctions are important in areas where torts are likely to be repeated, such as in nuisance, trespass and defamation. The granting of an injunction is at the discretion of the courts, and this is a wide discretion. It will not usually be granted where damages are perceived as offering a perfectly adequate remedy.

Interlocutory injunctions
These are provisional orders issued prior to the final trial of the case, usually with the aim of preserving assets or preventing further harm occurring pending the outcome of the trial itself. A plaintiff who obtains such an injunction against the defendant, only to lose his case when it comes to trial, may then have to pay the defendant damages for losses suffered by him in consequence of complying with the injunction.

APPENDIX

Revision and Exam Techniques

Revision

1. Make life easier for yourself and spread your workload throughout the period for which you are studying. At the end of each new topic, try to assimilate the main legal points associated with the subject. The diagrams at the end of most chapters should help you to obtain an overview of most topics. Learning of details can take place closer to the examination.

2. In order to ensure that you have a good set of notes from which to revise, try to obtain access to old examination questions and see if you can answer them with the material which you have in your files. If not, then go back to the textbook and add more detail.

3. As the exams get closer, start to make a timetable of study. Do not leave studying until the last minute. Start well in advance, so that you can rest before the exam itself. Revision means going through each section of your notes at least three times before the exams. Each time you read your notes, you should learn something more. Remember that there is a lot of diverse information to assimilate with 'A' level law.

4. Do not learn your notes parrot-fashion. The main way to achieve successful results is to obtain a good, overall understanding of your work.

The exam

1. Read the instructions on the examination paper before you start. Make sure, for example, that you understand how many questions you have to

attempt, how many marks they are worth, and how long you have in which to answer them.

2.   Read all questions carefully and select those which you feel you can best answer.

3.   As you may be nervous to begin with, it might be prudent to start with the question which you feel you know the most about. This will help to settle your nerves.

4.   Take a good five minutes to plan your answer. Good planning is essential to a good answer. Everyone has different approaches to planning answers, but one way is to put down in note form everything that you know about the question. Then place numbers next to each point in the order in which they should appear in the answer.

5.   A good answer should identify the legal points raised by the question and then deal with those points in turn. For example, if answering a criminal law problem, the best approach is to list all of the possible offences with which the defendant may be charged. Then work your way through each offence indicating the essential elements of the crime and the *mens rea* required. Do the stated facts indicate that those essential elements are present?

6.   Wherever possible, back up your argument with relevant case law or statute. When citing a provision of a statute, it is usually enough to cite the provision briefly, not in detail.

7.   After stating the law, always apply the law to the facts and come to a conclusion on what you think the answer should be.

8.   After writing your essay, spend a couple of minutes reading over your answer. It is surprising what silly mistakes may be eliminated by a quick read.

9.   Always attempt the full number of questions required by the examining board. Do not spend all your time, for example, on three questions if the exam requires you to answer a fourth.

10.   Keep your sentences short and concise. Do not ramble. Make sure your work is divided into paragraphs. There should be a new paragraph for each new point dealt with.

Index